Y0-BUP-073

Government Contracting Manual

GOVERNMENT CONTRACTING MANUAL

Timothy J. Healy

PRENTICE HALL
Englewood Cliffs, New Jersey 07632

Prentice-Hall International (UK) Limited, *London*
Prentice-Hall of Australia Pty. Limited, *Sydney*
Prentice-Hall Canada, Inc., *Toronto*
Prentice-Hall Hispanoamericana, S.A., *Mexico*
Prentice-Hall of India Private Limited, *New Delhi*
Prentice-Hall of Japan, Inc., *Tokyo*
Simon & Schuster Asia Pte. Ltd., *Singapore*
Editora Prentice-Hall do Brasil, Ltda., *Rio de Janeiro*

10 9 8 7 6 5 4 3 2 1

Library of Congress Cataloging-in-Publication Data

Healy, Timothy J. (Timothy Joseph)
Government contracting manual / Timothy J. Healy.
p. cm.
ISBN 0-13-361031-4
1. Public contracts--United States. 2. Government purchasing--Law and legislation--United States. 3. Government purchasing--United States. I. Title.
KF849.H427 1989
346.73'023--dc20
[347.30623] 89-71131
CIP

ISBN 0-13-361031-4

Printed in the United States of America

To my wife, Annette, who managed to keep her sterling sense of humor during her long tenure as a book widow, and to those many unsung government servants without whose efforts this book would not have been possible.

ABOUT THE AUTHOR

Timothy Healy received his MBA from Hofstra University in 1963, and gained extensive project management background with major defense aerospace and electronics companies. Later, he satisfied his entrepreneurial drives as founder and CEO of Clipper Air International, a commuter airline serving the Caribbean Islands of St. Croix, St. Thomas, St. Martin and Puerto Rico. After selling the airline, he applied his extensive government contracting knowledge as a consultant to a variety of Houston companies.

Currently he is a Vice President with Sigma Enviro-Serve Inc., a Houston company specializing in the handling of hazardous environmental waste, and he also maintains his government contracting consulting practice. He also founded Foster-Allen, Ltd. and Doyle Dunn and Associates, executive search firms serving on a national level. He is listed in the 1988–89 edition of *Who's Who in the South and Southwest*.

Future plans include a series of seminars on government contracting and another book.

He resides in Friendswood, Texas with his wife Annette, his son-in-law, daughter, and two grandchildren.

How This Book Can Help You Succeed in Government Contracting

This book will show you how to quickly and profitably sell to the U.S. government. You will learn what to do when the unexpected happens, what pitfalls to avoid, how the procurement system works, and, perhaps best of all, how to finance the contracts you will receive.

Whether you're a one-person business operating out of a garage or a high-level executive from the military-industrial complex, you'll find this book offers an abundance of timely and informative material. Government contracting officials will find this a handy reference to supplement their work, while minority-owned business owners will find it invaluable in expanding their horizons.

Here are just some of the topics covered:

- where to obtain financial aid for fulfilling your contracts
- key sources for finding government contracting opportunities
- guidelines on preparing your bid and negotiating a contract award
- government standards for ensuring fair and complete formal advertising—and when negotiation can be used instead
- six vital requirements of a responsible bidder
- tips on handling mistakes on bids
- how to read and understand a defense contract
- how to clearly interpret and comply with federal and military specifications
- bidding strategies that can help you gain the edge on your competition
- how to develop and submit unsolicited proposals that get accepted

- how to make the most of free government assistance
- when to subcontract, and how to do it profitably
- how to make the most out of the many programs and opportunities offered by the Small Business Administration (SBA)
- contract, financial, management, and other specialized program opportunities for minority businesses
- contract law and its impact on you as a government contractor
- fixed-price and cost-reimbursement contracts: when and how they are used, their similarities and differences, and special requirements for fulfilling your contractual obligations
- how the government measures contract performance—and how you must comply
- how to modify a government contract
- guidelines for appeals and resolving disputes

A unique approach to indexing is used. Instead of a total book index format, a chapter index system is employed. By tieing the index directly to the chapter subject, specific information is more quickly located.

In addition, three comprehensive appendices offer detailed information on government procurement programs and the Walsh-Healey Public Contracts Act, as well as an informative and up-to-date listing of key products and services bought by military and federal purchasing offices.

In short, this book completely demystifies the government contracting mechanism. You will learn what is required of you, the contractor, and what is required of your customer, the U.S. government.

If you have a product or service to sell, the federal government has a need for it and will buy it. This book shows you how to get the government to buy from you—how to join the ranks of smart, successful government contractors—quickly and profitably.

A Word from the Author

Every 17 seconds of each working day the U.S. government awards a contract with an average value of $440,000. And every year thousands of these contracts worth billions of dollars bypass both large and small companies and individuals because they are either unaware of this treasure trove of business, or because they do not know how to participate. Sometimes contractors bypass government contracts because they have heard that the government is a "slow payer," or there is the feeling that, despite everything, they really couldn't be competitive on government contracts anyway.

In reality, these preconceived notions could not be further from the truth. There is room for everyone in government contracting, from the ordinary citizen to the largest industrial complexes, even foreign-owned companies!

Figure 1 (page x) shows the total amount spent by various departments and agencies of the federal government during fiscal year 1988 (the latest available data). These figures include every item purchased, representing thousands of awards, ranging from a box of pencils on a small local purchase to an aircraft carrier. Let's take a look at some typical contract awards made from $25,000 and up.

- *Magnum PI*, various episodes, plus episodes of other hit TV shows; $330,820
- Official sports services at Fort Benning, Georgia; $189,292
- Writing paper for a federal correctional institution; $113,530
- Gold for NASA; $350,000
- Electric hospital beds for a VA medical center; $370,059
- Credit card and order processing services for the Treasury Department; $19,250,694
- Legal services for the Department of Housing and Urban Development; not to exceed $840,000
- Replace the roof, officer's club, Fort Bragg, North Carolina; $129,476
- Electric fans for the GSA; $2,751,964
- Mini-computer system for Aberdeen Proving Ground; $112,092

FEDERAL PROCUREMENT TOTALS BY AGENCY – FY 1988

AGENCY	DOLLARS (IN BILLIONS)
DOD - Department of Defense	$149.4
DOE - Department of Energy	14.5
NASA - National Aeronautics and Space Administration	8.5
GSA - General Services Administration	2.6
VA - Veterans Administration	3.3
DOI - Department of the Interior	1.5
USDA - Department of Agriculture	3.0
DOT - Department of Transportation	1.8
TVA - Tennessee Valley Authority	.8
EPA - Environmental Protection Agency	1.1
All Other	8.5
Total: 59 procurement Agencies	$194.4

Data courtesy of the Federal Procurement Data Center, 4040 N. Fairfax Drive, Ste. 900, Arlington, VA 22203. 703-235-1326. Fax: 703-235-2875.

Figure 1

Fascinating stuff, agreed? And the list goes on and on, covering thousands of awards on an almost unlimited array of products and services. They are the success stories of the many companies, both large and small, that helped themselves from that great smorgasbord of business known as government contracting! Consider the food business. Here are some typical requirements that have been solicited: Spaghetti, 1,111,200 pounds; bakery products, 82,000 pounds of various kinds of bread and rolls for daily delivery; meat and meat products (frozen) for the month of March, for delivery to the VA medical center at Palo Alto, California, 11,708 pounds. Requirements such as these should get your serious attention. Not for me, you say? Too rich for your blood? Agreed—not everyone is in a position to handle requirements on that scale. But let's take another example. Suppose you were the proprietor of an office supply store. Would you be interested in supplying 5,000 bottles of correction fluid to the General Services Administration (GSA)? Probably yes. By the way, that's 5,000 bottles at one time, not 100 a week for 50 weeks. That's not a bad size order for a small business that may sell only 100 or so bottles of the same product across the counter in the course of a year.

At this point you should be starting to get the picture. It can be safely said that the U.S. government is the largest customer for both goods and services in the world! Visualize yourself in a huge shopping mall—the world's most complete shopping mall. It is vast, with stores of every conceivable variety abounding in all directions, in which you can buy anything you could ever need. If you required medicine, computers, food, flags, fuel, pencils, clothing, cooking utensils, bearings, tools and machinery, air conditioners, locks, fire fighting equipment, communications equipment, and more, you could buy it all in this mall. This should begin to give you an idea of what types of items the government buys, both in large and small quantities. But this isn't the full picture! The government also buys services of all types—from engineering, to legal, to management, to consulting, to many others.

Keep in mind: The government wants to spread its business around, and not offer it to just a handful of companies or individuals. You've heard those stories about big defense contractors working on megabuck orders for sophisticated items. From this, it's easy to get the impression that the smaller business doesn't have a chance to compete. But this type of thinking is not supported by the facts. First, the giant suppliers are actually very few in number. Second, the vast majority of contracts are awarded to "average" companies, many of which are in the small business category. There are even items and services that the government *insists* must be bought from either small or minority-owned businesses. And this book will show you how to tap into this profitable pipeline.

Timothy J. Healy

TABLE OF CONTENTS

1

WHAT YOU MUST KNOW ABOUT GOVERNMENT CONTRACTING BEFORE YOU PLUNGE IN

WHERE TO FIND CONTRACTING OPPORTUNITIES: THREE KEY SOURCES

The first thing to do is to find out what is being bought, and when. You should subscribe to the *Commerce Business Daily* (*CBD*), which is published Monday through Friday and occasionally on Saturday by the U.S. Department of Commerce. An annual subscription by first-class mail costs $243. A subscription by second-class mail costs $173 per year. A six-month trial subscription costs $122 by first-class mail, $87 by second-class mail. Two-year subscription rates are available on request. Your order, including remittance in full, should be sent to

Superintendent of Documents
Government Printing Office
Washington, DC 20402–9325
Telephone (202) 783–3238

Your check or money order should be made payable to the Superintendent of Documents. VISA and MasterCard are also accepted. Allow six weeks for delivery of the first issue.

An electronic edition of the *CBD* is also available at $50 per edition. There are approximately 250 electronic editions per year, and their rapid transmission offers the bidder the advantage of longer response times. The electronic edition is also available from 13 private telecommunications firms at a substantial cost saving. Detailed information on the electronic edition, including the names and addresses of the private telecommunications firms, may be obtained from the U.S. Department of Commerce, Office of the Secretary, Washington, DC 20230, or by calling 202–377–0632.

The second thing to do is get on a Bidder's List. This is done by filling out a mailing list application, Form 129, (Figure 1–1). This form was originally titled *Bidder's Mailing List Application*, but the most current editions are called *Solicitation Mailing List Application*. Only the new version may be used. Some government departments have customized versions of Form 129 (it still bears the same form number), and they will send you their version to fill out, if necessary, upon receipt of your original submittal. This may seem an unnecessary duplication of paper work, but go along with it, anyhow. If an agency doesn't have its records in the correct form, it can't service you, and you will miss out on a lot of business.

You will most likely have to send Form 129 to more than one buying office. An easy way to prepare multiple copies is to fill out the body of the form, make copies, and then enter the name of a different agency on each separate copy. Form 129 is used by all agencies, both civilian and defense, and it has been authorized to be reproduced locally. The General Services Administration (GSA) will require submittal of GSA Form 3038, *Bidder's Mailing List Application Code Sheet* (Figure 1–2). This is prepared from the GSA List of Commodities and Services reproduced in Appendix D.

All government forms are sold in packs of 100 at reasonable rates. SF forms are sold by the Government Printing Office, 202–783–3238. GSA forms may be ordered from the GSA, 202–653–6542 or 202–653–7886; DD forms may be ordered by calling the Department of the Army at 703–487–4884.

In order to stay on a Bidder's List, you must maintain communication with the government. Every time a bid request is received, you must either submit a bid, or write to the purchasing office stating that you are unable to bid but wish to remain on the list. If you do neither of these things, you may be dropped from the list. (Sometimes the solicitation may stipulate that a ''no bid'' response is not required.)

The third way to find out about contracting opportunities is to be included on a Qualified Products List (QPL). These lists are used only for products requiring lengthy or costly testing to determine if they meet government requirements. The QPL for each product identifies the specification and the manufac-

53.301-129

SOLICITATION MAILING LIST APPLICATION

1. TYPE OF APPLICATION ☐ INITIAL ☐ REVISION | 2. DATE | FORM APPROVED OMB NO. 3090-0009

NOTE—Please complete all items on this form. Insert N/A in items not applicable. See reverse for Instructions.

3. NAME AND ADDRESS OF FEDERAL AGENCY TO WHICH FORM IS SUBMITTED *(Include ZIP code)*

4. NAME AND ADDRESS OF APPLICANT *(Include county and ZIP code)*

5. TYPE OF ORGANIZATION *(Check one)*

☐ INDIVIDUAL ☐ NON-PROFIT ORGANIZATION

☐ PARTNERSHIP ☐ CORPORATION, INCORPORATED UNDER THE LAWS OF THE STATE OF:

6. ADDRESS TO WHICH SOLICITATIONS ARE TO BE MAILED *(If different than Item 4)*

7. NAMES OF OFFICERS, OWNERS, OR PARTNERS

A. PRESIDENT	B. VICE PRESIDENT	C. SECRETARY
D. TREASURER	E. OWNERS OR PARTNERS	

8. AFFILIATES OF APPLICANT *(Names, locations and nature of affiliation. See definition on reverse.)*

9. PERSONS AUTHORIZED TO SIGN OFFERS AND CONTRACTS IN YOUR NAME *(Indicate if agent)*

NAME	OFFICIAL CAPACITY	TELE. NO. *(Include area code)*

10. IDENTIFY EQUIPMENT, SUPPLIES, AND/OR SERVICES ON WHICH YOU DESIRE TO MAKE AN OFFER *(See attached Federal agency's supplemental listing and instructions, if any)*

11A. SIZE OF BUSINESS *(See definitions on reverse)*

☐ SMALL BUSINESS *(If checked, complete items 11B and 11C)* ☐ OTHER THAN SMALL BUSINESS

11B. AVERAGE NUMBER OF EMPLOYEES *(Including affiliates)* FOR FOUR PRECEDING CALENDAR QUARTERS

11C. AVERAGE ANNUAL SALES OR RECEIPTS FOR PRECEDING THREE FISCAL YEARS

$

12. TYPE OF OWNERSHIP *(See definitions on reverse) (Not applicable for other than small businesses)*

☐ DISADVANTAGED BUSINESS ☐ WOMAN-OWNED BUSINESS

13. TYPE OF BUSINESS *(See definitions on reverse)*

☐ MANUFACTURER OR PRODUCER ☐ REGULAR DEALER *(Type 1)* ☐ CONSTRUCTION CONCERN ☐ SURPLUS DEALER

☐ SERVICE ESTABLISHMENT ☐ REGULAR DEALER *(Type 2)* ☐ RESEARCH AND DEVELOPMENT

14. DUNS NO. *(If available)*

15. HOW LONG IN PRESENT BUSINESS?

16. FLOOR SPACE *(Square feet)*

A. MANUFACTURING	B. WAREHOUSE

17. NET WORTH

A. DATE	B. AMOUNT
	$

18. SECURITY CLEARANCE *(If applicable, check highest clearance authorized)*

FOR	TOP SECRET	SECRET	CONFIDENTIAL	C. NAMES OF AGENCIES WHICH GRANTED SECURITY CLEARANCES *(Include dates)*
A. KEY PERSONNEL				
B. PLANT ONLY				

CERTIFICATION — I certify that information supplied herein *(Including all pages attached)* is correct and that neither the applicant nor any person *(Or concern)* in any connection with the applicant as a principal or officer, so far as is known, is now debarred or otherwise declared ineligible by any agency of the Federal Government from making offers for furnishing materials, supplies, or services to the Government or any agency thereof.

19. NAME AND TITLE OF PERSON AUTHORIZED TO SIGN *(Type or print)*	20. SIGNATURE	21. DATE SIGNED

NSN 7540-01-152-8086
PREVIOUS EDITIONS UNUSABLE

129-106

STANDARD FORM 129 (REV. 10-83)
Prescribed by GSA
FAR (48 CFR) 53.214(c)

Figure 1–1

53.301–129

INSTRUCTIONS

Persons or concerns wishing to be added to a particular agency's bidder's mailing list for supplies or services shall file this properly completed and certified Solicitation Mailing List Application, together with such other lists as may be attached to this application form, with each procurement office of the Federal agency with which they desire to do business. If a Federal agency has attached a Supplemental Commodity list with instructions, complete the application as instructed. Otherwise, identify in Item 10 the equipment supplies and/or services on which you desire to bid. (Provide Federal Supply Class or Standard Industrial Classification Codes if available.) The application shall be submitted and signed by the principal as distinguished from an agent, however constituted.

After placement on the bidder's mailing list of an agency, your failure to respond (submission of bid, or notice in writing, that you are unable to bid on that particular transaction but wish to remain on the active bidder's mailing list for that particular item) to solicitations will be understood by the agency to indicate lack of interest and concurrence in the removal of your name from the purchasing activity's solicitation mailing list for the items concerned.

SIZE OF BUSINESS DEFINITIONS
(See Item 11A.)

a. Small business concern—A small business concern for the purpose of Government procurement is a concern, including its affiliates, which is independently owned and operated, is not dominant in the field of operation in which it is competing for Government contracts and can further qualify under the criteria concerning number of employees, average annual receipts, or other criteria, as prescribed by the Small Business Administration. (See Code of Federal Regulations, Title 13, Part 121, as amended, which contains detailed industry definitions and related procedures.)

b. Affiliates—Business concerns are affiliates of each other when either directly or indirectly (i) one concern controls or has the power to control the other, or (ii) a third party controls or has the power to control both. In determining whether concerns are independently owned and operated and whether or not affiliation exists, consideration is given to all appropriate factors including common ownership, common management, and contractual relationship. (See Items 8 and 11A.)

c. Number of employees—(Item 11B) In connection with the determination of small business status, "number of employees" means the average employment of any concern, including the employees of its domestic and foreign affiliates, based on the number of persons employed on a full-time, part-time, temporary, or other basis during each of the pay periods of the preceding 12 months. If a concern has not been in existence for 12 months, "number of employees" means the average employment of such concern and its affiliates during the period that such concern has been in existence based on the number of persons employed during each of the pay periods of the period that such concern has been in business.

TYPE OF OWNERSHIP DEFINITIONS
(See Item 12.)

a. "Disadvantaged business concern"—means any business concern (1) which is at least 51 percent owned by one or more socially and economically disadvantaged individuals; or, in the case of any publicly owned business, at least 51 percent of the stock of which is owned by one or more socially and economically disadvantaged individuals; and (2) whose management and daily business operations are controlled by one or more of such individuals.

b. "Women-owned business"—means a business that is at least 51 percent owned by a woman or women who are U.S. citizens and who also control and operate the business.

TYPE OF BUSINESS DEFINITIONS
(See Item 13.)

a. Manufacturer or producer—means a person (or concern) owning, operating, or maintaining a store, warehouse, or other establishment that produces, on the premises, the materials, supplies, articles, or equipment of the general character of those listed in Item 10, or in the Federal Agency's Supplemental Commodity List, if attached.

b. Service establishment—means a concern (or person) which owns, operates, or maintains any type of business which is principally engaged in the furnishing of nonpersonal services, such as (but not limited to) repairing, cleaning, redecorating, or rental of personal property, including the furnishing of necessary repair parts or other supplies as part of the services performed.

c. Regular dealer (Type 1)—means a person (or concern) who owns, operates, or maintains a store, warehouse, or other establishment in which the materials, supplies, articles, or equipment of the general character listed in Item 10, or in the Federal Agency's Supplemental Commodity List, if attached, are bought, kept in stock, and sold to the public in the usual course of business.

d. Regular dealer (Type 2)—In the case of supplies of particular kinds (at present, petroleum, lumber and timber products, machine tools, raw cotton, green coffee, hay, grain, feed, or straw, agricultural liming materials, tea, raw or unmanufactured cotton linters and used ADPE), Regular dealer means a person (or concern) satisfying the requirements of the regulations (Code of Federal Regulations, Title 41, 50-201.101(a)(2)) as amended from time to time, prescribed by the Secretary of Labor under the Walsh-Healey Public Contracts Act (Title 41 U.S. Code 35-45). For coal dealers see Code of Federal Regulations, Title 41, 50-201.604(a).

- COMMERCE BUSINESS DAILY—The Commerce Business Daily, published by the Department of Commerce, contains information concerning proposed procurements, sales, and contract awards. For further information concerning this publication, contact your local Commerce Field Office.

STANDARD FORM 129 BACK (REV. 10-83)

53–43

Figure 1–1, continued

BIDDER'S MAILING LIST APPLICATION CODE SHEET
(Please type or print all entries)

FORM APPROVED OMB NO. 29-R0248

TO: *(Self mailer on back of form)*

General Services Administration (8FFS)
Centralized Mailing Lists Services
Building 41, Denver Federal Center
Denver, CO 80225

FROM: *(Name and address to which bidding forms are to be mailed) (Include ZIP Code)*

CHECK ONE OR MORE BOXES AS APPLICABLE

☐ NEW APPLICATION ☐ ADD MAILING CODES ☐ CHANGE IN BUSINESS MINORITY DATA
☐ NAME AND/OR ADDRESS CHANGE ☐ DELETE MAILING CODES

PREVIOUS NAME AND ADDRESS *(If changed)*

REQUESTED BY *(Typed or printed name)*

TITLE

SIGNATURE | DATE

REQUESTED AREAS OF INTEREST FOR BIDDING

Examine the various General Services Administration geographic areas below, and indicate in the appropriate blocks, areas to which your firm can make deliveries and compete for contracts. Complete only if new applicant or if you are changing/deleting an area.

CHECK (✓)	AREA SERVED	CHECK (✓)	AREA SERVED
	REGION 1 - Connecticut, Maine, Massachusetts, New Hampshire, Rhode Island, Vermont		REGION 2 - New Jersey, New York, Puerto Rico, Virgin Islands
	REGION 3 - Delaware, District of Columbia, Maryland, Pennsylvania, Virginia, West Virginia		REGION 4 - Alabama, Florida, Georgia, Kentucky, Mississippi, North Carolina, South Carolina, Tennessee
	REGION 5 - Illinois, Indiana, Michigan, Minnesota, Ohio, Wisconsin		REGION 6 - Iowa, Kansas, Missouri, Nebraska
	REGION 7 - Arkansas, Louisiana, New Mexico, Oklahoma, Texas		REGION 8 - Colorado, Montana, North Dakota, South Dakota, Utah, Wyoming
	REGION 9 - Arizona, California, Hawaii, Nevada		REGION 10 - Alaska, Idaho, Oregon, Washington
	ALL AREAS *(Regions 1 through 10 except export)*		EXPORT *(To be checked by firms interested in bidding for contracts involving deliveries to other countries)*

BUSINESS SIZE

(Check either block (1) or (3).)

(1) ☐ Small business - A small business concern for the purpose of Government procurement is a concern, including its affiliates, which is independently owned and operated, is not dominant in the field of operation in which it is submitting offers on Government contracts, and can further qualify under the criteria concerning number of employees, average annual receipts, or other criteria, as prescribed by the Small Business Administration. *(See Code of Federal Regulations Title 13, Part 121, as amended, which contains detailed industry definitions and related procedures.)*

(3) ☐ Other than small business concern.

MINORITY INFORMATION

(Check either block (4) or (5).)

(4) ☐ Minority enterprise - A minority-owned business is a business, 50% of which is owned by minority group members, or, in cases of publicly-owned businesses, 51% of the stock of which is owned by minority group members. For purposes of this definition, the minority ethnic group include Negro, Mexican-American, Puerto Rican, Cuban, Oriental, American Indian, Aleut, and Eskimo.

(5) ☐ Non-minority

FOR GSA USE ONLY *(Do not write below this line)*

DOC. I.D. 0 8 B | MAIL LIST NO. 3 0 1 | MONTH | DAY | YEAR | IDENTIFICATION NUMBER

NAME AND/OR STATISTICAL DATA ACTION ☐ NEW ☐ CHANGE ☐ DELETE

STATISTICAL DATA: 1 2 3 4 5

AREAS OF INTEREST: 1 2 3 4 5 6 7 8 9 0 A E

CARD NUMBER 1 2 3 4

STATE | ZIP CODE

GENERAL SERVICES ADMINISTRATION — **GSA FORM 3038 PAGE 1** (6-77)

Figure 1–2

INSTRUCTIONS

In order to receive solicitations for the commodities/services which you provide, use the GSA Form 1382 "List of Commodities and Services" to enter the appropriate codes in the boxes below. Please exercise care in transcribing the correct numbers in sequence.

A. COMMODITIES: Find the FSC group number of the commodity in which you are interested in the index in the front of the GSA Form 1382. Within that group locate the 4-digit class and the Mailing List Code that corresponds to your commodity.

B. SERVICES: Locate the Standard Industrial Group in which you are interested in the listing on the last page of the GSA Form 1382. Within that group (4 digits, the first always a 0), locate the Mailing List Code that corresponds to your service.

C. ADDITIONS/DELETIONS: Complete all areas on the front of this form except Area of Interest. Indicate below the Class and/or Standard Industrial Group and applicable Mailing List Codes you are changing. Place an A (add) or D (delete) as appropriate in the asterisked (*) column. To be removed entirely from the Mailing List File, submit a request in writing to the address on the reverse of this form. If you are only changing name, address, area of interest or business size/minority data, do not annotate these 2 pages.

D. NEW APPLICANTS: Complete Standard Form 129 "Bidder's Mailing List Application" as indicated on the reverse of that form, disregarding the instruction on filing with "each procurement office". Leave item 8 blank. Attach original to completed original of this form. Fold, staple and stamp the back where indicated. Return originals only. Do NOT return the GSA Form 1382 booklet.

	*	CLASS/ INDUSTRIAL GROUP	MAILING LIST CODE
NEW BIDDER FOR NAILS		5315	4

	*	CLASS/ INDUSTRIAL GROUP	MAILING LIST CODE
CURRENT BIDDER ADDING RIVETS	A	5320	1

	*	CLASS/ INDUSTRIAL GROUP	MAILING LIST CODE
CURRENT BIDDER DELETING VISUAL ARTS	D	0733	7

*	CLASS/ INDUSTRIAL GROUP	MAILING LIST CODE	*	CLASS/ INDUSTRIAL GROUP	MAILING LIST CODE	*	CLASS/ INDUSTRIAL GROUP	MAILING LIST CODE	*	CLASS/ INDUSTRIAL GROUP	MAILING LIST CODE	*	CLASS/ INDUSTRIAL GROUP	MAILING LIST CODE	*	CLASS/ INDUSTRIAL GROUP	MAILING LIST CODE

GSA FORM **3038 PAGE 2** (6-77)

Figure 1–2, continued

*	CLASS/ INDUSTRIAL GROUP	MAILING LIST CODE	*	CLASS/ INDUSTRIAL GROUP	MAILING LIST CODE	*	CLASS/ INDUSTRIAL GROUP	MAILING LIST CODE	*	CLASS/ INDUSTRIAL GROUP	MAILING LIST CODE	*	CLASS/ INDUSTRIAL GROUP	MAILING LIST CODE	*	CLASS/ INDUSTRIAL GROUP	MAILING LIST CODE

GSA FORM 3038 PAGE 3 (6-77)

GPO 913-599

Figure 1–2, continued

Please Make Sure You Have:

1. Signed both the SF 129 (new applicants) and this form.
2. Attached the SF 129 (new applicants) to this form.
3. Placed a stamp in the space indicated below.
4. Retained the GSA Form 1382 booklet and a copy of the application(s) for your files.
5. CLINCHED STAPLE FOR MAILING.

(Fold here and staple below address) **GSA FORM 3038 PAGE 4** (6-77)

NAME

ADDRESS

CITY AND STATE

PLACE STAMP HERE

Figure 1–2, continued

turer or distributor of each qualified item. When there is a need to procure a product from this list, bids or proposals are usually accepted from listed manufacturers or distributors. In order to get on the QPL, you have to submit a sample to the appropriate office for testing and acceptance.

SOME RULES OF THE GAME: CONTRACTOR QUALIFICATIONS FOR SELLING TO THE GOVERNMENT

In order to sell a product to the government, you must already be selling that same product to the general public. In other words, you must already be either a manufacturer of that product or a regular dealer of that product. There can be exceptions to this rule, and the reasons will become apparent as you read the following chapters. Another good reason for this rule is to keep government business at the primary levels of the marketplace by avoiding dealing with brokers.

This rule is stated in the Walsh-Healey Public Contracts Act, 41 U.S.C. 35., which in essence requires that a contractor for items costing *in excess of $10,000* per contract total must

1. be either a manufacturer of, or a regular dealer in, those items
2. pay the prevailing minimum wage

3. not work its employees in excess of the maximum daily or weekly hours
4. observe certain minimum ages of employment
5. not permit contract performance under unsanitary, hazardous, or dangerous working conditions

Penalties for violations include liquidated damages, contract termination, and a three-year debarment from government contracts. Note those key words "in excess of $10,000" in the act. If you are bidding on items to be sold to the government for less than that amount, you are exempt from the provision of the act requiring you to be either a manufacturer of, or regular dealer in, those items. Since this act is so important in government contracting, Appendix B contains a complete discussion of the provisions of the act and their interpretations.

The Davis-Bacon Act, 40 U.S.C. 276a, also provides for payment of prevailing minimum wages, as determined by the Secretary of Labor, to workers under construction contracts in excess of $2,000. Penalties similar to those in the Walsh-Healey Act are provided for violations.

The Miller Act, 40 U.S.C. 270 a-e, covers the same types of contracts as the Davis-Bacon Act, and it requires contractors to furnish performance and payment bonds for the protection of the government and all persons supplying labor and material under each contract.

The Service Contracts Act of 1965, 41 U.S.C. 351, covers all service contracts in excess of $2,500, whether advertised or negotiated, and requires the contractor to pay wages not lower than those determined by the Secretary of Labor to prevail in the area for that type of work, to provide certain fringe benefits such as hospital care or the equivalent payment, and to see that the contract is not performed under unsanitary or hazardous conditions. Violations of this act may result in disbarment, contract termination, and withholding of contract funds.

Section 503 of the Rehabilitation Act of 1973 (Public Law 93-112) requires contractors to employ qualified handicapped individuals. Another labor policy of the federal government is enforced under the Wagner-O'Day Act (41 U.S.C. 46–86c) wherein all entities of the government are generally required to purchase certain listed products and services from workshops for the blind and severely handicapped.

CONTRACTING AUTHORITY AND RESPONSIBILITY

The authority and responsibility to contract for authorized supplies and services is vested in the agency head. The agency head may establish contracting activities, and delegate to these the broad authority to manage the agency's contracting function. Contracts may be entered into and signed only on behalf of the government by contracting officers. In some agencies, a relatively small number of high level officials are designated as contracting officers solely by virtue of their positions.

Contracting officers, who may be either administrative contracting officers (ACO) or termination contracting officers (TCO), have the authority to enter into, administer, and terminate contracts, as well as to make related determinations and findings (D&F). D&Fs are a special form of written approval, required either by statute or regulation, and are a prerequisite to taking certain contractual action. The "determination" is either a conclusion or a decision supported by the "findings." The findings are statements of fact and rationale essential to support the determination, and they must cover each requirement of the statute or regulation. Each D&F must set forth enough facts and circumstances so that the determination arrived at is well justified.

Class D&Fs provide authority for a class of contracting actions, and an expiration date for these is mandatory. Expiration dates on individual D&Fs are optional.

REQUIRED SOURCES OF SUPPLIES AND SERVICES

Certain acquisitions are required to be made from, or through, government supply sources. This includes jewel bearings, public utility service, printing and related supplies, automatic data processing and telecommunications services, leased motor vehicles, strategic and critical materials (from excess GSA inventories), and helium. Ordering from the Federal Supply Schedule program, which is managed by the GSA, is mandatory. This program provides federal agencies with a simplified process for obtaining commonly used supplies and services at prices associated with volume buying.

ACQUISITION OF COMMERCIAL PRODUCTS

All agencies must acquire commercial products when these products satisfy their needs, and commercial distribution systems be used when possible. In evaluating commercial items, the government will make the same analyses as a consumer would. Factors of price, reliability, performance, and logistics support requirements, among others, will be considered in purchasing a commercially available item. Needless to say, the acquisition of certain items, such as major weapons systems, will never be purchased from a catalog.

FEDERAL SUPPLY SCHEDULE CONTRACTING

The Federal Supply Schedule program provides federal agencies with a simplified process of acquiring commonly used supplies and services in varying quantities at lower prices, while obtaining discounts associated with volume buying.

Indefinite delivery contracts (including requirements contracts) are awarded to companies to provide supplies at stated prices for a given period of time. Competitive procedures are used in awarding these contracts. The Federal Supply Schedules are publications issued by the schedule contracting office. These contain information necessary to place an order with a contractor. Each schedule identifies specific agencies in designated geographic areas that are required to use these contracts as the primary sources of supply. Although the GSA awards most of the Federal Supply Schedule contracts, it may authorize other agencies to publish schedules. The Veterans Administration, for example, awards schedule contracts for certain medical and nonperishable subsistence items.

Single-award schedules cover contracts made with one supplier, at a stated price, for delivery to a geographic area specified in the schedule. All responsible companies may submit offers in response to a solicitation for a single-award schedule contract. Each single-award schedule lists either the supplies or services covered and the prices.

Multiple-award schedules are based on negotiated contracts established with more than one supplier for the delivery of comparable commercial supplies and services. Again, all responsible firms may compete for awards, with contracts being awarded to those firms that supply the same generic types of items and services at varying prices designated for delivery within the same geographic areas. Prices under multiple-award schedule programs are based on discounts from commercial price lists after the contracting officer determines that the prices, terms, and conditions are reasonable.

The *New Item Introductory Schedule* (NIIS) is used to introduce either new or improved products into the Federal Supply System. Potential suppliers submit applications on GSA Form 1171, *Application for Presenting New Articles*. This form may be submitted through any GSA Business Service Center (BSC). The BSC screens the applications, and then forwards them to the GSA, Office of Federal Supply and Services (FSS), for review, and either subsequent acceptance or rejection. This review considers factors such as possible duplication, anticipated demand, health, safety, and legal requirements.

The *International Federal Supply Schedule* (IFSS) has been established to provide sources of supplies and services to U.S. government activities located overseas. The use of the schedule is mandatory only on the GSA. Part A of the IFSS consists of those items awarded under sealed bid procedures, while Part B lists items awarded using negotiated procedures.

In order to justify establishing a FSS, the annual business volume expected from a single regional schedule should normally exceed $20,000. If the schedule is national, the annual business volume expected should be at least $200,000 for multiple-award schedules, and $50,000 for a single-award schedule. The types of items placed on FSSs are those that are impossible to forecast definite quantity requirements for, and where the price advantages are sufficient to warrant the cost of maintaining the schedules.

PRIORITIES AND ALLOCATIONS

Under Title I of the Defense Production Act of 1950, the President is authorized to require that contracts in support of national defense be accepted and performed on a priority basis over all other contracts. The President may allocate materials and facilities in such a manner as to promote national defense. As a result, the Defense Priorities and Allocations System (DPAS) was established. This is a Department of Commerce (DOC) regulation in support of authorized national defense programs. The Office of Industrial Resource Administration (OIRA), within the DOC, is responsible for administering and enforcing this system of allocations and priorities.

HOW THE GOVERNMENT LOOKS FOR POTENTIAL SUPPLIERS

When the government begins seeking potential suppliers, the channels it uses are the *Commerce Business Daily* (*CBD*) and the Bidders' Lists (also called Solicitation Mailing Lists, or SMLs). The *CBD,* with certain exceptions to be discussed later, will list all item and service requirements that the government estimates (or knows from previous experience) will cost in excess of $10,000. Publication of requirements must occur 15 days prior to issuing a solicitation for property or services, and 30 days prior to issuing a solicitation for research and development. The Bidders' Lists contain the names of specific firms or individuals who have advised a particular buying office that they want to bid on a specific item or group of items, and who have supplied the necessary data, via Form 129, showing their ability to fulfill contracts for a particular item, service, or project. If a list is particularly long, only a segment of the list will be solicited. In this case, the regulations require that a pro-rata number of small businesses be solicited.

In virtually all cases, the purchasing office may want to receive bids. (The word *bids* here and throughout this book, is used in the collective sense, and it is used not only to cover *Invitations for Bid*, or IFBs, but *Requests for Quotation*, or RFQs, as well as *Requests for Proposal*, or RFPs, from firms not listed on the Bidders' List.) Bids are solicited through public advertisements in the *Commerce Business Daily*, and also through advertisements in trade publications and newspapers, notices in Post Offices, and contacts by Small Business Association representatives. In addition, for certain types of procurement, the buyer will often contact suppliers he or she has dealt with in the past. This occurs most frequently when the size of the procurement is small or when there is an urgent need, but not enough time to follow routine procedures.

Occasionally it isn't possible for the buyer to follow the formal advertising route. This happens when it is impossible to draft adequate specifications or describe adequately the specific item, service, or project. The purchasing office involved will then dispense with formal advertising and purchase by negotiation. Quite often, negotiated contracts cover advanced technology not widely supplied by small businesses, and may include the very complex areas of research and development connected with sophisticated computer systems, missile programs, and aircraft and weapons systems. However, negotiated procurement can be used for more routine procurements also. Unlike awards made under formal advertising, purchasing by negotiation does not mandate award to the lowest responsible bidder. In negotiated purchases, the buyer may consider factors other than price, such as who has the best design or whose bid is most advantageous to the government.

Suppliers for a planned negotiated procurement are identified through Bidders' Lists and other sources. The bid solicitation will be in the form of an RFP or an RFQ. In order to ensure a competitive procurement, several potential suppliers will be selected to receive the bid packages.

HOW TO DEAL EFFICIENTLY WITH SPECIFICATIONS AND STANDARDS

The government, especially the Department of Defense (DOD), often establishes specifications and standards for the items it buys. Additional specifications and standards cover how the items are to be packaged and packed. There is nothing mysterious about specifications. They are almost invariably based on commercial product descriptions issued by manufacturers. Quite often they are not even as demanding as those commercial product descriptions! In other words, the specs can often give you a bit of leeway when supplying certain items. Despite their appearance, specifications are actually quite easy to read and use. They can also present a better way of doing something. I know of one manufacturer who eliminated one packing step—and realized substantial cost savings—by following government specs!

Keep in mind: Specifications usually are not included in the bid package you receive. Consequently, you may have some difficulty in making bids until you build up your own specifications and standards library. One thing you'll learn is that the government is a very prolific user of most of the things it orders, and it won't be very long before the same item comes around for bid again. Any small amount of business you lose now will be more than made up for in the future.

What to Include in Your Own Specifications and Standards Library

To start off your specifications and standards library, here is a list of some basic documents you'll need:

MIL–STD–129: *Military Standard Marking for Shipment and Storage*

MIL–STD–147: *Military Standard Palletized Unit Loads*

MIL–STD–2073–1A: *DOD Material Procedures for Development and Application of Packaging Requirements*

MIL–STD–2073–2B: *DOD Requirement Codes*

FED. SPEC. NN–P–71: *Pallets, Material Handling, Wood Stringer Construction, 2 Way and 4 Way, Partial*

DGSC Form P–101: *Master Solicitation Small Purchase/ Delivery Order, Clauses, Provisions, and Instructions*

Naval Publications and Forms Center

The Naval Publications and Forms Center keeps on file and distributes, free of charge, federal and military specifications. In addition, the Center is responsible for commercial item descriptions of items used by the Defense Department. Address your requests for this material to

Commanding Officer

Naval Publications and Forms Center

5801 Tabor Avenue

Philadelphia, PA 19120

Urgent requests should be submitted by Telex (834295), Western Union (710–670–1685), or telephone (215–697–3321). Telephone requests are serviced by an automatic answering device 24 hours a day, 7 days a week. Telephone requests are limited to five line items. The material you are requesting should be described completely, both by the identifying number and by proper title. Full ordering instructions will be provided when you call in.

All urgent requests for documents that are in stock will be shipped within five working days. Your mailed requests can be in any form; however, you will probably do best using a *Specifications and Standards Requisition*, DD Form 1425 (see Figure 1–3). You will find additional copies of this form enclosed with your order shipment.

The Department of Defense Index of Standards and Specifications (DODISS)

A complete index of Specifications and Standards is available titled the *Department of Defense Index of Standards and Specifications* (DODISS). It is available in printed book form or microfiche editions, and consists of three parts: an alphabetical listing, a numerical listing, and a listing by Federal Supply Classification. The printed version of the DODISS is available from the U.S. Government Printing Office, Washington, DC 20402–9325. Subscriptions may be obtained for the alphabetical, numerical, and Federal Supply Classification listings. Each has a bimonthly supplement. The annual subscription for both the alphabetical listings and numerical listings is $90. The Federal Supply Classification is available at an annual subscription rate of $55.

The microfiche edition of the entire DODISS (all three parts) is on sale by the Director, Navy Publication and Printing Service Detachment Office, 700 Robbins Avenue, Philadelphia, PA 19111; 215–697–2000. Cost of this edition is $30. Allow four to six weeks for delivery.

Having the DODISS on hand is a great convenience if you are trying to build your library quickly. You will be able to anticipate the documents you will require, order them, and have them on hand when your bid packages arrive. This will prevent lost opportunities to bid because you don't have the "specs."

Caution: Never submit a bid based on guesswork, for this will often prove costly. Always review the specifications first.

SERVICE CONTRACTING

Contracting for services can be divided into three categories: nonpersonal services contracts, personal services contracts, and service contracts. *Nonpersonal service contracts* are those in which the person rendering the service

DD Form 1425: Specifications and Standards Requisition

DEPARTMENT OF THE NAVY
NAVAL PUBLICATIONS AND FORMS CENTER
5801 Tabor Ave.
Philadelphia, Pa. 19120
OFFICIAL BUSINESS
PENALTY FOR PRIVATE USE $300

POSTAGE AND FEES PAID
DEPARTMENT OF THE NAVY
DOD - 316

U.S.MAIL

Please self address the above label

SPECIFICATIONS AND STANDARDS REQUISITION

Send the number of copies of documents listed below which are in the DoD Index of Specifications and Standards. Limit 5 line items per request. Requests submitted on this form will speed service. Reorder forms will be enclosed with each shipment. *FORWARD REQUEST TO:* Naval Publications and Forms Center, Code 3015, 5801 Tabor Avenue, Philadelphia, PA 19120.

1. QUANTITY	2. STANDARDIZATION DOCUMENT SYMBOL	3. TITLE *(From DoD Index of Specifications and Standards)*	4. NONAVAILABILITY CODE * *(NPFC use only)*

***NONAVAILABILITY CODE EXPLANATION**

B – Item temporarily not in stock. Resubmit request in 30 days.
E – Item not identifiable as an active document listed in the DODISS. Direct questions concerning this action to NPFC, Attn: Code 1052 or call (215) 697-3321.
I – For Official Use Only. Submit request via cognizant DoD Inspection Office or Contract Administrator for certification of "need to know."
L – Industry standardization documents will not be furnished by NPFC to commercial concerns. Copies may be purchased from the appropriate Industry Association.

5. SIGNATURE OF REQUESTOR	6. DATE PREPARED *(YY, MM, DD)*	7. CLOSING DATE *(YY, MM, DD)* *(IFB, RFQ, or RFP)*

DD FORM 1425
82 MAY

Previous editions of this form are obsolete

Figure 1–3

DD Form 1425 (Back): Instructions for Completing DD Form 1425

INSTRUCTIONS FOR COMPLETING DD FORM 1425

Item 1. **Quantity**: Enter the number of publications requested.

*2. **Standardization Document Symbol**: Indicate the appropriate Standardization Document Symbol for each document requested.

3. **Title**: Enter the title of the document requested.

*4. **Nonavailability Code**: (For NPFC use only): The Naval Publications and Forms Center will enter the appropriate code to indicate the reason the requested document is unavailable.

5. **Signature of Requestor**: Self-explanatory

*6. **Date Prepared**: Enter the date prepared in the sequence of year, month, day (e.g., July 1, 1980 would be entered 80/07/01).

*7. **Closing Date**: Enter the closing date in the following format: year, month, day.

"**General Note for Personnel Processing This Report**:

Items marked with an asterisk (*) have been registered in the DoD Data Element Program."

DD FORM 1425 *(Back)*

Figure 1–3, continued

is not subject to the supervision and control usually prevailing in relationships between the government and its employees. *Personal services contracts* are those under which the person rendering the service appears to be a government employee. *Service contracts* engage the time and effort of a contractor whose primary purpose is to perform an identifiable task, rather than to furnish an end item of supply. Service contracts can also cover services performed by either professional or nonprofessional personnel, on an organizational or individual basis. Some of the areas covered by service contracts include:

1. maintenance, overhaul, repair, servicing, rehabilitation, salvage, modernization, and modification of supplies, systems, and equipment
2. routine recurring maintenance of real property
3. housekeeping and base services
4. consulting services

5. engineering and technical services
6. operation of government-owned equipment, facilities, and systems
7. communications services
8. architectural and engineering services
9. transportation and related services
10. research and development

The government's policy is to rely generally on the private sector for commercial services; however, no contract may be awarded for the performance of an inherently governmental function.

Since personal services contracts are characterized by the employer-employee relationship, and since the government is normally required to obtain its employees by direct hire under competitive appointment and other procedures required by civil service laws, these types of contracts circumvent the law, and may not be entered into unless specifically authorized by Congress. The key factor in determining whether or not a contract constitutes one of personal services is the degree of supervision involved. Sporadic supervision of one of a large number of contractor employees would be considered not relevant, while the obverse would have to be strongly taken into account.

Contracts for services are awarded through either sealed bidding or competitive proposals. The latter is used when sealed bid procedures are inappropriate. In those service contracts where the government requires the highest competence obtainable, such as evidenced by a solicitation for either a technical or management proposal resulting in technical evaluation and source selection, the small business Certificate of Competency procedures may not be applicable.

Contracts with Pinkerton Detective Agencies or similar organizations are prohibited by 5 U.S.C. 3108. This prohibition applies to contracts with organizations offering quasi-military armed forces for hire, regardless of the contract's character. A company providing guard and protective services, however, does not become a "quasi-military armed force," even though the guards are armed, and the organization provides both general investigative and detective services.

Consulting services are those services of a purely advisory nature relating to topics of agency administration and management (including program management). The scope of this type of service is all-inclusive, covering topics ranging from organizational structures, mail handling procedures, and internal policies and procedures to management information systems, acquisition strategies, and mission and program analysis. It is the policy of the government to use consulting services at all organizational levels in order to help managers achieve maximum effectiveness and economy in their operations. This objective encompasses virtually any function, however it is not permitted to contract for consulting work of a policy-making, decision-making, or managerial nature. These are normally the direct responsibility of agency officials. Additionally, it is not permitted to contract for consulting services that:

1. bypass or undermine personnel ceilings, pay limitations, or competitive employment
2. are specifically intended to aid in either influencing or enacting legislation, and
3. afford preferential treatment to former government employees

TIPS ON SELLING ARCHITECTURAL-ENGINEERING SERVICES TO THE GOVERNMENT

The government is a buyer not only of products, but also a tremendous variety of services. The main channels it uses to notify service suppliers of contracting opportunities are, again, the *CBD* and the use of solicitation mailing lists (SMLs). The *CBD* lists, by regulation, every proposed procurement over $10,000 and the names and addresses of firms to be solicited for major procurements for the benefit of subcontractors. In addition, procuring agencies are required to search continually for competent sources to do research and development work. This effort includes publishing the procuring agency's research and development requirements in the *CBD* as early as possible, but not later than 30 days prior to issuing a solicitation.

Contracting for architect-engineering (A&E) services uses a special procedure that does not involve SMLs. In accordance with the provisions of 40 U.S.C. 541–544 and 10 U.S.C. 2855, all requirements for A&E services are publicly announced. In addition, contracts for A&E services must be negotiated on the basis of demonstrated competence and qualifications for the type of professional services required, and these services must be acquired at fair and reasonable prices. Although the specifics may vary slightly depending on the agency you are dealing with, the broad procedures for selecting contractors will remain relatively constant.

Projects in the United States, its possessions, and Puerto Rico with estimated A&E fees in excess of $10,000, are announced in the *CBD*. Projects with estimated A&E fees less than $10,000 are announced on the bulletin board at the local contracting office. An announcement consists of a brief description of the scope of the services required, the location of the project, and the criteria on which the selection will be made. The announcement also advises interested firms meeting the selection criteria to submit Standard Forms (SF) 254 and 255 (see Figures 1–4 and 1–5).

SF 254, *Architect-Engineer and Related Services Questionnaire*, (Figure

STANDARD FORM (SF) **254**

Architect-Engineer and Related Services Questionnaire

Form Approved
OMB No. 3090–0028

Purpose:

The policy of the Federal Government in acquiring architectural, engineering, and related professional services is to encourage firms lawfully engaged in the practice of those professions to submit annually a statement of qualifications and performance data. Standard Form 254, "Architect-Engineer and Related Services Questionnaire" is provided for that purpose. Interested A-E firms (including new, small, and/or minority firms) should complete and file SF 254's with each Federal agency and with appropriate regional or district offices for which the A-E is qualified to perform services. The agency head for each proposed project shall evaluate these qualification resumes, together with any other performance data on file or requested by the agency, in relation to the proposed project. The SF 254 may be used as a basis for selecting firms for discussions, or for screening firms preliminary to inviting submission of additional information.

Definitions:

"Architect-engineer and related services" are those professional services associated with research, development, design and construction, alteration, or repair of real property, as well as incidental services that members of these professions and those in their employ may logically or justifiably perform, including studies, investigations, surveys, evaluations, consultations, planning, programming, conceptual designs, plans and specifications, cost estimates, inspections, shop drawing reviews, sample recommendations, preparation of operating and maintenance manuals, and other related services.

"Parent Company" is that firm, company, corporation, association or conglomerate which is the major stockholder or highest tier owner of the firm completing this questionnaire; i.e. Firm A is owned by Firm B which is, in turn, a subsidiary of Corporation C. The "parent company" of Firm A is Corporation C.
"Principals" are those individuals in a firm who possess legal responsibility for its management. They may be owners, partners, corporate officers, associates, administrators, etc.
"Discipline", as used in this questionnaire, refers to the primary technological capability of individuals in the responding firm. Possession of an academic degree, professional registration, certification, or extensive experience in a particular field of practice normally reflects an individual's primary technical discipline.
"Joint Venture" is a collaborative undertaking by two or more firms or individuals for which the participants are both jointly and individually responsible.
"Consultant", as used in this questionnaire, is a highly specialized individual or firm having significant input and responsibility for certain aspects of a project and possessing unusual or unique capabilities for assuring success of the finished work.
"Prime" refers to that firm which may be coordinating the concerted and complementary inputs of several firms, individuals or related services to produce a completed study or facility. The "prime" would normally be regarded as having full responsibility and liability for quality of performance by itself as well as by subcontractor professionals under its jurisdiction.
"Branch Office" is a satellite, or subsidiary extension, of a headquarters office of a company, regardless of any differences in name or legal structure of such a branch due to local or state laws. "Branch offices" are normally subject to the management decisions, bookkeeping, and policies of the main office.

Instructions for Filing (Numbers below correspond to numbers contained in form):

1. Type accurate and complete name of submitting firm, its address, and zip code.
   1a. Indicate whether form is being submitted in behalf of a parent firm or a branch office. (Branch office submissions should list only personnel in, and experience of, that office.)
2. Provide date the firm was established under the name shown in question 1.
3. Show date on which form is prepared. All information submitted shall be current and accurate as of this date.
4. Enter type of ownership, or legal structure, of firm (sole proprietor, partnership, corporation, joint venture, etc.)
   Check appropriate boxes indicating if firm is (a) a small business concern; (b) a small business concern owned and operated by socially and economically disadvantaged individuals; and (c) Women-owned; (See 48 CFR 19.101 and 52.219-9).
5. Branches of subsidiaries of large or parent companies, or conglomerates, should insert name and addresss of highest-tier owner.
   5a. If present firm is the successor to, or outgrowth of, one or more predecessor firms, show name(s) of former entity(ies) and the year(s) of their orginal establishment.
6. List not more than two principals from submitting firm who may be contacted by the agency receiving this form. (Different principals may be listed on forms going to another agency.) Listed principals must be empowered to speak for the firm on policy and contractual matters.
7. Beginning with the submitting office, list name, location, total number of personnel and telephone numbers for all associated or branch offices, (including any headquarters or foreign offices) which provide A-E and related services.
   7a. Show total personnel in all offices. (Should be sum of all personnel, all branches.)
8. Show total number of employees, by discipline, in submitting office. (If form is being submitted by main or headquarters office, firm should list total employees, by discipline, in all offices.) While some personnel may be qualified in several disciplines, each person should be counted only once in accord with his or her primary function. Include clerical personnel as "administrative." Write in any additional disciplines—sociologists, biologists, etc.—and number of people in each, in blank spaces.
9. Using chart (below) insert appropriate index number to indicate range of professional services fees received by submitting firm each calendar year for last five years, most recent year first. Fee summaries should be broken down to

NSN 7540–01–152–8073 254-102 STANDARD FORM 254 (Rev. 10-83)
PRESCRIBED BY GSA, FAR (48 CFR) 53.236-2(b)

Figure 1–4

STANDARD FORM (SF) 254

Architect-Engineer and Related Services Questionnaire

reflect the fees received each year for (a) work performed directly for the Federal Government (not including grant and loan projects) or as a sub to other professionals performing work directly for the Federal Government; (b) all other domestic work, U.S. and possessions, including Federally-assisted projects, and (c) all other foreign work.

Ranges of Professional Services Fees

INDEX		INDEX	
1.	Less than $100,000	5.	$1 million to $2 million
2.	$100,000 to $250,000	6.	$2 million to $5 million
3.	$250,000 to $500,000	7.	$5 million to $10 million
4.	$500,000 to $1 million	8.	$10 million or greater

10. Select and enter, in numerical sequence, **not more than thirty** (30) "Experience Profile Code" numbers from the listing (next page) which most accurately reflect submitting firm's demonstrated technical capabilities and project experience. **Carefully review list.** (It is recognized some profile codes may be part of other services or projects contained on list; firms are encouraged to select profile codes which best indicate type and scope of services provided on past projects.) For each code number, show total number of projects and gross fees (in thousands) received for profile projects performed by firm during past few years. If firm has one or more capabilities not included on list, insert same in blank spaces at end of list and show numbers in question 10 on the form. In such cases, the filled-in listing **must** accompany the complete SF 254 when submitted to the Federal agencies.
11. Using the "Experience Profile Code" numbers in the same sequence as entered in item 10, give details of at least one recent (within last five years) representative project for each code number, up to a **maximum** of thirty (30) separate projects, or portions of projects, for which firm was responsible. (Project examples may be used more than once to illustrate different services rendered on the same job. Example: a dining hall may be part of an auditorium or educational facility.) Firms which select less than thirty "profile codes" may list two or more project examples (to illustrate specialization) for each code number so long as total of all project examples does not exceed thirty (30). After each code number in question 11, show: (a) whether firm was "P," the prime professional, or "C," a consultant, or "JV," part of a joint venture on that particular project (New firms, in existence less than five (5) years may use the symbol "IE" to indicate "Individual Experience" as opposed to firm experience); (b) provide name and location of the specific project which typifies firm's (or individual's) performance under that code category; (c) give name and address of the owner of that project (if government agency indicate responsible office); (d) show the estimated construction cost (or other applicable cost) for that portion of the project for which the firm was primarily responsible. (Where no construction was involved, show approximate cost of firm's work); and (e) state year work on that particular project was, or will be, completed.
12. The completed SF 254 should be signed by a principal of the firm, preferably the chief executive officer.
13. Additional data, brochures, photos, etc. should not accompany this form unless specifically requested.

NEW FIRMS (not reorganized or recently-amalgamated firms) are eligible and encouraged to seek work from the Federal Government in connection with performance of projects for which they are qualified. Such firms are encouraged to complete and submit Standard Form 254 to appropriate agencies. Questions on the form dealing with personnel or experience may be answered by citing experience and capabilities of individuals in the firm, based on performance and responsibility while in the employ of others. In so doing, notation of this fact should be made on the form. In question 9, write in "N/A" to indicate "not applicable" for those years prior to firm's organization.

2

STANDARD FORM 254 (REV. 10-83)

Figure 1–4, continued

Experience Profile Code Numbers for use with questions 10 and 11

001 Acoustics; Noise Abatement
002 Aerial Photogrammetry
003 Agricultural Development; Grain Storage; Farm Mechanization
004 Air Pollution Control
005 Airports; Navaids; Airport Lighting; Aircraft Fueling
006 Airports; Terminals & Hangars; Freight Handling
007 Arctic Facilities
008 Auditoriums & Theatres
009 Automation; Controls; Instrumentation
010 Barracks; Dormitories
011 Bridges
012 Cemeteries *(Planning & Relocation)*
013 Chemical Processing & Storage
014 Churches; Chapels
015 Codes; Standards; Ordinances
016 Cold Storage; Refrigeration; Fast Freeze
017 Commercial Buildings *(low rise)*; Shopping Centers
018 Communications Systems; TV; Microwave
019 Computer Facilities; Computer Service
020 Conservation and Resource Management
021 Construction Management
022 Corrosion Control; Cathodic Protection; Electrolysis
023 Cost Estimating
024 Dams *(Concrete; Arch)*
025 Dams *(Earth; Rock)*; Dikes; Levees
026 Desalinization *(Process & Facilities)*
027 Dining Halls; Clubs; Restaurants
028 Ecological & Archeological Investigations
029 Educational Facilities; Classrooms
030 Electronics
031 Elevators; Escalators; People-Movers
032 Energy Conservation; New Energy Sources
033 Environmental Impact Studies, Assessments or Statements
034 Fallout Shelters; Blast-Resistant Design
035 Field Houses; Gyms; Stadiums
036 Fire Protection
037 Fisheries; Fish Ladders
038 Forestry & Forest Products
039 Garages; Vehicle Maintenance Facilities; Parking Decks
040 Gas Systems *(Propane; Natural, Etc.)*
041 Graphic Design
042 Harbors; Jetties; Piers; Ship Terminal Facilities
043 Heating; Ventilating; Air Conditioning
044 Health Systems Planning
045 Highrise; Air-Rights-Type Buildings
046 Highways; Streets; Airfield Paving; Parking Lots
047 Historical Preservation
048 Hospital & Medical Facilities
049 Hotels; Models
050 Housing *(Residential, Multi-Family; Apartments; Condominiums)*
051 Hydraulics & Pneumatics
052 Industrial Buildings; Manufacturing Plants
053 Industrial Processes; Quality Control
054 Industrial Waste Treatment
055 Interior Design; Space Planning
056 Irrigation; Drainage
057 Judicial and Courtroom Facilities
058 Laboratories; Medical Research Facilities
059 Landscape Architecture
060 Libraries; Museums; Galleries
061 Lighting *(Interiors; Display; Theatre, Etc.)*
062 Lighting *(Exteriors; Streets; Memorials; Athletic Fields, Etc.)*
063 Materials Handling Systems; Conveyors; Sorters
064 Metallurgy
065 Microclimatology; Tropical Engineering
066 Military Design Standards
067 Mining & Mineralogy
068 Missile Facilities *(Silos; Fuels; Transport)*
069 Modular Systems Design; Pre-Fabricated Structures or Components
070 Naval Architecture; Off-Shore Platforms
071 Nuclear Facilities; Nuclear Shielding
072 Office Buildings; Industrial Parks
073 Oceanographic Engineering
074 Ordnance; Munitions; Special Weapons
075 Petroleum Exploration; Refining
076 Petroleum and Fuel *(Storage and Distribution)*
077 Pipelines *(Cross-Country—Liquid & Gas)*
078 Planning *(Community, Regional, Areawide and State)*
079 Planning *(Site, Installation, and Project)*
080 Plumbing & Piping Design
081 Pneumatic Structures; Air-Support Buildings
082 Postal Facilities
083 Power Generation, Transmission, Distribution
084 Prisons & Correctional Facilities
085 Product, Machine & Equipment Design
086 Radar; Sonar; Radio & Radar Telescopes
087 Railroad; Rapid Transit
088 Recreation Facilities *(Parks, Marinas, Etc.)*
089 Rehabilitation *(Buildings; Structures; Facilities)*
090 Resource Recovery; Recycling
091 Radio Frequency Systems & Shieldings
092 Rivers; Canals; Waterways; Flood Control
093 Safety Engineering; Accident Studies; OSHA Studies
094 Security Systems; Intruder & Smoke Detection
095 Seismic Designs & Studies
096 Sewage Collection, Treatment and Disposal
097 Soils & Geologic Studies; Foundations
098 Solar Energy Utilization
099 Solid Wastes; Incineration; Land Fill
100 Special Environments; Clean Rooms, Etc.
101 Structural Design; Special Structures
102 Surveying; Platting; Mapping; Flood Plain Studies
103 Swimming Pools
104 Storm Water Handling & Facilities
105 Telephone Systems *(Rural; Mobile; Intercom, Etc.)*
106 Testing & Inspection Services
107 Traffic & Transportation Engineering
108 Towers *(Self-Supporting & Guyed Systems)*
109 Tunnels & Subways
110 Urban Renewals; Community Development
111 Utilities *(Gas & Steam)*
112 Value Analysis; Life-Cycle Costing
113 Warehouses & Depots
114 Water Resources; Hydrology; Ground Water
115 Water Supply, Treatment and Distribution
116 Wind Tunnels; Research/Testing Facilities Design
117 Zoning; Land Use Studies
201 ______
202 ______
203 ______
204 ______
205 ______

3 STANDARD FORM 254 (REV. 10-83)

Figure 1–4, continued

STANDARD FORM (SF)

254

Architect-Engineer and Related Services Questionnaire

1. Firm Name / Business Address:

1a. Submittal is for ☐ Parent Company ☐ Branch or Subsidiary Office

2. Year Present Firm Established:

3. Date Prepared:

4. Specify type of ownership *and* check below, if applicable.

A. Small Business
B. Small Disadvantaged Business
C. Woman-owned Business

5. Name of Parent Company, if any:

5a. Former Parent Company Name(s), if any, and Year(s) Established:

6. Names of not more than Two Principals to Contact: Title / Telephone
1)
2)

7. Present Offices: City / State / Telephone / No. Personnel Each Office

7a. Total Personnel ______

8. Personnel by Discipline: *(List each person only once, by primary function.)*

____ Administrative	____ Electrical Engineers	____ Oceanographers
____ Architects	____ Estimators	____ Planners: Urban/Regional
____ Chemical Engineers	____ Geologists	____ Sanitary Engineers
____ Civil Engineers	____ Hydrologists	____ Soils Engineers
____ Construction Inspectors	____ Interior Designers	____ Specification Writers
____ Draftsmen	____ Landscape Architects	____ Structural Engineers
____ Ecologists	____ Mechanical Engineers	____ Surveyors
____ Economists	____ Mining Engineers	____ Transportation Engineers

9. Summary of Professional Services Fees Received: (Insert index number)

	Last 5 Years (most recent year first)				
	19____	19____	19____	19____	19____
Direct Federal contract work, including overseas					
All other domestic work					
All other foreign work*					

*Firms interested in foreign work, but without such experience, check here: ☐.

Ranges of Professional Services Fees

INDEX
1. Less than $100,000
2. $100,000 to $250,000
3. $250,000 to $500,000
4. $500,000 to $1 million
5. $1 million to $2 million
6. $2 million to $5 million
7. $5 million to $10 million
8. $10 million or greater

4

STANDARD FORM 254 (REV 10-83)

Figure 1–4, continued

10. Profile of Firm's Project Experience, Last 5 Years

Profile Code	Number of Projects	Total Gross Fees (in thousands)	Profile Code	Number of Projects	Total Gross Fees (in thousands)	Profile Code	Number of Projects	Total Gross Fees (in thousands)
1)			11)			21)		
2)			12)			22)		
3)			13)			23)		
4)			14)			24)		
5)			15)			25)		
6)			16)			26)		
7)			17)			27)		
8)			18)			28)		
9)			19)			29)		
10)			20)			30)		

11. Project Examples, Last 5 Years

Profile Code	"P", "C", "JV", or "IE"	Project Name and Location	Owner Name and Address	Cost of Work (in thousands)	Completion Date (Actual or Estimated)
		1			
		2			
		3			
		4			
		5			
		6			
		7			

6 STANDARD FORM 254 (REV. 10-83)

Figure 1–4, continued

		8			
		9			
		10			
		11			
		12			
		13			
		14			
		15			
		16			
		17			
		18			
		19			

6

STANDARD FORM 254 (REV. 10-83)

Figure 1–4, continued

		20			
		21			
		22			
		23			
		24			
		25			
		26			
		27			
		28			
		29			
		30			

12. The foregoing is a statement of facts

Signature: ______________ Typed Name and Title: ______________

Date:

7

STANDARD FORM 254 (REV 10-83)

Figure 1–4, continued

STANDARD FORM (SF) **255**

Architect-Engineer and Related Services Questionnaire for Specific Project

Form Approved
OMB No. 3090-0029

Purpose:

This form is a supplement to the "Architect-Engineer and Related Services Questionnaire" (SF 254). Its purpose is to provide additional information regarding the qualifications of interested firms to undertake a specific Federal A-E project. Firms, or branch offices of firms, submitting this form should enclose (or already have on file with the appropriate office of the agency) a current (within the past year) and accurate copy of the SF 254 for that office.

The procurement official responsible for each proposed project may request submission of the SF 255 "Architect-Engineer and Related Services Questionnaire for Specific Project" in accord with applicable civilian and military procurement regulations and shall evaluate such submissions, as well as related information contained on the Standard Form 254, and any other performance data on file with the agency, and shall select firms for subsequent discussions leading to contract award in conformance with Public Law 92-582. This form should only be filed by an architect engineer or related services firm when requested to do so by the agency or by a public announcement. Responses should be as complete and accurate as possible, contain data relative to the specific project for which you wish to be considered, and should be provided, by the required due date, to the office specified in the request or public announcement.

This form will be used only for the specified project. Do not refer to this submittal in response to other requests or public announcements.

Definitions:

"Architect-engineer and related services" are those professional services associated with research, development, design and construction, alteration, or repair of real property, as well as incidental services that members of these professions and those in their employ may logically or justifiably perform, including studies, investigations, surveys, evaluations, consultations, planning, programming, conceptual designs, plans and specifications, cost estimates, inspections, shop drawing reviews, sample recommendations, preparation of operating and maintenance manuals, and other related services.

"Principals" are those individuals in a firm who possess legal responsibility for its management. They may be owners, partners, corporate officers, associates, administrators, etc.

"Discipline", as used in this questionnaire, refers to the primary technological capability of individuals in the responding firm. Possession of an academic degree, professional registration, certification, or extensive experience in a particular field of practice normally reflects an individual's primary technical discipline.

"Joint Venture", is a collaborative undertaking of two or more firms or individuals for which the participants are both jointly and individually responsible.

"Key Persons, Specialists, and Individual Consultants", as used in this questionnaire, refer to individuals who will have **major** project responsibility or will provide **unusual or unique** capabilities for the project under consideration.

Instructions for Filing (Numbers below correspond to numbers contained in form):

1 Give name and location of the project for which this form is being submitted.

2 Provide appropriate data from the *Commerce Business Daily* (CBD) identifying the particular project for which this form is being filed.

2a Give the date of the *Commerce Business Daily* in which the project announcement appeared, or indicate "not applicable" (N/A) if the source of the announcement is other than the CBD.

2b Indicate Agency identification or contract number as provided in the CBD announcement.

3 Show name and address of the individual or firm (or joint venture) which is submitting this form for the project.

3a List the name, title, and telephone number of that principal who will serve as the point of contact. Such an individual must be empowered to speak for the firm on policy and contractual matters and should be familiar with the programs and procedures of the agency to which this form is directed.

3b Give the address of the specific office which will have responsibility for performing the announced work.

4 Insert the number of personnel by discipline presently employed (on date of this form) at office specified in block 3b. While some personnel may be qualified in several disciplines, each person should be counted only once in accord with his or her primary function. Include clerical personnel as "administrative." Write in any additional disciplines—sociologists, biologists, etc.—and number of people in each, in blank spaces.

5 Answer only if this form is being submitted by a joint venture of two or more collaborating firms. Show the names and addresses of all individuals or organizations expected to be included as part of the joint venture and describe their particular areas of anticipated responsibility, (i.e., technical disciplines, administration, financial, sociological, environmental, etc.)

5a Indicate, by checking the appropriate box, whether this particular joint venture has worked together on other projects.

1 NSN 7540-01-152-8074 255-102 STANDARD FORM 255 (Rev. 10-83) PRESCRIBED BY GSA, FAR (48 CFR) 53.236-2(c)

Figure 1–5

STANDARD FORM (SF) **255**

Architect-Engineer and Related Services Questionnaire for Specific Project

Standard Form 255
General Services Administration,
Washington, D. C. 20405
Fed. Proc. Reg (41 CFR) 1-16 . 803
Armed Svc. Proc. Reg. 18-403

Each firm participating in the joint venture should have a Standard Form 254 on file with the contracting office receiving this form. Firms which do not have such forms on file should provide same immediately along with a notation at the top of page 1 of the form regarding their association with this joint venture submittal.

6. If respondent is not a joint venture, but intends to use outside (as opposed to in-house or permanently and formally affiliated) consultants or associates, he should provide names and addresses of all such individuals or firms, as well as their particular areas of technical/professional expertise, as it relates to this project. Existence of previous working relationships should be noted. If more than eight outside consultants or associates are anticipated, attach an additional sheet containing requested information.

7. Regardless of whether respondent is a joint venture or an independent firm, provide brief resumes of key personnel expected to participate on this project. Care should be taken to limit resumes to only those personnel and specialists who will have major project responsibilities. Each resume must include: (a) name of each key person and specialist and his or her title, (b) the project assignment or role which that person will be expected to fulfill in connection with this project, (c) the name of the firm or organization, if any, with whom that individual is presently associated, (d) years of relevant experience with present firm and other firms, (e) the highest academic degree achieved and the discipline covered (if more than one highest degree, such as two Ph.D.'s, list both), the year received and the particular technical/professional discipline which that individual will bring to the project, (f) if registered as an architect, engineer, surveyor, etc., show only the field of registration and the year that such registration was first acquired. If registered in several states, do not list states, and (g) a synopsis of experience, training, or other qualities which reflect individual's potential contribution to this project. Include such data as: familiarity with Government or agency procedures, similar type of work performed in the past, management abilities, familiarity with the geographic area, relevant foreign language capabilities, etc. Please limit synopsis of experience to directly relevant information.

8. List up to ten projects which demonstrate the firm's or joint venture's competence to perform work similar to that likely to be required on this project. The more recent such projects, the better. Prime consideration will be given to projects which illustrate respondent's capability for performing work similar to that being sought. Required information must include: (a) name and location of project, (b) brief description of type and extent of services provided for each project (submissions by joint ventures should indicate which member of the joint venture was the prime on that particular project and what role it played), (c) name and address of the owner of that project (if Government agency, indicate responsible office), (d) completion date (actual when available, otherwise estimated), (e) total construction cost of completed project (or where no construction was involved, the approximate cost of your work) and that portion of the cost of the project for which the named firm was/is responsible.

9. List only those projects which the A-E firm or joint venture, or members of the joint venture, are currently performing under direct contract with an agency or department of the Federal Government. Exclude any grant or loan projects being financed by the Federal Government but being performed under contract to other non Federal governmental entities. Information provided under each heading is similar to that requested in the preceding Item 8, except for (d) "Percent Complete." Indicate in this item the percentage of A-E work completed upon filing this form.

10. Through narrative discussion, show reason why the firm or joint venture submitting this questionnaire believes it is especially qualified to undertake the project. Information provided should include, but not be limited to, such data as: specialized equipment available for this work, any awards or recognition received by a firm or individuals for similar work, required security clearances, special approaches or concepts developed by the firm relevant to this project, etc. Respondents may say anything they wish in support of their qualifications. When appropriate, respondents may supplement this proposal with graphic material and photographs which best demonstrate design capabilities of the team proposed for this project.

11. Completed forms should be signed by the chief executive officer of the joint venture (thereby attesting to the concurrence and commitment of all members of the joint venture), or by the architect-engineer principal responsible for the conduct of the work in the event it is awarded to the organization submitting this form. Joint ventures selected for subsequent discussions regarding this project must make available a statement of participation signed by a principal of each member of the joint venture. ALL INFORMATION CONTAINED IN THE FORM SHOULD BE CURRENT AND FACTUAL.

2 STANDARD FORM 255 (Rev. 10-83)

Figure 1–5, continued

OMB Approval No. **3090-0029**

STANDARD FORM (SF) **255** Architect-Engineer Related Services for Specific Project	1. Project Name / Location for which Firm is Filing:	2a. ***Commerce Business Daily*** Announcement Date, if any:	2b. Agency Identification Number, if any:

3. Firm (or Joint-Venture) Name & Address	3a. Name, Title & Telephone Number of Principal to Contact
	3b. Address of office to perform work, if different from Item 3

4. Personnel by Discipline: (List each person only once, by primary function.)

___ Administrative	___ Electrical Engineers	___ Oceanographers	___ ________
___ Architects	___ Estimators	___ Planners: Urban/Regional	___ ________
___ Chemical Engineers	___ Geologists	___ Sanitary Engineers	___ ________
___ Civil Engineers	___ Hydrologists	___ Soils Engineers	___ ________
___ Construction Inspectors	___ Interior Designers	___ Specification Writers	___ ________
___ Draftsmen	___ Landscape Architects	___ Structural Engineers	___ ________
___ Ecologists	___ Mechanical Engineers	___ Surveyors	___ ________
___ Economists	___ Mining Engineers	___ Transportation Engineers	___ Total Personnel

5. If submittal is by JOINT-VENTURE list participating firms and outline specific areas of responsibility (including administrative, technical and financial) for each firm: (Attach SF 254 for each if not on file with Procuring Office.)

5a. Has this Joint-Venture previously worked together? ☐ yes ☐ no

3 STANDARD FORM 255 (Rev. 10-83)

Figure 1–5, continued

6. If respondent is not a joint-venture, list outside key Consultants/Associates anticipated for this project (Attach SF 254 for Consultants/Associates listed, if not already on file with the Contracting Office).

Name & Address	Specialty	Worked with Prime before (Yes or No)
1)		
2)		
3)		
4)		
5)		
6)		
7)		
8)		

4

STANDARD FORM 255 (Rev. 10-83)

Figure 1–5, continued

7. Brief resume of key persons, specialists, and individual consultants anticipated for this project.	
a. Name & Title:	a. Name & Title:
b. Project Assignment:	b. Project Assignment:
c. Name of Firm with which associated:	c. Name of Firm with which associated:
d. Years experience: With This Firm ___ With Other Firms ___	d. Years experience: With This Firm ___ With Other Firms ___
e. Education: Degree(s) / Year / Specialization	e. Education: Degree(s) / Years / Specialization
f. Active Registration: Year First Registered/Discipline	f. Active Registration: Year First Registered/Discipline
g. Other Experience and Qualifications relevant to the proposed project:	g. Other Experience and Qualifications relevant to the proposed project:

5 STANDARD FORM 255 (Rev 10-83)

Figure 1–5, continued

7. Brief resume of key persons, specialists, and individual consultants anticipated for this project.	
a. Name & Title:	a. Name & Title:
b. Project Assignment:	b. Project Assignment:
c. Name of Firm with which associated:	c. Name of Firm with which associated:
d. Years experience: With This Firm ___ With Other Firms ___	d. Years experience: With This Firm ___ With Other Firms ___
e. Education: Degree(s) / Year / Specialization	e. Education: Degree(s) / Years / Specialization
f. Active Registration: Year First Registered/Discipline	f. Active Registration: Year First Registered/Discipline
g. Other Experience and Qualifications relevant to the proposed project:	g. Other Experience and Qualifications relevant to the proposed project:

6 STANDARD FORM 255 (Rev 10-83)

Figure 1–5, continued

7. Brief resume of key persons, specialists, and individual consultants anticipated for this project.	
a. Name & Title:	a. Name & Title:
b. Project Assignment:	b Project Assignment:
c. Name of Firm with which associated:	c. Name of Firm with which associated:
d. Years experience: With This Firm ___ With Other Firms ___	d. Years experience: With This Firm ___ With Other Firms ___
e. Education: Degree(s) / Year / Specialization	e. Education: Degree(s) / Years / Specialization
f. Active Registration: Year First Registered/Discipline	f. Active Registration: Year First Registered/Discipline
g. Other Experience and Qualifications relevant to the proposed project:	g. Other Experience and Qualifications relevant to the proposed project:

7 STANDARD FORM 255 (Rev 10-83)

Figure 1–5, continued

7. Brief resume of key persons, specialists, and individual consultants anticipated for this project.	
a. Name & Title:	a. Name & Title:
b. Project Assignment:	b. Project Assignment:
c. Name of Firm with which associated:	c. Name of Firm with which associated:
d. Years experience: With This Firm ___ With Other Firms ___	d. Years experience: With This Firm ___ With Other Firms ___
e. Education: Degree(s) / Year / Specialization	e. Education: Degree(s) / Years / Specialization
f. Active Registration: Year First Registered/Discipline	f. Active Registration: Year First Registered/Discipline
g. Other Experience and Qualifications relevant to the proposed project:	g. Other Experience and Qualifications relevant to the proposed project:

8 STANDARD FORM 255 (Rev 10-83)

Figure 1–5, continued

8. Work by firm or joint-venture members which best illustrates current qualifications relevant to this project (list not more than 10 projects).

a. Project Name & Location	b. Nature of Firm's Responsibility	c. Project Owner's Name & Address	d. Completion Date (actual or estimated)	e. Estimated Cost (in thousands)	
				Entire Project	Work for which Firm was/is responsible
(1)					
(2)					
(3)					
(4)					
(5)					
(6)					
(7)					
(8)					
(9)					
(10)					

9 STANDARD FORM 255 (Rev. 10-83)

Figure 1–5, continued

9. All work by firms or joint-venture members currently being performed directly for Federal agencies.

a. Project Name & Location	b. Nature of Firm's Responsibility	c. Agency (Responsible Office) Name & Address	d. Percent complete	e. Estimated Cost (In Thousands)	
				Entire Project	Work for which firm is responsible

10

STANDARD FORM 255 (Rev. 10-83)

Figure 1–5, continued

10. Use this space to provide any additional information or description of resources (including any computer design capabilities) supporting your firm's qualifications for the proposed project.

11. The foregoing is a statement of facts.

Signature: ____________________ Typed Name and Title: ____________________

Date:

11

STANDARD FORM 255 (Rev. 10-83)

Figure 1–5, continued

1–4) provides the contracting agency with the basic information on a firm. Generally only a single copy is required, since the information is computerized. Revised SF 254s should be filed on at least an annual basis, sooner if significant changes in your status warrant doing so. The SF 255, *Architect-Engineer and Related Services Questionnaire for Specific Projects* (Figure 1–5), provides the contracting office with specialized information indicating the qualifications of a firm to handle a specific project. The SF 255 is filed only when requested by the contracting office. The *CBD* notice will indicate when this form is required.

Six Criteria for Awarding an A&E Contract

There are six criteria used in awarding an A&E contract:

1. professional qualifications necessary for satisfactory performance of the required services.
2. specialized experience and technical competence in the type of work required.
3. capacity to accomplish the work in the required time.
4. past performance on contracts with government agencies and private industry in terms of cost control, quality of work, and compliance with required schedules.
5. the firm's location in the general geographical area of the project and knowledge of the locale of the project. This applies only if there remains a sufficient number of qualified firms, in relationship to the size and scope of the project, after application of this criterion.
6. the volume of work previously awarded by the contracting agency to the firm, with the objective of promoting equitable distribution of contracts among qualified firms, including small businesses, small disadvantaged businesses, and firms that have not had prior contracts.

Architects and engineers are selected by an Architect-Engineer Selection Board. This board reviews the qualifications of firms interested in performing the work, and, where the procurement is estimated to cost more than $10,000, oral or written discussions are conducted with a minimum of three firms. An order of preference is then determined, wherein the most qualified firm is listed first, and so on. Contract negotiations are conducted with the first firm on the list. In the event that a mutually satisfactory contract cannot be arrived at, then negotiations are conducted with the second firm. This procedure continues until a contract has been negotiated.

A&E contracts are always negotiated because the law prohibits competitive bidding. When adequate data concerning the character and extent of the services required are available in advance, fixed-fee contracts are awarded. When these data are not available because of time constraints or when substantial technical development makes it impractical to define the scope of the services required, other contract types may be negotiated.

Under 10 U.S.C. 2306(d), the fee paid to an architect-engineer under a cost-plus-fixed-fee contract for the production and delivery of the designs, plans, drawings, and specifications may not exceed 6 percent of the estimated cost of the related construction project, exclusive of the amount of the fee. Some government agencies will apply this statutory limitation to the fee paid to an architect-engineer for the performance of such services under a fixed price contract.

GUIDELINES FOR PREPARING YOUR BID

Here are some of the routine factors that you will have to consider thoroughly while preparing your bid. It would be impossible to cover all of the facets that could apply to the wide range of requests generated by the government annually. You, as an expert in your particular field, can best determine what does and does not apply to the bids you will be working on. Use this list as a memory jogger when you are first getting started in government contracting.

Bid Preparation Checklist

1. Read the bid document thoroughly. What you read may seem confusing at first. This is because you're looking at something new for the first time. Spend some time familiarizing yourself with the format. Once you know what all the different clauses mean, you'll be able to skip reading them on future bids.
2. Work up the cost of the item or service on which you are bidding. Make certain that what you are pricing out matches what the requirement is.
3. Think about what your ancillary costs will be, such as any trips you would have to make to fulfill contractual requirements. (No, you can't squeeze in a side trip to St. Croix!) If you're going to need the services of outside consultants or companies, don't forget to figure out what these will cost.
4. Have you figured in your overhead and general and administrative (G&A) costs? Remember, you've got to pay the rent and the employees.
5. If you don't have all of the details or specifications, get them! Never assume anything.
6. Have you provided for freight both inbound to you and outbound to the destination?
7. Will there be any special inspection costs you may have missed? In some cases, the government will charge you for performing inspection at your facility. Look into it.

8. Now that you've worked up your numbers, check them! Better yet, have a reliable associate go over them. Two heads are always better than one. Make certain that all of the blanks have been filled in on the bid, and that you have answered all of the questions.
9. Have you covered the costs of any special packaging, marking, and packing that may be required?
10. If it is necessary to submit a sample, have you properly tagged and identified the sample? Will it get to the required destination in time?
11. Will your bid get there in time? Don't take chances if the time is tight. Use an overnight delivery service, or telegraph your response if this procedure is authorized.

Double-Check to Avoid Costly Errors

It cannot be emphasized too strongly the importance of double checking everything in your bid. The reason is simple: *The contracting officer has no authority to revise a contract price to compensate for a mistake you made!* In other words, if your bid contains an error (one that is not apparent to the government) and the bid wins, you will be bound to fulfill every one of its terms, including the error! Naturally, under these circumstances even a small mistake can be quite costly. One actual example involved a contract for strawberry jam. For some reason, the winning bidder missed the requirement specifying that each jar should contain a certain number of strawberries on an average basis. The bid submitted was based on a jam with fewer strawberries and, consequently, a lower price. When the bidder discovered the error, he asked to be released from the contract. The government declined, and the poor fellow had to supply the higher quality jam at the agreed-upon lower price. The lesson here is not that the government is unfair, but that *you have to read the bid!*

Important: Don't take a shortcut by *assuming* that you know what the government wants to buy.

Read and understand the bid and specifications before preparing your response. Don't guess about anything and don't make assumptions. If something is not clear, call the contracting officer for clarification. They will gladly clear up anything you are unsure of.

Strive to Meet-or-Beat Delivery Dates

Another point to consider when bidding is whether or not you will be able to meet the delivery or completion schedule. Missing a delivery constitutes default in the eyes of the government. The severity with which this will be treated depends on the urgency of the product or service. For most routine procurements, a grace period of 30 days is built into the system. However, this does not mean that you can deliver everything 30 days late! It means that a late delivery will not be a major concern until it is more than 30 days late. If you have been awarded a contract with a tight schedule, you are contractually obliged to comply with that schedule. One of the biggest mistakes you can make is to take delivery dates lightly! Late deliveries are noted, and they could be a factor in future award decisions. There is a standard delivery clause in most contracts (it is definitely contained in the larger procurement contracts) that permits the contracting officer to declare you in default if you fail to perform on time without good reason, or if you fail to perform any portion or provision of the contract, or if you fail to make sufficient progress on the contract so that performance becomes unlikely.

Tip: If the date in the solicitation is unattainable for any reason, you can always ask the buyer to issue a modification. If you have valid reasons, your suggestion will be well received. After all, if everyone in your industry is faced with the same problem, what else can the buyer do? Next time, the buyer will order sooner. If the problem with the date resides only with you, good luck! But don't be afraid to try for a pushed back date.

Try to beat every delivery date you have to meet. Never get in the habit of shipping late. If you had prepared your response correctly in the beginning, following this edict shouldn't be difficult. When you gain a reputation as a reliable supplier, you'll be amazed at how often you will be called on to provide things on an emergency purchase basis. This is an ideal situation, because competition will be limited, and you will probably be the sole bidder. A sole source is justified in urgent or emergency situations.

Meeting the delivery date is your responsibility. If, for example, your subcontractor gets behind schedule, you are responsible. The customer will look to you for relief, not to your subcontractor. Excusable delays are discussed further in Chapter 3.

Late delivery can be costly, and for it to be acceptable you will probably have to offer the government consideration, which most frequently translates into a contract price reduction.

Delivery dates are tracked by computer and fall under official scrutiny when they become 30 days overdue.

Note: When it first seems that a delivery date is in jeopardy, you should call the buyer or contracting officer and alert him or her of the possible slippage. Ask for a contract modification calling out a new delivery date, preferably one reflecting a contingency factor. Consideration will be required, but it is usually minimal. Quite often the buyer will ask you to make an offer of how much you're willing to give up. You can probably get away with one-quarter of one percent if you act in a businesslike and polite manner. Dealing with the government isn't really that difficult after all!

Timeliness is important in bid submittal. So is accuracy. The procedures the government uses in dealing with timeliness and mistakes are covered in Chapter 2.

Pay Attention to Packaging Requirements

Pay special attention to very specific requirements regarding special containers, preservation, packing, packaging, and labeling. These occur most frequently on military contracts. For clarification purposes packaging is defined as the first container in which the item is placed, such as peas in a can. Packing is the placing of these individual containers in a shipping container. Preservation, packaging, and packing all have three levels—A, B, and C. These will be defined in the bid, so it's not necessary to go into detail on these here. *One common mistake to avoid*: Thinking level C means *commercial*. Don't fall into that trap!

CONFORMITY: KEY TO SUCCESSFUL SALES TO THE GOVERNMENT

A low bid is certainly a key factor in winning the award. However, the bid must also *conform*. That is, the bid must meet the requirements exactly.

Imagine for a moment that you are bidding to supply a particular material, and there is a requirement that the material be supplied in a 1–fluid-ounce bottle. By a stroke of luck, you discover a manufacturer producing the exact material in a 1.5–fluid-ounce bottle. Furthermore, it costs only half as much per ounce as the next competing brand. Certain that you have the competitive advantage, you carefully fill out the bid package, submit it prior to the bid opening date, and then settle back in joyful anticipation of a big contract award. Then, to your amazement, you find out that the award went to your fiercest competitor, who, to make things worse, actually submitted a higher price than you did!

You wonder how this could have happened. The reason that the government awarded the contract to your competitor was that your competitor bid on exactly what the government wanted, and you didn't. The lesson here is that the government has a pretty good idea of what it wants, whether that idea makes sense to you or not. In this situation, you forgot the basic business rule of ''Give the customer what it wants''—which in this case was 1 fluid ounce, not 1.5 fluid ounces. Later on in this book you'll see what you should have done to avoid this problem, but for now keep in mind that one fundamental rule in selling to the government is to submit a conforming bid.

Finally, the bidder must be responsible. In addition to his financial capacity, factors such as judgment, skill, and integrity play important roles. All of these considerations will be covered in greater detail in succeeding chapters, and I mention them here briefly so as to permit you to start gaining a perspective on the overall picture.

HOW CONTRACT AWARD PROCEDURES WORK: AN OVERVIEW

The principal procurement statutes, 41 U.S.C. 253 and 10 U.S.C. 2305, require that a contract award should be made with reasonable promptness through giving written notice to the responsible bidder whose bid conforms with the invitation and will be most advantageous to the United States, price and other factors considered. Awards are normally made by mailing to the bidder an executed award document, properly referred to as a Notice of Award. This action must be taken either within the time specified for acceptance of the bid, or within any extension of the bid acceptance period.

However, an award may also be made if, after expiration of the bid acceptance period, the bidder who has submitted the most advantageous bid elects to accept the award based on that bid, provided that no other bidder would be prejudiced. In other words, if the time has expired, and you have submitted the "best" bid, you have the option of accepting the award based on the price you submitted, provided that another bidder is unable to submit a lower price. The procedure generally followed by the buyer is to contact the bidders, asking them if their bid represents their best and final offer. You now have an opportunity to raise your price if conditions have changed, lower the price if you wish to become more competitive, or just stand pat.

This situation can lead to some very interesting strategy sessions on the part of the bidders involved. The government does not have any obligation to accept any of the bids Just because an invitation for bids had been issued. All bids may be rejected by the government if this course is determined to be in the government's best interest. However, the rejection must be for cogent and compelling reasons, not based on whim. The purpose of this rule is to preserve the integrity of the competitive bidding system and to avoid the damage that could be done by disclosing prices prior to an award. This would "telegraph your punch" to your competitors, who would then have knowledge of your position and be able to react accordingly.

VALUE ENGINEERING: THE COST-EFFICIENT APPROACH TO PERFORMING MORE ECONOMICALLY

Value engineering is a formal technique wherein a contractor may either voluntarily suggest methods for performing more economically, and share in any resultant savings, or be required to establish a program designed to identify and submit to the government methods for performing more economically. The first approach is called the *incentive approach*; you, the contractor, use your own resources to develop and submit the value engineering change proposal (VECP). The contract provides for the sharing of the savings, and for payment of your allowable development and implementation costs, provided the VECP is accepted.

The second approach, and one that is mandatory under a contract, requires a specific value engineering program effort. Under this requirement, you must perform value engineering of the scope, and to the level, required by the government's program plan, and it is included as a separately priced item of work in the contract schedule. Except in architect-engineer contracts, you share in the savings realized on accepted VECPs, but at a lower percentage rate than under the voluntary approach. The objective of the mandatory value engineering program is to ensure that your value engineering effort is applied to areas of the contract offering opportunities for considerable savings, consistent with the functional requirements of the end item of the contract.

The Contractor's Financial Incentive for Participating

It is the policy for agencies to offer contractors a substantial financial incentive to develop and submit VECPs. That is to say, a fair share of the resulting savings must be offered. They must also provide contractors with objective and expeditious processing of VECPs, with a 45–day limit imposed on either its acceptance or its rejection. Value engineering incentive payments do not constitute either profit or fee for contract cost negotiation purposes, and these payments cannot be used by the government in computing statutory fee limitations under a contract.

The sharing base, to the maximum extent possible, must be extended to include affected end items under other contracts issued by either the entire agency, or any part of it. This is accomplished by determining, in writing, that to do so would be either more equitable, or would significantly increase contractor participation. In the case of contracts for items requiring an extended period of production, such as ship construction and major systems production, an agency may prescribe the sharing of future contract savings on all future contract units that are realized under contracts awarded for essentially the same item, during the sharing period. This holds true even if the scheduled date is outside of the sharing period.

Acquisition Savings

Acquisition savings may be realized on the present contract, concurrent contracts, and future contracts. The contractor is entitled to a percentage share of any net acquisition savings. Net acquisition savings occur when the total acquisition savings become greater than the total of government costs and any negative current contract savings. This may occur on the current contract, or it may not occur until reductions have been negotiated on current contracts or future contract savings are calculated. The savings may be calculated in the form of a lump-sum, or as each future contract is awarded. The contractor's profit and fee are excluded from these calculations.

Contractor shares of the savings are paid through the contract under which the VECP was accepted. On incentive contracts, the contractor's share of the current and future contract savings and collateral savings is paid as a separate firm-fixed-price contract line item on the current contract. These payments are required within three months of the date after concurrent contracts have been modified to reflect the VECP price reductions. The contractor's share of future contract savings may be paid either as subsequent contracts are awarded, or in a lump-sum at the time the VECP is accepted. The lump-sum method may be used only when the contracting officer determines that this is the best way to proceed, and the contractor agrees.

Sharings on construction contracts apply only to savings on the current contract and to collateral savings. Collateral savings are those measurable net reductions, resulting from a VECP, in the agency's overall projected costs of operation, maintenance, logistic support, or government furnished property. They are exclusive of acquisition savings, and they apply whether or not the acquisition cost changes.

The contractor's share of collateral savings is 20 percent of the estimated savings to be realized during an average year of use, but it cannot exceed the contract's firm-fixed-price, target price, target cost, or estimated cost at the time the VECP was accepted; or $100,000, whichever is greater.

The message of this section is quite clear: The government is making every effort to reduce cost and improve efficiency, and if you help in achieving this goal, you will be rewarded for it.

EXTRAORDINARY CONTRACTUAL ACTION: HOW THE GOVERNMENT CAN ACT TO AID NATIONAL DEFENSE

Public Law 93–155 (50 U.S.C. 1431–1435) empowers the President to authorize agencies exercising functions in connection with the national defense to enter into, amend, and modify contracts, without regard to other provisions of law related to contracts, whenever the President considers such actions necessary in order to aid national defense. Executive Order 10789, dated November 14, 1958, authorizes the heads of major agencies to exercise the authority conveyed by the act.

The act may not be used in a manner that encourages carelessness and laxity, or be relied upon when other adequate legal authority exists within the agency. Annual reports of actions taken on requests for relief, including indemnity, are required to be made to Congress by March 15 of each year. Certain kinds of relief previously available only under this act, such as recision or reformation of mutual mistake, are now available under the Contract Disputes Act of 1978. Competent advice should be sought in order to determine whether or not relief from a specific situation may be obtained through application of this extraordinary emergency authority granted to the President and authorized to agency heads. The act does not permit the use of other than standard contracting procedures and making contracts that are against the law. Additionally, the act neither permits the waiving of any bid bond, nor providing other than full and open competition for the award of contracts for supplies and services. Also, authority under the act does not permit the omission of contract clauses against contingent fees and the examination of records, and the clauses covering the Walsh-Healey Act, equal opportunity, and the assignment of claims.

Contract amendments and modifications cannot be made under the act's authority unless it is determined that doing so would either facilitate the national defense, or it is determined that other legal authority within the agency concerned is deemed to be either lacking or inadequate.

The agencies are authorized to form contract adjustment boards with the authority to approve, authorize, and direct appropriate action under the act, and to make all determinations and findings. The decisions of these boards are not subject to appeal; however, the boards may reconsider, modify, correct, and reverse their previous decisions.

How to Seek an Adjustment for a Loss Incurred Due to Government Action

Losses incurred under a contract are not considered sufficient basis for exercising the authority conferred by the act. However, when an actual or threatened loss under a defense contract will either jeopardize or impair your productive ability, and the contractor's performance on present and future contracts is vital to the national defense, the contract may be amended without consideration, but only to the extent necessary to avoid impairment of your productive ability.

When you suffer a loss (not considered to be merely a reduction in profits) because of government action, the character of the action is used to determine whether or not any adjustment will be made in the contract, and its extent. The understanding here is that the government's action, while it may not be creating any additional liability, does require, in the interests of fairness, an appropriate adjustment.

Under certain circumstances, informal commitments may be formalized in order to permit payment to persons who have taken action without a formal contract. By way of example, this could occur when a person, responding to an agency official's written or oral instruction, and relying in good faith upon the official's apparent authority to issue them, has either furnished or arranged to furnish supplies to an agency, contractor, or subcontractor without formal contractual coverage. Formalizing commitments under these circumstances would normally facilitate the national defense by assuring these persons that they will be treated fairly and paid expeditiously.

Your request for contract adjustment under the act must be submitted in duplicate to either the contracting officer or an authorized representative. The request, normally in letter form, should state as a minimum:

1. the precise adjustment requested
2. the essential facts, summarized chronologically, in narrative form
3. your conclusions based on these facts, and when you considered yourself entitled to adjustment

Other information should be included, such as whether or not all obligations under the contract have been discharged, final payment has been made, and to whom the payment is to be either assigned or transferred to, if this is applicable. It must be also stated if adjustment is to be sought, or has been sought, from the General Accounting Office or any other part of the government, or if adjustment will be sought in the future.

Amendments without consideration may be requested to be supported by facts and evidence to the extent necessary to support a finding. The types of information requested will be based on whether or not essentiality to the national defense is a factor in seeking the amendment. Similar information will be requested when it is necessary to formalize informal commitments and when correcting mistakes.

How to Request Indemnification for Unusually Hazardous Risks

Contractor requests for the indemnification clause to cover either unusually hazardous or nuclear risks should be submitted to the contracting officer along with the following information:

1. the contract on which the clause is requested
2. a statement of the type of risk, the extent of the risk, and how you will be exposed to it
3. a statement, by a company official having contractual authority, of the types of insurance presently in effect, and the specific risks to be insured against, plus the coverage to be extended to persons and property

Review of a request is made by the contracting officer with the assistance of legal counsel, and approval of the request is made by a Memorandum of Decision. The clause is then inserted in the contract. Prompt notice of either approval or denial of a request is required.

PROTECTION OF PRIVACY AND FREEDOM OF INFORMATION

The *Privacy Act of 1974*, (5 U.S.C. 552a), requires that when an agency contracts for the design, development, or operation of a system of records on individuals, and these records are judged necessary to accomplish the agency's function, then the agency must apply the requirements of the act to you, the contractor, and your employees working on the contract. Criminal penalties for violation are provided by the act. The types of information protected by the act include, but are not limited to, education, financial transactions, medical history, criminal background, and employment history. This applies to any data identified by the employee's name, employee's number, or other symbol, including voice print, fingerprint, and photograph. Any agency, acting within the limits of its authority, and failing to comply with the act's provisions, is open to civil liability.

The Freedom of Information Act (5 U.S.C. 552) provides that information is to be made available to the public by publication in the *Federal Register*, by providing an opportunity to read and copy records at convenient locations, or, upon request, by providing a copy of a reasonably described record. The act imposes strict time standards for agency response and exempting certain records from public disclosure. Examples of exempted records include all classified information, trade secrets, and confidential commercial and financial information. Also included is interagency and intra-agency memoranda, as well as personal and medical information pertaining to an individual.

PAYMENT IN LOCAL FOREIGN CURRENCY

Contracts entered into and performed outside of the United States with local foreign firms will be priced and paid for in local foreign currency, unless an international agreement provides for payment in either U.S. dollars, or the contracting officer determines the use of local foreign currency to be inequitable or inappropriate.

COST ACCOUNTING STANDARDS

Public Law 91–379 (50 U.S.C. App. 2168) requires that certain national defense contractors and subcontractors comply with the Cost Accounting Standards (CAS) published by the Cost Accounting Standards Board (CASB), and disclose, in writing, their cost accounting practices. These practices must be followed consistently. The obligation to comply with the CAS is extended to certain nondefense contractors as a matter of policy. However, either the submission or the revision of a Disclosure Statement is not required for a nondefense contract. Nevertheless, if a Disclosure Statement has been submitted in connection with a CAS-covered defense contract, the contractor must also comply with the disclosed cost accounting practices under nondefense CAS-covered contracts as well.

Copies of the CASB standards and regulations are printed in Title 4 of the *Code of Federal Regulations*. These may be obtained either by writing the U.S. Government Printing Office, Washington, DC 20402, or by calling the USGPO Washington, DC ordering desk at 202–783–3238.

Disclosure Statement

A Disclosure Statement is a written description of a contractor's cost accounting practices and procedures in a format prescribed by the CASB. The currently used form is CASB-DS–1. The submission of either a new or revised Disclosure Statement is not required from any nondefense contractor and small business concern. Disclosure Statements will be required, however, of any contractor selected to receive a negotiated contract of $10 million or more having CAS provisions, and from any company that has received $10 million or more in CAS-covered contracts in its most recent cost accounting period. This amount would include both prime and subcontracts.

Foreign contractors and subcontractors, in lieu of filing Form CASB-DS–1, may make disclosures on forms prescribed by an agency of their government, provided the forms meet the requirements of Public Law 91–379. Alternative forms have been approved for the countries of Canada and the Federal Republic of Germany.

15 Contracts Exempt from CAS Standards

Contracts exempt from CAS requirements are

1. sealed bid contracts
2. negotiated contracts and subcontracts not in excess of $100,000
3. contracts and subcontracts with small businesses
4. contracts and subcontracts with foreign governments, their agents, and instrumentalities, and any contract or subcontract awarded to a foreign concern
5. contracts and subcontracts in which the price is set by law or regulation
6. contracts in which the price is based on established catalog and market prices of commercial items that are sold in substantial quantities to the general public

7. contracts and subcontracts of $500,000 or less, provided the company is not currently performing any national defense CAS-covered contracts
8. nondefense contracts on which an award is made based on adequate price competition
9. nondefense contracts and subcontracts awarded to a company that is not currently performing any CAS-covered national defense contracts
10. contracts and subcontracts with educational institutions, other than those to be performed by Federally Funded Research and Development Centers (FFRDC)
11. contracts awarded to labor surplus area companies, pursuant to a labor surplus area set-aside
12. contracts and subcontracts awarded to a United Kingdom contractor for performance substantially within the United Kingdom, provided that the contractor has filed Form CASB–DS–1 with the United Kingdom Ministry of Defence (If the contractor is required to adhere to *U.K. Government Accounting Conventions*, the disclosed statements must be in accordance with those conventions.)
13. subcontracts under the NATO PHM Ship program that will be performed outside of the United States by a foreign concern
14. contracts and subcontracts to be performed entirely outside of the United States, its territories, and possessions
15. firm-fixed-price contracts and subcontracts that are awarded without submission of any cost data, provided that the failure to submit these data is not attributable to a waiver of the requirement for certified cost and pricing data

In some instances, compliance with all of the CAS principles may not be feasible, and if the contracting officer determines that it is not practical to obtain the materials, supplies, and services from another source, a waiver may be authorized. Full justification for the waiver will be required.

INDEX - CHAPTER 1

2

GUIDELINES ON BIDDING AND NEGOTIATING A CONTRACT AWARD

This chapter presents an overview of the government buying process from the time the need is advertised through the actual contracting phase. Some of the topics covered include negotiations, preaward surveys, small purchases, and what you can do if you make a mistake on your bid. The government's method of deciding on a contract award is also discussed.

FORMAL ADVERTISING: THE GOVERNMENT'S PREFERRED METHOD FOR MAKING PURCHASES

The federal government's preferred method of procurement is through formal advertising. This means contracting by competitive bids and awards, as opposed to contracting through negotiation. Let's take a look at how the formal advertising method operates.

Five Standards for Ensuring Fair and Complete Formal Advertising

The standards that have been established for formal advertising are fair and complete, and they leave nothing to arbitrary action. These standards are

1. There must be enough time before the purchase to allow all bidders time to prepare their bids.

2. The specifications must be descriptive enough to permit full and free competition. There cannot be full and free competition unless all of the bidders know exactly what they are bidding on.
3. There must be a public opening of bids.
4. The award must be made with reasonableness by giving written notice.
5. The award must be made to the responsible bidder whose bid conforms with the requirement and will be the most advantageous to the United States, price and other factors considered.

Title 10 U.S.C. 2305 contains the most significant and far-reaching requirements concerning formal advertising for defense contracts. Title 10, sections 2301–2314, is the Armed Services Procurement Act of 1947, which has been codified into sections. Section 2305 provides for sufficient time for submittal of bids prior to purchase or contract, clarity and descriptiveness of specifications and attachments, and public opening of bids.

Two Main Differences Between Formal Advertising and Negotiation

In formal advertising, there is a prescribed public opening at which all bids are read and every bidder has the opportunity to learn exactly what everyone else has bid. In negotiation, there is no public opening, bargaining is permitted, and the offeror is usually afforded the opportunity to revise a bid before award of a contract. Under formal advertising, the award must be made to the lowest responsible, conforming bidder. Unless you bid on what was asked for, you will not receive the award, regardless of price. In negotiation, factors other than price may be considered in making an award. Bargaining in negotiation consists of discussion, persuasion, the alteration of initial assumptions and positions, and give-and-take, which may apply to price, schedule, technical requirements, type of contract, and to other terms of a proposed contract.

Note: Do not assume that negotiated procurements are not competitive. Whether a contract is negotiated or formally advertised, proposals must be sought from as many qualified sources of supply as deemed necessary by the contracting officer. This assures full and free competition, thereby obtaining for the government the most advantageous contract.

Four Points to Remember About Formal Advertising

There are four points to remember about formal advertising:

1. The *Commerce Business Daily* (*CBD*) is the primary source of advertising requirements; mailing lists and trade publications are also used. Newspapers and magazines may be used on occasion.

2. In all cases, the advertisement must be free of cost to the government. Paid advertisements are not permitted.
3. Oral solicitation may be used, especially with regard to perishables. However, reasonable publicity must be used so that all available competition is generated.
4. A telegraphic solicitation may be used when, in the judgment of the contracting officer, the date for bid opening will not allow bidders sufficient time to prepare and submit bids on prescribed forms, or when prices are subject to frequent changes.

Two Rules of Thumb on Advertising Sufficiency

The sufficiency of the advertising is of great concern, and it basically depends on the type of item or service to be procured. The rules of thumb on sufficiency require:

- That there be sufficient circulation of the need, and
- That adequate time be allowed to prepare and submit bids by prospective contractors.

Advertising will be considered insufficient where a procurement is intentionally restricted either to a geographic area or to a group of suppliers to whom the procuring agency desires to award the contract. However, since agencies have some discretion in determining the extent of competition that may be required, some intentional restrictions may and have been held valid. Where a prospective bidder is not solicited because of inadvertence or oversight by the contracting officer, the general rule is that such failure is not sufficient reason to require rejection of all bids or cancellation of an award and subsequent readvertisement.

Finally, while the current principal procurement statutes provide that advertisements for contracts must be made in sufficient time before the award date, none of the statutes define the term *sufficient*. It is left in the hands of the contracting office to make certain that adequate preparation time for bids is allowed. Unfortunately, this time can often seem uncomfortably short when there is a lot of work ahead to finish a bid, and the deadline is approaching.

The Invitation for Bids: How the Government Sets the Terms for Contract Formation

The Invitation for Bids (IFB) is not legally an offer. Rather, it is a standard form setting forth the terms and conditions under which the government is willing to contract. In essence, it is a request for those interested in entering the contract to submit sealed offers to the contracting agency by a certain date. Legally, the IFB has the same status as an advertisement in a newspaper, where a potential seller solicits offers for the items he or she is trying to sell. A response to the ad is an offer, which must in turn be accepted or rejected by the person who placed the ad.

In government contracting, an acceptance of a bid conforming with the material requirements and terms of the invitation for bids consummates a contract. This means that in formally advertised contracts the government, as offeree, dictates the terms for contract formation. This departure from the normal contract formation procedures with regard to offer and acceptance is necessitated by the statutory limits placed upon the means by which agents of the government may contract. These limits place restrictions on the bargaining procedure. In effect, the procedure is designed to give all prospective bidders an equal opportunity to do business with the government, and in return secure the best possible bargain for the public. All bidders must have the same opportunity to bid in the same manner, at the same time, on the same contract, and have their bids evaluated on the same predetermined basis.

The IFB describes the terms upon which the government will contract, and invites bids for the supplies or services in accordance with those conditions. Obviously, the IFB can promote or restrain competition to the extent of how well the government's need is described. If delineated too narrowly, competition is restrained. Likewise, competition will be impeded if the terms for contracting are too burdensome or unduly strict.

Restrictions in the IFB can also consist of many competition limiting conditions other than those just mentioned. Some of these restrictions are either associated with the goals of the appropriation act under which the contract is made, or are provided for by the general procurement authority involved. A good example of this is the need for the standardization of parts. Still other restrictive conditions are imposed by the statutes for public policy reasons. A few examples are the Walsh-Healey Act, the Davis-Bacon Act, and the Small Business Act.

Of equal concern are restrictions imposed upon competition through administrative discretion, especially those involving the manner in which the goods or services being procured are described in the specifications. Specifications will be discussed in detail in Chapter 4.

Three Restrictions on Competition That Can Occur When Specifications Are Lacking

There are three occasions when specifications may be lacking. The First is when the government is unable to draft a set of adequate purchase specifications, or when prebidding restrictions are involved. The use of the "brand name or equal" description is permissible where the particular features of a product are considered essential by the government. However, the salient characteristics of the product must be set forth so that bidders may offer an "or equal" item if so provided for in the bid. The "or equal" language in the bid may be eliminated if it is decided that only the named brand will satisfy the government's minimum needs. In such cases, negotiation should be used instead of formal advertising to place the contract.

A second restriction upon competition that may be imposed by the specifications involves the use of a Qualified Products List (QPL). Essentially, the use of a QPL limits consideration for contract award to bidders having their products either listed on the QPL or qualified for listing prior to bid opening.

The third generally permissible method for limiting competition by specifications is by two-step formal advertising. This procedure was designed to permit wider use of advertising in procurements that were previously negotiated. The first step of this procedure involves submittal of technical proposals by offerors for evaluation by the procuring agency. After the technical evaluation, those offerors determined to be qualified are solicited for price proposals in the customary advertised manner, with award being made to the low bidder under the second step. No other bidders may bid during the second step, and each bidder may bid only on his or her own technical proposals previously found acceptable.

BUYING THROUGH NEGOTIATION

Formal advertising is the preferred way of buying, for as a rule it reaps the advantages of a competitive marketplace. If competition either does not exist, or if circumstances are not normal, then there are no grounds for the government to pursue this preference. In cases where advertising has not proved adequate, the government must resort to negotiation.

The word *negotiate* means to carry on business. Negotiating is the process of discussing or bargaining with a view toward reaching an agreement, and in contracting, negotiation is any method of contracting without formal advertising. Negotiation implies a series of offers and counter offers until a mutually satisfactory agreement is concluded by the parties. Negotiation is used most frequently

- when there is insufficient evidence of a competitive price situation
- when urgency requires immediate initiation of the procurement, and
- when public policy considerations outweigh the benefits to be gained through advertising

In negotiated purchases the contracting officer, by means of his or her authority to negotiate, has the flexibility to deal with a variety of circumstances.

How the Contracting Officer Solicits Supply Sources: Two Types of Formal Requests

Prior to actually negotiating the contract, the contracting officer must solicit the maximum possible sources of supply to assure full and free competition. Usually this is done in writing either by means of a Request for Proposal (RFP) or Request for Quotation (RFQ). Both are similar in form to the Invitation for Bid (IFB). However, the RFQ differs from the RFP in that the response does not constitute an offer. It is informational in character, and it may be used when the government does not intend to award a contract on the basis of the solicitation, but wishes to obtain price, delivery, and market information for planning purposes. A principal difference among the RFP, RFQ, and IFB may be the type of contract offered to suppliers. Formal advertising employs the fixed-price contract, while negotiated contracts may be any type except cost-plus-a-percentage-of-cost. The RFP, like the IFB, should set forth all significant matters that affect the opportunity of suppliers to compete on an equal basis. These would include delivery schedules, type of contract, closing date, and special evaluation factors.

After the Initial Proposal: How the Negotiating Discussions Begin

The contracting officer is required, after receipt of initial proposals, to conduct written or oral discussions with all responsible offerors who submit proposals within a competitive range. This negotiation, depending on the complexity of the item, can range from a simple "Is this your final and best offer?" to elaborate and lengthy talks, supported by cost and pricing data, and accompanied by numerous experts in the disciplines being discussed.

Remember: All offers received late, although they may be most competitive, are not eligible for consideration.

In certain instances, discussions after receipt of the initial proposal are not required, and award may be made on the basis of the initial proposal. These occur when

- the aggregate amount of the procurement does not exceed $10,000
- when procurement is for supplies for which prices or rates are fixed either by law or regulation
- when time for delivery will not permit discussion
- when the procurement represents the set-aside portion for either small business or labor surplus area concerns
- when the procurement is for a product where it can be shown that acceptance of the initial proposal, based on previous history and experience, would result in a fair and reasonable price to the government

In negotiated procurement for a fixed-price contract, the failure to conduct discussions may result in a rather incongruous situation, since negotiation is generally used when formal advertising is neither practicable nor feasible. However, the procedure closely resembles advertising if the award is made without either oral or written discussions with the offerors.

The question of what information the contracting officer must take into consideration when deciding whether or not to conduct discussions can be a weighty one. The general rule is that the decision to make an award on the basis of original proposals is discretionary in nature. However, all facts have to be considered before a decision can be made as to the reasonableness of the price. In one situation, a contracting officer made an award decision based on the fact that the competition demonstrated, through their offers, that the award price was fair and reasonable. However, prior to actual award, one offeror reduced his offer by 15 percent of the intended contract price. The Comptroller General, in his decision, advised that although the late price modification could not be considered as a basis for award, it should have been considered by the contracting officer in deciding whether or not the initial proposals reflected a fair and reasonable price. If this were done, then negotiations would not have been necessary with all those within the certain competitive range.

Note: Under appropriate circumstances, an award based on the initial proposal may be made to other than the lowest priced offer. This would be the case where the RFP calls for the selection to be made in terms of the most favorable price/technical quality ratio.

Finally, negotiations must be conducted with all competitive offerors if, for any reason, any one of them is permitted to make a substantive modification after initial proposals have been submitted.

As in advertised purchases, the requirements for adequate publicity, proper proposal preparation time, nonrestrictiveness of the specifications, clear and plain solicitation, and justified use of the Qualified Offerors List apply. The Qualified Offerors List performs the same function as the QPL, but it relates to the technical ability of the offeror, as opposed to just the listing of products. Unlike advertised procurements, there is no public opening of bids on negotiated purchases.

The Competitive Range: How Price and Technical Factors Affect the Evaluation Process

The competitive range encompasses both price and technical considerations, and either factor can determine whether or not an offeror's proposal can be included in the final evaluation process. However, exclusion from the competitive range is not justified merely because a proposal is technically inferior. Negotiations have to be conducted in this case, unless the offeror's proposal is so technically inferior that meaningful negotiations are considered an impossibility.

Key Point: The competitive range has to include all meaningful proposals that have a reasonable chance of being selected for award. The contracting officer possesses a broad range of discretion when dealing with negotiated purchases, and this applies to selecting what he or she considers the competitive range to be. However, the contracting officer must be certain that both the proper technical and price evaluations are made before forming a decision.

If it is necessary for the government to rectify discrepancies in the RFP or RFQ, the appropriate amendment must be furnished to all offerors on a timely basis.

Once the proposal has been included in the competitive range, it may not be dropped unless either a meaningful opportunity to submit a revised proposal has been allowed, or if the sole reason for being included in the competitive range was because of a favorable interpretation of an ambiguity or omission, and it later develops that the offeror should never have been included at all.

Keep in Mind: Responsiveness does not play the same role in negotiated purchases as it does in purchases conducted by formal advertising. The flexibility of negotiations allows the supplier to change his or her initial proposal, both in the area of price and technical consideration. This serves the basic policy of encouraging as much competition as possible in negotiated contracts. In other words, lack of responsiveness may be clarified in the negotiation process, which may serve to bring the proposals within the terms of the specifications, provided they are considered to be within the competitive range from the standpoint of both price and technical considerations.

Information Restrictions: What Cannot Be Revealed to Offerors

There are certain restrictions on the information either the contracting officer or negotiator can reveal to offerors in the course of negotiations. After receipt of initial proposals, neither information contained in any proposal, nor information regarding the number or identity of bidders can be made available. The reason for this is obvious: If this information was revealed, it could offer a competitive advantage to any of the bidders. Auction techniques, such as advising bidders of their price relationship with others, is obviously not allowed. However, this does not bar the government from telling an offeror that his or her price is too high, but this statement cannot be made in context with other offers. However, if one offeror's price is inadvertently disclosed to another offeror, it may be necessary for the offeror to whom the price was disclosed to have his or her continued participation be conditioned upon a similar disclosure of price to the other bidder.

Discussions may be conducted with each offeror in succession. However, the exact nature of what is discussed depends on the subject of the procurement. Most certainly the discussion will cover any deficiencies or ambiguities in the offer, and the offeror will be given an opportunity to respond to the points raised by the government. However, this cannot be extended to the point where "technical transfusion" occurs; that is, there should be no disclosure to any offeror of a competitor's solution to a technical problem. Some agencies, such as NASA for cost-type contracts and the DOD for research and development contracts, will limit their discussions with offerors to clarifications only. Discussions of deficiencies are not included. In this situation, after the discussion and proposal revision phase, a prospective contractor is selected, and the definitive contract is then discussed only with that offeror.

At the conclusion of discussions a final common cutoff date is established, and all remaining participants are so notified. This notification will include notice that discussions have been concluded and that offerors are being given an opportunity to submit a best and final offer.

Cost/Technical Tradeoffs: What to Expect

In a negotiated procurement, the contracting officer can make certain cost/technical tradeoffs. The extent to which one may be sacrificed for the other is ruled by prearranged standards that have been established for that particular procurement. These standards assign a weight to each factor to be judged, and these will be called out in the initial request distributed to interested bidders. When an agency determines that two competing proposals are technically equal in their merits, then price or cost becomes the determining factor in making an award.

Price Analysis. The contracting agency will make a price evaluation of its own as part of the evaluation process. This is done to compensate for the inherent restrictions imposed by negotiation on the competitive process. This evaluation, then, serves as a measure of the fairness of the price reached in the procedure. Price analysis is performed in all cases where cost analysis is not required. Some of the methods used in price analysis consist of comparing the submitted price quotations either with each other or with prior quotations and contract prices for the same or similar items. Price may also be compared with published competitive price lists and market prices. Independent government estimates and rough mathematical formulas may also be used, such as dollars per pound or per horsepower.

Cost Analysis. Cost analysis involves a more detailed review of the offeror's proposal, and it is used when the government has less assurance of a fair and reasonable price. This analysis consists of the review and evaluation of both the offeror's cost and pricing data as well as the judgmental factors applied in projecting from the data to the estimated costs. The following list covers the cost factors and pricing data that will be verified by the government:

- the necessity of certain costs
- the reasonableness of the amounts allocated against cost elements
- the allowances for contingencies
- the basis for and the applicability of the indirect costs to be allocated against the contract
- the actual costs previously incurred by the offeror
- the prior estimates the offeror has made on the same or similar items

The impact of future cost trends may also be taken into account, but care will be taken not to project the effect of any past inefficiencies into the future.

The Impact of the Truth in Negotiations Act on Cost and Pricing Data

As part of the process of assuring that the government will receive a fair shake for its money, Congress enacted, in 1962, Public Law 87–653, commonly referred to as the Truth in Negotiations Act. The principal effect of the act was to require cost and pricing data to be furnished by the prospective contractors prior to agreement upon contract prices. Now codified as 10 U.S.C. 2306(f), the act requires ''accurate, complete, and current'' data, and certification that the data furnished meets those requirements. Further, the contractor must agree to a contract provision giving the government the right to unilaterally reduce the price by the amount it was increased as a result of defective cost and pricing data.

This act was initially applicable only to military contracts only, but it has now been applied to all contracts, where applicable, by regulation. In one court decision, a contract price reduction was upheld when a contractor failed to disclose lower vendor quotes, even though the contract price was not negotiated on those quotes.

Remember: honesty is the policy in government contracting.

When to Submit Cost and Pricing Data. Cost and pricing data must be submitted when the negotiated contract cost is estimated to exceed $100,000. It also applies to all contract amendments estimated to exceed $100,000, whether cost and pricing data were required initially or not.

In addition to furnishing his or her own data, the prime contractor is required to obtain cost or pricing data from subcontractors if the price of the subcontract is to exceed $100,000. This applies to each tier of subcontractor, provided the $100,000 figure is to be exceeded at any level of subcontracting.

Three Major Exceptions to the Act. There are three major exceptions to the requirement for cost and pricing data:

1. Data are not required when the negotiated price is based on adequate price competition
2. Data are not required on catalog or market prices for substantially the same items sold to the general public.

Under these two exceptions a price analysis, and not a cost analysis, normally will be made. However, the second exception is discretionary, and the contracting officer may require these data at his or her option.

3. Cost and pricing data are not required for a negotiated price based on prices set by law or regulation. In addition, the head of the procuring agency may waive the requirement for cost or pricing data in exceptional cases.

Determining if Pricing Data Are Reasonably Available to a Bidder. Cost and pricing data, by definition, refer to that portion of the bidder's submittal that is factual. Such data include all facts reasonably available to the bidder, up to the time of agreement, that might reasonably be expected to have an impact on the price negotiation. The facts on which a prospective contractor bases a judgment constitute data, but the judgment is not part of the cost or pricing data. Note the use of the word *reasonable* in describing the data. If data are not reasonably available to a contractor, they may not be used in the future to support a defective price adjustment. Whether or not certain data significantly impacted a final negotiated contract price must be weighed by the accumulated data, rather than individually.

The burden of proving price increases caused by defective pricing data rests with the government. On the other hand, if the situation involves a contract price reduction, and the contractor refuses to agree to it, then the government must establish that the data submitted by the contractor was inaccurate, incomplete, and not current, and that this was the cause of the increased price, as well as what dollar amount resulted from the defective data. When appropriate, a clause entitled *price reduction for defective cost or pricing data* will be included in the contract which supports the situation just discussed.

SIX REQUIREMENTS OF A RESPONSIBLE BIDDER

Don't confuse the words "responsible" and "responsive." Responsibleness refers to the bidder's capacity to perform. Responsiveness refers only to the bidder's willingness to perform.

The term "responsible bidder" refers to more than just the financial capacity of the bidder. Factors such as judgment, skill, and integrity play important roles. By regulation, a bidder is responsible when he or she meets all of the following requirements:

1. is a construction contractor, or, if the contract calls for supplies, is a manufacturer or regular dealer in the items required
2. has adequate financial resources or the ability to acquire them
3. has the necessary experience, organization, and technical qualifications, and has the facilities to perform the contract, or can acquire the facilities
4. is able to meet the performance or delivery schedule
5. has a satisfactory record of performance, integrity, judgment, and skills
6. is otherwise qualified and eligible to receive an award under applicable laws and regulations

Where a bid is rejected because the prospective contractor is found to be irresponsible, the contracting officer is required to file a report of nonresponsibility, which is supported by the necessary documents and surveys.

REGULATIONS GOVERNING LATE, MODIFIED, AND WITHDRAWN BIDS

Late Bids

Let's take an expanded view and see what the regulations provide regarding late receipt of bids.

No bid received at the office designated in the solicitation after the exact time specified for receipt will be considered unless it is received before award is made *and* either:

(A) it was sent by registered or certified mail not later than 5 calendar days before the bid receipt of bid date specified; that is, mailed by the fifteenth if due on the twentieth.

(B) it was sent by mail, or telegram if authorized, and it is determined by the government that the late receipt was due solely to mishandling by the government after receipt at the government installation.

The Time Frame for Modifying or Withdrawing Bids

Modifications and withdrawals of bids are subject to the same conditions as late bids. A bid may also be withdrawn in person by either the bidder or his authorized representative, provided his or her identity is made known, and a receipt is signed for the bid. The withdrawal must be made prior to the time set for opening of the bids.

The only acceptable evidence to establish timeliness of these actions is as follows:

1. the date of mailing by either registered or certified mail is the U.S. Postal Service postmark on the wrapper or the original receipt from the U.S. Postal service. If neither postmark shows a legible date, the bid, modification, or withdrawal shall be deemed to have been mailed late.
2. Notwithstanding the above, a late modification of an otherwise successful bid making the terms more favorable to the government will be considered at any time it is received and may be accepted.

How the Firm Bid Rule Determines Bid Withdrawal

The firm bid rule sets the guidelines for when you are permitted to withdraw your bid, whether or not it is a result of an error or any other reason. The rule is that bids, in response to an IFB, may not be withdrawn after the bids have been opened. This rule is contrary to the rule of commercial contract law, which allows revocation or withdrawal of an offer any time prior to its acceptance (unless there was an option exchanged for consideration).

The firm bid rule operates only after the opening of the bids has taken place. It does not prevent a bidder from withdrawing his or her bid prior to opening. Actually, there is neither any federal statute which expressly forbids withdrawing a bid prior to its acceptance, nor is there any Supreme Court case deciding the issue of withdrawal prior to acceptance. Nevertheless, both the Comptroller General and the Court of Claims follow the firm bid rule in their decision making.

Five Exceptions to the Firm Bid Rule

1. It does not apply to negotiated contracts.
2. It does not apply where there has been a mutual mistake of a material fact.
3. It does not apply where the invitation for bids is silent on the question of withdrawal.
4. It does not apply when it is in the best interests of the government to allow the bidder to withdraw his or her bid.
5. It does not apply in cases where government-mandated performance would be inequitable, unconscionable, or impossible for the contractor.

The handling of mistakes on bids is discussed in Chapter 12.

HOW TO PREPARE FOR A GOVERNMENT PREAWARD SURVEY

The preaward survey is used primarily by the military contracting agencies, and the intent of the survey is to satisfy the government's need to verify that the prospective contractor is capable of fulfilling the terms and conditions of the contract, either from a legal point of view (such as compliance with laws and regulations), or from a financial and technical point of view. Notification that a preaward survey will be conducted is good news, for it means that you are on the verge of selection for an award. However, preaward surveys are not conducted on all contracts, and the results of the survey are applicable only to the one contract for which the survey is being conducted. No blanket approval for future contracts is available to the contractor from a single preaward survey. Let's take a look at the preaward survey in detail, and see how best to prepare for it so that a successful conclusion has the best chance of being reached.

It is the policy of the government to evaluate business organizations who have submitted bids in light of their competence, capability, and responsibility. This can involve the evaluation of many factors, and specialists from various branches of the government may be asked to participate. For example, in addition to technical and production capability, an evaluation of your accounting system, quality control procedures, plant safety, past performance record, labor resources, and other factors may be considered. If the survey team is aware of a particular weakness in your company, then the survey will concentrate heavily on this area.

14 Key Areas of Evaluation for a Survey Team

There are 14 areas a survey team may evaluate, and they are selected by the procuring activity involved. If any of the factors evaluated are not in place at the time of the survey, the offeror must be prepared to demonstrate positively that these deficiencies will be resolved in time to meet contract requirements. Here are the 14 factors:

1. *Technical capability* is an assessment of the offeror's key management personnel in order to determine whether or not they have the basic skill and knowledge necessary to produce the required product or provide the required service.
2. *Production capability* is an evaluation of the offeror's ability to plan, control, and integrate manpower, facilities, and other resources necessary for successful contract completion.
3. *Plant facilities and equipment* evaluation consists of either an assessment of these facilities in the offeror's possession, or of the offeror's ability to acquire the facilities and equipment necessary for successful contract completion.

4. *Financial capability* must be determined as adequate to acquire the needed facilities, equipment, material, and personnel necessary for successful completion of the contract.
5. *Purchasing and subcontracting* will be evaluated in order to determine that the offeror's system provides for the timely placement of orders with reliable vendors and for vendor follow-up and control.
6. *Accounting system* assessment normally will be requested when conditions such as progress payments or a cost or incentive type contract are contemplated.
7. *Quality control capability* evaluation will be made to determine that the offeror will be able to comply with the quality assurance requirements of the proposed contract. It may involve an evaluation of the offeror's quality control system, personnel, facilities, and equipment.
8. *Transportation* assessments will consist of evaluating the offeror's capability to comply with the laws and regulations applicable to the movement of government material or overweight, oversized, and hazardous cargo.
9. *Plant safety* assessments will determine the offeror's capability to perform a proposed contract which may involve materials or processes hazardous to health and safety.
10. *Security clearance* evaluation will determine that the offeror's security clearance is adequate and current, if clearance is required.
11. *Labor resources* will be looked at to determine the offeror's ability to staff adequately for performance on the proposed contract in areas other than 1 and 7 above. These apply to the specific functions they address.
12. *Performance record* evaluation will take into account the offeror's security clearance is adequate and current if clearance is required.
13. *Ability to meet schedule* evaluation will consist of an assessment of the offeror's overall ability to meet the required delivery schedule, and plant loading, including government and commercial work.
14. *Other* is a catchall factor used in addition to the 13 covered above. The most frequent use of factor 14 is when there are questions concerning the offeror's eligibility under the Walsh-Healey Act. Factor 14 may also be used when an evaluation of such things as packaging is required.

The Preaward Survey Checklist: 22 Self-Help Questions

The best way to prepare for a preaward survey is to work from the following systematic listing of 22 questions which, if answered positively, will place you in the best possible circumstances in the eyes of the survey team:

1. Has a company official, who has been empowered to speak for the company, been selected to meet with the government team?

2. Is management completely familiar with the purchasing office solicitation, as well as the company's offer?
3. Do any disparities exist between the solicitation and the company's offer which should be resolved during the initial meeting with the survey team?
4. Does the firm qualify as either a manufacturer or regular dealer, as defined by the Walsh-Healey Public Contracts Act, if the contract is for supplies in excess of $10,000?
5. Can actual technical capability or its development on the proposed contract products be demonstrated?
6. Is a company production plan available for survey team review?
7. Are plant facilities and equipment available and operable? If not, can it be demonstrated that they can be developed or acquired in time to meet proposed contract requirements?
8. Are requirements for transportation necessary for contract performance either available or obtainable?
9. Can your company meet the preservation, packaging, and packing requirements of the solicitation, even if these requirements may be unusual?
10. If the solicitation requires industrial security clearance, is your company prepared to do so?
11. Are labor resources with the proper skills currently employed? If not, can they be hired in the local area or elsewhere expeditiously?
12. Does the company have documentation available for survey team review, such as previous government contracts, subcontracts, or commercial orders, which will demonstrate a past satisfactory performance record as to delivery, quality, and finances?
13. Is the company's production plan, with production resources and machine utilization phased-in, adequate to demonstrate to the survey team a capability to meet contract schedules?
14. Have plans been made to escort the survey team through plant facilities, and will technicians and other personnel be available to answer questions?
15. Is documentation available to provide the team financial analyst with the company's current profit and loss summary, balance sheet, cash flow chart, and other pertinent information?
16. Is a listing of tools and equipment on hand and available for review by the team industrial/production specialist?
17. Have tentative and verifiable plans for vendor supplies, materials, or subcontracts been made to assure that the final delivery schedule can be met? Is there a follow-up system?
18. Are requirements for technical data and publications under the proposed contract understood?

19. If the proposed contract is other than firm-fixed-price, or, if progress payments have been requested, is adequate accounting documentation available for review?
20. Does the company have a workable quality control organization, and are such personnel familiar with MIL-I-45208, *Inspection System Requirements*, if the award will be a DOD contract?
21. If either government-furnished property, equipment, or material is involved in the procurement, does the firm have procedures established in accord with the regulations?
22. Does the company have other information or data that might be pertinent in assisting the preaward survey team?

HOW CONTRACTS ARE AWARDED

In order to receive an award, a bidder must be found to be responsible. Responsibility may be determined by information supplied by the bidder, by information kept on file within the government department or agency, or learned in a preaward survey. In addition, the contracting officers must assure themselves that the prospective contractor has not been declared ineligible to receive an award. This is done by consulting a joint list of firms or individuals debarred, declared ineligible, or suspended under the provisions of the regulations.

Contracts are awarded not only on the basis of price, but on other factors such as transportation costs, business status (either large or small), and delivery dates. In determining which bid is lowest, any prompt payment discounts offered by the bidders must not be considered in the evaluation of the bids. However, any discount offered will become a part of the award, and will be taken by the payment center if payment is made within the discount period specified by the bidder. As an alternative to indicating a discount in conjunction with the offer, bidders may prefer to offer discounts on individual invoices.

The discounts clause of the solicitation sets 20 calendar days as the minimum period for prompt payment discounts as eligibility for consideration in bid evaluation.

Where the invitation permits bidders to include economic price adjustment provisions in their bids, and no bidder takes exception to the price adjustment provisions, the government will evaluate bids on the basis of quoted price plus the allowable price adjustment. If an invitation does not contain an economic price adjustment clause, and either some or all of the bidders include economic price adjustment provisions in their bids, these bids will be evaluated at maximum possible price adjustment when determining the lowest bid on the requirement.

Under ordinary circumstances, the acceptance of a bid by the government must be in writing. This is especially true where a statute requires the contract to be in writing. This is very similar to state statutes of frauds which apply to oral contracts. Under emergency conditions, however, oral contracts with the government have been upheld by the Boards of Contract Appeals.

Of course, the ultimate factor in selection of the contractor is the determination of which bid will be most advantageous to the government.

WHEN NONCOMPETITIVE BIDS ARE ALLOWED

Procurement by other than competitive procedures is authorized only for sole source situations, unusual and compelling urgency of need, maintenance of a mobilization source, purchases for foreign governments, brand name items for resale, and national security considerations.Contracts resulting from unsolicited proposals are considered sole source procurements. Contracts for repeat orders for either continued development or production of major systems or highly specialized equipment are also considered sole source procurements.

Use of other than competitive procedures usually begins with an RFQ. A detailed cost analysis will be performed by the contracting officer. The contract price is established by negotiations. Any contract in excess of $100,000 will require the contractor to certify as to the accuracy, currency, and completeness of all cost or pricing data used to establish the price.

How the Government Promotes Bids on Small Purchases

Small purchases are those that do not exceed $25,000. They are made using simpler contract forms, and often include fast payment procedures. Methods of payment will be discussed in detail in Chapter 7. Purchases of $1,000 or less may be made without securing competitive quotations provided the contracting officer considers the price to be reasonable. For purchases between $1,000 and $25,000, the general rule is that competitive quotations are solicited orally from potential suppliers in the local trade area. Written solicitations are used when suppliers are outside the local trade area, when unusual specifications or a large number of different items are required, or when oral quotes are impractical. Reasonableness of the price is generally determined by the competitive process.

For repetitive purchases of small quantities of supplies, a blanket purchase agreement (BPA) is used, and usually they are placed with two or more suppliers of the same item. The order is generally placed orally, and payments are made monthly on a summary invoice issued by the contractor.

INDEX - CHAPTER 2

3

HOW TO "DECODE" DEFENSE CONTRACT LANGUAGE

When the government buys, the contract can range from a one-page commercial item description to dozens of pages covering a wide range of requirements. Military and NASA procurements usually have more stringent requirements than any other agency. For example, the majority of military contracts contain special clauses requiring labeling, packaging, preservation, packing, and other requirements unique to military needs. This increases the cost to the government, and benefits the contractor by additional cash flow.

You may think these contracts are excessively complex, and question the need for some of the requirements. However, with experience, you will find that successive procurements for the same items have the same clauses, and the initial difficulty you experienced will fall into a predictable routine.

If you understand what is contained in a defense contract, all other forms of contracts will become quite simple. Please don't feel intimidated by contracting with the DOD. DOD business is good business, and it should be sought after with intensity.

The uniform contract format used by the DOD for most procurements (excluding construction, subsistence items, and shipbuilding) has four parts:

1. the schedule
2. the contract clauses

3. the list of documents, exhibits, and other attachments
4. the representations and instructions

The list of documents identifies all attachments to the solicitation or contract. The representations and instructions are those solicitation provisions required to be received from offerors, and they include instructions to guide offerors in preparing their submittal. The major parts of every contract are the schedule and contract clauses, often referred to as the ''boilerplate'' clauses. This chapter looks at these two parts in detail.

THE CONTRACT SCHEDULE: BLUEPRINT OF YOUR PROSPECTIVE DEAL

The *contract schedule* is tailored to each transaction and represents the substance of the deal. It includes the following:

- a cover sheet, usually Standard Form (SF) 33.
- statement of the work to be done or the supplies to be furnished and the prices
- specifications
- packaging and marking requirements
- inspection and acceptance requirements
- the delivery schedule
- any necessary contract data information not included in the SF 33
- any special conditions pertaining to the contract

Different items being purchased separately or requiring delivery to different destinations are given individual line item numbers. Every DOD contract has a uniform numbering system for line items, with the first item listed in a schedule being 001.

The list of supplies or services is followed by either the specifications or other descriptions with which the work must conform. Specifications are covered in detail in Chapter 4.

Note: It's essential that you read the specifications carefully because many of them refer to other requirements, generally known as referenced documents, that must be consulted in order to complete the contract satisfactorily. The packaging and marking requirements as well as the inspection and acceptance requirements may also include referenced documents. This may seem unnecessarily complex at first, but once you know the broad meaning of the specifications and how to fulfill them, it becomes routine.

The delivery section of the schedule specifies either the time, place, and method of delivery for supplies, or the place of performance for services. Most contracts will require either F.O.B. origin or F.O.B. destination. When F.O.B. destination is required, you deliver the goods to the government and pay all of the shipping charges. When F.O.B origin is specified, the government will take delivery of the goods at your facility and it will pay the freight charges to destination. You will have to deliver the goods to the carrier.

Finally, the schedule contains any special provisions applicable to the specific contract. Examples of this include use of government-owned property, options for additional quantities of supplies, special test procedures, and agreements regarding payment of fees under cost-plus-fixed-fee contracts.

The *boilerplate contract clauses* are standard clauses that further define the contractor's obligations. These clauses usually refer to ''routine'' contract performance requirements, and are used repetitively. Example: A certificate of conformance certifying that the items furnished meet the specifications. The clauses used tend to follow a pattern, and are generally the same clauses that were incorporated in previous contracts for the same or similar items. *Special caution*: Never assume that the clauses in one contract will always be the same as in another. Review each contract thoroughly to avoid inadvertent noncompliance.

SIX MAJOR TOPICS FOUND IN MOST DEFENSE CONTRACTS

The second part of the DOD contract consists of clauses required by either statute or regulation. Deviations from the requirements of these clauses involve tedious procedures, which puts a successful request for deviation in the highly unlikely category. A sealed bid contract is similar to an insurance policy in that you have no control over the clauses included. In contracts awarded in other than sealed bid procedures, you may be able to influence some of the terms.

Certain clauses require particular attention because they expose you to many of the peculiarities associated with government contracting. These clauses have either little or no counterpart in commercial dealings. They relate to changes, disputes, terminations, patent rights, examination of records, government inspection, and correction of defects. The regulations contain over 500 pages of contract clauses, and it is obviously impractical to include them here. However, the pattern established by the types of goods or services you plan to sell to the government will result in only a very few of these being used at any one time in your contracts, and after awhile you will know them verbatim. Additionally, many clauses cover similar topics. These topics consist of six major groups:

1. performance
2. payments
3. cost principles
4. contract changes
5. terminations
6. public policies

Contract clauses will be covered in greater detail in Chapter 13.

1. Contract Performance

DOD Procedures and Clauses That Can Affect Contract Performance. While performing a contract you may face issues such as DOD inspection and acceptance; subcontracts; use of government property; patents, data, and copyrights; bonds, insurance, and taxes. In addition, every DOD contract contains a provision for resolving disputes if any arise from the contract. Let's cover these in some detail.

Inspection and Acceptance

Inspection and acceptance places responsibility on the contractor for either delivering products or providing services on schedule, and for assuring that they conform with contract requirements. The government contract administration office is responsible for assuring that you fulfill your contract quality requirements, and the government may conduct inspections and tests in order to determine whether or not the goods are in conformance. The type and extent of inspection and testing depends largely on the type of items being procured, and the contract schedule will designate the place of inspection. If the goods are to shipped from the plant prior to acceptance, the contract will contain a clause assigning the risk of loss if the goods are damaged in transit.

Generally, when each delivery is made, the contractor must prepare and submit a *Material Inspection and Receiving Report*, DD Form 250 (Figure 3–1). Additional copies may be obtained at no cost from your contract administration office. They will also supply the detailed procedures used in its preparation. If the contract contains a fast payment procedure, you may submit your invoice in lieu of form DD 250.

Fixed-Price Contracts. While there are many versions of the inspection clause, certain uniform features prevail. The standard clause used in fixed-price contracts provides that items for delivery under the contract are subject to inspection and test by the DOD before acceptance. The DOD has the right to reject nonconforming items, have the defects corrected at the contrac-

MATERIAL INSPECTION AND RECEIVING REPORT

1. PROC. INSTRUMENT IDEN. (CONTRACT) | (ORDER) NO. | 6. INVOICE | 7. PAGE | OF

8. ACCEPTANCE POINT

2. SHIPMENT NO | 3. DATE SHIPPED | 4. B/L | TCN | 5. DISCOUNT TERMS

9. PRIME CONTRACTOR *CODE* | 10. ADMINISTERED BY *CODE*

11. SHIPPED FROM *(If other than 9)* *CODE* | FOB: | 12. PAYMENT WILL BE MADE BY *CODE*

13. SHIPPED TO *CODE* | 14. MARKED FOR *CODE*

15. ITEM NO.	16. STOCK/PART NO. DESCRIPTION *(Indicate number of shipping containers - type of container - container number.)*	17. QUANTITY SHIP/REC'D *	18. UNIT	19. UNIT PRICE	20. AMOUNT

21. PROCUREMENT QUALITY ASSURANCE

A. ORIGIN

☐ PQA ☐ ACCEPTANCE of listed items has been made by me or under my supervision and they conform to contract, except as noted herein or on supporting documents.

DATE | SIGNATURE OF AUTH GOVT REP

TYPED NAME AND OFFICE

B. DESTINATION

☐ PQA ☐ ACCEPTANCE of listed items has been made by me or under my supervision and they conform to contract, except as noted herein or on supporting documents.

DATE | SIGNATURE OF AUTH GOVT REP

TYPED NAME AND TITLE

22. RECEIVER'S USE

Quantities shown in column 17 were received in apparent good condition except as noted.

DATE RECEIVED | SIGNATURE OF AUTH GOVT REP

TYPED NAME AND OFFICE

** If quantity received by the Government is the same as quantity shipped, indicate by (✓) mark, if different, enter actual quantity received below quantity shipped and encircle.*

23. CONTRACTOR USE ONLY

DD Form 250, JUN 86 *Previous editions are obsolete.* *Form Approved / OMB No. 0704-0248 / Expires Apr 30, 1989*

★ U.S.G.P.O.: 1986-491-133/52563

Figure 3–1

tor's expense, or accept the nonconforming items at a reduced price. Acceptance by the DOD is final, except with regard to hidden or latent defects and fraud.

You are required to provide facilities for, and assistance to, DOD inspectors at your own expense, and you must maintain an acceptable inspection system and quality control. If the government inspection or test is made somewhere other than on your premises or those of your subcontractor, it is at the DOD's expense. The inspection and test must not unduly delay your work.

Cost-Reimbursement Contracts. The clause governing inspection and correction of defects in cost-reimbursement contracts differs from the standard fixed price clause in two major respects:

- First, you will be reimbursed for correcting any nonfraudulent defects.
- Second, the government may require you to remedy any defective items up to six months after acceptance.

Subcontracts

Subcontracts affect the price and performance of prime contracts. The DOD frequently requires that you obtain the contracting officer's consent to proposed subcontracts. The regulations require prime contractors to select subcontractors and suppliers on the most competitive basis possible. The terms and conditions of a subcontract generally are subject to negotiation between the subcontractor and the prime contractor. However, the regulations do stipulate certain mandatory provisions in subcontracts. The subcontractor's contractual agreement is with the prime contractor, and not with the DOD. The DOD cannot intervene in the relationship between you and your subcontractor.

In many instances, contractors must require prospective subcontractors to furnish complete, current, and accurate cost and pricing data before award of a subcontract. The DOD reserves the right to reduce a prime contractor's price because of a subcontractor's defective cost and pricing data. In such a case, the subcontractor may have to reimburse the prime contractor.

Government Property

With regard to use of *government property* in performing your contract, you are generally required to furnish all of the property required to perform the contract. However, sometimes your contract may require the DOD to supply you with government property. Government property can be either government-furnished or contractor-acquired. Government-furnished property is, as its name implies, property the government either owns or acquires directly, and then makes available to the contractor. Contractor acquired property is property provided by the contractor for use in performance of the contract, but to which the government has title.

Government property includes materials, special tooling, special test equipment, and facilities. Materials are property that may be either incorporated into, or attached to, an end item to be delivered under the contract. They also may be consumed or expended in performing a contract. Special tooling and special test equipment are manufacturing aids designed for use in production and test of the product being produced under contract. Facilities are industrial property used for production, maintenance, research, development, or testing (other than material, special tooling, and special test equipment), including real property, buildings, and other structures.

As a rule, the government assumes the risk of loss or damage to its property. However, there are exceptions to this rule, and they will be called out in your contract when they occur.

Government property in your possession may be used only for performance of the contract for which it is provided. Use for any other purpose must be approved by the contracting officer. If the DOD-furnished property is unsuitable for its intended use or if it creates production difficulties resulting in extra costs, you are entitled to an appropriate price adjustment.

Contractors already in possession of government property suitable for use in future contracts may have a competitive edge on their competition. In order to eliminate any such advantage, the DOD applies evaluation or rental factors to the offers of these contractors when reviewing bids and proposals.

Contractors are required to establish and maintain controls over government property. These include record keeping, control of scrap and salvage, identification requirements, and the contractor's duties and responsibilities with respect to the property.

Patents, Data, and Copyrights

Patents, data, and copyrights are often described as "intellectual property." How the government handles these on bids is covered in Chapter 5. For now, let us examine these in the context of the contract. Essentially, there are two aspects of this type of property that are pertinent to DOD contracting:

- the determination of who receives title to the property developed while performing a DOD contract, and
- second, the right to use existing property

If one purpose of a contract is to perform experimental, developmental, or research work, the contract will contain a patent rights clause. It is the

DOD's policy that small business firms, whether or not they are acting as prime contractors or subcontractors, should retain title to any invention conceived or first reduced to practice in performance of work under DOD contracts. The government retains an irrevocable, nonexclusive, nontransferable, royalty-free license to either practice, or to have these inventions practiced, on its behalf. You must disclose any such invention to the contracting officer, and if not disclosed you may forfeit title to the invention. You may elect not to retain title to an invention, in which case the government may assume title and provide you with a royalty-free license.

You must agree that any exclusive right to use or sell any invention in the United States will provide that any product embodying the invention will be manufactured in the United States. The patent rights clause also provides for "march-in rights" to the government. Under this clause you may be required to grant a license to a responsible applicant if the government determines that you have not taken steps to achieve practical application of an invention, or if the public interest otherwise dictates such action.

The standard practice with respect to existing patent rights is to include an "authorization and consent" clause in every contract in excess of $25,000. This clause authorizes you to use any invention patented by others in the United States. Its purpose is to prevent disruption of contract performance by court injunctions against patent infringement. In the event of an infringement, the patent owner must sue the DOD instead of suing you.

The authorization and consent clause does not mean that the DOD accepts final liability for a patent infringement. Most contracts in excess of $25,000 for either supplies or services normally sold or offered for sale in the commercial market, or for minor modifications of these supplies or services, will contain a patent indemnity clause requiring you to reimburse the DOD for any claims paid as a result of patent infringement. You are required to notify the DOD of any infringement claims arising from the performance of your contracts, and to assist the government in defense of these claims.

It is the DOD's policy to acquire only those technical data rights essential to meet the needs. The term "technical data" means recorded information of either a scientific or technical nature. It does not include computer software or financial, administrative, cost or pricing data, or other management data.

The DOD acquires unlimited data rights if the data are developed at public expense and identified as a contract requirement. Unlimited rights allow the DOD to use the data in any manner and for any purpose, including follow-on work with other contractors. (The term "follow-on" generally refers to additional reorders of the same item or further development of an item previously ordered.)

The DOD acquires limited rights to unpublished data pertaining to items, components, or processes developed at private expense. This means that the DOD may use, duplicate, or disclose the data only for internal government purposes. The data may not be released outside the government except in certain emergencies.

The DOD policy on rights to computer software generally parallels that on technical data. The DOD acquires unlimited rights to software developed directly either under, or as a necessary part of, a contract. Software developed at private expense may be acquired with limited use rights; that is, for internal government purposes. Software supplies for a specific computer may be acquired with restricted use rights, and the software may generally be used only with the computer for which it was acquired.

The copyright law, in general, gives the owner of a copyright exclusive rights to

1. reproduce the copyrighted work in the form of either paper copies or recordings
2. prepare derivative works
3. distribute copies of recordings to the public
4. perform the copyrighted work publicly
5. display the copyrighted work publicly

Although you may copyright data originated under a government contract, the government retains a nonexclusive, paid-up license to reproduce, translate, publish, and use these data.

Bonds, Insurance, and Taxes

With regard to *bonds, insurance, and taxes,* contracting officers may require either performance or payment bonds in appropriate circumstances. In practice, these bonds are generally required only in construction contracts. When performance bonds are required, bid guarantees, usually 20 percent of the bid price but not more than $3 million, are also required.

The government is not ordinarily concerned with the contractor's insurance coverage if the contract is a fixed-price contract. Contractors are required to carry insurance under fixed-price contracts only in special circumstances. Under cost-reimbursement contracts, you are normally required to carry only worker's compensation, employer's liability, and comprehensive general liability (bodily injury and property damage) insurance with respect to contract performance.

Contracts for research and development may provide for indemnification against unusually hazardous risks for you and your subcontractors. This includes claims by third parties (including employees), for death, bodily injury, or loss of or damage to property. The indemnification also covers your property to the extent that any liability, loss, or damage resulting from a risk that the contract defines as "unusually hazardous" arises out of direct performance of the contract, and these are not compensated by insurance or in any other way.

Key points to remember: The tax aspects of government contracting are many and varied; however, two main points should be remembered. First, include in your contract price all *applicable* federal, state, and local taxes. Second, the contract may include a price adjustment clause to compensate for any increases or decreases in taxes. A further discussion of taxes, as they apply to government contracts, will be found in Chapter 12.

Disputes

Disputes, which will be covered in greater detail in Chapter 17, may occur under a contract. All contracts normally contain a disputes clause that outlines the procedures to be followed in the event of any unresolved disagreements between you and the contracting officer. Under these procedures you must state your position, in writing, to the contracting officer, who must respond with a written decision, including supporting reasons and a statement advising you of your appeal rights. Unless appealed within certain time limits, the contracting officer's decision becomes final, and it is not subject to review. You have 90 days from the date of an adverse decision by the contracting officer to appeal to the Armed Services Board of Contract Appeals. The board's decision is final, unless you appeal to the U.S. Court of Appeals within 120 days. Alternatively, you may elect to appeal a contracting officer's decision directly to the Court of Claims, provided you do so within 12 months of the date of the decision.

Remember: During the appeal process you are required to continue performance under the contract, except when DOD breaches the contract.

2. Payment Provisions

This is one of the most important provisions of a contract, so let's take a look at this from a broad point of view.

Cost-Reimbursement Versus Fixed-Price Contracts. Payments under cost-reimbursement contracts are different from those under fixed-price contracts. Your contract will specify the DOD office responsible for payments, and it will also contain invoicing instructions. Regardless of the type of contract, *the time it takes to be paid is directly related to the accuracy and completeness of your invoices*. Therefore, it is worthwhile to understand thoroughly the payment process. Every fixed-price contract contains a clause entitled "invoices." This sets forth the information to be included in your invoice. If the required information is not supplied, your check will be delayed!

How a Cost Reimbursement Contract Works. You are reimbursed for the *allowable* costs you incur in performing the work. Any costs that you incur that are not allowable will be omitted from your payments. Every two weeks, more often if warranted, you may submit either an invoice for costs incurred, or a public voucher form obtained from your contract administration office. The contract should specify a payment date, expressed as a number of days after receipt of your invoice. If not specified, you will be paid 30 days after your invoice is received by the disbursing office.

You must negotiate the way the fee will be paid, and this will be set forth in the contract schedule under the section entitled "special contract requirements." After you have received 85 percent of the fee under the contract, the contracting officer may withhold a reserve to protect the government's interest pending completion of the work. This reserve may not exceed 15 percent of the total fee or $100,000, whichever is less.

How a Fixed Price Contract Works. The method of payment can vary with the contract dollar value. For small contracts with a single item of work, you generally will be paid the total contract price in one lump sum. Payment is made after you deliver the products or services, and the DOD accepts them. For larger contracts with many items, you can invoice and receive partial payments. For example, in a contract for 120 units with a delivery rate of 10 percent per month, you can invoice each month for the price of delivered and accepted items. A payment date, expressed as a number of days after receipt of a proper invoice, should be included in the "payments" clause of the contract. This may not be less than 5 days. In the absence of a date, you will be paid 30 days after receipt of a proper invoice.

When the value of either a single contract or group of contracts to be performed by a small business concern exceeds $100,000, and the first delivery is scheduled to occur at least four months after the award, the DOD recognizes your need for working capital. To help finance the work, these contracts may contain a clause allowing you to obtain progress payments on a monthly basis. Progress payments to a small business are usually made at 95 percent of the costs incurred. Payments on delivery are adjusted to reflect previous progress payments. Your contract should specify a payment date, expressed as a number of days after the receipt of a progress payment request.

Even with progress payments at 95 percent of costs incurred, invoice processing time may cause your investment in work in process to exceed 5 percent. If this appears to be the case, you may request flexible progress payments for any contract in excess of $100,000. This procedure allows the progress payment rate to vary between 95 and 100 percent of costs incurred as work progresses. Detailed cash flow analyses are required to demonstrate the need for flexible progress payments. The contracting officer will assist you in determining whether you need and qualify for flexible progress payments.

Because progress payments are an advance for work to be performed, you must repay them if you fail to complete the work. In order to protect its interests, the DOD takes title to your work in process for which progress payments have been made.

In order to qualify for progress payments, you must have an accounting system and controls for adequate and proper administration of these payments. In addition, the contracting officer must be satisfied that your financial condition is sound enough to protect the government against loss of these payments. In order to receive progress payments, you must submit Standard Form (SF) 1433 to your administrative contracting officer. (See Figure 8–1 in Chapter 8.)

Fast payment procedures normally apply to contracts of $25,000 or less. These are implemented when you submit an invoice showing that the supplies have been delivered to a Post Office, a common carrier, or the point of first receipt by the government. You agree to replace, repair, or correct supplies not received at destination, damaged in transit, or not conforming with purchase requirements. When the DOD receives the invoice, you may be paid without waiting for actual receipt and acceptance of the supplies. However, you won't be paid until 30 days after receipt of your invoice unless an earlier date is specified in the contract.

Special note: The government, if properly invoiced, will pay within the time allowed in the contract. This is the term you offered the government in your bid, and the Prompt Payment Act enforces this policy. On rare occasions, however, paperwork mishandling will delay your check. Remember, payment occurs after acceptance, so it is important to make certain the receiving destination has the necessary wherewithal to inspect or test your product. If it seems doubtful that they do, such as when a complex electronic item is sent to a field destination, then it is wise to request a change in the point of acceptance from destination to inspection at your facility.

In order to minimize the need for financial assistance to contractors, the DOD emphasizes prompt payment on all contracts. This includes both DOD payments to prime contractors and prime contractor payments to subcontractors. If the government fails to pay amounts due on valid invoices within the prescribed time limit, you may be entitled to interest on the amounts overdue.

3. Contract Cost Principles

Allowable Costs

Contract cost principles outline certain cost tenets to be applied in the following situations wherein you cannot recover all costs incurred, but rather only those costs deemed "allowable:"

1. pricing of contracts when cost analysis is performed
2. determining reimbursements under cost-reimbursement contracts
3. negotiating indirect cost rates
4. termination settlements
5. price revision of redeterminable and fixed-price incentive contracts
6. pricing contract modifications

In order to be considered allowable, an individual item of cost must be

1. reasonable
2. allocable to the contract
3. computed in accordance with generally accepted accounting principles and practices appropriate to the particular circumstance
4. consistent with any limitation or exclusion set out in the regulations or in the contract

Allocable Costs. A cost is reasonable if, in its nature and amount, it does not exceed what would be incurred by a prudent person in the conduct of competitive business. Generally, a cost is allocable if it can be charged to a contract, product, product line, and so forth, according to the relative benefits received. Specifically, a cost is allocable if it

1. is incurred directly for the contract
2. benefits both the contract and other work, and can be distributed among all work in reasonable proportion to the benefits received
3. it is necessary to the overall operation of your business

The regulations do not discuss every type of cost. Approximately 50 selected items of cost are defined and designated as either allowable or unallowable. For example, depreciation of plant and equipment is an allowable cost, while interest on borrowed money is not. The allowance of costs not explicitly covered by the regulations is based on the general principles stated above, and on the treatment of similar or related cost items.

In any given contract, the reasonableness and the allocability of certain items of cost may be difficult to determine. To avoid disallowances, you should seek advance agreement with the DOD regarding the treatment of these costs. This agreement should be negotiated before the costs are incurred, and it should be incorporated into the contract. The advance agreement cannot allow treatment of costs inconsistent with the cost principles set forth in the regulations.

Fifteen Specific Cost Items in Which Advance Agreements May Be Important

1. compensation for personal services
2. use charge for fully depreciated assets
3. deferred maintenance costs
4. precontract costs
5. independent research, development, bid, and proposal costs
6. royalties
7. selling and distribution costs
8. travel and relocation costs, as related to special or mass personnel movements
9. costs of idle facilities and idle capacity
10. costs of automatic data processing equipment
11. severance pay to employees on support service contracts
12. plant reconversions
13. professional services
14. allocations of general and administrative costs
15. under construction contracts, the cost of constructing plant and equipment

Contract Changes

These are covered by a change clause, which will vary according to the type of contract; however, all change clauses contain certain elements. The need for a change clause is a result of the DOD's needs, which may vary frequently.

A change clause authorizes the contracting officer to order you to make changes "within the general scope of the contract." A change is within contract scope if it can be regarded as fair and reasonable within the contemplation of the parties when the contract was entered into. This means that the DOD cannot use a change order to change the nature of the contract. In supply contracts, the changes are limited to drawings, designs, or specifications (if the goods are specially manufactured for the DOD); the method of shipment or packing; and the place of delivery. If the change causes an increase or decrease in the cost of the work, or the time of its performance, in whole or in part, then an equitable adjustment will be made in either the contract price, the delivery schedule, or both. Change orders are always issued in writing, and you must submit your claim for equitable adjustment to the contracting officer within 30 days after receipt of the change order.

Warning: You must perform your contract as changed, unless the change is beyond the general contract scope. If you fail to proceed under a proper change order, you are liable for breach of contract.

Terminations

These are covered by clauses allowing termination either for the convenience of the government or for default. The termination for convenience clause is designed to protect the government's interests by allowing cancellation of contracts for items that have either become obsolete, or are no longer needed. This type of termination does not come about because of any fault on the part of the contractor.

What Happens if the DOD Terminates Your Contract. The DOD must give you written notice of the termination, which will usually direct you to do the following:

1. stop work
2. terminate subcontracts
3. place no further orders
4. communicate similar instructions to subcontractors and suppliers

If you fail to follow these directions, you do so at your own risk and expense. Additionally, you will be given detailed instructions regarding the protection and preservation of all property that is, or may become, government owned.

Allowable Costs Incurred in Settling a Termination for Convenience. After termination, the DOD is required to make a fair and prompt settlement with you. Generally, settlement takes the form of a negotiated agreement between the parties. The object of the negotiation is to reach an agreement on the amount required to fully and fairly compensate you for the work you have done, and for any preparation you have made for the terminated portion of the contract. A reasonable allowance for profit is also included. Under cost-reimbursement contracts, the settlement is much simpler, since you have been reimbursed on a cost basis from the beginning of the contract. You are entitled to recover all allowable costs incurred in settling a termination for convenience. These costs may include the following:

1. preparation and presentation of claim
2. termination and settlement of subcontracts
3. storage and disposal of government-owned property
4. other termination activities

The DOD retains the right to approve or ratify any settlements made with subcontractors. When you and the DOD agree to all or part of your claim for compensation resulting from the termination, a written amendment, known as a settlement agreement, is made to the contract.

Generally, termination halts regular payments to you under the contract.

However, since money is tied up in work in process, inventory, materials, and labor, most termination clauses provide you with interim financing by means of partial payments.

Three Reasons for Termination by Default. Terminations for default are made if you:

1. fail to deliver the supplies or perform the services within the time specified in the contract
2. fail to perform any provisions of the contract
3. fail to make progress, and this failure endangers contract performance

Before terminating a contract for default because of your failure to deliver supplies or perform services, the contracting officer will usually send a show cause notice. This notice directs you to show why your contract should not be terminated for default. This will point out the seriousness of your predicament, and your reply to this notice will be the basis of evaluating whether or not circumstances warrant termination by default.

Before terminating a contract for default because of either failure to make progress or perform other provisions of the contract, the contracting officer must give you a written notice called a "cure notice." This notice allows you at least ten days to cure any defects, and unless the remedies are performed in ten days, the contracting officer may issue a notice of termination for default.

Termination for default is not an easy way to get out of a contract. You will be entitled to payment only for the items actually accepted by the DOD, and it reserves the right to repurchase the items elsewhere and charge the excess procurement costs to you.

How to Avoid Termination by Default—Ten Excusable Delays. If you can show that your failure to perform the contract is excusable, then default termination cannot take place. In order for the failure to perform to be excusable, the failure must be beyond your control, and not caused by your negligence. Here are ten examples of excusable delays:

1. acts of God
2. acts of the public enemy (as in war)
3. acts of the government
4. fires (as in a contractor's plant)
5. floods
6. epidemics
7. quarantine restrictions
8. strikes

9. freight embargoes
10. unusually severe weather

If for any reason after termination for default has taken place it is determined that you were not at fault, then the termination will be handled as one for the convenience of the government.

Public Policies

These clauses, in addition to promoting small business, serve other national goals of an urgent or beneficial nature. These are summarized below under six categories: labor standards, labor surplus areas, equal employment opportunity, preferred products and services, sanctions against improper conduct, and examination of records and audits. Let's look at these categories in some detail.

Labor Standards

Under the Contract Work Hours and Safety Standards Act, certain government contractors who employ laborers and mechanics are required to pay them time-and-a-half for work in excess of 8 hours a day and 40 a week. This requirement extends to all subcontracts.

Contractors who are either manufacturers of, or regular dealers in, the supplies required must comply with the regulations issued by the Secretary of Labor under the Walsh-Healey Public Contracts Act. This act governs minimum wages, maximum hours, and working conditions, and prohibits the use of convict or child labor. Contracts not subject to the Walsh-Healey Act must include a provision prohibiting convict labor. Contracts involving construction work must contain several additional clauses relating to construction industry labor standards. Contracts for services contain a clause required by the Service Contracts Act, stipulating minimum standards for wages, fringe benefits, and working conditions for service employees.

Labor Surplus Areas

The government encourages placing of contracts with firms located in areas of unemployment or underemployment. In all contracts over $25,000 (except those for personal services or with foreign firms), contractors must try to place subcontracts in accordance with this policy. If the contract exceeds $500,000, the contractor must organize and carry out a program for placing subcontracts with firms located in areas of high unemployment or underemployment.

Equal Employment Opportunity

The government ensures equal opportunity for all qualified persons either employed by or seeking employment with government contractors, regardless of race, color, religion, sex, or national origin. Unless exempted by the director, Office of Federal Contract Compliance Programs, all DOD contracts and subcontracts must contain an equal opportunity clause. Individual contracts and subcontracts are exempt from application of the clause unless the aggregate value of this business exceeds $10,000 in any 12-month period. This clause obligates the contractor to ensure nondiscrimination in hiring and in the terms and conditions of employment. If the contractor does not comply, the contract may be terminated.

In contracts over $1 million offerors are subject to preaward equal opportunity review in order to determine their eligibility for contract award. Offerors on a contract over $10,000 must certify that they maintain nonsegregated facilities. Contracts and subcontracts exceeding $2,500 must contain a clause prohibiting discrimination against any employee or applicant for employment because of a physical or mental handicap, provided that person is otherwise qualified for the position. Contracts and subcontracts exceeding $10,000 must contain a clause prohibiting discrimination against either any employee or applicant for employment who is a disabled veteran of the Vietnam era, if that person is otherwise qualified for the position.

An executive order prohibits discrimination by government contractors and subcontractors because of age. No contract clauses are used to implement this policy.

Preferred Products and Services

Many DOD contract clauses reflect public policies requiring that preference be given to certain products or services, such as the use of U.S. private vessels for shipment of certain supplies or the purchase of jewel bearings from domestic sources. The most frequently encountered preferred product procedures involve the Buy American Act. Under this act, the government favors domestic products over foreign products. A product is considered to be domestic if the cost of domestic materials used in the product exceeds 50 percent of the cost of all materials used in the product. The act requires that domestic products be acquired only for public use except when

- the articles, materials, or supplies are to be used abroad or for commissary resale
- domestic products of a satisfactory quality are unavailable in sufficient quantities
- a domestic purchase would be either contrary to public interest or its cost would be unreasonable

In order to determine the reasonableness of the lowest acceptable domestic offer when both domestic and foreign products are offered, the foreign offer is adjusted by adding 6 percent of the offer inclusive of duty. If the low domestic offeror is either a small business or a labor surplus area business, a 12 percent factor is used instead of 6 percent. If the adjusted foreign offer is lower than the lowest acceptable domestic offer, the domestic offer is unreasonable and award is made to the foreign offeror.

The requirements of the act are waived when the government purchases certain defense items from companies in NATO countries. It is also waived on certain U.S. purchases from countries with which the United States has trade agreements. Prospective contractors are advised in the solicitation that information concerning exceptions under the act is available on request.

Sanctions Against Improper Conduct. Several standard clauses protect the integrity of the government procurement process.

The *officials not to benefit* clause prohibits both members of Congress and resident commissioners from participating in any share or part of a contract.

The *gratuities* clause provides that a contractor may not offer or give any gratuity (such as entertainment or a gift) to a government employee to obtain a contract. This includes favorable treatment regarding contract awards and determinations.

A clause entitled *covenant against contingent fees* requires contractors to warrant that no persons, other than employees or established or commercial selling agencies, have been employed for the purpose of soliciting business upon a commission, percentage, brokerage, or contingent fee basis.

The anti-kickback law prohibits subcontractors from paying any fee, commission, or compensation to any prime contractor and higher tier subcontractor as an inducement or acknowledgment for the award of an order. No contract clauses are used to implement this law.

The regulations prescribe sanctions against those who violate or otherwise fail to conform with the standards required of government contractors. These sanctions consist of debarment, suspension, and ineligibility for award of contracts. Debarment is the most serious penalty. It generally results from the conviction of either a serious offense or willful violation of contract requirements, and it can last for up to three years. Suspension is temporary, pending completion of investigation and legal proceedings, if necessary. It is used when serious evidence of wrongdoing exists but has not been proven. Contractors may become ineligible, that is, excluded from government contracting because of violations of laws and regulations such as the Buy American Act, the Walsh-Healey Act, and the other acts previously mentioned. All government agencies maintain a consolidated list of debarred, ineligible, and suspended contractors.

Examination of Records and Audits. In order to ensure accuracy and honesty in the pricing, costing, and reporting under contracts awarded without benefit of full and open competition, the government often reserves the right to either examine or audit the contractor's records and data supporting cost proposals, claimed costs of performance, reports required by the contract, and similar items.

Virtually all contracts except small purchases and those awarded by sealed bids must contain a clause granting the Comptroller General the right to examine the contractor's records related to the contract for up to three years after final payment. A similar clause must be included in subcontracts under these contracts.

All contracts (other than small purchases) that are on a cost-reimbursement, incentive, time-and-materials, labor-hour, or price-redeterminable basis give the contracting officer the right to examine and audit books, records, documents, and other data relating to the claimed costs of performance. In addition, the cost or pricing data used in support of contract pricing and any cost, funding, or performance reports required by the contract may be audited.

INDEX - CHAPTER 3

4

HOW TO CLEARLY INTERPRET AND COMPLY WITH GOVERNMENT SPECIFICATIONS

Specifications play an important role in government procurement, and an even more important role in procurement through formal advertising. Unlike negotiated purchases, there is no opportunity to discuss exactly what is required after the opening of bids. In addition, the bidder cannot be expected to offer more than the minimum quality item that is responsive to the bid, since awards on sealed bid purchases are made on the basis of price alone.

Therefore, all bidders must fully understand what is being purchased, without further clarification, so that the product offered will meet the specifications, and will fulfill the government's need. In essence, the specifications allow all bidders to compete on an even footing. This requires that the language of specifications be clear and exact, and that technical terms and words of the trade be used. This is because the courts interpret specifications by the meaning they have in common or local usage. The construction of specifications is logical in that, if properly prepared, each feature of the product described is discussed in a single paragraph or sentence devoted exclusively to that feature. When fully covered, that feature is not mentioned again in the specification unless it is absolutely necessary. In order to avoid confusion, one feature per paragraph is the rule.

THE IMPORTANCE OF SPECIFICATIONS IN GOVERNMENT CONTRACTS

A specification is the transfer of knowledge between minds. When procurement by formal advertising is used, the bidder has to have clear in his or her own mind what the requirement is, without any help (unless requested) from the government. It is essential that specifications be crystal clear. Obviously, in order for the procurement to be fair to all bidders, specifications must be equally accessible to all.

Specifications have two purposes:

1. identify either an item, material, process, or service, and its preservation, packaging, packing, and marking
2. establish the criteria by which the government can determine whether or not the requirements of a contract have been met

The government has exact specifications for most of the products and services it buys repeatedly. These are in the form of written descriptions, drawings, prints, commercial designations, industry standards, and other descriptive references. Since they are based in part on industrial and technical society standards and specifications, they meet the requirements of the government without lessening the ability of business concerns to furnish the needed items or services.

TWO KEY PROVISIONS OF THE GOVERNMENT'S POLICY ON SPECIFICATIONS

The government's policy on specifications is simple and direct:

1. state only minimum needs
2. describe so as to get the most competition

Many items used by the government are highly specialized, and must be developed especially for its use. In this case, design specifications are used. These tell the prospective contractor just how the item is to be made. Commercial items are purchased under a performance specification. These permit every manufacturer of a suitable product to participate in the bidding.

Favoritism for a particular product or manufacturer is thereby avoided, and competition is fostered.

FOUR WAYS THAT CONTRACTOR AND GOVERNMENT MUST COMPLY WITH SPECIFICATIONS

There are four principles relating to the interpretation of specifications with which the contractor and the government must comply:

1. A contract must be read in its entirety. It is a rule of law that a contract must be read as a whole. It is also a rule that the meaning of a contract must, if possible, be given to all of the words used. Therefore, no word of a contract is to be either rejected or treated as meaningless if meaning consistent with the other parts of the contract can be given to it, or if the contract is capable of being construed with the word or words left in. Therefore, a review of just the statement of work is not advisable. All parts of the contract have to be looked at. This includes not only the contract document but also the matters either referenced or incorporated by reference.
2. The government has the right to require compliance with contract terms and specification. Therefore, deviation from the specifications as written is at best a dicey tactic. However, if a misinterpretation by the government requires a contractor to do work not really called for under the terms, then a change order should be issued. This will entitle you to an equitable price adjustment in accordance with the changes clause of the contract.
3. When the government furnishes a design specification to a contractor specifying the method of producing an item, there exists an implied warranty that the specification is adequate for the intended use. A demonstration of a flaw in a government-designed specification entitles you to an equitable adjustment.
4. Where a contractor is required to proceed under either defective or incomplete specifications, or under specifications that make the contract impossible to perform, he or she is entitled to a price adjustment under the changes clause.

Deviations from, and waivers of, a federal specification may be granted by an agency when its needs are not covered by the specification. These waivers and deviations must be justified by a designated official, and major or repeated deviations cannot be made unless specifically provided for. The procurement office is required to report repeated deviations to the General Services Administration on a prompt and timely basis, along with a justification.

The DOD permits deviations from federal or military specifications for acquisition of research and development, test and evaluation, laboratory equipment, items for authorized resale, and purchases on a one-time basis.

WHAT TO DO IF THE SPECIFICATIONS ARE IMPOSSIBLE TO FULFILL

Let's look at what happens if you undertake a contracted task and find that, after much time and effort, your product just won't work the way the specifications say it should.

First, when you set out to produce an item under a performance specification, you assume the risk that you can, in fact, do the job. When you agreed to perform, the government presumed you knew the "state of the art," meaning you had the necessary scientific or technological capability in your area of expertise. State of the art may also mean within the "realm of science," and ability to perform a certain task makes it "within the realm of science." Conversely, inability to perform makes it outside the realm of science.

The most frequent argument used by contractors when a design doesn't work out as planned is that the performance specifications were impossible to meet. In other words, the claim is that the "state of the art" is such that it just can't be done.

The government's test of this claim is whether or not the level of performance required by the contract is beyond the reach of any contractor in the field. If no one can do the work, then the state of the art is such that it can't be done. On the other hand, if others in the field can do the work, then the impossibility of the task rests strictly with the contractor, and the inability to perform is not excusable.

If a specification is defective, ambiguous, or creates a doubt about the work, the contractor has a duty to seek a clarification with the contracting officer. If the contractor fails to do this, he will be held liable for the erroneous interpretation. The courts have ruled that a contractor must seek clarification on defective specifications as soon as the defect becomes apparent. This prevents the reliance on the implied warranty of specifications previously discussed. If there is a doubt, you must inquire; otherwise, you will forfeit any rights for relief against the government. On the other hand, if you seek clarification with a contracting officer and are told to proceed in spite of the adequacy of the specification, the government will be held responsible.

GENERAL GUIDELINES ON CONTRACTOR PERFORMANCE AND SPECIFICATIONS

On occasion conflicts will arise between the contract and the specifications or drawings, or between the specifications and the drawings. Where there is a conflict between the contract and the specifications or drawings, the contract terms will prevail. If the conflict is between the specifications and the drawings, the specifications will prevail.

Lesser documents can prevail, but only if the matter is not in conflict with some other provision, and only if the document of precedence is silent on the matter. For example, if the drawings provide for something not in the specification, and it is not in conflict with either the specification or the contract document, the drawing would prevail to the extent of that provision. This falls under the rule that the contract must be read and interpreted as a whole.

Strict compliance with specifications is not your sole responsibility as a contractor. You also have the duty to perform in a workmanlike manner. This means a performance standard equal to that of a qualified, careful, and efficient person performing similar work. This requirement exists even if it is not set forth in the contract. When the contract does not contain detailed specifications, the test of "skillful and workmanlike" performance is the one that will be applied by the government.

Note: Where alternate methods of performance are permitted by the specifications, you have the freedom of choice. However, you are expected to follow the least costly method of performing the task.

The following is a list of ten general rules involving performance and specifications:

1. When the government provides complete design information, there is an implied warranty that an acceptable product will result if the specifications are met.
2. If problems in determining the meaning of conflicting or ambiguous specifications arise, interpretation will be in the favor of the contractor, provided the language was written by the government.
3. The government is entitled to strict compliance with quantitative specifications, although substantial compliance may be held to be sufficient.
4. Qualitative specifications are interpreted in light of custom and usage in the particular trade or profession.
5. If a contractor's proposal is included as part of the specifications, the contractor may be held to the performance suggested by the proposal.
6. A contractor may not sit back and rely on patent ambiguity in specifications and then demand a compensable change. He or she has an obligation to point out the ambiguity to the contracting officer at the earliest possible time.
7. Research and development contracts usually do not contain design specifications because the contractor is generally required to design and build the item to meet performance specifications.

8. In the event of a discrepancy between design and performance specifications, the performance specifications generally prevail.
9. Most contracts provide, in addition to what is shown on the plans and spelled out in the specifications, that the contractor will be compelled to furnish and do whatever is necessary to provide either a complete system or a complete job.
10. Where the language of the specification is indefinite, ambiguous, or of doubtful construction, the practical interpretation of the parties, as evidenced by either usage or course of dealing, will control.

THREE METHODS OF LIMITING COMPETITION BY SPECIFICATIONS

There are cases where the government is unable to draft adequate purchase specifications, or prebidding restrictions are involved. In these cases, certain restrictions on the competitive procurement process will be introduced. These generally fall into three categories.

1. The "Brand Name or Equal" Description

The first category occurs when the ''brand name or equal'' description is used. There is nothing wrong with this procedure; however, a problem of restriction does occur when the ''salient characteristics'' of the brand name are not properly set forth, thereby preventing an ''or equal'' response. The listing of salient features treads a fine line between restrictive competition and proper description. If too few features are listed, the government is deprived of its right to reject, as nonresponsive, a bid that meets all of the characteristics listed, even though it believes the offered product will not satisfy its needs. Again, care has to be taken by the government not to specify nonessential features, thereby limiting competition. The ''or equal'' language should not be used where it is determined that only the named brand will satisfy the government's needs. However, in such cases, a negotiated procurement would probably be preferable to an advertised one.

Note: You may know that the wording ''or equal'' should be in a specification. This would occur when new products have been developed after the specification was written. The way to correct the problem is to call the buyer and explain that there is a product equally as good as the one defined in the specification, and to please amend the solicitation to include the ''or equal'' wording.

2. The Use of the Qualified Products List

A second restriction on competition that may be imposed by the specifications involves the use of the Qualified Products List (QPL.) Use of the QPL limits consideration for contract award to bidders having their products listed on the QPL or eligible for listing at time of bid opening. This procedure has been sanctioned by the Comptroller General where testing before award is necessary, and when time, cost, or equipment required for testing is unusual.

3. Two-Step Formal Advertising

The last generally permissible method of limiting competition by specifications is two-step formal advertising. This procedure was designed to permit wider use of advertising in procurements previously negotiated. The first step of this procedure involves the submission of technical proposals by offerors for evaluation by the procuring agency. After the technical evaluation, those offerors determined to be qualified are solicited for price proposals in the customary advertised manner, with award being made to the low bidder under the second step. Each bidder may bid only on his or her technical proposal previously found acceptable.

Important: If something in a specification isn't clear or seems ambiguous, never be afraid to ask. You will find the government willing and able to assist you. Also, always put all your cards on the table when you have a problem. Correct solutions can be found only if the entire problem is known.

TWO MAIN CATEGORIES OF SPECIFICATIONS: FEDERAL AND MILITARY

Federal Specifications

Federal specifications are issued by the General Services Administration and cover ''civilian type'' materials, products, or services for general use by, or for potential use of, two or more federal agencies, one or more of which is civilian. When published, federal specifications supersede any previous specifications, and where applicable, their use by all federal agencies is mandatory. The assistant commissioner, Office of Standards and Quality Control, Federal Supply Service, General Services Administration, administers these specifications.

Federal specification numbers are made up of two nonsignificant groups of letters followed by numbers, such as:

H-R–550, Roller, kit, paint

GG-C–455, Clocks, portable watchman's

HHH-S–450, Slide, microscope

The specification symbol starts with a single, double, or triple letter. A single letter appears next. This is the first letter of the first word in the title. The last portion of the symbol is the assigned serial number. This permits rapid identification of the specification being looked for.

Revisions: Since documents are controlled by their basic number, a letter after the number is used as a revision indicator. H-B–51 would be the first issue for Broom, upright (corn). The first revision would be H-B–51A; the second revision would be H-B–51B. A revised federal specification supersedes entirely the previous issue, including amendments to it.

Amendments: Amendments affect minor yet essential changes in technical requirements in specifications. An amendment is part of the document with which it is identified, and determines the date of that document for indexing purposes. Amendments are cumulative and are numbered consecutively; that is, by the number "2," "3," and so forth. Each amendment bears the specification number and the specification date in the upper right hand corner. For example:

J-C–580A
Amendment–6 (GSA-FSS)
March 6, 1987

Superseding
Amendment–5 (GSA FSS)
June 10, 1986

Federal specifications are listed in the Index of Federal Specifications, Standards, and Commercial Item Descriptions. This contains three principal sections that list the documents alphabetically, numerically, and by Federal Supply Class (FSC). In all three sections, a brief explanatory title describes each specification or standard. The index also gives the price, if any, at which each document may be purchased from the General Services Administration. It also lists cancelled or superseded documents.

Military Specifications

Military specifications describe the items and services purchased by the DOD and its many subdivisions, as well as by other agencies concerned with national defense. They cover materials, products, or services used primarily by the military. These may also include commercial items modified to meet military requirements. Some items used by the DOD, particularly those without any special military characteristics, can be described satisfactorily by federal specifications.

As in the case of federal specifications, military specifications, once published, supersede all previous specifications for the same material, and their use is mandatory.

Military specifications are identified by a three part symbol:

1. the letters "MIL"
2. a single letter that is usually the first letter of the first word of the title
3. a nonsignificant serial number

For example:

MIL-M–2241, Microscope, stage micrometer

Revisions: A revision of a military specification supersede entirely the previous issue, including any amendments to it. As with federal specifications, a revision is indicated by the addition of a capital letter following the symbol in the upper right-hand corner of the first page and preceding any suffix. The first revision is indicated by the letter "A," and succeeding revisions are indicated by the other letters in alphabetical sequence, except that the letters "I," "O," and "S" are not used. For example:

MIL-I–24391A
April 10, 1983

Superseding
MIL-I–24391
September 29, 1980

Amendments: Brief changes in a military specification are printed in the form of an amendment. Amendments bear the specification symbol, the amendment number, and the date in the upper right-hand corner. Only one amendment is in effect at any one time for an individual specification. Superseding amendments are indicated by the numbers "2," "3," and so on.

When Specifications Are Not Used

The use of specifications are not always needed. For example, there is no requirement to use them when the purchase is a one-time need, or when the procurement covers items for authorized resale. In addition, they are not required for use in procurement of items for either test and evaluation, or if the item is incidental to research and development.

Interim or Limited Coordinated Specifications

When it is determined that neither a federal nor a military specification meets a particular need, then either an interim Federal Specification or a limited coordinated military specification is used. Interim specifications are basically those awaiting final processing before becoming either new or revised federal specifications. Limited coordinated specifications are those limited to a single military department. They are issued by a department to cover items in which it alone has an interest.

Purchase Descriptions

In cases when applicable detailed specifications are nonexistent, purchase descriptions are used. Purchase descriptions set forth the essential characteristics and functions of the item wanted. In the case of the procurement of services, an outline of the requirements will be given.

The minimum acceptable purchase description is the use of a brand name followed by the words "or equal." This is used only as a last resort when a more detailed description cannot be made in time for the purchase being contemplated. Obviously, when only a particular brand will meet the need, the words "or equal" are omitted.

Design specifications spell out in detail the types of materials to be used, the size and shape of the item, and how the item is to be made. If done correctly, the item is so well-described that it can be manufactured by any capable contractor in the industry.

Performance Specifications

Performance specifications state the characteristics of the required item in broad terms of capacity, function, or operation. The details of design, fabrication, and internal structure are left to the contractor. However, some features or parts of the item may be specified.

Caution: Never skim over specifications. They should be read thoroughly to ensure full understanding of the requirement. Remember that pertinent points are mentioned only once, and that helps the understanding process. Remember also that specifications do change; therefore, check newly revised specifications for changes that might affect your pricing.

INDEX - CHAPTER 4

5

TIPS ON SUCCESSFULLY OUTBIDDING YOUR COMPETITION

The path to success in government contracting is the path of successful competitive bidding. What constitutes competitiveness depends on the item or service being procured. Competition on some items is extremely tough, to the point where a supplier with a one-time competitive advantage has the only chance of being selected. It is not uncommon to find certain items that have been supplied for years by a single supplier, and the price the government is paying has a tendency to be well above a fair market price. The best way to capitalize on this type of situation will be covered in detail a little further on in this chapter. For now, let's take a look at some of the things you will want to consider in preparing future bids. Based on these discussions, you will be able to construct specific strategies that apply to your specific field.

The object of bidding is to be successful. By successful I don't mean winning all of the awards 100 percent of the time, but rather obtaining your fair share of business...and then some. There are many companies today in just this position, and they represent your prospective competition. Keep in mind, however, that there are very few companies who get *all* of the awards *all* of the time. And for these few companies it is probably a safe bet to say that their Achilles' heel is the high price they are charging the government because of no competition. What it all boils down to is that you, as a prospective new bidder on government contracts, have as good a chance of getting business as anyone, even if only because your chief competitor may have had a cold the day the CBD advertised a requirement, and wasn't up to the task of requesting the bid package. Also remember that the requirement often comes up for the same item several times a year, with only minor variations in what is needed at any given time. For example, salad oil in 5-gallon containers may not be your forte, but in 12-ounce bottles you may be dynamite! The field is large, and there is something for everyone to bid on.

HOW LOCATION AFFECTS BIDDING

In addition to the competition, location is a critical factor in determining how well you will fare in the bidding process. You might have a tough time submitting a competitive F.O.B. destination bid for delivery to Los Angeles if you are located in Philadelphia. But if you are in Los Angeles, just think of how competitive you're going to be! This is one way government business is able to be shared around the country. There are other ways, also. For example, your geographical location may give you a competitive advantage if you are in a labor surplus area. If you do qualify under a set-aside, you have a distinct advantage over your competition located in other areas not considered to be labor surplus. Your bid will be given preferential treatment in the sense that only those companies located in similar areas are qualified to submit a responsive bid. This narrows the field considerably. If your company falls into the category of being either socially or economically disadvantaged, you will have a similar advantage.

TRANSPORTATION

The preferred way of transporting supplies for the government is by means of commercial carriers. However, government-owned, leased, and chartered vehicles will be used if they are available and not fully utilized, and their use will result in substantial economies. The government does not wish to be in the transportation business, and therefore it will rely on readily available commercial services, unless they are either not available, or in instances of emergency.

Transportation Insurance

Transportation insurance is normally not required when transporting government property, for it is the government's policy to be self-insured and assume all risks involved with transportation. Remember, we're talking about government property here, and something doesn't become the government's property until it is accepted. So, if your contract reads "acceptance at destination," then you, as a prudent contractor, should insure the shipment.

On occasion, the government will either buy insurance, or require the contractor to assume full risk for the property during transportation. In the latter case, the cost of insurance becomes a part of the total transportation cost. Normally, insurance coverage will always be required when transporting valuables.

Common carriers, subject to the jurisdiction of the Interstate Commerce Commission, under the provisions of 49 U.S.C. 10721, may offer to transport either persons or property for the account of the United States without charge! They may also, under the same provision, offer transportation under reduced rates. Section 10721 rates are published in government rate tenders, and apply to shipments moving on:

1. government bills of lading (GBL)
2. commercial bills of lading that are endorsed to show that they are to be either exchanged for, or converted to, GBLs at destination, after delivery to the consignees
3. commercial bills of lading endorsed to show that total transportation charges are assignable to, and will be reimbursed by, the government commercial bill of lading

Negotiations for revised section 10721 rates may be conducted when volume movements are expected, and when shipments are made on a recurring basis between designated places.

Shipment Rates

Section 10721 quotations do not apply to fixed-price F.O.B. destination contracts. Under fixed-price F.O.B. origin contracts, shipments are normally made on GBLs. However, if it is advantageous to the government, the contracting officer may occasionally require you, the contractor, to prepay the freight charges to a specific destination. In these cases, you should use a commercial bill of lading, and then seek reimbursement for the transportation costs under a separate item on the invoice. Under this type of arrangement, the government will always seek the benefit of section 10721 rates.

With regard to cost-reimbursement contracts, the Interstate Commerce Commission has ruled that section 10721 rates may be applied to shipments other than those made by the government, if the total benefit accrues to the government. *Keep in mind*: The government must either pay the charges or reimburse the contractor, then section 10721 rates may be used for shipments moving on commercial bills of lading under cost-reimbursement contracts.

However, the transportation costs must be direct and allowable elements under the contract in order for this provision to apply. This is a good note to keep in mind when preparing your next cost-reimbursement solicitation response.

Section 10721 rates may also be applied to the movement of household goods and personal effects of contractor employees who are relocated for the convenience of, and at the direction of, the U.S. government.

SMALL BUSINESS SET-ASIDES

Some items are set aside for procurement solely from small businesses. These are known as small business set-sides, and they can offer unique opportunities to supply a wide variety of products to the government. Under this type of procurement, you are given a competitive advantage over your large business counterparts because they are prohibited from bidding. They may normally have the economies of scale on their side, but the odds are evened by keeping them out of the running. The *Commerce Business Daily* lists those procurements reserved only for small business competition. Just what constitutes a small business is discussed in Chapter 8.

USE OF GOVERNMENT SOURCES BY CONTRACTORS

If it is in the government's interest, and if supplies and services required in the performance of a government contract are available from government supply sources, a contracting officer may authorize you to use these sources in performing cost-reimbursement contracts, when it is determined that a substantial dollar portion of your awards are of the cost-reimbursement type. Fixed-price contracts may also be included under this provision when the protection of classified information may require security equipment provided through GSA sources.

The use of government interagency motor pool vehicles and related services is also authorized. The related services include fuel and lubricants, vehicle inspection, maintenance and repair, storage, and the use of commercially rented vehicles for short term use. Complete rebuilding of major components of either contractor-owned or leased equipment requires the approval of the contracting office in each instance.

Vehicles and related services are obtained by submitting a written request to the appropriate GSA Regional Customer Service Bureau, Attention: Motor Equipment Activity. If the request is for more than five vehicles, then it must be submitted to the General Services Administration, FTM, Washington, DC 20406. These requests must contain the following:

1. two copies of the agency authorization to obtain vehicles and related services from the GSA
2. the number of vehicles and related services required, and their period of use
3. a list of the contractor's employees who are authorized to request vehicles and related services
4. when service is required, a listing of the make, model, and serial number of the contractor-owned or leased equipment authorized to be serviced
5. billing instructions and address

Before authorizing a contractor to use government supply sources, the contracting officer is required to prepare a written finding supporting issuance of the authorization. Orders for materials and supplies under various established schedule and requirement contracts, and government stock, require that contractors follow all of the terms and applicable procedures that have been established, either under the contract or by the issuing authority.

Title to all property acquired under the contracting officer's authorization will be vested in accordance with the terms of the contract, unless specifically provided for otherwise. If the contract is with an educational institution, then title to property having an acquisition cost of less than $1,000 will vest with the institution. Agencies may specify higher thresholds, if appropriate.

CONTRACTOR TEAMS AND POOLS: BIDDING WITH STRENGTH THROUGH UNITY

Contractor Team Arrangements

A contractor team arrangement exists when two or more companies form a partnership or joint venture in order to act as a potential prime contractor. A team arrangement would also exist when a potential prime contractor arranges that one or more other companies act as subcontractors under a specified government acquisition program.

These types of arrangements are considered beneficial, for they enable companies to complement each other's unique capabilities, thereby offering the government the best combination of performance, cost, and delivery for the end item being acquired. They are particularly appropriate in complex research and development procurements, but they may also be used to good advantage in other appropriate acquisitions and acquisition phases, including production. Team arrangements can be entered into at any point in the acquisition process, but they are normally entered into before submitting the offer.

Team arrangements neither authorize the violation of antitrust statutes, nor limit the government's rights or the prime contractor's responsibilities under the contract.

Defense Production and R&D Pools

A "pool" is a group of companies that have joined together in order to obtain and perform, either collectively or in conjunction with each other, defense production and research and development contracts. A specific agreement between the pool members must exist, and approval of the agreement is required by either the SBA under Section 9 or 11 of the Small Business Act, or by a designated official specified under Part V of Executive Order 10480, August 14, 1953 (18 FR 4939, August 20, 1952), and Section 708 of the Defense Production Act of 1950 (50 U.S.C. App. 2158).

A pool is treated in the same fashion as any other contractor. A contract cannot be awarded to a pool unless the offer is either submitted by the pool, or submitted by an individual pool member. This pool member must expressly state that the offer is being made on behalf of the pool.

Contracts with pools are exempt from the "manufacturer or regular dealer" requirement of the Walsh-Healey Act, and pools approved by the SBA are entitled to the preferences and privileges accorded to small business concerns.

Pool members are free to submit individual offers, however the contracting officer must not consider an independent offer by a pool member if that pool member participates in a competing offer submitted by the pool.

DETERMINING THE PRICE HISTORY OF AN ITEM TO BE BID ON

The first thing you should do is find out what the price history of the item has been. The price history simply means what the government paid for the given item at various points in time and for varying quantities in the past. The price history gives an insight into how your competition has been bidding on the item in the past. It offers food for thought, and if you enjoy games of strategy, you can get satisfaction out of understanding the tactics your competition used in the past, and drawing conclusions on what they will do in the future.

Sometimes the procurement is for a requirement that has never existed before. In this case, your best judgment comes into play. You will go over all sorts of pricing possibilities, from what the fair retail price is, to whether or not you should give the government a volume discount, and if so, how much. You will think about your competition, and wonder if they are going to bid on this also, and if they do, how they would logically apply their pricing strategy. By the way, you should now know that a discount offered the government for prompt payment has no effect on the award decision, so that's one less thing you will have to consider. Sometimes your competition may not bid directly, but will allow their distributors to take care of it. Sometimes the reverse will be true, and you could get crunched by a bigger company. Often, especially when the procurement for a given item has been made at irregular intervals or in varying quantities and package sizes, the problem of evaluation of previous history becomes complex.

What this all adds up to: Bidding is more than a numbers exercise; it can take on the proportions of a military campaign, with you as the general, wondering what your opponent can muster for the battle.

Where to Look for Information on Past History

Sometimes it is possible to get information easily from the buyers in charge of the procurement if they have the information readily at hand, and are not under too much of a rushed schedule. This information may be in the computer, or in that particular buyer's files. The computerized information is usually purged after one year, so it may not always be available. However, it is retained at some point in the records of the government. A good place to find what you are looking for is in the information supplied by the Federal Supply Code of Manufacturers (FSCM). This is available in microfiche edition, and will be of great help if you are bidding on items described by an FSCM number. The availability of this information can be determined by inquiry to the agencies you will be contracting with.

Abstract Services. Generally good, reliable, and complete information on past procurement pricing is available from an abstract service. Abstract services have no connection with the federal government. They are private enterprises specializing in collecting and correlating data. It is made available for sale to anyone wanting to bid on a particular item. Abstract services are listed in the yellow pages of major metropolitan centers, and certainly in the Washington, DC area. *The best way to evaluate an abstract service*: Telephone and find out if it's way of doing business is a personal one. Ask how many military and civilian buying offices the service covers. The more that are covered, the better it is for you. Let the service know that you are new to government contracting, if that is truly the case, and if the service is serious about getting you for a customer, it will volunteer a lot of helpful information.

Inquire if the abstract service offers a bulletin service, which is an advanced notice of what the government will be buying, in what quantities, and when. This will give you a leg up on the CBD, which if it has any faults at all, often leaves much to be desired in the time allowed to prepare your bid. This may be because the vast sums the government spends just can't be spent quickly enough. The requirements have to be pumped out on an avalanche basis, with little time allowed for the gentlemanly art of bidding. Think of how long it would take one person to spend one million dollars. This should give you some insight into the task faced by the federal government!

When using an abstract service, send your requests by letter, if time permits. However, the advantages of a telephone call can be very significant, in that the person at the service will be able to give you a quick interpretation of what is shown in the data, and may give you an insight into how to better proceed. The abstract service will give you the information and send you a bill.

The information will generally be of two distinct types:

- *The bid abstract.* This is usually a one-page document giving the name and location of the most recent bidders. Obsolete information is not included, but stale information may be if the procurement for the item hasn't taken place for an extended period of time. The prices bid by the various players are also included. The cost of an abstract runs about $7 to $12, depending on the extent of the information it contains.
- *The second type of report is the past history of the dollar value of all the bids submitted over the past few years.* The cost of this type of report can usually range from between $15.00 and $20.00, again the price depending on the extent of the information being provided.

The Federal Procurement Data Center. Another good source of historical information is the Federal Procurement Data Center. This department of the General Services Administration generates standard and special reports that summarize and correlate information such as the product or service purchased, the dollar amount, the contractor's name and address, whether the award was competitive or not, where the item was manufactured or the service performed, the government contracting office involved, and much more. The system's data base contains information on 3.5 million transactions with a cumulative dollar value exceeding $1.1 trillion, and dates back to Fiscal Year 1979. Most executive branch agencies and departments report to the system. They submit specifics on all transactions exceeding $25,000 and summaries of procurements under $25,000.

Standard reports are published quarterly and are free to anyone. Special reports are customized to your needs for a fee. Further information may be obtained by writing to the Federal Procurement Data Center, U.S. General Services Administration, 7th and D Streets SW, Room 7109, Washington, DC 20407, or telephoning 703–235–1326.

Based on price history information, it can take only a very short period of time to find out on which items in your area of expertise you can be most competitive. Sometimes the revelations are startling! Items that you could supply at half the price, and at a hefty profit, sometimes show up. The reverse can also be true. Sometimes you will wonder how your competition could possibly make money at the prices they are charging the government. Often their bids are quite puzzling. Let's look at what is really behind the process of successful bidding.

HOW YOUR BID CAN IMPACT ON OTHERS BIDDERS

If you want to win contracts, you've got to bid. Let's assume that you are a baker, and you are great at baking a loaf of whole wheat, but you're out of the running when it comes to pumpernickel. Common sense dictates that the pumpernickel should be left to someone else, while you sell your specialty to the government. Then something unexpected comes up. There, right before your eyes in the CBD, is a requirement for pizza, with anchovies yet, for a post exchange in northern Alaska! And to think that you have just the right kind of pizza ovens to do the job. No problem with the Walsh-Healey Act, either. You are a baker selling similar items to the general public! So you go for it, and all of a sudden you've doubled your annual business. Does this sound far-fetched? Not on your life. It happens every day!

Example: The item in question was a commodity, and a new bidder entered the picture, discovering that the successful bids were in the range of $1.25 per pound. The new bidder wanted this business very much, and on the next round requirement, he bid $1.23 per pound. The winning bid was $1.21 per pound. On the second appearance of the requirement a few months later, the new bidder bid $1.19 per pound, but this was higher by three cents a pound than the winning bid. The new bidder could have been successful in the second round if he had not been so concerned about leaving money on the table. The new bidder's pattern of bidding telegraphed to the "regulars" that the new kid on the block was going to make things rough for them, and since they weren't about to relinquish their business to this upstart, they tightened their competitive position. The big winner was the federal government.

Eventually the new bidder recognized this escalation in the intensity of the competition, and backed off in his attempt to low ball the competition. After that, the level of the winning bid gradually increased. No collusion existed, just the give and take of the marketplace.

WHEN TO SUBMIT A HIGH BID

At times you may want to submit a bid somewhat higher than what has been accepted for award in the past, but not excessively. On the surface this may appear as one of the better ways of *not* getting a contract. This will be true if there is more than one bidder, but often there is only one bidder, and if the buyer finds the price to be within an acceptable range, the award will be made. It is doubtful that, under this situation, a new requirement would be issued. This adds to the buyer's workload, causes delays in the receipt of the needed item, and slows the process of spending money. Also, you are sending a signal to the competition that you are not going to try to drive him out of business through irresponsible low bidding. That situation helps no one, including the government! Again, high bidding does not mean collusion.

Remember: Collusion is not a permitted practice and has significant legal consequences. What you are saying is that you intend to bid within the fair limits of the marketplace, and that is all.

Often a high bid is submitted by a potential contractor who has no intention of being competitive. This is done when that bidder's facility is at 100 percent capacity, and there isn't room for additional business. The thought behind this is to either benefit from a high profit situation if there are no other bidders, or to send a message to the competition that says "let's not get silly about this thing and start a price war." This is not recommended literally, for that would be collusion. Rather it represents action and reaction in a competitive climate.

Note: Any bid you submit, whether high or low, certainly lets the government know that you are around and in business. You may not be successful on the solicitation you are submitting, but you may be successful on future business when contacted by the government on an emergency purchase for a similar requirement. The result of letting the government know that you are around is somewhat similar to institutional advertising. It can bring business at any time.

THREE BIDDING STRATEGIES THAT CAN HELP YOU BE MORE COMPETITIVE

When a bid is submitted as either *all or none*, it is qualified by the condition that the entire requirement must be awarded to you based on the total price of your bid, not on individual low line item prices. You can see the advantage here. If you are very competitive on prune juice, but mediocre when it comes to apple juice, then the lower price on prune can make up for your excessive price on apple, resulting in an award.

Following the example above, you may be so poor a competitor on apple juice, that you recognize the futility of bidding on apple at all. In this case, a *line item bid* is called for. In this type of bid, you submit figures for those line items you are well equipped to bid competitively on, and avoid bidding on those items you will have little or no chance of getting. *Remember*:

Your bid must be responsive, and it will not be so if line item bidding is not allowed. This is seldom the case, for the government is well aware that all bidders are not created equal, and that line item bidding most often gets it the most for its money.

F.O.B. Bids

F.O.B. bids are those that take advantage of freight rate differentials. For example, you may notice that all successful previous bids on a particular item have been awarded to your competition with terms of F.O.B. the contractor's facility. Because of your competitive position, you are certain that you can get the goods to the destination at a lower cost than the government, so you bid the next round as F.O.B. destination. Your hunch pays off, you've underbid your competitors, and as the reckless captain of industry you know you are, you end up laughing all the way to the bank. This is an excellent strategy to use when appropriate. *Remember*: Stay on the responsive side!

Socioeconomic Bids

Some mention has been made about labor surplus area bids and bids by socially and economically disadvantaged businesses. These can give you an advantage if the product, or a portion of the product, comes from a firm meeting these criteria. The reason is that the government is interested in fostering the economic well being of these companies, and may offer preferential bid consideration if products from these companies are incorporated in your response. Check the solicitation first to see if any advantage exists, and if there is any question, don't hesitate to discuss the matter with the buyer. The buyer will be most helpful, and tell you straight from the shoulder whether or not your bid will fit the criteria.

HOW FREIGHT RATES AFFECT BIDDING

Freight rates can play an important part in deciding who will or will not get the award. Government tariffs are usually lower than the rates you and I are expected to pay. However, smart shopping for a carrier can make a big difference in your bid/award ratio. Not all carriers are best for all destinations. Some will charge excessively to one destination, and then virtually give the trip away on the next. All of this stems from the deregulation of the trucking industry.

Shop around wisely before picking a carrier for your shipment. If you are shipping from a remote spot, well off the path of the bigger carriers, you may be able to get a better rate by waiting for the next scheduled pickup by the carrier in that area, rather than insisting on the shipment on a given day. Keep your contractual delivery schedule in mind, though, before you jump to this solution. Often a favorable rate can be had if your shipment will be carried by a truck that will be going home empty. Anything the trucker makes on that trip is profit, but the difficult part is finding this carrier just at the right time.

Tip: Avoid doing business with marginal operators. You will be plagued by missed pickups and elaborate excuses, and the risk of default just isn't worth it.

When to Use Rail Shipments

Rail shipments sometimes offer an advantage when it comes to moving either large quantities or very bulky items. Rail may be more competitive in price, and it can be higher. Usually the shipper with a siding has the best advantage. *Note*: Make certain that your delivery destination is capable of accepting rail shipments before taking any action in this area.

Drop Shipping: A Good Choice for Lower Costs

Drop shipping, from place of manufacture to destination, is one good way to lower shipping costs. If the manufacturer of the item you are a dealer for is out of the geographical area serviced by the contract administration office, you can request a contract modification requesting acceptance at the manufacturer's plant. The government quality assurance representative servicing that area will then assume responsibility for inspecting the items. Of course, this would apply only to a change of horses midstream. On the original solicitation, the place of shipment is requested, so any last-minute changes can be avoided. Obviously the proximity of the manufacturer to the destination is important. *Remember*: By following this procedure, you may be giving the manufacturer the idea that he or she should also become a government contractor, and then you've just shot yourself in the foot. This has happened many times, so it's best to move carefully.

Bulk Shipping: Limited but Effective

Bulk shipping can provide a freight advantage, but its applications are limited. For example, you may elect to ship your product in bulk, then perform the final processing and packaging at a point close to the destination. This is a viable option as long as you have confidence in the quality control capabilities of the plant doing the final steps for you. It's a good idea to have someone on site to supervise the operation. You'll be glad you did!

HOW TO ENSURE A REASONABLE PROFIT ON A BID

Two Key Questions to Ask About a Prospective Bid

When contemplating the percentage of profit you want to make on a given bid, two questions must be considered:

- What percentage of profit makes it worthwhile to sell an item on the commercial market?
- What percentage of profit makes it worthwhile to sell the same item to the government?

These are not necessarily one and the same figure. You know what your commercial market profit has to be in order to stay competitive. The answer on what to charge the government depends, first, on the size of the requirement, and, second, on the impact the government business will have on your overall operation. If you are used to selling potatoes at a ton at a time, then one profit figure would be appropriate. If the government awards you a contract for one thousand tons of potatoes, then obviously you had recognized in your bid that a different profit percentage was called for. *Key point*: The main consideration on how much profit to earn is the risk involved, and what it costs you to get out the larger order. This is the thinking that will also be in the minds of your competitors, and you will have to react in a manner best suited to your particular situation. Price histories can help quite a bit.

Determining the Impact of Increased Business on Your Overall Costs

A greater volume will be experienced by the seller with government business. Since this business is being handled by a common facility—that is, the same site serving both commercial and government contracts—what will be the impact of the overhead, per unit produced or sold, on your commercial pricing structure? Usually the effect is significant, and it puts the company in a position to be more competitive across the board by spreading fixed costs across a greater volume of business—the economy of scale, if you will.

What is applicable in one situation may not be applicable in another, so the material just covered could fit your particular situation perfectly, or serve as a basis for alternative strategies.

INDEX - CHAPTER 5

6

HOW TO DEVELOP UNSOLICITED PROPOSALS THAT GET ACCEPTED

Unsolicited proposals are the primary means by which the government obtains creative ideas from the private sector to satisfy the nation's basic and applied research programs. Rapidly changing technology requires the utilization of every available resource by the government so that its goals and objectives can keep pace, and this isn't always accomplished through solicited proposals. In order to tap into the vast supply of talent "out there," the policy of the government is to encourage everyone, contractor or private citizen, to submit their ideas in the form of an unsolicited proposal.

This chapter will show you how to tailor your proposal to the agency you are serving, and help pave the way for significant income for you and your company.

THE GOVERNMENT'S POLICY ON UNSOLICITED PROPOSALS

By regulation, each department and agency is encouraged to set up its own specific procedures for encouraging the submittal of proposals, and part of this process is informing the public of its overall needs. For example, the Department of Energy has produced a brochure outlining the types of programs supported, and the areas in which unsolicited proposals are most welcome. Topics such as the procedure for handling inventions, the content of the proposal document, where to get help in preparing the proposal, and other information are spelled out in detail. Interesting policy information is also contained in the brochure, such as the DOE will normally fully fund the early phases of basic research and development programs, as well as a listing of the basic areas of DOE interest. A DOE program office may also encourage researchers to submit unsolicited proposals by issuing a Notice of Program Interest. The Air Force guide on unsolicited proposals explains how and where to submit proposals, lists focal points of interest for the various R&D organizations, and who to contact. Virtually every government department and agency has a similar type of publication; you must contact the right people and request the specific information you require.

Unsolicited proposals may be submitted at any time. However, in order for them to get the best possible review, there are certain basic ground rules that must be followed in their preparation. The methods the government uses to do business are structured in a highly detailed fashion, and the area of unsolicited proposals is no exception. As a result, the ideas submitted are classified under various headings, and it is important to know what they are in order to be most effective in obtaining idea acceptance.

Five Types of Material That May Be Submitted for Government Review

Let's take a look at the definition of terms assigned to the various types of material that can be submitted for review. Only one of these is classed as an unsolicited proposal.

Advertising material means material designed to acquaint the government with a prospective contractor's present products or potential capabilities.

A *Commercial product offer* means an offer of a commercial product that is usually sold to the general public and that the vendor wishes to see introduced into the government's supply system as an alternate or replacement for an existing supply item.

A *Contribution* means a concept, suggestion, or idea presented to the government for its use with no indication that the source intends to devote any further effort to it on the government's behalf.

Technical correspondence means written requests for information regarding government interest in research areas, submissions of research descriptions, proposal explorations, and other written technical inquiries.

An *Unsolicited proposal* means a written proposal that is submitted to an agency on the initiative of the submitter for the purpose of obtaining a contract with the government, and that is not in response to either a formal or informal request, other than an agency request constituting a publicized general statement of needs.

SIX EXCEPTIONS WHERE OTHER THAN FULL COMPETITION IS ALLOWED

Up to this point, the award of contracts by full and open competition has been stressed as one of the key procurement policies of the government. In fact, it seems that nothing could ever take place without it. How does this apply to unsolicited proposals? It doesn't! As usual, the government has covered every contingency, and it has a method of procurement called *Procurement by Other than Full and Open Competition.*

The policy is governed by 41 U.S.C. 253(c) and 10 U.S.C. 2304(c). Each statute authorizes, under certain conditions, contracting without providing for full and open competition. The Department of Defense, the Coast Guard, and NASA are subject to 10 U.S.C. 2304(c). Other executive agencies are subject to 41 U.S.C. 253(c).

There are still certain restrictions imposed by these laws preventing a carte blanche approach to contracting. For example, contracting without full and open competition cannot be justified for either lack of advanced planning, or concern by the agency regarding the expiration of funds. Contracting officers are also required to solicit offers from as many potential sources as practical. However, there are six specific circumstances where procurement by other than full and open competition is allowed:

1. When only one responsible source exists, and no other supplies or services will satisfy the agency requirements
2. under circumstances of unusual and compelling urgency, where delay in awarding the contract would be injurious to the government
3. for either industrial mobilization or engineering, development, and research capability
4. under either international agreement or treaty, and as authorized by statute
5. for reasons of national security
6. if it is in the public interest

With regard to item 1, supplies and services may be considered to be from a sole source if that source has submitted an unsolicited research proposal that demonstrates a unique and innovative concept, the substance of which is either not available to the government, or does not resemble the substance of a pending competitive acquisition.

Item 3–industrial mobilization or engineering, development, and research capability–comes into play when it becomes necessary to award a contract to a particular source in order to maintain the availability of a facility, producer, manufacturer, or supplier in case of a national emergency. It also is used to achieve industrial mobilization. It would apply to cases where it is necessary to either establish or maintain an essential engineering, research, or development capability that is to be provided by an educational and other nonprofit institution, or by a federally funded research and development center.

Some of the applications of item 3 would be as follows:

- To keep vital facilities and suppliers in business, and to make them available in event of national emergency.
- To train a selected supplier in the furnishing of either critical supplies or services, to prevent the loss of a supplier's ability and employee's skills, and to maintain active engineering, research, and development work.
- To maintain properly balanced sources of supply for meeting the requirements of acquisition programs in the interest of industrial mobilization.
- To limit competition for current acquisition of selected supplies and services that are approved for production planning under the DOD Industrial Preparedness Program. Awards would then be made to those producers for which industrial preparedness agreements covering the specific items exist.
- To create and maintain the required domestic capability for production of critical supplies by limiting competition to items manufactured in the United States or the United States and Canada.
- To keep contractors in production, when there would otherwise be a break.
- To divide current production requirements between two or more contractors in order to provide an adequate industrial mobilization base.
- To acquire specific items, such as measuring tools, optical instruments, communications equipment, and items containing jeweled bearings.

FIVE REQUIREMENTS OF A VALID UNSOLICITED PROPOSAL

The easiest way to begin is to state what an unsolicited proposal is *not*: It is not advertising material, commercial product offers, a contribution, or technical correspondence. An unsolicited proposal, by definition, is a written proposal submitted on the initiative of the submitter for the purpose of obtaining a contract. In order for an unsolicited proposal to be valid, it must:

1. be innovative and unique
2. be independently originated and developed by the offeror
3. be prepared without government supervision
4. include sufficient detail to permit a determination that government support could be worthwhile, and that the proposed work could benefit either the agency's R&D work, or other mission responsibilities
5. not be an advance proposal for a known agency requirement that can be acquired by competitive methods

Unsolicited proposals in response to a publicized general statement of agency needs are considered to be independently originated. If the proposal does not fit a particular agency's requirements, that agency may identify other agencies who might have an interest in the subject matter. *Advice*: Do your homework and make certain that the proposal is submitted to the proper agency in the first place.

HOW TO MAKE THE MOST OF FREE AGENCY ASSISTANCE

You are encouraged to make preliminary contact with the agency staff before preparing a formal proposal or submitting data to the government. These contacts should include, as a minimum, inquiries into the general need for the type of effort contemplated. They should also include discussions with agency technical personnel to try and understand the agency's mission and responsibilities relative to the proposal.

As a minimum, the agency is required to offer the following written information at no cost:

1. guidance on what would constitute an acceptable unsolicited proposal, and the suggested content
2. the requirements necessary to meet the criteria of becoming a successful contractor and potential organizational conflicts of interest
3. the role technical correspondence will play before proposal preparation
4. agency contact points for information regarding advertising, contributions, solicitation mailing lists, and other types of transactions frequently mistaken for unsolicited proposals
5. procedures for submission and evaluation of unsolicited proposals
6. information sources on agency objectives and areas of potential interest
7. instructions for identifying and marking proprietary information with the correct restrictive legends

Item 2 mentions potential organizational conflicts of interest. These exist when the nature of the work to be performed under a proposed government contract may, without some restrictions on future activities, result in an unfair competitive advantage to the contractor, or impair the contractor's objectivity in performing the contract work. However, an agency head may waive any rule and provision with regard to an organizational conflict of interest, if it is determined that its application would not be in the government's best interest. *Keep in Mind*: You may have to do a little creative selling if the topic of conflict of interest comes up.

WHAT TO INCLUDE: A PROPOSAL CONTENT CHECKLIST

Although there is no one, acceptable format for an unsolicited proposal, the following checklist will help you get started.

Basic Information

- your name and address and type of organization, such as profit, nonprofit, educational, or small business
- the names and telephone numbers of technical and business personnel to be contacted for evaluation and negotiation purposes
- the identity of proprietary data to be used only for proposal evaluation purposes
- the names of other federal, state, local agencies and parties who have received the proposal, and whether or not they are willing to fund it
- when applicable, reference the appropriate agency document that resulted in the proposal; for example, a *Notice of Program Interest* or other similar document
- the date of submission
- the signature of the person authorized to represent and contractually obligate the offeror

Technical Information

- a concise title and abstract of approximately 200 words describing the proposed effort
- a reasonably complete discussion stating the objectives of the proposed effort, the method of approach and the extent of effort to be expended, the nature and extent of the anticipated results, and the manner in which the work will help to support accomplishment of the agency's mission
- the names and biographical information of your key personnel, and their alternates, if any
- the type of support needed from the agency, including facilities, equipment, materials, and personnel resources

Supporting Information

- the proposed price and total estimated cost of the project presented in enough detail to permit meaningful evaluation
- the period of time the proposal is valid (a six-month minimum is suggested)
- the type of contract preferred
- the proposed duration of the effort
- a brief description of either the company or organization, its experience in the field, and the facilities that will be used in performing the work

- any required statements concerning organizational conflicts of interest, security clearances, and environmental impacts

Tips on Organizing Your Proposal

All proposals are usually divided into three parts:

a technical section

a business management section

a cost section

Current financial statements should be included in the cost section.

Elaborate proposals are neither required nor desired. However, if you were going to submit an unsolicited proposal, you should take care to present a readable, understandable document. It's OK to use technical terms, but don't try to dazzle them with footwork.

After you've completed a draft copy, give it to someone who is reasonably well-qualified to brush up the syntax. Technically gifted personnel are notoriously inept in using the King's English. Ask someone to play the devil's advocate. Try to find any holes in the proposal before sending it in. You will have too much riding on its successful outcome not to take this final precaution.

Written Government Notices That Must Be Included in Your proposal

Before starting a comprehensive evaluation of the proposal, the person you are dealing with on an initial contact basis in the agency will review the proposal for completeness, and if it passes muster, prompt review will be initiated. A notice will be attached to your proposal indicating that the information in it cannot be disclosed outside of the government, and cannot be duplicated, used, or disclosed in whole or in part for any purpose other than to evaluate the proposal.

Important: Each page of the proposal must bear this legend:

Use or disclosure of proposal data is subject to the restriction on the title page of this proposal.

If this legend is missing or is worded in any other fashion, the proposal will be returned to you along with a friendly reminder stating that if you fix it up with the correct wording, it will be acceptable for review.

Unless you state in writing that no restrictions are imposed on either the disclosure or use of the data contained in the proposal, the coordinating office will place a restriction notice in the form of a cover sheet or clear marking on the face of the proposal that reads as follows:

UNSOLICITED PROPOSAL

USE OF DATA LIMITED

All government personnel are required to use **EXTREME CARE** to ensure that the information in this proposal is not disclosed outside the government and is **NOT DUPLICATED, USED, OR DISCLOSED** in whole or in part for any purpose other than evaluation of the proposal, without the written permission of the offeror. If a contract is awarded on the basis of this proposal, the contract's terms shall control disclosure and use.

Important: In your proposal you must positively identify trade secrets, commercial and financial information, and other privileged and confidential information to the government. The notice just presented is used only to control the document while it is in the agency's hands. However, it does not justify an agency withholding information and improperly denying the public access to information when the Freedom of Information Act, 5 U.S.C. 552, is invoked.

Rest easy; your idea will be safe and sound, provided you follow all of the correct procedures.

How Unsolicited Bids Are Evaluated

The evaluation process includes weighing the following factors that are appropriate for the particular proposal:

1. the unique and innovative methods, approaches, and concepts demonstrated by the proposal
2. the overall scientific, technical, or socioeconomic merits of the proposal
3. the potential contribution of the proposal to the agency's specific mission
4. the offeror's capabilities, related experience, facilities, and techniques that are integral factors for achieving the proposed objectives
5. the qualifications, capabilities, and experience of the proposed principal investigator, team leader, or key personnel who are critical in achieving the proposal objectives

Prior to initiating the reviewing process, the proposal will be examined in order to ascertain that it contains sufficient technical and cost information, that it complies with the marking requirements explained above, and that it has the necessary responsible company signatory approvals.

A favorable comprehensive evaluation of an unsolicited proposal does not, in itself, justify the awarding of a contract without providing for full and open completion. Before any award is made, it will first be determined whether or not the item is either available to the government from another source, or closely resembles a pending competitive acquisition requirement.

It must also be determined that an innovative and unique method, approach, or concept exists.

If disapproved, the proposal will be returned to you. If it is accepted, the contracting officer will begin negotiations only after the agency technical office sponsoring the anticipated contract supports its recommendations with facts and circumstances that preclude competition, provides the needed funds, and supports the project with all of the necessary justification.

12 Government Requirements for Justifying a Project

This justification is somewhat extensive, and knowing the factors considered will assist you in shaping your proposal, each justification is required to contain at least the following information, only some of which are controllable by you:

1. The identification of the agency and the contracting activity, and specific identification of the document as a justification for other than full and open competition.
2. The nature and/or description of the action being approved.
3. A description of the supplies or services required to meet the agency's needs, including the estimated value.
4. An identification of the statutory authority permitting other than full and open competition.
5. A demonstration that the proposed contractor's unique qualifications and the nature of the acquisition requires the use of the authority cited.
6. A description of the efforts made to ensure that offers are solicited from as many potential sources as practical, including whether or not a CBD notice was or will be publicized, and if not, the reason why.
7. A determination by the contracting officer that the anticipated cost to the government will be fair and reasonable.
8. A description of the market survey conducted, and either its results or a statement of the reasons why a market survey was not conducted.
9. Any other facts supporting the use of other than full and open competition. This could consist of the reasons technical data packages, specifications, engineering descriptions, statements of work, and purchase descriptions suitable for full and open competition have not been developed, or the reasons why they are not available.
10. A listing of the sources, if any, that have expressed, in writing, an interest in the acquisition.
11. A statement of any actions that the agency may take to remove or overcome any barriers to competition before any subsequent acquisition of the supplies and services required

12. Contracting officer certification that the justification is accurate and complete to the best of the contracting officer's knowledge and belief.

Six CBD Advertising Exceptions That Apply to Unsolicited Proposals

Items 6 and 8 require some further discussion. With regard to item 6, the exceptions to CBD advertising, there are six basic considerations that apply to an unsolicited proposal:

1. that a disclosure in the CBD would compromise national security
2. that serious injury to the government would result from delays
3. that publication of the notice would jeopardize the unique and innovative research concept
4. that the contract action will be by a defense agency
5. that the contract will be performed outside of the United States, its possessions including Puerto Rico, and that local sources will be solicited only
6. when the head of the agency determines in writing that advance notice is neither appropriate nor reasonable.

Market Surveys: Justification Can Be More Flexible

By regulation, a procuring agency is required to conduct market surveys and acquisition planning for all acquisitions for the purpose of promoting full and open competition. The minimum effort would consist of obtaining competition to the extent that is practical, taking into account the nature of the supplies or services to be acquired. Market surveys and planning are synonymous in their application. The planning aspect requires an anticipation of what the agency's needs will be in the future, and taking the appropriate action necessary to solicit prospective suppliers in fulfilling these needs. The planning methods used are lengthy and complex, and they devote themselves to the mechanics of the process. *Keep in mind*: The odds will be in your favor that a government official has not dreamed up the type of thing you will submit in your unsolicited proposal. So move ahead, and don't be too concerned about this aspect of the justification.

SECURITY AND UNSOLICITED PROPOSALS: HOW TO PROTECT YOUR CLASSIFIED INFORMATION

If at all possible, an unclassified proposal should be submitted. If this is not feasible, and it is known that a proposal contains or may contain classified information, it should be classified in accordance with its content.

The proposal should indicate if it contains restricted data, formerly restricted data, or other classified information. Registered mail should be used to transmit any secret proposal and secret papers related to the proposal. Either certified or first-class mail may be used for confidential proposals and papers. In all cases, double opaque envelopes should be used. The outer envelope should be addressed in the same manner as any other mail, and it must not give any indication that it contains classified documents. If you have further questions, contact the Director of Security of the agency you will be dealing with.

If you do have a better mouse trap, and it fits all the guidelines, why not submit an unsolicited proposal? The amount of effort involved is minimal, and you just cannot afford *not* to take advantage of waiting business opportunities.

INDEX - CHAPTER 6

7

SUBCONTRACTING: WHEN IT MAKES SENSE AND HOW TO DO IT

Subcontracting is encouraged, even required in some cases, because of its consistency with many collateral policies of the contracting process. Subcontracting provides a larger distribution of funds, broadens the mobilization base, makes available a greater number of decentralized production facilities, and can be an aid to small businesses and labor surplus areas. This chapter offers an overview of subcontracting, and examines some of the considerations and opportunities relating to both contractors and subcontractors.

MAKE-OR-BUY PROGRAMS

All negotiated acquisitions in excess of $2 million will require that prospective contractors submit make-or-buy programs unless:

1. The contract is for research and development, and no significant future contracts for the production of prototypes and hardware under the same contract are anticipated.
2. The contract is set on the basis of either adequate price competition or established catalog and market prices of commercial items.
3. The contract involves work that, in the judgment of the contracting officer, is not complex.

The prime contractor is responsible for managing contract performance, including planning, placing, and administration of subcontracts, as necessary, to assure the lowest overall cost and technical risk to the government. Although it doesn't expect to participate in every management decision, the government may reserve the right to review and agree on the contractor's make-or-buy program. This is done so as to ensure reasonable prices, satisfactory performance, and the implementation of socioeconomic programs. All of this should be considered by the contractor in formulating any make-or-buy decision.

THE GOVERNMENT'S LIMITATIONS IN CONTROLLING SUBCONTRACTS

In the absence of a contractual relationship (privity of contract), the government has no legal basis on which to directly control or administer a subcontract. This matter is left solely with the prime contractor. In most cases, however, the subcontract clauses of the prime contract will require contracting officer approval prior to placement of any subcontracts. Although this may be the requirement, the no-privity rule still applies. It even applies where the subcontract is subject to all of the same terms and conditions as the prime contract, and it applies to all contracts, regardless of type. Approval is required in order to determine the necessity for the subcontract, the capabilities of the proposed subcontractor, the proposed type of subcontract, and the scope of the solicitation used by the prime contractor before the selection of the subcontractor.

As in many things applying to government contracting, there is an exception to the no-privity rule. This occurs when a prime contractor acts as an agent of the government (that is, acts on behalf of the government) for the purpose of buying goods and services. There is such a close relationship, contractually, between the seller and the government in this situation that it is doubtful the vendor could be classed as a subcontractor.

WHEN TO SEEK SUBCONTRACT CONSENT

''Consent to subcontract'' means the contracting officer's written consent for the prime contractor to enter into a particular subcontract. Consent is required when the work to be performed is complex, the dollar value is substantial, or the government's interest is not adequately protected by competition. The type of contract, and the resulting subcontracts, are also taken into account in determining the need for consent.

Consent to subcontract is not required under prime contracts that are either firm-fixed-price, or fixed-price with economic price adjustment provisions. If you have an approved purchasing system, then consent to subcontracts is not required under other fixed-price prime contracts, except for any subcontracts selected for special surveillance.

If you do not have an approved purchasing system, then consent to subcontracts will be required:

1. under fixed-price incentive prime contracts
2. under fixed-price redeterminable prime contracts
3. under firm-fixed-price prime contracts
4. under fixed-price prime contracts having economic price adjustment provisions, when a new subcontract results from an unpriced modification to the prime contract
5. for a cost-reimbursement, time-and-materials, or labor-hour prime subcontract estimated to be over $25,000, including any fee
6. for one of a number of subcontracts with a single subcontractor for either the same or related supplies and services that in the aggregate are estimated to be over $100,000

Cost-reimbursement and letter prime contracts require consent to subcontracts for:

1. the fabrication, purchase, rental, installation, or other acquisition of special test equipment, test items, or test facilities valued at more than $10,000
2. contracts having experimental, developmental, or research work as one of their purposes

If you do not have an approved purchasing system, consent is also required under cost-reimbursement and letter prime contracts for:

1. cost-reimbursement, time-and-materials, or labor-hour subcontracts
2. fixed-price subcontracts exceeding either $25,000 or 5 percent of the total estimated cost of the prime contract; except that for the DOD, Coast Guard, and NASA, the amounts will be either the greater of the small purchase limitation currently in effect or 5 percent of the total estimated cost of the prime contract

These requirements also apply to the acquisition of major systems, subsystems, and their components, even if you have an approved purchasing system. You must notify the government in advance if you plan to subcontract utilizing these types of contracts.

Finally, except for the purchase of raw material and commercial stock items, consent is required for all subcontracts under time-and-material contracts, and for subcontracting architect-engineer services, mortuary services, and the shipment and storage of personal property (when an agency requires prior approval of the subcontractor's storage facilities).

Time and material subcontracts for architect-engineer services require approval, and so do subcontracts for mortuary services, refuse services, as well as the shipment and storage of personal property, if that approval is required by the purchasing agency.

Any other specific requirements for approval will be called out in the subcontract clause of your contract.

Approved Purchasing Systems

The Administrative Contracting Officer is responsible for granting, withholding, and withdrawing approval of a contractor's purchasing system. Approval is granted after a Contractor's Purchasing Systems Review (CPSR) is conducted, and the results indicate that the purchasing policies and practices are efficient, and that they provide adequate protection of the government's interests. The CPSR is required when a contractor's sales to the government are expected to exceed $10 million during any following 12-month period. These sales can be in the form of prime contracts, subcontracts, or modifications to existing contracts. If the negotiated price is based on either established catalog or market prices of commercial items that are sold in substantial quantities to the general public, or the prices are set by law or regulation, then the $10 million figure is not applicable.

Generally, a CPSR is not performed for a specific contract, and the $10 million review level can be raised or lowered by an agency head if it is in the best interests of the government. Under a CPSR, specific attention will be given to:

1. degree of price competition obtained
2. pricing policies and techniques, including methods of obtaining accurate, complete, and current cost and pricing data and certification, as required
3. methods of evaluating a subcontractor's responsibility
4. treatment accorded affiliates and other concerns that have a close working arrangement with the contractor
5. policies and procedures pertaining to labor surplus area businesses, small business, and disadvantaged business

6. planning, award, and postaward management of major subcontracting programs
7. compliance with cost accounting standards in awarding subcontracts
8. appropriateness of the types of subcontracts used

Either the withholding or withdrawal of approval will occur when there are major weaknesses, or when the contractor is unable to provide sufficient information on which to base an affirmative determination.

Factors Used in Evaluating a Subcontract Proposal

In any solicitation requiring information for a proposed make-or-buy (that is, subcontract) program by the contractor, it should clearly set forth any special factors that will be used in evaluating the contractor's plan. Essentially, what will be required is that the contractor should evaluate the capabilities, capacities, and availability of small business and labor surplus area concerns as subcontract sources. Other factors, such as schedules, integration control, proprietary processes, and technical superiority or exclusiveness will also come into play. Finally, after making these considerations, the bidder will have to identify in his or her proposed make-or-buy program:

1. that work which will be performed by the contractor
2. that work which will be performed by the subcontractor
3. that work which can either be made or bought by the contractor; that is, optionally subcontracted

The prospective contractor must state the reasons for the make-buy decisions in sufficient detail so that the contracting officer may easily determine that sound business and technical judgment have been applied to each major element of the program. Since the contractor has the basic responsibility for the make-or-buy decisions, the contracting officer will usually accept the contractor's decisions unless they will harm the government or be inconsistent with government policy.

If the contracting officer determines that the proposed subcontract is unacceptable to the government, he or she will notify the contractor of consent refusal. It's then up to the contractor to make other arrangements for the proposed work. This may be accomplished by changing some of the terms of the subcontract, or it may require the choice of another subcontract source. Of course, the exact solution will hinge on the contracting officer's reasons for denying consent in the first place.

Consent by the contracting officer does not constitute approval of the terms and conditions of the subcontract. These are the responsibility of the prime contractor. One thing that will automatically bring about denial of consent is a clause in the subcontract purporting to give the subcontractor the right of direct appeal to an appeals board. As you are now aware, this is not legally possible, and disputes between the prime and subcontractor are expected to be handled by those parties directly, without any involvement by the government.

Subcontracting: A Special Benefit for Many Smaller Businesses

Probably the greatest benefit from subcontracting accrues to the smaller firms. They do not usually have the resources necessary to carry out the more involved work required by some government procurements. *Note*: In some cases, this can be the most practical way, and even the only way, a small business can initially participate in government purchasing. However, if you are a small business, please don't interpret this last sentence as a statement of absolute fact. There are many opportunities for small businesses to obtain prime contracts. The limiting factor for some will often be their capabilities in terms of plant, equipment, and personnel. A close review of the government's requirements in the *Commerce Business Daily* will give you a pretty good idea where you can best fit in from a prime contractor standpoint.

HOW THE GOVERNMENT ENCOURAGES SMALL BUSINESS SUBCONTRACTING OPPORTUNITIES

Before 1961, the opportunities to participate in government procurement as a subcontractor were limited. However, the growing complexity of some government procurement was dramatically reducing certain segments of the small business share. Thus, Congress amended the Small Business Act requiring the Small Business Administration (SBA), the General Services Administration (GSA), and the Department of Defense (DOD) to develop a subcontracting program. This is reflected by a contract clause, which is included in most prime contracts in excess of $1 million and in subcontracts in excess of $500,000. It requires the prime contractor to establish a program assuring that small business is solicited for subcontract opportunities, that appropriate records are maintained, and that regular reports covering subcontract status and activities be submitted to the contracting officer. In addition to these requirements, any contractor receiving a contract for more than $10,000 is required to agree in the contract that small business concerns and small disadvantaged business concerns will have the maximum practical opportunity to participate in contract performance consistent with efficient contract performance.

Subcontracts with small business may be made either by the prime contractor or the SBA. Authorization for the SBA to perform in this manner is found in 15 U.S.C. 637(a) (1). The SBA, in implementing this authorization, may enter into a direct contract with any procuring agency and subsequently subcontract work to small business concerns.

Another significant development was Public Law 95–507, October 24, 1978, 92 stat. 1757. Among other things, this law amended U.S.C. 637(d) so as to require apparently successful offerors on supply and service solicitations in excess of $500,000, as well as apparently low bidders for construction contracts over $1 million, to have prepared, before award, their subcontracting plans. These plans require the setting forth of percentage goals for the utilization, as subcontractors, small business concerns, and small business concerns controlled by socially and economically disadvantaged individuals as subcontractors.

WHAT TO CONSIDER BEFORE YOU AGREE TO SUBCONTRACT

Subcontracting has its own unique set of requirements and considerations that you must be aware of before entering into any firm arrangements. As a subcontractor, you will not enjoy the opportunity to deal directly with the government in the event of a problem. In many cases the government will extend to the contractor the benefit of every element of doubt, and fair play will often accompany any decision to what may seem an excess. The subcontractor, however, will be held to the more stringent rules of the marketplace, and will have to toe a narrower line in his or her dealings with the prime contractor. Often government specifications and standards can exceed what is acceptable under the rules of good commercial practice. *Caution*: Before you sign on the dotted line make certain you have all of the necessary wherewithal required to do the job, and that your cost estimates cover all of the elements involved.

If you are certain of your capabilities, then the subcontract shouldn't pose any problem. Of course, you should have a thorough understanding of the requirements of the prime contract as it applies to your portion of that work. This should be called out verbatim as either an inclusion or exhibit to your contract. As the subcontractor, it is up to you to assist in defining the scope of the job you have to do. If you rely on the prime contractor's definition, and an error is made, then it could cause problems for all concerned. *Keep in mind:* In addition to the work described, there may be assumed obligations under the subcontract.

Before you have gotten to this point, however, the prime contractor will have reviewed detailed information about you and your company, and your capabilities. Your management staff and key personnel will have been looked at, as well as your manufacturing, quality control, and administrative functions. An overall appraisal of your ability to do the work will have been made, including a review of your financial capability to carry the work through completion, with the help of either advance or progress payments, if necessary.

Key point: Your profitability, or lack of it, under the subcontract will be a result of how well you estimated your costs and how well you allowed for potential problem areas and contingencies.

THE RESPONSIBILITIES OF LARGE BUSINESS IN SUBCONTRACTING

The main thrust of the subcontracting program begins with the larger companies having contracts in excess of the limits previously described. These companies have a requirement to designate, either within the company or division, a small business liaison officer whose job is to represent the interests of the small business community for subcontracting purposes. The responsibility of the small business liaison officer is to assist the small business in becoming qualified on the company bid lists, and to assist the small business in meeting the buyers for the large company's goods and services. A list of these large companies, along with the name of the small business liaison officer, is contained in the *Small Business Subcontracting Directory*. This is published by the SBA and is for sale through the U.S. Government Printing Office. *Note*: Virtually every product line or service is covered in this directory, and it is must reading for the small business owner who wants to become a serious subcontractor. Some of the product lines and services listed include construction, electronic systems, forgings, castings, overhaul of aircraft, boots and shoes, pyrotechnics and ordnance, solid propellant rocket motors, transportation, potatoes—white instant granule, diving and salvage, data processing, gyroscopes, and dredging. This is only a very small example of the categories covered, but it should indicate that there is something there for everyone. The number of companies listed in this directory exceeds 1,200.

There is another good directory published by the GSA that lists the large manufacturers corresponding with the regions covered by the GSA Service Centers. The company name, address, telephone number, and name of the person to contact are all included, as well as a brief description of the company's primary product lines. This directory is titled *GSA Subcontracting Directory*, and it is prepared annually. Again, it is recommended reading. Both directories may be obtained through your nearest GSA Office of Small and Disadvantaged Business Utilization or the Superintendent of Documents, U.S. Government Printing Office, Washington, DC 20402–9325, or call 202–275–2051.

Six Requirements Larger Companies Must Include in Their Subcontracting Plans

The larger companies are required to devise a subcontracting plan that includes the following specific considerations:

1. The separate percentage goals for using small business concerns and small disadvantaged business concerns as subcontractors.
2. The name of the individual employed by the offeror who will be responsible for administering the offeror's contracting program, and a description of the duties of the individual.
3. A description of the efforts the offeror will make in order to ensure that small business concerns and small disadvantaged business concerns will have an equitable opportunity to compete for subcontracts.
4. Assurance that the offeror will include the clause providing for utilization of small and disadvantaged business concerns in all subcontracts that offer further subcontracting opportunities. It also requires all subcontractors, with the exception of small business concerns, who have received subcontracts in excess of $500,000 ($1 million for construction) to adopt a subcontracting plan similar to that of the prime contractor.
5. Assurances that the offeror will cooperate in any studies and surveys required, submit periodic compliance reports, and submit SF 294, *Subcontracting Report for Individual Contracts*, and SF 295, *Summary Subcontract Report*. See Figures 7–1 and 7–2.
6. A recitation of the types of records the offeror will maintain to show that the procedures adopted are designed to comply with the subcontract plan.

Subcontracting plans are not required from small business concerns, for personal services contracts, for contracts to be performed outside of the territorial limits of the United States and its possessions, and for modifications of contracts that do not contain the necessary subcontract clauses.

SUBCONTRACTING REPORT FOR INDIVIDUAL CONTRACTS
(Report to be submitted semi-annually. See back of form for instructions)

FORM APPROVED OMB NO. 3090-0052

1. REPORTING PERIOD FROM (Date)	TO (Date)	2. REPORT NO.	3. TYPE OF CONTRACT ☐ PRIME CONTRACT ☐ SUBCONTRACT	4. DATE SUBMITTED

GENERAL INFORMATION

5. AGENCY/CONTRACTOR AWARDING CONTRACT *(Name & Address)*	7. REPORTING CONTRACTOR *(Name and Address)*	
6. PRIME CONTRACT NO. *(And Subcontract No., If applicable)*	8. BUSINESS CLASS. CODE	9. DUNS NO. *(If applicable)*
10. ADMINISTERING AGENCY	11. DATE OF LAST GOVERNMENT REVIEW	12. REVIEWING AGENCY

13. DOLLAR VALUE OF PRIME OR SUBCONTRACT.	14. ESTIMATED DOLLAR VALUE OF COMMITMENTS AS IN PLAN.	15. GOALS	DOLLARS	PERCENT
		a. SMALL BUSINESS CONCERNS		
		b. SMALL DISAD. BUSINESS CONCERNS		

SUBCONTRACT AND PURCHASE COMMITMENTS

COMMITMENTS	THIS REPORTING PERIOD		CUMULATIVE	
	DOLLARS	PERCENT	DOLLARS	PERCENT
16. TOTAL DIRECT SUBCONTRACT COMMITMENTS *(Sum of a & b)*		100		100
a. TOTAL SMALL BUSINESS CONCERNS				
(1) SMALL DISADVANTAGED BUSINESS CONCERNS *(% of 16)*				
(2) OTHER SMALL BUSINESS CONCERNS *(% of 16)*				
b. LARGE BUSINESS CONCERNS *(% of 16)*				
17. TOTAL INDIRECT COMMITMENTS *(Sum of a & b)*				
a. TOTAL SMALL BUSINESS CONCERNS				
(1) SMALL DISADVANTAGED BUSINESS CONCERNS *(% of 17)*				
(2) OTHER SMALL BUSINESS CONCERNS *(% of 17)*				
b. LARGE BUSINESS CONCERNS *(% of 17)*				

18. REMARKS:

19. TYPE THE NAME AND TITLE OF THE INDIVIDUAL ADMINISTERING CONTRACT	SIGNATURE	TELEPHONE NO. *(and Area Code)*
20. TYPE THE NAME AND TITLE OF THE APPROVING OFFICER	SIGNATURE	

NSN 7540-01-152-8078
PREVIOUS EDITION USABLE

294-102

STANDARD FORM 294 (REV. 10-83)
Prescribed by GSA
FAR (48 CFR) 53.219(a)

Figure 7–1

INSTRUCTIONS

GENERAL INSTRUCTIONS

1. This reporting form is prescribed for use in the collection of subcontract data from all Federal contractors and subcontractors which, pursuant to the Small Business Act of 1958, as amended by Public Law 95-507, are required to establish plans for subcontracting with small and small disadvantaged business concerns. Reports shall be submitted to the contracting officer semiannually as of March 31 and September 30, as well as at contract completion. This report is due by the 25th day of the month following the close of the reporting periods, in accordance with instructions contained in the contract or subcontract, or as directed by the contracting officer.

2. This report is not required to be submitted by small business concerns.

3. This report is not required for commercial products for which a company-wide annual plan has been approved. The Summary Subcontract Report is required for commercial products in accordance with the instructions on that form.

4. Only subcontract and purchase commitments involving performance within the U.S., its possessions, Puerto Rico, and the Trust Territory of the Pacific Islands will be included in this report.

SPECIFIC INSTRUCTIONS

ITEM 1 – Specify the period covered by this report (e.g., April 1, 1981 - September 30, 1981).

ITEM 2 – Specify the sequential report covering this contract. The initial report shall be identified as Report Number 1. Add "Final Report" for the last report being made.

ITEM 3 – Specify whether this report covers either a Prime Contract awarded by a Federal Department or Agency or a Subcontract awarded by a Federal prime contractor or subcontractor.

ITEM 5 – Enter the name and address of the Federal Department or Agency or Prime Contractor awarding the Prime or Subcontract.

ITEM 6 – Enter the prime contract number. If this report covers a subcontract, enter both the prime contract and subcontract numbers.

ITEM 7 – Enter the name and address of the Prime Contractor or Subcontractor submitting the report.

ITEM 8 – Enter the Business Classification Code as follows:

Code	Definition
LB	Large Business
NP	Non-Profit Organization (including Educational Institutions).

ITEM 9 – Enter Dun and Bradstreet Universal Numbering System (DUNS) number (if available).

ITEM 10 – Identify Federal agency administering the contract. For Department of Defense, identify appropriate military department; i.e., Army, Navy, Air Force, or Defense Logistics Agency. Civilian agencies should be identified as noted in the contract award document; i.e., NASA, DOE, GSA, HHS, SBA, etc.

ITEM 11 & 12 – Enter the date of the last formal surveillance review conducted by the cognizant Department or Agency Small and Disadvantaged Business Specialist or other review personnel. For DOD, also identify the military department or Defense Contract Administration Service, as appropriate, that conducted the review. In those cases where the Small Business Administration conducts its own review, show the date and "SBA".

ITEM 13 – Specify the face value of the Prime or Subcontract covered by this report. If the value changes, the face value shall be adjusted accordingly.

ITEM 14 – Enter the estimated dollar value of subcontract and purchase commitments as set forth in the Subcontract Plan.

ITEM 15 – Specify in the appropriate blocks the dollar amount and percent of the reporting contractor's total subcontract awards contractually agreed upon as goals for subcontracting with Small Business and Small Disadvantaged Business concerns. NOTE: Should the original goals agreed upon at contract awards be either increased or decreased as a result of a contract modification, the amount of the revised goals shall be indicated.

ITEM 16 – Specify in the appropriate block the total amount of all direct subcontract commitments and the dollar amount and percentage of the total placed with the subcontractor classification indicated in a and b, both for this period and cumulative. Do not include in this report purchase commitments made in support of commercial business being performed by reporting contractor.

ITEM 17 – Complete Item 17 only if indirect contract commitments were included in establishing the small and small disadvantaged business goals for the contract being reported. Specify in the appropriate block the total allocable dollar amount of indirect commitments and the dollar amount and percentage of the total placed with the subcontractor classifications indicated in a(1), a(2), and b, both for this period and cumulative.

ITEM 18 – Enter any remarks. If the goals were not met, explain why on the final report.

ITEM 19 – Enter name and title of company individual responsible for administering contract.

ITEM 20 – The approving officer shall be the senior official of the company, division, or subdivision (plant or profit center) responsible for contract performance.

DEFINITIONS

1. A Small Business Concern is a concern that meets the pertinent criteria established by the Small Business Administration.

2. (a) A Small Disadvantaged Business means any small business concern:

(1) which is at least 51 per centum owned by one or more socially and economically disadvantaged individuals; or, in the case of any publicly-owned business, at least 51 per centum of the stock of which is owned by one or more socially and economically disadvantaged individuals; and

(2) whose management and daily business operations are controlled by one or more of such individuals.

(b) The contractor shall presume that socially and economically disadvantaged individuals include Black Americans, Hispanic Americans, Native Americans, Asian-Pacific Americans, and other minorities, or any other individual found to be disadvantaged by the Small Business Administration pursuant to Section 8(a) of the Small Business Act. "Native Americans" include American Indians, Eskimos, Aleuts, and native Hawaiians. "Asian-Pacific Americans" include U.S. citizens whose origins are from Japan, China, the Philippines, Vietnam, Korea, Samoa, Guam, the Trust Territory of the Pacific Islands, Northern Marianas, Laos, Cambodia, and Taiwan.

(c) Contractors acting in good faith may rely on written representations by their subcontractors certifying their status as either a small business concern or a small business concern owned and controlled by socially and economically disadvantaged individuals.

(d) The Office of Minority Small Business and Capital Ownership Development in the Small Business Administration will answer inquiries from prime contractors and others relative to the class of eligibles and has final authority to determine the eligibility of a concern to be designated as a small disadvantaged business.

3. Commercial Products means products sold in substantial quantities to the general public and/or industry at established catalog or market prices.

4. Commitments as used herein is defined as a contract, purchase order, amendment, or other legal obligation executed by the reporting corporation, company, or subdivision for goods and services to be received by the reporting corporation, company, or subdivision.

5. Direct Commitments are those which are identified with the performance of a specific government contract, including allocable parts of awards for material which is to be incorporated into products under more than one Government contract.

6. Indirect Commitments are those which, because of incurrence for common or joint purposes, are not identified with specific Government contracts, these awards are related to Government contract performance but remain for allocation after direct awards have been determined and identified to specific Government contracts.

STANDARD FORM 294 BACK (REV. 10-83)

Figure 7–1, continued

SUMMARY SUBCONTRACT REPORT
(Report to be submitted quarterly. See Instructions on reverse) (Type or Print)

FORM APPROVED OMB NO. 3090-0053

1. CONTRACTING AGENCY
2. ADMINISTERING AGENCY
3. DATE OF LAST GOVERNMENT REVIEW
4. REVIEWING AGENCY
5. DUNS NO.
6. REPORT SUBMITTED AS: ☐ PRIME CON-TRACTOR ☐ SUBCON-TRACTOR ☐ BOTH
7. CORPORATION, COMPANY, OR SUBDIVISION COVERED *(Name, Address, ZIP Code)*
8. MAJOR PRODUCTS OR SERVICE LINES:
a.
b.
c.

CUMULATIVE COMMITMENTS

Subcontract and Purchase Commitments for the Period October 1, 19 ____ through ____________________, 19 ____

COMMITMENTS	CURRENT FISCAL YEAR *(To date)*		SAME PERIOD LAST YEAR	
	DOLLARS	PERCENT	DOLLARS	PERCENT
9. TOTAL *(Sum of a and b)*		100		100
a. SMALL BUSINESS CONCERNS				
b. LARGE BUSINESS CONCERNS				
10. SMALL DISADVANTAGED BUSINESS CONCERNS *($ & % of 9)*				
11. LABOR SURPLUS AREA CONCERNS *($ & % of 9)*				

SUBCONTRACT GOAL ACHIEVEMENT

GOALS	NO. OF CON-TRACTS	$ VALUE OF SUBCONTRACTS (000)	$ VALUE OF SUBCONTRACT GOALS	ACTUAL GOAL ACHIEVEMENT	
				DOLLARS	%
12. CONTRACTS WITH SMALL BUSINESS SUBCONTRACT GOALS					
a. ACTIVE CONTRACTS					
b. CONTRACTS COMPLETED THIS QUARTER WHICH MET GOALS					
c. CONTRACTS COMPLETED THIS QUARTER NOT MEETING GOALS					
13. CONTRACTS WITH SMALL DISADVANT. BUS. SUBCONTRACT GOALS					
a. ACTIVE CONTRACTS					
b. CONTRACTS COMPLETED THIS QUARTER WHICH MET GOALS					
c. CONTRACTS COMPLETED THIS QUARTER NOT MEETING GOALS					

14. REMARKS *(Enter a short narrative explanation if: (a) Zero is entered in Blocks 9a or 10 for current fiscal year, (b) the percent entry in Block 9a for current fiscal year is more than 5 percentage points below the percent reported for same period last year, or (c) the percent entry in Block 10 for current fiscal year is lower than the percent reported for same period last year.)*

15. NAME AND TITLE OF LIAISON OFFICER	SIGNATURE	DATE	TELEPHONE NO. *(and Area Code)*
16. NAME AND TITLE OF APPROVING OFFICIAL	SIGNATURE	DATE	

NSN 7540-01-152-8079
PREVIOUS EDITION USABLE

295-102

STANDARD FORM 295 (REV. 10-83)
Prescribed by GSA
FAR (48 CFR) 53.219(b)

Figure 7–2

INSTRUCTIONS

GENERAL INSTRUCTIONS

1. This reporting form is prescribed for use in the collection of subcontract data from Federal contractors and subcontractors which hold one or more contracts over $500,000 ($1 million for construction) and are required to subcontract with small and small disadvantaged business concerns under a subcontract plan as required by the Small Business Act of 1958, as amended by Public Law 95-507. (See items 9 and 10 of Specific Instructions).

2. The report may be submitted on a corporate, company, or subdivision (e.g., plan or division operating as a separate profit center) basis unless otherwise directed. After submission of the first report on this form, succeeding reports shall be submitted on the same basis.

3. Reports shall be submitted by the 25th day of the month following the close of the reporting period, as follows: (a) quarterly, in accordance with instructions below, or as directed by the contracting activity, or (b) annually for subcontracts covered by an approved company-wide annual subcontracting plan for commercial products. The annual report should summarize all Federal contracts for commercial products performed during the year and should be submitted in addition to required quarterly reports, for other than commercial products, if any. Show in Item 14 or in an attachment to the report, the share of this total attributable to each agency from which contracts for such commercial products were received. Send a copy of this report to each listed agency.

4. If a contractor is performing work for more than one Federal agency, a separate report shall be submitted to each agency covering its contracts. However, for DOD contracts, see paragraph 5, below.

5. (a) For reports covering contracts awarded by the military departments or agencies of the Department of Defense (DOD) or subcontracts awarded by DOD prime contracts, each reporting corporation, company, or subdivision (except contractors involved in maintenance, repair, and construction) shall report its total DOD business on one report (i.e., it shall not segregate subcontracts arising from work for the Army, Navy, Air Force, or Defense Agencies). All contractors shall submit:

(i) The original of each report directly to the Office of the Deputy Secretary of Defense, Attention: Director of Small and Disadvantaged Business Utilization, The Pentagon, Washington, DC 20301.

(ii) A copy of the report to the office listed below whose military activity is responsible for contract administration of the contractor:

ARMY — Director of Small and Disadvantaged Business Utilization, Office of the Secretary of the Army, Washington, DC 20360

NAVY — Director of Small and Disadvantaged Business Utilization, Office of the Secretary of the Navy, Washington, DC 20360

AIR FORCE — Director of Small and Disadvantaged Business Utilization, Office of the Secretary of the Air Force, Washington, DC 20330

DLA — Staff Director of Small and Disadvantaged Business Utilization, HQ Defense Logistics Agency (Attention U) Cameron Station, Alexandria, VA 22314

(iii) A copy of the report, in accordance with instructions contained in the contract or subcontract, to the Federal agency or military department or defense agency, which is administering the prime or subcontractor.

(b) Contractors involved in maintenance, repair and construction shall also submit this report, similarly on a quarterly basis, to the appropriate construction contract administration activity. If a construction contractor is involved with more than one contract administration activity, this report should be submitted to each activity reflecting the contract awards under the supervision of the particular contract administration activity.

6. For NASA contracts forward reports to NASA - Office of Procurement (HM-1) Washington, DC 20546. For Department of Energy, forward reports to DOE - Small Business Division, Washington, DC 20585. For reports covering contracts awarded by other Federal Departments or Agencies and subcontracts placed by prime contractors of such departments or agencies, the original copy shall be sent to the Department or Agency Director of Small and Disadvantaged Business Utilization or as otherwise provided for in instructions issued by the Department or Agency.

7. Only subcontract or purchase commitments involving performance within the U.S., its possessions, Puerto Rico, and the Trust Territory of the Pacific Islands will be included in this report.

8. This report is not required to be submitted by small business concerns.

SPECIFIC INSTRUCTIONS

ITEM 1. Enter the agency which awarded the prime contract (e.g., DOD, HUD, GSA, etc.)

ITEM 2. Enter the department or agency administering the contracts (if different from item 1). For DOD contracts enter the military department or agency which has responsibility for the subcontracting program of the corporation or plant (i.e., Army, Navy, Air Force, or Defense Logistics Agency), not the "Office of the Deputy Secretary of Defense."

ITEMS 3 & 4. Enter the date of the last formal surveillance review conducted by the cognizant department or agency Small and Disadvantaged Business Specialist or other review personnel. For DOD, also identify the military department or Defense Contract Administration Service, as appropriate, that conducted the review. In those cases where the Small Business Administration conducts its own review, show "SBA" and the date.

ITEM 5. Enter Dun and Bradstreet Universal Numbering System (DUNS) number (if available).

ITEM 6. Check whether reporting business is performing as a prime or subcontractor or both.

ITEM 7. Enter the name and address of the reporting corporation, company, or subdivision thereof (e.g., division or plant) which is covered by the data submitted.

ITEM 8. Identify the major product or service lines of the reporting corporation, company, or subdivision.

ITEMS 9 & 10. Report all commitments and purchase orders, regardless of dollar value, made by the reporting organization under all Federal prime contracts and subcontracts (whether or not prime contracts are over $500,000 ($1 million for construction) and small and small disadvantaged business subcontracting plans and goals are required). Report on a quarterly cumulative basis until the end of the fiscal year on September 30 after which a new quarterly reporting cycle is to be initiated commencing with the first quarter from October 1 through December 31. Dollar amounts reported should include direct awards and the appropriate prorated portion of the prime contractor's indirect awards (see definition below) contracted with small and small disadvantaged business concerns and other than small business concerns. The indirect award portion should be based on the percentages of the Federal department or agency work being performed by the reporting contractor in relation to other work performed for other departments or agencies. Particular care should be taken not to include in quarterly reports purchase commitments made in support of commercial business being performed by the contractor.

ITEM 11. Show dollar amount of commitments valued over $10,000 placed with labor surplus area (LSA) concerns (i.e., those that will perform substantially in labor surplus areas). Prime contractors are also encouraged to include awards valued less than $10,000 if such additional reporting does not impose a burden upon the contractor. LSA's are identified in the Department of Labor (DOL) publication "Labor Surplus Area Listings" which can be obtained from the Federal Agency contracting officer or by writing to Employment and Training Administration, (Attention: TPPL), Department of Labor, 601 "D" Street, NW, Washington, DC 20213.

ITEMS 12 & 13. Enter the information as indicated regarding contracts with small and small disadvantaged business goals. For each item (as applicable), enter the number of contracts, the dollar value of subcontracts, the dollar value of subcontract goals (as expressed in the subcontract plans) and actual goal achievement expressed in dollars and percent of goal. This item does not apply to reports covering commercial products.

ITEM 16. The approving official shall be the chief executive officer or, in the case of a separate division or plant, the senior individual responsible for overall division or plant operations.

DEFINITIONS

1. A Small Business Concern is a concern that meets the pertinent criteria established by the Small Business Administration.

2. (a) A Small Disadvantaged Business means any small business concern—
(i) which is at least 51 per centum owned by one or more socially and economically disadvantaged individuals; or, in the case of any publicly-owned business, at least 51 per centum of the stock of which is owned by one or more socially and economically disadvantaged individuals; and
(ii) whose management and daily business operations are controlled by one or more of such individuals.

(b) The contractor shall presume that socially and economically disadvantaged individuals include Black Americans, Hispanic Americans, Native Americans, Asian-Pacific Americans, and other minorities, or any other individual founds to be disadvantaged by the Small Business Administration pursuant to Section 8(a) of the Small Business Act. "Native Americans" include American Indians, Eskimos, Aleuts, and native Hawaiians. "Asian-Pacific Americans" include U.S. citizens whose origins are from Japan, China, the Philippines, Vietnam, Korea, Samoa, Guam, Trust Territory of the Pacific Islands, Northern Marianas, Laos, Cambodia, and Taiwan.

(c) Contractors acting in good faith may rely on written representations by their subcontractors certifying their status as either a small business concern or a small business concern owned and controlled by socially and economically disadvantaged individuals.

(d) The Office of Minority Small Business and Capital Ownership Development in the Small Business Administration will answer inquiries from prime contractors and others relative to the class of eligibles and has final authority to determine the eligibility of a concern to be designated as a small disadvantaged business.

3. Commercial Products means products sold in substantial quantities to the general public and/or industry at established catalog or market prices.

4. Commitments as used herein is defined as a contract, purchase order, amendment, or other legal obligation executed by the Reporting corporation, company, or subdivision for goods and services to be received by the reporting corporation, company, or subdivision.

5. Direct Commitments are those which are identified with the performance of a specific government contract, including allocable parts of awards for material which is to be incorporated into products under more than one Government contract.

6. Indirect Commitments are those which, because of incurrence for common or joint purposes, are not identified with specific Government contracts; these awards are related to Government contract performance but remain for allocation after direct awards have been determined and identified to specific Government contracts.

7. A contract is considered to be completed when the supplies or services which are required to be delivered under the contract have been provided to the Government.

STANDARD FORM 295 BACK (REV. 10-83)

Figure 7–2, continued

HOW THE SBA CONTRIBUTES TO THE SUBCONTRACTING PROCESS

The SBA is actively involved in the subcontracting process to the extent that its subcontracting specialists maintain close liaison with the major prime contractor's purchasing officers, and often recommend potential small business sources capable of bidding on requirements. In addition, the SBA maintains a Procurement Automated Source System (PASS) on a nationwide basis. This provides subcontracting potential sources to both large business and federal acquisition buying centers. The intent of this program is to improve potential government contract and subcontract opportunities for interested small business firms who want to do business with the government. There is no charge for this service. A copy of the SBA PASS company profile submittal form may be obtained from your nearest SBA office.

Another service of the SBA is the assistance and counseling offered by the subcontracting specialists as an aid in solving general or specific problems encountered during the performance of contracts and subcontracts. Your nearest SBA regional office will be pleased to give you the name of a local subcontracting specialist, and again there is no charge for SBA services.

SBA Assistance Programs for Subcontractors and Contractors

How Procurement Center Representatives (PCRs) Can Help You. The SBA Prime Contractor Program is designed to increase contract awards to small business, both in terms of dollar awards and number of contracts. Currently, approximately 20 percent of all federal procurement is awarded to small business, and slightly less than that is additionally awarded as subcontracts. It becomes the responsibility of the procurement center representatives, PCRs for short, to increase these figures. They are either stationed at, or in liaison with, all federal installations, both military and civilian, having major buying programs.

As contracting officers process procurement packages, the PCRs become part of the review process. Their objective is twofold:

- First, to recommend, where feasible, that the purchasing requirement be processed as a small business set-aside. This means that the procurement would be restricted only to small businesses, and that large businesses would not be eligible to bid.
- Second, if a set-aside is not possible, the PCR will recommend small business procurement sources. One of the contracting officer's responsibilities is to determine that a set-aside will not result in an unusual cost to the government. If that is the case, and the set-aside is not in the government's best interest,

the contracting officer may withdraw the set-side. The appeals procedure is available if the situation becomes an issue.

The PCRs are additionally available to advise, counsel and assist small firms that are having procurement and contracting problems with specific federal agencies.

PCRs also perform another important function in their screening duties, and that is to be on the lookout for provisions that may either restrict or discourage small business from submitting offers. These restrictions could be, for example, in the form of restrictive specifications and unrealistic delivery dates. *Keep in mind*: If you are a small business, you are not prevented from bidding on any solicitation on which you are competent. The small business set-aside means that large businesses cannot compete on those specific requirements.

The Certificate of Competency Program. Sooner or later, because of the experience and growth you will gain as a subcontractor, you will give serious thought to bidding on prime contracts yourself. The usual way this happens is through receiving a solicitation for an item similar to those you have been supplying as a subcontractor in the past. As an aid in transitioning subcontractors into prime contractor status, the government has established a program called the Certificate of Competency (COC) program. This is also administered by the SBA and it is essentially a validation of your capability to perform government contracts, which you knew you could all along, anyway! If a contracting officer proposes to reject the low bid of a small business firm because the firm's ability to perform is questionable, the contracting officer must refer the case to the SBA for Certificate of Competency (COC) action. Because of this referral, and if the firm files application for a COC, the SBA makes an on-site study of the firm's capabilities in order to determine whether or not it can perform under the terms of the pending contract. If the SBA appraisal is positive a COC is issued, and the contracting officer must then award the contract to the small firm. The SBA is also empowered to issue COCs in behalf of small concerns engaged in purchasing federal property, such as timber.

The SBA, through its independent evaluation, may issue a COC on behalf of a firm originally found ineligible by the contracting officer due to the provisions of the Walsh-Healey Act. The findings of the SBA can be quite liberal in this area. For example, there's a chemical company that was found eligible to supply subsistence (food) items to the DOD! Appendix B contains detailed information on the interpretation of the Walsh-Healey Act, and it will give you a precise idea of what can and cannot be done under this law.

A COC is valid only on the specific contract for which it is issued.

There is no such thing as a blanket COC, the reason being that you may be exceptionally capable of handling one type of contract, and not another. Each case is determined only after a contracting officer has made a negative finding on a company based on one particular solicitation. As with the COC, a negative finding does not have unlimited scope, and it cannot operate as a blanket blackball. It applies to only one contract. You are not permitted to apply for a COC in anticipation of a negative action by the contracting officer.

The Technology Assistance Program. Technological assistance is available to small companies in three primary areas: research and development, technology utilization, and assistance offered by the Experimental Technology Incentives Program (ETIP).

Under the R&D program, the SBA field office will survey a small business, if requested, for inclusion in the agency's R&D directory. This directory is made available to government agencies and prime contractors who have R&D requirements.

The technology utilization program assists small business concerns in obtaining the benefits of research and development performed under government contracts. *One main objective*: To shorten the time gap between the discovery of a new technology and its use in the marketplace.

The ETIP program conducts, in conjunction with the National Bureau of Standards, a series of studies designed to evaluate modifications that could be made in government acquisition policies and procedures designed to enhance government contracting for R&D with small firms.

One other phase of government acquisition is the SBA's objective of ensuring that a fair share of the surplus property sold by the government is available to the small business community. This surplus property contains numerous items, such as machine tools, automobiles, trucks, materials handling equipment, real property, and surplus commodities such as rubber, copper, quinine, nickel, zinc, and lead. The federal government also sells timber from its forests, as well as coal, gas, and oil from its mineral holdings. A good portion of this aid consists of informing small businesses where and when the material will be sold. The SBA will also prepare set-asides of surplus property for exclusive bidding purposes by small business when this action is essential to assure that small firms receive a fair share of the property.

When necessary, the SBA informs small firms performing government defense contracts about the priority system designed to help small businesses secure any scarce materials needed for the manufacture of defense products.

The contracting officer's responsibilities under the subcontracting assistance program require his or her general support, including the encouragement of increased subcontracting opportunities in negotiated acquisitions by providing monetary incentives. These include payments based on either actual subcontracting achievement or award fee contracting. This is covered by a contract clause that is inserted by the contracting officer when, during contracting by negotiation, he or she determines that it is necessary to increase subcontracting opportunities for small and disadvantaged business concerns. This clause allows the increased payment of up to 10 percent of the subcontracting goal price for the achievement of any goals in excess of those in the contractor's subcontracting plan. If the contract is a cost-plus-fixed-fee contract, the fixed fee and the incentive fee cannot exceed what is currently authorized.

When using contractual incentive provisions based on rewarding the contractor for exceeding subcontracting goals, the contracting officer must be assured that the goals are realistic, and that the rewards the contractor receives are commensurate with the efforts the contractor would not have otherwise expended. The incentive provisions are normally negotiated after reaching final agreement with the contractor on the subcontracting plan.

HOW THE GOVERNMENT DETERMINES THE NEED FOR A SUBCONTRACTING PLAN

In determining the need for a subcontracting plan, the contracting officer will first ascertain that the dollar amounts allow subcontracting, and then whether or not subcontracting possibilities exist. This latter consideration will take into account such factors as:

1. whether or not firms engaged in the business of furnishing the types of items needed customarily contract for performance of part of the work, or maintain sufficient in-house capability to perform the subcontract
2. whether or not there are likely to be product prequalification requirements

If it determined that there are no subcontracting possibilities, that determination requires the approval of the next higher level above the contracting officer.

In the review of the subcontracting plan by the contracting officer, questions of its adequacy will be addressed, making certain that the six required elements (which were previously described) concerning information, goals, and assurances are included. Because every situation is different, there are no definitive considerations that must be taken into account. Instead, the contracting officer will consider each plan in terms of the

1. Previous involvement of small business concerns as either prime contractors or subcontractors in similar acquisitions.
2. Proven methods of involving small business concerns as subcontractors in similar acquisitions.
3. Relative success of the methods the contractor intends to use in order to meet the goals and requirements of the plan. The relevant records of the contractor may be required for review by the contracting officer.

If, under a sealed bid solicitation, the bidder's plan does not contain the six required elements, the contracting officer will advise the bidder of the deficiency, and request a revised plan be submitted by a specific date. If this is not accomplished, the bidder will be ineligible for award. If the plan, although responsive, evidences the bidder's intention not to comply with its obligations, the contracting officer will find the bid to be nonresponsive.

In negotiated acquisitions, the contracting officer is required to determine whether or not the plan is acceptable based on the negotiation of each of the six elements of the plan. The subcontracting goals should be set at a level the parties can reasonably expect to be achieved through good faith efforts by the contractor. The contracting officer is not permitted to negotiate any goal upward if it is apparent that the higher goal will significantly increase the government's cost or seriously impede the attainment of acquisition objectives. The incentive subcontracting clause may be used when additional and unique contractor effort will significantly increase subcontract awards to small and small disadvantaged businesses.

Five Actions Taken by the Contracting Officer When Reviewing a Proposed Subcontracting Plan

The contracting officer must take the following five actions before accepting a proposed subcontracting plan:

1. Evaluate of the offeror's past performance in awarding subcontracts for the same or similar products and services. If information is not available on a specific type of product or service, the overall past performance of the offeror will be evaluated.
2. Evaluate the offeror's make-or-buy policy or program to ensure that it does not conflict with the offeror's proposed subcontracting plan, and that it is in the government's interest. If the contract involves either products or services that are particularly specialized and not generally available in the commercial market, the contracting officer will then consider the offeror's current capacity to perform the work, and the possibility of reduced subcontracting opportunities.
3. Evaluate subcontracting potential, considering the offeror's make-or-buy policies and programs, the nature of either the products or services to be subcontracted, and the known availability of small and disadvantaged business concerns in the geographical area where the work is to be performed. Also to be taken into account will be the contractor's longstanding contractual relationship with its suppliers.
4. Advise the offeror of available sources of information on potential small and small disadvantaged business subcontractors, and any specific concerns known to be potential subcontractors. If the proposed goals are questionable,

the contracting officer is required to emphasize that the information provided should be used to develop realistic goals.

5. Obtain advice and recommendations from the SBA procurement center representative and the SBA small and small disadvantaged business representative.

Contracts requiring a subcontract plan will be awarded on the contractor's compliance with subcontracting requirements on previous programs. Prior to the award, the contracting officer will advise the SBA resident procurement center representative of the opportunity to review the proposed contract with the intent of seeking his or her recommendations on the matter.

After award, any contractor or subcontractor who fails to comply in good faith with the requirements of the subcontracting plan will be considered in material breach of the contract.

The SBA's Responsibilities in Administering the Program

The SBA's role in carrying out the program includes the following:

1. Assist both the government agency and the contractor in carrying out their responsibilities with regard to the subcontracting plan.
2. Review solicitations, within five working days, to see if they meet small business and small disadvantaged business standards.
3. Review, before execution and within five working days, any negotiated contractual documents requiring a subcontracting plan, including the plan itself. Based on this review, the SBA may submit recommendations of an advisory nature to the contracting officer.
4. Evaluate compliance with subcontracting plans, either on a contract-by-contract basis or, in the case of contractors having multiple contracts, on an aggregate basis.

Note. The SBA is not authorized to prescribe the extent to which the contractor and subcontractor will subcontract, to exercise any authority regarding the administration of individual prime contracts and subcontracts, or to stipulate specific companies to which subcontracts will be awarded.

Subcontracting plan compliance reviews are one of the responsibilities of the SBA. The SBA also participates in the Contracting Opportunity Workshops, where federal contracting agencies and prime contractors present their requirements to small business. This gives small business an opportunity to evaluate anticipated subcontracts in advance and plan their bid. Your local SBA office can notify you of the next workshop in your area.

Details on how contracts are awarded to the SBA for subcontract to small disadvantaged business (the 8(a) program) are discussed in detail in Chapter 11.

INDEX - CHAPTER 7

8

FINANCING AND ASSISTANCE: HOW TO OBTAIN PRIVATE LOANS, ADVANCES, AND PROGRESS PAYMENTS

The government wants to deal only with responsible contractors. One of the measures of responsibility is the contractor's financial capability, and although quite important, it is not necessarily the controlling factor in contract placement. Let us assume for the moment that you have the capability to produce a device that is of great importance to national defense, but because you are just an ordinary citizen who stumbled on the discovery while puttering around in the garage one day, you feel that there is no hope of ever using your discovery to build a company on, and that the only option is to sell the idea for whatever you can get for it. Well, take heart, Uncle Sam is ready, willing, and able to help!

From the perspective of the government, financial aid to contractors can be instrumental in expanding production capacity that can help in fulfilling its procurement needs and increasing the overall competitive climate. It also speeds contract performance, and this has the side benefit of aiding the government's small business program. It is the policy of the government to reduce the need for financing as much as possible by means of prompt payment to prime contractors. Despite this, needs arise requiring the selection of contractors who will need additional financial assistance.

PRIVATE FINANCING: TWO MAIN TYPES TO CHOOSE FROM

Private financing usually takes one of two forms: a government-guaranteed loan (which is obtained by the contractor and guaranteed by the government), and the straight commercial loan. Under a commercial loan, the contractor executes an assignment, to the lending agent, of all or part of the monies due or to become due under the contract. Let's look at this latter situation first.

How to Obtain a Commercial Loan for a Government Contract

The Assignment of Claims Act of 1940, as amended, 31 U.S.C. 3727, 41 U.S.C 15, is one of the means made available for the contractor by supplying added collateral and/or security to a bank or other bona fide financial institution. Essentially, the act provides that an assignment of contract rights, which translates into monies due under a contract, is permissible to a lending institution. *Note*: Many bankers are not aware that this is possible, so you may have to do a bit of educating, and some of the material presented here should help in that respect. The stipulations of the act increase during time of war and other national emergency, providing additional protection to the lending institution. Under these situations, the government is prevented from withholding payments due under the contract because of other debts owed by the contractor to the government, as long as those debts arose independently of the contract.

Three Contract Conditions That Must Be Met. Under the Assignment of Claims Act, a contractor may assign either money due or to become due under a contract if the following conditions are met:

1. The contract specifies payments aggregating at least 1,000 or more.
2. The assignment is made to a bank, trust company, or other financing institution, including any federal lending agency.
3. The contract does not prohibit the assignment.

Unless otherwise expressly permitted in the contract, the assignment applies to all unpaid amounts covered under the contract, and the assignment can be made only to one party. It is permissible for assignment to be made to one party as either agent or trustee for two or more parties participating in the contract's financing. Finally, a reassignment of the original assignment cannot be made by the contractor.

How the Assignment Process Works. The process is quite simple. Once the assignee agrees to the deal, the contractor sends a written notice of assignment, together with a true copy (not a Xerox copy) of the assignment to the contracting officer or the agency head, the surety on any bond applicable to that contract, and the disbursing officer, designated in the contract, who will be responsible for making the payments against contract performance.

"No Setoff" Commitments. The financial institution to which the assignment is made may be further assigned and reassigned by it to other financial institutions. If the contract does not contain a "no setoff" commitment, the government may apply to the assignee (against the payments) any contractor liability to the government arising independently of the assigned contract, if that liability existed at the time notice of the assignment was received. This is the case even though the liability had not yet matured, and was not yet due and payable.

No payments made by the government to the assignee under any contract assigned in accordance with the act may be recovered because of any contractor liability to the government. This immunity of the assignee is effective whether or not the contractor's liability arises from, or independently of, the assigned contract. A no setoff commitment in an assigned contract entitles the assignee to receive contract payments free of reduction for setoffs for any contractor liability to the government. This is the case even if the liability arises independently of the contract, as well as any of the following contractor liabilities to the government that can result from the assignment:

1. renegotiation under any contract clause or statute
2. fines
3. penalties, exclusive of amounts that may be collected or withheld from the contractor under, or for failure to comply with, the terms of the contract
4. taxes and social security contributions
5. either withholding or nonwithholding of taxes and social security contributions

In some situations, a setoff may be appropriate even though the contract contains a no setoff commitment. This would apply when the assignee has neither made a loan under the assignment nor made a commitment to do so. It would also apply if the amount due on the contract exceeds the amount of any loans made or expected to be made under a firm commitment for financing.

Assignments by Corporations, Partnerships, and Individuals. Assignments by corporations must be executed by an authorized representative, attested to by either the secretary or assistant secretary of the corporation, and impressed by the corporate seal. In lieu of the seal, it may be accompanied by a certified copy of the resolution of the corporation's board of directors authorizing the signing representative to execute the assignment.

If the contractor is a partnership, the assignment may be signed by only one partner, provided it is accompanied by an acknowledged certification that the signature is that of a general partner.

If the contractor is an individual, the assignment must be signed by that individual and the signature acknowledged before a notary public or other person authorized to administer oaths.

Recommended Format for Notice of Assignment. The format recommended by the Federal Acquisition Regulation for an assignment notification is as follows:

NOTICE OF ASSIGNMENT

To . . . (contracting officer or agency head, the surety, and disbursing officer). . . .

This has reference to Contract Number . . . . dated . . . ., entered into between (contractor's name and address) and (government agency, name of office, and address) . . . , for . . . (describe the nature of the contract). . . .

Moneys due or to become due under the contract described above have been assigned to the undersigned under the provision of the Assignment of Claims Act of 1940, as amended, 31 U.S.C. 3737.

A true copy of the instrument of assignment executed by the contractor on . . . (date) . . . is attached to the original notice.

Payments due or to become due under this contract should be made to the undersigned assignee.

Please return to the undersigned the three enclosed copies of this notice with appropriate notations showing the date and hour of receipt, and signed by the person acknowledging receipt on behalf of the addressee.

Very truly yours,

. . . .

(Name of assignee)

By . . . .

(Signature of signing officer)

Title . . . .

(Title of signing officer)

Address of assignee . . . .

Receipt is acknowledged of the above notice and of a copy of the instrument of assignment. They were received at . . . . (A.M.) (P.M.) on . . . . , 19. . . . .

Signature . . . .

. . . .
(Title)

On behalf of . . . .

. . . .
(Name of addressee of this notice)

How to Obtain a Guaranteed or V Loan

Successful assignment of your claims under a contract will depend on how well your banker knows you, and how sound a track record you have in your area of expertise. *Note*: It will be quite difficult for a newly started business to get any financial institution to accept an assignment of claims under a government contract. However, there is another type of banking option this company can follow.

Guaranteed loans are commercial loans guaranteed by the government. Under this form of financial assistance, the agency or the government act as guarantors to banks that lend money to contractors and subcontractors for working capital. No federal funds are actually expended unless the borrower either defaults on his or her loan, or the bank demands that the government purchase all or part of the guaranteed percentage of the unpaid principal of the loan. These loans are known as "V" loans, so named after Regulation V of the Board of Governors of the Federal Reserve System. The process of acquiring the loan is a bit involved, but going through the process beats passing up contracts. Let's take a look at V loans in detail.

Seven Government Agencies Who Can Make Loan Guarantees. Congress has authorized the Federal Reserve Banks to act, on behalf of guaranteeing government agencies, as fiscal agents of the United States in the making of loan guarantees for defense production. By Executive Order 10480, dated August 15, 1953 (3 CFR 1949–53), as amended, the President has designated the following agencies as guaranteeing agencies:

1. Department of Defense
2. Department of Energy
3. Department of Commerce

4. Department of the Interior
5. Department of Agriculture
6. General Services Administration
7. National Aeronautics and Space Administration

Loan guarantees are authorized for contract performance or other operations related to national defense, subject to the amounts annually authorized by Congress on the maximum obligation of any guaranteeing agency under any loan, discount, advance, or commitment entered into in connection with national defense contracts.

The guarantees are less than 100 percent of the loan unless the agency determines that the circumstances surrounding the need are exceptional, the operations of the contractor are vital to national defense, and that no other source of financing is available.

Responsibilities of the Guaranteeing Agency. The loan is essentially the same as conventional loans made by private financial institutions. However, except as previously stated, the guaranteeing agency is obligated upon demand from the lender to purchase a stated percentage of the loan and to share any losses in the amount of the guaranteed percentage. It is the responsibility of the private financial institution to disburse and collect funds and to administer the loan. Under Regulation V of the Federal Reserve Board (12 CFR 245), any private financing institution may submit an application to the Federal Reserve Bank of its district for either guarantee of a loan or credit. These loan guarantee agreements will then be made on behalf of the guaranteeing agency.

Under section 302(c) of Executive Order 10480, all actions and operations of Federal Reserve Banks, as fiscal agents, are subject to the supervision of the Federal Reserve Board. The Federal Reserve Board is authorized to prescribe, after consultation with the heads of the guaranteeing agencies, the following:

1. regulations governing the actions and operations of fiscal agents
2. rates of interest, guarantee and commitment fees, and other charges that may be made for loans, discounts, advances, and commitments guaranteed by the guaranteeing agencies through the Federal Reserve Banks
3. uniform forms and procedures to be used in connection with the guarantees

The guaranteeing agency is responsible for certifying eligibility for the guarantee, as well as fixing the maximum dollar amount and maturity date of the guaranteed loan needed by the contractor to meet contract performance of the defense production contract. This contract must be in hand at the time the guarantee application is submitted. The procedure for applying for a guarantee is fairly straightforward.

If a contractor, subcontractor, or supplier needs operating funds to perform a contract related to national defense, he or she first applies to a financing institution for a loan. If the financing institution is willing to extend credit, but considers a government guarantee necessary, the institution may apply to the Federal Reserve Bank of its district for the guarantee. Application forms and guidance are available at all Federal Reserve Banks. *Keep in mind*: Your friendly banker, during his or her entire career, may never have had experience with V loans. This is not an unusual situation. A bit of empathetic education may be required. I would recommend this during your initial discussion with your banker. Please don't wait until after he or she says "no." The loan will be much easier to acquire if your banker is aware that federal guarantees are available. Nothing can top a guarantee by the federal government.

After the Federal Reserve Bank receives a copy of the application for guarantee from the contractor's bank, the Federal Reserve Bank promptly forwards a copy of the application, along with a list of the relevant defense contracts held by the contractor, to the Federal Reserve Board. The board will then transmit the application and the list of contracts to the interested guaranteeing agency. The agency reviews all of this in order to determine the contractor's eligibility. To expedite the process, the Federal Reserve Bank may, in accordance with instructions of a guaranteeing agency, submit lists of the defense contracts to the interested contracting officers.

When the eligibility is being determined, the Federal Reserve Bank will make any necessary credit investigations to supplement the information submitted by the financing institution. The purpose of these investigations is to expedite the financing (remember, we're talking about defense contracts) and to protect the government against potential monetary loss.

The Federal Reserve Bank will then send its report and recommendation to the Federal Reserve Board. The board will then transmit these to the interested guaranteeing agency. The agency reviews all the relevant data, including the certificate of eligibility described below, as well as the contractor's financial status and previous performance, to determine whether or not a loan guarantee would be in the best interests of the government.

The Certificate of Eligibility: When and How It Is Determined. The *certificate of eligibility* is prepared by the contracting officer when he or she determines the contract to be of material consequence, but it is prepared only when it is requested by the contract financing office, another interested agency, or the application for a loan guarantee relates to a contract or subcontract within the contracting officer's cognizance. If the contractor has several major national defense contracts, it would be unusual for the contracting officer to evaluate the eligibility of relatively minor contracts. This determination of eligibility is required to proceed without delay, and it is based on the preponderant amount of the contracts involved.

The certificate of eligibility is based on a long list of determinations, as follows:

1. Are the supplies or services to be acquired essential to the national defense?
2. Does the contractor have the facilities and technical and management ability required for contract performance?
3. Is there a practical alternative source for the acquisition without prejudice to the national defense?
4. What is the extent of the prejudice to national defense, and would reletting the contract conflict with another source conflict with a major policy on defense acquisition?
5. What is the urgency surrounding performance of contract schedules?
6. What are the technical abilities and facilities of other potential sources?
7. To what extent would the other sources need contract financing assistance?
8. Would other sources be willing to enter into the contract?
9. What would be the time and expense involved in repurchasing for contracts and parts of contracts? Considered here would also be either the effect of potential claims for termination for convenience or delays incidental to default at a later date.
10. What would be the comparative prices available from other sources?
11. Would there be the disruption of established subcontracting arrangements?
12. What other pertinent factors would apply?

The contracting officer is required to attach sufficient data to the certificate of eligibility to support the determinations made. The data should include the contractor's past performance, the relationship of the contractor's operations to performance of schedules, and factors 4 through 12 just listed, if relevant. If the contracting officer determines that a certificate of eligibility is not justified, the facts and reasons supporting that conclusion must be documented and furnished to the interested guaranteeing agency's contract finance office.

If it is determined that a loan guarantee is justified, the guaranteeing agency then reviews the proposed guarantee terms and conditions. If they are considered appropriate, the agency then completes a standard form of authorization as prescribed by the Federal Reserve Board. The agency then transmits the authorization through the Federal Reserve Board to the Federal Reserve Bank. The Bank is authorized to execute and deliver to the financing institution a standard form of guarantee agreement, including the terms and conditions approved for the particular case. The financing institution then makes the loan.

The procedure is essentially the same when an application is made by an offeror who is actively negotiating or bidding on a defense contract, except that the guarantee is not authorized until the contract has been awarded and signed by all parties.

The contracting officer is required to report to the agency contract finance office any information about the contractor that would have a potentially adverse effect on a pending guarantee application. However, the contracting officer has no obligation to initiate any special investigation for this purpose.

Finally, with regard to existing contracts, the contracting officer must not consider the percentage of guarantee requested by the financing institution in determining the contractor's eligibility.

The Asset Formula Method for Limiting Guaranteed Loans. Under guaranteed loans made primarily for working capital purposes, the agency is required to limit the guarantee by a method referred to as the asset formula. The amount of the guarantee should not normally exceed a specified percentage, but not more than 90 percent of the contractor's investment in defense contracts. This computation includes payrolls and inventories, and may also include all items under defense contracts for which the contractor would be entitled to payment on either performance or termination. The formula *does not* include:

1. the amounts for which the contractor has not done any work or made any expenditure
2. the amounts that would become due as the result of later performance under the contracts
3. the cash collateral and bank deposit balances

Progress payments are deducted from the asset formula.

If the contractor's working capital and credit are inadequate, the agency may relax the asset formula for an appropriate period of time actually necessary for contract performance.

The agency may change either the guarantee amount or maturity date for the following reasons:

1. If the contractor enters into national defense production contracts after the application for a guarantee, but before its authorization, the agency may adjust the loan guarantee or the maturity date to meet any significant increase in financing need.
2. If the contractor enters into defense production during the term of the guaranteed loan, the parties may adjust the existing guarantee agreements in order to provide for new financing for the new contracts. Pertinent information and

the Federal Reserve Bank reports will be submitted to the guaranteeing agency under the procedures for the original guarantee application. Normally, a new certificate of eligibility will be required, if requested.

ADVANCE PAYMENTS: WHEN TO REQUEST, HOW THEY ARE AUTHORIZED

Advance payments are payments made directly by the government to a contractor without relation to progress or delivery. They are allowable if the action is appropriate under one of the following:

Section 305 of the Federal Property and Administrative Services Act of 1949 (41 U.S.C. 255)

Armed Services Procurement Act (10 U.S.C. 2307)

Public Law 85–804 (50 U.S.C. 1431–1435) and executive order 10789 of November 14, 1958 (3 CFR 1958 Supp. pp. 72–74)

An agency may authorize advance payments on prime contracts and subcontracts which were awarded either through negotiation or sealed bid, and they may be provided on any type of contract. Advance payments are considered the least preferred method of contract financing, and are used sparingly, only when other types of financing are not reasonably available to the contractor in adequate amounts. In the government's view, neither loans and credit (at excessive interest rates or other exorbitant charges) nor loans from other government agencies are considered reasonably available financing.

Three Requirements for Approving an Advanced Payment

Advance payments will be made only when the following statutory requirements are met:

1. The contractor must give adequate security.
2. The advance payments will not exceed the unpaid contract price.
3. Either the agency head or his or her designee determines that, based on written findings, the advance payment is in the public interest or facilitates national defense.

Seven Standards for Deciding How Much of an Advance Is Needed

There are seven standards for determining the amount of the advance payment required.

1. The first is that the payment will not exceed the contractor's interim cash need based on:

- analysis of the cash flow required for contract performance
- consideration of either the reimbursement or other payment cycle
- employment of the contractor's working capital to the greatest extent possible

2. The advanced payment must be necessary to supplement other funds or the credit line available to a contractor.
3. The recipient of the funds must be qualified as a responsible contractor.
4. The government must benefit from making either the advanced payment, or from other practical advantages.
5. The case must fit one or more of the following categories:
   - Contracts for experimental, research, or developmental work with nonprofit educational or research institutions.
   - Contracts solely for the management and operation of government-owned plants.
   - Contracts for acquisition, at cost, of facilities for government ownership.
   - Contracts of such a highly classified nature that the agency considers it undesirable for national security to permit assignment of claims under the contract.
   - Contracts entered into with financially weak contractors whose technical ability is considered essential to the agency. In these cases, the agency will closely monitor the contractor's performance and financial controls in order to reduce the government's financial risk.
   - Contracts for which a loan by a financial institution is not practical, whether or not a loan guarantee has been issued. This would occur when either the financing institution will not assume a reasonable portion of the risk, when loans with reasonable interest rates or finance charges are not available to the contractor, or the contract involves operations so remote from a financial institution that the institution could not be expected to administer suitably a guaranteed loan.
6. Contracts with small business concerns may be eligible, under which circumstances often occur that make advance payments appropriate, such as prompt and efficient contract performance. Incidentally, the award of a Certificate of Competency from the Small Business Administration has no bearing on the contractor's need for, or entitlement to, contract financing.
7. The final standard is contracts under which exceptional circumstances make advance payments the most advantageous contract financing method for both the government and the contractor.

Advance payments are authorized by law for items in addition to contract financing per se. These include payments for rent, tuition, insurance premiums, expenses of investigations in foreign countries, the extension and connection of public utilities for government buildings or installations, and subscriptions to publications. Also included is the purchase of supplies or services in foreign countries if the purchase price does not exceed $10,000, or the equivalent amount in foreign currency, and the advance payment is required by the laws and regulations of the foreign country concerned. In addition, they are available for enforcement of either the customs or narcotics laws, as well as other types of transactions excluded by agency procedures under statutory authority.

The items just discussed are covered by individual procedures developed and issued by the individual agencies under applicable statutes. The Department of Defense's policy on guaranteed loans, for example, is not to continue this form of assistance over an extended period of time, unless it is reasonably necessary in order to obtain required products.

Public Law 85–804 allows designated agencies to take actions to facilitate the national defense without regard to other provisions of law relating to contracts. The act empowers the President to authorize agencies in connection with the national defense to enter into, amend, and modify contracts, without regard to other provisions of law relating to making, performing, amending, or modifying contracts, whenever the President considers these actions necessary for the national defense.

Authorized advance payments may be made either at, or after, the award of sealed bid contracts, as well as on negotiated bid contracts. Bidders may request advance payment before or after award, even if the invitation for bids does not contain an advance payment provision. However, the contracting officer is required to reject any bid requiring that advance payments be provided as a basis for acceptance.

When advance payments are requested under this situation, the agency may enter into the contract and provide for the advance payments, enter into the contract without providing advance payments if the contractor does not really need them, or deny contract award if the request for advanced payments has been disapproved, and funds adequate for performance are not available to the offeror.

How a Letter of Credit Can Benefit the Contractor

The advance payments may be made in the form of a letter of credit issued to contractors by the contracting agency if that agency expects to have a continuing relationship with the contractor for a period covering a year or more, and having advances totaling at least $120,000 a year.

If the agency has entered into multiple contracts with a contractor, resulting in the issuance of multiple letters of credit, the agency is required to either consolidate funding for these contracts under just one letter of credit, or replace multiple letters of credit with just one letter of credit. The Department of Defense calls this latter situation a "pool arrangement."

The letter of credit allows the contractor to withdraw, through its bank, the necessary funds to cover or disburse cash required for contract performance. Only when it is feasible, the agency will probably require the contractor not to withdraw the government funds until the contractor's checks have been mailed to the payees or presented to the contractor's bank for payment. If any of these requirements are imposed, it is essential that they be followed. The government may terminate the advance financing arrangements if the contractor is either unwilling or unable to minimize the elapsed time between receipt of the advance and disbursement of the funds for contract performance.

If this termination of advance financing arrangements is enacted, it will be replaced by a method of financing called a working capital advance. This type of advance will be limited to only the estimated disbursements for a given initial period, and only for actual cash disbursements.

How Interest Is Computed on Advance Payments

The contracting officer is required to charge interest on the daily unliquidated balance of all advance payments at the higher of either the published prime rate of the banking institution in which the special bank account is established, or of the rate set by the Secretary of the Treasury. This interest rate will be adjusted, as needed, to reflect as applicable, changes in the prime rate or the semiannual determination by the Secretary of the Treasury. Interest is computed at the end of each month by the contracting officer on the daily unliquidated balance of the advance payments at the established rate.

Interest is required on all contracts that are for acquisition, at cost, of facilities for government ownership if these contracts are awarded in combination with, or in contemplation of, supply contracts or subcontracts.

Four Types of Contracts That May Be Authorized Without Interest. If it is in the government's interest, either the agency head or designee may authorize advance payments without interest under the following types of contracts:

1. contracts with either nonprofit education or research institutions for experimental, research, and developmental work, including studies, surveys, and demonstrations in socioeconomic areas
2. contracts solely for the management and operation of government-owned plants
3. cost-reimbursement contracts with governments, including state and local governments, or their instrumentalities

4. other classes of contracts and unusual cases, for which the exclusion of interest on advances is specifically authorized by agency procedures

If the contract provides for interest-free advance payments, the contracting officer may require the contractor to charge interest on either advances or down payments to subcontractors and credit the government for these proceeds. If this is the case, the interest rate is determined as previously discussed. It is optional with the contracting officer whether or not to require interest on advance payment to subcontractors who are in any of the four categories previously described.

Finally, the contracting officer is not allowed to consider interest charges as a reimbursable cost under the cost-reimbursement type of contract, regardless of whether or not the interest was incurred by the prime contractor or the subcontractor.

Six Essential Items to Include with Your Application for an Advance Payment

You, the contractor, may apply for advance payments either before or after the award of a contract by submitting your request, in writing, to the contracting officer. Six essential pieces of information must be included with this request:

1. Either the contract number, if the contract has been issued, or the solicitation number, if the request concerns a proposed contract.
2. A cash flow forecast showing estimated receipts and disbursements for the duration of the contract. If the contract is either for experimental, research, or developmental work with a nonprofit or research institution, or a contract solely for the management and operation of government-owned plants, the forecast should be limited to the portion of the contract that is to be funded by advance payments.
3. The proposed total amount of advance payments required.
4. The name and address of the bank at which you expect to establish a special account as depository for the advance payments. If advance payments in the form of a letter of credit are anticipated, you must identify the specific account that will be used at the bank. If an alternate agency procedure is being used, the provisions of that agency will be used instead.
5. A description of your efforts to obtain either unguaranteed private financing or a V loan for the contract. Again, this does not apply to the types of contracts mentioned in 2, above.
6. Any other information required that will facilitate an understanding of your financial standing and need. This would include ability to perform the contract without loss to the government, as well as the financial safeguards that will

be provided in order to protect the government from loss. If you are the type of contractor described in item 2, then it is necessary only to provide information on your reliability, technical ability, and accounting system and controls. Needless to say, a discussion of these and other strong points should be a part of every request.

After examination of the application, the contracting officer will recommend approval or disapproval, and will transmit the request and recommendations to the approving authority.

Tip: Part of the recommendation procedure by the contracting officer will include obtaining a report of your past performance, responsibility, technical ability, and plant capacity. He or she will then include the potential government benefits from the advance payments, as well as the proposed security requirements. It would therefore be wise to address these matters in your request. Probably the best advice is to include as much positive information in the request as possible.

The Contractor's and Government's Obligations with an Advance Payment

The approval is supported by a written document, prepared by the contracting officer, titled *Findings, Determinations, and Authorization for Advance Payments*, ordinarily referred to as the D&F. This document contains all of the legal wording and the authorization citation under which the funding will be granted. It also contains the covenants to which the parties (you and the government) will agree. These covenants typically will contain the following:

1. That the government will have a lien on the credit balance in the account in order to secure repayment of all advance payments made to the contractor. This lien is paramount to either any lien or claim of the bank regarding the account.
2. The bank is bound by the terms of the contract relating to the deposit and withdrawal of funds in the special bank account, but is not responsible for the application of these funds. The bank is required to act on written directions from the contracting officer, the administrative officer, or their duly authorized representative, and the bank is not liable to any party to the agreement for any action that complies with the written directions.
3. Either the government, or its authorized representative, will have access to the books and records maintained by the bank regarding the special bank account at all reasonable times and for all reasonable purposes, including, but not limited to, either the inspection or copying of the books and records and any and all pertinent memoranda, checks, correspondence, or documents.

The bank is required to preserve the books and records for six years after closing of the account.

4. In the event of the service of any writ or attachment, levy or execution, or commencement of garnishment proceedings regarding the special account, the bank is required to notify promptly the administering office named in the document.
5. While the special bank account exists, the bank is required to inform the government each month of its published prime interest rate and changes to that rate that have occurred during the month, and it will be transmitted on the last day of the month.

These covenants put a burden on the bank, but in exchange the bank receives a healthy cash flow. Since banking is a regulated industry, your banker will be used to dealing with the ways of the government, and these covenants should not appear to him or her as burdensome as they probably appear to you.

PROGRESS PAYMENTS: HOW TO PROVE YOUR NEED

Progress payments are made to the contractor as work progresses under a contract, even though the supplies or services have not been delivered. They are used only on fixed-price contracts and fixed-price subcontracts issued under cost-reimbursement prime contracts. For most acquisitions, progress payments are based on actual costs incurred. However, construction, shipbuilding, ship repair, and ship conversion contracts usually use other criteria, such as the percentage of work completed, or the stage of work completion at time of payment.

Customary Progress Payments

There are two types of progress payments: customary progress payments and unusual progress payments. Customary progress payments are made when a fixed-price contract has either a long lead time, usually six months or more for the first delivery, or when the cost outlay for the procurement will have a sharp impact on the contractor's working capital. Customary progress payments are granted as a matter of course under these conditions, provided that the contractor has an approved accounting system. Progress payments are not generally authorized on small contracts with the stronger and larger contractors. It is presumed that they are either capable of obtaining their own financing, or that their working capital is adequate to finance the procurement through delivery. From the government's point of view, contracts under $1 million are considered small. The size of the contract, however, has no bearing on progress payment authorization to small business concerns when the contract otherwise meets the standards for this type of payment.

Unusual Progress Payments

Unusual payments are progress payments that are other than the "usual" type described above. Included in the unusual category would be cases where payments exceed the standard percentage customarily used, where lead time is less than six months and predelivery expenditures may hurt the contractor, or where the contractor's finances are overextended.

Keep in Mind: The government's overall position on progress payments is that private financing is preferred. If you require progress payments, then it is up to you to prove actual need by showing that suitable progress cannot be made without them. If approved, the payments provide only the minimum amount that, along with other sources of funds, will meet contract needs.

Payment Rate: What to Expect

The customary progress payment rate is 90 percent of the total cost associated with the performance of the contract. For small business concerns, this rate is increased to 95 percent. Other rates may be established by the Department of Defense for foreign military sales and for flexible progress payments. Any rate higher than those provided for under these conditions would fall into the unusual progress payment category.

When progress payments and advance payments are authorized under the same contract, a progress payment rate higher than the customary rate will not be authorized.

The specific requirements for authorization by the contracting officer of unusual progress payments are

1. the contract necessitates predelivery expenditures that are large in relationship with the contract price or out of line with contractor's working capital and credit
2. the contractor fully documents the actual need to supplement any private financing available, including guaranteed loans
3. the contractor's request is approved by either the head of the contracting activity or a designee

If the progress payment rate exceeds the customary rate, the increment above the ordinary rate will be the lowest amount possible under the circumstances.

Progress payments will not be considered unusual merely by their inclusion in letter contracts or the definitive contracts superseding letter contracts.

How the Contract Price for Progress Payments Is Determined

For the purpose of making progress payments and determining the limitation on them, the contract price is defined as follows:

1. Under firm fixed-price contracts, the contract price is the current price plus any unpriced modifications for which funds have been obligated.
2. If the contract is either redeterminable or subject to economic price adjustment, the contract price is the initial price until it is modified.
3. Under a fixed-price incentive contract, the contract price is the target price plus any unpriced modifications for which funds have been obligated. However, if the contractor's properly incurred costs exceed the target price, the contracting officer may provisionally increase the price up to the ceiling or maximum price.
4. Under a letter contract, the contract price is the maximum amount obligated by the contract as modified.
5. Under an unpriced order issued under a basic ordering agreement, the contract price is the maximum amount obligated by the order, as modified.
6. Any portion of the contract specifically providing for reimbursement of costs only will be excluded from the determination of the contract price.

The contracting officer is not allowed to make progress payments or increase the contract price beyond the funds obligated under the contract, as amended.

How the Government Benefits from Allowing Progress Payments

Occasionally unanticipated circumstances arise during contract performance that require the contract to be amended in order to provide progress payments. Under these circumstances, the government will require ''consideration''; i.e., something of benefit to it for bailing the contractor out of a jam. This consideration should be considered adequate, and it may be provided in the form of either monetary or nonmonetary means. A monetary consideration could be a reduction in the contract price. A nonmonetary consideration could be the incorporation of terms in the contract modification giving the government new and substantial benefit.

A fair and reasonable consideration should approximate, as nearly as possible, the reduced amount of the contract price if the progress payments clause had been originally contained in the contract. If this figure is either unknown, or impossible to arrive at definitively, then the contracting officer will apply one of the following criteria in evaluating whether or not the proposed new consideration is adequate:

1. the value to the contractor of the unliquidated amount of the progress payments anticipated, as well as the duration of the progress payments, in relation to the estimated financial cost of the equivalent working capital
2. the estimated profit rate to be earned through contract performance

The contracting officer is not allowed to provide for any other type of specific charges for progress payments, such as interest.

If the contracting officer finds it necessary, terms protecting the government's interest may be used in addition to the terms of the progress payments clause. These would include personal or corporate guarantees, subordination of indebtedness, and special bank accounts.

Note: If in doubt as to whether or not the customary progress payments clause should be included in a solicitation, the contracting officer is required to resolve his or her reasonable doubts in favor of its inclusion. Bids conditioned on progress payments, when the solicitation did not provide for them, will be rejected as nonresponsive.

Contractor requests for progress payments must be submitted on Standard Form (SF) 1443, *Contractor's Request for Progress Payment* (Figure 8–1). The contracting officer may also request any additional information pertinent to your particular situation.

In evaluating your request, the administrative contracting office will take into account your reliability, competency, and ability to perform satisfactorily. In addition, the adequacy of your accounting system as well as its fiscal state of health will be considered. If it has been found that, in the previous 12 months, all of these elements were satisfactory, the approval of progress payments should be routine.

How Progress Payment Requests Are Approved

Formal audit may be required by the administrative contracting officer to establish your suitability to receive progress payments, but only when there is a question as to the reliability or accuracy of the contractor's certification, or if it is believed that the contract will involve a loss. Audit is not the preferred method to use, and every effort should be made to rely on the accounting and upon the contractor's certification.

If there is ever any doubt regarding the progress payment amount, the administrative contracting officer may withhold only the doubtful amount. This amount is subject to later adjustment after review or audit. All other

CONTRACTOR'S REQUEST FOR PROGRESS PAYMENT

Form Approved
OMB No. 3090–0105

IMPORTANT: This form is to be completed in accordance with Instructions on reverse.

SECTION I – IDENTIFICATION INFORMATION

1. TO: NAME AND ADDRESS OF CONTRACTING OFFICE *(Include ZIP Code)* *PAYING OFFICE*	2. FROM: NAME AND ADDRESS OF CONTRACTOR *(Include ZIP Code)*		
	3. SMALL BUSINESS ☐ YES ☐ NO	4. CONTRACT NO.	5. CONTRACT PRICE $

6. RATES		7. DATE OF INITIAL AWARD		8A. PROGRESS PAYMENT REQUEST NO.	8B. DATE OF THIS REQUEST
A. PROG. PYMTS.	B. LIQUIDATION	A. YEAR	B. MONTH		
%	%				

SECTION II – STATEMENT OF COSTS UNDER THIS CONTRACT THROUGH ____________ *(Date)*

9. PAID COSTS ELIGIBLE UNDER PROGRESS PAYMENT CLAUSE		$
10. INCURRED COSTS ELIGIBLE UNDER PROGRESS PAYMENT CLAUSE		
11. TOTAL COSTS ELIGIBLE FOR PROGRESS PAYMENTS *(Item 9 plus 10)*		
12. a. TOTAL COSTS INCURRED TO DATE	$	
b. ESTIMATED ADDITIONAL COST TO COMPLETE		
13. ITEM 11 MULTIPLIED BY ITEM 6a		
14. a. PROGRESS PAYMENTS PAID TO SUBCONTRACTORS		
b. LIQUIDATED PROGRESS PAYMENTS TO SUBCONTRACTORS		
c. UNLIQUIDATED PROGRESS PAYMENTS TO SUBCONTRACTORS *(Item 14a less 14b)*		
d. SUBCONTRACT PROGRESS BILLINGS APPROVED FOR CURRENT PAYMENT		
e. ELIGIBLE SUBCONTRACTOR PROGRESS PAYMENTS *(Item 14c plus 14d)*		
15. TOTAL DOLLAR AMOUNT *(Item 13 plus 14e)*		
16. ITEM 5 MULTIPLIED BY ITEM 6b		
17. LESSER OF ITEM 15 OR ITEM 16		
18. TOTAL AMOUNT OF PREVIOUS PROGRESS PAYMENTS REQUESTED		
19. MAXIMUM BALANCE ELIGIBLE FOR PROGRESS PAYMENTS *(Item 17 less 18)*		

SECTION III – COMPUTATION OF LIMITS FOR OUTSTANDING PROGRESS PAYMENTS
***SEE SPECIAL INSTRUCTIONS ON BACK FOR USE UNDER THE FEDERAL ACQUISITION REGULATION.**

20. COMPUTATION OF PROGRESS PAYMENT CLAUSE *(a(3)(i) or a(4)(i))* LIMITATION*	$	
a. COSTS INCLUDED IN ITEM 11, APPLICABLE TO ITEMS DELIVERED, INVOICED, AND ACCEPTED TO THE DATE IN HEADING OF SECTION II.		
b. COSTS ELIGIBLE FOR PROGRESS PAYMENTS, APPLICABLE TO UNDELIVERED ITEMS AND TO DELIVERED ITEMS NOT INVOICED AND ACCEPTED *(Item 11 less 20a)*		
c. ITEM 20b MULTIPLIED BY ITEM 6a		$
d. ELIGIBLE SUBCONTRACTOR PROGRESS PAYMENTS *(Item 14e)*		
e. LIMITATION a(3)(i) or a(4)(i) *(Item 20c plus 20d)* *		
21. COMPUTATION OF PROGRESS PAYMENT CLAUSE *(a(3)(ii) or a(4)(ii))* LIMITATION *		
a. CONTRACT PRICE OF ITEMS DELIVERED, ACCEPTED AND INVOICED TO DATE IN HEADING OF SECTION II		
b. CONTRACT PRICE OF ITEMS NOT DELIVERED, ACCEPTED AND INVOICED *(Item 5 less 21a)*		
c. ITEM 21b MULTIPLIED BY ITEM 6b		
d. UNLIQUIDATED ADVANCE PAYMENTS PLUS ACCRUED INTEREST		
e. LIMITATION *(a(3)(ii) or a(4)(ii)) (Item 21c less 21d)* *		
22. MAXIMUM UNLIQUIDATED PROGRESS PAYMENTS *(Lesser of Item 20e or 21e)*		
23. TOTAL AMOUNT APPLIED AND TO BE APPLIED TO REDUCE PROGRESS PAYMENT		
24. UNLIQUIDATED PROGRESS PAYMENTS *(Item 18 less 23)*		
25. MAXIMUM PERMISSIBLE PROGRESS PAYMENTS *(Item 22 less 24)*		
26. AMOUNT OF CURRENT INVOICE FOR PROGRESS PAYMENT *(Lesser of Item 25 or 19)*		
27. AMOUNT APPROVED BY CONTRACTING OFFICER		

CERTIFICATION

I certify that the above statement (with attachments) has been prepared from the books and records of the above-named contractor in accordance with the contract and the instructions hereon, and to the best of my knowledge and belief, that it is correct, that all the costs of contract performance (except as herewith reported in writing) have been paid to the extent shown herein, or where not shown as paid have been paid or will be paid currently, by the contractor, when due, in the ordinary course of business, that the work reflected above has been performed, that the quantities and amounts involved are consistent with the requirements of the contract That there are no encumbrances (except as reported in writing herewith, or on previous progress payment request No. ____________) against the property acquired or produced for, and allocated or properly chargeable to the contract which would affect or impair the Government's title, that there has been no materially adverse change in the financial condition of the contractor since the submission of the most recent written information dated ______________________ by the contractor to the Government in connection with the contract, that to the extent of any contract provision limiting progress payments pending first article approval, such provision has been complied with, and that after the making of the requested progress payment the unliquidated progress payments will not exceed the maximum unliquidated progress payments permitted by the contract.

NAME AND TITLE OF CONTRACTOR REPRESENTATIVE SIGNING THIS FORM	SIGNATURE
NAME AND TITLE OF CONTRACTING OFFICER	SIGNATURE

NSN 7540-01-140-5523 1443-101

STANDARD FORM 1443 (10-82)
Prescribed by GSA (FPR 1-16.808)
FAR (48 CFR 53.232)

Figure 8–1

INSTRUCTIONS

GENERAL - All entries on this form must be typewritten - all dollar amounts must be shown in whole dollars, rounded up to the next whole dollar. All line item numbers not included in the instructions below are self-explanatory.

SECTION I – IDENTIFICATION INFORMATION. Complete Items 1 through 8c in accordance with the following instructions.

Item 1. TO – Enter the name and address of the cognizant Contract Administration Office. PAYING OFFICE – Enter the designation of the paying office, as indicated in the contract.

Item 2. FROM - CONTRACTOR'S NAME AND ADDRESS/ZIP CODE – Enter the name and mailing address of the contractor. If applicable, the division of the company performing the contract should be entered immediately following the contractor's name.

Item 3. Enter an "X" in the appropriate block to indicate whether or not the contractor is a small business concern.

Item 5. Enter the total contract price, as amended. If the contract provides for escalation or price redetermination, enter the initial price until changed and not the ceiling price; if the contract is of the incentive type, enter the target or billing price, as amended until final pricing. For letter contracts, enter the maximum expenditure authorized by the contract, as amended.

Item 6A. PROGRESS PAYMENT RATES – Enter the 2-digit progress payment percentage rate shown in paragraph (a)(1) of the progress payment clause.

Item 6B. LIQUIDATION RATE – Enter the progress payment liquidation rate shown in paragraph (b) of the progress payment clause, using three digits - Example: show 80% as 800 - show 72.3% as 723.

Item 7. DATE OF INITIAL AWARD – Enter the last two digits of the calendar year. Use two digits to indicate the month. Example: show Janaury 1982 as 82/01.

Item 8A. PROGRESS PAYMENT REQUEST NO. – Enter the number assigned to this request. All requests under a single contract must be numbered consecutively, beginning with 1. Each subsequent request under the same contract must continue in sequence, using the same series of numbers without omission.

Item 8B. Enter the date of the request.

SECTION II – GENERAL INSTRUCTIONS. DATE. In the space provided in the heading enter the date through which costs have been accumulated from inception for inclusion in this request. This date is applicable to item entries in Sections II and III.

Cost Basis. For all contracts with Small Business concerns, the base for progress payments is total costs incurred. For contracts with concerns other than Small Business, the progress payment base will be the total recorded paid costs, together with the incurred costs per the Computation of Amounts paragraph of the progress payment clause in FPR 1-30.510-1(a) or FAR 52.232-16, as appropriate. Total costs include all expenses paid and incurred, including applicable manufacturing and production expense, general and administrative expense for performance of contract, which are reasonable, allocable to the contract, consistent with sound and generally accepted accounting principles and practices, and which are not otherwise excluded by the contract.

Manufacturing and Production Expense, General and Administrative Expense. In connection with the first progress payment request on a contract, attach an explanation of the method, bases and period used in determining the amount of each of these two types of expenses. If the method, bases or periods used for computing these expenses differ in subsequent requests for progress payments under this contract, attach an explanation of such changes to the progress payment request involved.

Incurred Costs Involving Subcontractors for Contracts with Small Business Concerns. If the incurred costs eligible for progress payments under the contract include costs shown in invoices of subcontractors, suppliers and others, that portion of the costs computed on such invoices can only include costs for: (1) completed work to which the prime contractor has acquired title; (2) materials delivered to which the prime contractor has acquired title; (3) services rendered; and (4) costs billed under cost reimbursement or time and material subcontracts for work to which the prime contractor has acquired title.

SECTION II – SPECIFIC INSTRUCTIONS

Item 9. PAID COSTS ELIGIBLE UNDER PROGRESS PAYMENT CLAUSE – Line 9 will not be used for Small Business Contracts. For large business contracts, costs to be shown in Item 9 shall include only those recorded costs which have resulted at time of request in payment made by cash, check, or other form of actual payment for items or services purchased directly for the contract. This includes items delivered, accepted and paid for, resulting in liquidation of subcontractor progress payments.

Costs to be shown in Item 9 are not to include advance payments, downpayments, or deposits, all of which are not eligible for reimbursement; or progress payments made to subcontractors, suppliers or others, which are to be included in Item 14. See "Cost Basis" above.

Item 10. INCURRED COSTS ELIGIBLE UNDER PROGRESS PAYMENT CLAUSE – For all Small Business Contracts, Item 10 will show total costs incurred for the contract.

Costs to be shown in Item 10 are not to include advance payments, downpayments, deposits, or progress payments made to subcontractors, suppliers or others.

For large business contracts, costs to be shown in Item 10 shall include all costs incurred (see "Cost Basis" above) for materials which have been issued from the stores inventory and placed into production process for use on the contract; for direct labor; for other direct in-house costs; and for properly allocated and allowable indirect costs as set forth under "Cost Basis" above.

Item 12a. Enter the total contract costs incurred to date; if the actual amount is not known, enter the best possible estimate. If an estimate is used, enter (E) after the amount.

Item 12b. Enter the estimated cost to complete the contract. The estimate may be the last estimate made, adjusted for costs incurred since the last estimate; however, estimates shall be made not less frequently than every six months.

Items 14a through 14e. Include only progress payments on subcontracts which conform to progress payment provisions of the prime contract.

Item 14a. Enter only progress payments actually paid.

Item 14b. Enter total progress payments recouped from subcontractors.

Item 14d. For Small Business prime contracts, include the amount of unpaid subcontract progress payment billings which have been approved by the contractor for the current payment in the ordinary course of business. For other contracts, enter "0" amount.

SECTION III – SPECIFIC INSTRUCTIONS. This Section must be completed only if the contractor has received advance payments against this contract, or if items have been delivered, invoiced and accepted as of the date indicated in the heading of Section II above. EXCEPTION: Item 27 must be filled in by the Contracting Officer.

Item 20a. Of the costs reported in Item 11, compute and enter only costs which are properly allocable to items delivered, invoiced and accepted to the applicable date. In order of preference, these costs are to be computed on the basis of one of the following (a) The actual unit cost of items delivered, giving proper consideration to the deferment of the starting load costs or, (b) projected unit costs (based on experienced costs plus the estimated cost to complete the contract), where the contractor maintains cost data which will clearly establish the reliability of such estimates.

Item 20d. Enter amount from 14e.

Item 21a. Enter the total billing price, as adjusted, of items delivered, accepted and invoiced to the applicable date.

Item 23. Enter total progress payments liquidated and those to be liquidated from billings submitted but not yet paid.

Item 25. Self-explanatory. (NOTE. If the entry in this item is a negative amount, there has been an overpayment which requires adjustment.)

Item 26. Self-explanatory, but if a lesser amount is requested, enter the lesser amount.

SPECIAL INSTRUCTIONS FOR USE UNDER FEDERAL ACQUISITION REGULATION (FAR).

Items 20 and 20e. Delete the references to a(3)(i) of the progress payment clause.

Items 21 and 21e. Delete the references to a(3)(ii) of the progress payment clause.

STANDARD FORM 1443 BACK (10-82)

Figure 8–1, continued

amounts clearly due and payable must be paid without awaiting resolution of the differences.

During the contract's course, several areas will be looked at on an ongoing basis:

- There will be postpayment reviews or audits designed to determine that the unliquidated progress payments are supported fairly by the value of the work remaining on the contract, and that the applicable limitation on progress payments in the progress payments clause has not been exceeded.
- The unpaid balance of the contract price will be reviewed to see if it is adequate to cover the balance of the work required.
- The resources of the contractor will be looked at in order to determine that they are adequate for completion.
- The adequacy of the contractor's accounting controls will also be reviewed to ascertain that they are performing as required.

Progress payments made under multiple-order contracts should be administered under each individual order, as if the order constituted a separate contract. If you so request, and it is agreed to by the contracting officer approving the individual progress payments, the progress payments may be administered based on either the overall contract or agreement. Under this method, you must provide a supporting schedule with each request for a progress payment. This schedule should identify the costs associated with each order, and the group of orders will be treated as one for payment purposes.

Six Conditions for Suspending or Reducing a Progress Payment

The progress payments clause permits the government either to reduce or suspend progress payments, or to increase the liquidation rate, based on the specific remedies discussed under the following conditions or occurrences:

1. Noncompliance by the contractor with all of the material requirements of the contract. These would include the failure to maintain efficient accounting systems and controls adequate for the administration of progress payments. If such a situation does occur without fault by the contractor, and overpayments have been made, the contracting officer is empowered either to adjust future payments or collect amounts due from the contractor.
2. If the contracting officer finds that contract performance is endangered either by the contractor's financial condition or by failure to make progress, the contracting officer will require the contractor to make any additional operating and financial arrangements adequate for completing the contract without loss to the government. If the contracting office concludes that further progress payments would increase the probable loss to the government, he or she

will suspend progress payments and all other payments until the unliquidated balance of progress payments is eliminated.

3. If the inventory allocated to the contract exceeds reasonable requirements, including a reasonable accumulation of inventory for continuity of operations, the contracting officer will, in addition to requiring the transfer of excessive inventory from the contract, eliminate the costs of the excessive inventory from the costs eligible for progress payments. This will be applied to any progress payments outstanding, and will reduce that figure. In addition, the contracting officer may apply additional deductions to billings for deliveries; that is, increase liquidation.
4. If the contractor becomes delinquent in paying his or her bills due either under the contract or in the normal course of business, the contracting officer will review the situation, but he or she is not permitted to deny progress payments if the contractor cures the delinquencies and avoids future delinquencies, and makes any adequate arrangements necessary to prevent loss to the government. Good faith disputes may not be taken into account until settled one way or the other by any means selected.
5. If, in the course of the contract, it is determined that the fair value of the undelivered work is exceeded by the progress payments, the contracting officer will take any appropriate steps necessary to eliminate this excess. The considerations used in reaching a judgment will be the degree of completion of contract performance, the quality and the amount of work performed on the undelivered (work in process) portion of the contract, the amount of work yet to be done as well as the estimated costs to completion, and the amount remaining unpaid under the contract.
6. If the contracting officer determines that a loss will occur—that is, the costs to complete the contract will exceed the contract price—the contracting officer will compute a loss ratio factor and adjust future progress payments to exclude the element of loss. This ratio is determined by adding together all of the pending changes to the contract price plus all costs to be incurred by future amendments, and dividing this revised contract price by the total costs incurred to date, plus the estimated costs to completion. This ratio will then be applied to the sum of costs paid that were eligible for progress payments.

Two Methods of Determining Liquidation Rates. In the first method, the ordinary method, progress payments are recouped by the government through the deduction of liquidations from payments that would otherwise be due the contractor for completed contract items. In order to determine the amount of the liquidation, a liquidation rate is applied to the contract price of the items delivered and accepted. The ordinary method of doing this is to assume that the liquidation rate is the same as the progress payment rate. This obviously applies at the beginning of the contract. With regard to General and Administrative (G&A) costs, the ordinary method includes the use of an adjusted liquidation rate to reflect the applicable G&A suspense account. This adjusted rate is established by dividing the unbilled G&A by the contract price, multiplying the quotient by the progress payment rate stated in the contract, and subtracting the resulting rate from the progress payment rate.

The second, or alternate liquidation rate method, permits the contractor to retain the earned profit element of the contract prices for completed items in the liquidation process. The alternate method is used only if the contracting officer determines that a reduction in the rate is required if:

1. The contractor requests a reduction in the rate.
2. The rate has not been reduced in the preceding 12 months.
3. The contract delivery schedule extends at least 18 months from the contract award date.
4. The data for the actual costs are available for either the products delivered, or if no deliveries have taken place, for the performance period of at least 12 months.
5. The reduced liquidation rate would result in the government recouping under each invoice the full extent of the progress payments applicable to the allocable costs of the invoice.
6. The contractor would not be paid for more than the costs of items delivered and accepted, less allocable progress payments, and the earned profit on those items.
7. The unliquidated progress payments would not exceed the limit prescribed in the progress payment clause.
8. The parties agree on an appropriate rate.
9. The contractor agrees to certify either annually, or more often if requested by the contracting officer, that the alternate rate conditions meet the conditions of items 5, 6, and 7 of this list.

The liquidation rate will be increased for both previous and subsequent transactions by the contracting officer if you experience a lower profit rate than the one anticipated at the time the liquidation rate was established. The contracting officer will then accordingly adjust the progress payments associated with items already delivered, as well as subsequent progress payments. The rate will be changed to reflect the changes in the contract, such as changes in the target profit under a fixed-price incentive contract having successive targets, or when a redetermined price involves a change in the profit element under a contract having price redetermination at stated intervals.

Changes in the liquidation rate are reflected in a contract modification specifying the new rate in the progress payments clause. Generally, the consideration provided by the progress payments clause is considered adequate. Either the payment or liquidation required under the situation must be made promptly by the parties.

How Alternate Liquidation Rates Are Computed. The contracting officer is required to ensure that the liquidation rate is high enough to result in the government's recouping of the applicable progress payments on each billing, and that they are supported by all the required documentation. The minimum liquidation rate is the expected progress payments divided by the contract price.

Usually the contracting officer will compute the expected gross payments by multiplying the estimated costs of performing the contract by the progress payment rate. For purposes of computing the liquidation rate, the contracting officer may adjust the estimated cost and the contract price in order to include the estimated value of any work authorized but not yet priced, as well as any economic price adjustments. However, this adjustment is not allowed to exceed the government's estimate of the price of all authorized work or the authorized funds obligated for the contract.

If a retroactive downward price reduction occurs under a redeterminable contract that provides for progress payments, the contracting officer is required to calculate the excess payments made for delivered items, determine the refund due the government, and make the necessary collection of the refund. The contracting officer will also increase the unliquidated progress payments amount for overdeductions made from the contractor's billings for items delivered.

The contracting officer will also increase the unliquidated progress payments amount if the contractor makes either an interim or voluntary price reduction under a redeterminable or incentive type of contract.

Any excess payments will be promptly corrected by increasing the liquidation rate, reducing the progress payment rate, or suspending progress payments. An excess in the unliquidated progress payments is most likely to occur when the costs of performance exceed the contract price; when actual costs of performance exceed the cost estimates used to establish the alternate liquidation rate; when the rate of progress or contract quality is unsatisfactory; and when the rate of rejection, waste, or spoilage is excessive.

How the Government Protects Its Right to Title

Since the progress payments clause gives the government title to all of the materials, work in process, finished goods, and other items described in the progress payments clause, the administering contract officer (ACO) must be assured that title to these is not compromised. If there is no reason to believe otherwise, the contractor's certification contained in the progress payment request may be relied on. If the ACO becomes aware of any arrangement or condition that would impair the government's title to the property affected by the progress payments, the ACO will require additional protective provisions as deemed necessary.

The existence of these encumbrances is a violation of the contractor's obligations under the contract, and the ACO may, if necessary, suspend or reduce progress payments. This is authorized by the progress payments clause.

Risks Incurred by the Contractor with Progress Payments

Under the progress payments clause, and except for normal spoilage, you, the contractor, bear the risk for loss, theft, destruction, and damage to the property affected by the clause, even though title is vested in the government. However, this may be negated if the government has expressly assumed the risk. If a loss occurs for which you are responsible, you are obligated to repay the government the amount of unliquidated progress payments based on costs allocable to the property. If the government has assumed the risk, and a serious loss affecting contract performance occurs, the contracting officer may have to take the necessary steps provided in the clause to cover that situation.

Subcontracts and Progress Payments

Subcontracts providing progress payments in accordance with the same provisions as the prime contracts are encouraged by the government. Your request for progress payments may include the full amount paid to subcontractors as progress payments under the contract and subcontracts.

If you are considered to be making unusual progress payments to a subcontractor, the parties will be required to follow the policies for unusual payments as they apply to the prime contractor. If the unusual progress payments are approved by the government, the necessary contract modification will take place authorizing the progress payments to the subcontractor, and they will be included in the cost basis for progress payments by the government.

The progress payments clause under subcontracts should contain the same substantive clause provisions as the progress payments under the prime contract. Vesting of property by the subcontractor will be with the government, and not the prime contractor, and the right to reports and access to records should be expanded to include the prime contractor as well as the government. If you make progress payments to a subcontractor under a cost-reimbursement prime contract, the contracting officer must accept the progress payments as reimbursable costs if the payments are made under the criteria for customary progress payments, and they do not exceed the usual rates unless they have been approved. The subcontractor must also comply with the same liquidation principles as they apply to the prime contractor.

HOW TO OBTAIN GOVERNMENT-FURNISHED PROPERTY (GFP) AND REDUCE YOUR INVESTMENT COSTS

Government-furnished property (GFP) is property that is in the possession of, or acquired by, the government. It is then subsequently delivered to or made available to the contractor. GFP can include a broad range of things: material, military property, special tooling, special test equipment, or facilities. It does not include property on which the government has a lien resulting from advance, progress, or partial payment.

Material is considered anything that may be built into or attached to an item to be delivered under a contract. It may also be anything that is used up in performing the contract. For example, some of the types of items that are considered material include raw and processed material, parts, components, assemblies, and also small tools and supplies that may be consumed in normal use during contract performance.

Special tooling includes all jigs, fixtures, dies, molds, patterns, taps, gauges, and other equipment and manufacturing aids that are so specialized that, without substantial modification, their use is limited to the production of particular supplies or parts.

Special test equipment means single or multipurpose integrated test units engineered, designed, made, or changed in order to perform special testing required by the contract. Examples of some of the types of items falling into this category include any electrical, electronic, hydraulic, pneumatic, and mechanical assemblies and equipment that are modified in such a way as to become an entirely new piece of equipment.

Military property is that which is unique to military operations, and is kept track of by a military inventory control point. Included in this category would be weapons systems and their components, as well as the related support equipment. However, if the military property is consumed in the performance of the contract, it will be classified as material instead.

Facilities includes industrial property designed for production, maintenance, research, development, or tests. It may be real property and the rights invested in the property, or buildings, structures, improvements, and plant equipment.

The control of GFP is the responsibility of a property administrator, who has very little vested authority and who works essentially on behalf of the contracting officer. The property administrator will ascertain that the contractor maintains adequate records, that the contractor has an adequate control system, and that it is functioning as it should. Scrap write-off is one of the property administrator's functions, and he or she is permitted to write off scrap as long as it is reasonable; excessive scrap, losses, and damage to GFP may not be written off.

Two Rules Regarding Correct Usage of GFP

The question of legitimate usage comes up in all contracts where GFP is provided. Two rules pertaining to correct usage are used: one for material and one for equipment and facilities.

> *Rule 1*: With regard to material, the contract clause states that *the material may be used only for the contract under which it was provided*. You may not use the material for any other purpose, regardless of the merits of the alternate use.
>
> *Rule 2*: With regard to facilities, *it is usual for rent to be charged if that facility is used for nongovernment work*. The concern of the government in this case is not that the facility is being used for nongovernment work, but rather how much of the work performed in the facility is nongovernment. A problem arises if your record-keeping function does not delineate the exact amount of work being performed for other than government purposes. If there is any doubt, the property administrator can charge you as if the facility were being used full time for nongovernment work. The message here is quite clear.

There are two contract clauses pertaining to the contractor's risk under the use of GFP. Under the property clause in a fixed-price contract awarded through advertised bids, the contractor assumes total liability for loss of the GFP. Insurance is obviously the answer to any potential loss. Under fixed-price negotiated contracts where competition was light, or under cost-type contracts, the government will usually prefer to be self-insured.

Bailment Contracts: When and Why They are Used

The General Services Administration (GSA), under the Federal Property and Administration Services Act of 1949, has the exclusive right, power and duty to deal with all government property in a federal establishment. The GSA has delegated the right to deal with its property to the Department of Defense. Therefore, all property controlled by the Department of Defense is a result of this delegation. Because the Department of Defense may not sell property outright to a contractor, property is furnished under this situation by something called a ''bailment'' contract. A bailment applies only to personal property, and it is a contract where the legal and equitable titleholders are not the same person. Under a bailment, there is a delivery of property by the legal owner, called a bailor, to another person, called the bailee. During the specified time of use, the bailee becomes the equitable owner.

Bailments are used when the contractor's price, through use of the bailment, will be lower than it otherwise would be. The rule of thumb here is that normally the government will not bail property unless the item is not commercially available, or unless savings through use of the bailment will be reaped by both parties. All bailed property must be handled in accordance with the government property clause and any other applicable contract provisions. These other clauses will cover receipt, use, disposal, and other pertinent actions expected to apply to the property during the term of the bailment.

Your Rights if the Government Breaches Contract

The GFP clauses require the government to furnish the property on time and in a condition suitable for its intended use. If the government fails in any one of these responsibilities, it has breached an implied warranty. This entitles you to administrative relief under the equitable adjustment provisions of the GFP clause. You may not, however, sue the government for breach of contract.

Your Obligations as Contractor to Take Care of Government-Furnished Property

The GFP clause provides that you will have to carry out a sound program for the utilization, maintenance, repair, protection, and preservation of government property. This requirement continues until final disposition of the property is made. Any repair to, or replacement of, the GFE performed as your responsibility under the clause must be done at your own expense.

The government reserves the right to make changes in GFP. It may increase quantities, decrease quantities, or make alterations or substitutions in GFP. In any situation covered here, the government may have to make an equitable adjustment in the contract price, period of performance, or both.

Final disposition of the GFP is accomplished at the contract's completion. The contracting officer will require an inventory schedule of all items of GFP not consumed in the performance of the contract. The method of disposal is either determined by the contracting officer, or it is returned to the government. If the contracting officer directs you to sell the GFP, the net proceeds of the sale are credited toward the contract price. In some instances the contract may allow you to keep the GFP for a negotiated credit on the contract price. Finally, the government is not required to restore the premises from which the GFP is removed.

Note: It is easy for the dollar size of some government contracts to outstrip your established lines of credit, whether they be with your banker or suppliers. As a result, its best not to wait for a contract award before you start looking for financing. Take all of the necessary steps to establish your financing as soon as possible, so as not to endanger contract performance.

INDEX - CHAPTER 8

9

THE SBA AND GOVERNMENT CONTRACTING: HOW TO QUALIFY FOR FINANCIAL ASSISTANCE PROGRAMS

The Small Business Administration (SBA) was created by Congress in 1953 to help small business. Specifically it helps people get into business and stay in business, acts as a small business advocate, and helps small firms win federal procurement contracts. The SBA is an independent agency of the executive branch, and its administrator is appointed by, and reports to, the President. It has approximately 100 offices scattered across the country, and in Puerto Rico and Guam. Every state has at least one SBA office.

While there are other federal agencies providing assistance to small business, the SBA is the only agency whose sole responsibility rests in this area. Of approximately 14 million small businesses in the nation today, over 13 million, or approximately 93 percent, are classified as small. Obviously these small businesses play a vital role in the nation's economy. However, being small often makes it difficult for them to compete with larger businesses, who are better able to finance growth and research and to deal with government procurement and government regulations. Additionally, management difficulties have a more significant impact on smaller businesses.

In response to these problems, the SBA offers four types of assistance: financial, procurement, management, and advocacy. The SBA makes special efforts to help those facing unusual obstacles in raising capital and finding markets, and it extends itself especially to the socially and financially disadvantaged, women, veterans, the handicapped, and others determined from time to time to be in need. The SBA also offers a variety of loans and financial assistance to eligible small businesses, to privately owned Small Business Investment Companies (SBIC), and to Area Development Companies.

This chapter covers the general functions of the SBA and financial assistance programs as they relate to government contracting. Procurement, advocacy, and management assistance will be covered in Chapter 10.

Let's start with some definitions that will help you understand just where your company fits in from a classification point of view.

HOW THE SBA CLASSIFIES SMALL COMPANIES AND INDIVIDUALS

When a small company is not dominant in its field of operation, it means that the business, including its affiliates, does not exercise either a controlling or major influence, on a national basis, in the business activity in which it is competing. *Dominance* is determined by many factors, such as volume of business; number of employees; financial resources; competitive status and position; and the ownership and control of materials, processes, patents, license agreements, facilities, sales territories, and the very nature of the business activity.

A small *disadvantaged business concern* is defined as a small business concern that is at least 51 percent owned by one or more individuals who are both socially and economically disadvantaged, or a publicly owned company having at least 51 percent of its stock owned by one or more socially and economically disadvantaged individuals. It must be managed and controlled by one or more of these individuals.

A *socially disadvantaged individual* is one who has been subjected to either racial or ethnic prejudice or cultural bias resulting from membership in a group, without regard to his or her qualities as an individual.

An *economically disadvantaged individual* means a socially disadvantaged individual whose ability to compete in the free enterprise system is impaired because of diminished opportunities to obtain capital and credit, as compared with others in the same line of business who are not socially disadvantaged. Those groups qualifying under this standard include

- Subcontinent Asian (Asian-Indian) American (U.S. citizen with origins from India, Pakistan, Bangladesh, Sri Lanka)
- Asian-Pacific American (U.S. citizen with origins from Japan, China, The Philippines, Vietnam, Korea, Samoa, Guam, U.S. Trust Territory of the Pacific Islands, Northern Mariana Islands, Laos, Cambodia, or Taiwan)
- Black American (U.S. citizen)
- Hispanic American (U.S. citizen with origins from South America, Central America, Mexico, Cuba, The Dominican Republic, Puerto Rico, Spain, or Portugal)
- Native American (American Indians, Eskimos, Aleuts, or native Hawaiians)

SBA BUSINESS SIZE STANDARDS FOR QUALIFYING AS A SMALL BUSINESS

What constitutes a small business? Size standards for different types of businesses have been established by the SBA, and by definition, Congress has defined a small business as one that is independently owned and operated, and not dominant in its field of operation. However, the SBA is charged with the responsibility of establishing definitive size standards.

By general definition, a small business concern is a company, including all of its affiliates, that is independently owned and operated, not dominant in the field of operation in which it is bidding on government contracts, and qualified as a small business under the criteria and size standards in 13 CFR Part 121. Size standards are established by the SBA on an industry-by-industry basis, and they are applied by

1. classifying either the product or service being acquired in the industry whose definition, as found in the Standard Industrial Classification (SIC) manual, best describes the principal nature of the product or service being acquired, and
2. by specifying in the solicitation the size standard SBA established for that industry

The size standards defining small business for contract and subcontract bidding purposes are as follows:

Manufacturing: A concern is considered small if, including its affiliates, its number of employees does not exceed 500 persons, and large if the number of its employees exceeds 1,500. Within this range, the size standards vary from industry to industry. For example, in the petroleum industry, a company is considered small if its number of employees does not exceed 1,500 persons, and its crude oil capacity does not exceed 50,000 barrels per day.

General Construction: A concern is considered small if its annual average receipts for the preceding three fiscal years did not exceed $17 million. If you are in dredging, the figure is $9.5 million.

Special Trade Construction: If average annual receipts for the preceding three fiscal years did not exceed $7 million, the company is considered small.

Nonmanufacturing: A company in this category is considered small if its number of employees does not exceed 500 and it furnishes products manufactured in the United States by small business manufacturers.

Services: A company is considered small for the purposes of a procurement of a service if its average annual receipts for the preceding three fiscal years did not exceed $3.5 million, and large if its average annual receipts exceed $9 million. Again, within this range the size standards vary from industry to industry.

Transportation: A company is small if the total number of employees does not exceed 500, except if the company is engaged in air transportation, and then the number increases to 1,500. Trucking, packing and crating, and warehousing are considered small if annual receipts do not exceed $12.5 million.

Research, Development, and Testing: A concern is considered small, for the purposes of a contract that does not require delivery of a manufactured product, if its number of employees does not exceed 500. If the contract requires the delivery of a manufactured product, a concern is considered small if it either meets the definition of a small business manufacturer of the product being procured, or qualifies as a small business nonmanufacturer.

Various formulas are used by the government in determining small business size when a contract either crosses SIC lines of demarcation, or when the company proposes to furnish a product that it did not manufacture. The size standards are equitably arrived at, and once reduced to writing in a solicitation, they are considered final. If, during the preparation of your response to a solicitation, there is any doubt about whether or not you are either a small or large business, the contracting officer will be pleased to give you a precise answer.

Key Point: It is important to represent your company properly as either a large or small business in your bids, or in determining your eligibility for the various assistance programs that are available.

How Specific Size Standards Vary According to Industry

In order to be eligible for either loans or help in winning government procurement contracts, annual receipts, depending on the industry the company operates in, cannot exceed between $100,000 and $17 million. Staffing size considerations, where applicable, vary in a range of up to 1,500 employees.

- If you are in the wholesale business or a nonmanufacturing business, you are considered small if your average annual number of employees does not exceed 500.
- Construction varies by industry, and dollar volume is the determining factor. In general construction, in order to be considered small, annual receipts should not exceed $17 million. If you are in dredging, this figure cannot exceed $9.5 million. If you are in special trade construction and annual receipts for the preceding three fiscal years did not exceed $7 million, you are considered small.
- If you are a farmer, or in a related industry, your annual receipts should not exceed $100,000.
- If you are a manufacturer, you will be considered a small business if your average annual employees do not exceed between 500 to 1,500. Within this range, the size standards vary from industry to industry. For example, in the petroleum industry, a company is considered small if its number of employees does not exceed 1,500 persons, and its crude oil capacity does not exceed 50,000 barrels per day. If your company is in a labor surplus area, the size standards for loan eligibility and help with government contracting increase by 25 percent.
- A nonmanufacturing company is considered small if its number of employees does not exceed 500 and it furnishes products manufactured in the United States by small business manufacturers.
- If you are a retailer, you will be considered small if your annual sales are $3.5 million or less, and large if sales exceed $13.5 million. The classification for the middle ground depends on the type of retailing you are doing.
- If you are in a service business, you are small if your annual receipts do not exceed $3.5 million. You are large if your receipts exceed $14.5 million. Within this range the size standards vary by industry.
- If you are in transportation you are small if your annual receipts do not exceed $3.5 mullion, except air transportation, where small is defined as a staffing of less than 1,500. Trucking, packing and crating, and warehousing are considered small if annual receipts do not exceed $12.5 million.
- If you are in research, development, and testing you are considered small, for the purposes of a contract that does not require delivery of a manufactured

product, if your employees do not exceed 500. If the contract requires the delivery of a manufactured product, you are considered small if you meet the definition of a small business manufacturer of the product being procured, or qualify as a small business nonmanufacturer.

Keep in mind: These standards are subject to change, and the list is not all-inclusive. If you want to verify your status, contact the nearest SBA Field Office for the most current information.

GUIDELINES FOR DETERMINING WHO CONTROLS THE BUSINESS

With regard to determining just who controls a business, there is a sweeping collection of definitions. For example, *an affiliate* is a business concern having the power to either directly or indirectly control another business concern, or group of business concerns. In determining whether or not affiliation exists, consideration is given to all of the appropriate factors, including common ownership, common management, and contractual relationships. However, the constraints imposed by a franchise agreement are not considered in determining whether or not a franchiser either controls or has the power to control a franchisee. Control may be active or passive, and it is immaterial whether or not the control is exercised as long as the power to control exists. Control through stock ownership exists if a party owns 50 percent or more of a concern's voting stock, or the stock that is owned or controlled is large compared with any other outstanding block of stock. However, if it can be shown that a large block of stock does not truly control the company, it effectively removes this standard of evaluation.

Stock options and convertible debentures that may be exercised at any time after the determination of size status, or agreements to merge in the future, are considered to constitute control over a company.

Control through common management is considered to consist of interlocking management, where the officers, directors, employees, or principal stockholders of one concern serve as a working majority of the board of directors of another concern.

Common facilities control exist when one concern shares common office space, employees, and other facilities with another concern, particularly where the concerns are either in the same industry or related field of operation. This would also apply to firms that were formerly affiliated.

A newly organized concern is considered to be in control where former officers, directors, principal stockholders, or key employees of one concern organize a new concern in the same or related industry or field, and the first concern furnishes to the other, for free or a fee, subcontracts, financial-technical assistance, and facilities.

Control through joint venture, for size determination purposes, is an association of persons and concerns with common interests defined by a contract, express or implied, for the purpose of carrying out a specific business venture for joint profit. A joint venture exists when the parties combine their efforts, property, money, skill, and knowledge, but not generally on a continuing and permanent basis.

ELIGIBILITY REQUIREMENTS FOR FINANCIAL AND PROCUREMENT ASSISTANCE

If you require a loan or procurement assistance, the SBA has set up specific eligibility requirements. Procurement assistance, by the way, means advice regarding which government agencies are prospective customers, assistance in getting on the bidders' lists, and help in obtaining drawings and specifications for specific contracts. The eligibility requirements for loans and procurement assistance are based on the business size standards just discussed and certain general credit requirements. For example, as required by the Small Business Act (15 U.S.C. 637), a loan must be of "such sound value or so secured as reasonably to assure repayment." An applicant must be of good character, and must have enough capital in the business so that, with SBA assistance, it will be possible for him or her to operate on a sound financial basis.

The assistance standard for SBICs, Minority Enterprise Small Business Investment Companies (MESBIC), Development Companies, and pollution control guarantees—for all industries—net worth should not exceed $6 million, and net income, after taxes, should not exceed $2 million. This standard also increases by 25 percent if you are located in a Labor Surplus Area.

If you require assistance with surety bonds, and you are a service company, your gross income cannot exceed $3.5 million in order to be eligible. The standards for retailers, wholesalers, and manufacturers are the same as those for loans and government contracting assistance. If you are in general construction, annual receipts should not exceed $5 million.

As a public agency responsible for taxpayer money, the SBA has additional responsibilities as a lender. For example, it will not make loans to an individual who derives any part of his or her gross income from gambling activities. It will also not make loans for the purpose of speculation in either real or personal property.

HOW SBA FINANCIAL ASSISTANCE OPTIONS CAN HELP YOU

In providing financial assistance through the umbrella of the Business Loan program, the SBA has many different alternatives at their disposal that put about $3 billion annually into the small business community. One of these programs, the 7(a) program, consists of a direct assistance by the SBA. However, the SBA is not in business to compete with private lenders.

By law, borrowers first have to apply at a bank or other private financing source and be turned down before applying to the SBA for a loan. If, however, a small business needs money and cannot borrow it on reasonable terms from conventional sources, the SBA is permitted to extend help.

One way the SBA assists is by participating with a lender in a loan, or a loan guarantee of up to 90 percent of the amount agreed to by the lender. Applicants for the loan programs must agree to comply with the SBA regulations stating that there will be no discrimination in employment and services to the public based on either race, color, religion, sex, age, or marital status.

A key item of the SBA's financial assistance program is in the area of counseling. Quite often the SBA can demonstrate to a businessman that there may be another way to go instead of borrowing. If borrowing is required, however, and the lender is not able to furnish the money under the guarantee program, the SBA can lend the entire amount up to a maximum of $150,000 as a direct government loan. This is a somewhat rare occurrence, for about 90 percent of the SBA's loans are conducted through the guarantee program.

The largest and oldest SBA loan program is the 7(a) regular business loan, with 7(a) referring to the authorization section under the Small Business Act. Under this section, loan proceeds may be used for business construction, business expansion or conversion—relative to the purchase of machinery, equipment, supplies, facilities, and materials—and for working capital. Most small businesses, including farms and ranches, are eligible for SBA business loans. There are exceptions, however. Speculative firms, nonprofit businesses, newspapers, and businesses primarily engaged in lending and investing do not qualify under the program.

Repayment Guidelines

The basic lending purposes have remained virtually unchanged throughout the agency's history; however, loan ceilings, maximum maturity, and interest rates have varied over the years. Presently the ceiling for any one borrower under the guarantee program is $500,000. A repayment period of up to 25 years is permitted when the purpose of the loan is to acquire real property or construct facilities. Generally, however, business loans are made with a

10–year maturity. The interest rate is governed by a statutory formula based on the cost of money to the government when it borrows on the open market. Banks set the interest rates on guaranteed loans and their portion of immediate participation loans, with a maximum set from time to time by the SBA.

The SBA Guaranty Loan Program

Business loans are made either in immediate participation with a bank, where the bank provides at least 25 percent of the funds and the SBA the balance, or under the guaranty plan. Under this plan either the bank or other lending institution provides all of the funds, with the SBA guaranteeing up to 90 percent of the loan in case of default. Bankers love the guaranty plan; if they are successful in receiving principal and interest payments for at least one year prior to any borrower default, they will come out way ahead. Naturally, default is not advocated here. For one thing, it can certainly foul up your business career for a long, long time. *Key point*: A loan under the SBA guaranty program is looked on very favorably by the bank, and is usually approved without much ado.

Credit Requirements for an SBA Loan

Generally, credit requirements for an SBA loan are similar to those of a private lending institution. Applicants must be of good character, and they must have, and show, the ability to operate the business successfully. Additionally, they must invest enough capital in the company so that the business can operate on a sound financial basis and demonstrate that the proposed loan is either of such sound value, or so well secured, that repayment is reasonably assured.

The applicant must be able to show that the past earnings record and the future prospects of the company are a strong indication of thc ability to repay the loan, and other fixed debt, if any, out of gross profits. The applicant's personal resources will be looked at, in order to verify that sufficient funds are available to withstand possible losses. This is of concern mainly during the early stages of the venture.

Collateral for an SBA loan may consist of any one of the following:

1. a mortgage on land, building, or equipment
2. the assignment of warehouse receipts for marketable merchandise
3. a mortgage on chattels, such as furniture, automobiles, livestock, farm equipment, and related items
4. either a guarantee or personal endorsement, and an assignment in some instances, of receivables

THREE WAYS TO SECURE INDIRECT FINANCING BY THE SBA

Indirect financing is carried out by the SBA in three basic ways; through the agency's SBICs, through loans to state and local development programs, and through the surety bond program.

1. Small Business Investment Companies (SBICs)

Under the Small Business Investment Act, the SBA licenses, regulates, and helps to provide financing of privately and publicly owned Small Business Investment Companies, commonly termed SBICs. These investment companies provide equity capital and long-term loans to small business, and they may furnish management consulting services as well. An SBIC may begin operations with as little as $1 million in paid-in capital and paid-in surplus.

How an SBIC Obtains Funds. An SBIC may obtain long-term funds from both government and private sources. When 65 percent of its private funds are invested or committed, an SBIC may request the SBA to either lend, or guarantee, 100 percent of the financing from private lending institutions, and other sources, in an amount equivalent to 300 percent of its capital. The debentures issued by the SBIC for these funds may be subordinated to other debts and obligations. For an SBIC with private capital in excess of $500,000, additional funds become available through the matching of 400 percent of its private capital, provided 65 percent of the total funds available for investment are either invested in, or committed to, venture capital investments. The maximum available to a qualified SBIC is $35 million.

Interest Rates and Financing Agreements. The interest rate on SBIC debentures that are either purchased or guaranteed by the SBA, must be not less than the current average market yield on outstanding marketable obligations of the United States having comparable periods of maturity.

Financing agreements by an SBIC must provide, generally, for at least a five-year period, and loans having no equity features may be for a period as long as twenty years. This twenty-year period may be extended for additional periods not exceeding ten years. Financing agreements of less than five years' maturity may be made when they are reasonably necessary either to protect previous SBIC investments or, to a limited extent, when they are part of a sound small business financing package. Also taken into account is whether or not this financing constitutes a reasonably necessary part of the overall financing required, and whether or not it facilitates ownership by persons whose participation in the free enterprise system is hampered because of social and economic disadvantages.

An SBIC may furnish assistance to a single small enterprise in an amount not exceeding 20 percent of the investment company's combined paid-in capital and paid-in surplus. If a small firm needs more funds than one SBIC can provide, several SBICs may participate in meeting the firm's requirements.

Five SBIC Methods for Financing a Small Business. An SBIC may finance a small business by one or more of the following methods:

1. by purchasing debentures that are convertible into stock in the company
2. by purchasing capital stock in the small business, both with and without warrants to purchase additional stock
3. by purchasing debt securities, either with or without warrants to purchase stock
4. by any other acceptable instrument of equity financing
5. through long term loans to the business

Your local SBA office can put you in touch with various SBICs who may have an interest in your particular venture.

How a Small Business Can Qualify for SBA Financing. For purposes of SBA financing, a business is classified as small if:

1. together with its affiliates it is independently owned and operated, and is not dominant in its field of operation
2. it does not have a net worth in excess of $6 million, if it meets the business loan standards previously described, and does not have a post-tax average net income in excess of $2 million for the preceding two years

Programs relating to the Small Business Investment Act and those governing special examination of loans made under the financial assistance programs of the SBA, including liquidation and disposal, are subject to examination and postexamination. The idea here is to prevent unscrupulous business practices, and the SBA welcomes any notification of these.

The SBA also maintains liaison with the Securities and Exchange Commission (SEC), the Federal Deposit Insurance Corporation (FDIC), the Comptroller of the Currency, the General Accounting Office (GAO), the Federal Home Loan Bank Board, and other agencies where investigative findings are either of mutual interest, or involve matters affecting the operations of the SBA.

2. State and Local Development Programs

A *State Development Company* (SDC) may receive financing from the SBA under the provisions of the Small Business Investment Act of 1958, Title V, Section 501 (a) and (b). The purpose of this act, as expressed by the Congress, is "to improve and stimulate the national economy in general, and the small business segment thereof in particular, by establishing a program

. . . of long term loans for the sound financing of the operations, growth, expansion, and modernization of small business concerns.''

A State Development Company is a corporation organized under a special act of a state legislature to promote and assist in the generation, growth, and development of business and industry within the state. Typical members of SDCs are banks, insurance companies, and other financial institutions that are committed to lend funds to the SDC in amounts measured by the size of the lending institutions.

In order to be eligible to borrow from the SBA, an SDC must be an independent, privately owned corporation, organized on a profit or nonprofit basis. An official state or municipal corporation is not eligible.

A State Development Company may borrow from the SBA an amount equivalent to the total outstanding debt from other sources. The SDC is required to maintain a portfolio of small business loans and investments having an outstanding principal value of not less than 133-1/3 percent of the loan from the SBA.

The funds borrowed from the SBA must be used by the SDC to assist small business concerns by equity investment or long term loans that stimulate the flow of private capital for the sound financing, growth, expansion, and modernization of small business. Funds obtained from other sources may be used for the purpose permitted by the development company charter.

The maximum term for a loan to an SDC under Section 501 is 20 years. Repayment without penalty may be made on any interest date. Normally payments are scheduled in annual installments over the life of the loan. The terms, security, and rate of repayment are the same as are applicable to other borrowing by the SDC. The interest rate is reviewed annually to make certain that it conforms with the cost of money to the Treasury on borrowings to maturity.

While State Development Companies (sometimes called Business Development Corporations or Development Credit Corporations) are established primarily to bolster the economies of the various states through the use of a specially created private fund for all sizes and levels of business, most of their financial aid has gone to smaller businesses, mainly because they are the concerns more likely to seek the kind of assistance offered.

Local Development Company. The *Local Development Company* (LDC or 502) program is similar to the SDC in structure except that the LDC has less than statewide coverage and does not require a special act by the state legislature. While an SDC receives a loan from the SBA, an LDC may make 7(a) guaranteed loans, in addition to loans guaranteed under the 502 program. The 502 program assists eligible small businesses in acquiring fixed assets that contribute to the economic base of the community.

Certified Development Company. The Small Business Administration's *Certified Development Company* (CDC) program was enacted on July 2, 1980, as an amendment to the Small Business Act of 1958. The program's purpose is to help communities by stimulating the growth and expansion of small businesses within a defined area of operation. SBA-Certified Development Companies organized under provisions of Section 503 will provide long term, fixed asset financing. By providing this service, the program will enable communities to create jobs, increase their local tax base, expand business ownership opportunities, and offer improved community services. In addition, the program is a flexible economic development tool that can be used for other purposes such as city and regional development, neighborhood revitalization, and minority enterprise development. Through this joint federal government-private sector program, financing for the acquisition of land and building construction, expansion renovation, and equipment is available to small business concerns for a period of up to 25 years.

A CDC may operate on a local, regional, or statewide basis. It may be organized as either a private nonprofit corporation, or as a "for profit" stock corporation. The requirements are broad, requiring government participation at the appropriate level, a private lending institution, a community organization, or a business organization.

The CDC's members and stockholders must be geographically representative of the area of operations, and must include representation from the appropriate level of government reflecting the 503 development company's area of operation.

The CDC must have a professional staff with the capacity to package, process, close, and service its loans. Furthermore, the development company must be able to provide professional accounting and legal services to small business concerns. These functions may be provided either by the CDC's membership or on a contractual basis, subject to SBA approval. The services provided under contract must be performed by qualified firms and individuals who either live or do business in the 503 company's area of operation.

The CDCs must contain a five-member board of directors that meets at least bimonthly, and at least one private lending institution must be represented on the board.

Members, shareholders, and groups of shareholders and members of the CDC owning a direct financial interest in the project are limited in their control. They may not have either a combined individual or voting control in the CDC, or more than 10 percent of either the total outstanding stock or membership.

Another requirement is that its charter must indicate that its chief purpose is to "promote and assist the growth and development of business concerns including small business,'' and ''any monetary profit or other benefits that flow to shareholders (members) shall be incidental to the corporation and shareholders.''

CDCs are authorized to sell debentures pertaining to an identifiable small business concern with the SBA's 100 percent guarantee. The proceeds from the sale of a debenture can be used for plant acquisition, construction, conversion, or expansion for the particular small business involved.

The amount of each debenture guaranteed by the SBA may not exceed one half of the cost of each project. The remaining one half will have to be provided from nonfederal sources.

A CDC can provide assistance to small business under two basic plans:

1. The Re-Lend Plan, under which the small business buys the property being financed, where the CDC is a conduit through which the SBA-guaranteed debentures and the nonfederal financing flow to the small business concern.
2. The Lease Plan, under which the CDC owns the property and leases it to the small business. The arrangement can be a lease, a lease-purchase, or a lease with an option to purchase.

Under the *Re-Lend Plan*, the business has title to the property, and under the first mortgage formula, the bank is entitled to make a loan to the business in exchange for a first mortgage. Proceeds from the CDC debenture, which are guaranteed by the SBA, are reloaned to the small business in exchange for a second mortgage. This is then assigned to the SBA.

Under the *Lease Plan*, the CDC uses the proceeds from the sale of the debenture, along with the funds borrowed from nonfederal sources. These funds may be used by the company to purchase property, renovate property, or build on the property, as required.

A CDC is required to inject into the project an amount equal to 10 percent of the funds necessary to complete a given project. The 10 percent injection may come from a variety of sources, including from the small business company receiving the assistance.

3. The SBA Surety Bond Guarantee Program

The SBA Surety Bond Guarantee Program is unique in the federal government in that it helps bridge a surety bonding gap among small contractors, private commercial sureties, and public governmental bodies contracting for public bodies.

To induce sureties to bond more small contractors, the SBA can guarantee up to 90 percent of the surety's loss in event of contractor default. The guarantee is for contracts up to $1 million, and they can be placed on both bid bonds and the actual contract bonds, such as performance bonds and payment bonds for suppliers and labor.

In exchange for the SBA guarantee, a surety pays the SBA a percentage of the surety's normal bond premium; the contractor pays the SBA a fee of $5 per $1,000 of the contract amount. In order to participate, sureties must be eligible by U.S. Treasury standards, and any other standards set by the SBA.

How the Surety Bond Program Works. The secondary market is designed to permit participating lenders to sell the SBA-guaranteed portion of a loan to an investor. A participating lender makes a loan to a small business and obtains the SBA's guaranty. The lenders then elect to sell the guaranteed portion and seek a buyer, normally through a broker dealer. An agreement is executed by the lender, the buyer, and the SBA after the loan is closed and fully dispersed. This agreement extends the SBA guaranty from the lender to a subsequent good faith customer.

Although some lenders have set up their own marketing operation, most lenders sell the guaranteed portion either to, or through, a broker. Typically, brokers and others bid on the guaranteed portion, and the lender accepts the best bid. The broker may then convert the guaranty portion, through the use of the SBA-appointed fiscal and transfer agent, into a certificate. This certificate, in turn, permits resale to a new buyer. The new buyer is usually a pension fund or other institutional account. As an alternative to using the SBA-appointed fiscal and transfer agent, many secondary market sales can occur by direct placement.

The principal benefit accrues to small business borrowers by virtue of the increased availability of funds through local lenders. This is made possible by providing funds directly from sources that would not otherwise be accessible for investment in small businesses.

The funds available for the financing of small concerns come from a broader base, and therefore the supply of funds is less likely to be interrupted by cyclical fluctuations in the financial markets. Competition is made possible in the origination and servicing of small business loans without large commitments of capital from lenders. The increase in competition should result in more favorable terms for the business community.

The lenders have greater financial flexibility because of the liquidity provided by the secondary market. Therefore their ability to providing financing for small concerns is enhanced.

Lenders can substantially broaden their customer base with moderate capital commitments, and therefore realize operating and financial leverage leading toward improved profits from small business financing.

Under the Federal Action Loan program the SBA is authorized to make loans to small businesses in bringing about additions to, alterations in, or reestablishment in the same or a new location. This assistance, resulting from direct action by the federal government, can be used to restore plant, facilities, or methods of operations. Similarly, this assistance would also flow from endeavors by state governments acting in accordance with federal law.

Public Law 97–35 mandates that loans to businesses that are able to obtain credit elsewhere may have a maximum maturity of only three years. Loans to those who are unable to obtain credit elsewhere may be made for up to a maximum of 30 years. All loan maturities, however, are ultimately based on the applicant's ability to repay.

INDEX - CHAPTER 9

10

SBA OFFICE OF ADVOCACY: KEY SERVICE PROGRAMS THAT BENEFIT CONTRACTORS

This chapter examines the Small Business Administration (SBA) Office of Advocacy and how it serves the contractor, as well as the general assistance available from the SBA.

Many of the programs presented here can be of great benefit to all classes of business.

HOW THE OFFICE OF ADVOCACY OPERATES

Six Responsibilities of the Chief Council for Advocacy

The SBA Office of Advocacy was established when Congress, in 1976, passed legislation that authorized the Chief Counsel for Advocacy within the SBA. This person, who is appointed by the President and confirmed by the Senate, is charged with an impressive collection of responsibilities:

1. to act as a primary spokesperson for small business, and represent its views and interests before Congress and other federal bodies
2. to serve as a conduit through which suggestions and policy criticisms are received

3. to inform the small business community of issues that affect it, and to assist the entrepreneur with questions and problems regarding federal law, regulations, and assistance programs
4. to examine the role of small business in the economy with regard to competition, innovation, productivity, and entrepreneurship
5. to measure the impact of federal regulation and taxation on small business, and to make policy recommendations designed to enhance the performance of small business
6. to evaluate the credit needs of small business, particularly with regard to the free flow of capital to minority and women-owned enterprises

The Office of Advocacy, which is supported by 12 regional advocates, contains four divisions: Interagency Affairs, Economic Research, Information, and State and Local Affairs. These are described in more detail below.

The Office of Interagency Affairs. The Office of Interagency Affairs provides professional support for the Chief Counsel's advocacy for small business on a wide variety of issues. Appropriate policy recommendations are made to the White House, Congress, and federal agencies. One of the more interesting functions is that of assisting the entrepreneur with specific problems he or she may face in dealing with the federal bureaucracy. One of its key functions is to monitor federal agency compliance with the Regulatory Flexibility Act (RFA) of 1980. This act recognizes that the impact of government regulation is especially burdensome on small business. The RFA does much to temper this burden by requiring federal agencies to anticipate the effects of contemplated rules that would apply to small business. In addition the act mandates that, in order to reduce the burden on small business, every agency must review existing regulations to determine whether or not they should be continued, modified, or eliminated. The Chief Counsel reports frequently to the President and Congress on federal agency compliance with RFA requirements.

The Office of Economic Research. The Economic Research Division coordinates and conducts applied research on such topics as taxes, credit availability, innovation, procurement, and regulation. These studies form the factual basis used in strengthening its arguments for particular policies designed to promote the interests of small business. This office has also developed a data base that is used in determining the trends and conditions of individual segments of the small business community, or the sector as a whole. This data base is also used by policy makers for predicting the economic effect their decisions will have on small business.

This office also plays a leading role in drafting the *President's Annual Report on Small Business and Competition.* This report incorporates data from numerous statistical sources on small business productivity, competition, economic trends, innovation, and job growth. It describes changes in the economy and the small business sector, and details the impact of federal policy on small business.

The Office of Information. The Office of Information facilitates communication with government officials, lawmakers, organizations representing small firms, and small business owners. This communication is carried out by means of special publications covering the current topics of interest, research summaries, and briefs of current issues. Meetings and conferences, personal contact with trade and business groups, and correspondence with individuals seeking information and assistance are also an integral part of their operation.

Office of State and Local Affairs. The Office of State and Local Affairs is responsible for coordinating and assisting states and localities with their special needs affecting small business. One of the functions the office performs is conducting an annual conference at which state and local government officials discuss small business policy initiatives at their respective levels of government. Through workshops and panel discussions, information regarding small business problems and possible solutions to those problems are shared between states. This office also has an ongoing responsibility to promote small business legislation and to provide information on state initiatives that have been successful in encouraging small business development. A directory of these state and small business programs is published by this office as one of the means of aiding communication.

An information and referral service is also maintained. This directs callers to appropriate government agencies, trade associations, and other applicable offices and resources. The toll free number is 1–800–368–5855. In Washington, DC, call 653–7561.

THE PROCUREMENT AUTOMATED SOURCE SYSTEM (PASS)

Over the years many source lists and bidders' lists evolved within federal agencies and major corporations. Some were manual, others were partially automated. The need to have this information centralized led to the Procurement Automated Source System (PASS), which is under the jurisdiction of the SBA.

PASS is a computer-based inventory and referral system of small businesses interested in being a prime contractor or subcontractor for government contracts. The system operates by computerized matching of key words small companies have used to describe their capabilities. When an agency or prime contractor requests small business sources, SBA makes available the names of companies capable of meeting the requirements.

This information is available on terminals in all SBA Regional Offices and most of the major government purchasing agencies. The expansion of the PASS network is continuing, and private industry has access to the system on a cost sharing basis. An application for the PASS program is available through your nearest SBA office. It is a simple, one-page form that can be completed in minutes. Your company will be profiled in the system within a few weeks from the day the completed form is received by the SBA. PASS registration does not guarantee contracting opportunities, but small firms within the data base have their capabilities available for review by government and industry when the need arises.

SURPLUS PROPERTY SALES: HOW THE SBA MAKES SURE SMALL BUSINESS GETS A FAIR SHARE OF THE MARKET

Surplus property sales help make certain that a fair share of the property on the market is available to small business. Included in the surplus category, in addition to the things that we are all familiar with, are the sale and lease of timber lands and related forest products, oil, minerals, and vegetation. The SBA and other agencies work together in ensuring opportunities for small business to bid on these items. *Note*: Frequently, this cooperation leads to either small business set-asides, or the sale of the material in smaller quantities, which attracts smaller businesses.

To qualify as a small business for purposes of purchasing government-owned property, the small business standards discussed in Chapter 9 apply.

THE SMALL BUSINESS INNOVATION RESEARCH PROGRAM (SBIR): TO PROMOTE TECHNICAL AND SCIENTIFIC NEEDS

The Small Business Innovation Development Act (SMIDA) of 1982, Public Law 96–219, 15 U.S.C. 631, set into being the most profound change in the acquisition of federal research and development in over 20 years. This act's stated purposes are as follows:

1. to stimulate technical innovation
2. to use small business to meet federal research and development needs
3. to foster and encourage participation by minority and disadvantaged persons in technological innovation
4. to increase private sector commercialization innovations derived from federal research and development

This act led to the formation of the Small Business Innovation Research Program (SBIR). Under the act each agency having either an outside research or R&D budget in excess of $100 million is required to establish an SBIR program. This program is funded by setting aside a set percentage of dollars each fiscal year. The maximum percent is 1.25. Participating agencies include the Departments of Agriculture, Defense, Energy, Health and Human Services, Interior, and Transportation, the Environmental Protection Agency, the National Aeronautics and Space Administration, the National Science Foundation, and the Nuclear Regulatory Commission.

The SBIR's Three-phase Process for Awarding Funds

Under the law, the SBIR program is a three-phase process.

Phase 1: Awards of approximately $50,000 will be made for research projects in order to evaluate the scientific and technical merit of an idea.

Phase 2: As a result of Phase 1, those projects with the most potential will be funded, for either one or two years, up to approximately $500,000. The purpose is to further develop the proposed idea.

Phase 3: Private sector investment and support will bring an innovation to the marketplace. Where appropriate, this phase can also involve future production contracts with a federal agency for future use by the federal government. No SBIR funds may be used in Phase 3.

The law designated the SBA as the lead agency for program implementation, governing policy, and monitoring analysis of program performance. These functions are performed by the SBA Office of Innovation, Research, and Technology. This office is responsible for

1. developing, coordinating, issuing, and updating policy directives for the government-wide conduct of the SBIR program
2. developing and administrating an SBIR program information and outreach program
3. developing and maintaining a mailing list file of qualified small-business, high-tech firms
4. developing, coordinating, and publishing agency presolicitation announcements for the public
5. surveying and monitoring agency SBIR programs
6. coordinating with the private sector on the commercialization of SBIR programs

To get on the SBIR mailing list and receive these presolicitation announcements, contact the U.S. Small Business Administration, Office of Technology, Research, and Innovation, Room 500, 1441 L Street NW, Washington, DC 20416; 202–623–6458. Actual solicitations are received from the specific agency then contacted.

THE SMALL BUSINESS RESEARCH AND DEVELOPMENT (R&D) PROGRAM

The Small Business Innovation Development Act also created the Research and Research and Development (R&R&D) goaling program. This program is designed for agencies with an R&D budget in excess of $20 million in any one fiscal year, establishing small business goals for R&R&D funding agreements. The goal to be set annually cannot be less than an agency's achievement last year.

The SBA also has the responsibility to assist small business concerns in obtaining the benefits of federally financed research and development. The SBA provides technology information to small businesses that may assist them in solving particular technological problems, improving their processes, or providing state-of-the-art information in areas with new product potential.

The SBA has entered into cooperative agreements with the University of Connecticut and the University of Southern California in order to provide a fast reaction technology information service for small business interested in participating in the SBIR program. This service provides, within five days, state-of-the-art information useful in preparing either SBIR proposals or in guiding SBIR research efforts. The output is a comprehensive bibliography derived from a computerized search of a wide variety of data bases. The cost of this service to small businesses is approximately $125 per inquiry. The addresses of these universities are

University of Southern California
Western Research Applications Center
3716 South Hope Street, No. 200
Los Angeles, CA 90007

University of Connecticut
New England Research and Applications Center
Mansfield Professional Park
Storrs, CT 06268

THE MANAGEMENT ASSISTANCE PROGRAM: TO IMPROVE THE MANAGEMENT SKILLS OF SMALL BUSINESS

The Management Assistance Program of the SBA provides training, counseling, and information to small business through a community-based network of small business resources created and managed by the agency. Its objective is to improve the management skills of small business owners in order to support the growing economic impact and job creation potential of the small business sector, and to reduce the number of failures caused by poor management practices.

A closely allied program provides management counseling to small business owners, where expertise is offered in the areas of marketing, buying, producing, selling, record keeping, financial management, financing, and administration. Advice is also available on starting a business the right way initially, and on the most suitable businesses to enter.

Management Counseling Resources Used in the Program

The resources used to provide this and other program information consist of the Service Corps of Retired Executives (SCORE), the Active Corps of Executives (ACE), the Small Business Institute program (SBI), Small Business Development Centers (SBDC), community and junior colleges and their small business resource centers, chambers of commerce resource centers, and professional and trade associations. Some of these programs will be discussed in greater detail shortly.

Essentially, these SBA programs are well received, for annually close to 200,000 small business men and women participate in them. There is a widespread negativism toward SBA programs in general, probably because of a misunderstanding regarding the quality of the programs, which are often thought to be created for the lowest common denominator. Nothing could be farther from the truth, however, for the SBA-generated information is generally excellent. *The best advice*: Give the programs a try. If you feel that they offer nothing for you, then just drop out. Avoid the temptation to make a decision without having the facts.

Service Corps of Retired Executives (SCORE). SCORE was developed by the SBA in order to increase management counseling to small business. The corps is composed of thousands of retired business executives who have volunteered their services to help small business solve problems. The idea is to match the needs of the business with the talents of a particular SCORE volunteer, who makes a detailed analysis of the business and comes up with a plan to help.

The collective experience of SCORE volunteers spans the full range of business enterprise. Experts in the areas of retailing, production, office management, law, engineering, accounting, economics, banking, advertising, public relations, sales, wholesaling, procurement, science, foreign trade, and more comprise SCORE. There is no charge for this service.

Active Corps of Retired Executives (ACE). ACE was organized in 1969 to supplement the talent available in the SCORE program. ACE volunteers are recruited from major industry, trade associations, educational institutions, and the professional ranks. In working as a team with SCORE, the ACE volunteer shares current business understanding with the small business community.

Small Business Institute Program (SBI). The SBI program was begun in 1972, and it is a three-way cooperative among more than 500 college level schools of business administration, members of the nation's small business ranks, and the SBA. Under the supervision of the university and the SBA staff, senior and graduate students of business administration work directly with owners of small firms in order to give them on-site management counseling at no charge.

Small Business Development Centers (SBDC). The SBDC program, which was begun in 1976, is a major management assistance program developing and coordinating a wide variety of resources. Universities, community colleges, the private sector, state and local government, and federal agencies provide management training, counseling, and technical assistance to small business.

SBDCs offer a variety of problem solving assistance in areas ranging from basic business management skills to assistance requiring highly specialized technical expertise. SBDCs do not limit their activities to training and counseling. They are also actively involved in the development and coordination of research into problem areas affecting small business, they develop and disseminate state and local small business information, conduct surveys, promote small business interests throughout the state, and provide guidance to both present and future business owners and managers. Several SBDCs are offering innovation and assessment services, computer and related technology assistance, international trade assistance, legal assistance, procurement assistance, and local economic development assistance. SBDCs located in agricultural areas are emphasizing a full range of services to small business in agricultural-related industries. SBDCs receive partial funding from the SBA, which is matched by state and local governments and private sector contributions.

Local Practical Management Training Instruction Sponsored by the SBA

In 1982, a survey of small business owners indicated that there was a growing need for practical, hands-on management training adapted to the small business environment and available on a local basis. In response, the SBA developed a supporting network of cosponsoring institutions and trainers designed to provide this type of instruction to small business owners. The types of training cosponsored by the SBA are described below.

Prebusiness Training on How to Start Your Own Business. Prebusiness training provides basic information on how to start your own business on a sound footing, and is available to new business owners as well. Topics covered usually include the personality traits required, management skills, success and failure factors, market analysis, legal aspects, record keeping, financial factors, sources of capital, regulations, taxes, and insurance. This training is usually presented in a one-day workshop format. Other formats include multiple mini-workshops and courses covering various topics, including how to start and succeed in a business of your own, and managing your own business.

Follow-up training is conducted for the 20 percent of the prebusiness training participants who want further information. The main topic covered centers on how to do in-depth business planning. This covers the marketing plan, the financial plan, and the operation and administrative control plan. This training can be presented in either a one-day workshop or multiple conference format.

Basic Training Courses for Managers. A management basics training course is also available. It covers the key functional areas essential to successfully running a small business, providing students with all of the practical tools and skills for identifying and solving small business problems. Typical topics of instruction include small business management, business planning, marketing and sales, record keeping, financial management, and legal and risk management.

Specialized Instruction. Instruction in specialized topics is also available. These are categorized into three topical areas and a special emphasis area. The three topical areas are functionally related, industry related, and time related.

Functionally related topics cover the individual tools and specialized processes applicable to any business, such as inventory control, pricing, cash flow, and computers. Industry-related topics include those related to a specific industry, such as manufacturing, wholesaling, retailing, service, export, restaurants, art, trucking, and home-based business owners. Time-related topics refer to new information needed quickly by small business. These topics have a short life span, and typically include tax law changes, hazardous waste disposal, Small Business Innovative Research Act implementation, survival during a recession, and expansion during an economic upswing.

Special emphasis training is designed for groups that have been designated for special attention by either the President or Congress; for example, minority 8(a) clients, SBA borrowers, the handicapped, women, artists, and international trade.

These courses are available as either half-day or full-day conferences, or as specialized, in-depth instruction. They are cosponsored by the SBA with community colleges, universities and colleges, vocational educational institutions, chambers of commerce, trade associations, libraries, SCORE/ ACE chapters, and private sector organizations. The cosponsors promote and administer their training programs, select and pay instructors, and are permitted to charge nominal attendance fees in order to cover expenses. Presently, over 400,000 small business persons participate annually in the SBA Cosponsored Management Training Program.

Workshops for Discussing Management Problems. The SBA also runs workshops for prospective small business owners where management problems are discussed and good management practices are emphasized. These workshops may be conducted either as a one-day session or as a series of evening meetings. The training consists of discussions, scripts for role playing, worksheets, and visual aids.

The Office of International Trade. A recent survey conducted by the Senate Small Business Committee indicated a lack of current information on how to export, and a need for sources of assistance and financing. As a result, the Office of International Trade was established, whose goal was to continue to facilitate financial assistance and other appropriate management and technical aid to those firms with the potential to become successful exporters. The basic export counseling includes one-on-one counseling by SCORE and ACE volunteers with significant international trade expertise, access to university research and counseling, and assistance from professional international trade management consulting firms. Referrals are also made to other public and private sector experts, such as an attorney having international trade experience. Business management training is also available, as are international trade and export marketing publications.

MINORITY SMALL BUSINESS AND CAPITAL OWNERSHIP DEVELOPMENT

In October 1978, Public Law 95–507 was signed into law amending the Small Business Act and the Small Business Investment Act. Public Law 95–506 specified that section 8(a) was to be used to assist socially and economically disadvantaged individuals. It identified the type of management and technical assistance to be provided to them, and required the establishment of a Small Business and Capital Ownership Development program. The Associate Administrator for Minority Small Business and Capital Ownership Development is charged with managing and utilizing the 8(a) program to assist existing, newly organized, or prospective profit-oriented small businesses that are owned, controlled, and operated by socially and economically disadvantaged persons in order to help them to compete effectively in the marketplace. Incentives are designed to foster rapid development and successful entry of these businesses into the commercial marketplace. This objective is accomplished by providing government contracts, along with management, technical, and financial assistance, and business development expense and advance payments. Additionally, this office is involved with various projects, including business development seminars, minority trade associations, and special projects designed to benefit the small business owner.

The thrust of this office is to identify and address opportunities for minority-owned businesses to enter markets, access equity and debt financing, and to obtain management assistance and technological knowledge. Emphasis is placed on the barriers, and how they may be overcome, as well as the deficiencies inherent in minority business enterprises. These can best be addressed through specialized training programs and individual counseling.

One of the aids available, the 7(i) program, offers loans to small business concerns located in high unemployment, low income areas, or owned by low income individuals. It applies to businesses located in both rural and urban areas.

The 7(j) program provides management assistance to small business concerns eligible to receive contracts under Section 8(a) of the Small Business Act. Eligibility is based on social and economic disadvantage, as well as if the business is located in an economically depressed rural or urban area having a high proportion of unemployed or low income individuals.

The amendments provided by Section 203 of the law authorizes the procuring authority under Section 8(a) to be used as a tool for developing business ownership among groups that own or control little productive capital. Previously, the award of contracts could be made only to "small business concerns and others." Public Law 96–481 was enacted in October 1980. It amended the Small Business Act by requiring the SBA to establish a fixed period of time for participation in the Minority Small Business and Capital Ownership Development program for its 8(a) participants. A detailed look at the 8(a) program follows this section.

The *Code of Federal Regulations* indicates that a fixed program participation term will establish the maximum time period during which a concern may remain in the program, and the conditions for staying in the program, regardless of whether or not competitiveness is reached or the program is completed.

The Minority Small Business and Capital Development program is responsible for actively promoting and assisting other agencies by means of its interagency agreements. These are designed to provide a doubling and tripling of government procurement to small businesses. Additionally, the office of Minority Small Business actively continues to implement an extensive marketing program in order to assist 8(a) firms and other minority-owned small businesses in selling their goods to the private sector. There are two components to the Office of Minority Small Business and Capital Ownership Development. These are the Office of Business Development and the Office of Capital Ownership Development. The functions of these offices are tied closely to the 8(a) program.

To meet these objectives, the SBA maintains procurement center representatives in each major buying activity. It is also required to assign a breakout procurement center representative to each major purchasing center. A major purchasing center is defined as a buying office of the Department of Defense, or other entity designated by the SBA, that awarded contracts for items, other than commercial items, totaling at least $150 million in the preceding fiscal year. The function of the breakout procurement center representative is that of an advocate for full and open competition, and to identify items for future acquisition from small and small disadvantaged business concerns.

The contracting officers cooperate fully with the breakout procurement center representatives, by making available all reasonably obtainable contract information relating to current procurements. The breakout center representative participates as an integral member of the procurement center, attending provisioning conferences, reviewing restrictions on competition, and making recommendations on how to eliminate them. These restrictions, incidentally, can result from rights of the United States in technical data and the various acquisition methods under contemplation. They would also include the other restrictions discussed in previous material. The breakout center representatives will also make available any technical data necessary to prepare a competitive solicitation package on any previous noncompetitive procurement resulting from lack of this data. They also review unsolicited engineering proposals in order to see if they will result in lower cost to the government.

THE 8(a) PROGRAM: TO HELP SOCIALLY AND ECONOMICALLY DISADVANTAGED SMALL BUSINESSES

Section 8(a) of the Small Business Act established a program that authorized the SBA to enter into all types of contracts for goods and services with other government agencies, and to in turn award subcontracts for these to socially and economically disadvantaged small businesses.

When acting under the authority of this program, the SBA certifies to the agency that it is competent and responsible to perform a specific contract, and it is on the contracting officer's discretion that the contract is awarded to the SBA on mutually agreeable terms and conditions. If for some reason the contracting officer and the SBA fail to agree, the matter may be referred to an agency head for review by the SBA administrator.

In theory, the subcontracts awarded by the SBA to a company under the 8(a) program provides the capacity necessary for the company to operate at or above the break-even point, while permitting it to concentrate on the development of commercial and non-8(a) government sales.

The goals of the 8(a) program are:

1. to foster business ownership by socially and economically disadvantaged individuals
2. to promote the competitive viability of these companies by providing available contract, financial, technical, and management assistance as may be necessary
3. to clarify and expand the program for the procurement by the United states of articles, equipment, supplies, services, materials, and construction work from small business concerns owned by socially and economically disadvantaged individuals

Seven Criteria Used in Determining 8(a) Program Eligibility

Until the passage of P.L. 95–507, eligibility for participation in the 8(a) program was determined by an individual's social and economic disadvantage. The amendments now provide for 8(a) subcontracts to be let to socially and economically disadvantaged business concerns as well. The new criteria cover seven major areas:

1. The applicant must complete and execute a statement of social disadvantage.
2. Those applicants who are socially disadvantaged must be evaluated to determine whether or not they are economically disadvantaged.
3. The company must be at least 51 percent owned, daily managed, and controlled by one or more socially and economically disadvantaged individuals who are residents of the United States. Resident aliens are specifically excluded.
4. It must be determined that the applicant company, in conjunction with contract, technical, management, and financial support, has reasonable prospects for success executing the contract.
5. The company must have a reasonable chance for success competing in the private sector once 8(a) eligibility expires.
6. It must be determined that the applicant company is a small business concern within the applicable SBA regulations, as previously discussed.
7. The individual's character will be reviewed, and if any adverse information is obtained from a credible source regarding criminal conduct, this will be included as part of the evaluation. Prior criminal conviction is not automatically grounds for rejection, however.

Emphasis on the dollar value of contracts awarded, as a measure of the program's success, has been replaced by objectives for increasing the firm's competitiveness during its period of participation in the 8(a) program.

How the Contracting Procedure Works

The contracting procedure used by the government to implement the 8(a) program has four facets:

1. The proposed acquisitions may be divided into reasonably small lots, but not less than economic production runs, in order to permit offers on less than the total requirement.
2. The acquisition plan, where practical, and only if the work exceeds the amount for which a surety may be guaranteed by the SBA, may include more than one small business.
3. Delivery schedules can be established on a realistic basis which will encourage small business participation.
4. The contracting officer, when contracting by negotiation, may insert a clause requiring the subcontracting plan be designed to increase subcontracting opportunities for small and disadvantaged business. Of course this must not jeopardize efficient and economical contract performance.

The last requirement can be modified when the inclusion of a monetary incentive is, in the judgment of the contracting officer, necessary to meet the stated goals. The contracting officer may include small- and small-disadvantaged business concern subcontracting as one of the factors to be considered in determining the award-fee in a cost-plus-award-fee contract. However, the incentive should not award the contractor for results other than those that are attributable to the contractor's efforts under the incentive subcontracting program.

The matchup of the agency's requirements with the capabilities of the 8(a) firm are a cooperative effort between the SBA and the buying agency. The SBA identifies acquisition opportunities based on its knowledge of the capabilities of the companies in the program, and the agency recommends to the SBA those acquisitions suitable for 8(a) firms. When a suitable acquisition is identified, the SBA requests the agency's commitment to support the 8(a) company's business plan. Part of this request contains background information on the company and its technical capability, its production facilities, capacity, and how additional needed facilities will be provided in order to ensure that the company will be fully capable of fulfilling the contractual requirements.

Agency evaluation of the SBA request for commitment is based on its current and future acquisition plans, based on the quantities required, the number of construction projects planned, and the likelihood of the company being able to meet the performance schedule requirements. Any previous problems will be taken into account, and if sufficient information is not available on the company, then the agency will conduct its own independent evaluation of the company's capabilities. If the company passes muster, the next step is the pricing of the 8(a) contract.

How an 8(a) Contract Price Is Negotiated

Pricing is negotiated based on the data obtained from the company by the SBA. A cost analysis is performed, comparing it with the current fair market price of the work on the open market. Any excess of the negotiated price of the contract over the estimated current fair market price is eligible for funding as business development expense. This outlay may include the costs of start-up, training, and similar investment, as well as learning costs in excess of those normally incurred by established concerns engaged in the same business. If a contract including business development expense is awarded, that expense will be funded by the SBA. The negotiated contract price, the estimated current fair market price, and the amount of any business development expense are subject to SBA review and concurrence.

Any business development expense that the SBA agrees to fund is made to the contracting activity prior to award of the contract to the 8(a) concern. If the SBA does not agree to fund the business development expense, the contract cannot be awarded unless the negotiated contract price is reduced by the amount of that expense.

Remember: the eligibility of either an individual or business may be used only once in qualifying for the 8(a) program. Ineligible businesses are brokers and packagers, as well as debarred and suspended individuals and concerns.

Every 8(a) program participant is subject to a fixed program participation term. This term must be negotiated between the SBA and the applicant, the maximum allowable being five years. Not less than one year prior to the expiration of this term, a concern may request that the SBA extend the term for a period not to exceed the difference between the term requested in the original business plan and the maximum fixed term of five years, plus two years. In this negotiation for extension, the SBA will look at continued economic disadvantage, the progressively decreasing importance of 8(a) contract support in the future, and the effect this support has had in the past, including the estimated length of time it will be necessary for the concern to become competitive in the open marketplace.

Actual contract negotiations may be conducted by the procuring agency and the SBA. Where practical, the SBA's contractor should participate in these negotiations. On occasion, the SBA may authorize the contracting officer to negotiate directly with the company. Regardless of the format, the SBA has the final responsibility for approving the resulting contract before award, and determining whether or not the contractor is required to post a performance bond. A preaward survey of the contractor will be requested of the contractor whenever it is considered useful.

SMALL BUSINESS SET-ASIDES: TO AWARD CERTAIN ACQUISITIONS SOLELY TO SMALL BUSINESS

The Office of Advocacy is also charged with the responsibility of seeing that every small business gets its fair share of government business. One of the key programs accomplishing this objective is the small business set-aside.

The purpose of small business set-asides is to award certain acquisitions exclusively to small businesses. A set-aside may be open to all small businesses or, except for the Department of Defense, restricted to small businesses located in labor surplus areas. This set-aside may be total or partial.

A set-aside may be created by either a unilateral or a joint determination. A unilateral determination is one made by the contracting officer. A joint determination is made by the SBA procurement center representative, and concurred with by the contracting officer. The contracting officers are well aware of the SBA's small and disadvantaged business utilization program, and if a seemingly obvious set-aside is not made, the reasons must be fully documented. Agencies may establish threshold levels in unilaterally determining their set-aside programs, depending on their needs. In automated contracting systems, all proposed acquisitions are considered for small business set-asides. However, ultimately only those qualifying will be so designated.

At the request of an SBA procurement center representative, the contracting officer makes available for review all proposed acquisitions in excess of $10,000 that have not been unilaterally set aside for small business. If the value of the procurement is less than $10,000, a category of procurement known as small business-small purchase set-asides has been established. A company in the nonmanufacturing category may respond to these requirements with any domestically manufactured product. Once successful procurement by the set-aside method has been established, it may become a repetitive set-aside, if authorized by the agency's regulations. This can remain in effect as long as at least two companies bid on the procurement, and the price of the procurement remains fair.

If a proposed small business set-aside is estimated to exceed $1 million in value, and if a bond is required, the contracting officer is obliged, to the extent practical, to divide the requirements so that more than one company can perform the work.

Three Criteria for Establishing a Unilateral Set-aside

Determining whether or not to establish a unilateral set-aside is based on three primary considerations. First is to evaluate the set-aside in relation to the need to either maintain or mobilize the nation's full productive capacity; second, the impact of the set-aside on national defense programs; and third, an assurance that a fair proportion of government contracts are placed with small business. Whether or not to make the set-aside a total set-aside for small business is a judgment call, based on experience. Remember, it is necessary to obtain offers from at least two offerors at reasonable prices. Past history is a factor in the decision-making process, and in making R&D set-asides. Therefore, there has to be a reasonable expectation of obtaining from small business the best scientific and technical sources, consistent with the demands of the proposed acquisition, for the best mix of cost, performance, and schedules.

How a Partial Set-Aside Is Determined

Partial set-asides are established when a total set-aside is not appropriate, and the requirement can be severable into two or more production runs or lots. Either one or more small businesses are expected to have the technical competence and productive capacity to satisfy the requirement at a reasonable price. Generally, construction set-asides are not placed in the partial set-aside category. Partial set-asides can also be established for a class of acquisitions, and they may be used in conjunction with multiyear contracting procedures.

Procedure for Negotiating a Set-Aside

When contracting by negotiation, the usual procedure followed for partial set-asides is to conduct negotiations after all awards have been made on the nonset-aside portion of the requirement. Negotiations will be conducted only with those companies who have submitted responsive offers. An offeror who receives an award for a nonset-aside portion of a requirement, and who then accepts an award on the set-aside portion, is not required to accept a lower price because of the larger number of items involved in his or her contract. Similarly, negotiations cannot be conducted by the contracting officer with a view of obtaining a lower price because of the increased quantities.

The government is committed to the set-aside program. A contracting officer may not decline to make a set-aside because a large proportion of the previous contracts placed for the item were with small business, or because small business was already receiving a fair share of the agency's business. Likewise, it is not excusable to establish a set-aside because the item is on a QPL, because the contract is classified, or because another contracting activity has established a set-aside for the same item or service.

The SBA's Order of Preference in Implementing Set-Asides

In carrying out the Small Business Set-Aside program, contracting officers, with the exception of DOD contracting officers, must follow an order of preference. These are as follows:

1. a total set-aside for small business concerns in labor surplus areas
2. a total set-aside for small business concerns
3. a partial set-aside for small business concerns located in a labor surplus area
4. a partial set-aside for small business concerns
5. a total labor surplus area set-aside for concerns that are not considered small business

DOD Procedures for Carrying Out Set-Asides

The DOD procedures vary slightly from those just described. For example, architectural and engineering service contracts in excess of $85,000 cannot be set aside for small business. Those A&E contracts expected to run less than that amount are considered on a case-by-case basis. Every proposed acquisition for construction, including maintenance and repairs, in excess of $5,000 and under $2 million (except dredging under $1 million), are considered individually for set-aside applicability. Construction projects expected to run in excess of $2 million, and dredging contracts expected to run in excess of $1 million, are considered for set-aside on an individual acquisition basis.

The DOD attempts to divide set-asides so that a portion of the procurement will be made available to small business, and a portion will be made available to small business in a labor surplus area.

The order of preference used by the DOD in implementing set-asides is as follows:

1. combined small business/labor surplus area set-asides
2. partial set-asides for labor surplus area firms

3. total set-aside for small business concerns
4. partial set-asides for small business

Contracting officers are permitted to reject recommendations by the SBA procurement center representative regarding proposed set-asides. The representative may appeal this decision, and during this time period the contracting officer must suspend action on the acquisition unless it is in the public interest to proceed.

How a Set-Aside Can Be Modified or Withdrawn

Set-asides may be either modified or withdrawn by the contracting officer if it is determined that an award to a small business concern would be detrimental to the public interest. This could be represented by an unreasonable price, for example, and this license applies to joint set-asides as well. Again, if there is a difference of opinion regarding this decision, an appeal may be filed by the procurement center representative.

If a set-aside is not awarded, either the unilateral or joint determination leading to the set-aside provision is automatically dissolved. Reissuance of a set-aside provision will depend on schedule demands for either the item or service required. If, in the contracting officer's judgment, a set-aside would not best serve the interests of the United States, the set-aside in the new solicitation will be eliminated.

HOW THE SBA HELPS WOMEN AND VETERANS

The Women's Business Ownership Program, administered through the Office of Women's Business Ownership, has the responsibility of increasing the strength, profitability, and visibility of women's business enterprises through enhancing equal opportunities and access to government and private sector resources and programs.

The emphasis is on educational development, improving financial access, and increasing federal and private sector marketing opportunities. Some of the specific programs include:

- assisting women business owners in surviving business crises
- providing SBA personnel with the skills necessary to respond to the needs of women business owners
- increasing federal marketing opportunities
- negotiating an annual goal with federal agencies for procurement from women business owners

- collecting and analyzing data on women-owned firms and developing appropriate programs based on these studies

The SBA seeks to utilize the private sector in meeting the needs of women entrepreneurs. It also provides administrative and staff support to the Interagency Committee on Women's Business Enterprise. This committee was established under Executive Order 12138. The President's Advisory Committee on Women's Business Ownership was established by Executive Order 12426.

Programs to Help Businesses Owned and Operated by Veterans

The SBA has a number of programs designed to help foster and encourage businesses either owned or operated by veterans. It also assists veterans to become owners of their own small businesses. The type of help available includes advocacy, management, and financial assistance, with most of the SBA loans being made to veterans under its Loan Guarantee Program. In 1983, Congress authorized a loan program for Vietnam era vets and disabled veterans. Under this program, either a Vietnam era or disabled veteran meeting the SBA's credit criteria, may qualify for a direct loan if he or she is unable to obtain financing from commercial and other lenders. All of these programs are administered by a veterans affairs officer who is located in each SBA field office. Check your telephone directory for the current telephone number of the office nearest you.

INDEX - CHAPTER 10

11

MINORITY BUSINESS DEVELOPMENT: CONTRACT, FINANCIAL, AND OTHER SPECIALIZED PROGRAM OPPORTUNITIES

There are three important ingredients to any successful business: first, there has to be the right person; second, there must be a realistic opportunity; third, there must be adequate capital coupled with adequate management and technical assistance.

The first ingredient is supplied by the entrepreneur willing to take the risks associated with the competitive marketplace and the rewards it may bring. The remaining ingredients, as shown in this chapter, can be and are being supplied by the federal government. The purpose is to give members of minority groups an equal place on the entrepreneurial starting line.

This chapter is organized into three sections: the first section covers the Minority Business Development Agency (MBDA) of the Department of Commerce and the various contracting opportunities and business and technical assistance offered by various departments and agencies of the government; the second section covers the various financial assistance programs; and the third section outlines the specialized programs that are available to minority group members.

The programs mentioned here do not reflect the entire spectrum of programs offered by the various departments and agencies of the federal government, but rather those applying most directly to minority-owned businesses and individuals. Many of the programs do apply equally to all individuals, so you are advised to review this material, regardless of whether or not you are a member of a minority group. Some of these programs may appear far afield from government contracting, but any one of them could provide the resources necessary to become a government contractor, or the right catalyst to become more competitive in your area of business. Also, the availability of government ADP software through the National Technical Information Service, NASA, and the Department of Energy, all covered later in this chapter, can be a major help in running a dynamic business.

THE MBDA AND BUSINESS CONTRACT ASSISTANCE

The Minority Business Development Agency (MBDA), a part of the Department of Commerce, provides broad assistance to minority businesses and individuals so that they may achieve equitable and effective participation in the economy, as well as overcome social and economic disadvantages that have limited their participation in the past. Upon request, all minority group members are eligible for general business information and referral services, plus the services provided through business and trade associations.

Who Can Qualify for MBDA Aid

All other MBDA assistance services are available to minority firms that meet the following criteria:

1. either gross annual sales of at least $150,000, or, if a new business or expansion, a projection of sales of this amount by the end of the second year after assistance is provided
2. either five paid employees, or a projection of five paid employees by the end of the second year after assistance is provided
3. being in an industry or trade in which minority business participation has been historically minimal

MBDA promotes and coordinates the efforts of the other federal agencies in providing market opportunities for minority firms in the private sector. This assistance is provided primarily through the National Minority Supplier Development Council and its affiliates. MBDA promotes the participation of federal, state, and local governments, as well as business and industry, in directing resources designed to develop strong minority businesses.

12 Ways the Minority Business Opportunity Committee (MBOC) Can Help You

The types of assistance provided are comprehensive, and represent more than what the average good business consultant could provide on a fee basis. The programs are implemented throughout the government by the Minority Business Opportunity Committee (MBOC). The MBOC consists of a group of local federal agency officials involved in the development and commitment of resources for minority business in various cities throughout the country. Many of these MBOCs have a permanent executive director. The primary minority business goals of the MBOC program are procurement, education and training, capital development, business ownership, outreach, technical assistance, and economic development. A detailed look at these follows.

General Business Information and Referral Services: Current data are provided on business conditions and available resources in various areas, including finance, technical assistance, education, and training. Business opportunities in the area of concessions and franchises are also available.

General Business Counseling: Assistance in this realm primarily includes personal counseling on problems encountered in operating a business, and how to expand an existing business.

Obtaining Financial Assistance: Help is offered in preparing loan applications, securing credit from suppliers, obtaining bank lines of credit and bonds, and applying for other forms of capital assistance, such as equity participation and federal loan guarantees.

Management and Technical Assistance: Assistance and guidance is offered in a wide variety of areas, including accounting, marketing, inventory control, sales, promotion, and personnel management.

Obtaining Contracts: The purchasing needs of federal agencies, state and local governments, and major corporations, including subcontract requirements on prime government contracts, are identified. Aid is offered in qualifying minority firms to meet these needs, including help in preparing responsive bids.

New Business Starts and Expansions: Evaluations of proposed new ventures and expansions are offered. Feasibility studies, location analysis, and market analysis are also provided.

Construction Contracting: In this area, specialized support is offered on cost estimating. This includes labor, materials, materials scheduling, bid preparation, and assistance in either obtaining bonds or raising bond levels.

Construction Contractor Assistance Centers (CCAC) work with federal, state, and municipal agencies playing a major role in the construction industry. They also interface with sureties, insurance companies, commercial banks, and other groups whose support of the construction contractor is essential to his or her success. CCACs also provide expert service regarding other matters pertaining to the construction industry. For example, estimating, labor scheduling, and bid preparation could be included.

Technology Commercialization: Help is offered on maximizing technology-based business opportunities, including product identification, technological modifications, market feasibility, and distribution channels. This program is designed to assure that the greatest opportunities exist for minority businesses to utilize the unrealized commercial potential of new technologies. It functions throughout the Department of Commerce and at Technological Commercialization Centers, which provide the actual services. It is also linked to the resources of other federal agencies and the private sector.

Special Assistance for Larger Minority Firms: Help is available on various topics, such as business acquisitions and mergers, entering the export market, participating in international joint ventures, production, quality control, and engineering. Contracted Support Services (CSS) supplies management and technical assistance to large businesses with complex problems that cannot be resolved effectively by other MBDA-funded organizations.

Franchises: Identification of the availability of franchise opportunities, income estimates, operating issues, financial requirements, and other requisites are available.

Business Group Assistance: Groups of minority businesses, consisting of manufacturers and minority industry organizations, may receive information and aid considered unique to the group's needs. There are minority business and trade associations providing cooperative services designed to enhance the competitive positions of their members. These programs include dissemination of information on techniques to improve the member's operations, and seminars and other activities designed to improve the viability of firms in a particular industry.

State and Local Government Assistance: These groups help in procurement opportunities, concessions in state facilities, tax incentives permitted under state and local law, and help in meeting special licensing, bonding, zoning, and insurance requirements.

State Offices of Minority Business Enterprise (SOMBE)

State Offices of Minority Business Enterprise (SOMBE) provide, at the local level, basic functional activities similar to those mandated by the MBDA.

These offices are located in either the office of the governor, the state's Department of Commerce, or the state economic development unit. The scope of activities of the SOMBEs, although similar to those of the MBDA, vary according to the perceived requirements of the individual state programs. They are charged with developing state procurement activities for minority entrepreneurs, and promoting business opportunities for minority entrepreneurs through concessions in state facilities, tax incentives, and revisions of licensing, bonding, insurance regulations, and other matters.

Business Development Organizations (BDOs)

Business Development Organizations (BDOs) are the major sources of MBDA assistance to minority-owned firms. They provide direct support, thereby helping business candidates develop and implement business plans, evaluate proposed business ventures, and advise clients on the realistic potential for profit and growth. They also help the client submit his or her business package to an appropriate financial institution, help negotiate the best possible terms, and provide direct management and technical assistance in the fields of marketing, accounting, financing, inventory control, and procurement.

The BDOs additionally provide referrals of clients for special assistance to public and private organizations, including banks, business resource centers, trade associations, and regional business consultant contractors for in-depth specialized assistance. Information services are also provided, covering topics that include current business data on financial, technical, training, and educational resources. These are provided to assist the business person in making sound and reasonable decisions.

Maritime Business Opportunities for Minorities

The Department of Commerce, through the Maritime Administration (MARAD), also maintains the MARAD Minority Business Enterprise program and the Coastal and Energy Impact program. The main thrust of MARAD's program is that of providing subsidies to support and promote the development of an adequate U.S. merchant fleet. This is partially achieved by helping minority businesses become subcontractors to the recipients of MARAD subsidies. Any minority business either now engaged, or seeking to become engaged, in some aspect of the U.S. maritime industry is eligible.

There are two programs designed to provide financial assistance to minority businesses. The first is the Maritime Research and Development program, designed to stimulate the development and maintenance of the U.S. merchant fleet. The second program, Federal Ship Financing Guarantees, helps finance vessels which are designated for either research or commercial use. Any ship of more than five net tons and floating dry docks, may be eligible for assistance under this program. The ship owner must provide either 12½ or 25 percent of the actual cost, depending on the method of construction.

These programs are open to any qualified citizen. Contact the Assistant Administrator for Maritime Aids, Maritime Administration, U.S. Department of Commerce.

The Coastal and Energy Impact program, under the auspices of the National Oceanic and Atmospheric Administration (NOAA), offers contract opportunities involving:

1. Grants to states that have Outer Continental Shelf (OCS) oil and gas leasing and development activities. These may be used in planning and developing public facilities and services, including environmental and recreational resources.
2. Grants to help states and local governments plan for the social, economic, and environmental consequences on the coastal zone of new or expanded energy facilities, including housing, public safety, public facilities, and environmental impacts.
3. Grants to develop and implement projects designed to either prevent or reduce environmental losses in the coastal zone resulting from siting, constructing, expanding or operating equipment or facilities required by energy activities.
4. Loans to provide financial assistance for public facilities that are required as a result of increased populations stemming from coastal energy activity, including the construction of highways and roads, mass transit, docks, waste collection and treatment, schools, and hospitals.

The SBA, while not a part of the Department of Commerce, will assist anyone interested in accessing any of these Department of Commerce programs.

NON-SBA GOVERNMENT AGENCY PROGRAMS THAT CAN ASSIST SMALL BUSINESS

The business contract opportunities offered by the SBA have been discussed in great detail in Chapter 10, and therefore will not be mentioned here. As you remember, the SBA is the only agency charged with the sole responsibility of assisting small and minority businesses in a wide variety of ways. However, many other agencies have programs designed to assist the small business community. Let's take a look at these on an agency by agency basis.

General Services Administration

The General Services Administration (GSA), through its Business Service Centers, provides contracting opportunities through the 8(a) program and assistance in subcontracting with GSA prime contractors. Public Law 95–507 requires that each federal agency with procurement authority establish an Office of Small and Disadvantaged Business Utilization (OSDBU) to coordinate its small business, disadvantaged business, and labor surplus area programs. In the GSA this office reports to the Deputy Administrator, and it is responsible for policy formulation and overview of the agency's socioeconomic acquisition programs. Additionally, the Business Service Center counselors are a very valuable resource for small business concerns, women-owned businesses, disadvantaged businesses, and labor surplus area companies. *Tip*: If you are a small business operator, don't miss the opportunity to take advantage of this resource. It can make a big difference in your bottom line.

The GSA is an excellent customer because it is a very large purchaser of items used in common by many departments and agencies. Included are a broad assortment of nonpersonal services and "off-the-shelf" types of supplies and equipment, including office supplies, office furniture and equipment, household furniture, hardware, handtools, motor vehicles, refrigerators, air conditioners, water coolers, firefighting equipment, paper and paper products, waxes, adhesives, brushes, janitorial supplies, floor coverings, and many other items. It also lets contracts for the design and construction of government buildings and contracts for supplies, equipment, and services needed for their repair, remodeling, and maintenance.

The GSA, through its purchasing activities, is responsible for the appraisal, leasing, and disposal of real estate and government surplus personal property. It awards contracts for the acquisition and disposal of strategic and critical stockpile materials, as well as contracts for services, such as protection (guard) service, janitorial service, trash removal, window washing, stenographic reporting, furniture repair and refinishing, sound and video recording and reproduction, the repair of tires, tubes, office machines, and many other similar services.

Also on the GSA list of acquisitions is the lease and purchase of automatic data processing supplies, equipment, and services, as well as telecommunications equipment and services. Appendix D provides a complete listing of all of the GSA services and articles purchased in conjunction with their mailing list program. The GSA is an excellent customer to serve, primarily because of the wide variety of items purchased in very large quantities. It is also an easy customer to serve, for its requirements fit nicely into the commercial way of doing things, as opposed to the requirements of the Department of

Defense, which frequently needs items specially packaged and packed. Occasionally these requirements can exceed the cost of the items being purchased, and to the first time DOD contractor they can present an uncommon challenge.

The GSA also provides dissemination of technical information through its federal Information Centers. These centers provide information about any department or agency of the federal government, and they operate as a single point in each major metropolitan area for public questions about federal agencies. For further information, contact the General Services Administration. Information may also be obtained from the nearest GSA Service Center. Consult your telephone directory.

Department of Defense

The Department of Defense (DOD) is the largest purchaser of supplies, services, and construction in the federal government. The DOD *wants* to do business with all competent companies. Becoming a ''defense contractor'' is quite simple; all you have to do is sell something to this very big customer. Even pencils will do! This department's purchasing offices welcome small business firms, companies in labor surplus areas, small disadvantaged businesses, and small women-owned business firms who offer their products in support of defense needs. This permits purchasing at the best possible price, and it serves to distribute this business throughout the economy.

Assistance to small business is provided by each military service, the Defense Logistics Agency (DLA), and the Defense General Supply Center (DGSC), through their Small Business offices maintained in Washington, DC. Additionally, the SBA, GSA, and Department of Commerce Business Assistance offices provide guidance and help.

The DOD policy toward small business is to increase the involvement of socially and economically disadvantaged business concerns in as many defense procurement programs as possible. The basic interest is to focus attention on competitive contract and subcontracting opportunities. A significant aspect of this is the awarding of noncompetitive contracts to the SBA under the 8(a) program. Major support for disadvantaged business development is provided by the Department of Commerce's Office of Minority Business Development.

The DOD maintains a Minority Group Products and Services Program, which advises prospective minority vendors on contracting and procedures for doing business with the Army and Air Force Exchange Service (AAFES). This program monitors the stock assortment of minority-group-oriented products and services that are made available to minority group customers. The project officer attends minority trade shows and business conferences in order to review products and services offered either by minority-owned firms, or those firms offering minority-group-oriented products that could possibly be of use to the service. Any minority enterprise wishing to do business with the AAFES is eligible.

Department of Housing and Urban Development

The Department of Housing and Urban Development (HUD) administers the principal programs that provide housing assistance for the development of the nation's communities. HUD has six programs that fit into its minority business development goals.

1. The Small Purchases Program: The small purchases program emphasizes the need to develop business opportunities for minority firms on a large number of products and services valued under $10,000. Any minority business is eligible.

2. Public Housing Modernization: HUD has emphasized the need to cultivate increased minority business opportunities in constructing, rehabilitating, and modernizing public housing and services and supplies for public housing. In conducting its public housing modernization program, HUD makes direct loans annually for capital improvements. Any minority business is eligible.

3. Nonprofit and Consumer Organizations: Direct loans to nonprofit corporations and consumer cooperatives are made available by HUD in order to provide rental, cooperative housing, and related facilities for the elderly and the handicapped.

4. Contracting: Contracting opportunities from housing management offer minority businesses the chance to construct and rehabilitate these buildings and to provide the services and supplies necessary to operate them.

5. Property Repair: The Office of Property Disposition offers contracts for the repair of properties and contracts for the management of individual properties and groups of properties and commissions on the sale of holdings. Competitive bid contracts for repair and management by appropriate minority businesses are encouraged. These are placed through open competition and 8(a) procurement. The office also maintains an open listing of properties for sale by licensed real estate brokers. Acquired multifamily projects are placed for sale on the market by a sealed bid procedure. Further information on any of the preceding HUD programs may be obtained from any HUD regional office.

6. Community Planning and Development: The Community Planning and Development Agency offers Community Development Block Grants (CDBG) and Urban Development Action Grants (UDAG) for cities and localities nationwide. While the CDBG grants can be used for a variety of locally determined purposes, such as housing and public facilities, the UDAG grants, targeted for severely distressed cities and urban counties, are specifically allocated to help alleviate physical and economic deterioration through economic development and neighborhood revitalization. UDAG is also aimed at generating private sector involvement in these projects. In both types of grants, minority businesses can obtain contracts from the public agencies receiving these grants. In addition, minority businesses can apply to a grantee under UDAG for direct assistance in business development. For further details, contact the appropriate local government agencies in your telephone directory.

Department of Labor

The U.S. Department of Labor (DOL), through its Employment and Training Administration, offers the Employment and Training Research Program. Project contracts and grants are available for planning, developing, and conducting a comprehensive series of studies, as well as experimental, demonstration, and pilot projects designed to provide information necessary for improving the effectiveness of employment and training programs. Models of new program techniques are an integral part of this policy. These activities address industry-wide skill shortages, the training of workers for job opportunities in areas of high employment, developing information networks to serve the particular needs of specialized client groups, and assisting in eliminating artificial barriers and advancing affirmative action goals.

You enter this program by submitting a proposal following specific guidelines obtainable from the Employment and Training Administration, Office of Research and Development. All academic institutions, state and local government bodies, business organizations, and minority businesspersons capable of fulfilling the objectives of the program are eligible.

The LSA Set-Aside Program for Severe Economic Need. Companies located in labor surplus areas (LSA) can be given preference in bidding on federal procurement contracts. The purpose of the LSA set-aside program is to direct procurement dollars into areas where people are in the most severe economic need. These set-asides apply to both large and small businesses located in areas of high unemployment. The areas currently designated as LSAs appear in official lists issued by the Employment and Training Administration (ETA), and are published in *Area Trends in Employment and Unemployment*. This publication is available on a subscription basis from the Superintendent of Documents, U.S. Government Printing Office.

The DOL's Office of Small and Disadvantaged Business Utilization. This office is responsible for implementing and executing the department's responsibilities under sections 8 and 15 of the Small Business Act.

The Women's Bureau. The Women's Bureau seeks to promote the welfare of women workers. In cooperation with public and private agencies, it explores ways to expand women's training, resulting in employment opportunities in higher paying jobs. Additionally, it promotes the establishment of employee-sponsored child care services for working mothers, and develops models of innovative programs that effectively address the employment needs of women. This office also cooperates with the SBA's Office of Women Business Ownership on special initiatives designed to expand entrepreneurship for women.

Further information on these programs may be obtained from the U.S. Department of Labor.

Department of the Interior

The U.S. Department of the Interior (DOI), through its Minority Business Enterprise Program, which is administered through the Office of Small and Disadvantaged Business Utilization, offers assistance in developing markets for minority businesses within the department. This program provides counseling and advice to minority businesses on developing business opportunities within the DOI. It also helps the various bureaus and offices of the DOI in developing new business requirements for minority businesses. This applies to direct contracting and subcontracting opportunities, the SBA's 8(a) program, construction and concessions, training and education, financing and banking, grants and loans, permits, and rights-of-way assistance.

Any minority business is eligible. Contact the Office of Small and Disadvantaged Business Utilization, Division of Minority Business Utilization, U.S. Department of the Interior.

Indian and Tribal Enterprises. Assistance is available to Indian and tribal enterprises on reservations in the preparation of economic development plans, the establishment of business enterprises, manufacturing, economic development committees, corporations, and other programs designed to carry out economic development. A wide variety of businesses and industries have located near reservations in order to avail themselves of this labor supply. They include manufacturers of plastic pipe, automobile floor mats, agricultural products, wood products, and many others, as well as diversified recreational centers, including motels and ski resorts.

For further information on these programs, contact the U.S. Department of the Interior.

Veterans Administration

The Veterans Administration (VA) offers assistance counseling on contract awards and contracting through its supply service agency. The VA purchases thousands of items and services, including hospital items, office equipment, data processing equipment, supplies, services, communications equipment, and contractor and maintenance services. Minority businesses are provided with advice and counseling on the techniques and processes involved in this procurement. Included are 8(a) contracting, architect and engineering procurements, and standard competitive procurement.

Most of the VA's large purchases are made by the marketing divisions located at the VA Marketing Center, P.O. Box 76, Hines, IL 60141. Each division determines acquisition source and method of distribution, using both competitive sealed bids and competitive proposals in fulfilling their requirements. Local purchasing is conducted by each of the 172 VA medical centers located throughout the country. Large purchases by the VA include maintenance supplies, food, and services, including exterminator, laundry, maintenance, repair, and construction under $2 million.

Any minority business is eligible. For further information, contact the Office of Supply Services, Veterans Administration.

Department of Energy

The U.S. Department of Energy (DOE) has numerous activities designed to assist minority businesses, ranging from acting as an advocate for the preference program to active involvement in all phases of the set-aside programs. The DOE screens requests for their applicability to minority business contracting on an ongoing basis, and offers information, advice, and counseling to small business, disadvantaged business, LSA and women-owned businesses on doing business with the DOE.

For further information on these and other programs, contact the Department of Energy.

Department of Transportation

The U.S. Department of Transportation (DOT) has various programs within each of its various agencies dedicated to minority business enterprise. The Federal Aviation Administration (FAA) has established a group of minority business coordinators at FAA headquarters and regional offices. The FAA also requires that local agencies receiving federal funds for aviation and airport development provide opportunities for minority contracts and concessions at airports.

Federal Highway Administration. The Federal Highway Administration (FHWA) focuses on the need to establish and maintain a minority bidders list, plus the need to develop minority business contract opportunities. Assistance is also provided so that minority businesses can contact appropriate state highway departments. These activities by the FHWA ensure participation by minority businesses in procurement programs.

Urban Mass Transportation Administration. The Urban Mass Transportation Administration (UMTA) program includes direct federal procurement and procurement by local government agencies receiving federal grants. These programs include the preparation of minority bidders' lists and an information program aimed at attracting minority bidders. This latter program is based on the UMTA requirement that minority business participation be included in any grant application awarded by the local agencies receiving these grants. Prime and subcontracts are included.

Federal Railroad Administration. The Federal Railroad Administration (FRA), through the Minority Business Resource Center (MBRC) program, provides procurement opportunities for minority businesspersons in railroad projects funded either in whole or in part by the federal government. Twenty-seven outreach centers have been established. A Research and Training program, a Prime Railroad Supplier program, and a Marketing Assistance Clearinghouse also have been set up. Their function is to identify minority businesses for the procurement process. The MBRC also actively invests in selected Minority Enterprise Small Business Investment Companies (MESBIC).

Contact the Department of Transportation for information on these programs.

Environmental Protection Agency

The Environmental Protection Agency (EPA), through its Minority Business Enterprise program, offers counseling on contract awards and business opportunities, thereby providing advice to minority-owned-and-operated firms on how to strengthen their contracting opportunities in the EPA procurement process. This counseling covers contracts awarded under the 8(a) program, the Subcontracting program, the Competitive Procurement program, and contracts awarded to minority business organizations. The full range of EPA socioeconomic programs covers small businesses, socially and economically disadvantaged individuals and businesses, women-owned businesses, and LSA businesses.

Further information on these programs may be obtained from the U.S. Environmental Protection Agency.

Department of State

The U.S. Department of State has established an automated file of minority businesses that is used to match minority vendor capabilities with pending requirements. Minority businesspersons can submit data on their capabilities for consideration and possible inclusion in this file. This file is keyed to Standard Industrial Codes (SIC) and Dunn and Bradstreet identification numbers.

Any minority business may obtain further information from the U.S. Department of State.

Department of Health and Human Services

The Department of Health and Human Services (HHS) fulfills many of its responsibilities through nonfederal organizations using either contracts or grants. The department encourages its grantees to be aware of, solicit, and make use of small business concerns in the acquisition of goods and services, including construction, alteration, renovation, supplies, equipment, and consulting services.

It is HHS's policy that grants be awarded to profit-making and nonprofit organizations, institutions, individuals, agencies, and state and local governments.

The type of items purchased is quite varied, for they must meet the needs of HHS's four principal operating components; the Office of the Secretary, the Public Health Service, the Office of Human Development Services, and the Health Care Financing Administration. Under these offices are a wide array of familiar organizations, such as the National Institute of Health, the Centers for Disease Control, and the Social Security Administration.

Contact the Department of Health and Human Services for further information.

United States Postal Service

The United States Postal Service (USPS), through its Business Opportunity program, offers procurement assistance by providing information geared to help small businesses and minority enterprises obtain contracting opportunities. Included are procurements for supplies, services, construction, and mail transportation. Contact the Postal Service for further information.

WHERE TO OBTAIN FINANCIAL ASSISTANCE

The programs described in this section represent direct loan, loan guarantees, insurance, and other types of financial assistance. A minority business applicant must be able to satisfy the individual requirements of any of these programs in order to obtain appropriate financial benefits. Some of these programs are available only to minority businesspersons. There are two Indian loan programs; one in the Department of Agriculture, the other in the Department of the Interior. A much larger number of the programs are generally available to any small business applicant, and they can include minority businesses. Some of these programs have very specific requirements, while others can serve broad and general business needs.

Housing Loans for New and Older Buildings

The Office of the Assistant Secretary for Housing offers mortgage loan insurance and guarantees to help finance the development of homes incorporating either new or untried construction concepts designed to reduce housing costs, raise living standards, and improve neighborhoods. This experimental housing program addresses the restoration and fabrication of homes and multifamily housing by minority businesses. The program also applies to the purchase, refinancing, and construction of single family housing, rental housing, cooperative housing, condominiums, and manufactured homes. Provisions also include property insurance loans, housing for the elderly, nursing homes, intermediate care facilities, nonprofit hospitals, and group practice medical facilities. Special programs include loan and mortgage insurance for land development, manufactured home (trailer) parks, housing in urban renewal areas, armed services housing, and single family housing for home ownership subsidized by interest assistance payments.

Some of these programs are described in greater detail below.

Property Rehabilitation Loans for Designated Areas. The Community Planning and Development Agency, through its Community Planning and Development Housing Rehabilitation Loan program, makes direct loans to either residential and nonresidential property owners or tenants for the purpose of financing the rehabilitation of property in designated areas. The loans may be used to finance existing debt on property. The limits are $27,000 for a dwelling unit and $100,000 for nonresidential property. Minority businesses can be involved in any of the resulting rehabilitation contracts, and they can use these funds for their business premises.

Eligibility for this program is broad. Owners of property and tenants of nonresidential property in federally assisted code enforcement, urban renewal,

CDBG, and urban homestead areas may apply to HUD. Individual minority businesses can apply to recipients of these loans for contract opportunities.

Property Improvement Loans. The Property Improvement Loan program offers guaranteed and insured loans against losses on loans made to finance alterations, repairs, and improvements on existing structures and to erect new nonresidential structures. The maximum amount of this loan is $15,000. These funds can be used for the facility of a minority business. This program is offered by the Office of the Assistant Secretary for Housing. Eligibility requirements include any minority businessperson who owns the property or has a lease extending at least six months beyond the maturity of the loan.

Additional information on all of these HUD programs can be obtained from the U.S. Department of Housing and Urban Development.

Economic Development Loans

The U.S. Department of Commerce has several programs available through its various agencies. The Economic Development Administration (EDA) offers the Trade Adjustment Assistance program, the Special Projects program, the Grants and Loans for Public Works and Development Facilities, and the Business Development Assistance programs. These are open to all minority groups. Trade Adjustment Assistance consists of direct loans, guaranteed insured loans, and a technical information dissemination service. A company adversely affected by import competition can petition EDA for certification enabling the applicant to seek EDA recovery help. The company must demonstrate that the increased importation of articles that are the same or similar to those produced by the firm, contributed to the decline in sales and the potential threat of loss of the company's work force. A complete proposal for its economic recovery must also be submitted.

Aid for Minority Businesses in Distressed Neighborhoods. The Special Projects program of grants and contracts, which supports local economic development strategies, seeks to generate economic development in distressed neighborhoods and communities through the major EDA financial assistance programs. These include public works, business development, technical assistance, and long-term economic deterioration (Title IX). All projects receiving EDA financial assistance must be consistent with the local Overall Economic Development Strategy program, and they must support local regional programs designed to create jobs and break long term cycles of unemployment and underemployment.

Industrial and Commercial Development. Grants and Loans for Public Works and Development Facilities helps to attract new industry and encourage business expansion. The projects must either directly or indirectly improve the opportunities for the successful establishment and expansion of industrial and commercial plants and facilities, or otherwise help create additional jobs for the long-term unemployed and members of low income families. Examples of eligible projects are industrial park development, port facilities for industrial expansion, community infrastructure, and tourism.

Applicants may be states, local subdivisions, Indian tribes, and private and nonprofit organizations and associations located in either EDA development areas or economic development district growth centers and areas. Large businesses are not eligible. Small private businesses can be included, but they must repay the government for technical assistance.

Long-Term Loans for Private Investment. The Business Development Assistance program encourages private investment by providing low interest long-term loans. These may be required by businesses for either expansion or the development of plants in designated redevelopment areas. These loans come into play when these projects cannot be financed through banks or other private lending institutions. Long-term business development loans for up to 65 percent of the cost may be used only to acquire fixed assets. Working capital loans are also available for short periods of time, and guarantees for up to 90 percent of the loan are also authorized.

Any individual, private or public corporation, and Indian tribe is eligible, provided that the project is located in a qualified area at the time of the application. Funds will not be made available to applicants who have relocated within the previous three years, or are contemplating relocation. An allocation under these conditions would result in either loss of employment or the encouragement of production of a product having an excess of supply over demand. If the project involves the reporting and dissemination of news, it is also not fundable.

International Development

The U.S. International Development Cooperation Agency, through its Overseas Private Investment Corporation, offers direct loans and guaranteed loans. These are made available to ventures in less developed countries having U.S. equity interests. Loans are generally made for a term of between seven and ten years. Any minority-owned business is eligible, as are firms of mixed private and public ownership. Further information may be obtained from the

U.S. International Development Cooperation Agency, Overseas Private Investment Corporation.

Management Assistance and Information Services

General Business Services. The General Business Assistance Program is offered through the Industry and Trade Administration Agency (ITA). ITA's mission is to provide general business services designed to promote the growth of business. The services provided cover government regulations, market data, help with government procurement, data on business and industry growth, foreign trade administration, and foreign and domestic manufacturing and performance data. Any minority business is eligible.

Patents and Trademarks. Patent and trademark technical information and dissemination is offered through the Patent and Trademark Office. Patent applications are examined for patentability, and information, including copies of patents, can be obtained and public searches may be made in a patent room. Any interested party is welcome.

Technical Dissemination. The National Bureau of Standards (NBS) conducts the technical information dissemination program, which provides technical information and services regarding standards, measurement techniques, calibration services, reference materials, and reference data.

Government-Sponsored Research. The National Technical Information Service (NTIS), a division of the Department of Commerce, serves as a central source for the public sale of government-sponsored research, development, engineering reports, and other analyses prepared by national and local government agencies, their contractors and grantees, and by special technology groups. Information is available in machine processible data files. NTIS also promotes U.S. government-owned patents for licensing by U.S. manufacturers, and has established the Center for Utilization of Federal Technology (CUFT). This group alerts industry of selected federally owned technology having immediate practical value. NTIS also manages the Federal Software Exchange Center. The center makes available to the public federal computer software, programs, data files, and the planned systematic acquisition of generally unpublished foreign technology of particular interest to U.S. industry.

NTIS is a government agency sustained solely by its customers, and it operates very much as a business, but in the public service. All costs of NTIS products and services, including rent, telephones, marketing costs, postage, and other usual costs are paid from sales income, not from tax-supported congressional appropriations.

Full summaries of current U.S. and foreign research reports and other specialized information in hundreds of subject categories are published regularly in weekly newsletters, a biweekly journal, an annual index, and in various subscription formats for other federal agencies. A complete bibliographic index of unique subject groups and abstracts is available for search on line using the services of organizations that maintain the data base through contract with NTIS. The more timely abstracts are continually grouped by NTIS into paperbound *Published Searches*. These cover 4,000 subject areas.

Additional Computer Software. Computer software is also available from the Department of Energy and NASA. NASA software is available from the Computer Software Management and Information Center (COSMIC), which is administered under contract by the University of Georgia. Address information is in Appendix A. COSMIC is a unit of NASA's Technology Utilization Network, distributing software developed under NASA funding. Over 1000 computer programs are available, covering computer graphics, structural mechanics, aerodynamics, thermal analysis, control systems design, trajectory determination, and many more. The *COSMIC Software Catalog*, issued annually, contains detailed abstracts describing the programs, which are made available at a fraction of their actual development cost. For example, the median prices for software by type of computer are: mainframe computers, $900; microcomputers, $300. Purchase of the catalog entitles you to the quarterly publication *COSMIC UPDATE*, which describes new additions to COSMIC's inventory. A customized search for programs in your area of interest is available on written or telephone request, and the abstracts describing these programs are sent for your evaluation at no charge.

DOE software is available through The National Energy Software Center (NESC). The NESC is operated by Argonne National Laboratory for the DOE Office of Scientific and Technical Information (OSTI). Over 1400 packages, covering primarily scientific and engineering subjects, are on hand to support DOE and the Nuclear Regulatory Commission (NRC) research and development programs. Any organization can use NESC. If you are interested in using the center on a regular basis, an annual subscription fee covers the cost of NESC publications, special information services, and two library software packages requested during the year. If you are not interested in a subscription, you may choose a single program package license on a one-time basis.

Appendix A contains contact information for all of these programs.

SPECIALIZED PROGRAMS

These programs cover a wide variety of activities with potential for minority business assistance. They include the sale of federal surplus property, concessions in civilian and military installations, investments and deposits in minority banks, educational programs for business owners and employees, programs to promote the growth of companies, programs in agriculture, fish production, minerals leasing, grazing, and surface transportation. Also included are Indian programs for the development of arts and crafts, Indian acquisition of federal property, Indian employment, and Indian business enterprise development. About half of the programs listed operate solely for minority business. The balance are open to any other eligible groups and individuals.

Surplus Personal Property Donations and Sales

The Office of Federal Supply and Services donates excess personal property to minority and other eligible individuals, and conducts sale of this property on the open market. This program allows individuals, businesses, and other organizations to enter purchase bids on a wide variety of items, ranging from medical equipment, motor vehicles, and computers, to boats and mobile homes. Examination of the lists of items purchased in Appendix D of this book will give you a good idea of the variety of items that are eventually available for resale when they become surplus. The government also generates a substantial quantity of scrap that is made available for public sale. Normally, there are no usage restrictions imposed on property purchased from the government. Competitive bid sales are open to the general public, and names can be placed on mailing lists in GSA regional offices for certification when the types of property desired are for sale.

The Public Buildings Service administers the Minority Business Concessions Program. It presents minority entrepreneurs with opportunities to operate business concessions in GSA-controlled buildings. Any minority business is eligible to apply.

Further information on surplus property sales and the Minority Business Concessions Program is available from the General Services Administration.

Concessionaire Contracts and Economic Adjustment Programs

The U.S. Department of Defense (DOD), through the Army and Air Force Exchange Service (AAFES), and the Navy Resale System Office, offers concessionaire contracts with minority business concerns through reservation, and with no competition, as they become available on an individual basis. Any qualified minority business referred to these groups through a MBDA is eligible.

The Office of Economic Adjustment is responsible for planning and managing DOD economic adjustment programs, and for assisting federal, state, and local officials in cooperative efforts to alleviate any serious social and economic side effects resulting from major DOD realignments, such as either base closings or contract changes, and other actions. This office coordinates other federal resources, which can include advice and technical assistance, and grants and loans. Guidance is given on converting facilities, and technical assistance is provided in order to develop strategies for growth. State and local governments, public organizations, and responsible community leadership groups are eligible.

For further information on these programs, contact the Department of Defense.

Employment Services and Job Training

The U.S. Department of Labor, through its Employment and Training Administration (ETA), offers a variety of programs, including employment services and job training. The United States Employment Service (USES) provides assistance to states in maintaining a system of local public employment offices throughout the country and the territories. Through the Internal Revenue Service, it provides tax credits to employers who hire workers from certain target groups, and gives special recruitment assistance to employers. It also provides individuals with counseling, guidance, referral, and placement in apprenticeship training opportunities.

The Office of Job Training Programs, under the Job Training Partnership Act (JTPA), makes block grants to the 50 states, the Virgin Islands, Puerto Rico, the Commonwealth of the Northern Marianas, American Samoa, the Trust Territory of the Pacific Islands, and the District of Columbia. The goal of the JTPA is to train, retrain, and place eligible individuals in permanent, unsubsidized employment, preferably in the private sector. Eligible individuals are primarily economically disadvantaged individuals who have either been, or are about to be, displaced from their employment. The JTPA also provides that a fixed percentage of the block grants be used for programs for older individuals. In addition to the block grants, the JTPA provides for national programs for special target groups, including Native Americans and migrant and seasonal farm workers. It also provides authority for the job corps, a residential training program for disadvantaged youth.

Apprenticeship training is available through the encouragement and assistance of sponsors and potential sponsors in the development, expansion, and improvement of apprenticeship and other forms of allied industrial training. Technical information on training methods, public training facilities, and successfully demonstrated programs are made available to industry. The program addresses the national requirements for fully skilled workers in promoting economic growth.

For further information on these programs, contact the U.S. Department of Labor.

Energy-Related Inventions

The U.S. Department of Energy, in conjunction with the Commerce Department's National Bureau of Standards (NBS), conducts the Energy-Related Inventions program. This provides grants, the use of facilities, advisory services, and technical information in order to encourage nonnuclear energy technology among individuals and small businesses. The assistance provided includes evaluating ideas, inventions, funding, and advice on engineering, marketing, business planning, licensing, and patents. Any interested party is eligible. For further information, contact the Office of Energy Related Inventions, National Bureau of Standards.

Technological Innovations

The National Aeronautics and Space Administration (NASA) offers the Technology Utilization program, which involves the dissemination of technical information. Under this program, innovation, inventions, and improvements to existing technology are brought to the attention of both industry and the public. Technology transfer to private industry is a major goal. The NASA Computer and Software Management and Information Centers offer government computer programs to the public. Any interested party is welcome. Contact the National Aeronautics and Space Administration.

Telecommunications

The Department of Commerce, through the National Telecommunications and Information Administration (NTIA), offers business development to minority businesses in the form of the Minority Telecommunications program. This program develops and coordinates federal finance, procurement, and regulatory policies and programs designed to increase and sustain minority ownership of telecommunications firms. Any minority person or group is eligible. Further information may be had from the U.S. Department of Commerce.

INDEX - CHAPTER 11

12

GOVERNMENT CONTRACT LAW: YOUR RIGHTS AND OBLIGATIONS

This chapter examines the government procurement structure with regard to this principle, as well as the procurement structure that has evolved over the years into the surprisingly efficient process that is today. Keep in mind that this is not a legal text, and all references made to law are made with the intent of being casually informative, not with the intent of defining and interpreting the law. You are advised to consult an attorney for any definitive legal interpretation of any legal concepts contained in this chapter and throughout the book.

SIX PRIMARY SOURCES OF GOVERNMENT CONTRACT LAW

There are six sources of government contract law, the Constitution is the primary one. But this really doesn't account for the wide variety of laws and regulations that regulate our government's contracting activities. The six sources of government contract law, in order of importance, are:

1. the Constitution
2. statutes passed by Congress

3. executive orders issued by the President
4. administrative rules and regulations
5. decisions of the courts
6. common law

NINE RESTRAINTS THAT LIMIT THE GOVERNMENT'S POWER TO CONTRACT

There are nine main restraints on the government's authority to contract. These nine curbs basically limit the conditions under which it is legal for the government to enter into contracts. They are as follows:

1. the Anti-Deficiency Act
2. nonapplicability of the doctrine of apparent authority
3. statutory restrictions on fees
4. restrictions on types of contracts
5. restrictions relating to kickbacks
6. the requirement to advertise for contracts
7. "square corners" restrictions
8. the requirement that there be beneficial consideration
9. the requirement that all essential elements of a contract exist

Let's look at these nine restraints in detail.

1. The Anti-Deficiency Act: This act states that "no contract or purchase on behalf of the United States shall be made unless the same is authorized by law and is under appropriation adequate to its fulfillment." Contracting for more money than is appropriated is thus prohibited. A contracting officer may neither contract for a project unless Congress has appropriated the money, nor exceed the statutory dollar limitations set by Congress on the project.

2. Nonapplicability of the Doctrine of Apparent Authority to Government Contracts: This means that the government cannot be bound by a person who only *appears* to the contractor to have authority to make such contracts. For example, assume that you are an engineering contractor working on a government construction project. A project engineer employed by the government and assigned to the project requests that you make some fairly expensive changes to your work plan. This project engineer appears to you to have the authority to order a change in the contract, so you proceed. Later you learn that, despite appearance, the project engineer had no legal authority over the contract. As a result, you will not be paid for the changes you made. (A similar case involving a civil contract between two individuals may have a different outcome.)

3. Statutory Restrictions on Fees: The statutory restrictions on the size of fees prevent a contracting officer from agreeing to pay either an architect or an engineer more than 6 percent of the total cost of the project, not including the fee. Assuming that the agency was bound by this statutory restriction, payment of more than 6 percent for A&E services would be illegal.

4. Restrictions on Types of Contracts: There are restrictions on the types of contracts that the government can enter into. You could not enter into a cost-plus-a-percentage-of-the-cost type of contract, for example. Such an agreement would be null and void.

5. Kickback Restrictions: Kickback restrictions prevent government officials and members of Congress from using their position to influence a contract award in exchange for a fee. Again, a contract awarded under these circumstances would be null and void.

6. Advertising Requirements: Formal advertising requirements mean that the government cannot normally award a contract unless it has advertised for contractors. Purchasing by negotiation, the other method of procurement, can also be accomplished through the use of formal advertising.

7. "Square Corners" Restrictions: The Rule of "square corners" means that the government must play fair. Originally, the rule was applied only to the contractor, and it meant that the contractor had to perform ethically when dealing with the government. Now the courts have decided that this rule applies equally to the government.

8. Beneficial Consideration: Beneficial consideration means that the government must receive a benefit from the bargain. This does not mean that the benefit must be a bargain! There is a major difference between these two concepts. It also doesn't mean that the government must benefit more than the contractor.

9. Meeting Essential Contract Elements: In order for an agreement to be considered a binding contract and enforceable by the courts, certain essential elements must be present.

1. there must be an offer and an acceptance.
2. there must be competency of the parties.
3. there must be legality of purpose.
4. there must be clarity of terms.
5. there must be beneficial consideration.

THE FIVE VITAL ELEMENTS OF A VALID CONTRACT EXPLAINED

For an agreement to be considered a binding contract and enforceable in court, the five essential elements must be present. In most cases the law determining the validity of government contracts is very much like that governing private contracts. *Keep in mind*: The U.S. government acts as a sovereign power designed for the overall benefit of society at large, and because of this sovereignty it receives special treatment in contract law. Let's look at these five points in detail.

1. The Concept of Offer and Acceptance

Offers may be either express or implied. The vast majority of offers are express, although many offers are implied in many subtle ways. They are nonetheless capable of being accepted, thereby forming a valid contract.

Offers made under duress, in jest, or in pain cannot be considered to be accepted, as they fail to meet the test of serious intent to be bound.

A properly communicated offer remains open until it either lapses, is revoked, is rejected, or is finally accepted.

Determining How Long an Offer Remains Open. An offer does not need to contain a stated period of time for acceptance. In many offers, nothing is said about how long an offeree may have to consider the terms and conditions of the offer. Such an offer remains open for a ''reasonable period'' of time, depending on the nature of the offer. Whether or not an offer has lapsed because of the passage of time is a question of fact, and each case must stand on its own. Sometimes the answer is found in the subject matter of the offer. For example, an offer to deal in perishables will remain open for a far shorter period than an offer on nonperishables. The best test overall, however, is the answer to the question whether or not the offeree has taken unfair advantage of the offeror. The courts will rule that the offer has lapsed if unfair advantage has been taken. An attempt to accept an offer beyond the time period stated in the offer amounts to nothing more than a counteroffer, and a counteroffer is a rejection of the original offer.

In government procurement, the IFB, RFQ, and RFP constitute a request by the government for offers of a certain nature. The bid or proposal submitted in response to the solicitation is in fact the offer, and the subsequent contract award constitutes acceptance.

Revoking an Offer. Under common law, offers can be revoked at any time before acceptance. This is still true today, except in the case of government contracts. In government contracting, a contractor may not withdraw or revoke his or her bid between the time set for opening of bids and the award, except under certain situations that will be discussed later in this chapter. This is known as the *firm bid rule*. Indiscriminate allowance of bid withdrawal could lead to collusion, conflicts, and a variety of illegal actions that would threaten the whole system of competitive bidding.

Once an offer has been rejected by the government, it cannot be reconsidered and accepted. This would amount to a counteroffer, and that constitutes rejection.

Requirements for Accepting an Offer. Once a bona fide offer has been made and accepted, the offer then becomes a contract, provided, of course, that all of the necessary requirements for a binding and valid contact have been met. Once the contract exists, that specific requirement for the product, commodity, or service is no longer available for consideration by other bidders. An acceptance cannot be conditional. Such an acceptance, which would contain additional terms and conditions becomes, again, a counteroffer. Acceptance, as it applies to government contracting, is effective as soon as it is dispatched by the offeree, provided that the offeree communicates the acceptance by a means authorized by the offeror. Therefore, offers sent by mail and accepted in the same way become binding the moment the acceptance is placed in the mail box. If an unauthorized means of acceptance is used, it is effective only when it is received by the offeror. Acceptance by the U.S. government follows a rule laid down by a Supreme Court decision, which states a government contract comes into being the moment the government mails its acceptance signed by the contracting officer to the contractor. This rule was established following a case brought by a contractor who claimed that he had never received a signed copy of the contract and was therefore not bound to perform it. The Court held that the signed copy of the contract together with its mailing constituted acceptance.

Acceptance may be express or implied. Express acceptance by the offeree is in the form of words, stating that he or she accepts the offeror's proposal. Implied acceptance consists of any conduct or action by the offeree implying acceptance. For example, if the offeree exercises physical control over property that is the subject of the offer, then acceptance is implied.

Silence in the absence of other circumstances will not constitute acceptance. If the offeror writes in the offer, "unless I hear from you to the contrary, I shall assume that you accept" and the offeree does not respond, this does not constitute acceptance. The offeror cannot place on the offeree the burden of rejecting an offer under the penalty of accepting it.

Acceptance subject to approval of a third party or higher authority is not an uncommon problem, especially in government contracting. Under this condition, the offer is looked on as a conditional agreement that is dependent upon such consent being given. Prior to that consent, the agreement is taken as not having become effective. Unless otherwise provided in the document, this third party acceptance need not be in writing and may be implied.

2. Competency of the Contracting Parties

Every contract must have two or more parties, all of whom are legally competent to enter into contractual relationships. These parties may be either individuals or entities created by law and authorized to enter into contracts. A corporation would be one such entity. The authorizations to enter into contracts are almost never unlimited, and even in the case of natural persons, there are restrictions as to legal competency. For example, contracts made by minors are voidable, persons of unsound mind lack the legal capacity to make a binding contract, and persons under the influence of alcohol or drugs are likewise incompetent to contract.

In government contracting, competency of parties becomes a serious matter in the award of any contract. One of the first things a contracting officer must determine is how reliable a proposed contractor is. In other words, the contracting officer must determine, before award, that a proposed contractor is financially sound, that he or she has facilities to do the job, and finally, that the proposed contractor can do the job. In the award of some kinds of contracts, competency of parties becomes even more specific. For instance, supply contracts over $10,000 are subject to the provisions of the Walsh-Healey Public Contracts Act. This law specifies that any proposed contractor must be a ''manufacturer or regular dealer'' in the items to be supplied. In contracts for special types of products, such as munitions, explosives, and nuclear energy supplies, a contractor must have the qualifications to deal in these goods.

3. Legality of Purpose: How It Affects Public Welfare

The right to contract is fundamental, but this right is not absolute. The liberty to contract is subject to the public welfare, and fair reasonable restrictions may be imposed by law when clearly required for the public interest. This point was touched on lightly previously. Now some specific statutory controls on the right to contract will be covered. Also, the courts have the power to declare certain types of contracts contrary to the public policy and to render them void.

Contracts That Break Statutes. As a general rule, a contract that breaks a statute is unlawful and void and will not be enforced. If a statute expressly declares that a specific type of contract is prohibited, such contracts are absolutely void. This is true whether or not the statute is a state or a federal law. Here are some examples: statutes prohibiting gaming and wagers, statutes prohibiting the taking of usury or interest in excess of that established by law, and statutes regulating the traffic in intoxicating liquors and drugs.

Contracts Against Public Policy. Even where there is no prohibitory statute, certain kinds of contracts are against public policy. Public policy is the common sense and conscience of the community extended and applied throughout the state to matters of public morals, health, safety, and welfare. Some types of contracts that have been deemed to be against public interests are an agreement to unreasonably restrain trade or business, an agreement for the sale of public office (the paying of a price to exercise political influence), and an agreement to obtain government contracts by either personal or political influence or other corrupt means.

Lawful Purpose. Lawful purpose is a vital provision in every contract awarded in the name of the United States. The law will therefore not aid either party to an illegal contract. If one party fails to perform an illegal contract, the other party cannot enforce it in court. If the contract has been performed, a court will not permit recision (rescinding) and recovery of what was given in performance. No court, in other words, will become a party to an illegal contract. It will simply dismiss the case and leave the parties in exactly the same position as it found them.

4. Clarity of Contract Terms and Conditions

For a contract to be enforceable, its terms must be clear enough to permit the courts to conclude that a contractual agreement was intended. The courts will apply well-established rules to construe the meaning of language used by the parties. It follows, then, that the agreement must be clear enough to let a court collect from the contract the full intention of the parties at the time that they entered into the contract. A lack of certainty concerning offer, acceptance, or consideration may render an agreement unenforceable. Uncertainty as to the time of performance, the amount of work to be done, the price to be paid, the services to be rendered, or the property to be transferred may invalidate a government as well as a private contract. A government contract, like a private contract, must be sufficiently definite to have exact meaning.

Four Rules Used in Determining Intent of Contract Language. In determining what the intention of the parties was at the time that they entered into a contract, the courts use four primary rules of construction:

1. The ordinary meaning of language as used throughout the country will be applied.

2. Technical terms and words of the art will be given their special meaning unless clearly indicated otherwise.
3. The contract must be read and interpreted as a whole.
4. Circumstances of the transaction will be taken into consideration in arriving at the intent of the parties. Such things as negotiations, letters, figures, and estimates will be used to shed light on the intention of the parties, and will be admitted as evidence.

Oral Statements and the Parol Evidence Rule. Oral statements made by the parties about what they intended the writing to mean are not allowed. That would violate the well-established principle of law known as the *Parol Evidence Rule*. "Parol" is French for "spoken word." The Parol Evidence Rule states that oral evidence is inadmissible to contradict, add to, or otherwise vary the terms of a written contract. Parol evidence may be used, however, to explain a contract or add a term not covered in the written agreement between the parties. An example would be if there is a written contract for the sale of goods that mentions price but fails to spell out the terms of payment. Oral evidence may be introduced to explain the terms of payment.

Ambiguity: Let the Writer Beware. There is one secondary rule of contract interpretation that is frequently applied to government contracting. This rule states that ambiguities in a contract will be most severely interpreted against the author who was responsible for drafting the agreement.

Frequently, lack of certainty in contract terms results in mistakes. If a mistake is bilateral, no contract will result because there has been no meeting of the minds of the contracting parties. This type of mistake usually occurs when the contract language used is clearly subject to contrary interpretations and each party interprets it differently. Unilateral mistakes usually afford no basis for relief. The reason is that most of the mistakes result from carelessness on the part of the party making the mistake. This should not affect the rights of the other party who entered into the contract without misconduct and good faith.

If a mistake is apparent upon its face, or if the government contracting officer knew or should have known of the mistake, a different rule applies. The contracting officer must request the contractor to "verify the bid." The contracting officer must also point out the area suspected to be in error. If the contractor verifies the bid, the contract may be awarded as is.

5. Beneficial Consideration in a Contract

Consideration is that something of value that changes hands between the parties to a contract. Consideration may also consist of doing something that one is not normally bound to do, or refraining from doing something that one has a legal right to do. Refraining from doing something, also called forbearance, has the same force as a physical act in the eyes of the law. Consideration can take the form of money, property, services, or other things.

Contracts may be considered as being executed or executory. An executed contract is one that has been fully performed, or carried out, by both of the contracting parties. An executory contract is one that is yet to be performed. An agreement may be executed on the part of one party, and executory on the part of another party. For example, in purchases made on credit, the commitment has been fulfilled by the seller. However, the buyer is still required to make payment for the goods.

If there is no exchange or consideration involved, then the offer is that of a gift rather than that of a contract. If you offer something to someone without demanding anything in return, you cannot be held to your promise for there was no true contract. In a true contract, the agreement to the exchange is known as the bargain. Without this bargain, or agreement to the terms of the exchange, there is no contract.

Measuring Gain or Loss. Benefit and detriment, meaning gain and loss, are terms used for an exchange of consideration. For example, Jones agrees to pay Smith $10,000 to build a tennis court. The consideration promised by Jones is the $10,000. Smith, on the other hand, by promising the tennis court, stands to receive the $10,000. The $10,000 is Smith's benefit from the bargain, which in turn is a detriment to Jones. The tennis court is a benefit to Jones and a detriment to Smith because of its cost in materials and labor. Thus a contract is an exchange of benefits versus detriments.

It was stated earlier that a promise is not binding unless a bargain has been made for consideration in return. Now it is necessary to add that a promise is not binding unless the consideration offered qualifies as a detriment. In other words, for a promise to be binding on the party making the promise, the promise must cost the promisor something. It must be detrimental to the promisor. Usually a government contract is not divisible into exchanges of individual promises. *Key Point*: The whole benefit or obligation of one party is the consideration for the benefit or obligation of the other party. Moreover, a single obligation or benefit can be consideration for more than one promise.

Four Ways Consideration Can Be Fulfilled in a Contract. Consideration is sometimes called the price paid for a promise. This price can take many forms:

1. a promise for a promise
2. an act for a promise
3. forbearance for a promise
4. creation, modification, or destruction of a legal relationship

Consideration in a bilateral contract involves at least two promises, one made by each of the parties to the agreement. In a bilateral contract, both parties are bound to perform. In a unilateral, or one-sided, contract, only one party makes a promise, so only one party is bound by the contract. An example would be the promise of a reward if something is found. Those who read the reward notice are free to act by finding the item or not. Unilateral contracts do not become binding until the second party begins performance. At that point it is too late for the offeror to revoke or cancel the promised offer. Let us assume that you post a promise in your front yard to pay $20 to anyone who shovels the snow out of your walkway. Michael sees the sign, and relying on the promise, goes out and buys a snow shovel and then shows up for work. You cannot now revoke the offer because it would be ruled that performance was begun with the purchase of the shovel. The obvious disadvantage to the offeror in one-sided contracts is that the offeror doesn't have to be notified that work has begun and the contract has been accepted unless a requirement for notification of acceptance is contained in the contract. In addition, the offeror in a unilateral contract is the only one under a legal duty.

Adequacy and Sufficiency: Two Critical Points in Contract Consideration. Adequacy and sufficiency of the consideration are two points that sound similar but have two quite different meanings in law. Twenty dollars would be probably more than adequate to shovel snow off a walk. Sufficiency of consideration means that the consideration in a contract, and particularly in a government contract, has value in the eyes of the law. Therefore, value must be received. If the consideration offered costs the offeror no detriment, it will not be judged sufficient. There are many types of consideration that will prove insufficient to support a contract. For example, a promise not to do something you have no right to do in the first place is insufficient.

Past Promises Versus New Promises. "Past consideration" will not support a new promise. For example, a homeowner and a roofer enter into a contract for a new roof at a fixed price. After the agreement is signed, the roofer claims that he is unable to do the job at the agreed-upon price because of a rise in the cost of materials. The roofer wants $500 more, and the homeowner promises to pay. When the job is done and the bill is presented, the homeowner refuses to pay the extra sum on the grounds that her promise was not supported by any additional consideration from the roofer. In this case a court would rule in the homeowner's favor because the idea behind contract formation is bargain and exchange. The owner would not be receiving a fair exchange for the extra sum, and for this reason she cannot be held to her promise.

What has just been said about sufficiency of consideration really deals with "mutuality of consideration." Simply stated, mutuality of consideration means that either both parties must be bound, or neither is bound. In bilateral contracts, the mutuality comes about by the exchange of promises. In unilateral contracts, the consideration becomes mutual when the offeree initiates substantial performance of the offeror's requested act of performance. In each situation, the parties receive a fair exchange.

Past favors from contractors for which there is no legal obligation may not constitute consideration for present promises by the government. In other words, a contractor who gave free goods to the government could not claim this as consideration for slipping on the delivery schedule of a later contract.

The requirement for sufficient consideration in contracts stems from the theory that the parties to an agreement will be more likely to perform according to promise if they stand to receive something of value in return. Thus, it will not be necessary for the courts to force compliance. Furthermore, the courts feel that there is more likelihood that a promise has in fact been made where there is consideration supporting it than where the promise has no consideration.

The requirement of consideration is equally applicable to supplemental agreements or contract amendments. The general rule is that in the absence of a statute specifically so providing, no agent or officer of the government has the power to give away or surrender a vested contractual right of the government.

THREE CRITERIA FOR A VALID GOVERNMENT CONTRACT

The requirements for meeting the essential elements of a civil contract differ from the test for validity of a government contract. The criteria for a valid contract have been established by law and by the decisions of the Comptroller General. They are as follows:

1. Availability of Funds Test
2. Definite and Certain Contract Terms
3. Bona Fide Need Rule

1. Availability of Funds Test

This covers both time and subject matter restrictions. No contract can be written unless it is covered by funds appropriated for a specific purpose.

2. Definite and Certain Contract Terms

This is a clear test, since a contract whose terms and conditions are too vague is voidable. For this reason, an indefinite contract, or one in which the amount of the government's obligation is uncertain at the time of entering into the contract, is not enforceable.

3. Bona Fide Need

The Bona Fide, or Good Faith Rule, means that the items or services ordered by the government must serve a bona fide need of the fiscal year in which the need arises, in order to replace what was used in the previous year.

THE LAW OF AGENCY: THREE WAYS OF ENTERING A CONTRACT RELATIONSHIP

The federal government has both inherent and implied powers to enter into contracts. *Agency* is a device whereby one party, known as the principal, appoints another party, known as the agent, to enter into a contractual relationship with a third party. An agent is created in three ways:

1. by mutual agreement between the principal and the agent, which is known as *appointment*
2. by the doctrine of ratification
3. by the doctrine of estoppel

1. Appointment. An agent, appointed as a representative of the government, receives certain power through the appointment. The contracting officer, as an appointed agent of the government, also has a fiduciary responsibility toward the government in carrying out the government's instructions. This role of trust requires loyalty and good faith, obedience, skill, diligence, and proper accountability. If the instructions are discretionary, then the agent must use the best possible judgment.

In civil matters, an agent can have four main kinds of authority: express, implied, customary, and apparent. However, a government agent can never have apparent authority. Express authority consists of what has been spelled out. It may be oral or written. When authority is express, both principal and agent know exactly what power is granted.

Implied authority flows from express authority. Since it is impossible to cover in detail with the agent all of the powers required to perform his or her duties, implied authority is defined as anything necessary to do the job. Any agent who is given express authority is also given implied authority.

Customary authority belongs, by custom, to a particular profession or trade.

2. Ratification. Ratification is the process used by the government contracting officer to correct or "legalize" unauthorized acts that have occurred during the performance of a contract. If it is determined that a certain occurrence, although outside of the contract's scope, should be ratified for the good of the parties, then the action by the unauthorized agent is ratified, thereby making the act by that individual one of true agency. In some agencies, contracting officers have no authority to ratify unauthorized acts, and these requests must be submitted to higher authority for approval.

3. Estoppel. The third way an agency can be created is by estoppel. The word *estoppel* means to stop, prohibit, or deny the existence of something. Under the law there are two types of estoppel, equitable and legal. An equitable estoppel prevents a person from denying responsibility for the acts of his or her agent. This occurs when the contracting officer may not have actually given an agent authority or ratified the agent's actions. When a person denies this responsibility, the court can create an agencyship even where one had never been contemplated by the contracting officer. An equitable estoppel is usually invoked when the party who is denying responsibility for an alleged agent is likely to be unjustly enriched by this action. In government contracting, this means that if some link can be found between a contracting officer and a person ordering a contract change, the contractor can recover her claims. This situation is termed a *constructive change* to a contract.

In a legal estoppel, by contrast, the court can rule that no agency exists at all. This usually occurs, in the case of a government contract, when a government representative has taken unauthorized actions regarding the contract work. If these actions lead the contractor to seek additional compensation, the court can rule that the government representative is not a true agent, and therefore his or her unauthorized actions are not binding on the government.

THE WAYS TO CLASSIFY CONTRACTS

There are three classifications of contracts. These are express, implied, and quasi-contracts.

Express Contracts

An express contract is an agreement in which all of the detailed terms and conditions are set forth clearly either in writing or orally. In other words, the intent to contract is clearly spelled out in writing. As a general rule, a contract need not be in writing to be enforceable. However, there are some very important exceptions to this general rule. Some of these apply to government contracting: promises by an executor or an administrator to answer damages of the estate out of his own estate, promises to answer for the debt of another, contracts for the sale of land or any interest in land, and contracts not to be performed within one year of their making.

Implied Contracts

An implied in fact contract arises from an offer and acceptance that have to be inferred from the conduct or actions of the parties. The phrase *implied in fact* means that there is in fact a contract, but it is implied rather than express. In such contracts, the agreement of the parties is shown by the parties' actions and not by express words. The intent to contract can be judged from the surrounding facts and circumstances, coupled with the action and conduct of the parties. The criterion used here is to look at what happened, not at what was said. For example, if store owner Heather delivers goods to Michael in circumstances showing that she expects payment, and if Michael accepts and uses the goods, there is an implied contract that payment will be made for the goods. The contract is evidenced by the conduct of the parties in the delivering of goods on one side, and in accepting and using them on the other. Delivery of the goods is the offer to sell, and accepting and using the goods is the acceptance of the offer. The only difference between an express contract and an implied in fact contract is the evidence by which the agreement is proven.

Quasi-Contracts

Quasi-contracts, or implied in law contracts, come about out of obligations that are not based upon a contract. Quasi-contracts are implied in law on the theory that no one should be unjustly enriched at the expense of another. For example, if a doctor aids an unconscious man in an emergency, an obligation to pay the doctor may be imposed on the man by law, even though he never gave consent. Such an obligation is not an *actual* contract, because there was no intent to enter an agreement. However, it is a quasi-contract. In a quasi-contract, the parties to a transaction never intended to create a contractual relationship, but their transaction is nevertheless clothed with the semblance of a contract for the purpose of providing a remedy.

VOID, VOIDABLE, AND UNENFORCEABLE AGREEMENTS: THE LEGAL CONSEQUENCES

An agreement that is void has no legal effect whatsoever. In fact, it is a misuse of the term to call it a contract at all. The word *void* means that something never existed, and cannot therefore give rise to any rights or obligations under any set of circumstances. Typical examples would be contracts to commit crime, contracts contrary to public policy, and contracts that are prohibited by law.

Voidable Contracts

Voidable contracts can be affirmed or rejected at the option of just one of the parties, but remain binding on the other party at all times. A voidable contract is without a legal defect, as is a void contract, and it can become legal and binding. This happens when the party having the right to disavow the contract chooses instead to affirm it. In other words, a voidable contract is one marked by a legal flaw, which is curable. The legal flaw consists of one of the parties suffering from some sort of legal disability. An example is a contract entered into between a minor and an adult. The minor is incapable of making a perfect contract before reaching the legal age of majority. The courts then provide a second opportunity: the minor may either choose to be bound by the contract or disavow the contract. Contracts that were induced by fraud or fraudulent misrepresentation, and contracts that are induced by drugs or alcohol are likewise voidable.

Unenforceable Contracts

Unenforceable contracts are contracts that are valid but incapable of being sued upon or proven by one or both of the parties to the agreement. This type of contract cannot be set aside at the option of just one of the parties. The obstacles to the contract's enforcement have nothing to do with the contract. These obstacles create their difficulties in establishing either sound proof or sound legal action in support of the agreement by either party. Unenforceable contracts fail to comply with some provision of the law and therefore cannot be proven as valid. Two examples are as follows:

1. Contracts that are in violation of the statute of frauds, such as oral contracts for the sale of real estate, are unenforceable because they have not been put in writing.

2. Contracts that are barred by statutes of limitations are unenforceable. Statutes of limitation require parties to file actions to recover upon contracts within a given time period. If this action is delayed beyond the stated period of time, there is no longer a legal obligation to pay, although the moral obligation to do so may still exist. In government contract cases, a contractor must sue the United States Government within six years, commencing from the date the contract was completed and accepted by the government. If the contractor delays beyond the six-year limitation, the action will be summarily dismissed by the court.

FOUR GUIDING PRINCIPLES OF CONTRACT LAW

There are four guiding principles that will help you to understand certain aspects of contract law: contract conditions, divisibility, substantial performance, and discharge of contracts.

1. Contract Conditions

Contract conditions may be those that precede or are subsequent to the contract. A condition that must happen before a duty to perform arises is called a condition precedent. This could consist of a condition that a contract must be approved by a higher authority. A condition that follows a promise is called a condition subsequent. It defeats a contract on the subsequent happening of an event. For example, in a contract to sell goods, a provision that the contract shall be of no effect if the factory is destroyed is a condition subsequent.

Likewise, there may be constructive conditions. These are promises in a contract that are not expressly conditioned, but the law may imply one or more of these promises as conditions. In a contract for the purchase of a building site that requires the delivery of the deed before a fixed date, tender of payment must be made prior to the fixed date.

2. Contract Divisibility

Problems frequently arise whether a contract is entire or divisible. No formula has been found that furnishes a test for determining, in all cases, which contracts are divisible and which are entire. The primary criterion for determining the question is the intention of the parties. Intent is determined by a fair construction of the contract's terms and provisions, both by the subject matter and the circumstances. The best test is whether or not all of the elements, viewed as a whole, are the essence of the contract. That is to say, if it appears that the contract's purpose is to take the whole, or none, then the contract is entire. Otherwise it is divisible.

Where the execution of the contract is capable of being divided into several distinct performances and counter-performances, it is a matter of how the contract is written as to whether the parties intended it to be a divisible or indivisible contract. Stated another way, a contract is divisible where the part to be performed by one party consists of several distinct and separate items, and the price to be paid by the other is apportioned to each item.

3. Substantial Performance

With regard to substantial performance of a contract, the general rule is that such performance will support recovery of the contract price, less allowances for defects in performance or damages for failure to comply strictly with the contract. Substantial performance can prevent termination of a contract for default. If the government can make substantial use of a substantially completed item, then the contract may not be defaulted. The contractor would be entitled to payment, less deductions for delay and final completion. This principle of law is generally applied to construction contracts. Here are two examples of what does and does not constitute substantial performance:

1. a building may be complete with the exception of trim work and doors, and if the building is complete enough to allow occupation, substantial performance has occurred.
2. On the other hand, a bowling alley could be fully completed except for the final finishing coats of varnish on the alleys. In this case, since no use could be made of the bowling alley, the contract is not substantially complete.

4. Contract Discharge

The discharge of a contract means that the obligations incurred by the parties when they entered into the agreement are excused. No longer are they bound to perform as they had promised. Discharge can be accomplished in a number of ways, performance by both parties being the most obvious. However, an agreement to rescind the contract is another form of discharge, as is the writing of a new contract that provides for setting aside of the original contract. The original parties may agree to substitute a new party for any one of them. Assuming the consent of the new party, he or she assumes the obligations of the original party. Finally, an accord and satisfaction will discharge a contract. The contracting parties may have had a series of dealings between themselves concerning the sale and purchase of goods, and it may have become doubtful what the exact amount due really is. Under these circumstances, if a bona fide legitimate dispute arises as to the exact amount that is due under the contract, the party who owes the other party may make out a check in an amount that she feels to be a reasonable final payment, and mark the check as payment in full. If this check is cashed, this discharges any remaining obligations.

Tip: The key to accord and satisfaction is that it may be used only in those cases where there is a bona fide legitimate dispute over the sum owed. If there is no question about the amount of money owed, then this means may not be used to discharge an obligation. Even if the check is marked "paid in full," it may still be cashed and the party may sue for the remaining amount due.

SIMILARITIES AND DIFFERENCES BETWEEN PRIVATE AND GOVERNMENT CONTRACTS

There are many similarities between commercial and government contracts. The principal, from the government's side of the deal, is the one who acts for the government, or is the government's agent. As in private contracting, the government is bound by the acts of its agents committed within the scope of their authority.

In many cases the problem is to ascertain the authority of the officer or person acting on the part of the government. Fortunately, in most cases, the authority of the agent is expressed; that is, it is a matter of statute or regulation. When the duties, powers, responsibilities, and authority of an agent are statutory, any authority exercised that is not in conformance with the statute or regulation is not binding on the government. This situation could lead to some unanticipated results. *Keep in mind*: Ignorance of the law is no excuse.

There are many cases where the government may be bound by acts of its agents even though the authority of the agent, as exercised, is not spelled out in a statute or regulation. When a contracting officer, by his warrant, has express authority to act, he may have the implied authority to implement the responsibilities charged to him. If an agent of the government needs to act in order to carry out his express authority, then the agent has the implied authority to perform the act. This implied authority is said to be incidental to express authority. The rules about this type of authority in government contracts are no different from those in private contracts.

Five Key Stipulations Shared by Government and Private Contracts

Government contracts are the same as private contracts in the following respects:

1. Government contracts, like private contracts, must have all the essential elements of a contract.
2. Standards of contract interpretation are by and large the same for both.
3. Bilateral contracts are recognized and used by the government.
4. Unilateral contracts are used for small purchases by the government.
5. The rules for ratification are about the same as for private contracts. A contract that was not binding because the officer lacked the authority to act, may become binding on the government by ratification. Ratification can be by a principal or by a superior agent who had the power to grant the authority at the time the unauthorized act was committed.

Ratification and approval of contracts are two entirely different things. When an approval of a contract is required by statute or other regulation, the proposed contract must be submitted to superior authority as a condition precedent to binding effect. At all times, a contracting officer has the authority to enter into a contract, subject to the condition precedent. In a situation requiring ratification, the contracting officer does not have the power to enter the contract.

How the Right of Sovereignty Separates Government Contracts from Commercial Contracts

There are major differences separating government contracts from commercial contracts. Let's look at these in some detail.

1. The Government Is Immune from Most Lawsuits. Because of its sovereignty, the government is immune from suit except to the extent that it voluntarily consents to be sued. Only the legislative branch may waive this sovereign immunity. In the case of government contracts, Congress enacted the Tucker Act in 1887. This statute allows contractors to sue the U.S. government in all actions founded upon either express or implied in fact contracts, or in cases where liquidated damages have been assessed.

In determining questions arising from government contracts, the courts are not bound by the law of any particular state. Federal common law will be applied wherever the question is not answered by the Constitution or by federal statute or regulation. In other words, federal law controls.

2. The Government Is Not Liable for Acts That Indirectly Obstruct Other Government Contracts. Because of its sovereignty, the government also enjoys immunity from acts originating within the government that have the effect of obstructing the government's contracts. In other words, the government is not liable for the effects of sovereign acts. An example of this type of obstruction would be where one branch of the government, for instance, the legislative branch, obstructs the performance of another agency, such as the executive branch. This immunity is subject to one exception: where the obstruction is of a direct rather than an indirect nature. An act committed for the general public good would be considered an indirect obstruction, while an act committed solely for the purpose of a particular contract would be considered a direct one.

3. The Government Is Immune from State and Local Taxes. The federal government and its agencies and property are immune from state and local taxation under the supremacy clause of the Constitution. The government must have the right to deal with its own property free from any interference that state or other forms of local taxation might cause. Accordingly, state and local statutes cannot directly tax the property or functions of the U.S. government and its agencies or instrumentalities unless immunity from such taxation has been expressly waived by an act of Congress. All goods and services purchased by a contractor or subcontractor for use on a government contract are therefore tax exempt. See Appendix B for further details.

4. The Government Is Not Bound by the Doctrine of Apparent Authority and Estoppel. The doctrine of apparent authority and estoppel does not apply to government contracts. As stated before, the government is not bound by the unauthorized acts of its agents, even when the contractor is misled in the process by the appearance of authority in the agent. This principle is based on the doctrine that a party entering into arrangements with representatives of the United States has an absolute responsibility to ascertain whether the representative acts within the bounds of his or her authority. Since apparent authority and estoppel are both based on the concept of reliance, a party doing business with an agent of the government does so at his or her own risk. *Remember*: If the agent does not have actual authority to act, the agent will not be found to have apparent authority.

There are certain clauses that must be contained in government contracts that are not required in private contracts. These clauses are discussed in Chapter 3.

TWO MAIN LEGISLATIVE ACTS THAT REGULATE FEDERAL CONTRACTING

There are two legislative acts that form the basis of federal contracting regulations: the *Federal Property and Administrative Services Act of 1949* and the *Armed Services Procurement Act of 1947*. The first covers contracting by all other departments and agencies of the government except the military; the second covers contracting by the military.

Federal Property and Administrative Services Act

The Federal Property and Administrative Services Act applies to contracting by the General Services Administration (GSA) and by any other executive agency of the government except military ones. The Federal Acquisition Regulation (FAR) is based on this act. The FAR establishes uniform contracting policies and procedures for all federal agencies. The net result is that the government presents a uniform face to business and industry. The FAR also provides simplicity and comprehensibility, establishes zero-based (new) procedures, curtails the proliferation of regulations, standardizes contract clauses, makes use of the Uniform Commercial Code (UCC) where possible, and reduces paperwork. Best of all, the FAR makes it much easier to do business with the federal government!

The FAR is an integral part of the procurement system prescribed by the administrator of the GSA under the authority of the act and other laws. Within the system are other sets of regulations for individual agencies. These supplement the basic FAR. The provisions of the FAR are developed in cooperation with the contracting agencies, such as the Departments of Energy or of the Treasury.

The FAR is divided into subchapters, parts, subparts, sections, and subsections. All of these are defined by a well-thought-out numerical identification system that organizes this rather massive document into a very manageable and organized format. The FAR comprises approximately 2,000 pages. While the basic FAR provisions are used by all agencies of the government, certain agencies, such as NASA and the DOD, have modified many of the procedures extensively in order to meet their requirements. The *DOD FAR Supplement*, for example, contains approximately 3,000 pages! Other agencies have developed somewhat less extensive modifications of the FAR suitable for their needs. These variations could have a significant impact on how you should do business with any given agency; doing your homework first will prevent starting out on the wrong foot.

Also, the FAR is constantly being updated to reflect new legislation, regulations, and policies. However, this doesn't mean that you must rush out and acquire a set of these regulations right now. They are costly, and you won't need to refer to them often. If the need does arise to research something in detail, you can obtain what you need from a good library system or from the nearest government purchasing office.

Agency-wide acquisition regulations, as required by law, are published in the *Federal Register*, and are codified under *Title 48, Code of Federal Regulations*.

Armed Services Procurement Act

The Armed Services Procurement Act applies to the Army, Navy, Air Force, Coast Guard, and the National Aeronautics and Space Administration (NASA). It covers all contracts for property except land, and it applies to all services for which payment is made from appropriated funds. This act is the basis of the *Department of Defense* (*DOD*) *FAR Supplement*, which establishes uniform contracting regulations within the DOD.

HOW TO CORRECT MISTAKES ON BIDS

By now you are aware that all government operations are conducted in accordance with law and regulation, and with mistakes you may make on a bid, there are definite procedures to be followed to correct them. Let's take a detailed look at them.

After determining which bids are responsive, the contracting officer examines them for mistakes. Let us say, for example, that the invitation called for a bid acceptance period of 60 days and the low bidder only offered a 30-day acceptance period. Here the issue of mistakes would never occur, for the bid was nonresponsive on its face.

The general rule: In the submittal of a bid on which the bidder has made a mistake that was strictly his or her own fault, and the bid has been accepted, the bidder must bear the consequences. Chapter 1 contains a bid checklist that can help you avoid costly errors. *Warning*: Government contracting is not a game in which you can talk your way out of a bad situation. The government will be deaf to all pleas of mercy resulting from either a misunderstanding or omission in preparing your bid. However, if the contracting officer knew, or should have known of the mistake at the time the bid was accepted, a valid, binding contract cannot result.

Where there is either an obvious mistake, or where there is reason to believe that a mistake may have been made, the contracting officer must ask the prospective contractor for verification of the bid, and state the reason for the verification request, which in this case is a suspected mistake. *Key point*: If the bidder certifies his bid, or if the bidder *fails or refuses to furnish evidence in support of an alleged mistake,* then the contracting officer will consider the bid as submitted.

Any clerical mistakes apparent on the face of the bid may be corrected by the contracting officer, prior to award, provided that the contracting officer has first obtained from the bidder either written or telegraphic verification of the bid as actually intended. Examples of clerical mistakes are errors in discounts, or misplacing a decimal point.

The GAO has set forth the following guidelines to handle other than apparent mistakes on bids. These are in supplement of the regulations, which carry specific actions to be taken in various cases.

1. Where the bidder requests permission to withdraw his or her bid, and clear and convincing evidence establishes the existence of a mistake, the contracting officer may permit a bidder to withdraw the bid.
2. If the evidence is clear and convincing, both as to the existence of a mistake and the bid actually intended, and this bid is the lowest received, the contracting officer may correct the bid and not permit its withdrawal.
3. Where the bidder asks permission to correct a mistake in the bid, and clear evidence establishes both the existence of a mistake and what the intended bid should have been, the bidder may be permitted to correct the mistake provided the correction will not displace one or more lower bids. In this case, the existence of the mistake and the bid actually intended must be ascertained from the invitation and the bid. If the evidence is only clear as to the mistake, but not to the intended bid, the bidder may be permitted to *withdraw* his or her bid.
4. Where the evidence is not clear and convincing that the bid as submitted was not the bid intended, the contracting officer may require the bid to be considered for award in the form submitted.
5. Where a mistake in bid price is alleged after the award, it cannot be corrected unless it can be shown that the mistake was mutual or that the contracting officer had notice of the mistake. In such a situation, however, there is no authority for payment of any amount in excess of the next low bid.

Important: Retain in your files all material and data used in preparing a submittal. When a mistake occurs, and you want to take corrective action, the government isn't going to just say "OK" without substantiated proof from you that a mistake did indeed occur. The government will request copies of work sheets and other data in order to satisfy this requirement. Obviously, there is a need to make certain that the reason for seeking corrective action is truly based on error, and not for any other reason. A mistake, in order to be correctable, must be one of fact rather than of law. Ignorance of the law is never a defense. Where the mistake is mutual, a valid contract does not result and the bidder will be allowed to withdraw or correct the bid, or the existing agreement will be reformed to reflect the true intent of the parties. Virtually all of the mistakes made in government contracting are made by the bidder, and they are typically discovered after bid opening when the bid may no longer be changed or withdrawn at will. While the mistake rules apply equally to negotiated and advertised procurement, the primary concern is with advertised procurement. A negotiated procurement permits changing of offers to correct errors.

Mistakes Discovered on a Bid Prior to Award

When a mistake is discovered by a bidder prior to award, the bid may be withdrawn *if the bidder presents evidence sufficient to reasonably support the error*. However, for correction of a bid, a higher burden of proof is placed on the bidder, and the mistake cannot relate to the responsiveness of the bid. A bid will be corrected only if clear and convincing evidence is presented that a mistake has been made, the nature of the mistake, how the mistake was made, and finally, what the bid would have been except for the mistake. Further, if bid correction will displace a lower bidder, this evidence must be found in the invitation and bid documents, and not by extrinsic evidence supplied by the bidder.

The Comptroller General will not question an agency's denial of correction of an alleged bid mistake unless the agency's action is without a reasonable basis.

Mistakes Discovered After Contract Award

Generally the contract, as awarded, represents the final understanding of the parties as well as all rights and liabilities thereunder. Even when a mistake exists in the favor of the contractor, the government may not waive the right of strict performance of contract terms in the absence of adequate consideration. The term *adequate consideration* most often means a downward adjustment of the contract price. However, where the mistake is so apparent that it is presumed the contracting officer had knowledge of it, or where it can be shown that the contracting officer did have knowledge of the mistake, the government is not allowed to take advantage of the contractor by holding him or her to a contract the contractor had no intent of making in the first place.

The mistake must be a patent or open one, since the contracting officer does not have the duty to be certain that a low bid was computed correctly with regard to economic conditions, past procurement, or other matters purely incidental to the written bid. Additionally, the contractor must waive the right to relief by verifying the bid prior to award, by executing the contract with knowledge of the mistake, or by fully performing the contract before seeking relief.

INDEX - CHAPTER 12

13

KEY TYPES OF CONTRACTS USED BY THE GOVERNMENT FOR PURCHASING GOODS AND SERVICES

This chapter explores the types of contracts used by the government to buy the goods and services it requires. The government employs two main types of contracts: fixed-price and cost-reimbursement. However, several variations of these have developed over the years.

When purchasing through use of advertising, some form of firm fixed-price contract is used because the specifications are (or should be) definitive, and competition is present. The government may also award a fixed-price contract with economic price adjustment or escalation clauses in certain circumstances.

When procurement is conducted through negotiation, the contract type, while selected by the government, may be changed to facilitate contract price negotiation. Obviously, the firm-fixed-price or lump-sum type of contract places the greatest risk, in terms of performance, on the contractor. The cost-plus-a-fixed-fee type of contract, at the other extreme, places either the cost or maximum performance risk on the government, with the contractor receiving a guaranteed fee. A cost-plus-a-percentage-of-cost type of contract is prohibited under the two principal procurement statutes, 10 U.S.C. 2306 and 41 U.S.C. 254(b). These statutes prohibit a system of contracting whereby a contractor may increase his or her fee by increasing the government's cost.

FIXED-PRICE CONTRACTS

Firm-fixed-price contracts are characterized by a lump-sum price not subject to adjustment. Adjustment in this case does not include contract change orders or modifications. The risk of performance falls on the contractor, and is used where competition is present and specifications are available. These contracts are used when there is adequate price competition, and the available cost and pricing data permit realistic estimates by the government of probable costs of performance.

Fixed-price-contracts with economic price adjustments are characterized by a lump-sum price subject to upward or downward adjustment, dependent on contingencies contained in the contract. These contingencies will involve matters beyond the parties control, such as labor rates or market price indices.

Fixed-price with price redetermination contracts are essentially lump-sum with provision for adjustments within specified limits that are negotiated as the actual costs become known. As in fixed-price escalation contracts, the government assumes the risk of contingencies that may occur. The price redetermination may be made either at specified times during performance or after completion of performance.

Fixed-ceiling-price contracts with retroactive price redetermination provide a fixed-ceiling price and retroactive price redetermination within the ceiling after contract completion. They are found to be most appropriate for use in research and development acquisitions when total cost is estimated to be $100,000 or less, and when a firm fixed price cannot be negotiated for any reason.

Firm-fixed-price level of effort term contracts describe the required work in general terms, which is usually either an investigation or research task, and the contractor is required to expend a specified level of effort for a stated period of time for a fixed dollar amount. These contracts are suitable for investigations and studies in a specific research and development area. The contract usually requires a report showing the results achieved.

COST-REIMBURSEMENT CONTRACTS

Cost-reimbursement contracts provide for payment of allowable incurred costs, to the extent prescribed in the contract. These contracts establish an estimate of total costs for the purpose of obligating funds, and establish a ceiling a contractor may not exceed without the approval of the contracting officer. If the ceiling is exceeded, it is at the contractor's risk. These contracts are suitable only when uncertainties involved in contract performance do not permit costs to be estimated with sufficient accuracy, thereby permitting the use of any type of fixed-price contract.

Cost contracts are cost-reimbursement contracts in which the contractor does not receive a fee. They are appropriate for use in research and development work with nonprofit institutions and in facilities acquisitions.

Cost-sharing contracts are used when the benefits of a research and development effort will accrue to both parties. The contractor does not receive a fee and is reimbursed only for a portion of the costs. This is an excellent contract to receive if there is expectation of substantial compensating advantages.

Cost-plus-award-fee contracts involve a target cost, a fixed base fee, and evaluation criteria to assess the contractor's performance in areas such as quality, timeliness, ingenuity, and cost effectiveness. If the contractor's performance meets the stipulated criteria, an adjustment is added to the base fee up to a specified maximum limit. The government's subjective evaluation of the contractor's performance is not appealable under the contract disputes clause.

Cost-plus-fixed-fee contracts reimburse the contractor for all costs allowable under established cost principles, and provide for a set fee. The fees allowable are set by statute.

INCENTIVE CONTRACTS

Incentive contracts are used when a firm-fixed-price contract is not appropriate. They are used when either the required supplies or services can be acquired at lower cost, and when either improved delivery or technical performance can be achieved by relating the contractor's profit to the contractor's performance.

Most incentive contracts include only cost incentives, which take the form of either a profit or fee adjustment formula. They are intended to motivate the contractor to manage costs effectively. No incentive contract may provide for other incentives without also providing either a cost incentive or a cost restraint.

Technical performance incentives may be considered in connection with specific product characteristics, such as the performance of an end item. Incentive contracts are therefore particularly well-suited for major systems procurements.

Delivery performance incentives will be considered when improvement of a standard delivery date becomes a government objective.

Fixed-price incentive contracts provide for adjusting profit and establishing the final contract price by applying a formula based on the relationship of final negotiated total cost to total target cost. The contractor's profit either increases or decreases, in accordance with this formula, as the actual costs vary upward or downward from the target cost. The fixed-price incentive contract is distinguished from the cost-incentive contract by the inclusion of a ceiling price. Costs in excess of this ceiling are borne entirely by the contractor.

Cost-plus-incentive-fee contracts are similar to the fixed-price-incentive contract, except there is no ceiling price. There is a target cost, target fee, minimum and maximum fee, and a fee adjustment formula. These provide, within limits, for fee increases above target fee when total allowable costs are less than target costs. Conversely, the fee may also be decreased. This type of contract provides an incentive for good and efficient management on the contractor's part.

Cost-plus-award-fee contracts are a cost reimbursement type of contract providing for a fee consisting of a base amount fixed at the inception of the contract, and an award amount the contractor may earn, either in whole or in part, during performance. These provisions are intended to promote excellence in the areas of quality, timeliness, technical ingenuity, and cost-effective management. These contracts are used when it is neither feasible nor effective to devise predetermined incentive targets applicable to cost, technical performance, or schedule; and the likelihood of meeting acquisition objectives will be enhanced by using a contract that effectively motivates the contractor toward exceptional performance.

Fixed-price incentive (firm target) contracts specify a target cost, a target profit, a price ceiling (but neither a profit ceiling nor floor), and a profit adjustment formula. These elements are all negotiated at the outset. The price ceiling is the maximum that may be paid to the contractor, except for any adjustment allowable under the contract clauses. When the contractor completes performance, the parties negotiate the final cost, and the final price is established by applying this formula. The reward is based on how well the contractor has performed. This type of contract is appropriate when the parties can negotiate, at the outset, a firm target cost, target profit, and profit adjustment formula that will provide a fair and reasonable incentive and ceiling, and provide for the contractor's assumption of an appropriate share of the risk.

Fixed-price incentive (successive targets) contracts specify an initial target cost, an initial target profit, and an initial adjustment formula to be used for establishing the firm target profit, including a ceiling and a floor for the firm target profit. This formula normally provides for a lesser degree of contractor cost responsibility than would a formula for establishing final profit and price. Additionally, there is a production point at which the target costs and profits will be negotiated, as well as a ceiling price that is the maximum that may be paid to a contractor, except for allowable adjustments.

INDEFINITE-DELIVERY CONTRACTS

There are three types of indefinite-delivery contracts: definite quantity contracts, requirements contracts, and indefinite quantity contracts. They are used when either the exact times or quantities of future deliveries are not known at time of contract award. These types of contracts may provide for firm-fixed prices with economic price adjustment, fixed prices with redetermination, and prices based on catalog or market prices.

Definite quantity contracts provide for delivery of a definite quantity of supplies or services for a fixed period, with deliveries to be scheduled at designated locations upon order.

Requirements contracts provide for filling of all actual purchase requirements for specific supplies and services during a specified contract period. The deliveries are scheduled upon placement of the order.

Indefinite quantity contracts provide for an indefinite quantity, within stated limits, of specific supplies and services during a contract period. Again, deliveries are scheduled by placing orders with the contractor.

TIME-AND-MATERIALS, LABOR-HOUR, AND LETTER CONTRACTS

Time-and-materials contracts provide for acquisition of supplies and services on the basis of direct labor hours at specified, fixed, hourly rates. These rates include wages, overhead, general and administrative expense, materials cost, materials handling costs, and profit. This type of contract may be used only when it is not possible to estimate accurately the extent and duration of the work at the time of placing the contract. Use of this contract falls into the "last resort" category. Its use requires a prior determination and finding exercise by the contracting officer.

Labor-hour contracts are a variation of the time-and-materials contract, differing only in that the materials are not supplied by the contractor.

Letter contracts are written preliminary contractual instruments authorizing the contractor to immediately begin manufacturing supplies or performing services. These are used when the government's interest demands that the contractor be given a binding agreement so that the work can begin immediately, and when negotiating a definitive contract is not possible in time to meet the requirement. When a letter contract award is based on price competition, it will also include a price ceiling.

AGREEMENTS: TWO MAIN TYPES AND HOW THEY DIFFER FROM CONTRACTS

There are two types of agreements: the basic agreement and the basic ordering agreement.

Basic agreements are written instruments of understanding, negotiated between the procuring agency and the contractor. They contain contract clauses applying to future contracts between the parties during their term, and contemplations of separate future contracts that will incorporate, either by reference or attachment, the required and applicable clauses agreed upon in the basic agreement. These may best be used when a substantial number of separate contracts may be awarded to a contractor during a particular period, and where previous negotiation problems have been experienced. These agreements neither obligate funds, nor do they imply any agreement by the government to place future contracts and orders.

Basic ordering agreements are written instruments of understanding that are negotiated between a procuring activity and a contractor. They include terms and clauses that will apply to future contracts between the parties, a specific description of the supplies and services to be provided, and the method for pricing, issuing, and delivering future orders under the basic ordering agreement. The contracting officer can neither make any final commitment nor authorize the contractor to begin work on an order under a basic ordering agreement until prices have been established. This could take the form of a specified ceiling price. Additionally, the need for the supplies and services must be compelling and unusually urgent.

SMALL PURCHASES

Small purchases are those that do not exceed $25,000. They are made using simpler contract forms, and often include fast payment procedures. Methods of payment will be discussed in detail in Chapter 17. Purchases of $1,000 or less may be made without securing competitive quotations provided the contracting officer considers the price to be reasonable. For purchases between $1,000 and $25,000, the general rule is that competitive quotations are solicited orally from potential suppliers in the local trade area. Written solicitations are used when suppliers are outside the local trade area, when unusual specifications or a large number of different items are required, or when oral quotes are impractical. Reasonableness of the price is generally determined by the competitive process.

For repetitive purchases of small quantities of supplies, a blanket purchase agreement (BPA) is used, and usually they are placed with two or more suppliers of the same item. The order is generally placed orally, and payments are made monthly on a summary invoice issued by the contractor.

INDEX - CHAPTER 13

14

CONTRACT PERFORMANCE: HOW YOU AND THE GOVERNMENT MUST COMPLY

Performance of government contracts, as in all contracts, should be carried out in strict accordance with the terms of the contract as written. Prior negotiations, understandings, or other forms of parol evidence are not permitted to alter the terms of performance as set out in the contract. As a result, you assume the full responsibility of performing your obligations under the contract along with the duty to compensate the government for the failure to perform. This strict rule of performance has been modified considerably in government contracts by including several contract clauses allocating certain performance risks between the contractor and the government, and allowing the government to unilaterally change, delay, or terminate contract performance.

FIVE BASIC RULES OF CONTRACT INTERPRETATION

Government contracts are subject to the same common law rules of interpretation applied to other contracts. These rules include:

1. The intention of the parties must be gathered from the whole contract.
2. Contract provisions should not be interpreted so as to render either one or more provision meaningless, unless it is otherwise impossible to do so.

3. The interpretation that gives reasonable meaning to the whole document is preferred.
4. The dominant purpose of the interpretation adopted by the parties will be used to ascertain the meaning of the contract provisions.
5. When there is a conflict, specific provisions prevail over general provisions.

How to Resolve Inconsistencies: A Five-Point "Order of Precedence" Clause

Government contracts usually provide for resolution of a conflict between the various provisions by the inclusion of a clause entitled order of precedence. This clause provides that inconsistencies within the contract provisions shall be resolved by giving precedence in the following order:

1. the schedule that contains information on price and delivery
2. solicitation instructions and conditions
3. general provisions containing the standard contract terms
5. other contract provisions, such as the specifications describing the material to be procured

How the Government Interprets Contract Ambiguity

One of the most important common law rules of interpretation, as far as government contracts are concerned, is that involving an ambiguous provision that is open to more than one interpretation. In this situation, the ambiguity will be interpreted against the party creating it. In government contracts, this is inevitably the government, for it prepares the contract provisions. The interpretation adopted by the contractor in such cases need not be the only one, just a reasonable one. However, the ambiguity may be resolved against the contractor when he or she knew of the ambiguity and failed to seek clarification from the contracting officer prior to bidding.

Contract Specifications and Performance

Contract specifications dictate the very nature and degree of performance required of the contractor, and when those specifications are accurate, complete, and realistic, the issue becomes one of either performance or failure to perform. As discussed in Chapter 13, there are essentially two types of contracts: the fixed-price type and the cost-type. In the latter type contract, the government undertakes the responsibility for reimbursing the contractor for the cost of meeting the specifications, while in the fixed-price type of contract, the contractor assumes the risk and cost of meeting the specifications. Since the government to some degree drafts the specifications for all of its contracts, the courts and boards of contract appeal have attached a certain legal responsibility for doing so. As the complexity of the design or performance specifications increases, the legal difference between the two decreases. However, when a general performance specification is used, less responsibility for that specification rests with the government.

In those cases where the government has drafted a detailed set of specifications to be followed by you, the contractor, in fulfilling your contractual obligation, the courts have held that the government impliedly warrants that, if those specifications are followed, the expected results will be obtained. This warranty of specification may be limited by the government when it notifies prospective contractors that the specifications may be defective. Additionally, you may have assumed the risk if it can be shown that you had knowledge that impossibility of performance existed. Impossibility of performance as an excuse for contract nonperformance does not require either actual or literal impossibility, only commercial impracticality. This occurs when something can be done, but only at excessive and unreasonable cost.

Defective specifications may entitle you to additional compensation if the cost of performance is increased. Similarly, a mutual mistake of fact may result in an adjustment to the contract price. In this situation, there must be a mistaken concept by both parties as to a material fact which results in more costly performance. To recover the extra cost of performance, you must show that the contract did not allocate to it the risk of this type of a mistake, and that the government received a benefit from the extra work for which it would have been willing to contract, if the facts had been known. All of these matters relate to problems inherent in all contracts. Problems peculiar to government contracts arise when the government, by means of authority granted in a contract clause, unilaterally alters the time, method, or cost of performing the contract as awarded.

THE CHANGES CLAUSE: A UNILATERAL POWER UNIQUE TO GOVERNMENT CONTRACTING

The contract clause entitled *changes*, together with the *default*, *termination for convenience*, and *disputes* clauses, distinguishes government contracts from other contracts by the control over performance vested in one of the contracting parties. Unlike other contracts, the changes clause allows the government to alter the work to be performed without the contractor's consent. This is done by written order. Changes of this type may also result in either an appropriate upward or downward equitable adjustment in the contract price, delivery schedule, or time of performance. Additionally, the changes clause provides that if a dispute over the equitable adjustment is a question of fact under the clause, then nothing in the clause will excuse the contractor from proceeding with the contract as changed. This unilateral power, which is unique to government contracting, allows the contracting officer to alter performance without unnecessary interruption, and to subsequently determine the appropriate contract price adjustment.

Requirements for Issuing a Valid Change Order

The standard changes clause imposes certain requirements for issuing a valid change order. The first requirement is that the change order must be issued by the contracting officer. This literal requirement has been relaxed in certain circumstances, permitting changes directed by engineers and inspectors to be incorporated into the work scope, either through the theory of ratification by the contracting officer, or through an actual or implied delegation of authority. The clause also states that the change must be made by written order: however, this requirement generally has been ignored by the courts. This is especially true since the development of the theory of constructive change orders. Constructive change orders occur when the contracting officer, either through his or her actions or directions, has changed the contract work scope but has failed to issue a change order. Further discussion of contract changes is found in Chapter 16.

TITLE AND RISK OF LOSS CLAUSE: HOW THE CONTRACTOR CAN BE HELD RESPONSIBLE

Fixed-price supply contracts have a clause called title and risk of loss. It is used to keep down the risk of loss that may occur while goods are in transit from the contractor's facility to the delivery point. Under common law, the risk of loss is incurred either by the owner or person who has taken title to the goods at the time of loss. However, under government contracting, this is not the case. Ownership is transferred most often at the contractor's facility as soon as the government inspector signs off on the acceptance document. It does not include the risk of loss, which is transferred to the government when the goods are delivered. The title and risk of loss clause states that, unless provided otherwise in the contract, the contractor is responsible for the supplies until they are delivered to the designated destination, regardless of the fact that they were inspected and accepted. This means that:

1. Goods shipped F.O.B. origin places responsibility on the government.
2. Goods shipped F.O.B. destination places responsibility on the contractor.
3. If supplies fail to meet contract requirements, risk of loss remains with the contractor until a cure is effected or the government otherwise accepts.
4. The contractor will not be held liable for either loss or damage caused by, or due to, the negligence of the government, its agents, or employees.

The title and risk of loss clause has been interpreted by the Armed Services Board of Contract Appeals as follows:

> We find it highly significant that the title and risk of loss clause separates these concepts; that is title, and risk of loss, into two paragraphs. This makes it clear to us that the latter does not rely on the former. In other words, risk of loss does not follow and does not depend on, or is even related to title. While title may have passed to the government at the time of acceptance, if the items accepted failed to conform to the contract requirements so as to give the government a right of rejection, the risk of loss or damage to these items remains with the contractor.
>
> Until the advent of the Uniform Commercial Code (UCC), which this court and boards have relied upon as reflecting sound, up-to-date rules of commercial law, title to property was the governing factor in many situations, including upon whom the risk of loss fell. Under the UCC, title is not the governing factor in the majority of situations. The UCC contains specific provisions delineating the rights and duties between sellers and buyers, and in many of these situations such ownership considerations do not play a part. Risk of loss is one such area.
>
> It is clear to us that the contract clause has adopted the UCC concept that risk of loss is related more to performance, or lack of it, than to title in the historic sense. In both the UCC and the armed services procurement regulation clause incorporated in these contracts, the contractor immediately shifts the risk of loss from himself to the government by delivering conforming supplies to the carrier, if delivery is F.O.B. origin, and shifts it at a later time when the delivery is F.O.B. destination. But when the contractor delivers nonconforming goods so that the government has the right of rejection, the risk of loss does not shift until the deficiencies which caused them to be nonconforming are cured, corrected or until the government accepts the goods.

THE INSPECTION CLAUSE: CONTRACTOR OBLIGATIONS FOR ENSURING A TIMELY DELIVERY AND QUALITY PERFORMANCE

The responsibility for inspection and correction of defects rests with you, the contractor. Failure to meet specifications or make delivery on time may be cause for default of the contract. Although you are fundamentally responsible, the government also plays a role in ensuring a quality product. This is accomplished through inspections and inspection requirements that are included in every contract. Essentially, the type of inspection conducted varies with the contract cost and with the type of product. For commercial items purchased "off the shelf," usually only simple verification that the correct item and quantity was shipped may be required. On the other hand, a contract for either sophisticated equipment or research will require a complete inspection system, starting with the raw materials and purchased components, continuing through the various stages of production, and ending with the acceptance testing of the completed item.

The basic policy on quality states that you are ultimately responsible for product quality; that is, you may offer for acceptance only those items that meet contract requirements. The inspection clause sets specific contractor inspection responsibilities, and vests in the government certain rights. Let's take a look at these concepts now, with a view of understanding your responsibilities and avoiding the necessity for costly defect correction. Defects may occur if all of the proper steps aren't taken to ensure a quality product.

Inspection is the examination and testing of either supplies or services in order to see whether or not they meet contract requirements.

Acceptance denotes the government's assertion of ownership over products or articles, and the approval of services rendered.

Delivery consists of the physical transfer of items from the contractor to the government. It has nothing to do with the transfer of ownership from the contractor to the government.

Four Ways a Contractor Must Control Product Quality

There are four basic requirements that oblige you, the contractor, to inspect and control the quality of your product. These requirements are also the basis for government inspection of supplies and services.

1. The Standard Inspection Requirement

The "standard inspection requirement" mandates that you must maintain an inspection system acceptable to the government over the life of the contract. The exact details of what to include in this inspection system are not spelled out, but it must include both the procedures employed and the maintenance and storage of records. Records retention is required during the life of the contract and for a reasonable period thereafter. Probably the best term of storage would be for the length of the statute of limitations. Often this inspection requirement is referred to as the "boilerplate" inspection clause, and it is the foundation on which all other inspection specifications are based. This clause is all-encompassing, making you liable for all hidden (and latent) defects, as well as for fraud perpetration and gross mistakes. In addition to the standard inspection requirement, the contract may stipulate that you must have an inspection system operating in accordance with government specification. An acceptable inspection system will be denied by the government through reference to the applicable standards and specifications, and by specific recommendations made by the QAR personnel. If you are currently producing a commercial product requiring a quality control procedure, chances are very good that what you are now doing inspection-wise will either meet or exceed government expectations. In most cases, the only additional requirement imposed is the definite marking and segregation of defective items. The primary concern is that if this is not done definitively, the defective items may inadvertently find their way back into the production process.

Latent Defects. A latent defect is one that existed at the time of government acceptance, but could not be discovered by reasonable inspection. If, in the government's opinion, the inspection is judged to have been reasonable under the circumstances, and the defect was not discovered, the defect was latent. However, if a reasonable examination of an article would have revealed a defect, but the examination was not made, the defect will not be ruled a latent one.

A reasonable inspection is one that would normally be performed as a custom of the trade or industry. In the examination of shoes, for example, just looking them over would be sufficient. X-ray testing would not be expected. However, in the examination of welding on structural steel, a radiograph would be required, because it is a custom of the industry.

The burden of proof is on the government to show that defective material and workmanship is the most probable cause of the failure of a product. Under the standard inspection clauses, you are responsible for latent defects discovered at any time after final acceptance; however, the extent of your liability is prorated over the useful life of the item.

Latent defects apply not only to supplies and services, but also to design. A good example of this is a contract for the design and manufacturing of a certain item, where the design is defective in an undiscoverable manner. Manufacturing is then performed under the defective design criteria, and the resulting defective articles must be repaired or replaced by you at no cost to the government. This concept applies only to fixed-price contracts. Under a cost-reimbursement contract, the repairs would be performed at the expense of the government.

Patent Defects. A patent defect is one that is apparent on its face. In other words, it is obvious by ordinary inspection, such as a heel missing on a shoe. Regardless of the type of contract, patent defects are corrected solely at your expense. The government's position on these types of defects is that your inspection system should have been up to the task of discovering them prior to submittal of the goods for inspection.

Correction of Defects. If you fail to promptly remove defective items of supply or lots of supplies, or fail to promptly replace or correct these supplies (or lack of supplies), the government may replace them at your expense. If necessary, the government may also either terminate the contract for default, or require delivery at an equitably reduced price. If you fail to agree to the reduced price, it will be construed as a dispute. Disputes are covered in detail in Chapter 17.

Note: The actions just mentioned will be used only in the most severe cases as a last resort, where there is no hope for getting the contractor back on the right path. To the serious businessman and businesswoman, such actions should cause absolutely no concern.

Fraud and Gross Mistakes. Fraud and gross mistakes have virtually no statute of limitations. You are responsible, for the useful life of the product, for any defects found resulting from fraud and gross mistakes. The government cannot seek relief under a situation of fraud unless it can prove an intent to deceive by the contractor and a misrepresentation of material fact, which the government relied upon at time of acceptance of the product. This would apply to events occurring at any stage of the design and manufacturing process. Since it is very difficult to prove intent, proof of fraud is not often achieved.

In order to establish a gross mistake that amounts to fraud, it is necessary to prove that the error was so gross that it should be considered as fraud. However, it is not necessary to prove intent to deceive.

2. The Product Inspection Requirement

The second type of quality control is the "product inspection requirement." This is the simplest type, and the basic responsibility for conformance rests with you, the contractor. In this situation, you follow the federal product specification called out in the contract, and you document all tests required. Only those supplies and services meeting the requirement can be offered to the government for acceptance. Evidence of conformance must be supplied concurrently with the articles. The government's role under this process is that of determining how much it should inspect in order to ensure the effectiveness of your procedures. This determination is usually made after various considerations, such as:

1. your integrity and reliability, especially in previous government contracts
2. the adequacy of your inspection system, which would include coverage of incoming material, lab testing, in-process inspection, packaging, packing, crating, and marking
3. the nature and value of the item involved
4. inspections performed by government inspectors

3. Inspection Carried Out by the Government

The third type of inspection consists of inspection carried out by the government. There are several methods that can be employed under this procedure; the most commonly used ones are as follows:

1. Visual checks are done by eye, wherein the inspector simply uses his or her own judgment, looking for surface defects, missing pieces, and parts out of alignment. Dimensional checks are performed with appropriate measuring equipment and gauges.
2. The conduction of, or witness of, a physical or performance test, such as the proper operation of the item involved. Chemical tests necessary for determining composition and physical tests designed to determine hardness are in this category.

4. Production Points of Inspection

The fourth method used by the government to assure quality is through "production points of inspection." Under this procedure, inspection is performed at several strategic points along the production line. For example, the quality and type of raw materials used may affect the quality of the end product, therefore the company's incoming inspection program will be monitored. In some cases, the raw materials will be inspected at the plant of the supplier. At other points in the manufacturing process, inspections of the various physical properties of the item in production will be conducted. This could include checks of malleability, machinability, brittleness, hardness, and other factors that could change as a product moves down the line. This would additionally include the inspection of subassemblies if they are subject to change or damage during manufacture.

Although this in-process inspection is performed by the government, the responsibility still rests with you, the contractor, for inspection of the completed items. This is accomplished by performing all inspections and tests called out in the specifications.

The Government's Rights Under Inspection Clauses

Inspection clauses allow the government to inspect all supplies, including raw materials, components, intermediate assemblies, and end products. These clauses also allow the testing of the product, to the extent that is practical, at all times and places. This could involve any point in the production process, and most certainly prior to final acceptance by the government. The government is also allowed to inspect all materials and workmanship at any time and place where work on the contract is being performed. Although inspection clauses place test requirements and responsibilities on the contractor, the government reserves the right to perform any tests and inspections necessary to assure itself that the contractor is performing in the required manner, and that the contract will be fulfilled as expected.

First Article Testing. The government may also want to conduct first article testing, formally named first article approval rights. The term ''first article'' carries a broad definition, and may include preproduction models, initial production samples, first lots, pilot models, and pilot lots. The purpose of the evaluation is to ascertain the suitability of the product either before, or in, the initial stages of production.

The first article approval clause is used primarily by the government when it is necessary to verify confidence about a product that has not been previously furnished to it by you. Once you have established a good track record, the request for this type of testing will diminish. This testing will also be used if the item is to serve as the manufacturing standard.

The testing procedure used is to confirm that the item being supplied conforms with contract requirements, and it may be required when you have either not previously furnished the item to the government, or:

1. There have been subsequent changes in processes and specifications.
2. Production has been discontinued for an extended period of time.
3. The product acquired under a previous contract developed a problem during its life.

Normally, first article testing and approval is not required in contracts for research and development, when an applicable Qualified Products List exists, for products normally sold in the commercial market, and for products covered by complete and detailed technical specifications, unless the requirements are so exacting that it is doubtful that the products would meet requirements without testing and approval.

To reduce the risk to the contractor in conforming with the testing and approval requirement, the contracting officer should provide sufficient lead time for the contractor to acquire the materials and components, and for production after receipt of first article approval. However, delivery schedules may interfere with this provision. If this is the case, the contracting officer may authorize the contractor, prior to first article approval, either to acquire specific materials and components, or to begin production to the extent necessary to meet the schedule.

Additional Provisions. The inspection clause further provides that if either any inspection or test is made by the government on the contractor's or subcontractor's premises, the contractor will, without any additional charge, provide all reasonable facilities and assistance for the safety and convenience of the government inspectors in the performance of their duties. If inspections are performed at places other than the contractor's or subcontractor's facility, the inspections will be at government expense.

All inspections and tests must be made by the government so as not to unduly delay the work. For practical purposes, the level of staffing at any one time in the government Quality Assurance office assigned to your contract is the governing factor on how promptly inspections will be performed. From a contractual point of view, however, if the contract specifies a test schedule requiring performance of testing within a given number of days after submission of the item to be tested, and the government unreasonably delays the test, you may request a delivery time extension or recovery of costs incurred by the delay, or both. If the contract does not specify a test schedule, the government is expected to complete its tests within a reasonable length of time.

This street runs two ways. Just as you may seek relief for government-caused inspection delays, the government may charge you for any costs resulting from either contractor-caused delays or for government reinspection of rejected items. It then becomes mandatory, from a sound business point of view, that you submit for test and inspection only items conforming with the contractual requirement. In essence, the government is saying that if you have a problem, don't hope the government will do a second-class inspection and allow shoddy goods to pass. Get your act together first. This makes good sense, and it conforms with good commercial practice, and should not pose any problem for you whatsoever.

How Inspection Clauses Differ from Contract to Contract

With one noted exception, the discussion to date has addressed inspection clauses as they apply to firm-fixed-price contracts only. The following will point out the primary differences in inspection clauses as they apply in other types of contracts.

Fixed-Price Construction Contracts

Under this type of contract, the government testing and inspection of materials and workmanship are made at the construction site. The clause also provides that the materials going into final construction may be inspected at the place of production or shipment.

Inspection and tests should be made by the government so as not to unreasonably delay the work. This is similar to the supply contract clause, except it is designed to address the suspension of work clause. Under this clause you may be compensated for unreasonable inspection and testing delays caused by the government.

Before acceptance, the government may require the removal or tear-out of completed work. If the work is defective, you pay for the inspection costs and rework. If the work is acceptable, you are compensated for the inspection time and for the reconstruction of the work. Again, this inspection procedure will be used only for good cause. If you have a good track record, it will probably never be used. It may be used, however, regardless of your reputation, to inspect critical aspects of the construction project if no record of previous in-work inspection exists.

Finally, acceptance is the same as in a supply contract, except that if any other warranty is applicable, government acceptance is not final and conclusive.

Cost-Reimbursement Supply and Research and Development Contracts

Inspection clauses for these types of contracts have the same basic provisions as the fixed-price supply clause, with the exception that in the cost-reimbursable contract:

1. The government may inspect the premises of the contractor and subcontractor.
2. Unless otherwise provided, the acceptance will have been deemed to have occurred not later than 60 days after delivery for the supply clause, and 90 days for the R&D clause.
3. The government may require you to either repair or replace supplies at any time up to six months after acceptance, if at the time of delivery the supplies were found to be defective. Your cost will be paid by the government, but no fee will be allowed on this inspection.
4. At any time after acceptance you may be required to replace or correct defective supplies if the defects resulted from fraud, lack of good faith, or willful misconduct of your supervisors.
5. You have no continuing obligation for correction of either latent or hidden defects.

Fixed-Price Incentive Contracts

The inspection clause under this type of contract is the same as in the basic fixed-price supply contract except for the following provision, here quoted in part:

> Prior to the establishment of total final price, all replacements or corrections made by the contractor shall be accomplished at no increase in total price.

This clause also provides for either contractor replacement or correction of defective supplies. If you fail to comply, the government may either replace or correct the supplies, and reduce the final price. The government may alternatively choose to terminate for default.

FINAL ACCEPTANCE: HOW TITLE PASSES FROM CONTRACTOR TO GOVERNMENT

As previously stated, acceptance is the act of the government asserting ownership, and, in the case of services, approving them. The procedure of acceptance is well-defined and of great importance, for it is at that point that title passes from the contractor to the government.

The contract terms state where the items will be accepted. In most cases requiring government quality assurance at a plant, acceptance will be done at the plant. When quality assurance actions are performed at destination, acceptance will ordinarily be performed there.

After delivery is made, the government has a reasonable period of time for either acceptance or rejection. Even though the government may not have formally accepted the items, acceptance may be implied by either the government's delay or the government's conduct. The burden, then, of prompt inspection and acceptance falls upon the government. Unless a notice of rejection is transmitted to the contractor promptly, acceptance may be implied, in certain cases, as a matter of law.

The conduct of the government may also be judged to imply acceptance even though formal acceptance has not yet been accomplished. For example, if the government consumes either part or all of the defective items delivered, an acceptance of the consumed portion is generally considered to have taken place. Alteration of items prior to rejection, as well as use of the items, also constitutes acceptance.

In certain instances, the contracting officer may require a contract to include a clause entitled "certificate of conformance" (COC). This certificate must state that all supplies delivered under the contract conform with contract drawings and specifications, and it may be the only basis for government acceptance of the item and payment of your invoice. The COC may also be used as further assurance that the supplies meet contract performance prior to acceptance.

The government's acceptance is final only if there are no latent defects, fraud, or gross mistakes tantamount to fraud. If any of these conditions are proven, even after final payment has been made, you are still responsible. The government, in these situations, will pursue the same remedies available to it where the items are found defective prior to acceptance.

Tip: If you look at commercial practice, many of the same procedures are followed in day-to-day transactions, albeit in a somewhat different fashion. You may feel that the presence of a government inspector in your facility is an undue intrusion on your privacy. However, just as you can look at a glass as half full or half empty, the presence of a government inspector can be considered an unpaid quality control "hand" who is there to assist you in performing your job correctly. You would not deliver poor quality or defective goods to the commercial market. Likewise, you shouldn't want to deliver the same type of merchandise to the government. If you do your job correctly, the impact of government inspection can be positive.

THE DIFFERING SITE CONDITIONS CLAUSE: HOW YOU CAN GET AN EQUITABLE ADJUSTMENT FOR UNANTICIPATED DELAYS OR COSTS

There is a unique clause that is mandatory for inclusion in all fixed-price construction contracts. It is unique in that it entitles you to an equitable adjustment if you encounter unknown and unanticipated physical conditions at the work site that may either delay or increase the cost of the work. One of the purposes of the clause is to eliminate excessively high bids resulting from anticipation of problems by the bidder that may not actually occur. This makes the job of bidding much simpler, and allows much closer pricing. Under the clause, the government assumes liability for changed conditions and will give quick relief.

The clause requires that the contracting officer be given prompt notification in writing of any changed condition. This allows the government to investigate the site and possibly change the location in order to avoid the problem. *Keep in mind*: Failure on your part to comply with this requirement may bar future claims for equitable adjustment. However, your claim must be considered by the government regardless of whether or not the government is able to show that it was hurt by the late or nonexistent notice.

This clause provides assistance under two different types of problems.

Category I claims involve subsurface and hidden physical conditions at a work site that differ from those indicated in the contract documents. In other words, the government failed to include "special information" that it had at the time of contract award. Category II claims involve unknown physical conditions that no one knew of or anticipated. Essentially they are unusual conditions that are not foreseeable. Please note that recovery would not be allowed if you ignored the warnings in the specifications and all warning signs that would have been apparent on a site investigation. In order to fall into Category II, the condition need not have existed at time of award. It may be the result of a man-made change after the award. The concept here is that the government could have corrected the conditions, but failed to do so.

The site clause offers a magnanimous approach by the government to problems frequently faced in construction, and it represents as safe a bet as available anywhere to the contractor for performance within budget.

HOW THE GOVERNMENT ENFORCES FAIR LABOR POLICIES WITH CONTRACTORS

We are all aware of the federal government's concern with fair labor policies in the United States. In its ongoing efforts to bring about social and economic changes in areas requiring them, the federal government has two powerful tools at its disposal. One is the government contract, and the other is the power given Congress under the Interstate Commerce Clause of the Constitution. Its purpose is to "regulate commerce with foreign nations, and among the several states, and with the indian tribes." It is an all-powerful and all-encompassing clause, with a history of long-standing precedent. What is important to you as a government contractor are the provisions that have been established to ensure compliance. Part I of President Nixon's Executive Order 11478 of August 8, 1969 applies to federal employees, providing for complaint procedures to the Civil Service Commission (now the Office of Personnel Management), with appeal provisions to the commission and the establishment of all necessary regulations to carry this out. Parts II and III made the Secretary of Labor responsible for administration of the order relative to government contracts, and the issuance of rules and regulations considered to be necessary and appropriate in achieving program objectives. In order to assist in the administration of this order, the Office of Federal Contract Compliance (OFCC) was established.

The OFCC monitors, coordinates, and evaluates the government-wide contract compliance program, which carries out the provisions of the Executive

Order. Included under the provisions of the order is the Small Business/Labor Surplus Area program, which was covered in Chapter 10.

Compliance with all of the provisions of the Civil Rights Act and all of the provisions of the executive orders is carried out by means of compliance and preaward reviews. The Equal Employment Opportunity Commission (EEOC) compliance review is a thorough on-site analysis of the personnel policies, procedures, and practices of both prime and subcontractors, while a preaward review is a regular compliance review generated as a result of a request from a procurement activity for preaward clearance of a contractor to whom a contract award is contemplated. These apply to contracts, and their modifications, anticipated to be in excess of $1 million.

Equal Employment Opportunity Act

The *Equal Employment Opportunity Act* applies to all government contractors and first tier subcontractors. The exceptions cover individual contracts or subcontracts of $10,000 and less, unless the sum total of all contracts in a 12–month period are expected to exceed $10,000. Also excluded is work performed outside the United States, contracts with either state or local governments, work on Indian reservations, contracts exempted by the Secretary of Defense in the interest of national security, and specific contracts and facilities exempted by the Director, Office of Federal Compliance programs.

The act requires that all government contractors and subcontractors provide equal opportunity for all persons, regardless of race, religion, color, sex, or national origin. The policy on age discrimination is set forth in Executive Order 11141, dated February 12, 1964. Discrimination for reason of age is not permitted.

The Act is enforced through compliance review, certification that the contractor conforms with the act, and posting of the Act in conspicuous places. The contractor is required to furnish all information and reports required by the government and permit access to its books, records, and accounts.

Violations can cause the contract to be cancelled, terminated, or suspended in whole or in part, debarment of the contractor for up to three years, and submittal to either the Justice Department or the Equal Opportunity Commission for institution of appropriate civil or criminal proceedings.

The Davis-Bacon Act

This act covers construction projects in excess of $2,000 and contracts for nonappropriated fund activities, and is applicable both to prime contractors and subcontractors. It places a minimum on wages paid to laborers and mechanics, the minimums being decided by the Secretary of Labor, and provides for paid vacations, sick leave, and hospitalization benefits.

The act is enforced in the contract by the specifications containing minimum wage rates, the requirement to post wage rates at the work site, and the requirement to submit certified payrolls weekly.

Violations of the act carry severe penalties, which include termination plus excess costs of reacquisition, debarment from government contracting for a maximum of three years, and the suspension of contract payments for continued violations. The contracting officer has the right to withhold payments from the contractor or the subcontractor in order to correct any violations of the wage provisions, as applicable to mechanics and laborers. The act also authorizes and directs the Comptroller General to pay directly to laborers and mechanics any accrued payments of wages due them under terms of the contract. In addition, the employees may sue either the contractor or subcontractor directly for wages that are underpaid.

The Anti-Kickback Enforcement Act of 1986

This act was passed to deter subcontractors from making payments, and contractors from accepting payments, for the purpose of improperly obtaining or rewarding favorable treatment in connection with either a prime contract or subcontract relating to a prime contract.

The Contract Work Hours Standards Act of 1962

This act applies to all contracts utilizing laborers or mechanics on public works contracts. It applies to all contracts to which the U.S. government is a party, or to all contracts made on behalf of the government, and to all contracts financed either in whole or in part by the United States. Exceptions include contracts covered by the Walsh-Healey Act, contacts of $2,500 or less, and construction contracts of less than $2,000. Under this act, no laborer or mechanic doing any part of the work contemplated by the contract can be either required or permitted to work more than 8 hours in one day or 40 hours in one week, unless hours worked in excess of these limits are compensated at not less than time and one-half of the basic rate.

Enforcement is carried out by means of examination of the contractor's and subcontractor's weekly payroll records. These must be retained for three years after completion of the work.

Intentional violations are enforced under criminal penalties that include a fine of $1,000 or imprisonment for up to six months, or both. Willful violations are punished by debarment for up to three years. In addition, the contractor is liable for liquidated damages both to the employee and the United

States for any amounts due. Liquidated damages are computed with respect to each individual laborer or mechanic employed at the rate of $10 for each 8-hour calendar day or excess of a 40-hour week, whichever is the greater number of hours. In addition, the contracting officer may withhold from the prime contractor all sums determined necessary to satisfy the contractor's (and subcontractor's) liability for unpaid wages and liquidated damages.

The Walsh-Healey Act

This act applies to supply contracts exceeding $10,000, and provides that the contractor must be either a contractor or regular dealer in the items required by the contract. Minimum wages as determined by the Secretary of Labor must be paid, without reduction or rebate, and time and one-half pay is required for each hour worked in excess of 8 in one day or 40 in one week. Work under unsanitary, hazardous, or dangerous conditions is not permitted, and the employment of persons under 16 years of age and convict labor is not permitted.

The contractor is required to furnish proof of eligibility as either a manufacturer or regular dealer in the items under contract, and a copy of the law must be posted in a readily accessible place at the work site. In addition, all employment records must be retained and made available for inspection for three years from the time of contract completion.

Violations are punished by means of liquidated damages of $10 per day on child or convict labor, plus a sum equal to the amount of any deductions, rebates, refunds, or underpayment of wages due any employee. As under the acts mentioned previously, funds may be withheld to cover underpayments. In addition, contract termination and assessment of reacquisition costs are permitted, as well as three-year debarment of the contractor from any federal contracts. All suits must be brought in the name of the United States by the Attorney General, not by individuals.

The Walsh-Healey Act is the basic labor statute for supply contracts exceeding $10,000. It is very comprehensive and covers all of the areas that the several statutes do for construction. It is highly volatile with regard to its provisions that a contractor must be either a regular dealer in, or manufacturer of, the items required by the contract. Appendix C is devoted to the Walsh-Healey Act and its interpretation, which clarifies what can and cannot be done legally under the act's provisions.

The Service Contracts Act of 1965

This act became effective on January 19, 1966, and it extended the federal minimum wage, fringe benefits, and working condition standards to all contracts and subcontracts thereunder for services in excess of $2,500.

Both the contractor and the subcontractor must pay his or her employees the prevailing wage rate for the locality, as determined by the Secretary of Labor. Fringe benefits must also be included. The law also covers performance of the work under safety standards and sanitary conditions. Posting of wage rates is required at the job site, and records must be retained for inspection on request for three years.

The act covers all United States and District of Columbia contracts and subcontracts over $2,500 for services. Service contracts for less than $2,500 are covered under the Fair Labor Standards Act. Excluded under this act are contracts covered by the Davis-Bacon Act, the Walsh-Healey Act, transportation contracts to be performed under published tariffs, postal contracts for substations, and services performed outside the United States.

Punishment for violations follows the pattern of the other acts, providing for the withholding of funds for wage underpayments, termination and assessment of reacquisition costs, up to three-year debarment, and the bringing of suit by the government for wage underpayments.

The Fair Labor Standards Act

This act applies to all employees engaged in either interstate or foreign commerce, or the production of goods for interstate or foreign commerce, and any process or occupation essential to the production of these goods. It applies specifically to service contracts not exceeding $2,500, and provides that contractors and subcontractors must pay the minimum wages specified in the Fair Labor Standards Act of 1938.

Under this act, minimum wages and maximum hours are established, oppressive child labor is prohibited, and wage and hour divisions within the Department of Labor are established for purposes of interpretation and enforcement. The Secretary of Labor enforces this law, and employees may sue in a civil action for unpaid wages or overtime wages, plus an equal amount in liquidated damages.

A clause covering this law need not be in the contract since the law applies to industry in general, and that automatically includes government contracts.

Acts Promoting Employment of the Handicapped

The Rehabilitation Act of 1973 requires contractors to employ qualified handicapped individuals, while the Wagner-O'Day Act requires all entities of the federal government to purchase certain listed products and services from workshops for the blind and other severely handicapped individuals.

Probably the most extensive and complex social policy in government procurement is that favoring small business. The Small Business Act of 1953 states that it is the policy of congress that a fair proportion of government procurement must be placed with small business concerns. This, along with the provisions for labor surplus area procurements, were covered in detail in Chapter 10.

OTHER KEY AREAS OF CONCERN FOR CONTRACTORS WHEN COMPLYING WITH GOVERNMENT CONTRACTS

The Buy American Act

The Buy American Act (41 U.S.C. 10a-d) as implemented by Executive Order 10582, requires, with certain exceptions, that the end product of all supply and services contracts be a domestic product. This law applies even if it raises the price of the low bidder. The act is quite complex, and should be interpreted only by a qualified person. Essentially it requires that all articles, material, and supplies acquired for use within the United States, its territories, and possessions must be either mined or manufactured in the United States, or must be manufactured for the most part in the United States. Executive Order 10582 provides standards for preferential treatment of domestic supplies, and not total exclusion of foreign products. Under this order, there are two key statements of policy:

1. Under section 2(a) it is determined that a material is foreign if the cost of the foreign products (and components) used constitutes 50 percent or more of the cost of the product.
2. Section 2(c) (1) establishes 6 percent as the normal evaluation factor to be added to bids offering foreign products. This means that for the purposes of bid evaluation, an amount equal to 6 percent of the foreign product bid will be added to that bid. This evaluation factor may be increased by the procuring agencies to 12 percent where the low domestic bid was submitted by a small business or Labor Surplus Area concern.

Exceptions are made if the articles are for use abroad, and if the supplies are not satisfactorily available domestically. Exceptions are also made if the head of an agency determines that the domestic purchase would be either too expensive or not in the public interest.

Enforcement of the act generally takes the form of either flat bid rejection by the contracting officer, or rejection of the bid if the offending component is not replaced. Special consideration is made for Canadian, NATO, and Allied Nation products.

A large number of GAO bid protest cases involves the application of the act and implementing regulations formulated to cover specific procurement situations. Many of these involve the distinction between an end product and component. *Key point*: Once the appropriate determinations have been made, and the proper evaluation factors have been applied, the Buy American Act does not provide authority to disregard the low responsive bid.

If at any time a question arises regarding the appropriateness of the source of either the materials or supplies you are contemplating offering to the government, consult the contracting officer in charge of the solicitation. He or she usually can give you an immediate response as to whether or not your bid will be responsive.

Bonds, Insurance, and Bid Guarantees

A *bond* is a written instrument that is executed by either a bidder or a contractor, who is the principal, and a second party, which is the surety. A bond assures fulfillment of the principal's obligations to a third party, the obligee. Bonds are usually in an amount equal to 100 percent of the contract price at time of award, although the contracting officer may set a lesser amount, but normally not less than 50 percent of the contract price. The obligee, for our purposes, is the government. Contract modifications resulting in a price increase require that the contractor furnish additional performance bond protection.

A *performance bond* is a guarantee that the work will be performed to completion.

A *payment bond* assures payment to persons supplying labor and materials in the course of a contract. The amount for this type of bond varies.

The requirement for these bonds is called out in the Miller Act. However, your failure to furnish the required bonds will not necessarily either stop payment or invalidate the contract if the work has been satisfactorily completed, and all required wages paid. The Comptroller General has even permitted claims to be paid on the theory of *quantum meruit*, where a contracting officer exceeded his authority by awarding the contract without requiring the furnishing of performance and payment bonds.

The Miller Act. All fixed-price contracts over $2,500 for the construction, alteration, and repair of any public buildings or public work of the United States are subject to the provisions of this act. It places two conditions on the awarding of contracts, the first requiring the prime contractor to furnish a performance bond, the second requiring the prime contractor to furnish a payment bond. Since protection under the Miller Act is limited to materials and labor, unrelated claims, such as damages for breach of contract or loss of profits to one covered by the act, are not recoverable. The Comptroller

General has no authority to assist a subcontractor, materials supplier, or laborer in collecting amounts due him under a payment bond because there is no privity of contract between any of these persons and the government. In case of a claim, civil suit must be pursued. *Keep in mind*: Essentially, the Miller Act is a remedial statute, and the courts have consistently applied a liberal construction to it.

Insurance is defined as a contract that provides, for a stipulated consideration, the indemnification of one party by another against loss, damage, or liability arising from either an unknown or contingent event.

Bid guarantees are a form of security assuring that the bidder (a) will not withdraw a bid within the period specified for acceptance, (b) will execute a written contract and furnish required bonds, including any necessary coinsurance and reinsurance agreements. Bid guarantees must be executed on the specified forms within the time stipulated in the bid, unless a longer time is allowed. A bid guarantee is required only when a performance bond or a performance and payment bond are required.

All types of bid guarantees are acceptable for supply and service contracts. Single bid bonds are acceptable with construction contracts. A bid guarantee amount must be at least 20 percent of the bid price, but need not exceed $3 million. When a penal sum or penal amount—which is either the money specified in a bid bond or the percentage of the bid price—is expressed as a percentage, then a maximum dollar amount must be stated.

The penal amount of performance bonds is required to be 100 percent of the original contract price, unless the contracting officer determines that a lesser amount would be adequate for the protection of the government.

The penal amount of payment bonds must equal 50 percent of the contract price for contracts under $1 million, 40 percent of the contract price if it is more than $1 million but less than $5 million, and $2.5 million if the contract price is more than $5 million. The government will require additional protection if the contract price is ever increased above these limits.

Performance bonds are required, when necessary, to protect the government's interest when certain situations exist.

1. When either government property or funds are to be provided to the contractor for use in performing the contract. A performance bond will also be required when either property or funds will be used as partial compensation (as in the retention of salvaged material).
2. When a contractor either sells assets to, or merges with, another company, and the government recognizes the latter concern as the successor in interest, and wants assurance that it is financially capable.
3. When substantial progress payments are made before the delivery of the end item begins.

4. When the contract is for the dismantling, demolition, or removal of improvements.

A payment bond is required only when a performance bond is required, and if the payment bond is in the government's interest. In this situation, the contracting officer determines the amount of the bond.

Annual performance bonds apply only to nonconstruction contracts, and they must provide a gross penal sum applicable to the total amount of all covered contracts. When the penal sum obligated by contracts either approximates or exceeds the penal sum of the annual performance bond, an additional bond will be required to cover additional contracts.

The head of an agency may approve other types of bonds, such as advance payment bonds. These are required when the contract contains an advance payment provision and a performance bond is not furnished. The amount is discretionary with the contracting officer. Patent infringement bonds are required when the contract provides for patent indemnity, and a performance bond is not furnished, or the financial responsibility of the contractor is unknown or doubtful. Again, in this situation, the contracting officer determines the sum.

The SBA provides bond guarantees for surety companies. These are available to small businesses, and no charge is made to the applicant. Once the contract is obtained, however, the contractor is required to pay the SBA a guarantee fee of $6 per thousand of the contract amount. Space does not permit covering all of the SBA bonding procedures here, but let it be considered words to the wise that, at the first sign of a problem, consult with your nearest SBA office. You'll be glad you did!

A surety is either an individual or corporation considered legally liable for debt, default, or failure of a principal to satisfy a contractual obligation. An individual surety is one person, as distinguished from a business entity, who is liable for the entire penal amount of the bond. A corporate surety is licensed under various insurance laws and, under its charter, has legal power to act as a surety for others. Sureties require that agencies obtain adequate security for bonds. Acceptable forms of security include either corporate or individual sureties, and options in lieu of sureties, such as United States bonds and notes in an amount equal, at their par value, to the penal sum of the bond. Either certified and cashier's checks, bank drafts, Post Office money orders, or currency, in an amount equal to the penal sum of the bond, may also be furnished.

Contractors may be required to carry insurance. This insurance may be in the form of self-coverage, if so desired. It is required to counterbalance the perils facing the contractor, except when the government agrees to indemnify the contractor, or the contract specifically relieves the contractor of liability for either the loss of, or damage to, government property. Other insurance requirements exist, such as for work performed under war hazards. Additionally, there are assorted types of insurance required by the various types of contracts that can be awarded.

Compliance with Workers' Compensation and employer's liability, general liability, automobile liability, and aircraft public and passenger liability are all required when performing government contracts.

The Convict Labor Law of 1887

There are two additional laws that are worth looking at before moving on. One of these, the Convict Labor Law of 1887, is mentioned purely from the point of academic interest, for it is doubtful that you would be in a position to ever perform a government contract with prisoner labor. This law applies mainly to state and local governments who are eligible to bid on and receive federal government contracts!

The coverage of the law is sweeping. It applies to all government contracts. As in most laws, there are exceptions, and the ones that apply here include contracts covered by the Walsh-Healey Act, purchases from federal prisons, purchases from state prisons, and most important, persons on parole, probation, and pardoned personnel who have served their term.

The law prohibits any representative of the U.S. government from entering into a contract for the purpose of hiring any prisoner confined for violation of any law of the United States. This was modified in 1905 by Executive Order 325A, which was intended to cover any person undergoing sentence or imprisonment at hard labor imposed by any state, territory, or municipality having criminal jurisdiction. Violations, upon conviction, are punishable by a fine of $1,000, imprisonment for three years, or both.

Occupational Safety and Health Act

Finally, the Occupational Safety and Health Act (OSHA)—passed on the basis that it would contribute to the general welfare by reducing accidents caused by unsafe working conditions—is a requirement in the government contract. This shouldn't pose any problem now, since the provisions of OSHA have been in existence a good number of years. The purpose of the act is to encourage employers and employees to reduce hazards in the workplace and create new, and improve existing, safety and health programs. Mandatory job safety and health standards were developed—and are continuing to be developed—as well as the requirement to establish reporting and record keeping on job related accidents and illnesses. It also established separate but independent responsibilities and rights for employers and employees to ensure better safety and health conditions. The authority was vested in the states to establish their own version of OSHA, requiring these programs to be at least as effective as the federal program.

This act covers all employers and their employees in all states, territories, the District of Columbia, and all other territorial areas under federal jurisdiction.

A wide variety of fields, such as construction, longshoring, agriculture, law, medicine, charity and disaster relief, organized labor, and private education, are covered by the act. Even religious groups are included to the extent that they employ workers for secular purposes. It is probably easier to mention what is not covered under the act: self-employed persons, family-owned farms, and work places already protected by other federal agencies under other federal statutes. However, even when another federal agency regulates safety and health conditions in a particular industry, but it does not do so in specific areas, then OSHA regulations apply.

Taxation: Immunity from Price Adjustments

As a general rule, the federal government is immune from state and local taxes with respect to both real and personal property owned by the United States. However, where a contractor purchases materials and supplies that are going to be incorporated into a contract end item, state and local taxes are usually included in the price paid by the contractor. They are subsequently paid for by the federal government. In addition, contractors are sometimes required to pay certain federal taxes. Because of these situations, certain tax clauses are included in government contracts. Some of the more pertinent provisions of these clauses as they apply to different types of contracts are covered below.

Price adjustments for federal taxes must be provided for on all fixed-price contracts through the inclusion of the *federal, state, and local taxes* clause. It is required for all contracts procuring goods through formal advertising and in all competitively negotiated fixed-price contracts in excess of $10,000.

The clause provides that the contract price will include all applicable federal, state, and local taxes and duties, except social security and employment taxes. It further provides that equitable price adjustments be made if there is either a corresponding increase or decrease in an applicable tax, imposition of a new tax, or elimination of a tax. These adjustments cannot be less than $100, either in the contractor's favor or in favor of the government.

Price adjustment for state and local taxes in negotiated fixed-price contracts in excess of $10,000 are made using the same clause, but only after the contracting officer is satisfied that the contract price excludes all contingencies for state and local taxes. Provisions include an increase or decrease in the contract price to compensate for changes in these taxes. Adjustments of less than $100 are not made. Social Security, income, and employment taxes are excluded.

Insurance Requirements

Contracts for supplies and services require that the contractor carry insurance if it is mandatory by law, or if the government considers it desirable to utilize the services of the insurance industry, such as underwriting services for safety purposes. It will also be required in special instances if it is considered either necessary or desirable in connection with contract performance. Normally, the government acts as it own insurer. However if a contractor is performing construction work on a government installation, insurance would be required.

Keep in mind: Either cancellations to, or modifications of, a policy affecting the interests of the government are not effective unless written approval by the contracting officer is given.

Let's take a look at how insurance requirements apply to various types of contracts.

Fixed-Price Contracts: Under these types of contracts, the government normally acts as a self-insurer, and is not concerned with the contractor's insurance program. Under special circumstances, however, the government may require insurance coverage of some type. For example, insurance would be a requirement if the contractor is either engaged principally in government work, such as construction contracts, or where government-furnished equipment is involved.

Cost-Reimbursement Contracts: Under these types of contracts, there is a requirement to carry workers' compensation, employer's liability, general liability including property damage, automobile liability, and any other type of insurance specified. The limits of liability on the various types of insurance will be set by the procuring agency concerned.

Covenant Against Contingent Fees: A covenant against contingent fees clause is mandatory in fixed-price and cost-reimbursement type contracts. Generally the clause contains the contractor's warranty that no persons, other than employees and established commercial and selling agencies, have been employed for the purpose of soliciting business on a commission, percentage, brokerage, or contingent-fee basis. A violation of the warranty gives the government the right either to annul the contract without liability, or to deduct the amount of the fees from the contract price.

What the contingent fee clause really means is that no contractor may pay a contingent fee to any person for the purpose of obtaining government business. This eliminates any temptation for anyone to arrange the award of a contract to either a favored individual or firm, and maintains the integrity of the competitive procurement process.

The Economic Price Adjustment Clauses: As they apply to the fixed-price contract, these clauses provide for various pricing arrangements to cover contingencies and price increases and decreases. They provide for either upward or downward revision of the contract price based on certain contingencies or the change in the cost of components used in the end item. This reduces the risk assumed by the contracting parties. If the price of a commodity causes the price of the item to go up, the contractor is protected. Under the reverse situation, the government is protected.

WARRANTY PROVISIONS IN GOVERNMENT CONTRACTS

Many of the items purchased by the government will be covered by warranties that convey your assurance as contractor that the goods or property sold comply with contractual requirements. The warranty allows the government additional time, after acceptance, in which to assert its rights of defect correction. Warranties may be either express or implied, and may cover compliance with contract specifications, performance, or fitness of purpose. Whether or not a warranty will be a contractual requirement depends on past experience with that item, and the anticipated cost addition this warranty will have on the procurement.

Express Warranties: Three Conditions for Compliance

To provide protection to buyers of goods and services, uniform legal provisions have been enacted in every state, with the exception of Louisiana, and the Commonwealth of Puerto Rico. This law is known as the Uniform Commercial Code (UCC), and since there is no federal law conflicting with the UCC, the government has felt free to adopt this code as a common law guide for government contracts. The UCC provides that express warranties are created by a seller as follows:

1. Any affirmation of fact or promise made by a seller to the buyer that relates to the goods and becomes a part of the basis of the bargain, creates an express warranty that the goods do conform with what was promised.
2. Any description of the goods that is made part of the basis of the bargain creates an express warranty that the goods will comply with that description.

3. Any sample or model that is made a part of the basis of the bargain creates an express warranty that all of the goods will conform with that sample.

When the seller creates an express warranty it is not necessary that the seller use formal words such as "warranty" or "guarantee," or that the seller have any specific intention of making a warranty. However, a warranty is not created either by the seller's affirmation of the value of the goods, or by a statement claiming to be the seller's opinion or commendation of the goods.

Implied Warranties: Five Factors Determining Marketability

Unless either excluded or modified, a warranty that the goods will be marketable is implied if the seller is a merchant with respect to goods of that kind. The factors determining marketability are as follows:

1. They must pass in the trade, without objection, under the contract description, and in the case of fungible goods—which are goods with all units identical, such as grains of corn—they must be of fair average quality within the contract description.
2. They must suit the ordinary purpose for which the goods are intended to be used.
3. They must, within the variations permitted in the contract, be of even kind, quality, and quantity in their individual characteristics, as well as among all of the units involved.
4. They must be adequately contained, packaged, and labeled as required by the contract.
5. They must conform with either the promises or affirmations made on the container or label, if any.

Where the seller—at the time of contracting—knows the best purposes for which the goods are suited—and the buyer is relying on the seller's skill and judgment to select or furnish suitable goods—there is, unless excluded, an implied warranty that the goods will be fit for the purpose required.

Although implied warranties provide protection to buyers, an implied warranty may be specifically excluded by calling to the buyer's attention, in clear, understandable language, that warranties are excluded and that there is no implied warranty. In addition, an implied warranty is excluded when a buyer has examined the goods, sample, or model as fully as she wanted to at the time, or if she refuses to examine the goods. Also, by agreement between buyer and seller, the extent of the remedies under the warranty may be restricted or limited.

15 Cost-Risk Factors to Consider When Evaluating a Warranty

Except for commercial warranty clauses, the decision to require a warranty on a government contract is reserved for the head of the contracting activity. This is the case because warranties may be used only if economically feasible and administratively practical. Usually a contract committee is set up to advise on these decisions. Warranties are not free, and the cost-risk factors must be evaluated. Specific factors that will be taken into consideration include the following:

1. nature of the item and its end use
2. cost of the warranty and the degree it will affect price and cost
3. degree of criticality involved in achieving design and performance specifications
4. cost of replacement by the government, contractor, or other source in the absence of a warranty
5. administrative cost and degree of difficulty in enforcing the warranty
6. ability to take advantage of the warranty, as conditioned by storage time, distance of the agency using the item, and similar factors
7. operation of the warranty as a deterrent against furnishing either defective or nonconforming supplies
8. extent to which government acceptance will be based on the contractor's quality control
9. nature of the items, and whether or not the government's inspection system could provide protection without a warranty
10. contractor's quality control reliability, and whether or not it is sufficient to provide adequate protection without a warranty, and if not, whether or not a warranty would cause the contractor to institute an effective and reliable quality program
11. degree of reliance on "brand name" integrity
12. extent to which a warranty is given for a commercial component of a more complex end item
13. critical requirement for the item to protect personnel, such as safety in flight
14. stage of development of the item and the state of the art
15. practices customary in the trade

Warranty clauses are not used in cost-reimbursement contracts because the inspection clause for those contracts has sufficient warranty provisions included. In addition, under this type of contract, the government would have to pay for repairs anyway.

Five Types of Warranties for Which Contractors Are Responsible for Correcting Defects

In general, there are five basic types of warranties that impose responsibilities on contractors for correction of defects:

1. The failure-free warranty (generally known as the hardware warranty) is one under which the contractor accepts responsibility for correcting any failure or defect that occurs during a specified period of time or measured amount of operation. The cost to the government of this type of warranty is usually very high in terms of contract price and administrative control.
2. The correction of deficiencies warranty, under which the contractor agrees to correct any design, material, and workmanship deficiencies that become apparent during test and early operation. In weapons systems contracts, the warranty clause usually applies to spare parts and other supplies included in the contract.
3. The supply warranty, under which the contractor is responsible for reworking or replacing items found to be defective at the time of acceptance. The clause incorporating this warranty usually gives the government a specified period of time in which to discover any defects.
4. The service warranty, under which the contractor agrees to correct or reperform defective services, provided the defects in workmanship existed at the time of acceptance and are discovered within a specified time.
5. The construction warranty, which is used in construction contracts, requiring the contractor to remedy, at its own expense, any work not conforming with the specifications, and any defect of material, workmanship, and contractor design.

The government will require strict compliance with the warranty provisions in order to assure its protection. Timely notice of defects must be given to you in writing by the government before the period in the warranty clause expires.

CONTRACT AUDITS

Audits of government contracts are performed by two separate agencies for different purposes. The contracting agency performs audits in order to assure that the contract is being performed according to its terms and legal requirements, and to determine the propriety of contract payments. The General Accounting Office (GAO) performs independent audits for the purpose of ascertaining whether government agencies are making procurements in the most efficient, economical, and effective manner, and to advise Congress of

GAO's recommendations for legislative or administrative actions necessary to improve agency contracting practices and procedures. In addition, the GAO may review individual contracts to determine whether or not excessive and unreasonable payments have been made to contractors. The GAO has limited manpower resources, and pursues this latter situation sparingly.

Agency audits are normally based on the authority of a clause contained in the contract. However, in many instances there is statutory authority for these audits. Statutes 10 U.S.C. 2313(a) and 41 U.S.C 254(b) provide for audits, by the procurement activity, of any cost or cost-plus-a-fixed-fee contract made by that agency. This authority extends to subcontracts issued under the prime contract.

Authority to audit other forms of contracts formerly was obtained solely through contract clauses. The regulations require the inclusion of an audit clause in most contracts. The exceptions are contracts for less than $100,000 or contracts awarded under formal advertisement procedures. The military agencies have the statutory right to audit the books and records of contractors and subcontractors for the purpose of evaluating the accuracy, completeness, and currency of cost or pricing data required to be submitted under 10 U.S.C. 2306(f).

Audits by the GAO take the form, primarily, of a review after the contract is completed. The purpose is to inform Congress of the manner in which the procurement centers are administering appropriated funds. The authority of the GAO to conduct these audits in negotiated contracts is statutory: 10 U.S.C 2313(b) and 41 U.S.C. 254(c). The right to conduct audits of contracts issued under advertising is by virtue of a contract clause included by the contracting officer. The regulations, both military and civilian, require the insertion of the Comptroller General's audit rights in all negotiated contracts for all procurements exceeding $10,000. The Comptroller General's right to examine records extends to first-tier subcontractors and covers all records that directly pertain to the contract subject matter, whether they were used in the negotiation or not.

HOW THE GOVERNMENT HANDLES PATENTS, DATA, AND COPYRIGHTS IN THE BIDDING PROCESS

Some bidders may be concerned that their "trade secrets" will be jeopardized if they are made known to the government through the bidding and contracting process. Actually, more than adequate safeguards have been established to protect the bidder from any potential loss. Additionally, the policies exercised in this area are quite fair and are designed to be of benefit to you, the contractor, as well as to protect the government's interests.

Patent rights, technical data, copyrights, and trade secrets fall under the heading of proprietary information; that is, information protected by the law. Broadly stated, it is the policy of the government to foster the public interest by acquiring the principal rights to inventions. This applies where either the nature of the work, or the government's past investment in the field of the work, favors full public access to resulting inventions. But policy also recognizes that the public interest might better be served at times by according exclusive rights to the contractor. This would be the case in situations where a contractor has an established nongovernmental commercial position, and where there is a greater likelihood that an invention can be better put to use in a commercial environment, rather than having it freely accessible to all. Under this situation, the government acquires an irrevocable, royalty-free license to use the invention in any of its contracts.

Eight Guidelines the Government Follows Regarding Patents, Data, and Copyrights

1. The government encourages the maximum practical commercial use of inventions made while performing government contracts.
2. Generally, the government will not refuse to award a contract on the grounds that the prospective contractor may infringe a patent.
3. Generally, the government encourages the use of inventions in performing contracts and, by appropriate contract clauses, authorizes and consents to their use. This is the case even if the inventions are covered by U.S. Patents and indemnification against infringement may be appropriate.
4. Generally, the government should be indemnified against infringement of U.S. patents resulting from performing contracts when either the supplies or services acquired under the contracts are normally offered for sale or sold to the public. This would also apply to supplies and services that are much the same as commercial supplies and services sold to the government.
5. Even though the government acquires supplies and services on a competitive basis, it is important that the efforts directed toward full and open competition not improperly demand or use data relating to private developments.
6. The government honors the rights in data resulting from private developments, and limits its demands for use of the data to those essential for government purposes.
7. The government honors rights in patents, data, and copyrights, and complies with the stipulations of the law in using or acquiring these rights.
8. Generally, the government requires that contractors obtain permission from copyright owners before including privately owned copyrighted works in data required to be delivered under government contracts.

How Patent Rights Are Upheld in Government Contracts

The government and the contractor must know and exercise their rights in inventions conceived under government contracts in order to ensure their expeditious availability to the public. This is essential in order to avoid the unnecessary payment of royalties and to defend themselves against claims and suits for patent infringement. As an aid in attaining these objectives, the government administers contracts containing patent rights clauses in a way that will:

1. ensure that inventions are identified, disclosed, and reported as required by the contract
2. protect the rights of the government
3. make certain that, where appropriate, the necessary patent applications are filed on a timely basis
4. document the rights of the government in filed patent applications through formal instruments, such as licenses and assignments
5. bring about expeditious commercial utilization of the inventions

You, the contractor, should follow any effective procedures required to make certain that your patent rights obligations are met, and that all inventions are disclosed on a timely basis. It is expected that you will have written procedures delineating how to proceed when an invention is made. The government will, through its follow-up procedures, verify that you are performing as required with regard to inventions. The government will make every effort to correct any deficiencies on your part with regard to inventions, and in cases where every avenue of obtaining compliance has been exhausted, the government may invoke the withholding of payment provisions clause of the contract.

In cases where the government, through its contract, acquires the entire right, title, and interest in an invention, the government's interest is normally protected by an assignment from each coinventor to the contractor, and from the contractor to the government. The assignment may be made directly to the government, however, and if you consent to this procedure, it clearly establishes the chain of title from the inventor to the government. When the government's rights are limited only to a license, a confirmatory instrument to that effect will also be required.

When Invention Disclosures Are Published

Publication of invention disclosures will be withheld by the government until the first filing of patent application. If a disclosure release is eminent, the government must expedite the patent filing process. The government will also withhold from disclosure to the public any information indicating an invention that has been included in any data delivered under a contract; however, you are expected, when the data are delivered, to notify the government that the data contain an invention disclosure. This notification can be made either to the contracting officer or the patent representative to whom the invention has been reported.

Since the publication of information disclosing an invention by any party before the filing of a patent application may prevent a valid patent, an agency is also required to withhold release of copies of any document that is part of a domestic or foreign patent application.

You, the contractor, have the right, after disclosure of an invention, to elect to retain title to it. However, for various reasons, such as national defense considerations, the government may request greater rights to the invention. When you retain title to the invention, the government will require at least a nonexclusive, nontransferable, irrevocable, paid-up license to use the invention throughout the world, and may have additional rights to sublicense the invention either to foreign governments or other international organizations. The licensing of patent rights to third parties by the government is not a preferred practice. However, it may be done with the approval of the agency head when it has been determined that doing so will either expedite the work being performed under the contract, or expedite the commercial application of the invention.

How the Government Can Receive Title to an Invention

In cases where the contract so authorizes, the government has the right to receive title to an invention. This will usually be the case when the contract is for the operation of a government-owned research or production facility. It will also apply under conditions where either the restriction or elimination of your right to retain title is necessary to protect the security of intelligence and counterintelligence activities.

To the extent provided for in the patent rights clause, the government also has the right to receive title to an invention:

1. when the contractor has not disclosed the invention within the time period specified in the clause
2. in any country where the contractor either does not elect to retain rights or fails to elect to retain rights to an invention within the specified time period of the clause
3. in any country where the contractor has not filed a patent application within the time specified in the clause

4. in any country where the contractor decides not to continue pursuing a patent application, pay maintenance fees, or defend in either a reexamination or opposition proceeding on the patent
5. in any country where the contractor no longer desires to maintain title

March-in Rights

The government maintains march-in rights to any invention with which you, the contractor, have acquired title if you refuse to grant any type of license to any field of use, or to a responsible applicant under reasonable terms. Under its march-in rights, the government may force you to comply with licensing of the invention in order to bring about its most productive application. This right of an agency is exercised only after you have been given a reasonable time period in which to submit the facts and show cause why the proposed agency should not take these steps. You have the right to appeal the agency's proposed action.

Nonexclusive Versus Exclusive Rights

Unless otherwise stated, contracts provide that no contractor who receives title to an invention, including the contractor's assignee, may grant the exclusive right to either use or sell the invention in the United States unless it is agreed that the products resulting from the invention will be manufactured substantially within the United States. Waiver of this requirement may be granted by an agency if either the contractor or assignee show that reasonable but unsuccessful efforts were made to grant the appropriate licenses.

Securing a License for the Invention

When the government acquires title to an invention, you, the contractor, are normally granted a revocable, nonexclusive, royalty-free license to that invention throughout the world. This license extends to your subsidiaries and affiliates, and includes the right to grant sublicenses of the same scope required of you at time of contract award. This license is transferable only with the approval of the contracting officer, except when it is transferred to your successor, relative to the business to which it pertains.

Your domestic license may be revoked or modified to the extent necessary to bring about expeditious practical application of the invention. The revocation may be partial. It will not pertain to those geographical areas in which you have achieved practical application, and continue to make the benefits of the invention reasonably accessible to the general public. A foreign license may either be revoked or modified to the extent that you or licensees have failed to achieve practical application in that country.

In those cases where the government has either authorized or consented to the manufacture or use of an invention described in, or covered by, a patent of the United States, any suit for infringement of the patent based on the manufacture and use of the invention by the government, through a contractor or subcontractors, can be maintained against the government only in the U.S. Claims Court, and not against either the contractor or subcontractor.

How the Government Protects Against Patent Infringement

To ensure that the work of a contractor and subcontractor are not enjoined because of patent infringement, the government gives authorization and consent to use the invention in accordance with the established rules and regulations. The liability of the government for damages in a suit against it must be borne by either the contractor or subcontractor in accordance with the terms of the patent indemnity clause of the contract. An authorization and consent clause does not detract from any patent indemnification commitment by the contractor and subcontractor. Therefore, both a patent indemnification clause and an authorization and consent clause may be included in the same contract.

The contracting officer is not permitted, however, to include in any solicitation and contract any type of clause expressly indemnifying the contractor against liability for patent infringement, or any authorization and consent clause, when complete performance and delivery are outside of the United States, its possessions, and the commonwealth of Puerto Rico.

The contractor is required to notify the contracting officer of any claims of infringement received in connection with contract performance. The contractor is also required to assist the government, when requested, with any suit against the government, as well as with claims made against the government before suit has been instituted.

When Patent Indemnity Clauses Are Used

The government will require reimbursement for liability for patent infringement, and various patent infringement clauses will be required as the situation requires. The general rules governing when the clauses are to be inserted depends on the type and cost of the procurement. They are somewhat complex, as you will see from the following examples.

Patent indemnity clauses are inserted in sealed bid contracts for supplies and services if the contracting officer determines that they have been either offered for sale or sold by any supplier, in whole or in part, on the commercial market. They are also inserted in sealed bid contracts in order to obtain an indemnity regarding specific components, spare parts, and services not previously sold on the open market. The clause will be used in solicitations and contracts for communication services and facilities, where performance is by a common carrier and the service is unregulated and not priced under a tariff schedule. Negotiated contracts, other than for construction, do not normally require an indemnity clause, the determination not to include it being based on price considerations to the government.

These are only some of the situations where the contracting officer is required to use the appropriate clause. Because of the multitude of considerations involved, deep and serious evaluation will be made before a decision is reached one way or the other.

The payment of royalties under a contract is governed by the appropriate clauses. These include clauses addressing payment of foreign royalties, and the procedures covering the adjustment and refund of royalties. If royalties are paid when the government has a royalty-free license, and if they are either excessive or improper in any way, a refund will be required under the refund of royalties clause. When a fixed-price contract is negotiated under circumstances making it questionable as to whether or not substantial amounts of royalties will have to be paid by the contractor or subcontractor, they may be included in the target price, provided the provision of refund of the unpaid royalties is made to the government.

Copyright Regulations

Compared with the area of patents, there is very little specific material pertaining to copyrights. Essentially all that is mentioned in the regulations on copyrights is that it is necessary for government departments, in performance of their duties, to acquire access to many types of data. It is recognized that the contractor may have a proprietary right or other valid economic interest in certain data resulting from private investment, and that protection of these rights from unauthorized use and disclosure is required in order to preclude compromise of these rights and interests. If these rights are not protected, the contractor's commercial position could be harmed, and the government's ability to obtain access to the data would be impaired.

As a result, it is essential that these types of data be protected to encourage qualified contractors to participate in government programs and the application of innovative concepts to these programs. Individual agencies are encouraged to prepare specific regulations that will strike a balance between the government's need and the contractor's economic interest.

INDEX - CHAPTER 14

15

CONTRACT TERMINATION: WHAT YOU SHOULD KNOW

Contract termination can be initiated by the government for a variety of reasons. The need for an item may no longer exist or there may be a breach of contract terms and conditions by the contractor. When breach (or anticipated breach) occurs, the government is entitled to relief. However, in addition to any remedies the government may have under the terms of its contracts and under law, it also has a specific responsibility not to act imprudently. Termination cannot be initiated without good cause, but when termination is necessary, proper procedures designed to protect the contractor must be followed. Additionally, the contractor must receive proper financial compensation for work performed and for costs incurred during the termination phase. This chapter will examine the default termination clauses, termination for convenience, procedures to be followed in lieu of termination, and other contract remedies available to the government.

DEFAULT TERMINATION CLAUSES

Default clauses are invoked by the government in order to regain control of a procurement that is going badly. For example, you may fail to deliver as required, fail to perform other contract provisions, or fail to make progress. In order to obtain either the goods or services on time, it may be necessary for the government to declare you in default and to procure from some other source. If this is done, you can be held liable for excess costs. Each type of contract is designed for different procurement purposes, therefore you must read the default clause to understand just what its provisions are. There is no universal default clause. Additionally, termination for default is not a routine practice of the government.

Note: Default provisions are included solely for the purpose of protecting the government from loss. They are not intended to be used for arbitrary, coercive, or punitive purposes. This will become readily apparent when we examine the equitable duties imposed by the government for resorting to any of the actions designed to minimize damages.

In essence, the government desires to acquire goods and services to meet specific requirements. Neither government nor industry is in the business of litigation.

Situations requiring use of the provisions of the default clause, the liquidated damages clause, and the disputes clause are, fortunately, the exception rather than the rule. Contracting officers are required to exercise these remedies with good judgment and in such a manner as to fully protect the best interests of the government.

How the Government Defines "Excusable Cause" for Breach of Contract

Under the traditional concept of law, if one party fails to perform his or her contract, the other party recovers money damages for breach of contract. This basic concept has been modified when the breach occurs because of some *excusable cause*. Recognition of this principle should be apparent from the language of the default clause, which states:

> The contractor shall not be liable for any excess cost if the failure to perform the contract arises out of causes beyond the control and without the fault or negligence of the contractor.

Further on it provides:

> If after notice of termination of this contract under the provisions of this clause, it is determined...that the default was excusable...the rights and obligations of the parties shall, if the contract contains a clause providing for termination for the convenience of the government, be the same as if notice of the termination had been issued pursuant to such clause.

The philosophy of excusable breach of contract is evidenced, even in those government contracts not containing a termination for convenience provision, by the enabling clause's continued wording:

> ...and if this contract does not contain a clause providing for termination for convenience of the government, the contract shall be equitably adjusted to compensate for such termination and the contract modified accordingly.

The Default Clause: How It Works

The government is empowered to terminate either all or any part of a contract if you, as contractor, fail to perform within the time specified in the contract. Termination may be considered when you fail to make progress so as to endanger contract performance, or fail to perform any other provision of the contract. However, termination proceedings are not automatic. Termination is a discretionary process by the government that exists regardless of how slight the delay may be. However, for practical purposes, the government does not indiscriminately terminate immediately, for doing so would often be irresponsible and counterproductive.

Often the question arises in the mind of the contracting officer as to what point in time notice of termination for default for nonperformance should be given, and what type of notice should be used. This is answered by the fact that a contractor already in default is not entitled to any prior notice, unless there is a contract provision requiring notice, and the contract may be terminated immediately.

When a notice of failure to perform any provision of a contract or to make progress on the contract is required by the contract, the contracting officer must notify the contractor, citing the failure, and the contractor must be given the opportunity to correct the situation within ten days, or longer if so authorized. This must be done before termination can occur. This notice and advice of the opportunity to correct the situation must be in writing. An oral notice is insufficient, and any termination for default initiated by oral means is improper.

If the opportunity to correct the situation (''cure'' notice), is less than the ten-day minimum, termination for default would likewise be improper. The contracting officer would be in error if the time remaining for delivery is less than ten days and he or she used the notice of termination as a means of accelerating the contractor's performance.

The Armed Services Board of Contract Appeals has repeatedly required the government to adhere strictly to the notice provision of the clause where the time available prior to delivery is greater than 10 days.

If the time required to remedy the deficiency exceeds the period of time allowed by the cure notice, then a ''Show cause'' notice may be issued instead. This directs the contractor to show why it should not be terminated for default.

Use of this notice is not mandatory, however it is considered advisable from the contracting officer's perspective since the existence of an *excusable* cause would result in the default termination being changed to a convenience termination.

In order for a delay to qualify as excusable, the cause must be beyond your control and not your fault. Causes listed in the default clause and considered excusable include, but are not limited to, acts of God, acts of the government (either sovereign or contractual), acts of the public enemy, fires, floods, epidemics, quarantine restrictions, strikes, freight embargoes, and unusually severe weather. The key determination as to whether or not an event is beyond your control is based on its *foreseeability*. If a strike is foreseen, then any delays caused by it may not be interpreted as being beyond your control. This type of situation could occur, for example, if historically the contractor had experienced a strike every two years. You would be considered at fault if the anticipated delays to be caused by the next strike were not included in the schedule.

Under the excusable delay provisions of the default clauses, you, as contractor, have the burden of showing that performance was actually delayed and the extent of that delay. If you fail to do this, a time extension will not be granted.

The provisions of the default clauses provide only for performance time extensions, not for an adjustment in the contract price to compensate for delay. Normally, government contracts do not contain any other clause providing for price adjustment due to delay, if the delay is caused by a party other than the government.

There is, however, an implied obligation in every contract that one party to the contract will not hinder or prevent the performance of the other party. Several acts that have been held as breach of this implied duty by the government include issuing faulty specifications, delay in furnishing government property or making the site available, delays in inspection, and delays in approval or notice to proceed with performance. However, where the government acts as the sovereign rather than as the contracting party, it does not breach the contract for delay.

How You Can Recover for Government-Caused Delays

Recovery of costs incurred for government-caused delays requires you to show three things:

1. that the government expressly or impliedly promised to either do or not to do something
2. that the government inexcusably failed to keep that promise
3. that the government's breach of promise was the approximate cause of your increased costs

Often the government's act, which would constitute a breach of the contract, is held to constitute a change under the changes clause. In construction contracts it is recognized under the differing site conditions clause of the contract.

With regard to excusable delays caused by the failure of a subcontractor to perform, the delay must be shown to have been caused by forces outside both the prime contractor's and subcontractor's control, and not because of negligence by either party. Even if this requirement is met, the cause of the delay will not be excusable if the delayed supplies were obtainable from another source in sufficient time for the contractor to make delivery on time.

Forbearance: The Government's Policy of Avoiding Immediate Contract Termination

Many matters must be considered in arriving at the decision to terminate. Causes for delay, either excusable or inexcusable, must be determined, the nature of the item involved must be considered, and whether or not it is available from other sources of supply. The time it will take to initiate a new procurement in relationship to the urgency of need for the item must be taken into account. An evaluation must also be made of the contractor's ability to perform if additional time is allowed. Thus, the government frequently takes no immediate action and the contractor continues to perform even though the original performance period has passed. If the government ultimately decides to terminate, it may be faced with a situation where it has effectively waived its rights to terminate for default. This waiver is often called an "election" by the government to allow a contractor to continue performance, notwithstanding the passage of the delivery date.

Since termination causes loss of all hope of performance, it is usual for the government to pause and reflect before taking such drastic action. This process is called forbearance, and in so doing, the government determines whether or not termination is in its best interest. It has generally been recognized that the government is entitled to this pause and reflection time, which is not construed as a waiver of its right to terminate, but rather forbearance of that right. The regulations provide for several courses of action in lieu of termination for default when it is determined to be in the best interests of the government. These include:

- permitting either the contractor, or its surety or guarantor, to continue performance under a revised delivery schedule
- permitting the contractor to continue performance by means of a subcontract or other acceptable third party
- if the requirement for either the supplies or services no longer exists, allowing a no-cost termination settlement agreement to be executed

This period of forbearance must be a reasonable one, otherwise the inaction can constitute a waiver. A waiver has been defined as the intentional or voluntary relinquishment of a known right. Under a condition of waiver, the government can be presumed to have elected to allow the contractor to continue performance.

In addition to time lapses, other actions by the government may constitute waiver. First of all, the exact period of time and actions that constitute a waiver have not been clearly defined by court decisions. The period of time involved depends on the facts of the case. Forbearance times ranging from one week to over three months have been considered not to be a waiver, while periods of over three months have been determined to constitute a waiver.

Actions that have been considered a waiver by the government are urging the contractor to continue, accepting samples and preproduction models, performing an acceptable inspection, accepting deliveries, and issuing change orders and supplemental agreements. With regard to urging the contractor on, it is clear that when the government induces a contractor to continue performance, and the contractor relies on this inducement to continue, a waiver will exist.

Actions not constituting waiver constitute topics of progress discussions with the contractor. These include failure to answer the contractor's request for more time, accepting partial deliveries, and limited tests by government inspectors.

However, if any action by the government constitutes a waiver, a new delivery schedule must be established that allows reasonable performance time in light of all the facts.

There is an optional "stop work" clause that can be used. This clause permits the government to suspend work for a limited and specified period of time without causing the government to incur any liability for the delay. This could be used to limit the costs incurred during a forbearance period, if so required.

How the Default Clause Applies to Various Types of Contracts

Fixed-Price Supply Contracts

If this type of contract is terminated either in whole or in part for default, you may be required to transfer title and deliver all completed and partially completed supplies, tools, materials, fixtures, parts, dies, drawings, information, and contract rights to the government. The contract price will be paid for the items delivered. Except for defaults by subcontractors at any tier, supplies similar to those terminated may be acquired from another source, and you will be held liable to the government for any excess costs for those supplies. The excusable delays listed in the default clause exempt the contractor from this liability. You are obligated to continue work on any portion of the contract that is not terminated. The provisions of the disputes clause applies if any problem affecting equitable settlement occurs.

Fixed-Price Research and Development

If this type of contract is terminated in whole or in part, the government may acquire, under the terms and manner the contracting officer considers appropriate, work similar to the work terminated. You will be held liable to the government for any excess costs for this similar work. Treatment of default by subcontractors and excusable delays is similar to fixed-price supply contracts. If the termination is partial, you are obliged to continue the work not terminated.

The default clause is similar to the fixed-price supply contract, not only with regard to the reasons for default, but with regard to the ten-day cure notice, repurchase and excess costs, and excusable cause provisions.

Fixed-Price Construction Contracts

Under this type of contract, the provisions of the default clause permit the government to terminate the contractor's right to proceed with either the work, or any "separable" part of it, for two reasons:

1. if the contractor either refuses or fails to undertake the work in such a way that completion within the time specified in the contract is assured
2. if the contractor fails to complete the work within the time specified in the contract

These provisions are similar to the "failure to make progress" and "failure to deliver" provisions of fixed-price supply contracts previously discussed.

Once a contract has been terminated, the government may take over the work and either complete it, or have it completed by another contractor. This includes taking possession of and using any materials, appliances, equipment, or plant that may be on the work site, and which is considered necessary for contract completion. In addition, you are liable to the government for any damages caused by your failure to complete the work on time. This latter situation is a matter of fact, whether or not the contract is terminated.

Under the previously discussed differing site clause, you are eligible for an equitable price adjustment if the site conditions either materially differ from what the government warrants, or what is usual for the area in question.

When Suspension of Work Is Allowed. In addition to the differing site clause, construction contracts contain a mandatory clause entitled "suspension of work.'' Under this clause, the government is unilaterally allowed to suspend work for its convenience, and to adjust the contract price to reflect the cost of the work unreasonably delayed. This adjustment in the contract price does not cover a profit on an increased cost. This is similar to the optional ''stop work clause'' found in supply contracts. Both clauses include a time period within which you must assert its claim for delay, and this period is rigidly enforced. Under the stop work clause, the government is restricted in the period of time it can unilaterally delay the work.

Service Contracts

Violations of the mandatory clauses covering minimum wage and fringe benefits required by the Service Contracts Act make the responsible party liable for an amount equal to that of any deductions, rebates, refunds, or underpayments due employees engaged in work on the contract. The government may withhold and place on deposit a sum equal to the accrued payments due the contractor that are necessary to pay the employees. If these withheld payments are insufficient to reimburse all employees to whom compensation is due, the government may bring action for the remaining amount against the contractor, subcontractor, or sureties.

When any of the contract stipulations are violated, the contracting officer may cancel the contract upon written procedural notice. Upon cancellation, the government may then enter into other contracts necessary to complete the original contract, and may charge the original contractor with any additional costs incurred in its completion.

The Comptroller General is directed by the Service Contract Act to distribute to all government agencies a list of the names of persons and firms that have been found to have violated the Act. This amounts to disbarment for up to three years.

Cost-Reimbursement Contracts

The default termination provisions for this type of contract permit the government to terminate the contract either in whole or in part, both for actual default or failure to make progress. Failure to make progress endangers performance, and this could result in default. The ten-day cure notice is required by the clause, with the same restrictions on its use as in the other types of contracts.

In the event of termination, you are reimbursed for your allowable costs in accordance with the clause, and appropriate reduction is made in the total fee. There is no provision for the recovery of excess costs or reprocurement after termination. However, in those cost-reimbursement supply contracts that include a clause covering the inspection of supplies and the correction of defects, the situation is somewhat different. Under this circumstance, the government may at any time within the contract's performance period, but not later than six months after acceptance, request either replacement of the supplies or correction of the defects. In addition, the government may either repurchase the supplies and charge the excess costs to the contractor, or equitably reduce the fee.

Excusable causes for cost-reimbursement type contracts are set forth in a special clause titled Excusable Delays. These delays are recognized to the same extent as in fixed-price supply contracts, and are stated in the clause. There is a requirement to revise the delivery schedule to accommodate an excusable delay. This does not appear in any other termination for default clause.

If either the supplies or services are obtainable from other sources, the excusable cause for delay will remain intact unless the government orders the contractor, in writing, to obtain them from that other source and the contractor fails to ''reasonably comply'' with that order.

TERMINATION FOR CONVENIENCE

The right to terminate a contract for convenience of the government is essentially the right of the government to refuse to continue with contract performance, to stop the work, and to settle with the contractor at the point of the termination. The provisions of the termination for convenience clause are covered in the contract, and the actual termination is carried out by the contracting officer. Unlike the default termination process, the termination for convenience is not based on fault by the contractor, and it is designed to promote the best interests of the government. It provides the flexibility the government requires over its vast procurement programs, however in exercising this control many procedural factors must be recognized, and a fair settlement arrived at.

The right to terminate for convenience of the government is usually based on the fact that the contractor and the government have agreed to the clause as written in the contract. However, there are two other facets that must be recognized: incorporation by operation of law and breach of contract.

Even though the termination for convenience clause is omitted from the contract, the right of termination for convenience may still bind the parties. This is based on a court decision that stated the procurement was governed by the regulations, and since the regulations were promulgated pursuant to law, they had the effect of law. Since the regulations required that the clause be in the contract, and no authorized deviation was granted, the court concluded that the clause is operative as if it were physically incorporated in the contract. This is not to say that the clause need not now be incorporated in the contract. Government policy and good business practice dictate otherwise, Nevertheless, this definitely extends the termination for convenience coverage.

Limitation on the Right to Terminate for Convenience

There is a limitation on the right to terminate for convenience, which requires the contracting officer not to terminate arbitrarily and to justify his or her actions. Practically speaking, however, you would have great difficulty disputing the right to terminate, as the grant of authority under the clause is very broad. By comparison, in commercial contracts, termination is normally possible only by mutual consent of the parties, otherwise a contract breach occurs. There is no unilateral right to terminate, as is given the government in its contracts.

Factors Involved in Allowing a Termination for Convenience

In reaching a decision to terminate for convenience, many of the same factors involved with default termination must be considered. Some of these include technological considerations in the state of the art, budgetary constraints, the effect of the procurement on either subsidiary or related procurements, the requirements of other government activities, and the estimated cost of the termination. Generally, heavy consideration is given to the facts before a decision is reached. Good planning is also essential, so that the process can be completed in the least costly way possible.

How the Termination Process Works

The notice of termination is usually first given by telegraph and then confirmed by letter. In some cases, only a letter will be used. In these notices, certain information and instructions must be included, such as the effective date of the termination, whether or not all work is to be stopped, and the specific work to be terminated, if the termination is partial. The notice may also include special instructions about the continuation of certain work, disposition of inventory, and other matters. For example, even though the work on the main piece of equipment is terminated, the government may still want to order spare parts and other supply support items for delivered equipment.

On the option of the government, these supply support items are often ordered under special contract provisions, and these may be reflected in the notice of termination. In addition, the notice must contain recommended action that would minimize subcontractor expenses.

One of the contracting officer's responsibilities is to arrange a meeting with the contractor so that a definite plan is developed for bringing about equitable termination settlement. All topics related to the principles, policies, and procedures governing the settlement are discussed. For example, a list of the potential items to be covered would be the extent of the termination, the status of plans, drawings, and other data; as well as the status of continuing work. Other topics included might consist of the termination of subcontracts, the transfer of title to material to the government, interim financing, inventory schedules, accounting data, and the subcontractor's submission of a settlement proposal. The purpose of all of this is to protect the government's interests. If you find yourself in this situation, be prepared to present your side of the case properly so that a truly equitable settlement for both sides will be arrived at.

The contractor's duties are defined in the notice of termination and the contract termination clause. Generally sound business judgment dictates that you must immediately stop work as directed. Any continuation beyond the stage authorized by the notice of termination can be at your risk, with the additional costs incurred coming out of your pocket. In addition, you must terminate all unperformed or partially performed subcontracts and purchase orders related to the termination and settle, with the contracting officer's approval, all outstanding liabilities and claims arising from the termination. It is essential that all steps necessary to cancel all terminated work in process be done on a timely basis. Any questionable situations will be reviewed for prudent and reasonable action under the circumstances.

Settling a Fixed-Price Contract

After a termination for convenience, the government is under the legal obligation to make a fair and prompt settlement with the contractor. Generally speaking, settlement of terminated contracts takes the form of either negotiated agreements between the parties, or unilateral determinations by the contracting officer. When the parties cannot agree on the terms of the settlement, a formula settlement may be used. You may appeal to the Boards of Contract Appeal if it is felt that this formula is not equitable.

Total Costs Versus Inventory Method of Settlement. Settlements of fixed-price contracts may be based on either total cost or inventory. Each method of settlement has its advantages and disadvantages. From the government's point of view, the inventory basis settlement is usually preferred.

The total cost method of settlement requires the contracting officer's approval. Any other method of settlement, such as a percentage of physical completion, is rare because of the necessity of having this and similar methods approved by the Secretary or his duly authorized representative.

Under the inventory method of settlement, you list only those costs applicable to the terminated parts of the contract. Inventory is priced and listed in the settlement proposal at either purchased or manufactured cost, or both, and other proper charges are added. These charges would include initial costs allocable to the terminated portion of the contract, general and administrative expenses, settlement expenses, cost of settlements with subcontractors, and profit or adjustment for loss. End items that were completed but not delivered at the time of termination are paid for at contract price. The total of these amounts is your gross termination claim. From this sum are deducted inventory disposal credits, unliquidated progress payments, and advance payments.

The government favors the inventory method of settlement because only the costs relating to the terminated portion of the contract have to be considered. Another reason is that the cost of inventory listed on the schedule is priced at either purchased or manufactured cost at the time of termination. Any other costs, such as initial costs allocable to the termination, have to be listed individually.

Under the total cost basis of settlement, the entire contract must be reviewed and audited. If your accounting system is not up to the task of properly segregating cost, or if the contract was in its early stages at time of termination, with only preparatory costs incurred, then the total cost basis would be the best choice.

When the total cost basis is used under a complete termination, all costs incurred to the date of the termination are itemized, plus settlements with subcontractors and applicable settlement expenses. At this point, adjustment is made for either profit or loss. The contract price for accepted end items and other known payments and credits are then deducted from this total.

The use of the total cost basis of settlement on a partial termination requires you to defer submission of your settlement proposal until after completion of the continued portion of its contract. All costs incurred under the contract are then totaled, including costs applicable to the continued portion. In other respects, the settlement is similar to the settlement of a complete termination on a total cost basis.

How to Negotiate Profit Percentages. Virtually all settlements are arrived at by negotiation. However, this does not mean that the contractor and the government necessarily agree. Generally speaking, you are paid for goods already accepted under the contract. In addition, percentage profit factors might be used. For example, a 2 percent profit on the cost of materials not yet incorporated in the work, and 8 percent profit on the remaining work costs, could be agreed on. Additionally, it may be agreed that the entire profit will not exceed 6 percent of the total cost incurred in performing the terminated work, excluding the cost of completed supplies already paid for by the government.

The rule on profit in termination for convenience is that you will be allowed profit only on the preparations and work performed on the terminated portion of the contract. Anticipatory profits—what the contractor expected if the work had continued without termination—are not allowed. In addition, profit on post-termination and settlement expenses is not allowed. Included here are expenses incurred in protecting termination inventory and in the settlement of subcontracts.

There is no hard and fast rule for determining the profit that should be allowed, but there are many guidelines followed by the government. One of these would be the percent of profit either agreed on or contemplated by the parties at the time the contract was negotiated. Another is the rate you would have earned if the contract had been allowed to continue to completion. These computations can be time consuming and costly, and the shortcut of comparing the work done on the terminated portion of the contract with the work completed on the entire contract may be an expeditious route to a fair settlement. This may also be more suitable because costs incurred do not accurately reflect the degree of difficulty of the work already performed.

If it appears that you would have suffered a loss on the entire contract, no profit will be allowed. Instead, the settlement figure will be adjusted to reflect the indicated rate of loss. Under this situation, on a total cost basis of settlement, the actual cost to date, exclusive of settlement expenses, is reduced by multiplying the cost by the ratio of the total contract price to your actual cost, plus the estimated cost to complete the entire contract.

Settling a Cost-Reimbursement Contract

The settlement procedure for a cost-reimbursement contract is different from that of the fixed-price contract because you have been reimbursed on a cost basis from the cost contract's beginning.

Vouchered Costs. On a complete termination, you may continue to voucher out costs incurred after termination, just as the pre-termination costs were vouchered out. Vouchered costs include costs for work done before termination and not previously vouchered, and costs relating to termination. The termination costs would include the expenses of settling subcontracts, the costs of preparing the settlement claim, expenses incurred in protecting and disposing of property allocable to the contract, and other expenses related to the termination.

As in the case of fixed-price contracts, settlements with subcontractors require review and approval by the contracting officer. This is necessary even when you elect to voucher out your costs. If costs are vouchered out, settlement negotiations are limited to adjusting only the fee. If costs are partially vouchered, the termination settlement will include unvouchered costs and fee.

Interim Financing with Partial Payments. Since termination for either one of the two reasons previously discussed effectively halts regular payments to the contractor, most termination clauses provide a means of interim financing by means of partial payments. This is obviously an essential requirement from your point of view as contractor, because of the funds tied up in work in process, inventory, and labor. Additionally, accounts payable will become due before the settlement agreement is reached, and these will require prompt attention.

The contracting officer may make partial payments on either a fixed-price or a cost-reimbursement type contract upon application by the contractor, in writing, any time after either the interim or final settlement proposal is submitted. With the contracting officer's approval, up to one 100 percent of the contract unit price may be paid for undelivered, acceptable items completed before the termination date. Additionally, if it had been so authorized by the contracting officer, this would apply to those items completed after the termination date.

A subcontract settlement made by the prime contractor and approved by the government may also be paid in full. The contractor may receive in partial payment an amount of up to 90 percent of the direct costs of the termination inventory. This amount includes costs of raw materials, purchased parts, supplies, and direct labor. A reasonable amount, but not more than 90 percent, may be paid for other allocable costs. Neither profit nor fixed-fee payments may be made.

ANTICIPATORY BREACH OF CONTRACT

Generally speaking, a contract is not breached until the time set for performance has arrived. However, under modern contract law, it is possible for a breach to occur prior to the time set for performance. In this situation, the breach is called an anticipatory breach. In theory, the anticipatory breach provides a remedy to one party to the contract when the other has repudiated his or her contractual obligations.

The purpose underlying this theory is that it is unjust to require a party who is ready, willing, and able to perform under the contract to stand by—perhaps to his or her detriment—under circumstances that indicate the other party clearly will not perform. This remedy is available to the government to the same extent that it is available to private parties.

Three Vital Elements for Claiming an Anticipatory Breach

There are three elements that are necessary to constitute an anticipatory breach:

1. There must be a positive intention not to perform.
2. There must be communication of this intent not to perform by either word or action.
3. There must be action by the aggrieved party based on the notice of intent not to perform.

Statements by the contractor indicating that the contract *may* not be performed are not sufficient grounds for the government to establish anticipatory breach. Neither would information received from a third party, such as a supplier or subcontractor, be considered adequate for establishing anticipatory breach unless proper opportunity is given to the contractor to set forth reasons why the contract should not be terminated for default.

In determining whether or not anticipatory breach has occurred, the government may take a contractor at his word and accept his statement that he does not intend to perform the contract. In this case, a ten-day notice prior to termination for default is not necessary. An anticipatory breach can also result from the contractor's conduct. For example, the petition for voluntary bankruptcy could establish a breach. Abandonment of the work by the contractor would definitely constitute breach.

In order to make the breach complete, the complaining party, in this case the government, must act either in anticipation of, or reliance on, the breach. If the government urged the contractor on, this would be inconsistent with the later claim that the government relied upon the contractor's repudiation of its obligations under the contract.

Tip: The anticipatory breach may be repudiated by the contractor at any point in time until the government has changed its position. In other words, if in a moment of indiscretion you tell the government to take this job and shove it, tomorrow you can still say you're sorry and go on as if nothing had happened, provided that the government hasn't taken action to find you in default.

CONTRACT REMEDIES AVAILABLE TO THE GOVERNMENT TO ENSURE CONTRACTOR COMPLIANCE

The government has many remedies that may be used to compel compliance with its needs, the contract, federal law, or the regulations.

Stop Work Order

With regard to the needs of the government, the contract may be either changed or modified, or work stopped or suspended, if the items being purchased are no longer needed by the government, and continued production would be wasteful. A stop work order is not permitted unless the contract contains the stop work clause. In fact, improper use of the stop work order may be considered a breach of contract by the government. Even when the contract contains the clause, stop work orders are specifically prohibited when a decision to terminate has been made. Before the stop work order may be issued, prior approval at a level higher than the contracting officer is required. Stop work orders may be effective for a period of 90 days, and while the order is in effect, the contractor must take all reasonable steps to minimize costs. The stop work period may be extended by agreement of the parties. It is required that either within the 90–day period, or within the period agreed to, the contracting officer must either cancel the stop work order or terminate the contract for the convenience of the government. If the stop work order is canceled, the contractor must then resume work.

Suspension of Work Order

Suspension of work provisions on construction contracts provide that work may be suspended for an unlimited period of time; however you are entitled to an equitable adjustment, excluding profit, for the unreasonable portion of the period when work was suspended. The clause neither applies to delays recognized by other contract clauses, nor to delays attributable to you. The clause requires you to give notice of any action that you regard as falling within the coverage of the clause, even though no actual order had been issued by the contracting officer. In these situations, properly called ''constructive suspension'' situations, you will be barred from recovery of costs incurred more than 20 days prior to the date the written notice was given. In those cases when an actual suspension order is given, but where you are given timely notice of a construction suspension, you are required to submit your claim as soon as practical after the termination of the suspension but not later than the date of final payment.

Miscellaneous Claims Against the Contractor

Claims against the contractor, such as for debt, may be taken to the U.S. District Court if suit is required. The administrative collection of debt is provided for in the regulations, and it is initiated by the contracting officer, usually by means of setoff of money due the contractor.

Contractor Debt. If contractor debt occurs, such as from excess cost of assessment following default termination, the contracting officer may seek out other contracting officers and agencies who owe the contractor money, and request them to setoff the claim against their debt owed the contractor. The government has the right, in addition, to refuse payment until it is paid what it is owed.

Deductions Resulting from Contractor Provisions Not Delivered

Deductions may arise from the contract terms themselves. These have been taken historically under the provisions covering defective pricing, the withholding of payment while awaiting technical data, and the patent clauses.

In the service contract area, deductions have been approved for services not rendered, reflecting the good business practice of not paying for something that is not delivered.

When the claim for any deduction is uncontested, and the parties agree on the settlement claim, a supplemental agreement reflecting the agreement generally will be issued by the contracting officer.

Damages: Two Main Forms. Damages for breach of contract by the contractor can be a remedy of the government even though a default termination is not contemplated. The government's acceptance of contract performance does not constitute a waiver of breach of contract claims. In these situations, the contracting officer will send you a letter referencing receipt and acceptance of supplies, but reserving breach claims.

Damages can take two forms: unliquidated and liquidated. Unliquidated damages are not determined in amount. That is, there has been no agreement by the parties, and a court determination has not been made. Unliquidated damages arise when you fail, in some substantial respect, to perform the contract as written, and harm to the government results.

Liquidated damages are predetermined in amount by agreement of the parties, and are contained in the contract. They are contingent upon the happening of a named event, which is usually either late delivery or nonperformance by the contractor. Liquidated damages should be provided for in the contract for two reasons only:

1. when the time of delivery or performance is such an important factor to the government that it may reasonably expect to suffer damages if either delivery or performance is delinquent
2. when either the extent or amount of the damages would be difficult to ascertain and prove

The rate of liquidated damages used has to be reasonable and considered on a case-by-case basis since liquidated damages fixed without any reference to probable actual damages may be considered a penalty, and therefore unenforceable.

Excessive Earning of Profits. The Examination of Records Clause is mandatory in all fixed-price contracts in excess of $10,000. The basic intent is to discourage certain contractors from earning excess profits. In addition, the clause applies to subcontracts in excess of $10,000, and to small business restricted advertised contracts in excess of that figure. The provisions of the clause allow either the Comptroller General or his duly authorized representative the right to examine the books, documents, papers, and records of both the contractor and subcontractor for a period of three years after final payment has been made.

Debarment Due to Misconduct or Other Cause. Debarment places the contractor in an ineligible status regarding receipt of further government contracts because of either misconduct or other cause. Debarment is based on the findings of either the Secretary of Labor, or the secretaries of the various departments. The grounds for placing a prospective contractor in the debarred bidders' classification usually include findings by the Comptroller General that the contractor has violated the provisions of either the Walsh-Healey or the Davis-Bacon Act, whichever may be applicable.

Department secretaries are also authorized to place a contractor's name on the debarred bidders' list for convictions of criminal offenses involving government contracts. Included in this category are embezzlement, theft, forgery, bribery, and any other serious offense that indicates a lack of business integrity, and which seriously affects the responsibility of the bidder as a government contractor.

Debarment may also result from an administrative determination that the contractor has willfully failed to perform according to the terms of a government contract. This would include the Buy American Act and noncompliance with the Equal Opportunity Act. Repeated acts of failure to perform or unsatisfactory performance may result in debarment. Debarment can also result from violations of the gratuities clause and the covenant against contingent fees clause of the contract.

The period of debarment is usually three years. If the contractor had been previously suspended because of these violations, this suspension time will count toward the three-year debarment period. The contractor must be given notice of the proposed debarment, including the reasons for it, and a 30-day period of time within which to present evidence in opposition to the proposed debarment. Notice of actual debarment must be given within 10 days after determination has been made to debar. Debarment may be extended to all of the contractor's affiliates if it is determined to be appropriate.

IMPROPER BUSINESS PRACTICES AND PERSONAL CONFLICTS OF INTEREST

The standards of conduct imposed by law and regulation require that government business be conducted in a manner that is above reproach, and, except as authorized by statute or regulation, with complete impartiality and with preferential treatment for none. Some of the things that cannot be done fall under the category of routine business ethics. These are the routinely adhered to, common standards of the marketplace. Some of the others may be somewhat of a surprise. Major pieces of legislation prohibiting specific behavior were covered in Chapter 1. Some of the less visible ethical standards that must be adhered to when dealing with government business are discussed here.

Gratuities for Special Treatment

The gratuities clause is required in all government contracts, with the exception of contracts with foreign governments and contracts for personal services entered into with an individual. This clause gives the government the right to terminate a contract if it is found, after notice and hearing, that gratuities in any form were either given or tendered to government employees, by contractors or their agents, in order to secure a contract or obtain favorable treatment under a contract. The government is entitled to the same remedies it would have against a contractor for a breach of the contract, and also any exemplary damages it may have by law. Exemplary damages are recoverable in an amount not less than three times but not more than ten times the cost of the gratuity provided by the contractor.

No government employee may solicit or accept, either directly or indirectly, any gift, favor, entertainment, loan or anything of monetary value from anyone either seeking government business with the employee's agency, or anyone who conducts activities that are regulated by the employee's agency. Additionally, accepting gratuities from someone having interests that may substantially affect the employee's performance of his or her duties is likewise prohibited.

Legislation prohibits officials, specifically Congressional members, delegates, and commissioners, from being admitted to any share or part of any contract. The contract, under these circumstances, can be voided, and all payments to the contractor may have to be returned. Debarment and exemplary damages are also provided for. Exemplary damages are recoverable in an amount not less than three times but not more than ten times the cost of the gratuity provided by the contractor. Criminal penalties also apply.

Contractor Fraud

Fraud is covered under the False Claims Act, Title 31 U.S.C. 231. Any person not in military service or employed by the United States, who makes a false claim against the government and knows it to be false, may be required to forfeit $2,000 plus double the amount of damages caused the United States by his or her indiscretion. The provisions of this act are broad, and although used most frequently in the area of defective pricing data, it is not limited to these situations.

Criminal fraud is defined as either knowingly and willfully making a false statement, or submitting a false document to a government agency. Punishment can consist of a fine of $10,000 or imprisonment of up to five years, or both. Fraud is considered a federal crime according to Title 18 U.S.C. Section 1001. False representations in government bids and negotiations are covered by this act as well.

Conflict of Interest

Conflict of interest by government employees is covered under Title 18, U.S.C. Section 203. This bars government officers and agents from either directly or indirectly soliciting, receiving, or agreeing to receive any payment for services relating to any government contract, claim, or other matter of interest to the United States. The penalty is a maximum fine of $10,000, imprisonment for two years, and mandatory disqualification from federal office. Section 203 does not apply to retired military officers who have not been recalled to active duty, or to those who are otherwise in government service or employment.

Part-time consultants, who are defined as special employees working for the government for a period not exceeding 130 days out of 365 consecutive days, are treated separately under Section 203 of the act. They are subject to it only in two matters: those in which they have participated personally and substantially in their government capacities, and those pending in the department or agency in which they served. This second restriction does not apply if the part-time employee has served no more than 60 in the preceding 365 days.

Title 205 of the same code prohibits officers and employees from acting as either agents or attorneys for, and aiding or assisting in, the prosecution of any claims against the United States. They also may not represent any person as agent or attorney before the government in any matter of government interest. Special part-time employees are subject to Section 205 in matters in which they have participated personally and substantially in a government capacity. If the employee has served in his or her agency more than 60 days during the year, Section 205 covers all matters pending before that agency. There are also provisions for limited waivers of this section for part-time employees. This is granted by the head of the agency after publication of the request in the *Federal Register*.

Organizational Conflicts of Interest

An organizational conflict of interest exists when the nature of the work to be performed under a proposed government contract, without some restrictions in future activities, results in an unfair competitive advantage to you, the contractor, or impairs your objectivity in performing the work.

Some examples clarifying the cans and cannots relative to organizational conflicts of interest are quite interesting.

1. Company A agrees to provide systems engineering and technical direction for the Navy on the power plant on a group of submarines. Company A should not be allowed to provide any power plant components; however, it may supply components unrelated to the power plant.
2. On a certain system, Company A is the systems engineering and technical direction contractor. After some progress, but before completion, the system is canceled. Later, Company B assumes the same role as Company A on a substantially different system to produce the same results. Company A may provide either this new system or its components.
3. Company A develops new electronic equipment and, as a result of this development, prepares specifications. Company A may provide that equipment.
4. Company A, along with Company B, representing Company C, work under government supervision and control to refine specifications and clarify requirements of a defined acquisition. These companies may supply the item.
5. Company A is awarded a contract to prepare specifications and performance criteria that will be used as the basis for the equipment competitive bid. Company A cannot participate in the competition for the hardware award.
6. Company A receives a contract to define the detailed performance characteristics an agency will require in purchasing rocket fuel. Company A has not

developed the particular fuel. It is clear to both parties that the performance characteristics arrived at will be used to competitively choose a contractor to either develop or supply the fuel. Company A may not be awarded this follow-on contract.

7. Company A receives a contract to prepare a detailed plan for scientific and technical training of an agency's personnel. Company A suggests curricula endorsed by the agency, and subsequently these curricula are incorporated in the agency's RFQs sent to institutions to establish and conduct the training. Company A may not be awarded a contract to conduct the training.
8. Company A is selected to study the use of lasers in communications. The agency conducting the study intends to ask other companies doing research in this field to make their proprietary information available to Company A. Later, when the research contract is awarded to Company A, it must require Company A to enter into agreements with the other firms in order to protect any proprietary information they might provide, and to refrain from using this information in supplying lasers to the government, or using it for any purpose other than what it was intended.
9. An agency regulates an industry and wishes to develop a system for evaluating and processing license applications. Company A helps to both develop the system and process the applications. Company A cannot act as a consultant to any of the license applicants during its period of performance and for a reasonable period thereafter.

Collusive Bidding

Collusive bidding practices are specifically prohibited. This is stated in a clause titled *Certificate of independent price determination* which is a requirement of all firm-fixed-price contracts and all fixed-price contracts with economic price adjustment provisions. This clause is not used if the acquisition is to be made under the small purchase procedures, or when the work is to be performed by foreign suppliers outside of the United States, its possessions, and Puerto Rico. It is also not used when the solicitation is either a request for a technical proposal under two-step bidding procedures, or when the solicitation is for utility services for which rates are set by law and regulation.

Offers suspected of being collusive will be rejected, and the situation is required to be reported to the Attorney General. It is also required that suspected antitrust violations be reported to the Attorney General. Some of the practices and events indicating probable violation of antitrust legislation include the existence of either an "industry price list" or "price agreement," to which contractors refer in formulating their offers. Also, a sudden change from competitive bidding to identical bidding can be indicative of antitrust activity, as can simultaneous price increases and follow-the-leader pricing. The rotation of bids or proposals, so that each competitor takes a turn in sequence as either the low bidder can be a tip-off. Bidding where certain competitors are low on a given size contract and high on others is another indication. Division of the market, wherein certain competitors bid low only for contracts in certain geographical areas or certain products, and bid high on all others, is also prohibited.

Collusive price estimating systems are also violations of antitrust legislation, as is joint bidding by two or more competitors, when one alone has sufficient technical capability and productive capacity for contract performance. Incidents suggesting direct collusion among competitors, such as identical calculations and spelling errors in two or more competitive offers, and the submission by one firm of offers for another firm, will result in agency reports to the Attorney General, as will assertions by either employees or former employees and competitors that an agreement to restrain trade exists.

Payment of Contingent Fees

Payment of contingent fees by contractors for either soliciting or obtaining government contracts has long been considered contrary to public policy, because these arrangements may lead to either the attempted or actual exercise of improper influence. Contingent fees are considered to be any commission, percentage, brokerage, or other fee that is contingent upon the success that a person or company has in obtaining a government contract. The statutes prohibiting this practice, 10 U.S.C. 2306(b) and 41 U.S.C. 254(a), affirm the public policy but permit certain exceptions.

These statutes require, in every negotiated contract, a warranty by the contractor that contingent fee arrangements do not exist, but they do permit, as an exception to the warranty, contingent fee arrangements between the contractor and bona fide contractors, bona fide employees, and bona fide agencies. In order to be ''bona fide,'' an agency must be either an established commercial or selling agency that is maintained by the contractor for the purpose of securing business. A bona fide employee is one employed by the contractor and subject to the contractor's supervision. It goes without saying that neither an agency nor an employee may exert improper influence in obtaining government business. They may not hold themselves out as being able to obtain any government contracts through improper influence.

Buying In

Buying in, which means submitting an offer below anticipated costs and later expecting to increase the contract amount after award with either unnecessary or excessively priced change orders, is not permitted. Another aspect of buying in consists of submitting an artificially low initial offer in anticipation of receiving future contracts at high prices that would cover the loss. The government is sensitive to the effects buying in produces. These result in reduced competition and reduced contract performance. This is especially important when you stop to realize that contracting officers rely on multiyear contracting to a great extent, and the impact of buying in can have a significant dollar impact over the life of the contract.

The contracting officer's primary concern is the price the government actually pays; the contractor's eventual cost, profit, and fee are of secondary concern. When the purchase is negotiated, a contract with a price offering the contractor the greatest incentive for efficient and economical performance is the goal. The negotiation of a contract type and price are related, and are considered together with the issues of risk and uncertainty to both the contractor and the government. Consequently, if you insist on either a price or fee considered unreasonable by the contracting officer, and all other options, including alternative sources, have been exhausted, then the matter is referred to higher authority by the contracting officer.

Subcontractor Kickbacks

Subcontractor kickbacks were covered in Chapter 1, and quite obviously this practice is not permitted. Associated with this issue would be a contractor's unreasonable demand that a subcontractor be precluded from making direct sales to the government of any supplies and services furnished under the prime contract. However, this does not preclude contractors from asserting rights otherwise authorized by both law and regulation.

Government Employees Cannot Participate

It is not permitted to award a contract to a government employee or to any company either substantially owned or controlled by one or more government employees. This policy is intended to avoid conflicts of interest between an employee's interests and government duties, and to avoid the appearance of favoritism and preferential treatment by the government toward its employees.

Laws prohibiting fraud, graft, conflict of interests, and gratuities will most likely continue to be severely pursued. The implication of these are great, to the extent that some government QAR personnel have even refused a cup of coffee on a facilities visit.

INDEX - CHAPTER 15

16

GUIDELINES FOR MODIFYING A GOVERNMENT CONTRACT

Once a contract has been entered into, it may seem to be a definite and finite act, and any thoughts on changing it are, at best, remote. This is often true in commercial contracts, but it is not the case with government contracts, especially those in either the R&D area, or systems contracts with a high dollar value. Changes can be introduced for several reasons, such as to correct omissions, to reflect changes in procurement goals, and to incorporate new technological developments. Essentially, the object of a contract change is to produce a better end product for the government.

In this chapter, the effects of modifications and changes will be discussed in relation to the rights and obligations of the government and contractor, who is authorized to make a change, the form of the change, and how changes are brought about.

TWO BASIC METHODS OF CONTRACT MODIFICATION AND HOW THEY AFFECT CONTRACT PERFORMANCE

Let's take a look at the two basic types of changes, and see how they affect contract performance.

Change Orders

There are two types of modification: *unilateral* and *bilateral*. In the unilateral, or one-sided change, the contracting officer makes a change without the consent of the contractor. This type of change must be within the scope of the contract. However, in a bilateral (two-sided) modification, the consent of both parties is needed to bring about the change.

By definition, a change order is a unilateral modification. In an opinion from the Armed Services Board of Contract Appeals it was stated that:

> Changes are issued pursuant to the changes clause in the contract, and they are evidenced by written orders from the contracting officer to the contractor. Since the contract at the time of its execution contained a changes clause, no new consideration is required to support a change order, nor need the consent of the contractor be obtained.

In other words, as long as the proposed change is within the *general scope* of the work contemplated by the contract, a unilateral order may be issued by the contracting officer. Your failure as a contractor to perform a unilateral change would be considered a contract breach. If the change order is valid, you must perform the work and adhere to the contract standards. If not, the contract can be terminated for default.

A change order is not the same as an amendment to a contract. Essentially, an amendment to a contract is a new agreement upon different terms from those contained in the original contract. Obviously an amendment that is a two-party agreement requires the contractor's consent, and it cannot be issued unilaterally by the government.

A change order should not be confused with an excusable delay. Facts and circumstances that do not give rise to a claim for a price increase under the changes clause may constitute an excusable cause of delay under the default clause.

Essentially, the change order is a right reserved for the government, and consideration need not be given the contractor for the change immediately. The change may, however, entitle the contractor to equitable relief, referred to as equitable adjustment. It is most important that the change order be issued by a person in authority. If the change is issued by an unauthorized party, there is an excellent chance that you, the contractor, will not be paid for it.

Supplemental Agreements

Bilateral modification creates a supplemental agreement, which is an entirely new, negotiated contract entered into by the parties and issued as an addendum to the existing contract. Again, your assent as contractor is required. A supplemental agreement would be used, for example, in a case where you had an inexcusable delay. The contracting officer will request consideration (generally an agreed to reduction in contract price). Excusable delay falls under the termination clause, not the changes clause.

Limitations in Modifying a Contract

The use of modifications has certain limitations. For example, a modification change order may not be used to negate formally advertised requirements, and it is not an allowable means by which the government can permit a bid modification. Contracts awarded through formal advertising may neither be modified using the change order, nor may the change order be used to add new items or revised quantities to the contract performance. In addition, the changes clause may be used only if an authorized party, which would be either the contracting officer or his or her duly authorized representative, makes either a written or oral order directing the change. *Remember*: The change must be within the contract scope and within the scope of the pertinent changes clause.

Further limitations on the use of the change order prohibit its use in bringing about either partial or complete termination, or for repurchases. Additionally, the change order may not be used to relieve a contractor of his or her own mistake in figuring the amount of a bid.

Key point: Change orders may not be used to make major changes outside of the contract's general scope. If you are required to comply with a unilateral order for extra work outside of or beyond contract scope, you may sue the government for breach.

A supplemental agreement is not made pursuant to any specific authority provided in the contract, and it is therefore essential that the contracting officer receive your acceptance in writing.

Nine Situations Where Supplemental Agreements Are Commonly Used. Supplemental agreements are commonly used in the following situations:

1. to finalize change orders
2. to redetermine price in a fixed-price redeterminable contract
3. to raise contract price in accordance with economic price adjustment provisions in the contract
4. to accommodate decisions of the Boards of Contract Appeal
5. to finalize other equitable adjustments in connection with other contract clauses
6. to finalize a termination for convenience or letter contract

7. to allow a contractor to complete a construction contract after nonexcusable delay, provided that the contractor assumes liability for all damages caused by the delay
8. to obtain additional performance under a contract where the work is outside the scope of the contract, but is of such an inseparable nature that no one but the original contractor could perform it
9. to change contract price, delivery schedule, quantity, quality, or other terms, that may not be changed unless the contractor so agrees

Three Reasons Why the Government Prefers the Supplemental Agreement Instead of the Change Order

The supplemental agreement releases and discharges the government of any further liability to the contractor. The supplemental agreement is preferred by the government, as opposed to the change order, for three reasons.

1. The supplemental agreement puts the government in a much better bargaining position. The change order permits you to come to the negotiating table "armed" with actual costs, which are assumed to be reasonable, thereby preventing the government from getting a "fair" price.
2. The supplemental agreement permits coordinated plans for bringing about the needed change. If problems in implementing the change are likely to appear, they will usually be revealed in negotiations.
3. The supplemental agreement removes the possibility of any claim by you that the government may have issued an illegal change, such as one that would be outside the contract scope.

How to Show That Modifying a Contract Is in the Best Interests of the Government. Effectively, the supplemental agreement is a new contract. It must therefore be based on the essential ingredients of a contract, which are offer, acceptance, and consideration, as well as the ancillary requirements of competency of the parties, lawful purpose, and clarity of terms and conditions. From the government's point of view, all of these are secondary in importance to the primary concern of price. This will be based on the considerations of the original contract, and from your point of view, it must be fair.

A contract may be modified only when it is found to be in the best interests of the government. Therefore, if the supplemental agreement either lessens your original obligation or in any way improves your bargain, the government must receive something called beneficial consideration. For example, your request for a time extension is, in effect, a request to improve your original bargain with the government. Before the contracting officer may consider this request, he or she must first determine whether or not it is in the best interests of the government. If it is decided that the extension is feasible, the contracting officer must then find out what you are prepared to offer the government by way of beneficial consideration.

Whatever you offer must cost you a legal detriment, and this in turn must benefit the government. In other words, the government must acquire some new right (consideration) that was not provided for in the original contract. If you want to refresh your memory on these concepts, they are explained in detail in Chapter 12.

Examples of consideration that the government would consider beneficial are as follows:

1. price reduction
2. better end product
3. additional quantities, if a need exists
4. release or partial release of a pending claim
5. change of an F.O.B. point from origin to destination
6. the catchall statement of anything else that would be of benefit to the government

With regard to item 5, the government is not permitted to use this as a club to beat the contractor into releasing a claim.

If, for any reason, the government fails to obtain a beneficial consideration for a supplemental agreement, the GAO will probably be able to either block payment or obtain recovery if payment has already been made. This ability is founded on the rule that the contracting officer may not waive a vested right of the government without beneficial consideration. Your action in so doing is not binding on the government because the contracting officer acted outside of the scope of his or her authority.

Lastly, the supplemental agreement may not be used to purchase additional items in order to avoid the use of additional formal advertising. In addition, if the supplemental agreement will make any substantive change in a construction contract, consent of surety is required.

There are other ways to change a contract:

1. Public Law 85–804
2. constructive change
3. stop work order
4. suspension of work
5. extra clauses in a supply contract

These and many of the points discussed above will be covered in greater detail as we progress through this chapter. Public Law 85–804, however, will be covered in greater detail in Chapter 17.

HOW TO AVOID MAKING UNAUTHORIZED CHANGES

A change being authorized by the contracting officer or his or her duly authorized representative. The courts have defined the contracting officer as the person who effects changes under the changes clause. The definition as set forth in the supply contract reads:

> The term contracting officer names the person executing this contract in behalf of the government and any other officer or civilian employee who is a properly designated contracting officer, and the term includes except as otherwise provided in this contract, the authorized representative of a contracting officer acting within the limits of his authority.

Warning: Not every government officer and employee who appears either at your plant or on the construction site is an authorized representative of the contracting officer, and a person able to make changes. Be wary of overly zealous engineers and inspectors.

What should you do if you find out that you've made an agreement with an unauthorized person? As soon as possible, discuss the matter with the contracting officer, and seek ratification of the agreement or change. The smart contractor, however, would never get into this situation. *Play it safe*: Talk with the contracting officer first before executing any changes not emanating from his or her office.

HOW TO INTERPRET—AND ACT ON—A CONTRACT'S CHANGES CLAUSE

The authority for the government to modify its contracts is contained in the contract's changes clause. There are several variations of this clause, and each must be interpreted within its own meaning; however, typical initial wording of the clause will start off as follows:

> The contracting officer may, at any time, by a written order, and without notice to sureties, make changes, within the general scope of the contract, in any one or more of the following: . . .(and) if any such change causes an increase or decrease in the cost of, or the time required for, the performance of any part of the work...the contracting officer shall make an equitable adjustment in the contract price...(and) the contractor shall maintain separate accounts of all costs of work,... both changed and not changed...(and) the contractor shall diligently

> continue performance of this contract to the maximum extent possible in accordance with its terms...(and) failure to agree to any adjustment shall be a dispute under the disputes clause...

Let's look at the key phrases given in this typical changes clause more closely.

Oral Versus Written Changes

It is risky to proceed with an oral change because, in a 1913 court decision, the court decided that an oral change, although emanating from the contracting officer, could not be recovered against because either the new or extra work was not agreed on as set out in the contract. The requirement that the change be made by the *written order* of the contracting officer was considered essential. However, in a 1943 court decision, it was found that performance of work without a written change order gave rise to an implied contract to pay when the government received the benefit of the work, and when the change was performed at the oral direction of a responsible officer. A similar decision was rendered in a case where the change order by an authorized representative was overruled by the responsible officer after the work was completed. It was held that the work should be paid for on the grounds that an implied in fact contract existed. In effect, the 1913 decision had been overturned.

In certain cases, the administrative appeals boards have decided that the contracting officer had in fact issued a change order, and that not putting it down in writing was an administrative error that could be corrected. These boards have also said that they will regard as done that which should have been done. This can give an oral order the effect of the written order. This is sometimes referred to as the "constructive changes doctrine," and more will be discussed on this topic shortly.

Tip: From the prudent contractor point of view, it is probably a wise choice to "get it in writing" before working on a change. Although an oral change may be acceptable, it could lead to much wasted time proving that the change was indeed issued. If the press of time makes the short delay required for a written change to be received intolerable, then you're doing something wrong!

Surety Requirements

"Without notice to surety" means that the bondsman has waived notice to the changes. The wording is there in order to retain the full obligation of the surety. Consent of surety, however, is required for supplementary agreements if the modification changes the contract price upward or downward by more than a certain amount or percent, as specified in the contract.

Contract Scope

The meaning of the phrase "make changes if within the general scope of the contract" is defined by the Supreme Court as what was "fairly and reasonably within contemplation of the parties when the contract was entered into." The determination of what was contemplated by the parties is at best a difficult situation. Much depends on the circumstances of the individual contract. A change involving a relatively high increase in cost may still be well within contract scope.

If the change order is written within the scope of the contract, it is a change contemplated by the parties, and thus binding on the government and the contractor. If the change is not within the original scope of the contract, however, it represents extra work that the contractor can legally decline to perform.

Keep in mind: If the work is beyond the scope of the original contract, make sure funds are available for the extra work. Remember that one of the tests of a valid contract is the availability of funds. Get all confirmation in writing.

The magnitude and quality of the change rather than the number of changes made, is more of a determinant in deciding whether or not the change falls within contract scope. By way of simple example, the addition of new units to a construction contract would be considered outside the scope of the original contract. If the change is neither a supplemental agreement nor a change order, then it falls into the category of a new acquisition.

As you can see, much needs to be considered in determining whether or not a change is within the original scope of the contract. What was "reasonably contemplated" is the best test, but the courts are likely to ask if it is a "cardinal change." If the change is of great magnitude, it will then be ruled as a new acquisition.

For example, a contract called for a vinyl tile floor in two rooms of a building. Later, the decision was made to carpet the office. Should the contracting officer use a change order or supplemental agreement, or is the change entirely outside the contract scope? If you decided that the work was outside the scope of the contract, you were wrong! In this case a supplemental agreement is the best selection. But interestingly enough, if you, the contractor, did not have the means of installing the carpeting within your capability, the change cannot be forced on you by the contracting officer.

As another example, the specifications for a building in a construction contract omitted the requirement for a large hangar type door for a loading dock. Later, the specifications were changed to include the door. This situation clearly illustrates a new acquisition. In addition, a further change adding fire escapes to the building was a new acquisition.

You must submit claims for changes on a timely basis. The reason for this is twofold:

- First, if the claim is very late, and it comes as a surprise to the government, the claim may be referred to one of the administrative boards, and payment could be delayed.
- Second, the lateness in filing the claim could be construed as prejudicial or harmful to the government, and again payment could be delayed.

As a rule of thumb, submit all claims as promptly as possible, but never more than 30 days after the change. Usually the 30-day time limit is specified in the changes clause. This may be extended by the government if necessary. Needless to say, all requests for adjustment should be submitted prior to final contract settlement.

Cause and Effect

Causation means what has caused the change to be brought about. Implied in the word is the meaning ''cause and effect.'' In order to be entitled to equitable relief, you must establish that your increased costs were caused by the changes, not by something else.

Equitable Adjustment

Equitable adjustment normally includes the actual added direct cost to the extent that it is reasonable, the applicable overhead or indirect cost, and a fair profit. What constitutes a fair profit is an open question, for there is very little basis for prescribing an exact formula.

If a change is of a relatively small dollar amount, and it is for the same kind of work contained in the basic contract, the government will use a method called the ''weighted guidelines'' method of computing the amount of the adjustment. This will generally result in a profit margin similar to the one in the original contract. In other words, the basic profit rate is applied to the change.

In a situation where the change calls for a different kind of work, the government will then do a detailed analysis in order to determine what is appropriate. Additionally, this same analysis will be made of overhead expenses. An analysis will also be performed if the cost of the change is large in relation to the cost of the original contract.

There is a rule handed down by the court, known as the Bruce Case Rule, which states that the proper measure of the value of an equitable adjustment is the contractor's cost, reasonably incurred. This means that the government will reimburse you for only those costs associated with the change. A contract change, then, does not represent an opportunity for you to gain extra profit. This is both simple and broad in scope. What it does is strike a compromise between the reasonable and specific costs concepts. The rule gives weight to the objective standard in that costs must be reasonably incurred, but it does not otherwise set aside the contractor's actual costs. As a result, you must exercise close control of all costs associated with a contract change. There is no *carte blanche*. This rule is the prevailing rule now being used by the courts and appeal boards.

Changed Versus Unchanged Work

The changes clause provides that the effect on unchanged work may be taken into consideration in arriving at an equitable adjustment. This is sometimes referred to as the "ripple effect" or "impact costs." This is based on recognition that a change will usually have both a cost and schedule effect on the work that has been changed and the balance of the work under the contract.

The work not changed may be affected by the need to make extensive revisions in plant scheduling of equipment, or there may be disruption in the flow of materials. Associated delays in your overall efficiency may result, and the contracting officer is obliged to take all of these effects into account when working out an equitable adjustment. Of course, it is your responsibility to substantiate the impact costs associated with the change. The contracting officer will not do this for you, and don't be ashamed to submit even the most trivial costs.

Duty to Proceed

After receipt of a change, you are legally required by the contract to proceed with the work as changed, and to work out the problem of compensation later. This is true regardless of how long the change will take, or how difficult the change will be. The government has the right to terminate the contract for default if you do not proceed with legal contract changes. One tough part about the effect of changes is that you will have to finance the change until equitable adjustment can be worked out. Government contracting on the larger scale is not for those who are either short of cash or who don't have a friendly banker knowledgeable about the ins and outs of government contracting.

Failure to Agree

What happens when you, the contractor, cannot arrive at an equitable compensation figure for the change? When the contractor and government cannot reach agreement, it is treated as a "question of fact," and the contractor must process his appeal through the disputes clause contained within his respective contract. Refer to the specific wording of the clause in your contract in order to be certain that you are following the correct procedure. Disputes and protests will be covered in detail in Chapter 17.

CONSTRUCTIVE OR IMPLIED CHANGES

The word "constructive" is derived from the word "construe," meaning to interpret. A constructive change is made based on either some action, or lack of action, on the part of the government, and it applies to all government contracts. The theory of constructive change is often used to allow administrative settlement of cases involving defective or impossible specifications, and for acceleration of performance situations, where you encounter excusable delays known to the government, but for which the government refuses to extend the performance time. The normal time period of 30 days, unless extended by the government, for the assertion of claims resulting from a change does not apply to constructive changes on supply contracts. The requirement here is that the claim be asserted only within a reasonable time period.

A constructive change, by its nature, is an informal change. A formal change would be made in accordance with the changes clause. The constructive change falls into the gray area between change orders and supplemental agreements. As you remember, the contracting officer, under the changes clause, has the unilateral right to make any change within the scope of the contract. Supplemental agreements may be used if you are willing to agree to the change. Constructive changes are those that come about in none of these two ways.

How the Supreme Court Defines a Constructive Change

The Supreme Court has clearly stated what constitutes a constructive change: "It is an informal request for additional work or services caused by some act or omission to act on the part of the government that causes the contractor extra work, delay, money..."

An example would be a contracting officer who sends his agent to order the contractor to stop burning trash because of complaints from the surrounding community that are addressed to the base commander. When the contractor submits his or her claim for the additional cost of hauling the trash away, the contracting officer refuses to pay. The contractor files suit, and the court allows recovery of the added cost on the grounds that the banning of the burning amounted to a limitation of work methods; that is, a constructive change.

If you look at the Supreme Court's definition of constructive change, you find that all of the elements have been met in our example just given. The request by the contracting officer, via his messenger, amounted to "an informal request." A change order was neither issued, nor was a supplemental agreement entered into. The requirement "for additional work or services" was certainly met when the contractor had to hire extra men and trucks and haul the debris several miles to the dump. That part of the definition reading "caused by some act or omission to act on the part of the government" was met by the request that the burning on base be stopped. Finally it is clear that the change caused the contractor "extra work, delay, [and] money..."

How the Law of Equity Applies to Government Contracting

The theory of constructive change is based on the law of equity. Essentially this means doing what is fair and just under given circumstances. Under the U.S. court system, the judge must first hear and decide the legal issues. If the ruling shocks the court's conscience, then the judge can use the equitable powers with which he or she is vested and overrule the decision based on law.

For example, let's look at a hypothetical case where a salesman approaches your great-grandmother, who is 92 years old, and convinces her to sign a contract for 15 years' worth of dance lessons for $15,000. Later, after you have a conversation with great-grandmother on the subject, she realizes that she perhaps has made a foolish mistake, and she refuses to pay the money.

The dance studio sues, and wins the case on the legal ground that a valid contract was entered into. It may have been a foolish contract, but it is still a valid one. However, this decision shocks the court's conscience, so the judge removes his legal hat and puts on the equitable one. Because great-grandmother has a poor chance of reaching age 107, and an even poorer chance of using dancing lessons at that age, the dance studio is forbidden to exercise its legal right to collect the $15,000. Whether or not to invoke vested equitable powers is the judge's choice.

If great-grandmother had signed a two-year legal contract for only $2,000, then the judge would probably let stand the legal decision; that is: ''you must dance because you have a contract.''

Any conduct by the contracting officer or other government representative that has the effect of requiring the contractor to perform additional work can, under the right circumstances, be considered a constructive change order. The mention of constructive change to an overly zealous government employee can do wonders in getting things back on track.

Often, constructive changes are letters, telegrams, and other documents written by government people other than the contracting officer. Not infrequently, letters are written by engineers and technicians who have no idea that they are issuing a change order. Here are actual examples that were held to be constructive changes.

Example 1: Improper Action. Two supervisory engineers at an Air Force base told the contractor to make some changes in the contract drawings. The engineers were not contracting officers, and they had no authority to issue change orders. Nonetheless, the contractor obeyed their instructions and changed the drawings. This resulted in costly extra work, for which the contractor sought an equitable adjustment. The Board of Contract Appeals awarded an equitable adjustment, stating that the engineer's orders to the contractor constituted a constructive change to the contract, since the changes forced the contractor to do extra work beyond that called. The order was imputed (attributed) to the contracting officer, because it was decided that he either knew, or should have known, about them.

Example 2: Lack of Action. In another example the contract called for the contractor to write some technical manuals based on data provided by the government. As it turned out, the government failed to provide some of the data, and furnished other data that was incomplete, inapplicable, or inaccurate. The engineer in charge of the project directed the contractor to do work necessary to make the data adequate. The contract expressly said that the engineer did not have the authority to order changes. Despite this, the Board of Contract Appeals held that the engineer's order did in fact constitute a constructive change to the contract. Hence, the contractor was entitled to an equitable adjustment.

The board noted that the engineer had been permitted to make changes and was not rebuffed by the contracting officer. The contracting officer's lack of action was construed to mean approval of the engineer's orders. This amounted to a constructive change order coming from the contracting officer.

The Board of Contract Appeals will tend to find a way to pay the contractor whenever the need to spend extra money results from the action and/or lack of action by a government official.

Six Reasons for Initiating Constructive Change Orders

Constructive change orders can arise in many ways. Here are six examples:

1. Acceleration: If you encounter an excusable delay entitling you to a time extension (another form of equitable adjustment), and the government either fails or refuses to grant a time extension, which results in your being required to perform within the original performance period, then a constructive change order to accelerate performance takes place. You are entitled to an extension of both immediate schedules and overall completion date.

2. Defective Specifications: If a contract contains design specifications, there is an implied warranty that, if the specifications are followed, the item will meet contract performance. Constructive change results if these specifications either prove to be defective or incomplete, or if they impose impossible requirements.

3. Government-Furnished Property: If the contract requires the government to furnish certain property or information, and one or the other proves to be defective, you are able to recover either under the government-furnished property clause, or under the changes clause on the basis of a constructive change. A constructive change has been held to result from the furnishing by the government of a defective model, erroneous drawings, defective patterns, erroneous data or information, and erroneously marked parts.

As an example, a contractor was required to produce wind measuring equipment in accordance with a performance specification and a government-furnished model. The contract stated that, in the event of conflict between the specification and the model, performance requirements would govern over the model.

During contract negotiations, the contractor was told by a government engineer that the model would meet specification requirements. When the contractor manufactured the set according to the model, it failed to meet the performance specification.

Upon appeal, the board said that the model was equivalent to a design specification. It was therefore held that, when the government specifies the design to be followed and also specifies performance requirements, the contractor is entitled to relief if design will not meet performance requirements.

4. Method of Work: If the contract permits you freedom of choice between various methods of doing the work, and the government later insists that the more expensive way of doing the job be used, then a constructive change results. In addition, if government action results in you having to alter the planned sequence of performance, it is a constructive change.

5. Interpretation of the Specifications: If the government interprets the specifications one way and you interpret them another way, and it turns out that the government was in error, then a constructive change results.

This would occur most likely in the case where the government underestimated the effort required to bring about an acceptable end item, while you insisted that it couldn't be done that way, but it was mandated that the government approach be used.

If the government interprets the specifications one way, and then later changes that interpretation, a constructive change results. According to the board, ''a change in the interpretation of the meaning of a contract provision is equivalent to a change in the provision itself.''

6. Rejection and Rework: If the government unjustifiably rejects your work, requiring you to perform rework of the acceptable item, then a constructive change results.

Other actions by the government that have been held to constitute constructive change include requiring the contractor to perform excessive or repetitive testing, changing the time and manner of inspection, tests, or quality control, and requiring the contractor to meet a standard of performance higher than that required by the contract. If no particular standard is prescribed, the minimum acceptable standard of the industry applies. Additionally, the ordering of the use of substitute materials, making an ''irresistible suggestion'' concerning the direction a contractor's efforts should take, and government-ordered changes to drawings, designs, and plans that have already been submitted and approved by the government are constructive changes.

A constructive change can have many faces, and the problem of identifying them is crucial to obtaining equitable adjustment. Since events leading to constructive change can seem benign in character, it is essential that you and all your key personnel become sensitive to what can often be obscure events leading to constructive change. This would be especially true with regard to your engineering staff, who are usually in the best position to spot constructive change in even the slightest alteration of technical requirements.

The government is very sensitive to the impact of constructive changes, not only from the cost point of view, but also from the point of maintaining a cohesive project effort. This is impossible if anybody is permitted to voice an opinion on what either he or she thinks is the best way to proceed. Remember, the contracting office is the final authority for issuing changes. If a government employee suggests that he or she has a better way of doing something, or suggests something that doesn't sound as if it were originally agreed to in either the contract or specifications, then the best policy is to request that the suggestion, which may be quite valid, be authorized through the contracting officer's office.

The chances of getting equitable adjustment for constructive change has proven to be excellent. However, the time lost in letters and appeals makes the effort extremely costly, so it's best to stick to the principle of ''getting it in writing'' in all situations.

INDEX - CHAPTER 16

17

HOW TO HANDLE CONTRACT DISPUTES AND PROTESTS

Most contracts are completed as planned. Unfortunately, disagreements do arise from time to time. The majority of these disputes do not come about by reason of bad faith on the part of the contractor or the government. They arise out of the normal performance of the work by the contractor, plus many other reasons, and are unavoidable in all cases regardless of how carefully a contract is written, how carefully a contract is administered, or how carefully a contractor performs. They may also occur prior to contract award.

Under commercial work, the contractor might either refuse to continue with the work until the matter is settled, or pursue the option of suit against the other party for not fulfilling his or her bargain. If these remedies were used in government contracting, essential work could be crippled over extended periods of time. One way of avoiding this situation is through the contract's disputes clause. Decisions are reached based on hearings before an administrative board. This is the most widely used procedure when disputes cannot be settled amicably between the contractor and the contracting officer.

Other remedies available include a request for relief from the General Accounting Office (GAO), a suit in the U.S. Court of Claims, a request for relief under Public Law 85–804, and the request for relief in the form of a private bill through Congress. Let's take a detailed look at disputes and protests, and some of the ways to reach their resolution.

HOW TO SUBMIT A FORMAL PROTEST

A protest is defined as a written objection by an interested party to a solicitation for the proposed acquisition of either goods or services, or to a proposed award or actual award of a contract. Contracting officers are required to consider all protests, whether or not they are submitted before or after award, and whether or not they were filed with the procuring agency, the GAO, or the General Services Board of Contract Appeals (GSBCA). Appeals to the GSBCA are normally made with regard to automatic data processing acquisitions. In all appeals cases, the protestor is required to be notified in writing of the final decision on the protest.

Protesting Size Standards

An offeror and any other interested party may protest the small business representation of an offeror in a specific offer. For example, at any time after the offers are opened, a contracting officer may question the small business representation of any offeror by filing a contracting officer's protest. This protest, and any other protest filed by any other interested party, such as a competing bidder, is required to be forwarded to the SBA regional office on a timely basis. The protest must describe the basis of the complaint with specific, detailed evidence in support of the allegation that the offeror is not a small business.

In order for the protest to be timely, it must be received at the SBA regional office by the close of the fifth business day after opening the sealed bids. Under negotiated acquisitions, it must be received by the fifth business day after receipt of the special notification from the contracting officer identifying the apparently successful offeror.

Oral protests may also be made. However they must be confirmed in writing within the five-day period, with the letter postmarked no later than one day after the oral protest is voiced.

Written protests may be delivered to the contracting officer by hand, telegram, or letter postmarked within the five-day period. A protest under a multiple award schedule will be timely if received by the SBA at any time prior to the expiration of the contract period, including renewals.

The appropriate action by the SBA after receipt of a protest is to furnish, by certified mail to the protested firm, a copy of the protest and an application for *Small Business Determination*, SBA Form 355.

The challenged offeror must file the form with the SBA within three business days, including a statement answering the allegations in the protest and the appropriate supporting evidence. The final determination is made by the SBA within ten business days.

Meanwhile, the contracting officer is not permitted to make an award decision until either the SBA determination is received, or until the ten-day response time required of the SBA lapses. This procedure may be overridden by the contracting officer when he or she determines, in writing, that the delay of the award is not in the public interest. It is optional with the contracting officer, in the absence of any adverse information, to extend the ten-day period if it is not disadvantageous to the government.

Appeal of any SBA size determination may be filed when either a protest has been denied, or the SBA decision has adversely affected the protestor. These appeals must be filed with the Office of Hearings and Appeals, Small Business Administration, Washington, DC 20416.

Protesting Eligibility Under the Walsh-Healey Act

Protests of eligibility under the Walsh-Healey Public Contracts Act have a longer interval of applicability than protests for size standards. If a protest is made prior to award, the contracting officer will notify the apparently successful offeror of the protest, and inform the protestor and the offeror that evidence concerning the matter must be submitted to the contracting officer within ten working days. Additionally, the other offerors who may become eligible for award will be notified of the protest, requesting them to extend their offers, if necessary. If the contracting officer's determination is disputed by either party, the case will be referred to the Department of Labor if a large business is involved, and to the SBA if a small business is involved.

The contracting officer may take decisive action, awarding the contract immediately if the required items are urgently needed, and delays in either delivery or performance will result in substantial hardship to the government. In this situation, full documentation by the contracting officer is required.

If the eligibility protest under the Walsh-Healey Act is received by the contracting officer after contract award, but before final completion, it will be handled as if it were a protest received prior to award. If the contract has been completed prior to the receipt of the protest, the contracting officer will inform the protestor that no action will be taken.

In cases where the offeror did not act in good faith in representing that it was a regular dealer or manufacturer of the supplies offered, the contracting officer may immediately terminate the contract, make open market purchases, or enter into new contracts for completing the original contract, and charge any additional cost incurred to the original contractor.

Protesting Solicitations and Awards

When protests against an agency solicitation for supplies or services, or objections to proposed or actual contract awards are filed, the protesting party is encouraged to seek resolution within the agency before filing protests with the GAO or the GSBCA. When a protest is filed only with an agency, an award cannot be made until the matter is resolved, or until it is determined that the protest should be countermanded because of urgency of need or performance, or that prompt award is advantageous to the government. The same notification procedures as applicable to Walsh-Healey type protests will be followed when the protest is received prior to award. If the protest is received after award, the contracting officer need not suspend contract performance or terminate the contract unless it appears that the award may be invalidated and delay in performance is not prejudicial to the government's interest. In this event, the contracting officer will seek a mutual agreement with the contractor to suspend performance on a no-cost basis.

Protesting to the GAO

Protests to the GAO require that the protestor furnish a copy of his or her complete protest as specified in the solicitation. In the absence of this information, it should be submitted through the contracting officer no later than one day after the protest is filed with the GAO. Failure to supply this information may result in dismissal of the protest. Any protest, whether or not it is pre- or postaward, will require the GAO to prepare a report covering all of the relevant aspects of the protest, and to advise all parties, including offerors, who may be affected by the protest. This report will be supported by an ancillary report prepared by the contracting officer covering all of the facts of the case.

Protests filed directly with the GAO before award prohibit contract award unless the head of the agency finds urgent and compelling circumstances that will significantly affect the interests of the United States, and these do not permit waiting for the GAO decision. Likewise, this decision can be made if it appears that the protest lacks merit, and the award will be made as originally determined within 30 days.

Postaward protests require the contracting agency to either suspend performance or terminate the contract, unless the usual conditions of urgency and need prevail, when protests are received from the GAO within ten working days after award. Again, a no-cost termination will be the desired objective of the government. If the notice of protest is received after the ten-day period, there will be no requirement for the contracting officer to terminate or suspend unless he or she believes that the award may be invalidated, and the delay in receiving the supplies will not be prejudicial to the government.

The GAO may declare an appropriate interested party to be entitled to the costs of filing and pursuing the protest, including any reasonable attorney's fees, and the cost of bid and proposal preparation.

Protesting to the GBSCA

Protests to the GBSCA may be made by any interested party regarding an ADP acquisition conducted under Section 111 of the Federal Property and Administrative Services Act (40 U.S.C. 759). ADP acquisitions not covered under this statute may not be heard by the GBSCA, so check your status before filing. If not covered by the statute, the protest will be heard by the agency, the courts, or the GAO. Filing with the GBSCA requires that a copy of the protest be submitted simultaneously to the official and location designated in the solicitation, as well as to the contracting officer if this information is not included. Any request for a hearing on either a suspension of procurement or on the merits of the procurement must be contained in the protest.

The agency will, within one working day after receipt of the protest, give either oral or written notice of the protest to all parties who responded to the solicitation. If the solicitation has closed, notice will be given only to those who have submitted a sealed bid or offer. Written follow-up in confirmation of the notice and a listing of all persons and agencies receiving notice must be given to the board by the agency within five working days after receipt of the protest.

The GBSCA will establish a file containing all of the pertinent information on the case within ten working days after the filing of the protest, and within five days after that it will submit its answer setting forth its defenses to the protest and its findings, actions, and recommendations in the matter. If the protest contains a timely request for suspension of the procurement, a hearing will be conducted within ten days and suspension will be instituted unless there are urgent and compelling circumstances making suspension unwise, or regardless of circumstances, the award will be made within the next 30 calendar days. This latter situation requires a *Determination and Finding* (D&F) executed by either the agency head or designee. The GBSCA may also declare an interested party eligible for filing and pursuit costs and reasonable attorney's fees, in addition to bid and proposal preparation costs.

DISPUTES AND APPEALS: GUIDELINES FOR ASSERTING AND RESOLVING CLAIMS

The Contract Disputes Act of 1978 (41 U.S.C. 601–613) establishes procedures and requirements for asserting and resolving claims by or against contractors arising out of contracts subject to the act. In addition, the act requires payment of interest on contractor claims, certification of contractor claims in excess of $50,000, and a civil penalty for either fraudulent contractor claims or claims based on misrepresentation of fact. A misrepresentation of fact is considered to be a false statement, as is any other conduct that is designed to either deceive or mislead. If the contracting officer suspects fraud, he or she will refer the matter to the agency official responsible for investigating fraud.

Interest is paid on claims found due and unpaid from either the date the contracting officer receives the properly prepared claim or the date payment would otherwise be due. The simple interest rate is set by the Secretary of the Treasury.

What Is—And Is Not—Legally Considered a Claim

A claim is defined as either a written demand or assertion by one of the contracting parties seeking the payment of money, the adjustment or interpretation of contract terms, or other relief arising either under a contract or relating to the contract. A claim arising under a contract, unlike a claim relating to a contract, can be resolved under a contract clause that provides for the relief sought by the claimant. However, either a written demand or written assertion by the contractor seeking the payment of any money exceeding the sum of $50,000 is not a claim under the Contract Disputes Act until certified. This certification must state that the claim is made in good faith, that the supporting data are accurate and complete to the best of the contractor's knowledge and belief, and that the amount requested accurately reflects the contract adjustment for which the contractor feels that the government is liable. A voucher, invoice, or routine request for a payment due, which is not in dispute when submitted, cannot be considered a claim.

The disputes clause recognizes the "all disputes" authority established by the act, and states certain requirements and limitations of the act for the guidance of contractors and contracting agencies. The clause is not intended to affect the rights and obligations of the parties, or to constrain the authority of Boards of Contract Appeals (BCA) in the handling and deciding of contractor appeals under the act.

The policy is to try to resolve all contractual issues by mutual agreement at the contracting officer's level, without litigation. Where appropriate, and as an aid in resolving the differences, the contracting officer will attempt to set up informal discussions between other individuals who have not substantially participated in the dispute. This could mean any person even remotely concerned, such as employees, suppliers, subcontractors, and other government employees. The object is to get the facts, and all approved methods will be followed.

Time-Frame for the Final Disposition

When a claim by or against a contractor cannot be satisfied or settled by mutual agreement, and a decision on a claim is necessary, the contracting officer is required to seek assistance from other advisors, usually legal, and prepare a final disposition based on the facts of the case and his or her own independent judgment. If the claim is under $50,000, the final disposition is required to be furnished within 60 days after receipt of the contractor's request. If the claim is over this amount, and the decision cannot be reached within 60 days, then the date on which it will be issued must be stated by the contracting officer.

How the Appeals Process Works

The contractor has the right to appeal this decision to the BCA. However, the contractor must continue contract performance during this appeal period. The appeal must be filed within a reasonable time period. Not to do so within a maximum of 90 days may be considered untimely. Filing the appeal by registered or certified mail, return receipt requested, will stop the running of the clock. Normally, the contracting officer is required to forward the appeal to the BCA within ten working days of its receipt. Within 30 days the contracting officer must compile and submit to the board all documents pertaining to the case, including the findings of the original decision, the correspondence between the parties, and transcripts of any testimony that was taken. Copies of these documents will also be forwarded to the contractor in order to give him or her the opportunity to make any supplements deemed necessary.

If the contractor is successful on appeal, he or she must then contact the contracting officer requesting that a supplemental agreement be entered into. This will be forwarded to the finance officer, who will then make payment to the contractor. The supplemental agreement is used to release the claim and to prevent any future litigation.

Disputes Involving National Defense Contracts

Public Law 85–804 and its amendments, along with Executive Order 10789 of November 14, 1958, covers disputes involving national defense contracts. Under this law, extraordinary action is allowed with regard to amending and modifying contracts without regard to other provisions of the law. However, the President must determine that this action will facilitate the national defense. The Executive Order expands coverage of the law by authorizing the heads of all of the major departments and agencies of the government to exercise the authority conferred by the act. Since the powers of the act are so extraordinary, it is required that an annual report on actions taken on requests for relief, including indemnity, be made to Congress by March 15 of each year.

Under the act, an agency may establish a contract adjustment board having the authority to approve, authorize, and direct the appropriate action, and to make the appropriate determinations and findings. The decisions of these boards are not subject to appeal; however, a board may reconsider and modify, correct, or reverse its previous decision.

Under the act it is not permitted to provide for other than open competition, the waiver of a bond, or other illegal contractual arrangements. It is also not permitted to make either any contract amendment or modification unless it is found by the approving authority that it will aid national defense, that it is within the limits of the amounts appropriated, that it is necessary because of inadequate legal authority within an agency, or that it will obligate the government for any amount over $25 million.

HOW TO MODIFY A CONTRACT DUE TO A MISTAKE

A contract may not be modified or amended unless you, the contractor, submit a request before all obligations, including final payment under the contract, have been discharged. Generally, under negotiated contracts, an increase in the contract price to an amount higher than the lowest rejected bid of a responsible bidder is allowed.

Informal commitments cannot be formalized unless you submit a written request for payment within six months of furnishing, or arranging to furnish, supplies or services in reliance upon that commitment. The approving authority must also find that, at the time of the commitment, it was impractical to use normal contracting procedures. For example, in the course of performing a contract, a government official may have orally requested that certain supplies be furnished, and this was not done in connection with the existing contract. This would constitute a mistake, and mistakes obligating the government for over $1,000 cannot be corrected unless the contracting officer receives notice of the mistake before final payment. The correction of a mistake cannot raise the contract price above that of the next lowest responsible bidder.

Other examples of mistakes and ambiguities consist of the failure to express, in the contract, the agreement as both parties understood it. A mistake would also exist if it was so obvious that it either was, or should have been, apparent to the contracting officer. A mistake can also consist of a mutual misunderstanding about a material fact.

Remember: No amendment, traditionally, can be made without additional consideration flowing to the government.

Your requests, normally in the form of a letter, will include as a minimum the precise adjustment requested, the essential facts, summarized chronologically in narrative form, and your conclusions based on these facts. It should also be stated if any proceeds from the request will be assigned or transferred in any way, and to whom. If relief through the GAO or any other part of the government has been or will be sought, it should be so stated in the request.

Keep in mind: Either modification or amendment to correct mistakes is under the jurisdiction of the contracting officer, and relief is available under the disputes clause. This is probably the best route to follow initially when a mistake occurs.

RELIEF THROUGH PRIVATE BILL BY CONGRESS

An essential difference exists between the relief made possible by Public Law 85–804 and any action under the disputes clause. The disputes clause provides for settlement of disagreements having to do with the contract as written. Public Law 85–804 offers relief outside of the contract.

When all else fails, the contractor may seek relief by attempting passage of a private bill by Congress. Under this procedure, you seek out your Congressman and request passage of an appropriate bill. This bill may appropriate an amount in full satisfaction of your claim, direct the court of claims to take jurisdiction over the case, or direct the Comptroller General to settle and adjust the claim.

WHAT TO EXPECT FROM THE BOARDS OF CONTRACT APPEALS

The Department of Defense and the respective armed service secretaries have established the Armed Services Board of Contract Appeals. The Department of Energy; the Commodity Credit Corporation; the Veterans Administration; the General Services Administration; the Coast Guard; the Departments of Agriculture, Commerce, Transportation, and Interior; the National Aeronautics and Space Administration; the Postal Service; and the Federal Aviation Administration have similarly established contract appeals boards. The purpose of these boards is to provide a forum of equity in the hearing of appeals, under the disputes clauses, arising from contract performance.

The authority of these boards arises solely from the standard disputes clause. This clause provides for an appeal of the decision by the contracting officer on any contractual matter. The appeal may be made to the secretary or to the head of the contracting agency, as well as to the authorized representative. The various secretaries and heads of these agencies have delegated their decision making authority to these boards, which constitute their authorized representatives. They are therefore vested with the authority granted their secretaries by the contracts. The delegation of authority to the Armed Services Board of Contract Appeals is contained in a charter that defines the rules of procedures pertaining not only to this organization, but to other executive department and agency boards as well.

Each agency board has jurisdiction to decide any appeal, ranging from a decision by a contracting officer applicable to that officer's own agency, and any other agency when the primary agency's board so designates. In exercising this jurisdiction, the agency board is authorized to grant any relief that would be available to a litigant asserting a contract claim in the Court of Claims. At one time the boards were unable to grant relief based upon questions of law. Now they are authorized to do so, and this represents a major advantage to you, the contractor. A decision can now be reached substantially sooner than in the court, permitting all parties to get back to the business at hand as quickly as possible.

Agency boards provide, to the fullest practical extent, an informal, speedy, and inexpensive solution to disputes. They take prompt action on each appeal submitted, and issue their decision in writing, which is available to all concerned parties.

The decision of the board is final on any questions of fact unless it can be proven that the decision is fraudulent, capricious, arbitrary, so grossly erroneous as to imply bad faith, or unsupported by substantial evidence. Agency decisions based on questions of law are not considered conclusive. They may be appealed and heard in the U.S. Court of Claims.

The ability of the various boards to hear and review decisions of contracting officers is based solely upon the inclusion of a disputes clause in a government contract. In the absence of this clause, the board is without jurisdiction to hear a dispute.

One additional jurisdiction requirement is that there must actually be a case to hear and decide upon. Neither a moot question nor a mere academic discussion will vest the administrative board with jurisdiction.

Since the boards have jurisdiction by contract and not by statutory enactment, the procedural operations of the boards are not subject to the Administrative Procedures Act, which qualifies the procedural requirements for federal hearing boards.

Contractor's Appeal Checklist

An appeal before a board is similar to a civil case held without a jury. While not bound by formal rules of procedure as are the courts, the boards have formulated rules that must be followed on any appeal. These are designed to give you a just and speedy form for your appeal. The process is as follows:

1. The contractor files a notice of appeal with the board.
2. The board sends a copy of the rules and procedures to the contractor.
3. The appeals board dockets the case.
4. Within 30 days of docketing the appeal, the contractor must file a complaint. In this complaint, the contractor is required only to use simple language.
5. An answer to the complaint is filed by either the contracting officer or other government representative within 60 days of receipt of the complaint by the board.
6. A hearing is held, which is like a civil trial without a jury.
7. Transcripts of all hearings before the board are required under the standards of due process.
8. Briefs are submitted by both parties to the appeal.
9. The board renders its decision based upon the appeal file and the testimony of witnesses.
10. Within 30 days of decision, either party may file a motion for reconsideration.

In summary, the documents submitted to the board by both sides constitute the appeal file. It is open to examination by the parties. They have the right to amend their complaint or answer at any time, subject to the board's discretion. Provision is made for the taking of depositions of witnesses by either side. The board may also ask the parties to appear at prehearing conferences in order to simplify the issues.

HOW TO SUE THE U.S. GOVERNMENT ON A CONTRACT CLAIM

Contractors may sue the government in the federal courts on contract claims. The Tucker Act of 1887 permits the government to be sued upon any contract, whether it be either express or implied in fact. This right has always been separate from, and independent of, the disputes clause.

Legal actions must be filed within the time-frame specified in the statute of limitations, which is six years. The purpose of this statute is to provide equality of treatment between the litigants by assuring that all claims are brought while the necessary witnesses, documents, and other evidence are still available, and memories are still fresh. The same six-year period applies to the government in any claims it may have against a contractor. The statute does not begin to run until the disputes procedure afforded by the contract have been exhausted. There are no statutory time limitations on the filing of claims and appeals with the boards of contract appeal, and final decisions under the disputes clause have no specific time limit.

INDEX - CHAPTER 17

APPENDICES

Appendix A

GOVERNMENT PROCUREMENT PROGRAMS

Federal purchases can be thought of in two broad classes: those for general use and those for special mission-oriented application. All agencies need items for general use, such as office equipment and office space, transportation, janitorial services, telephones, and computers. Many agencies need specialized supplies. Printing plants need ink and paper; the Army, Navy, and Air Force need weapons systems and supporting material; the Forest Service buys firefighting equipment, seeds, fertilizers, and insecticides. An overview of these procurement programs follows. Contact information for further information is listed at the end of this appendix.

MILITARY PROCUREMENT PROGRAMS

There are four basic methods of procurement for the Armed Forces: the individual departmental programs, interdepartmental consolidated purchasing programs, procurement by other government agencies (principally the GSA), and local sources of supply.

The Department of Defense (DOD) integrates policies and procedures and provides unified direction for the three military services (Army, Navy, and Air Force), for the Defense Logistics Agency (DLA), and for other groups.

The office of the Secretary of Defense does not ordinarily contract for procurements. Individual military departments and defense agencies award contracts to supply their respective needs and the combined needs of DOD activities when either a department or an agency is designated as an executive agent.

The Under Secretary of Defense for Research and Engineering is responsible for the development and acquisition of weapons systems, including procurement policy and production planning. The Assistant Secretary of Defense formulates procedures for military supply and related fields. All military departments and the DLA have small business specialists at their major procurement centers. These specialists are available to furnish detailed information on how to do business with the DOD.

U.S. Army Material Command

The Department of the Army, as represented by the U.S. Army Material Command, is responsible for the material functions of the Army, including research and development, product improvement, human factors engineering, testing and evaluation, procurement and production, new equipment training, scientific and technical intelligence production, international logistics programs, storage, distribution, transportation, maintenance, demilitarization, and disposal.

The command consists of a nationwide network of 66 military installations and 250 separate units. It directs subordinate commands, installations, and activities. The development of logistics management services and technical guidance and assistance are also two of its responsibilities.

Naval Material Command

The Department of the Navy requirements are the responsibility of the Naval Material Command. This command has subordinate commands for air, electronics, sea, supply systems, and facilities engineering. It also makes limited procurements for the Marine Corps. The Military Sealift Command contracts for ocean shipping services, including ship chartering and ocean towing, and contracts for the repair of ocean-going ships. The Office of Naval Research contracts for studies in electronics, materials, chemistry, physics, the earth and ocean sciences, biological sciences, and psychological sciences. It also coordinates the research programs of the Navy's technical commands.

The Bureau of Naval Personnel is responsible for personnel research programs, special studies, and recruiting and training services. Procurement for the Bureau of Naval Personnel is handled by Naval Material Command supply activities.

Air Force Logistics Command

The Air Force Logistics Command buys all supplies and services for weapons support and other operations systems. The Air Force Systems Command procures all Air Force systems and makes the initial purchase of related support equipment. It is also responsible for all research and development. In general, all other Air Force commands purchase supplies and services needed to operate Air Force bases. Additionally, the Military Airlift Command procures services to provide airlift and air taxi service, while the Air Training Command procures services for flight training. The Air Force Communications Command operates and maintains ground communication services.

Defense Logistics Agency (DLA)

The Defense Logistics Agency (DLA), formerly the Defense Supply Agency, manages approximately two million general supply items for the military services. Some of the typical items the DLA buys are food, clothing, textiles, medical and dental equipment, industrial and chemical equipment, electrical equipment and electronics, food preparation equipment, construction equipment, automotive equipment and fuel, and petroleum products and services.

There are six DLA supply centers that purchase and manage specific commodities: the Defense Construction Supply Center, the Defense Electronics Supply Center, the Defense Fuel Supply Center, the Defense General Supply Center, the Defense Industrial Supply Center, and the Defense Personnel Support Center.

Management and administration of most defense contracts are consolidated under the DLA through the Defense Contract Administration Services (DCAS) regional offices. These regional offices are also staffed by small and disadvantaged business specialists, who are responsible for arranging subcontracting opportunities with prime contractors. Prime contractors interested in subcontracting should contact the nearest DCAS regional office.

The DLA, through the Defense Property Disposal Service (DPDS), has worldwide responsibility for the disposal of military surplus personal property. DPDS maintains a centralized bidder's mailing list.

CIVILIAN PROCUREMENT PROGRAMS

A large volume of goods and services utilized by civilian agencies and military departments is contracted for by the GSA. The GSA has six major subdivisions: the Automated Data and Telecommunications Service (ADTS), the Public Buildings Service (PBS), the Office of Federal Supply and Services (FSS), the Transportation and Public Utilities Service (TPUS), the Federal Property Resources Service (FPRS), and the National Archives and Records Service (NARS).

Automated Data and Telecommunications Service

Automated Data and Telecommunications Service (ADTS) negotiates ADP/communications schedules for most types of commercially available ADP/ communications equipment. These fixed-price, indefinite quantity schedules are used by federal agencies for the rental, purchase, and maintenance of ADP equipment. These schedule contracts allow the continuation of rental and maintenance and the addition of peripherals and features to existing equipment. This eliminates the expenditure of time and money that normally would be used to purchase by separate contract.

The ADP schedules cover computer systems and on-line peripherals, proprietary software, and accessorial ADP equipment used off-line or in a stand-alone mode. Examples of these are analog instrumentation records, tape cleaners/certifiers, key-to-key preparation equipment, terminals, modems, multiplexers, disk packs, and computer output microfilm equipment.

The communications schedules cover radio, telephone, telemetry, recording/reproducing video equipment, as well as recording and instrumentation tapes.

ADP equipment requirements contracts are awarded by ADTS for a wide variety of items such as disk drives, terminals, and even punch-card machines. The use of requirements contracts must be used when the equipment available will meet the agency's needs. They simplify the agency's procurement procedures and provide savings over commercial rates. Under this program. ADTS awards annual fixed-price indefinite schedule contracts that are mandatory sources for federal agencies. ADTS also negotiates basic agreements with vendors for agencies needing customized services in order to support specific requirements.

ADP service contracts for obtaining systems analysis, programming, data entry, key punch, and computer-output microfilm are awarded nationwide for those federal agencies requiring them. Additionally, contracts for telecommunications transmission facilities with common carriers and the purchase and lease of teletype terminals for data and facsimile transmission are negotiated by this agency. Contracts are also awarded for installation and maintenance services on this equipment.

Public Buildings Service

Public Buildings Service (PBS) awards negotiated contracts to architect-engineer firms for a variety of projects. These include office buildings, courthouses, and research centers. Negotiated design contracts for air conditioning systems, elevators, repairs, and alterations are also awarded. The GSA's policy with regard to design services is to acquire them from the most highly qualified architect-engineer firms. The notices of pending work appear daily in the CBD, and selection is based on the established criteria for the job and the demonstrated competence and qualification for the type of professional service required. Negotiations are conducted following an evaluation of Standard Form 254 plus photos of completed projects previously filed with GSA central and regional offices. Generally, those firms within the geographical area of the project are considered, although exceptions are made for projects of national significance.

Subcontracts with consulting engineers are subject to GSA approval. If the project is basically of an engineering nature, the prime contract is negotiated with an engineering firm.

Topographic surveys, soil tests, and soil analysis are generally subcontracted by the architect-engineer, and are reimbursable items exclusive of the design fee.

GSA regional offices commission murals and sculptures for placement in public buildings. Artists for these works are selected in cooperation with the National Endowment for the Arts (NEA). NEA-appointed panels, consisting of local civic and art-oriented representatives, and the project architects recommend artists to the GSA.

Construction and alteration contracts are awarded to the lowest responsive and responsible bidder on the basis of competitive bids. When competitive bids are solicited, a notice is placed in local newspapers, various trade journals, technical publications serving the construction industry, and the CBD. Each of the GSA's PBS regional offices maintains mailing lists of interested prospective bidders. Firms may apply by contacting the nearest Business Service Center. Bid bonds are required for construction contracts in excess of $25,000. Standard Form 24, *Bid Bond*, accompanied by a certified cashier's check, bank check, or money order is acceptable. Successful bidders must provide a performance bond for the total amount of the bid and a payment bond for half that amount. These bonds are available from any surety or bonding company. The SBA can be of help in this area, if requested.

Leasing of space in urban centers is a responsibility of the GSA. However, there are certain exceptions. The Departments of Agriculture, Commerce, and Defense may lease their own building space after GSA clearance. The GSA does not lease space for either post offices or space in foreign countries. Leases are normally obtained by negotiation, however occasionally invitations for sealed bids are issued.

PBS operates buildings under the control of the GSA. In order to perform this function, items such as tools, hardware, paint, janitorial supplies (including uniforms), shop, and cafeteria equipment are necessary. Purchases from non-government sources are usually contracted for by authorized building managers, who can spend up to $2,500 per purchase for equipment, supplies, and materials. The Office of Contracts procures a wide range of services. These include security guards; janitorial, window cleaning, and utility services; cafeteria operation; garbage removal; and dry cleaning. For more information contact the nearest GSA Business Service Center. No bid bond is required for maintenance contracts.

Appraisals of fair market value and fair rental rates of properties are performed by the GSA's own staff, independent appraisal companies, and other individuals. A period of between 30 and 90 days is usually required for appraisals, although the actual time depends on the size and complexity of the property. Appraisers are selected from the GSA Register of Available Real Estate Appraisers. Interested appraisers should contact the nearest GSA Business Service Center and request an application (Form 1195) for placement on the register.

Surveying and related cadastral services are obtained from civil engineers, surveyors, and land development firms. Since this need is limited, the GSA has not established a listing. Regional offices usually employ local surveyors under a selective professional services Contract. Surveyors should inform the Business Service center of their interest.

Federal Supply Service

The Federal Supply Service (FSS) is responsible for supplying thousands of commonly used items such as office supplies and furniture, equipment and books; hardware, refrigerators, air conditioners, and water coolers; and laboratory, medical, photographic, and audio-video recording equipment and supplies.

These items are procured under four basic programs: the stock program, federal supply schedules, consolidated purchase contracts, and direct order purchasing.

Under the *stock program*, approximately 20,000 items in routine use throughout the various departments and agencies are stored in warehouses

strategically located to provide quick service when items are needed. Agencies submit their requisitions to the GSA regional office serving their area. The orders are then directed to the appropriate supply distribution facility for shipment from stock. If the order is large enough, direct shipment from the supplier may be used instead. Examples of the types of items available under this program are paint, tools, and office supplies.

Federal supply schedules are used where economies can be realized. This program supplies federal agencies with sources for products and services such as furniture, electric lamps, appliances, photographic, laboratory and duplicating supplies, athletic equipment, and supplies and equipment for audio and video recording.

Schedules are indefinite quantity contracts usually established for a term of one year. They permit agencies to place orders directly with suppliers, and payment is made directly to the contractor by the ordering agency. Solicitations for bids under federal supply schedules are advertised in the CBD. Under certain conditions, contracts are negotiated in lieu of sealed bidding.

Consolidated purchase contracts are used when items are not suitable for inclusion in either the stock or federal supply schedule programs. Agency requirements for these items are consolidated by the GSA and special definite quantity contracts are executed. Direct delivery is made from the contractor to the agency involved. These contracts are usually formally advertised, but, as in federal supply schedule requirements, negotiation may at times be used.

Direct order purchasing is performed by the GSA for those agencies requesting this service. These requests usually occur when an agency either lacks the technical personnel or expertise to do its own purchasing, has unique requirements, or feels that the GSA can buy more advantageously because of its knowledge of the market.

Transportation and Public Utilities Service

Transportation and Public Utilities Service (TPUS), through a central purchasing program, procures goods and services ranging from cars and trucks through discount motel accommodations for federal travelers. This service also rents passenger vehicles and trucks, and either directly purchases or sets the standards for acquiring automotive parts, accessories, services, and fuel. Actual procurement of these items is through the managers of its more than 100 motor pools in the 50 states and Puerto Rico. Information on TPUS automotive purchases can be obtained from the nearest GSA Business Service Center. However, since the TPUS motor pools reflect about 20 of the total federal fleet, other agencies should be contacted directly for information concerning vehicles and related procurements.

TPUS, through a central purchasing program, negotiates and contracts for special discount air and rail fares for federal passengers on high traffic routes. It also sets policies on the procurement of travel and travel services by all executive agencies, the purchase of rail, truck, ocean, and air freight, and the settlement of travel and freight loss and damage claims. It is also responsible for the procurement of public utilities, such as gas, electricity, water, steam, and sewage services for individual executive agencies and government-run buildings. Individual purchases of $10,000 and up may be made for a term of up to ten years.

Federal Property Resource Service

Federal Property Resource Service (FPRS) is the arm of the GSA charged with the repair and rehabilitation of personal property, such as furniture and office machines, carpets and drapes, motor vehicles, tires, household appliances, and fire extinguishers. Contracts are also awarded for recycling activities. This salvage could, for example, include the recovery of silver from used photographic solutions and scrap film, and the collection of wastepaper for remilling. Federal agencies may contract for their own repair and maintenance services only if an FPRS contract is not available.

A majority of the contracts are set aside for small and minority businesses, workshops for the blind and severely handicapped, and Federal Prison Industries, Inc. Further information may be obtained from your nearest GSA Business Service Center.

National Archives and Records Service (NARS), through its trust fund, makes special procurements related to the audiovisual field, including photographic supplies and related equipment, microfilm services, and film processing.

DEPARTMENTAL CIVILIAN PURCHASING PROGRAMS

U.S. Department of Agriculture

The U. S. Department of Agriculture (USDA) has more than 200 local offices purchasing throughout the United States on a decentralized basis. The Office of Operations and Finance exercises general responsibility for all phases of the department's procurement, supply, and property management functions. This office also acquires management for its leased and owned real estate, and is responsible for its proper utilization and disposition. Formally advertised and negotiated purchases are used when it is estimated that the cost of filling a requirement will exceed $10,000. When filling requirements for less than this amount, the purchasing offices generally use small purchasing procedures.

These procedures are less structured than either formally advertised or negotiated contracting, and are characterized by informally solicited quotations from a limited number of qualified sources. The number of sources actually contacted usually depends on the anticipated size of the purchase. Final vendor selection is based on price, delivery schedule, quality of product, and other pertinent factors.

Each purchasing office maintains bidders' lists for the items it buys. The purchasing offices also maintain copies of outstanding solicitations for ready reference by interested bidders. Business firms are encouraged to have their representatives visit the various agency purchasing offices to pick up copies of these solicitations and to discuss the use of articles and services they have to offer the programs of the agencies. There are 27 major service programs and purchasing activities under the jurisdiction of the USDA, and further information on these is available through your nearest USDA office. Four of the more widely known are discussed next.

Agricultural Research Service

The Agricultural Research Service (ARS) procurement is decentralized and on a regional level. It buys special laboratory, scientific, and testing equipment; light trucks and laboratory-equipped trailers; farm equipment and supplies; refrigerating and dehumidifying equipment, as well as furniture and supplies.

Its construction requirements include animal pens, insectarias, and greenhouses; storage sheds, permanent and prefabricated laboratory buildings; windmills, wells, dock and harbor repairs, and soil moisture tanks; fences, roads, driveways, and parking areas.

Animal and Plant Health Service

The Animal and Plant Health Service (APHIS) buys laboratory supplies, vehicles, farm equipment, aircraft, office equipment and supplies, radio transmitters and receivers, insecticides, data processing, as well as service and construction contracts.

Forest Service

The Forest Service (FS) buys petroleum products; building and construction supplies; transportation equipment including motor vehicles, aircraft, parachutes and boats; engineering, laboratory test, scientific, photographic, and radio equipment; refrigerators and heavy equipment including tractors, graders, compressors, concrete mixers, truck tractors, trailers, cranes, explosives, chemicals, and insecticides; seeds and fertilizers; hardware, including hand tools, machine tools, barbed wire, and paints; as well as firefighting tools, lookout towers, and binoculars.

Its public works projects include the construction of roads, bridges, and buildings. Forestry work projects include insect control, tree planting, range vegetation, and brush disposal.

FS procurement is decentralized, and is handled by national and regional forest staffs.

Soil Conservation Service

The Soil Conservation Service (SCS) procurements are decentralized, and are on the state level. SCS buys architect, engineering, and construction services (including core drilling); laboratory, photographic, radio, and soil sampling equipment; laboratory and office furniture and supplies; data processing equipment; office machines and supplies; vehicles and other transportation equipment, as well as drafting and engineering equipment and supplies. It also purchases farm equipment and supplies such as feed, insecticides, and fertilizers.

Construction requirements include small dams, reservoirs, channels, debris basins, and other water use and control structures. The agency also rents construction equipment.

Department of Commerce

The Department of Commerce (DOC) provides centralized procurement for a variety of supplies, equipment, and services used in support of the National Bureau of Standards, the Bureau of the Census, and the National Oceanic and Atmospheric Administration.

Department of Education

The Department of Education procures articles and services for both the staff and operation of programs of education from elementary school through post-graduate and vocational courses. Purchases include EDP material, educational research and improvement programs, and education for the handicapped and minorities. The procurement responsibility is divided between two offices in Washington, DC.

Department of Energy

The Department of Energy (DOE) was established in 1977 to develop and execute a national energy program. It acquires research and development through contracts and interagency agreements and assists both private and public institutions through grants and agreements. A wide variety of solicitations are used in addition to the standard IFB and RFP formats.

The *Program Opportunity Notice* (PON) is used principally to solicit competitive proposals relating to nonnuclear energy demonstration projects when there is a stated general objective and an urgent public need. A definitive statement of work is usually not available, for a variety of approaches are desired. PONs may result in the award of contract grants and cooperative agreements. Multiple awards may be made.

A *Program Research and Development Announcement* (PRDA) is used to solicit a broad mix of research, development and related nonnuclear energy project proposals. As opposed to the PON, which is used for projects utilizing existing, commercially available technology, a PRDA solicits proposals for projects in areas where R&D is required, but where it is difficult to describe in detail the nature of the work to be undertaken. A PRDA may be used to solicit proposals for procurement contracts, grants, and cooperative agreements. Multiple awards on proposals with dissimilar approaches are generally made. This allows for a large number of approaches and many organizations in solving a problem in whole or in part, and it supports new and creative solutions.

A *Program Solicitation* (PS) is a notice used to request either proposals or applications to be competitively evaluated for DOE financial assistance awards. Usually the program needs are clearly defined. It is also used to support applications for support grants except when proposals on these are obtained as the result of program regulation. A *Solicitations for Cooperative Agreement Proposal* (SCAP) is used exclusively to solicit cooperative agreement proposals for financial assistance. SCAPs are prepared jointly by the program office and the procurement office. They contain the objectives, specifications, schedule, instructions, and other conditions applying to the solicitation and the resulting proposal. In many respects the SCAP contains a level of detail comparable to that of an RFP. Unsolicited proposals are also encouraged.

The PON, PRDA, PS and SCAP are negotiated procurements, and quite often involve a substantially longer and more complex evaluation process.

Department of Health and Human Services

The Department of Health and Human Services (DHHS) buys goods and services for programs involving health, social security, and general welfare. The greatest dollar volume goes to the Public Health Service, and this includes architectural, engineering, and construction services. Grants are also available.

Since the procurement responsibilities are decentralized, business should also direct inquiries to either the constituent agencies of DHHS or the regional office nearest them. Complete information will be available in the literature.

Department of Housing and Urban Development

The Department of Housing and Urban Development (HUD) administers programs concerning housing needs and the improvement and development of the nation's communities in general. The headquarters office procures water and space heaters, ranges and refrigerators, lawn mowers, paint, screen wire, toilet seats, ash and garbage cans, hot air furnace filters, window shades, cloth, and furniture.

Supplies and services for the repair, rehabilitation, management, maintenance, sale, and demolition of properties are contracted for by the area offices of HUD, provided the requirements do not exceed $10,000. If you want to be put on the HUD regional source lists, contact your nearest HUD regional office. These bidders' lists are not maintained at the national level. A list of HUD regional and area offices may be obtained by requesting HUD Form 788, *Field Office Jurisdiction,* from the HUD Publications Services Center.

Department of the Interior (DOI)

The Department of the Interior (DOI) fulfills its needs through the individual bureaus. Central office procurements are arranged by the Division of Property and Records.

The *National Park Service* contracts for physical improvements and concessions. A list of offices that issue bid invitations is available from the Division of Contracting and General Services. Contact the Chief, Office of Public Affairs.

The *Bureau of Mines* makes purchases at field research centers, laboratories, area and district offices, and helium plants. Many of the purchases are related to laboratory needs and helium production. File Standard Form 129 at any field office. For a list of offices issuing bid invitations, write to the Chief, Branch of Procurement, Bureau of Mines.

The *Fish and Wildlife Service* buys small boats, outboard motors, construction and farming equipment, two-way radios, and fish foods. Inquiries may be addressed to any one of the regional offices, or to the Chief of Contracting, Fish and Wildlife Service.

The *Bureau of Indian Affairs* purchases supplies and equipment for agriculture, building maintenance, and construction—especially roads and irrigation. It also buys subsistence items and school supplies. To get on the mailing list, send requests to the nearest office. Contact the Department of the Interior for addresses.

Geological Survey purchases include scientific and ADP equipment. The survey also enters into R&D contracts and a wide variety of service contracts. It administers certain federal grants and cooperative agreements, and as often as possible, awards are made to economically and socially disadvantaged firms. Address inquiries and mailing list applications to U.S. Geological Survey, Branch of Procurement and Contracts, Policy and Procedures Section.

The *Bureau of Land Management* purchases include fire fighting equipment, range grass seed, and tree thinning and planting services. The bureau also contracts for cultural resource studies, the construction of fences, roads, earthfill dams, and oceanographic environmental studies. Acquisitions are made by the Washington Office, the Denver Service Center, and the field offices. For more information, contact either the Bureau of Land Management, Branch of Contract Operations or the Denver Service Center.

The *Office of Surface Mining Reclamation and Enforcement* procures office supplies and equipment, special photographic supplies and equipment, two way radio mobile communication equipment, and automotive fleet maintenance. This office also contracts services applying to research, ecological investigation, environmental monitoring, geotechnical research, laboratory testing services, engineering support (exploratory drilling, testing, reclamation site specifications development), reclamation construction (dredging, contouring, backfilling, revegetation, mine sealing), training programs, and computer software and systems design. Inquiries may be directed to the Chief, Branch of Procurement, Office of Surface Mining.

The *Water and Power Resources Service* develops and manages water and related land resources in the 17 contiguous western states, construction accounts for about 70 percent of its total business. On construction projects, contractors furnish all equipment and materials necessary, except for special design components such as pumps, turbines, generators for hydroplants, and large transformers. These are purchased separately. Contracts for construction and architect-engineering services are handled by seven regional offices. Research, development, and automated data processing contracting is done primarily by the Engineering and Research Center in Denver, Colorado. Both the center and the regional offices procure supplies and services for their internal needs. Inquiries and mailing list applications should be mailed to one of the regional offices. Addresses can be obtained from the Department of the Interior.

Department of Justice

The *Department of Justice* purchases through its various bureaus and services. Requirements include paper and paper products, fingerprint supplies, arms and ammunition, handcuffs and leg irons, medical supplies and equipment, and miscellaneous office supplies and equipment.

The *Bureau of Prisons* procures a wide range of general commodities since many of them are, in effect, self-contained cities. Purchases are made by the individual prisons from local sources of supply or from national supply houses. Direct all inquiries and mailing list applications to specific penal institutions. Personal contact by company representatives are recommended. They should be arranged sufficiently in advance to permit appropriate technicians and interested officials to be present, particularly for demonstrations of new or improved products. All general inquiries about doing business with the federal prison system should be directed to the Bureau of Prisons, U.S. Department of Justice.

Federal Prison Industries, Inc. (FPI), also referred to as UNICOR, is a self-supporting, wholly owned government corporation of the District of Columbia. This agency purchases the raw material required in the various prison workshops. Most procurements are by negotiated contract. Materials purchased include steel for steel furniture construction, wool and cotton for textile production, textiles for the manufacture of clothing, and leather for the making of shoes. Bristles for making brushes, furniture lumber, and broom corn are also on the list. Federal prison products are available for sale to government agencies only, usually through the facilities of the GSA. FPI also provides training and employment for prisoners confined in federal penal and correctional institutions through the sale of its products and services to government agencies. These products and services are diversified in order to prevent unfair competition to private industry. However, it has turned out that FPI and the Workshops for the Blind and Other Severely Handicapped may produce identical supplies and services. When a particular need can be filled by either source, supplies and services are purchased in the following order of priority:

1. supplies:
   (a) FPI
   (b) workshops
   (c) commercial sources
2. services:
   (a) workshops
   (b) FPI
   (c) commercial sources

As you can see, the commercial supplier ranks third in each case; however, the motivation to purchase from FPI and the workshops is provided by the Javits-Wagner-O'Day Act (41 U.S.C. 46–48(c) and the rules of the Committee for Purchase from the Blind and Other Severely Handicapped (41 CFR Part 51). If you provide either products or services similar to those of FPI and the workshops, there will be times when you will be outgunned by legislation. However, through the philosophy of impartiality, you will be able to receive your fair share of the awards.

The *Drug Enforcement Administration* (DEA) interests focus mainly on communications equipment, laboratory equipment, guns, ammunition, automatic data processing equipment, and development contracts directly applicable to law enforcement activities. Contact the Drug Enforcement Administration, Administrative Services Division, U.S. Department of Justice.

The *Federal Bureau of Investigation* (FBI) procurements are mainly in the major commodity areas of radios and electronics, special laboratory equipment, guns and ammunition, and other types of law enforcement supplies. Inquiries with regard to FBI procurement, and visits by business representatives who are interested in selling their products, should be made to the Procurement and Administrative Services Section, Federal Bureau of Investigation, U.S. Department of Justice.

The *United States Marshals Service* purchases weapons, ammunition, communications equipment, and related services. It also leases special-purpose real estate. If you need more information on agency requirements, contact the Administrative Services Division, United States Marshals Service, U.S. Department of Justice.

Department of Labor

The *Department of Labor* (DOL) purchases health and safety equipment, including protective clothing and mine safety equipment, ADP hardware and software, and audiovisual equipment and services. Service requirements include architecture, engineering, and construction; research, evaluation, and training; auditing and statistical services; and publications, art, and graphics. Two offices may be contacted for general information. They are the Office of Procurement and the Office of Printing Management. Inquiries regarding business opportunities for small, minority, and women-owned firms should be addressed to the Director, Small and Disadvantaged Business Utilization.

The *Employment and Training Administration* is basically concerned with the purchase of statistical services, research, evaluation, and work experience and training for groups having difficulty entering or returning to the work force. This training may be classroom, on-the-job, or other job-related training. Block grants are made to train and place individuals in unsubsidized private employment. There are three offices that may be contacted with regard to these items: the Office of Administrative Services, the Office of Policy, Evaluation, and Research, and the Office of National Programs.

The *Mine Safety and Health Administration* is concerned mainly with health or safety equipment and services. It provides assistance to the states in the development of effective state mine safety and health programs, including training programs. Direct inquiries in this area to the Office of Public Affairs, Mine Safety and Health Administration, U.S. Department of Labor.

The *Department of the Treasury* purchases supplies and services primarily through the procurement offices at its 11 bureau headquarters. Additional purchases are also made at many field office locations, however these are generally limited to housekeeping and routine operational needs. For more information and a detailed listing of all of the department's procurement offices throughout the United States, obtain a copy of the booklet titled *Selling to the Department of the Treasury*. It may be purchased at nominal cost from the Superintendent of Documents, U.S. Government Printing Office.

The Bureaus of Government Financial Operations, Mint, Engraving and Printing, Customs Service, and Internal Revenue Service have the largest procurement activities of the Treasury. They issue the majority of the department's bid and proposal solicitations for a wide range of items. Contact the Chief, Procurement Division (Operations), Office of the Secretary of the Treasury and request the addresses of the major procurement offices. There are 8 centralized offices and three field offices involved in purchasing. Submit Form 129 to the offices most interested in your product or service.

Department of Transportation

The Department of Transportation (DOT) procurement activities are decentralized, and each operating administration takes care of their own needs. The Office of the Secretary of Transportation contracts primarily for studies and services relating to transportation management, research, and operations.

The *Federal Aviation Administration* (FAA) makes nationwide procurements of equipment needed for communications, air navigation, and air traffic control. These include computer hardware, supporting software, and software service. Purchases are made at headquarters for research and development and for the major electronics systems. Further information may be obtained from any FAA regional office or the Procurement Management and Services Branch, Contracts Division, Federal Aviation Administration.

The *Federal Highway Administration* procures supplies, materials, equipment, and services, including research and development, construction, and professional and technical services. For notification of contract opportunities, submit Form 129 to the Procurement Branch, Federal Highway Administration.

The *U.S. Coast Guard* district offices and other units procure ship repairs and ship replacement parts, aircraft repairs, aircraft replacement parts, buoys, and materials and construction needed to support Coast Guard operating units. The Washington DC office procures vessels, aircraft, electronics equipment, outfitting supplies and equipment for new vessels, and research services. Inquiries should be directed to the Commandant (G-FCP), U.S. Coast Guard, U.S. Department of Transportation.

The *Urban Mass Transportation Administration* (UMTA) contracts for research, development, and demonstration projects related to mass transportation. Information may be obtained from UMTA, Office of Procurement and Third Party Review, U.S. Department of Transportation.

The *Saint Lawrence Seaway Development Corporation* procures navigational lock operating equipment and related maintenance parts. They also buy heavy construction equipment and spare parts. Information may be obtained from the Administrative Services Officer, Saint Lawrence Seaway Development Corporation, U.S. Department of Transportation.

The *Federal Railroad Administration* (FRA) oversees the northeast corridor program to improve service between Washington, D.C. and Boston, Massachusetts, and is also responsible for the Alaska Railroad and management of the DOT Transportation Test Center at Pueblo, Colorado. This administration contracts for research in aerodynamics, vehicle propulsion, vehicle control, communications, and vehicle safety. FRA also purchases studies and demonstrations relating to the safety, environment, and efficiency of our national rail system. Information on FRA procurement can be obtained from the Federal Railroad Administration.

The *National Highway Traffic Safety Administration* (NHTSA) procures research, development, and test and evaluation services designed to promote vehicle safety. Information on all NHTSA procurements may be obtained from the National Highway Traffic Safety Administration, Office of Contracts and Procurement.

The *Research and Special Program Administration* procures studies and services to plan, develop, initiate, and manage programs in all fields of transportation research and development. Information may be obtained from the Procurement Division (DPA–14), Research and Special Program Administration.

The *Maritime Administration* contracting needs are in the areas of ship design and construction, development of advanced ship operations, port and intermodal development, and marine technology. For more information contact the Maritime Administration, Office of Administration and Contracts.

Environmental Protection Agency (EPA)

The Environmental Protection Agency (EPA) purchasing activities and requirements are wide and diversified because of the many types of programs the agency is responsible for. First and foremost, EPA is a regulatory agency responsible for establishing and enforcing environmental standards concerning air and water pollution, solid waste management, pesticides, radiation, noise, and toxic substances. Some of the data gathering and analysis required to develop effective standards and guidelines are obtained under contracts with experts or companies specializing in technical services. Most of the automated data processing equipment required is procured by negotiated contracts. These contracts may also cover software and support services.

EPA also requires construction, alteration, and repair of buildings, structures, and other real property. Construction is normally procured by means of formal advertising, and EPA has an architect-engineer selection board. For more detailed information, write to one of the three EPA addresses listed at the end of this appendix. Ask for the booklet *Contracting with EPA—A Guide for Prospective Contractors.*

National Aeronautics and Space Administration

The *National Aeronautics and Space Administration* (NASA) operations—essentially of a research and development nature—are performed at spaceflight centers, research centers, and other installations throughout the country. Each installation has a specifically prescribed mission, and each procures the material and services needed to carry it out. NASA awards contracts to universities, nonprofit research organizations and private industry. Further information may be obtained by writing to NASA's Washington, DC office.

The Tennessee Valley Authority (TVA)

The Tennessee Valley Authority (TVA) purchases are primarily for construction and operation of electric power plants and transmissions systems, construction of dams and locks, and development and experimental production of fertilizers. Items required include electrical generating equipment such as turbogenerators, steam generating units, nuclear plant equipment, hydraulic turbines and generators, transformers, boilers, piping systems, and switch gear. Coal, coke, and nuclear fuel are purchased, as are electric and electronic supplies, communications equipment, and a wide variety of spare parts. Supplies procured include structural and milled steel, chemicals, and items for medical, laboratory, and photographic purposes.

TVA has a centralized Division of Purchasing divided into branches. The Nuclear Procurement Branch buys nuclear fuel, turbogenerators, and nuclear steam supply systems. The Equipment Procurement Branch is responsible for all other nonnuclear equipment. The Materials Procurement Branch buys construction and structural and building materials, architect-engineer services, and general supplies. The Fuels Procurement Branch buys coal and coke; and transportation services are bought by the Traffic Branch. The Open Market Procurement Branch buys equipment and materials with requisition totals of $10,000 or less. Send requests for information and mailing list applications to the Chief of the branch responsible for the equipment or supplies of interest, Division of Purchasing, Tennessee Valley Authority.

United States Postal Service

The United States Postal Service (USPS) is a large buyer of both goods and services. Goods include mail processing and handling equipment; customer service equipment; office furniture, machines, equipment, and supplies; and custodial, protective, building, and vehicle maintenance equipment. Services purchased are building protection and maintenance and vehicle maintenance and repair. Procurements in excess of $10,000 are published in the CBD, including those for facilities, architect-engineering services, and specific research and development programs and projects.

The *Postal Contracting Manual*, Publication 41, outlines uniform policies and procedures for the procurement of mail transportation, facilities, equipment, supplies, and services. It is available at current rates under stock number 039–000–81003–4 from the Superintendent of Documents, U.S. Government Printing Office.

The Eastern Area Supply Center, U.S. Postal Service Contract Branch, purchases open market items such as bulletin boards, carrier satchel straps, conveyors, corrugated boxes, custodial supplies, envelopes, workroom and lobby furniture, gloves, hardware products, marginal punched forms, materials handling equipment, paper products, signs, and other postal supplies.

The Western Area Supply Center, U.S. Postal Service Contract Branch, purchases spare parts for electric, electronic, vehicle, and mechanical equipment assemblies and bulk conveyors.

In order to be placed on the appropriate bidder's list for supplies, services, and equipment, other than for construction and transportation of mail services, file PS Form 7429, *Bidder's Mailing List Application*, and Form 7429–A, *Commodity and Geographic Location Check-Off*, with the Data Automation Division, Bidders Mailing Lists, Western Area Supply Center. Additional information on contracts and small business activities may be had from the Procurement and Supply Department.

For information on construction and leasing, and to be placed on the appropriate bidders' list, as well as to obtain information on transporting mail, contact the General Manager, Facilities Procurement Division, Real Estate and Buildings Department. They will also direct you to the regional procurement activities in your area.

For information on transporting mail, contact the Office of Transportation Services.

Further details concerning postal service procurement programs are contained in Publication 151 titled *Selling to the Postal Service*. It is available free of charge from the Office of Contracts, Documents and Processing Branch, Procurement and Supply Department.

Veterans Administration

The Veterans Administration (VA) has a central purchasing facility, the Marketing Center, P.O. Box 76, Hines, IL 60141; 312–687–6782. It purchases medical, dental, and surgical supplies; drugs and chemicals; nonperishable foods; prosthetic and orthopedic aids; uniforms, flags, laundry equipment; and medical and radiological equipment. Some items are procured locally by individual VA medical centers. These types of items include perishable food, maintenance supplies, off-the-shelf drug items, medical supplies, a wide range of medical and maintenance services, and books.

The Office of Supply Services awards management consultant contracts. The Office of Construction awards contracts for building design, construction, and technology research. They are also responsible for the design and construction activities of the National Cemetery System.

All of the major contracting opportunities are advertised in the CBD, with awards being made to firms in the geographical work area based on competitive bidding. Address all inquiries to the Veterans Administration's Washington DC office.

DEPARTMENTAL AND AGENCY CONTACT INFORMATION

Federal Information Centers

Federal Information Centers (FIC) can eliminate the maze of referrals often experienced in contacting the federal government. They are clearinghouses for information about the government. If you experience difficulty contacting an agency or getting the information you want, call your nearest FIC. An FIC specialist will either answer the question or locate an expert who can.

Alabama	
Birmingham	202–322–8591
Mobile	205–438–1421
Alaska: Anchorage	907–272–3650
Arizona: Phoenix	602–261–3313
Arkansas: Little Rock	501–378–6177

California	
Los Angeles	213–894–3000
Sacramento	916–440–3344
San Francisco	415–556–6600
Santa Ana	714–836–2386
Colorado	
Colorado Springs	303–471–9491
Denver	303–236–7181
Pueblo	303–544–9523
Florida	
Fort Lauderdale	305–522–8531
Jacksonville	904–354–4756
Miami	305–350–4155
Orlando	305–422–1800
St. Petersburg	813–893–3495
Tampa	813–229–7911
West Palm Beach	305–833–7566
Georgia: Atlanta	404–221–6891
Hawaii: Honolulu	808–546–8620
Illinois: Chicago	312–353–4242
Indiana	
Gary	219–883–4110
Indianapolis	317–269–7373
Iowa: from all points	800–523–1556
Kansas: from all points	800–432–2934
Kentucky: Louisville	502–582–6261
Louisiana: New Orleans	504–589–6696
Maryland: Baltimore	301–962–4980
Massachusetts: Boston	617–223–7121
Michigan	
Detroit	313–226–7016
Grand Rapids	616–451–2628
Minnesota: Minneapolis	612–249–5333
Missouri	
St. Louis	314–425–4106
from elsewhere in Missouri	800–392–7711
Nebraska	
Omaha	402–221–3353
from elsewhere in Nebraska	800–642–8383

New Jersey	
Newark	201–645–3600
Trenton	609–396–4400
New Mexico: Albuquerque	505–766–3091
New York	
Albany	518–463–4421
Buffalo	716–846–4010
New York City	212–264–4464
Rochester	315–476–8545
Syracuse	315–476–8545
North Carolina: Charlotte	704–376–3600
Ohio	
Akron	216–375–5638
Cincinnati	513–684–2801
Cleveland	216–522–4040
Columbus	614–221–1014
Dayton	513–223–7377
Toledo	419–241–3233
Oklahoma	
Oklahoma City	405–231–4868
Tulsa	918–584–4193
Oregon: Portland	503–221–2222
Pennsylvania	
Philadelphia	215–597–7042
Pittsburgh	412–644–3456
Rhode Island: Providence	401–331–5565
Tennessee	
Chattanooga	615–265–8231
Memphis	901–521–3285
Nashville	615–242–5056
Texas	
Austin	512–472–5494
Dallas	214–767–8585
Fort Worth	817–334–3624
Houston	713–653–3025
San Antonio	512–224–4471
Utah: Salt Lake City	801–524–5353
Virginia	
Norfolk	804–441–3101
Richmond	804–643–4928
Roanoke	703–982–8591

Washington
Seattle 206–442–0570
Tacoma 206–383–5230

Wisconsin: Milwaukee 414–271–2273

Military Departments and Agencies

Department of Defense
The Pentagon
Washington, DC 20301–1155
202–545–6700.
(The Department of Defense telephone directory is available for sale by the Superintendent of Documents.)

Defense Logistics Agency
Cameron Station
Alexandria, VA 22314
202–274–6000 or 6001

Defense General Supply Center
(Contact the Defense Logistics Agency)

Defense Property Disposal Service (DPDS)
Department of Defense
P. O. Box 1370, Battle Creek, MI 49016.

Department of the Army
The Pentagon
Washington, DC 20350
202–545–6700

Department of the Navy
The Pentagon
Washington, DC 20350
202–545–6700

Department of the Air Force
The Pentagon
Washington, DC 20350
202–545–6700

Army and Air Force Exchange Service (AAFES)
Merchandising Support Branch
Merchandising Division, Dallas, TX 75222.

Civilian Departments and Agencies

Department of Agriculture
Fourteenth Street and Independence Avenue SW
Washington, DC 20250
202–447–2791

Agricultural Research Service
Department of Agriculture
Beltsville, MD 20705
301–344–2264

Animal and Plant Health Inspection Service
Department of Agriculture
Washington, DC 20250
202–447–2511

Forest Service
Department of Agriculture
P.O. Box 2417
Washington, DC 20013
202–447–3760

Soil Conservation Service
Department of Agriculture
Washington, DC 20250
202–447–4230

Department of Commerce
Fourteenth Street Between Constitution Avenue and E Street NW
Washington, DC 20230
202–377–2000

Maritime Administration
400 Seventh Street SW
Washington, DC 20590
202–426–5807.

National Bureau of Standards
Fourteenth Street Between Constitution and E Street NW
Washington, DC 20230
202–377–2000.

National Technical Information Service
Department of Commerce
5285 Port Royal Road
Springfield, VA 22161
703–487–4600

Department of Education
400 Maryland Avenue SW
Washington, DC 20202
202–245–3192

Department of Energy
1000 Independence Avenue SW
Washington, DC 20585
202–252–5000

National Energy Software Center
Argonne National Laboratory
9700 South Cass Avenue
Argonne, IL 60439
312–972–7250

Department of Health and Human Services
200 Independence Avenue SW
Washington, DC 20201
202–245–6296

Department of Housing and Urban Development
451 Seventh Street SW
Washington, DC 20410
202–655–4000

Department of the Interior
C Street between Eighteenth and Nineteenth Streets NW
Washington, DC 20240
202–343–3171

Bureau of Land Management
Department of the Interior
Washington, DC 20240
202–343–9435

Division of Minority Business Utilization
Department of the Interior
C Street Between Eighteenth and Nineteenth Streets NW
Washington, DC 20240
202–343–3171

National Park Service
Department of the Interior
P.O. Box 37127
Washington, DC 20013–7127
202–343–7394

Office of Surface Mining Reclamation and Enforcement
Department of the Interior
Washington, DC 20240
202–343–4719

U.S. Geological Survey
Department of the Interior
119 National Center
Reston, VA 22092
703–860–7444

Department of Justice
Constitution Avenue and Tenth Street NW
Washington, DC 20530
202–633–2000

Bureau of Prisons
Department of Justice
Washington, DC 20534
202–724–3198

Drug Enforcement Administration
Department of Justice
1405 I Street NW
Washington, DC 20357
202–633–1000

Federal Bureau of Investigation
Ninth Street and Pennsylvania Avenue NW
Washington, DC 20535
202–324–3000

Federal Prison Industries
Department of Justice
Washington, DC 20534
202–724–3198

United States Marshals Service
U.S. Department of Justice
One Tysons Corner Center
McLean, VA 22102
703–285–1131

Department of Labor
200 Constitution Avenue NW
Washington, DC 20210
202–523–8165

Employment and Training Administration (ETA)
Washington, DC 20213
202–376–6636

Office of Administrative Services
Department of Labor
Room 8400
601 D Street NW
Washington, DC 20213
202–376–6300

Office of National Programs
Division of Contracting Services
Department of Labor
Room 6320, 601 D Street NW
Washington, DC 20213.

Office of Policy, Evaluation, and Research
Department of Labor
Central Procurement Staff
Room 9002
601 D Street NW
Washington, DC 20213

Office of Public Affairs
Mine Safety and Health Administration
Department of Labor
Room 601
4015 Wilson Boulevard
Arlington, VA 22203
703–235–1452.

Office of Small and Disadvantaged Business Utilization
Room S–1004
200 Constitution Avenue NW
Washington, DC 20210.

Department of State
2201 C Street NW
Washington, DC 20520
202–655–4000.

Department of the Treasury
Fifteenth Street and Pennsylvania Avenue NW
Washington, DC 20220
202–5656–2000

Procurement Division (Operations)
Office of the Secretary of the Treasury
Fifteenth Street and Pennsylvania Avenue NW
Washington, DC 20220
(202) 566–2000

Department of Transportation
400 Seventh Street SW
Washington, DC 20590
202–426–4000

Federal Aviation Administration
Procurement Management and Services Branch
Contracts Division
Department of Transportation
Washington, DC 20591
202–426–8058

Federal Highway Administration
Procurement Branch
U.S. Department of Transportation
400 Seventh Street SW
Washington, DC 20590
202–426–0630

Federal Railroad Administration
Department of Transportation
400 Seventh Street SW
Washington, DC 20590
202–426–0881

Maritime Administration
Office of Administration and Contracts,
Department of Transportation
400 Seventh Street SW
Washington, DC 20590
202–426–5807

National Highway Traffic Safety Administration
Office of Contracts and Procurement
Department of Transportation
400 Seventh Street SW
Washington, DC 20590
202–426–2768

Research and Special Program Administration
Procurement Division Department of Transportation
400 Seventh Street SW
Washington, DC 20590
202–426–4934

Saint Lawrence Seaway Development Corporation
Administrative Services Officer
Department of Transportation
P.O. Box 520, Massena, NY 13622

U.S. Coast Guard
Department of Transportation
2100 Second Street SW
Washington, DC 20593
202–426–2158

Environmental Protection Agency
401 M Street NW
Washington, DC 20207
202–634–7740

Contracts Management Division
Environmental Protection Agency
Cincinnati, OH 45268

Contracts Management Division
Environmental Protection Agency
Research Triangle Park, NC 27771

Headquarters Contract Operations
Environmental Protection Agency
401 M Street SW
Washington, DC 20460

General Services Administration
General Services Building
Eighteenth and F Streets
Washington, DC 20405
202–655–4000

National Aeronautics and Space Administration
600 Independence Avenue SW
Washington, DC 20546
202–453–1000

Computer Software Management and Information Center (COSMIC)
The University of Georgia
382 East Broad Street
Athens, GA 30602
404–542–3265

Superintendent of Documents
U.S. Government Printing Office
Washington, DC 20402–9325
202–275–2051
Publications information: 202–275–3050

Tennessee Valley Authority
Chief, (name the branch of interest)
Division of Purchasing
Chattanooga, TN 37401
615–755–3011

U.S. International Development Cooperation Agency
Overseas Private Investment Corporation
1129 Twentieth Street NW., Washington, DC 20527
202 653–2920

United States Postal Service
475 L'Enfant Plaza SW
Washington, DC 20260–0010
202–245–4000

Eastern Area Supply Center
U.S. Postal Service Contract Branch
VA Depot, Sommerville, NJ 08877

Western Area Supply Center
U.S. Postal Service Contract Branch
Topeka, KS 66619

Director, Office of Transportation Services
Mail Processing Department
U.S. Postal Service
475 L'Enfant Plaza West SW
Washington, DC 20260
202–245–4000

Facilities Procurement Division
Real Estate and Buildings Department
U.S. Postal Service
475 L'Enfant Plaza West SW
Washington, DC 20260
202–245–4000

Office of Contracts
Documents and Processing Branch
Procurement and Supply Department
U.S. Postal Service
475 L'Enfant Plaza SW
Washington, DC 20260
202–245–4000

Procurement and Supply Department
U.S. Postal Service
Washington, DC 20260–3121
202–245–4215

Veterans Administration
810 Vermont Avenue NW
Washington, DC 20420
202 393–4120

Office of Supply Services
Veterans Administration
810 Vermont Avenue NW
Washington, DC 20420
202–393–4120

INDEX - APPENDIX A

APPENDIX B

THE WALSH-HEALEY PUBLIC CONTRACTS ACT

The Walsh-Healey Act (41 U.S.C. 35–45) has had the most significant impact on government contracting to date. It sets the playing rules governing who can sell, and what they can sell, to the U.S. government.

PROVISIONS OF THE WALSH-HEALEY ACT

The Walsh-Healey Act generally applies to all government contracts performed within the United States, Puerto Rico, and the Virgin Islands that exceed or may exceed $10,000. Some contracts are specifically exempted, by either statue or regulation. For purposes of clarification, all contracts, including indefinite-delivery contracts, basic ordering agreements, blanket purchase agreements, and subcontracts under Section 8(a) of the Small Business Act, are subject to the act's provisions, unless specifically exempted.

The act states that all contracts entered into by any executive department, independent establishment, and other agency or instrumentality of the United States, the District of Columbia, as well as any corporation whose stock is beneficially owned by the United States, for the manufacturing or furnishing of materials, supplies, articles, and equipment in excess of $10,000, shall:

1. be only with manufacturers or regular dealers in the supplies and equipment manufactured or used in performing the contract; and
2. include or incorporate by reference the representation that the contractor is either a manufacturer or a regular dealer of the supplies offered, and the

stipulations required by the act pertaining to matters regarding minimum wages, maximum hours, child labor, convict labor, and safe and unsanitary working conditions

EXEMPTIONS FROM THE WALSH-HEALEY ACT

Contracts for the acquisition of the following supplies and services are exempt from the act:

1. any item in those situations where the contracting officer is authorized by the express language of a statute to purchase generally "in the open market," or where a specific purchase is negotiated in circumstances where immediate delivery is required by the public exigency
2. perishables, including dairy, livestock, and nursery products
3. agricultural or farm products processed for first sale by the original producers
4. all agricultural commodities and derivative products thereof purchased under contract by the Secretary of Agriculture
5. when a contract is with a common carrier having published tariff rates for the carriage of freight and personnel by vessel, airplane, bus, truck, or rail
6. when the contract is for the furnishing of service by radio, telephone, telegraph, and cable companies subject to the Federal Communications Act of 1934

Contracts for the following types of acquisitions are fully exempt from the act:

1. public utility services, including electric light and power, water, steam, and gas
2. supplies manufactured outside of the United States, Puerto Rico, and the Virgin Islands
3. purchases against the account of a defaulting contractor, where the stipulations of the act were not included in the defaulted contract
4. newspapers, magazines, and periodicals that are contracted for with sales agents and publisher representatives, and which are to be delivered by the publisher

The following contracts are partially exempt from the act:

1. Contracts with certain coal dealers, specifically one who regularly buys and sells coal on his or her own account in lots of not less than either a cargo or railroad carload; or with an agent of a coal mining company who is authorized to negotiate and conclude contracts for the furnishing of coal in the lot sizes previously specified. The dealer must notify the mine that the purchaser is the United States, and the provisions of the act apply at the mines. The

dealer, apart from the mine's liability, will be liable for the observance in the mines of all of the labor standards required by the act.

2. Certain commodity exchange contracts entered into by the Commodity Credit Corporation under the Commodity Credit Corporation Charter Act.
3. Contracts with certain export merchants, specifically those who buy from manufacturers and resell exclusively for export. The items purchased by the government must be for export, and the export merchant must notify the manufacturer that the purchaser is the United States, and that the provisions of the Walsh-Healey Act apply.
4. Contracts with small business defense production pools and small business research and development pools.
5. Contracts with public utilities for the acquisition of certain uranium products, specifically uranium concentrates, uranium hexafluoride, and enriched uranium.

The partial exemptions applying to the first four types of contracts just listed exempts the contractor from the requirement of being either a manufacturer or regular dealer. Contracts with public utilities are exempt in the sense that they are regulated under local, state, and federal laws governing operations of public utilities. However, keep in mind all other provisions of the act apply.

Upon the request of an agency head, the Secretary of Labor may exempt specific contracts or classes of contracts from the application of one or more of the act's stipulations, provided the request includes a finding by the agency head stating why the conduct of government business will be seriously impaired unless the exemption is granted.

Other requests for exemption that relate solely to safety and health standards must be transmitted by the contracting officer to the Assistant Secretary for Occupational Safety and Health (OSHA).

RULINGS AND INTERPRETATIONS OF THE ACT

The Walsh-Healey Public Contracts Act was enacted for the purpose of "providing conditions for the purchase of supplies and the making of contracts by the United States." It is not an act of general applicability to industry. The Supreme Court has described it as an instruction by the government to its agents (contracting officers) who are selected and granted final authority to fix the terms and conditions under which the government will permit goods to be sold to it. Its purpose, according to the Supreme Court was

> . . . to impose obligations upon those favored with government business and to obviate the possibility that any part of our tremendous national expenditures

> would go to forces tending to depress wages and purchasing power and offending fair social standards of employment.

The Secretary of Labor is authorized and directed to administer the provisions of the act, to make investigations, findings, and decisions thereunder, and to make, amend, and rescind rules and regulations with respect to its application. The Supreme Court has recognized that the Secretary may issue rulings defining the coverage of the act when it ruled that under the statute, as originally enacted, that "Congress submitted the administration of the act to the judgment of the Secretary of labor, not to the judgment of the courts."

An amendment to the act in 1952 added specific provisions for judicial review, and subsequent rulings by the courts have held that the "interpretations of the Walsh-Healey Act and regulations adopted thereunder, as made by the Secretary of labor acting through his administrator, are both correct and reasonable."

One important fact about this act is that a contractor must be either "the manufacturer of or a regular dealer in" the items being purchased, making it quite clear that it is intended to eliminate the award of contracts to "bid brokers." The legislative history also provides labor standards protection for employees who actually engage in either the manufacture or furnishing of the goods to the government by requiring that the government award contracts only to bona fide manufacturers and regular dealers. A contractor who has been awarded a contract despite his or her failure to qualify as a manufacturer or regular dealer is not relieved of the obligation to comply with other requirements of the act and regulations. Incidentally, a contractor's eligibility status under either a previous Walsh-Healey contract or subcontract is not considered determinative evidence of the bidder's present eligibility.

How the Act Defines a Manufacturer

A *manufacturer* is defined as a "person who owns, operates, or maintains a factory or establishment that produces on the premises the materials, supplies, articles, or equipment required under the contract and of the general character described by the specifications." Under this definition, there should be no question regarding the bidder's eligibility. The bidder either has, or has not, the requisite plant, equipment, and personnel required to produce, on the bidder's own premises, the goods called for under the government contract. If assembly operations alone are contemplated, they will be considered to constitute manufacturing when a series of assembly operations utilizing machine tools and workers result in either a significant fabrication or production of the desired product. A bidder may also qualify as a manufacturer if the bidder has the facilities to produce, on his or her own premises, a significant portion of the required component parts needed for the final product, even if the bidder will perform only assembly operations under a particular procurement.

Packaging does not constitute assembly. For example, a bidder who proposes to supply bottles of aspirin, and whose operations would consist solely of purchasing in bulk the aspirin and bottles, transferring the aspirin from the bulk container into bottles, and then labeling, wrapping, and shipping the bottled aspirin, would not qualify as a manufacturer. As another example, a bidder proposing to purchase a hose and a clamp, and place the clamp on the hose to make a "hose assembly," and then package and ship them, is not a manufacturer within the intent of the act.

How to Qualify for an Award as a Manufacturer. If you are a bidder who wants to qualify for an award as a manufacturer, you must show, before the award, that you currently have the plant, equipment, and personnel to manufacture, on the premises, the items called for under the contract. Arrangements and proposals for subcontracting, and a bidder's affiliation or relation with another firm, even one having the same officers or ownership, are not considered to be commitments. Also, they are not evidence of the bidder's own eligibility as a manufacturer, even though the affiliate or subcontractor might be a qualified manufacturer in his or her own right.

If you are a new bidder entering into a manufacturing activity, and have made all necessary arrangements and commitments for manufacturing space, equipment, and personnel on your own premises, you must be able to show that the manufacturing operation is sufficient for contract fulfillment. If you are an offeror newly entering into a manufacturing activity, you must show that written, legally binding arrangements and commitments to enter a manufacturing business have been made. It is not the policy of the government, however, to bar an offeror from receiving an award because the offeror has not yet done any manufacturing, even if the arrangements and commitments are contingent upon the award of a government contract. The written and legally binding arrangements entered into prior to the award of the contract are considered to be evidence of a bona fide intent to establish a continuing manufacturing entity, and in so doing, become an eligible manufacturer. This requirement is intended to exclude from eligibility those bidders who make unsubstantiated assertions that they are eligible, and then either totally subcontract or broker the contract after award.

Manufacturing Space. Manufacturing space can be owned, or leased, by and in, the name of the bidder. Either a recorded deed or a bona fide lease agreement clearly identifying the manufacturing space and setting forth the terms of the lease are considered evidence of prior arrangements and definite commitments for space. If the space is leased, the term of the lease must be sufficient to permit the bidder to clearly fulfill the contract prior to lease expiration.

Manufacturing Equipment. In addition to the commitment for space, the bidder must also own the necessary manufacturing equipment. If this is not the case, then it must be shown that legally binding definite commitments to purchase or lease sufficient equipment to fulfill the contractual requirements have been made. If the equipment is leased, unrestricted control must be demonstrated. The requirements regarding either a bill of sale or purchase order for the necessary equipment may be satisfied by having the appropriate document dated and signed by the bidder, specifically identifying and describing the equipment and the terms of payment. This document must display the required date, or alternatively a promised delivery date, as appropriate.

Letters of intent for space and equipment, and vendor quotations and offers to lease space or equipment do not constitute the required legally binding contractual agreements. Nor does an affidavit stating that a sale or conveyance has occurred.

With regard to personnel availability, the best evidence is the presence on the payroll of manufacturing employees ready and able to fulfill the contract. However, if this is not possible, then affirmative evidence showing that prior arrangements and definite commitments have been made to hire personnel will be considered by the preaward survey team.

In order to fully qualify under the act's provisions, you as a new manufacturer must show that the operation has not just been set up solely to produce under a government contract, and that the operation will not be terminated after the contract is completed. Satisfactory evidence should exist that all of the proper arrangements have been made for establishing production of the items required under the contract on a continuing basis.

The requirement that a company is currently capable of manufacturing on its premises is not fulfilled by the use, rental, or sharing of the facilities of another legal entity. In other words, arrangements for equipment, personnel, and space on a time-and-material or "as needed" basis, does not meet the guidelines.

The mere representation or affirmation that all of the applicable conditions have been fulfilled is also considered insufficient. The evidence must show that all of the applicable conditions have been met *prior to* any award of a contract subject to the act. If it is discovered after award that a bidder did not act in good faith by actually fulfilling these acquisition requirements, the contract will be subject to immediate termination.

How the Act Defines a Regular Dealer

You, as bidder, may qualify as a *regular dealer* if you own, operate, and maintain either a store or warehouse, or other establishment, in which the goods of the general character described by the specifications, and required under the contract, are bought, kept in stock, and sold to the public in the usual course of business. The storage of goods in a public warehouse will not satisfy the place of business requirements unless there is a continuing right (that is, a bona fide written lease agreement) to a specified, identified amount of space in the warehouse. To qualify for award as a regular dealer you must show, to the satisfaction of the contracting agency and prior to any award, that you are engaged in an established regular business, and that you stock and offer for sale to the general public the articles of the same general character required under the contract. The stock maintained must be true inventory from which sales are made. A stock of sample goods, surplus goods from previous orders, stock unrelated to the supplies that are the subject of the bid, or stock maintained primarily for token compliance from which few, if any, sales are made, does not fulfill this requirement.

The dealer's business must be shown to be an established and going concern. It is not sufficient to show that arrangements have been made to set up a business with these characteristics.

For dealers in specific products, alternative qualifications have been established. Currently these products are listed as hay, grain, feed, and straw; raw cotton, lumber, and timber products; machine tools, green coffee, and petroleum; agricultural liming materials, tea, and cotton linters; certain uranium products; and used automatic data processing equipment. In recognition of the existing commercial and industrial practices in those industries, the requirement that the dealer maintain stock has been eliminated.

Authorized Agents

With regard to *agents*, if you as bidder qualify as a manufacturer or regular dealer within the meaning of the act and regulations, you may bid, negotiate, and contract through an authorized agent. It is necessary, however, that the agency be disclosed, and that the agent both bids and contracts in the name of the principal. Brokers, from whom foreign-made goods are purchased and consigned directly to the government, need not qualify as regular dealers, since the contract is not subject to the act.

DETERMINING ELIGIBILITY

The responsibility for applying the eligibility requirements rests first with the contracting officer. It is his or her responsibility to investigate and determine the eligibility of an offeror when there is a question about validity of a bidder's representation. This would also be the case if a protest has been lodged, and the offeror in line for the contract award previously has not been awarded a contract subject to the act.

The Department of Labor neither conducts preaward investigations nor renders final determinations of eligibility until the contracting officer initially has determined whether or not the requirements have been met, and any negative determinations involving small businesses have been confirmed by the Small Business Administration.

If an offeror's representation is not accepted, the contracting officer is required to make a determination as to whether or not all of the applicable eligibility requirements have been met by obtaining and considering all available factual evidence, including:

1. preaward surveys
2. the experience of other acquisition offices
3. information that is available from the cognizant contract administration office
4. information provided directly by the offeror
5. any other factual evidence necessary to help determine whether or not all of the applicable eligibility requirements have been met, including evidence obtained through an on-site survey conducted specifically for this purpose

If the contracting officer determines that an apparently successful large business offeror is ineligible, he or she will notify the company in writing, stating the reasons why it does not meet the eligibility requirements, and that the company may protest the findings by submitting substantiating evidence to the contrary within ten working days. If, after review of the evidence, the contracting officer's position has not changed, the offeror's protest must be submitted by the contracting officer to the Department of Labor, Administrator of the Wage and Hour Division, for a final determination.

If the apparently successful offeror is a small business concern, the same notification and protest procedures apply, with the big exception that any determination of ineligibility, whether or not protested, must be forwarded to the Administrator of the Small Business Administration, and the offeror must be so notified. If the SBA disagrees with the contracting officer's determination, it will reverse the determination and forward the contracting officer a certification of the offeror's eligibility. If the SBA agrees with the contracting officer's determination, it must forward the case to the Department of Labor for determination.

During this period, the award normally should be held in abeyance until a final determination from either the DOL or SBA is received. However, if a survey of the offeror's facilities is conducted, and it is found that the offeror is in compliance with the provisions of the act, the award may be made immediately by the contracting officer. When an award is held in abeyance, the contracting officer is required to notify other offerors whose awards may become eligible, asking them to extend their acceptance period, if necessary.

PROTESTS AGAINST ELIGIBILITY

When another offeror challenges the eligibility of the apparently successful offeror, the contracting officer must notify both parties that their respective substantiating evidence, supporting their respective positions, must be submitted to the contracting officer within ten days. The contracting officer then must investigate the facts, make a determination, and notify both parties of the procedure to be followed if either party disagrees with the decision. If there is disagreement, then notification to either the DOL or SBA is required. The same abeyance procedures apply, unless the contracting officer finds that the award should be made immediately, as described next.

AWARD PENDING FINAL DETERMINATION

If the items required are urgently needed, and the failure to make a prompt award will result in substantial hardship to the government, the contracting officer is permitted to make the award prior to any determination by either the DOL or SBA. Appropriate notification by the contracting officer to these agencies is required.

INDEX - APPENDIX B

APPENDIX C

LISTINGS FOR MAJOR PURCHASING OFFICES AND PRODUCTS

PRODUCTS AND SERVICES BOUGHT BY THE MAJOR MILITARY PURCHASING OFFICES

MAJOR MILITARY PURCHASING OFFICES

The following major military procurement offices make large purchases of materials, supplies and services in support of the Departments which they represent. In addition, each of these major offices frequently makes smaller purchases on behalf of the individual military installations in its area. Small business concerns should request information about these smaller purchases from the major purchasing offices nearest their communities.

Small business owners also should bear in mind that most military installations are authorized to make local purchases in smaller quantities, and to contract for such services as laundry, dry cleaning, shoe repairs, automotive repairs, maintenance and repair services. Therefore, it is important for small firms interested in supplying these local purchases to contact the individual military installations in their areas. A list of military installations, which is in addition to the listing of major purchasing offices given below, will be found in "Local Purchases by Military Installations."

Each Army, Navy, Air Force, and Coast Guard installation in this country establishes its own procurement requirements. Actual purchases of resale items are made at the installation level. In the case of Army and Air Force exchanges, the headquarters conducts negotiations for virtually all U.S.-origin retail merchandise, equipment and supplies for exchanges overseas and many of those items for exchanges in the U.S. Headquarters AAFES also procures most architect-engineer services and major construction for exchanges in the U.S. and some common services for exchanges worldwide. The five CONUS exchange regions purchase some retail merchandise, equipment, supplies and food for feeding activities for exchanges in their respective geographical areas. These regions also contract for concession and support services and some construction for their respective exchanges. Firms desiring additional information regarding selling to the Army and Air Force Exchange Service should write to Procurement Support Division, Army and Air Force Exchange Service, P.O. Box 22305, Dallas TX 75222, or contact one of the exchange regions in A-2 below. Firms wishing to sell to the overseas Navy and Marine Corps exchanges should write the Commanding Officer, Navy Resale and Support Office (AMD), Fort Wadsworth, Staten Island, NY 10305; and the Marine Corps Exchange Service Headquarters, U.S. Marine Corps (LFE), Washington, D.C. 20380.

Firms desiring information on selling to Coast Guard exchanges should write to Commandant (FSU), U.S. Coast Guard, 400 7th Street, S.W., Washington, D.C. 20590.

In selling to individual post exchanges in the United States, a firm may either arrange for representatives to call on the exchanges or may circularize them with descriptive literature, prices, discount terms, shipping data, and other pertinent information. However, personal calls are usually more effective than sales efforts by mail.

For information on selling to the commissary stores contact the Chief, Army Support Services, Department of the Army, Washington, D.C. 20315; Headquarters Air Force Commissary Service (HQAFCOMS), Kelly Air Force Base, San Antonio, TX 78241; the Commanding Officer, Navy Resale and Support Office (AMD) Fort Wadsworth, Staten Island, NY 10305; the Marine Corps Exchange Service Headquarters, U.S. Marine Corps (LFE), Washington, D.C. 20380, and Commandant (FSU), U.S. Coast Guard, 400 7th Street, S.W., Washington, D.C. 20590.

Department of the Army Major Purchasing Offices

A-1 Contracting Officer, Publications Directorate, TAGCEN, Washington, D.C. 20314.

A-2 Headquarters, Army and Air Force Exchange Service, Dallas, Texas 75222 Exchange Regions for the Army and Air Force Exchange Service are as follows:

Alamo Exchange Region, Army and Air Force Exchange Service, 5315 Summit Parkway, San Antonio, TX 78228.

Capitol Exchange Region, Army and Air Force Exchange Service, Bldg. No. 6, Cameron Station, Alexandria, VA 22314.

Golden Gate Exchange Region, Army and Air Force Exchange Service, Box 3553, San Francisco, CA 94119.

Ohio Valley Exchange Region, Army and Air Force Exchange Service, Indiana Army Ammunition Plant, Bldg. #2501, Charlestown, IN 47111.

Southeast Exchange Region, Army and Air Force Exchange Service, 12840 Kershaw Street, Montgomery, AL 36196.

A-4 Director, Defense Supply Service—Washington Office, Secretary of the Army, Washington, D.C. 20310.

A-11 U.S. Army Electronics Research and Development Command (ERADCOM), ATTN: DRDEL-SB, 2800 Powder Mill Road, Adelphi, MD 20783. Tel: 202/394-1076.

ERADCOM performs research, development, engineering and initial procurement of assigned items. As the principal electronics research, development and acquisition center of the Army, ERADCOM accomplishes programs in such areas as electronic signal intelligence, electric warfare, atmospheric sciences, target acquisition and combat surveillance, electronic fuzing, radars, sensors, night vision, radar frequency and optical devices, nuclear weapons effects, instrumentation and simulation, and fluidics. ERADCOM has direct control and management of seven major Army laboratories and four project managers.

Associated Installation/Procuring Activities

Atmospheric Sciences Laboratory (ASL), USA White Sands Missile Range, White Sands, NM 88002. Tel: 915/678-1401.

Engaged in the establishment of an atmospheric/environmental technology base for electro-optical military weapons systems, meteorological equipment systems, and intelligence applications; mission focuses upon the enhancement of combat and strategic operations in the following areas: ground combat, air-mobile operations; site defense; ground trafficability; nuclear, biological and chemical operations; and surveillance, target acquisition, night observation and high-energy lasers. ASL is also working to develop automated meteorological data, new atmospheric sensors, improved meteorological techniques, and upper-atmospheric-transmittance modeling.

Combat Surveillance and Target Acquisition Laboratory (CSTAL), Fort Monmouth, NJ 07703. Tel: 201/532-4511/12/13.

Areas of interest are radar, photography, remote sensing, acoustics, nuclear radiation detection and measurement, data links and identification of friend, foe or neutral (IFFN). CSTAL concentrates upon improving the Army's capability in battlefield surveillance, target acquisition and designation, radiological survey, nuclear burst detection and IFFN.

Electronics Technology and Devices Laboratory (ETDL), Fort Monmouth, New Jersey 07703. Tel: 201/532-4511/12.

Conducts a diversified electronics-oriented program focusing on critical barriers that inhibit the development of next generation systems. Maintains the Army's principal integrated circuit facility and executes broadbased internal and contractual program in the areas of microelectronics display devices, microwave and millimeter wave devices, power sources, frequency control and filter devices, high power subsystems, electron tubes, and electronic materials.

Electronic Warfare Laboratory (EWL), Fort Monmouth, NJ 07703. Tel: 201/532-4511/12/13.

Performs applied research and development in the following areas: intercept, direction finding, signal analysis, jamming, deception, signal intelligence, acoustic intelligence, self-protection, agent equipment security, counterintelligence, vulnerability, countermeasures, and counter-countermeasures. EWL responds to the Army's need for electronic countermeasure protection of aircraft, ground troops and combat vehicles by refining the capability to intercept, identify and locate the source of enemy emissions by facilitating Army operations in a hostile electronics warfare environment, and by confining the enemy's effective use of the electro-magnetic spectrum.

Harry Diamond Laboratories (HDL), ATTN: DELHB-SB, 2800 Powder Mill Road, Adelphi, MD 20783. Tel: 202/394-1076.

Performs basic and applied research, development engineering (including prototype model production and related industrial and maintenance engineering), development testing and evaluation, in the fields of radiating and influence fuzing, electronic delay or fluid time fuzing, selected command fuzing, and pure fluid systems; performs related studies of means of optimizing weapon effects through fuzing, of target signatures, of the effects of countermeasures, battlefield nuclear high altitude and space environments on systems performance, and of means of providing the maximum practicable immunity to such environmental effects as are adverse; performs related research and development on instrumentation, measurements, and simulation, and on materials, components & subsystems, including power supplies, transducers and control systems, lead laboratory for fluidics technology; lead laboratory for nuclear weapons effects to provide the Army with information, materials, and techniques necessary for the evaluation of the nuclear survivability, vulnerability, and hardening of Army weapons, communication and materiel systems; performs as the DARCOM countermeasure/counter-countermeasure (CM/CCM) focal point in order to provide Army equipment with the capability to function and survive in the battlefield environment.

Night Vision and Electro-Optic Laboratories (NVEOL), Fort Belvoir, VA 22060. Tel: 703/664-2482.

Provides the Army with equipment that will enable it to carry out nocturnal operations with daylight efficiency. The laboratory's attention is directed at image intensification, far infrared, radiation sources, visionics, lower-cost all-weather vision systems and electro-optical low-energy lasers, and associated research and development and first production buys related thereto.

Signals Warfare Laboratory (SWL), Vint Hill Farms Station, Warrenton, VA 22186. Tel: 703/347-6284.

Responsible for research, development, acquisition, and integration of electronics equipment required to support the Army's signal intelligence, electronic warfare, and signal security missions. SWL's efforts provide the Army with the defense capability of obstructing the enemy's use of electromagnetic emissions as well as the offensive capability to utilize those same enemy emissions for the purpose of acquiring tactical information. The laboratory's expertise is the development of equipment that will allow for jamming, deception or information leading to the destruction of hostile electronics devices and systems.

U.S. Army Communications and Electronics Material Readiness Command (CECOM), ATTN: DRSEL-SB, Fort Monmouth, NJ 07703. Tel: 201/532-4511 or 4512.

The US Army Communications-Electronics Command (CECOM) is responsible for research, development, engineering, and acquisition of assigned communications/ADP items/systems, including life cycle software support of assigned command, control, and communications systems; and for all materiel readiness functions associated with assigned communications-electronics systems/subsystems and related equipment. It also has the responsibility to execute assigned missions in support of other US Army Materiel Development and Readiness Command (DARCOM) or Department of Defense (DoD) elements having centralized management responsibilities for specific communications-electronics systems or items.

CECOM is the host command at Fort Monmouth, NJ, providing installation support to tenant commands and activities.

CECOM was activated 1 May 1981 with the merger of the

US Army Communications and Electronics Materiel Readiness Command (CERCOM) and the US Army Communications Research and Development Command (CORADCOM).
The CECOM mission covers the full spectrum of services to the US soldier in the field of communications-electronics. The first steps in converting concepts into new military materiel are taken in the CECOM Research and Development Center and its centers for Communications Systems (CENCOMS), Tactical Computer Systems (CENTACS) and Systems Engineering and Integration (CENSEI). These centers are responsible for research and development on military command, control and communications (C^3) systems designed to improve the ability of the battlefield commander to accomplish his assigned missions.
Along with making full use of its own scientists, engineers and laboratories, the Research and Development Center works closely under contract with the electronics industry in accomplishing its mission. Systems under development will help the commander to perceive the battlefield, plan operations, allocate and sustain forces in a timely manner and finally to engage the enemy. These systems will represent an all-important force multiplier.

U.S. ARMY MEDICAL DEPARTMENT

The U.S. Army Medical Department consists of two procuring activities one of which is Office of The Surgeon General and the other is the U.S. Army Health Services Command, a major command.

OFFICE OF THE SURGEON GENERAL

The Surgeon General is responsible for development, policy direction, organization, and overall management of an integrated Army-wide health services system. The Principal Assistant Responsible for Contracting for the Office of The Surgeon General is located at the following address:

A-12 Commander, US Army Medical Materiel Agency, ATTN: SGMMA-HCA, Frederick, MD 21701, Tel. 301/663-7477.
The contracting office under the Office of the Surgeon General is responsible for the acquisition of medical research and development; minor construction (repairs and rehabilitation of buildings); grounds keeping, custodial and mess attendant services; laboratory supplies and equipment; specialized research equipment; research animals; office supplies; equipment; machine rentals and repairs; electrical, plumbing and chemical supplies; and miscellaneous hardware and tools for various agencies under the Office of The Surgeon General, Fort Detrick Garrison, and its tenant activities.
Contracting office
Commander, US Army Medical Research and Development Command, ATTN: SGRD-RMA, Fort Detrick, Frederick, MD 21701, Tel: 301/663-2183

A-13 U.S. ARMY HEALTH SERVICES COMMAND

The Commander of the US Army Health Services Command (HSC) as the single manager for the delivery of health care for the US Army within the fifty states and Panama has procurement offices within selected medical centers to accomplish his mission. These procurement offices which are subordinate to HSC Procurement Office, DCSLOG, Ft. Sam Houston, Texas 78234, Tel 512/221-3568, are responsible for the local procurement of nonstandard medical supplies and equipment, specialized research equipment and research animals, limited quantities of drugs and biologicals and medical related services.
Walter Reed and Fitzsimons Army Medical Centers in addition to purchasing the above items, are authorized to buy a variety of supplies and services such as: Automotive spare parts, housekeeping supplies, office supplies, equipment, machine rentals and repairs, electrical, plumbing, chemical supplies, and miscellaneous hardware. Services include minor construction (repairs and rehabilitation of buildings) lawn mowing, grounds keeping, etc.
Those medical treatment facilities that do not have an organized procurement office are dependent upon the installation procurement office for procurement support.

PURCHASING OFFICES (Under HSC)

Brooke Army Medical Center, ATTN: HSHG-MDL-PC, Fort Sam Houston, Texas 78234, Tel: 512/221-5446.
William Beaumont Army Medical Center, ATTN: HSHK-MDLD-P, El Paso, Texas 79920, Tel: 915/568-6900.
Letterman Army Medical Center, ATTN: HSHH-MDLC, Presidio of San Francisco, CA 94129, Tel: 415/561-5474.
Madigan Army Medical Center, ATTN: HSHJ-MD-LOC, Tacoma, Washington, 98431, Tel: 206/967-6707.
Walter Reed Medical Center, ATTN: HSHM-LP, Washington, DC 20012, Tel: 202/427 5081.
Fitzsimons Army Medical Center, ATTN: HSHG-SPC, Denver, CO 80240, Tel: 303/341-8758.
Tripler Army Medical Center, ATTN: HSHK-LD, Tripler AMC, HI 96859.

A-21 U.S. Army Missile Command (MICOM), ATTN: DRSMI-B, Redstone Arsenal, AL 35809, Tel: 205/876-5441.
Areas of responsibility include (1) design and development, (2) product, production, and maintenance engineering; and (3) new equipment training design of pertinent training devices. The U.S. Army Missile Command is responsible for integrated commodity management of free rockets, guided missiles, ballistic missiles, targets, air defense, fire control coordination equipment, related special purposes and multisystem test equipment, missile launching and ground support equipment metrology and calibration equipment, and other associated equipment.

A-31 U.S. Army Tank-Automotive Command (TACOM), ATTN: DRSTA-CB, Warren, Michigan 48090, Tel: 313/573-5388/5406.
The U.S. Army Tank-Automotive Command (TACOM) is responsible for research, design, development, engineering, test management, modification, product assurance, integrated logistics support, acquisition, and deployment of the following items: Combat, tactical, special purpose vehicles, (e.g. automotive systems, subsystems, and engines, transmissions, suspensions, electrical, peculiar diagnostic test equipment, armor materials application and vehicle survivasbility, and miscellaneous vehicular components), carriers (e.g. personnel, cargo, missile, and rearm), trailers, tractors, special tools, and special purpose kits.
TACOM has the responsibility for the procurement production, maintenance, supply, and repair parts support of the US Armed Forces vehicle fleet, general purpose, construction equipment, material handling equipment, and tactical vehicles for the DoD and our foreign allies.

Associated Installations
Keeweenaw Field Research Center, Houghton, Michigan 49331.
Detroit Arsenal, Warren, Michigan 48090.
Pontiac Storage Facility, Pontiac, Michigan 48657.
Army Tank Center, Lima, Ohio 45804.
TACOM Support Activity-Selfridge, Selfridge ANG BASE, Selfridge, Michigan 48046.

U.S. Army Test and Evaluation Command (TECOM), Aberdeen Proving Ground, MD 21005, Tel: 301/278-4790.
The mission of the U.S. Army Test and Evaluation Command is to direct those assigned research activities, proving grounds, installations, boards, and facilities required to test equipment, weapons, and materiel systems to plan and conduct tests of materiel intended for use by the U.S. Army, or developed by the Army for use by other departments of the Government, and to assure efficient and economic use of test facilities.

Associated Installations
U.S. Army Aberdeen Proving Ground, ATTN: STEAP-DC-S, Aberdeen Proving Ground, MD 21005.

Tel: 301/278-3878.
U.S. Army Dugway Proving Ground, ATTN: STEDP-PR, Dugway, Utah 84022, Tel: 801/522-2102.
U.S. Army Jefferson Proving Ground, ATTN: STEJP-LD-P, Madison, Indiana 47250, Tel: 812/273-7226.
U.S. Army White Sands Missile Range, ATTN: STEWS-PR, White Sands Missile Range, NM 88002, Tel: 915/678-1401.
U.S. Army Yuma Proving Ground, ATTN: STEYP-PC, Yuma, Arizona 85364, Tel: 602/328-2825.
U.S. Army, Natick Research and Development Laboratories (NLABS), Natick MA 01760, Tel: 617/633-4995.
NLABS is responsible for research and development of items/systems to include: air drop equipment (platforms, parachutes and packaging); organizational equipment; refrigeration equipment; non-powered heaters; DoD tactical shelters; individual field sanitation equipment; biological materials (germicides, insecticides); tentage and equipage; clothing and personnel equipment; DoD food and food service equipment; containers and packaging (excluding HME containers physical security (safes and padlocks); materials (textiles, rubber, leather, plastic, paper and chemicals); field support equipment (printing, composing and duplicating); hand tools; office equipment and supplies and furnishings; appliances; and cleaning equipment.

A-32 U.S.Army Aviation Research and Development Command, (AVRADCOM) ATTN: DRDAV-V, Bldg. 105, 4300 Goodfellow Blvd., St. Louis, MO 63120, Tel: 314/263-1400.
AVRADCOM is responsible for research and development of new helicopter systems, support of qualification testing of turbine engines, development and evaluation of prototype hardware for fueling and defueling equipment for use in combat areas and solving of fuel contamination problems. Conducts research in both explanatory and advanced development is subsonic areas of application.

Associated Installations:

Aeromechanics Laboratory, NASA Ames Research Center, Moffett Field, California 94035, Tel: 415/965-5584/5837.
The Mission of Research and Development Laboratory (RTL) is to plan, develop, manage, and execute, for AVRADCOM, the research and explanatory development programs, and the advanced development programs through demonstration of technology to provide a firm technical base for future development of superior airmobile systems.
Applied Technology Laboratory, Fort Eustis, Virginia 23604, Tel: 804/878-4828.
RTL achieves its mission through in-house studies, utilization of the resources of academic institutions and commercial research organizations, close cooperation with other Government agencies, and the award of contracts to aerospace industrial firms, colleges, and universities.
Aviation Engineering Flight Activity, Edwards AF Base, California, 93523, Tel: 805/277-3756.
NASA Langley Research Center, Hampton, Virginia 23605, 804/827-1110.
Propulsion Laboratory, NASA Lewis Research Center, Cleveland, Ohio 44135, Tel: 216/433-4000.
U.S. Army Troop Support and Aviation, Materiel Readiness Command, (TSARCOM) ATTN: DRSTS-V, 4300 Goodfellow Blvd., St. Louis, MO 63120, Tel: 314/263-2222.
Integrated commodity management and procurement responsibility for the following types of equipment: surface transportation (other than tactical wheeled and general purpose vehicles); aircraft both fixed and rotary wing; electric power generation, and services; barrier equipment (including mine and dispensing; general support and supplies (fire fighting, industrial engines, heating and air conditioning, water purification, etc.); test equipment that is apart of, or used with assigned materiel, and aerial delivery equipment.
After a communications-electronics system of item passes the research and development stage, CECOM must procure and manage it. As the Army's direct link with the electronics industry, CECOM contracts for the full range of communications-electronics equipment and systems, along with spare parts, tools, and special items for maintenance and repair.
CECOM also is responsible for keeping fielded communications-electronics equipment in a high state of readiness. This task includes worldwide distribution of materiel and integrated materiel management of C-E systems and repair and support items. CECOM also provides maintenance support for communications and electronics equipment and systems in the field.
The fourteen DARCOM major subordinate commands listed below include eight research and development commands (responsible for developmental contracts) five readiness commands (responsible for most production contracts), and one test and evaluation command. The major subordinate commands are:

A-45 U.S. Army Armament, Research and Development, Command (ARRADCOM), ATTN: DRDAR-SB, Dover, N.J. 07801, Tel: 201/328-4106.
The U.S. Army Armament Research and Development Command is responsible for the conduct of management of research, development, life-cycle engineering, product-assurance, initial acquisition, and acquisition through transition to the U.S. Army Armament Materiel Readiness Command (including product engineering, production engineering, maintainability engineering, value engineering, human factors engineering) and surety of: Weapons and ammunition, nuclear and nonnuclear (including artillery weapons, infantry weapons, crew served weapons, mortars and recoilless rifles, gun type air defense weapons, surface vehicles mounted weapons, and aircraft mounted weapons); weapons systems and support equipment; turrets, cupolas and mounts required for weapon installation and operation; fire control equipment; rocket and missile warhead sections; demolition munitions, mines, bombs, generades, pyrotechnics, boosters, JATO's; offensive and defensive chemical materiel, flame and incendiary systems and defensive biological and radiological materiel as assigned; and special tools and test equipment which are a part of or used with assigned materiel.

Associated Installations

Chemical Systems Laboratory, Edgewood Area, Aberdeen Proving Ground, Maryland 21010, Tel: 301/671-2309.
Research and development in the fields of chemical, smoke and flame weapons, including defensive aspects; development, production and maintenance engineering related to new and standard chemical, smoke, incendiary flame and special weapons systems and CBR defense items.
Benet Weapons Laboratory, Watervliet Arsenal, Watervliet N.Y. 12189, Tel: 518/266-5005.
Research, development, engineering and design of mortars, recoilless rifles and cannon for tanks, towed and self-propelled artillery.
Balistics Research Laboratory, Aberdeen Proving Ground, Maryland 21010, Tel: 301/671-2309.
Basic and applied research in mathematics, physics, chemistry, biophysics, and the engineering sciences related to the solution of problems concerned with ballistics and vulnerability technology.
US Army Armament Materiel, Readiness Command (ARRCOM), ATTN: DRSAR-SB, Rock Island, Illinois 61299, Tel: 309/794-5145.
The US Army Armament Materiel Readiness Command is responsible for Integrated logistics (materiel readiness) management, including follow-on procurement, production, engineering in support of production, industrial management, product assurance, maintenance, value, and logistics engineering, international logistics, and transportation and traffic management of: Artillery weapons systems (towed and self propelled) Components of weapons systems including: tube and breech, gun, ammunition (including fill and fuze), fire control, and recoil; also infantry weapons systems (individual and crew-served), Air defense weapons systems (gun type) aircraft weapons systems, rocket warheads and non-nuclear munitions, chemical systems, protective equipment, tools, and test equipment. ARRCOM has responsibility of Single Manager for conventional ammunition for the Department of Defense. Also control over four arsenals, 27 government owned—contractor operated army ammunition plants (AAP), and two government owned—government operated AAP/activities.

Associated Installations

Rock Island Arsenal, ATTN: DRSAR-SB, Rock Island, Illinois 61299, Tel: 309-794.
Performs manufacturing, fabrication, engineering support to

production and product assurance of assigned materiel. Manages Dept. of Army Tool Set program. Procures equipment, services and supplies in support of above.

Watervleit Arsenal, ATTN: SARWV-SB, Watervliet, NY 12189, Tel: 518/266-5765.

Performs process engineering and value engineering for morters, recoilless rifles, cannon, and cannon components. Procures cannon and cannon components including equipment, services, and supplies in support of fabrication mission.

Pine Bluff Arsenal, ATTN: SARPB-SU, Pine Bluff, AR 71611, Tel: 501/541-3159.

Specialization in the manufacture, assembly, and demilitarization of chemical munitions.

Rocky Mountain Arsenal, Denver, CO 80022, ATTN: SARRAM-TSP, Tel: 303/288-0711 Ext 274.

Specialization in the manufacture, assembly, and demilitarization of chemical munitions.

McAlester Army Ammunition Plant, ATTN: SRRMC-DLP, McAlester, Oklahoma 74501, Tel: 918/421-2422.

Produce/renovate conventional ammunition and related components, perform industrial engineering and product assurance; store, ship, demilitarization & disposal of conventional ammo; operate a calibration lab.

A-60 USA Ballistics Missile Defense Systems Command, PO Box 1500, Huntsville, Ala., 35807.

Project Manager, ballistics missiles

A-61 USA Communications Command, Procurement Division, PO Box 748, Fort Huachuca, Az., 85613.

Communications engineering services.

A-62 USA Troop Support Agency, Building P-12400, Fort Lee, Va., 23801.

Troops subsistence and commisary resale items.

A-63 U.S. Army Mobility Equipment Research and Development Command (MERADCOM), ATTN: DRDME-ZV, Fort Belvoir, Virginia 22060, Tel: 703/664-2482.

MERADCOM is responsible for integrated commodity management (research, development, procurement, initial production, integrated logistics management, maintenance and quality assurance) of mobility equipment in four areas: mobility/countermobility; survivability; energy; and logistics. These include countermine, counterobstacle/construction equipment, gap crossing/bridging, obstacles/barriers, field fortifications, camouflage, physical security, tunnel detection, topographic equipment, tactical sensors electric power, fuels and lubricants, heaters and air conditioners, water supply, fuels handling, materials handling equipment, marine craft, and railway and utility equipment. As Department of Defense lead agency for terrestrial applications of solar energy, MERADCOM is responsible for developing photovoltaic solar systems for use by all military services. The command is also responsible for the development of the Army Energy Plan. As DARCOM lead laboratory for countermine and camouflage, it is responsible for coordinating and directing related efforts at all DARCOM laboratories. MERADCOM also engineers and procures topographic equipment, landing mats, and insect and rodent control equipment developed by other Army organizations. In addition, it performs the R&D procurement functions for other Fort Belvoir-based organizations including: Night Vision and Electro Optics Laboratory, (NV&EOL), U.S. Army Engineer Topographic Laboratories (ETL), U.S. Army Facilities Engineering Support Agency (FESA), the DoD Project Manager for Mobile Electric Power, the Product Manager for Physical Security Equipment, and the U.S. Army Computer Systems Command.

U.S. ARMY CORPS OF ENGINEERS

The corps of Engineers contracts with civilian contractors for construction, maintenance, and repair of buildings, structures, and utilities for the Department of the Army. The Corps of Engineers is also responsible for civil works such as river and harbor improvement, flood control, hydroelectric power, and related projects. Inquiries concerning military construction or civil works should be sent to the following offices:

A-77 Office of Chief of Engineers, Department of the Army, Washington, D.C. 20314.

U.S.A. Engineer Division, Europe, APO New York 09757.

U.S.A. Engineer Division, Huntsville, P.O. Box 1600 West Station, Huntsville, Alabama 35807.

U.S.A. Engineer Division, Lower Mississippi Valley, P.O. Box 80, Vicksburg, Mississippi 39180.

U.S.A. Engineer District, Memphis, 668 Clifford Davis Federal Building, Memphis, Tennessee 38103.

U.S.A. Engineer District, New Orleans, P.O. Box 60267, New Orleans, Lousiana 70160.

U.S.A. Engineer District, St. Louis, 210 North 12th Street, St. Louis, Missouri 63101.

U.S.A. Engineer District, Vicksburg, P.O. Box 60, Vicksburg, Mississippi 39180.

U.S.A. Engineer Division, Middle East, APO New York, 09038.

U.S.A. Engineer Division, Middle East (Rear), P.O. Box 2250, Winchester, Virginia 22601.

U.S.A. Engineer District, Al Batin, APO New York 09038.

U.S.A. Engineer District, Riyadh, APO New York 09038.

U.S.A. Engineer Logistics Command, Saudi Arabia, APO New York 09038.

U.S.A. Engineer Division, Missouri River, P.O. Box 103 Downtown Station, Omaha, Nebraska 68101.

U.S.A. Engineer Division, New England, 424 Trapelo Road, Waltham, Massachusetts 02254.

U.S.A. Engineer Division, North Atlantic, 90 Church Street, New York, New York, 10007.

U.S.A. Enginner District, Baltimore, P.O. Box 1715, Baltimore, Maryland 21203.

U.S.A. Engineer District, New York, 26 Federal Plaza, New York, New York 10278.

U.S.A. Engineer District, Norfold, 803 Front Street, Norfolk, Virginia 23510.

U.S.A Engineer District, Philadelphia, U.S. Custom House, 2nd & Chestnut Street, Philadelphia, Pennsylvania 19106.

U.S.A. Engineer Division, North Central, 536 S. Clark Street, Chicago, Illinois 60605.

U.S.A. Engineer District, Buffalo, 1776 Niagara Street, Buffalo, New York 14207.

U.S.A. Engineer District, Chicago, 219 S. Dearborn Street, Chicago, Illinois 60604.

U.S.A. Engineer District, Detroit, P.O. Box 1027, Detroit, Michigan 48231.

U.S.A. Engineer District, Rock Island, Clock Tower Building, Rock Island, Illinois 61201.

U.S.A. Engineer District, St. Paul, 1135 USPO & Custom House, St. Paul, Minnesota 55101.

U.S.A. Engineer Division, North Pacific, P.O. Box 2870, Portland, Oregon 97208.

U.S.A. Engineer District, Kansas City, 700 Federal Building, Kansas City, Missouri 64106.

U.S.A. Engineer District, Omaha, 6014 USPO & Courthouse, Omaha, Nebraska, 68102.

U.S.A. Engineer District, Seattle, 4735 East Marginal Way South, Seattle, Washington 98134.

U.S.A. Engineer District, Walla Walla, Bldg. 602, City-County Airport, Walla Walla, Washington, 99362.

U.S.A. Engineer Division, Ohio River, P.O. Box 1159, Cincinnati, Ohio 45201.

U.S.A. Engineer District, Huntington, P.O. Box 2127, Huntington, West Virginia 25721.

U.S.A. Engineer District, Louisville, P.O. Box 59, Louisville, Kentucky 40201.

U.S.A. Engineer District, Nashville, P.O. Box 1070, Nashville, Tennessee 37202.

U.S.A. Engineer District, Pittsburgh, Federal Building, 1000 Liberty Avenue, Pittsburgh, Pennsylvania 15222.

U.S.A. Engineer Division, Pacific Ocean, Bldg. 230, Ft. Shafter, Hawaii 96558.

U.S.A. Engineer District, Far East, APO San Francisco 96301.

U.S.A. Engineer District, Japan, APO San Francisco 96343.

U.S.A. Engineer Division, South Atlantic, 510 Title Building, 30 Pryor Street, S.W., Atlanta, Georgia 30303.

U.S.A. Engineer District, Alaska, P.O. Box 7002, Anchorage, Alaska 99510.

U.S.A.Engineer District, Portland, P.O. Box 2946, Portland, Oregon 97208.
U.S.A. Engineer District, Charleston, P.O. Box 919, Charleston, South Carolina 29402.
U.S.A. Engineer District, Jacksonville, P.O. Box 4970, Jacksonville, Florida 32201.
U.S.A. Engineer District, Mobile, P.O. Box 2288, Mobile, Alabama 36628.
U.S.A. Engineer District, Savannah, P.O. Box 889, Savannah, Georgia 31402.
U.S.A. Engineer District, Wilmington, P.O. Box 1890, Wilmington, North Carolina 28401.
U.S.A. Engineer Division, South Pacific, 630 Sansome Street, Rm. 1216, San Francisco, California 94111.
U.S.A. Engineer District, Los Angeles, P.O. Box 2711, Los Angeles, California 90053.
U.S.A. Engineer District, Sacramento, 650 Capitol Mall, Sacramento, California 95814.
U.S.A. Engineer District, San Francisco, 211 Main Street, San Francisco, California 94105.
U.S.A. Engineer Division, Southwestern, 1114 Commerce Street, Dallas, Texas 75242.
U.S.A. Engineer District, Albuquerque, P.O. Box 1580, Albuquerque, New Mexico 87103.
U.S.A. Engineer District, Fort Worth, P.O. Box 17300, Fort Worth, Texas 76102.
U.S.A. Engineer District, Galveston, P.O. Box 1229, Galveston, Texas 77553.
U.S.A. Engineer District, Little Rock, P.O. Box 867, Little Rock, Arkansas 72203.
U.S.A. Engineer District, Tulsa, P.O. Box 61, Tulsa, Oklahoma 74102.
U.S.A. Corps of Engineers, MX Program Agency, Norton AFB, California 92409.

A-96 Eastern Area, Military Traffic Management Command, Bayonne, NJ 07002

A-97 Western Area, Military Traffic Management Command, Oakland Army Base, Oakland, CA 94626

A-98 Military Traffic Management Command, 5611 Columbia Pike, Falls Church, Va., 22041
Stevedoring and Related Terminal Services; Truck and rail tariffs/tenders; passenger traffic; household goods moves and storage.

A-99 USA Computer Systems Command, Fort Belvior, Va., 22060
Computer hardware

Department of the Navy Major Purchasing Offices

N-1 Commander, Naval Air Systems Command, Department of the Navy, Washington, D.C. 20361.

N-3 Commander, Naval Sea Systems Command, Department of the Navy, Washington, D.C. 20362.

N-4 Commander, Naval Facilities Engineering Command, Department of the Navy, 200 Stovall St., Alexandria, VA 22332.

N-5 Commandant of the Marine Corps (Code LB), Headquarters, U.S. Marine Corps, Department of the Navy, Washington, D.C. 20380.

N-6 Commanding Officer, Naval Regional Contracting Center, Washington Navy Yard, Washington, D.C. 20390.

N-7 Chief of Naval Research, Department of the Navy, 800 N. Quincy St., Arlington, VA 22217.

N-8 Commander, Naval Electronic System Command, Department of the Navy, Washington, D.C. 20363.

N-9 Commanding Officer, Navy Aviation Supply Office, 700 Robbins Avenue, Philadelphia, Pennsylvania 19111.

N-11 Commanding Officer, Navy Ships Parts, Control Center, Mechanicsburg, Pennsylvania 17055.

N-12 Commanding Officer, Naval Regional Contracting Center, Long Beach, California 90822.

N-14 Commanding Officer, Naval Regional Contracting Center, Philadelphia, Pennsylvania 19112.

N-19 Director, Naval Research Laboratory, 4555 Overlook Avenue, S.W., Washington, D.C. 20390.

N-19a Commanding Officer, Naval Training Equipment Center, Orlando, Florida 32813.

N-21 Commanding Officer, Navy Resale and Support Office (AMD), Fort Wadsworth, Staten Island, NY 10305.
This Office provides support and administrative and technical guidance and assistance to exchanges, commissary stores and ships stores afloat of the Navy Resale System and purchases equipment for these activities. Resale merchandise and supplies are generally purchased at the local level by individual exchanges, commissary stores and ships stores afloat based on Price Agreement Bulletins negotiated by the Navy Resale System Office and, for commissary items, contract bulletins developed by the Defense Personnel Support Center, Philadelphia, Pennsylvania. Interested business concerns may obtain a listing of Navy Resale activities and information concerning procedures to follow to receive consideration as potential suppliers of resale items from the Navy Resale System Office in Brooklyn.

N-21a Marine Corps Exchange Service Headquarters, U.S. Marine Corps (LFE), Washington, D.C. 20380.
This office exercises management and technical control of Marine Corps exchanges. However, needed equipment and material and merchandise for resale to military personnel are purchased on a local decentralized basis by individual Marine Corps exchanges and commissaries. A listing of Exchanges to contact for sales opportunities may be obtained from the Marine Exchange Service, Headquarters, U.S. Marine Corps (LFE), Department of the Navy, Washington, D.C. 20380.

N-24 Commanding Officer, Naval Administrative Command, Naval Training Center, Great Lakes, Illinois 60088.
Commanding Officer, Naval Supply Center, Oakland, California 94625.
Commanding Officer, Naval Supply Center, Charleston, S.C. 29411.
Commanding Officer, Naval Supply Center, Building W 143, 6th Floor, Norfolk, Virginia 23512.
Commanding Officer, Naval Suply Center, 937 North Harbor Drive, San Diego, California 92132.
Commanding Officer, Naval Supply Center, Pearl Harbor, Hawaii; Mailing Address: Box 300, FPO San Francisco 96610.
Commanding Officer, Naval Supply Depot (Guam), Mailing Address: FPO San Francisco 96630.
Commanding Officer, Naval Supply Center, Puget Sound, Bremerton, Washington 98314.

N-25 Commander, Charleston Naval Shipyard, Code 530, Building 198, Charleston, South Carolina 29408.
Commander, Portsmouth Naval Shipyard, Portsmouth, N.H. 03801.
Commander, Pearl Harbor Naval Shipyard, Box 400, FPO San Francisco 96610.
Commander, Norfolk Naval Shipyard, Portsmouth, Virginia 23709.
Commander, Mare Island Naval Shipyard, Vallejo, Calif. 94592.

N-26 Commanding Officer, Naval Air Station, Patuxent River, Md. 20670.
Commanding Officer, Naval Air Station, Jacksonville, Florida 32212.
Commanding Officer, Naval Air Station, Pensacola, Florida 32508.
Commanding Officer, Naval Air Station, Memphis (84), Millington, Tennessee 38054
Commanding Officer Naval Air Station, Corpus Christi, Texas 78419.
Commanding General, Marine Corps Air Station, Cherry Point, N.C. 28533.
Commanding Officer, Naval Air Station, Alameda, California 94501.
Commanding Officer, Naval Air Station, North Island, San Diego, California 92135.
Commanding Officer, Naval Air Station, Norfolk, Virginia 23511.

N-27 Commanding Officer, Naval Avionics Center, Indianapolis, Indiana 46218.

Officer in Charge, Naval Ocean Systems Center, San Diego, California 92152.
Commanding Officer, Code NA4, Naval Underwater Systems Center, Newport, R.I. 02840.
Commander, Naval Surface Weapons Center, White Oak Laboratory, Silver Spring, Maryland 20910.
Commanding Officer, Naval Ordnance Station, Indian Head, Md. 20640.
Commanding Officer, Naval Ordnance Station, Louisville, KY. 40214.
Commanding Officer, Naval Coastal Systems Center, Panama City, Fla. 32401.
Commanding Officer, Naval Torpedo Station, Keyport, Washington, 98345.
Commander, Naval Surface Weapons Center, Dahlgren Laboratory, Dahlgren, Virginia 22448.

N-27a Commanding Officer, Naval Weapons Support Center, Crane, Indiana 47522

N-28 Superintendent, Naval Academy, Annapolis, Md. 21402.
Commanding Officer, Naval Station, Key West, Fla. 33040.

N-29 Commanding Officer, Naval Submarine Base, New London, Box 00, Groton, Conn. 06040.

N-29a Commanding Officer, Naval Air Engineering Center, Lakehurst, New Jersey 08733.

N-29b Commander, Naval Oceanographic Office, NSTL Branch, HTT: Code 4130, Bay St. Louis, Miss. 39522.

N-29c Commander, Naval Air Development Center, Warminster, Pa. 18974.

N-31 Commanding General, Marine Corps Logistics Support Base, Albany, Georgia 31704.
Commanding General, Marine Corps Supply Center, Barstow, Calif. 97312.

-N-77 Officer in Charge of Construction, NFEC Contracts, Madrid, Spain. Mail: Officer in Charge of Construction, Naval Facilities Engineering Command Contracts, APO New York, N.Y. 09285.
Commander, Pacific Division, Naval Facilities Engineering Command, FPO San Francisco, Calif. 96610.
Officer in Charge of Construction, NFEC Contracts, Far East, FPO San Francisco, Calif. 96662.
Officer in Charge of Construction, NFEC Contracts, Southwest Pacific, FPO San Francisco, Calif. 96528.
Commanding Officer, Northern Division, Naval Facilities Enginnering Command, Philadelphia, Pennsylvania 19112.
Commander, Atlantic Division, Naval Facilities Engineering Command, U.S. Naval Base, Norfolk, Virginia 23511.
Commanding Officer, Chesapeake Division, Naval Facilities Engineering Command, Washington Navy Yard, Washington, D.C. 20390.
Commanding Officer, Southern Division, Naval Facilities Engineering Command, 2144 Melbourne St., Charleston, South Carolina 29411.
Commanding Officer, Western Division, Naval Facilities Engineering Command, P.O. Box 727, San Bruno, Calif. 94067.

N-79 Commander, Military Sealift Command, Department of the Navy, Washington, D.C. 20360.

N-79a Contact one of the following Officers: Commander, Military Sealift Command, Atlantic Military Ocean Terminal, Bldg. 42, Bayonne, N.J. 07002.
Commander, Military Sealift Command, Pacific Naval Supply Center, Oakland, Calif. 94625.

N-80 Naval Air Technical Services Facility, 700 Robbins Ave., Philadelphia, Pennsylvania 19111.

N-81 Navy Publications and Printing Service Management Office. Address inquiries to Director, Navy Publications and Printing Service, Management Office, Washington Navy Yard, Bldg. 157-3, Washington, D.C. 20374.

United States Air Force Major Purchasing Activities

AF-1 Ogden Air Logistics Center, Hill Air Force Base, Ogden, Utah 84056.
a. Generally assigned to the Army or Navy for procurement
b. For the following missiles: CIM-10, LGM-30, LGM-25c, AGM-65.
c. For the following aircraft: F-101, F-4, F-16.
d. For the following engines: LR-59, LR-87, LR-91, J-43, LR-58.

AF-2 Oklahoma City Air Logistics Center, Tinker Air Force Base, Oklahoma City, OK 73145.
a. Purchases services and commodities for the following missiles: AGM-69A, AGM86B, AGM-109H, BGM109G.
b. Purchases services and commodities for the following aircraft: A-7D, A-7K, B-1B, B-52, C-135, EC-135, WC-135, C-137B/C, E-3A, E4A/B, KC-10, KC-135, NC-135, NKC-135, RC-135, C-18.
c. Purchases services and commodities for the following engines: J-79, J-402, F-101, F-107, F-108, TF-30, TF-33, TF-41, JT-3D, JT8D, T-58, T-64.

AF-3 Sacramento Air Logistics Center, McClellan Air Force Base, Sacramento, CA 95652.
a. For use with the Atlas, Titan, and Thor missiles.
b. Purchases services and commodities for the following aircraft. A-1, A-10, C-12, C-121, F-84, F-86, F-100, F-104, F-105, F-111, FB-111, T-28, T-33, T-39, and communication-electronics systems - non airborne, meteorological, microwave command guidance, surveillance and warning and air-to-air recovery systems.

AF-4 San Antonio Air Logistics Center, Kelly Air Force Base, San Antonio, TX 78241.
a. For the following aircraft: A-37A/B, O-2A, T-37, T-38, T-41, Lockheed C-5, Douglas C-9A, Convair C-131, F-102, F-106, T-29, Northrop F-5, F-51, OV-10A, VC-6, C-6, T-43, 627-A.
b. For the following aircraft engines: IO-360, IO-520, O-470, J-69, O-480, T-53, R-985, R-1340, R-1830, R-2000, R-2800, R-4360, J-52, R-1300, R-3350, J-65, J-44, J-85, TF39, T56, T76, Pratt and Whitney (Canada) T400-CP-400, O-290, O-300, J-100, R-1820, F-100, T55 JT8D, TPE331, J-62.

AF-5 Warner Robins Air Logistics Center, Robins Air Force Base, Warner Robins, GA 31098.
a. Purchases services and commodities for the following missiles: AIM4/AIM26, AIM7, AIM9, AGM12/ATM12, AGM45, AGM78A/ATM78A, BQM34, MQM13, AQM91, XQM93A.
b. Purchases services and commodities for the following aircraft: B-57, B-66, RB-57F, C-7A, C-8A, C-46, C-47/C-117, C-54, C-118/DC-6B, C-119, C-123, C-124, C-130, C-133, C-140, C-141, C-142, CH-47, F-15, H-1, H-3, H-13, H-19, H-21, H-23, H-34, H-43, H-53, HU-16, O-1, U-3, U-4, U-6, U-10, U-17.

AF-6 Aeronautical Systems Division, Wright-Patterson AFB, Dayton, OH 45433.

AF-7 2750th Air Base Wing, Wright-Patterson AFB, Dayton, OH 45433.

AF-9 Aerospace Audio-Visual Service (AAVS), Norton Air Force Base, California 92409.

AF-10 Headquarters Military Airlift Command, Scott Air Force Base, Belleville, Illinois 62225.

AF-12 Electronic Systems Divison, L. G. Hanscom Field, Bedford, Massachusetts 01730.

AF-13 Air Force Flight Test Center (AFSC), Edwards Air Force Base, CA 93523.

AF-14 Armament Division, Eglin AFB, FL 32542.

AF-15 Arnold Engineering Development Center, Arnold Air Force Station, TN 37389.

AF-17 Eastern Space and Missile Center, Patrick AFB, FL 32925.

AF-16 Ballistic Missile Office, Norton AFB, CA 92409.

AF-19 Air Force Contract Management Division, Kirtland Air Force Base, NM 87115.

AF-77 Air Force architect-engineer construction contracts and Construction Materials may be let by individual Air Force Bases, major Air Commands, Army Corps of Engineers, Air Procurement Districts, and Navy District Public Works Offices. Firms desiring such contracts should contact the offices designated or described below which are in their areas or in areas in which they wish to perform work:
1. *Army Corps Engineers Offices.* See code A-77.
2. *Navy District Public Works Offices.* See code N-77.
3. *Local Air Force Bases.* See Air Force Installations listed in

the local purchases section of this Directory, page 41.
4. *Deputy Director for Facilities Support, Housing Construction Division, Headquarters, U.S. Air Force, Washington, D.C.*

Defense Logistics Agency Major Purchasing and Contract Administration Offices

D-1 Commander, Defense Personnel Support Center, 2800 South 20th Street, Philadelphia, Pennsylvania 19101
In addition to contacting this Headquarters, contact the Subsistence Regional Headquarters listed below:
Defense Subsistence Regional Headquarters, DPSC, 2155 Mariner Square Loop, Alameda, California 94501

D-4 Defense General Suppy Center, Bellwood, Petersburg Pike, Richmond, Virginia 23297

D-5 Defense Industrial Supply Center, 700 Robbins Avenue, Philadelphia, Pennsylvania 19111

D-6 Defense Defense Fuel Supply Center, Cameron Station, Building 8, 5010 Duke Street, Alexandria, Virginia 22314

D-7 Defense Construction Supply Center, 3990 East Broad Street, Columbus, Ohio 43215

D-9 Defense Electronics Supply Center, 1507 Wilmington Pike, Dayton, Ohio 45444

D-10 Defense Contract Administration Services (DCAS) has taken over the function of some 200 Army, Navy, Air Force, and DCA field contract offices for quality assurance, production expediting, industrial security, and payment of contractors. DCAS is divided into various geographical regional and management area offices known as DECASR'S and DECASMA'S
Subcontracting: A Market for Small Business
Defense prime contractors require the supplies and services of many capable small business firms. DCAS (a part of the Defense Logistics Agency) has offices located nationwide in every principal industrial concentration. To assist small businessmen in locating suitable subcontracting opportunities, DCAS has Small Business Specialists assigned to their 9 Regional and 14 of the management area offices shown below. Specifically, DCAS Small Business Specialists are available at the following listed offices to assist small businessmen:

Commander, DCASR, Atlanta; 805 Walker St., Marietta, Georgia 30060.
Commander, DCASMA, Birmingham; 908 South 20th Street, Birmingham, Alabama 35205.
Commander, DCASMA, Orlando; 3555 Maguire Blvd., Orlando, Florida 32803.
Commander, DCASR, Boston; 666 Summer Street, Boston, Massachusetts 02210.
Commander, DCASMA, Hartford; 96 Murphy Road, Hartford, Connecticut 06114.
Commander, DCASMA, Rochester; US Courthouse & Federal Office Bldg., 100 State St., Rochester, New York 14614.
Commander, DCASR, Chicago; O'Hare International Airport, P.O. Box 66475, Chicago, Illinois 60666.
Commander, DCASMA, Indianapolis; Finance Center, U.S. Army, Building 1, Ft. Benjamin Harrison, Indiana 46249.
Commander, DCASMA, Milwaukee; 744 North 4th Street, Milwaukee, Wisconsin 53202.
Commander, DCASR, Cleveland; Federal Office Building, 1240 East Ninth Street, Cleveland, Ohio 44199.
Commander, DCASMA, Dayton; c/o Defense Electronics Supply Center, Bldg. 5, Dayton, Ohio 45477.
Commander, DCASR, Dallas; 500 South Ervay Street, Dallas, Texas 75201.
Commander, DCASMA, Detroit; McNamara Federal Office Bldg., 477 Michigan Avenue, Detroit, Michigan 48226.
Commander, DCASR, Los Angeles; 11099 South LaCienega Blvd., Los Angeles, California 90045.
Commander, DCASMA, Phoenix; 3800 N. Central Avenue, Phoenix, Arizona 85012.
Commander, DCASR, New York; 60 Hudson Street, New York, New York 10013.
Commander, DCASMA, Garden City; 605 Stewart Avenue, Garden City, L.I., New York 11533.
Commander, DCASMA, Springfield; 240 Route 22, Springfield, New Jersey 07081.
Commander, DCASR, Philadelphia; 2800 South 20th Street, Philadelphia, Pennsylvania 19101.
Commander, DCASMA, San Francisco; 866 Malcolm Road, Burlingame, California 94130.
Commander, DCASMA, Seattle; Building 50, U.S. Naval Air Station, Seattle, Washington 98115.
Commander, DCASR, St. Louis; 1136 Washington Avenue, St. Louis, Missouri 63101.
Commander, DCASMA, Twin Cities; Federal Building, Fort Snelling, St. Paul, Minnesota 55111.

Major Coast Guard Purchasing Offices

Code	Title and Address
CG-1	Chief, Procurement Division (G-FCP), U.S. Coast Guard, 2100 Second St., S.W., Washington, D.C. 20593
CG-2	Commanding Officer, U.S. Coast Guard Supply Center, 830 Third Avenue, Brooklyn, New York 11232
CG-3	Commanding Officer, U.S. Coast Guard Yard, Curtis Bay, Baltimore, Maryland 21226
CG-4	Commanding Officer, U.S. Coast Guard Aircraft Repair and Supply Center, Elizabeth City, North Carolina 27909
CG-5	Superintendent, U.S. Coast Guard Academy, New London, Connecticut 06320
	Commanding Officer, U.S. Coast Guard Training Center, Cape May, New Jersey 08204
	Commanding Officer, U.S. Coast Guard Reserve Training Center, Yorktown, Virginia 23490
	Commanding Officer, U.S. Coast Guard Training Center, Petaluma, California 94952
CG-6	Commander, First Coast Guard District, 150 Causeway St., Boston, Massachusetts 02114
	Commander, 2nd Coast Guard District, Federal Building, 1430 Olive Street, St. Louis, Missouri 63103
	Commander, 3rd Coast Guard District, Governors Island, New York, New York 10004
	Commander, 5th Coast Guard District, Federal Building, 431 Crawford Street, Portsmouth, Virginia 23705
	Commander, 7th Coast Guard District, Federal Building, Room 1018, 51 S.W. 1st Avenue, Miami, Florida 33130
	Commander, 8th Coast Guard District, Hale Boggs Federal Bldg., 500 Camp St., New Orleans, Louisiana 70130
	Commander, 9th Coast Guard District, 1240 East 9th Street, Cleveland, Ohio 44199
	Commander, 11th Coast Guard District, Union Bank Bldg., 400 Oceangate Blvd., Long Beach, California 90802
	Commander, 12th Coast Guard District, 630 Sansome Street, San Francisco, California 94126
	Commander, 13th Coast Guard District, 915 2nd Avenue, Seattle, Washington 98174
	Commander, 14th Coast Guard District, Prince Kalanianole Federal Bldg., 300 Ala Moana Blvd., 9th Floor, Honolulu, HI. 96850
	Commander, 17th Coast Guard District, P.O. Box 3-5000, Juneau, AK 99802

SUBCONTRACTING OPPORTUNITIES

Firms which desire subcontracting work should consult the following offices and publications:

1. Small Business Administration field offices will counsel small business owners desiring subcontracting opportunities, and furnish them lists of prime con-

tractors in their areas to contact for possible subcontract work. Of prime importance is the work of these offices in developing specific subcontract opportunities for qualified small firms. The small business owner should request assistance from the Small Business Administration office which is nearest his place of business.

2. The following Navy representatives counsel business firms on Navy procurement procedures, including subcontract opportunities in the facilities to which they are assigned:

Naval Plant Representative Office, Lockheed California Company, P.O. Box 551, Burbank, CA 91520
Naval Plant Representative Office, McDonnell Douglas Corp., Douglas Aircraft Company, P.O. Box 516, St. Louis, MO 63166
Supervisor of Shipbuilding, Conversion & Repair, Long Beach Naval Shipyard, (Code 1400B), Building 300-2, Long Beach, CA 90822
Naval Plant Representative Office, General Dynamics Pomona Division, (Code COA-3), 1675 West Mission Blvd., P.O. Box 2505, Pomana, CA 91766
Supervisor of Shipbuilding, Conversion and Repair, Naval Station, Box 119, (Code 415), San Diego, CA 92136
Supervisor of Shipbuilding, Conversion and Repair, (Code 430), San Francisco, CA 94135
Naval Plant Representative Office (Special Projects), Lockheed Missiles & Space Company, Inc., (Code SPL-501), P.O. Box 504, Sunnyvale, CA 94086
Supervisor of Shipbuilding, Conversion and Repair (Code 424), General Dynamics Corporation, Electric Boat Division, Groton, CT 06340
Naval Plant Representative Office, Pratt and Whitney Aircraft Division, United Technologies Corporation, East Hartford, Connecticut 06108
Naval Plant Representative Office, Sikorsky Aircraft Division, United Technologies Corporation, Stratford, CT 06497
Supervisor of Shipbuilding, Conversion and Repair, Drawer T, Mayport Naval Station, (Code 420), Jacksonville, FL 32228
Naval Plant Branch Representative Office, Pratt & Whitney Aircraft Group, Company Products Division, P.O. Box 2691, West Palm Beach, Florida 33402.
Supervisor of Shipbuilding, Conversion and Repair, (Code 425), New Orleans, LA 70142
Supervisor of Shipbuilding, Conversion and Repair, (Code 410), 574 Washington Street, Bath, ME 04530
Naval Plant Representative Office (Code COC-2) Applied Physics Laboratory, Johns Hopkins Road, Laurel, MD 20707
Supervisor of Shipbuilding, Conversion and Repair, (Code 420B) 495 Summer Street, Boston, MA 02210
Naval Plant Representative Office (CODE SPG005) 100 Plastics Avenue, Pittsfield, MA 01201
Supervisor of Shipbuilding, Conversion and Repair (Code 424) Pascagoula, MS 39567
Naval Plant Representative Office, Grumman Aircraft Corporation, Bethpage, Long Island, New York 11714.
Supervisor of Shipbuilding, Conversion and Repair (Code 433), Flushing & Washington Avenues, Brooklyn, NY 11251
Naval Plant Representative Office (CODE COA), Sperry Corporation, Great Neck, NY 11020
Naval Plant Representative Office, Goodyear Aerospace Corporation, Akron, Ohio 44305.
Naval Plant Representative Office, Rockwell International Corp., 4300 East 5th Avenue, Columbus, Ohio 43216.
Supervisor of Shipbuilding, Conversion and Repair, (Code 412), Naval Base, Bldg. 76, Charleston, SC 29408
Naval Plant Representative Office, Vought Corporation, P.O. Box 225907, Dallas, TX 75265
Naval Plant Branch Representative (Code SPLB-712), Hercules Aerospace Division, P.O. Box 157, Magna, UT 84044
Supervisor of Shipbuilding, Conversion and Repair, (Code 402), Newport News, VA 23607
Naval Air Systems Command Representative, Atlantic Naval Air Station, Norfolk, VA 23511.
Supervisor of Shipbuilding, Conversion and Repair (Code 410), P.O. Box 215, Portsmouth, VA 23705
Supervisor of Shipbuilding, Conversion and Repair, (Code 426), 7500 Sandpoint Way, N.E., Seattle, WA 98115
Supervisor of Shipbuilding, Conversion and Repair, (Code 400), 61 North 2nd Ave., Sturgeon Bay, WI 54235

3. The Chief of Engineers Offices listed under Code A-77, and the Officers in Charge of Construction listed under Code N-77, will furnish, upon request, lists of construction prime contractors to firms seeking construction subcontracting work.

4. The following publications are useful to firms seeking guidance in obtaining subcontracting work:

The Air Force Contract Management Division, located at Kirtland Air Force Base, New Mexico, has contract administration cognizance of 29 major defense contractor operations. The following Air Force locations can provide the small business owner assistance in how to do business with the major prime contractor. A pamphlet (AFCMDP 70-30) is available on Selling to Air Force Prime Contractors and may be obtained upon request from:

Air Force Contract Management Division
AFCMD/BCE
Kirtland AFB NM 87117

Air Force Plant Representative Office (AFPRO) locations:

AFPRO (Det 4), Pratt & Whitney Aircraft, Government Products Div, PO Box 2691, West Palm Beach FL 33402
AFPRO (Det 5), Pratt & Whitney Aircraft Gp, East Hartford CT 06108
AFPRO (Det 9), Martin Marietta, Denver Aerospace, PO Box 179, Denver CO 80201
AFPRO (Det 12), Rockwell Intl Corp, Rocketdyne Div, 6633 Canoga Avenue, Canoga Park CA 91304
AFPRO (Det 13), Lockheed Missile & Space Co, Space Systems Div, PO Box 504, Sunnyvale CA 94086
AFPRO (Det 15), Rockwell Intl, NAAO, PO Box 92098, Los Angeles CA 90009
AFPRO (Det 16), Rockwell Intl Corp (AB02), 3370 Miraloma Ave, Anaheim CA 92803
AFPRO (Det 21), Lockheed-Georgia Co, Marietta GA 30063
AFPRO (Det 27), General Dynamics Fort Worth Div, PO Box 371, Fort Worth TX 76101
AFPRO (Det 28), GE Company, Caller No. 1615, Cincinnati OH 45215
AFPRO (Det 34), Boeing Military Airplane Co, 3801 S. Oliver St, Wichita KS 67210
AFPRO (Det 35), Aerojet-General Corp, PO Box 15846, Sacramento CA 95852
AFPRO (Det 36), Hughes Aircraft Co, PO Box 92463, Los Angeles CA 90009
AFPRO (Det 37), Northrop Corp, Hawthorne CA 90250
AFPRO (Det 38), GE Co, Space Systems Div, PO Box 8555, Philadelphia PA 19101
AFPRO (Det 40), AVCO Systems Div, 201 Lowell Street, Wilmington MA 01887
AFPRO (Det 43), Thiokol Corp, PO Box 524, MS-250, Brigham City UT 84302
AFPRO (Det 44), Fairchild Republic Co, Farmingdale NY 11735
AFPRO (Det 45), Westinghouse Electric Co, Defense and Electronics Cen, PO Box 1693, Baltimore MD 21203
AFPRO (Det 46), TRW Electronics and Defense Sector, One Space Park, E2-2015, Redondo Beach CA 90278

AFPRO (Det 47), Douglas Aircraft Co, 3855 Lakewood Blvd, Long Beach, CA 90846
AFPRO (Det 48), Hughes Missile Systems Gp, PO Box 11337, Tucson AZ 85734
AFPRO (Det 49), Eaton Corp, AIL Div, Commack Road, Deer Park NY 11729
AFPRO OL AB, Rockwell Intl, North, American Aircraft Operations, PO Box 1259, Columbus OH 43216
AFPRO OL AA, Fairchild Republic Co, Showalter Road—Plant 4, Hagerstown MD 21740
AFPRO OL AA, Hughes Missile Systems Gp, 8433 Fallbrook Ave, Canoga Park CA 91304
AFPRO Northrop/FO, AF Plant 42 (Site 5), Palmdale CA 93550
CSD, AFPRO (Det 13), PO Box 50015, Sunnyvale CA 95150
AFPRO OL AA, Rockwell Intl, NAAO, 3000 30th St. E., Palmdale CA 93550

Commerce Business Daily. This publication (issued Mondays through Fridays, except on Federal legal holidays) is a useful guide for firms seeking subcontract work since it provides names of companies receiving current defense contracts and gives the item, quantity and dollar value for each contract. The "Commerce Business Daily" is available on a subscription basis for $88.00 per year via second class mail and $160.00 via first class mail from the Superintendent of Documents, Government Printing Office, Wshington, D.C. 20402. Purchase order must be accompanied by payment. All remittances (check or money order) should be made out to the Superintendent of Documents, Government Printing Office, Washington, D.C. 20402.

PRODUCTS AND SERVICES BOUGHT BY THE MAJOR MILITARY PURCHASING OFFICES

Abrasive materials, AF-1, AF-5, N-24, N-25, N-27, N-28, AF-4, CG-3, CG-4.
Abrasives, belts, disks, wheels and stones, A-45, N-25, N-26, N-28, N-29, CG-3, CG-4.
Abrasive Cleaning, sandblasting equipment, A-45, N-6, N-24.
Acceleration equipment, N-26, N-29c.
Accelerometers, N-1, N-26.
Accumulators, aircraft, N-9, N-26.
Acetylene, D-4, CG-3, CG-4.
Accounting & calculating machines, A-2, AF-5, N-26, N-27.
Acid, Sulfuric, N-14, N-24, N-25, N-26, N-27.
Acoustic Devices, N-1, N-3, N-14, N-19, N-24, N-26, N-27, N-29b, N-29c
Activation, mothballed ships, N-3.
Actuators, electric motor, pneumatic, rotary, solenoid, thermal, AF-15, N-9, N-24.
Actuators, Hydraulic, AF-1, AF-15, N-9, N-12, N-24, N-25, N-26, AF-4.
Adapters, A-45, AF-15, N-9, N-11, N-24, N-25, N-26, D-4, D-7, AF-4.
Addressing, mailing equipment, A-4.
Adhesives, AF-1, A-2, N-26, N-27, N-29c, D-6.
Aerial delivery containers (See Containers).
Aerial delivery slings (See Slings, aerial delivery).
Agricultural machinery, components & accessories, D-7.
Aiming circles, A-45.
Aiming posts, A-45.
Air cargo terminal services, N-6, N-24.
Air circulators, N-3, N-11, N-12, N-24, N-26, AF-4, D-4.
Air conditioning equipment, A-2, A-4, A-32, N-3, N-6, N-9, N-11, N-12, N-14, N-19, N-21, N-24, N-25, N-26, N-27, N-27a, N-28, N-29, N-29a, AF-1c, AF-2, AF-4, AF-6, AF-17, D-4.
Air filters, aircraft, A-32, A-45, N-9, AF-2, AF-4, CG-4.
Air filters, automotive, A-2, A-31, N-26, AF-4, D-7.
Air gauging equipment, N-26.
Air hose, N-9, N-24, N-26.
Air purification equipment, A-32, A-45, N-3, N-24, N-26, D-7, AF-5, AF-15.
Air Weapons, A-45, N-26, AF-1a
Aircraft, A-32, N-1, N-26, AF-6, CG-1.
Aircraft, fixed wing, A-32, N-26, AF-1c, AF-2b, AF-3, AF-4a, AF-5b, AF-6.
Aircraft, rotary wing, N-26, AF-6.
Aircraft, Armament, A-45, N-9, N-26.
Aircraft accessories & components, miscellaneous, A-32, N-9, N-24, N-26, AF-1c, AF-3b, AF-5, AF-4, AF-6, CG-4.
Aircraft actuators, electric, A-32, N-9, N-12, N-14, N-26, AF-4, CG-4, AF-1.
Aircraft air conditioning systems, N-9, N-26, AF-1, AF-2, AF-4, AF-6.
Aircraft air filters, N-26, AF-2, AF-4.
Aircraft arresting and barrier equipment, N-5, N-9, N-14, N-26, N-29a, AF-4.
Aircraft auxiliary fuel tanks, A-32, N-1, N-9, N-26, AF-1, AF-3, AF-4.
Aircraft belts, safety, A-32, N-9, N-26.
Aircraft cargo tie-down equipment, A-32, N-9, N-24, N-26, AF-4, AF-5.
Aircraft de-icing system, components only, N-9, N-26, AF-1, AF-2, AF-4, AF-6.
Aircraft electrical system components, A-32, N-9, N-12, N-26, AF-1c, AF-4, AF-6.
Aircraft engine control quadrants, A-11, A-31, A-32, N-9, N-26, AF-4.
Aircraft engine cowling mounts, A-11, A-31, A-32, N-9, N-26, AF-4.
Aircraft food cooking, baking & warming equipment, N-26.
Aircraft fuel system components (See Fuel system components).
Aircraft ground handling equipment, A-32, N-9, N-14, N-24, N-26, N-29a, AF-1c, AF-6, D-7, AF-4, D-4, CG-1, CG-2, CG-3, CG-4.
Aircraft gyroscopes, N-9, N-26, N-29b, AF-1.
Aircraft heaters, cabin & cockpit, A-32, N-9, N-26, AF-1, AF-2, AF-4, AF-6.
Aircraft hydraulic, vacuum & de-icing system components, A-32, N-9, N-26, N-29c, D-7, AF-1, AF-2, AF-4, AF-6.
Aircraft, inspection, overhaul & repair, A-32, N-1, N-12, N-14, N-26, N-29a, AF-2, AF-3b, AF-4, CG-1, CG-4, AF-1c.
Aircraft instruments, N-9, N-26, AF-1, AF-6.
Aircraft landing gear components, D-7.
Aircraft landing systems, A-32, N-9, N-14, N-26, AF-1, CG-1.
Aircraft launching equipment, N-9, N-14, N-24, N-26, N-29a, AF-4, AF-12.
Aircraft lighting fixtures (See Lighting fixtures).
Aircraft maintenance & engine change stands, A-32, N-9, N-14, N-26, AF-4, CG-1, CG-4.
Aircraft maintenance & repairshop equipment, A-32, D-4, N-9, N-24, AF-4, CG-4.
Aircraft meters, miscellaneous (See Meters).
Aircraft oil filters, N-9, N-26, AF-1c, AF-2, AF-4.
Aircraft pressurizing & breathing equipment, A-32, N-9, N-26, AF-2, AF-4, AF-6, CG-1.
Aircraft propellant actuated devices, N-12, N-26, AF-1, AF-4, AF-6.
Aircraft propeller components, A-32, N-9, N-26, CG-4.
Aircraft propellers, A-32, N-9, N-26, AF-5, CG-4, D-7.
Aircraft receivers, N-9, N-26.
Aircraft refueling services (NAVY), D-6.
Aircraft releases, tow target, A-32, N-9, N-26, AF-1, AF-4.
Aircraft, small, A-32, N-26, CG-1.
Aircraft shoulder harness, A-32, N-9, N-26, AF-1e, AF-4.
Aircraft specialized trucks and trailers, D-7.
Aircraft structural components, A-32, N-1, N-9, N-12, N-26, AF-1, AF-2b, AF-4, CG-4.
Aircraft traget drones, N-12, N-26
Aircraft training equipment, N-19a, AF-1
Aircraft weapons, automatic, A-45, N-1, N-26.
Aircraft wheels & brake systems, A-32, N-9, N-26, AF-1, AF-6, CG-4, D-7.
Aircraft windshield wipers, A-32, N-9, N-26, CG-4, AF-4.
Airfield specialized trucks & trailers, N-26, AF-4, CG-1.
Airframe, structural components, N-9, N-26, AF-1c, AF-2b, AF-3, AF-4a, AF-5b, AF-5c, AF-5d, AF-6, D-5.
Airlift, AF-10.
Airmunitions, AF-1.
Airport signal systems & components (See Signal systems & components, airport).
Alarm & signal systems, aircraft, A-32, N-9, N-26, AF-4.
Alarm & signal systems, miscellaneous, A-4, A-32, A-44, A-45, N-3, N-6, N-9, N-11, N-14, N-19, N-24, N-28, AF-4, AF-7, AF-12, D-4.
Alarm & signal systems, shipboard, N-3, N-4, N-11, D-4, N-24, N-25, N-26.
Alcohol, indistrial, D-4.
Alidades, N-27, AF-4.
Altimeters, N-1, N-9, N-26, CG-1, AF-2.
Ammunition, A-2, A-45, N-11, AF-1a.
Ammunition, artillery, A-45.
Ammunition boxes, metal, A-45, N-6, AF-1, AF-6.
Ammunition boxes, wood, A-45, AF-1.
Ammunition gun, including components, A-45, N-3, N-5.
Ammunition maintenance & repair equipment, AF-1, D-4.
Ammunition, rocket, A-45, N-3, N-11, AF-1a.
Ammunition, small arms type, complete rounds, A-45, N-26, CG-1.
Amplifiers, audio, N-6, N-9, N-14, N-26, AF-7.
Amplifiers, direct current, N-9, N-26, AF-1.
Amplifiers, radio, N-9, N-26, AF-1, AF-7.
Amplifiers, radio frequency, N-9, N-24, N-26, AF-7, AF-17.
Amplifiers, synchro, gyrocompass, N-9, N-26, AF-1.
Amplifiers, (test instrument), A-11, A-45, N-11, N-12, N-14, N-19, N-24, N-26, N-27, N-27a, AF-1, AF-4, AF-17, CG-2, CG-4.
Amphibious craft, A-32, N-3.
Analogue recorder readout, wide band, N-26, N-29b, AF-7, AF-8, AF-17.
Anchors, N-9, N-11, N-13, N-29b, CG-1, CG-2, CG-3, CG-6.
Anhydrators, thermal, N-26, AF-6.
Animal equipment, saddles, harness, whips, leashes, A-32, D-7.
Animals laboratory, N-29, AF-4, AF-7.
Anodes, plating, N-26.

Anodizing equipment, N-26.
Antennas & related equipment, A-2, A-11, A-45, N-1, N-3, N-4, N-5, N-6, N-8, N-9, N-11, N-12, N-14, N-19, N-24, N-25, N-26, N-27, N-29c, AF-2, AF-3, AF-7, AF-1, AF-8, AF-12, AF-16, AF-17, D-9, CG-1, CG-6.
Antenna testers, A-11, N-12, N-19, N-24, N-26, AF-17
Antifreeze compounds, A-2, D-4.
Antisubmarine warfare equipment, N-1, N-3, N-12, N-24, N-26.
Apparel findings, D-1.
Appliances, A-2, N-21, N-21a, N-24, N-26, D-4, CG-3, CG-4, CG-5, CG-6.
Appraisal services, A-77, N-77.
Architect, engineering services, A-2, A-4, A-77, N-4, N-24, N-77, AF-7, AF-13, AF-17, CG-1, CG-4, CG-5, CG-6.
Architectural & related metal products, N-6, D-7.
Arm racks, A-45.
Armament training devices, A-45, D-4, N-9, N-19a.
Armor, naval ordnance, steel, N-3, N-6, N-12, N-24, N-25, D-5.
Armor, personal, D-1.
Asbestos fabricated materials, N-24, D-5.
Asphalt (See Construction materials, minerals).
Astronomical instruments, A-11, AF-4, D-4.
Athletic clothing (See Clothing, athletic).
Athletic equipment, A-2, AF-7, N-5, N-21, N-21a, N-26, N-28, N-31, D-4, CG-2, CG-5.
Athletic footwear, A-2, N-21, N-21a, N-26, N-28, D-1, CG-5.
Atlases, AF-7, D-4.
Atomic ordnance, A-45, N-2.
Attenuators, fixed and variable, N-24, N-26, N-27, N-27a, AF-17.
Audio visual equipment, A-4.
Automatic Data Processing systems, A-4, A-99, N-6, N-12, N-14, N-19, N-26, N-27, N-27a, AF-5, AF-6, AF-7, CG-1.
Automatic pilot mechanisms & airborne gyro components, N-9, N-12, N-26, N-29a, AF-2, AF-6, D-4, CG-1.
Automotive electrical system components, A-31, A-32, N-21, N-28, N-30, N-31, D-7.
Automotive fuel system components (See Fuel system components).
Automotive lighting fixtures (See Lighting fixtures).
Automotive oil filters (See oil filters).
Automotive type lighting fixtures (See Lighting fixtures).
Aviation lighting fixtures (See Lighting fixtures).
Azimuths, A-11, A-45, N-9, N-11.
Azimuth indicators, AF-5.

Badges, insignia & emblems, A-2, N-6, N-26, D-1, AF-17, CG-2.
Bags, cases, covers, various, A-2, A-45, A-62, AF-5, AF-7, N-14, N 27, D-1, D-4.
Bags, grocery, A-2, N-26, AF-7.
Bakery & cereal products, A-2, A-62, N-24, N-26, D-1.
Baking & kitchen equipment & miscellaneous machinery, A-2, A-32, N-24, N-26, N-28, N-29, AF-5, AF-7, D-4.
Balances, A-45, N-5, N-6, N-26, AF-4.
Ballast, lead and stone, N-14, N-27a, AF-13.
Ballasts, lampholders & starters, N-24, AF-4, D-4.
Ballast, tubes, AF-3.
Balloons, meteorological, AF-3, AF-17.
Bandages and Surgical Dressing, D-1.
Bandoleers, A-45.
Barber supplies & equipment, A-2, N-21, N-21a, D-4.
Barges, lighters, A-32, N-3.
Barges, special purpose, N-3, N-4.
Barrels, gun, A-45, N-19.
Barrier deck lighting fixtures (see lighting fixtures).
Bars, iron and steel, A-32, A-45, N-14, N-24, N-25, N-26, N-27, N-29a, AF-5, AF-17, D-5, CG-3, CG-4.
Bars, nonferrous base, A-31, A-45, N-24, N-25, N-27, N-29a, AF-5, AF-7, AF-17, D-5, CG-3, CG-4.
Batteries, dry cell (JAN type), A-11, A-44, N-11, N-14, N-19, N-27, N-27a, AF-1, AF-7, AF-17, CG-2.
Batteries, primary, N-3, N-27a, AF-1, AF-4, AF-7, D-4, CG-6.
Batteries, secondary, A-2, A-11, A-32, A-44, D-4, N-3, N-5, N-6, N-9, N-11, N-12, AF-1, AF-4, AF-7, CG-6.
Batteries, torpedo propulsion, N-3, N-27, D-4.
Batteries, wet, N-9, AF-17, D-4.
Bayonets and bayonet knives, A-45.
Bearings, A-31, A-32, A-45, N-9, N-11, N-24, N-25, N-26, N-27, N-29c, AF-1, AF-4, AF-5, AF-17, D-5.
Bearings, antifriction, A-32, A-45, N-9, AF-1, AF-5, D-5.
Bearings, ball, A-31, A-32, AF-1, D-5.
Bearings, roller, A-31, A-32, A-45, A-84, N-9, N-29c, AF-1, D-5, CG-1, CG-3.
Bearings, sleeve, mounted or unmounted, N-9, AF-1, AF-5.
Bearings, split, N-9, AF-1.
Bedding mattresses & related items, N-6, N-24, N-26, D-1.
Belting, A-31, A-32, N-31, AF-4, D-7.
Belts, aircraft, safety (See Aircraft belts, safety).
Belts, drive, A-31, A-32, N-31, AF-4, AF-7, D-7.
Belts, fan, A-31, A-32, N-19, N-31, AF-4, AF-7, D-7.
Benches, work, N-14, N-26, AF-7, AF-13.
Bending & forming machines (metalworking), A-45, N-6, N-24, N-27, AF-5, AF-7, D-4.
Berths, aluminum, N-11, N-14.
Beverages, non-alcoholic, A-2, A-62, N-21, N-21a, N-24, N-29, D-1, CG-3, CG-4, CG-5, CG-6.
Binoculars, A-2, A-45, N-3, N-11, N-21, AF-4.
Binding & related products, A-1, N-81, AF-7.
Binding of periodicals, N-14, AF-7.
Bins, storage, N-14, N-24, N-26, D-4, AF-17.
Biological agents, military, AF-1a.
Biological protective equipment (See Protective equipment).
Blanket, electric, rocket, A-2, A-45.
Blasting sands & media, N-24, N-25, N-26.
Blocks, electrical distribution, N-24, N-25, AF-4.
Blocks, tackle, N-13, D-5, CG-3.
Blowers, forced draft, N-3, N-24, AF-4, D-7, CG-3.
Blueprint & photocopy service, A-4, N-14.
Blueprinting machines & equipment, N-80, CG-1, CG-3, CG-4, CG-5, CG-6.
Boards, bulletin, N-24, N-26.
Boards, printed circuit, N-6, N-9, N-26, N-27a, N-29b.
Boat davits, A-32, N-3, CG-1, CG-3.
Boat propulsion components, A-32, N-3, N-11, N-24, CG-1, CG-3.
Boats, small, A-32, N-3, N-6, N-11, CG-1, CG-3, CG-6, AF-4.
Boats, tow, A-32, N-3, CG-1.
Boiler uptakes & stackes, A-32, N-3.
Boilers, industrial, N-3, N-6, AF-5, AF-7, D-7, CG-1.
Bolometers, A-11, N-10, AF-4.
Bolts, A-31, A-32, N-9, N-24, N-25, N-29a, AF-4, D-5.
Bombs, A-45, AF-1a.
Bombs, nuclear, AF-4.
Bombsights, aircraft, N-9.
Booby traps, A-45.
Bookbinding equipment, N-31.
Books & pamphlets, except medical books, A-1, A-2, A-4, N-3, N-5, N-6, N-9, N-14, N-19, N-24, N-26, N-81, AF-7, AF-17, D-4, CG-1.
Books, medical, A-45, N-26, D-1, AF-7, CG-1.
Boom, oil recovery, N-6, N-24.
Booms and nets, harbor defense only, N-2.
Booths, spray painting, N-6, N-24, N-26, N-27a.
Boring machines, A-45, N-6, N-24, AF-5, D-4.
Bottles & jars, N-26, D-4, AF-5.
Box, battery, A-32.
Boxes, ammunition, wood (See Ammunition boxes).
Boxes, ammunition, metal (See Ammunition boxes).
Boxes, cartons, crates, A-2, AF-1, AF-5, N-24, N-26, D-4.
Boxes, metal, A-32, A-45, N-9, N-11, N-14, D-4, AF-1.
Boxes, tool and hardware, N-14, D-4, AF-1.
Boxes, wood, A-45, N-14, N-24, N-26, D-4.
Boxes, wood, cargo, A-32, N-24, D-4.
Brazing alloys, A-45, N-11, N-24, N-25, AF-5, D-4.
Breathing apparatus, A-45, N-9, N-24, N-29c, AF-2.
Brick, D-7.
Bridges, fixed & floating, A-32, N-4, D-7.
Bridges, impedance, A-11, N-11.
Bridges, pontoon, gear types, Navy, D-7.
Briquets, D-6.
Broaching machines, A-45, A-82, A-84, N-6, AF-5.
Brooms, A-2, N-21, N-21a, N-28, D-4, AF-1.
Brushes, A-2, A-45, N-12, N-21, N-21a, N-24, N-25, N-26, N-27, N-28, D-4, AF-1.
Brushes, carbon, N-12.
Brushes, contact, electrical, AF-3.
Building block, D-7.
Building glass, N-24, D-7.
Building panels, prefabricated, A-77, N-24, N-27a, D-7.
Building paper, D-7.
Buildings, complete, panelized, ready-cut, A-77, N-14, N-77, D-7.
Bulldozer blades, parts & equipment, for tanks, N-4, N-12, D-7.
Buoys, A-32, D-4, N-4, N-11, N-24, N-27, CG-1, CG-6.
Buoys, plastic, N-3.
Burster casings, A-45.

Cabinets, electronic equipment, N-3, N-11, N-19, N-24, N-25, N-27, AF-7, AF-15, AF-17.
Cabinets, lockers, bins, & shelving, N-12, N-14, N-24, N-26, N-27, N-29b, D-4, AF-5, AF-7, AF-14.
Cable assemblies, A-11, A-45, A-84, N-11, N-14, N-19, N-24, N-25, N-26, N-27, N-27a, N-29a, N-29b, D-4, D-5, D-7, CG-1, CG-2, AF-3, AF-1, AF-4, AF-6, AF-17.

Cable, cord & wire assemblies communication equipment, N-12, N-14, N-24, N-25, N-26, N-27a, N-29b, AF-3, AF-4, D-4, AF-1, AF-14, AF-17.
Cable, electrical, A-2, A-11, A-45, N-9, N-11, N-12, N-14, N-19, N-24, N-25, N-26, N-27, N-27a, N-28, N-29b, AF-1, AF-3, AF-4, AF-7, AF-17, D-5, D-7, CG-1, CG-2.
Cable, electrical & mechanical, N-14, N-19, N-24, N-26, N-27, N-27a, N-29b, AF-1, AF-4, AF-17, D-7.
Cable fittings (See Fittings for rope, cable, chain).
Cable, steel, A-32, N-24, N-27, N-29a, D-5, CG-1, CG-3, AF-17, D-4.
Calcium chloride, A-45, D-4.
Calcium Hypochlorite, A-45, D-4.
Calibrators, A-11, A-45, N-11, N-24, N-26, AF-4.
Cameras, motion picture & still, A-2, A-44, A-45, D-4, N-21, N-24, N-26, N-27, AF-1, AF-7, AF-13, AF-17, CG-1, CG-6.
Cameras, submarine periscope, N-3, N-26.
Cameras, television, N-19, N-26, N-27, AF-17.
Cameras, underwater, N-1, N-3, N-6, N-19, N-24, N-27, N-29b.
Camouflage & deception equipment, A-32, A-45, D-4.
Cams, A-41, D-7.
Candy & confections, A-2, N-21, N-21a, D-1, CG-3, CG-4, CG-5, CG-6.
Cans & drums (See Drums and cans).
Capacitor Testers, A-11, N-11, N-19, N-24, N-26, AF-4, CG-2.
Capacitors, A-32, A-45, N-4, N-9, N-11, N-19, N-24, N-26, N-27, AF-1b, AF-3, AF-4, AF-17, D-9, CG-2.
Capstans, (marine use), N-3, N-24, N-27, N-29b, D-7, CG-1, CG-3.
Carbon dioxide, N-14, N-19, N-24, D-4.
Cargo, ocean transport, N-79.
Cargo & tanker vessels, supply & repair parts, A-32.
Carriages & mounts (towed) field, anti-aircraft & anti-tank, A-45, N-27a.
Carry cases, all types, A-2, A-45, A-81.
Cartridge cases, A-45, N-6, N-11, N-27a.
Cartirdge clips, A-45.
Carts, hand, A-45, N-24, N-27, D-4.
Cases, canvas, A-45, N-9, D-4.
Castings (machined), A-45, N-12, N-24, N-25, N-27, N-27a, N-29a, AF-1, AF-16.
Castings, nonferrous investment and die, N-27, AF-1.
Castings, steel precision, A-45, N-24, N-25, N-27, AF-1, N-27a, CG-1.
Cataloging, A-2, A-11, A-21, A-32, N-3, AF-7.
Cells, fuel (aircraft), AF-1, AF-3.
Cement (See Construction materials, minerals).
Centrifugals, A-32, N-24.
Centrifugals, separators, & pressure & vacuum filters, D-7, AF-5.
Chain, AF-4, D-5, AF-17, CG-2, CG-3.
Chain Fittings (See Fittings for rope, cable, chain).
Chain pipes, CG-3.
Chain, welded & weldless, A-32, A-45, N-11, N-24, N-27, D-5, CG-1, CG-2.
Charcoal, A-2, A-45, N-21, D-4, D-6.
Chargers, Ba.tery, All types, A-2, N-5, N-6, N-8, N-11, N-14, N-24, N-26, AF-3, AF-7.
Charts, N-29b, AF-17.
Chemicals, A-45, N-11, N-12, N-24, N-25, N-26, N-27, N-28, AF-4, D-4.
Chemical agents, A-45, A-44, AF-1a.
Chemical composition determining instruments, A-45, N-19, N-24, N-27, AF-4.
Chemical protective equipment (See Protective equipmenet).
Chemical specialties, miscellaneous, A-45, AF-4, AF-7, AF-17, D-4.
Chemical weapons & equipment, A-45, A-81, A-82, A-84, D-4.
Chemicals, basic, A-45, A-43, AF-4, D-4, AF-1.
Chemicals, photographic (See Photographic chemicals).
Chocks, A-32, N-9, N-24, AF-4.
Chokes, electronic, AF-3.
Chronographs, A-45, N-26.
Circuit breakers, A-11, A-32, A-45, N-3, N-6, N-14, N-24, N-25, N-26, N-27, N-27a, AF-1b, AF-3, AF-15, D-9, CG-1.
Clay & Concrete Products, machinery, D-4.
Cleaners, engine, aircraft, AF-2, AF-4.
Cleaners, engine, non-aircraft, A-2, AF-1, AF-4, D-4.
Cleaners, steam, N-9, N-12.
Cleaning compounds & preparations, A-2, A-45, N-24, N-25, N-27a, D-4.
Cleaning machines, A-2, A-45, N-6, N-12, N-24, N-26.
Cleaning services, carpet/furniture, A-4.
Clean room equipment, N-26, N-27a.
Clocks, various types, A-2, A-45, N-9, N-11, N-31, AF-4, D-4.
Cloth, nylon coated, N-14, N-24, D-1.
Clothing, A-2, N-21, N-21a, D-1, CG-2.
Clothing, athletic, A-2, N-21, N-21a, N-28, N-31, D-1, CG-5.
Clothing, protective, A-45, N-14, N-15, N-24, N-26, D-1, CG-2.
Clothing, special purpose except flight, A-45, N-24, N-26, D-1, CG-2.
Clothing, special purpose, flight, N-9, AF-4, D-1.
Clothing, Utility items, D-1.
Coal, anthracite and bituminous, AF-7, D-6.
Coal testers, A-11.
Coils, electrical, A-11, A-32, N-11, N-19, N-27, AF-1b, D-9.
Coils, electronic, AF-3, AF-15.
Coils, ignition (See ignition coils).
Coils, torpedo wire guidance, N-2.
Coke, D-6.
Cold type composition services, N-14.
Collector's items, D-4.
Collets, taps, dyes, hand & machine, N-24, AF-5.
Combat ships & landing vessels, repair parts, operating & supply kits, A-32, N-3, N-12, N-24, N-26.
Communication equipment, airborne, miscellaneous, A-11, A-32, A-44, N-1, N-9, N-12, N-19, N-26, N-27, AF-4, AF-5, AF-12, AF-13, AF-16, AF-17, CG-1.
Communication equipment (cable, cord and wire assemblies), AF-3, AF-5, AF-17, AF-16.
Communication equipment, marine & shore, A-11, N-3, N-6, N-8, N-11, N-12, N-19, N-24, N-25, N-26, N-27, N-29b, AF-5, AF-6, CG-1, CG-2.
Communication equipment (miscellaneous), AF-3, AF-7, AF-12, AF-13, AF-17.
Communication services, A-11, A-21, A-44, A-61, N-4, N-26, CG-1.
Communication test sets, N-9.
Communications, invisible, & visible lights, A-11, A-44, N-8, N-11, N-12, AF-2, AF-3.
Comparators, optical, A-45, N-29, AF-1, AF-4.
Compasses (Includes Terrestrial types, except aircraft), A-45, N-3, N-9, N-11, AF-1, AF-4, CG-1.
Compasses, aircraft, A-32, N-9, N-26, AF-1, AF-2, CG-4.
Compilation & printing of instructions, operations & maintenance manuals, A-1, A-11, A-21, A-32, A-45, N-1, N-3, N-6, N-14, N-19a, N-24, N-27, AF-4, CG-1.
Components & spare parts for cooking, heating, & electric equipment, N-24.
Compound, asphaltic, N-27a, AF-7.
Compounds, industrial, A-45, A-81, N-24, N-27, AF-1, AF-7.
Compound, paint stripping, N-26, AF-1.
Compound, sealing, N-27a.
Compressors, air, N-14, N-24, N-26, AF-7.
Compressors, aircraft, N-9, N-26, AF-5.
Compressors, portable, A-32, A-45, N-26, D-7.
Compressors, rotary, A-32, N-19, D-7.
Compressors (special), N-24.
Computers, A-4, A-45, N-1, N-3, N-19, N-26, AF-1, AF-17, AF-7, CG-1.
Computers, analog, A-45, N-3, N-29c, AF-1, AF-7.
Computers, gun direction, A-45, N-12.
Computers, missile control, A-21, N-1, N-3, N-12, N-24, AF-16, AF-17.
Computers, navigation & stabilization, N-3, N-12, N-19, N-26, N-29b, AF-1.
Concrete, bituminous, N-14, AF-7.
Concrete, ready mixed, N-14, N-24, N-26.
Concrete forms, AF-5, D-7.
Concrete machines, A-32, A-63, D-7.
Condensers, air cooled, N-6, N-26, AF-17.
Condensers, steam, A-32, N-3, N-19, AF-5, D-7.
Conduit, nonmetallic, N-14, N-24, D-4.
Connectors, electrical, A-11, A-32, A-45, N-5, N-6, N-9, N-11, N-12, N-19, N-24, N-25, N-26, N-27, N-27a, N-28, N-29, N-29b, AF-1b, AF-3, D-4, D-9.
Connectors, flexible, N-9, N-11, N-25, N-26, D-4, D-7.
Construction, A-77, N-4, N-77, AF-1, AF-17, AF-77, CG-3, CG-4, CG-5, CG-6.
Construction machinery, A-63, N-4, D-7.
Construction machinery, miscellaneous repair parts & attachments, A-32, N-31, D-7.
Construction materials, minerals (asphalt, crushed stone, gravel, road oil, sand, etc.), A-32, A-77, N-4, N-12, N-14, N-24, N-25, N-26, N-27, N-27a, N-28, N-29, N-77, AF-1, AF-17, AF-77, D-7.
Contractors, (See Relays, contractors, & solenoids).
Containers, aerial delivery, A-32, A-36, N-5, N-24, AF-7.
Containers, engine & instruments shipping, A-32, AF-2, AF-4c, CG-4.
Containers, fiber, fiberboard, plywood, A-2, A-45.
Containers, jet engine, N-9, N-24, N-26, N-27, N-28, D-4, AF-1, AF-2, AF-4.
Containers, metal fabricated, A-31, A-32, A-45, N-3, N-5, N-9, N-11, N-25, N-27, N-27a, D-4, AF-1, AF-6.
Containers, missile, wood, metal, fiber, N-1, N-12, N-24, N-27, N-27a, N-29a, AF-1, AF-5, AF-6, AF-14.
Containers, specialized, A-32, AF-1, AF-5, AF-14, D-4.
Contractual maintenance services, A-4, A-11, A-21, A-31, A-32, A-44, A-45, A-61, A-77, N-1, N-24, N-77, CG-1.
Control equipment, electrical, A-11, A-32, A-45, N-1, N-3, N-5, N-9, N-11, N-12,

N-14, N-19, N-24, N-26, N-27, AF-1, AF-3, AF-17, D-4.
Control equipment, fire (See Fire Control equipment).
Control equipment, inertial & automatic, N-1, N-26, N-29c.
Conversion kits, nuclear ordnance, AF-4.
Converters, electrical, A-32, A-45, D-4, A-41, N-11, N-12, N-19, N-24, N-26, AF-4.
Converters, electrical, non-rotating, and rotating, A-3, AF-6, D-4.
Converters, torque, N-26, AF-4.
Conveyors, A-2, N-6, N-27a, D-7.
Conveyors units, portable, A-2, N-3, N-6, N-24, N-27, N-27a, D-7.
Conveyors, coal, aggregate, etc. D-7.
Cookers, steam pressure, N-6, N-24, D-4.
Cooking, baking & heating equipment, N-24, N-26, N-28, AF-5, D-4.
Cooling systems, aircraft, N-1, N-9, N-26, AF-2, AF-4, AF-6.
Cooling systems, automotive, A-2, A-31, A-32, N-31, AF-4, D-7.
Cooling systems, marine, A-32, N-3, N-24.
Corrosion preventatives, A-45, N-11, N-24, N-26, N-29c, D-6.
Counter measures devices, N-1, N-3, N-8, N-12, N-19, N-26, AF-4, AF-5.
Counters, particle, N-26.
Counters, preset, N-26.
Couplings, N-3, N-5, N-11, N-24, N-25, N-26, N-27, D-7, AF-17.
Court Reporting, A-4.
Cranes (marine use), N-3, N-4, N-6, N-14, N-19, N-24, N-26, CG-1, CG-3.
Crane & crane shovel attachments, D-7.
Cranes & crane shovels, A-32, D-7.
Cranes & derricks, A-32, D-7.
Cyrogenic equipment, N-9, D-4, AF-13, AF-17.
Cryptographic equipment, A-11, A-44.
Crystals, piezo-electric, A-11, N-10, N-26, N-27, N-27a, AF-1b, AF-2, AF-3, AF-5, D-9.
Crystals, rectifying, A-11, N-10, N-26, N-31, AF-1b, AF-3, D-9.
Cutlery & flatware, A-2, D-4.
Cutting & forming tools (metalworking), A-45, N-6, N-11, N-24, N-26, N-27, AF-5, D-4.
Cutting equipment, flame (See Flame cutting equipment).
Cycles (Special purpose only), A-31.
Cylinder blocks, A-31, N-9, D-7, CG-1, CG-3.
Cylinder, electrically cast, N-25.
Cylinder head gaskets, A-2, A-31, A-32, N-9, N-11, D-7, CG-2, CG-3, CG-4, CG-5, CG-6.
Cylinders, gas, compressed gases (See Gas cylinders, compressed gases).

Data processing & card punching services, N-6, N-9, N-14, N-24, N-25, N-26, N-27, N-29b, N-29c, AF-1, CG-1, CG-2, CG-3, CG-4, CG-5, CG-6.
Data processing equipment, A-2, A-4, A-11, A-44, A-45, N-1, N-3, N-6, N-12, N-19, N-26, N-27, N-27a, N-29b, N-29c, AF-1, AF-5, AF-7, AF-13.
Data procuring equipment, automatic, A-11, N-3, N-12, N-19, N-26, N-29b, AF-1, AF-7, AF-13, CG-1.
Deburring machines, N-26.
Decalcomania, N-24, N-27, N-27a, N-81, CG-1, CG-2, CG-4, CG-6.
Deck machinery, A-32, N-3, N-6, N-11, N-24, CG-1, CG-3, D-5.
Decontaminating agents, A-45.
Decontaminating & impregnating equipment, A-45, D-4.
Decontaminating equipment, A-45, N-3, AF-6.
Degasifiers, water treatment, N-26.
Degaussing equipment, N-3, N-24, CG-1.
Degreasers, vapor and ultrasonic, N-6, N-14, N-26.
Dehydrators, thermal, N-3, D-7.
Delivery, courier, A-4.
Demolition charges, AF-1a.
Demolition equipment & destructors, A-45, N-2.
Demolition materials, underwater, N-3, AF-1a.
Demounter, tire, A-45, N-31.
Dental equipment & supplies, N-24, N-26, AF-7, D-1.
Dentifrices, A-2, N-21, N-21a, N-26, D-4.
Depth charge tracks, release mechanism & hydraulic controls, N-3.
Depth charges, N-3.
Derricks, (marine use), N-4, N-19, D-7.
Design services, marine, N-3, N-12, N-14, N-24.
Detergents, N-21, N-28, D-4.
Detonators, nuclear ordnance, AF-4.
Development & research, See Part V.
Die cast products, A-45, N-12, N-24, N-27, N-27a.
Dies, (metalworking), A-45, N-24, AF-5.
Diesel Engines and Components, D-7.
Direction finding equipment, A-45, N-3, N-8, N-24, CG-1.
Dishes, A-2, N-21, N-21a, D-4, CG-2.
Dishwashing machines, A-2, N-12, N-14, N-24, N-26, D-4.
Disinfectants, A-2, A-45, D-4.
Distributors, A-11, A-31, A-32, N-11, N-26, D-7, AF-17.
Diving apparatus, A-32, N-3, N-11, N-24, D-7, CG-1, CG-6.
Docks, floating, A-32.
Dollies, A-4, N-6, N-27, D-4.
Doors, metal joiner, N-14, N-24, N-25.
Drafting equipment, fire control, A-32.
Drafting instruments, surveying & mapping, A-32, N-29b, AF-4, D-4.
Drafting services, (mechanical, topographic, etc.), A-4, A-45, A-77, N-29b.
Draperies, awnings, and shades, A-2, N-12, N-24, N-26, AF-5, D-4.
Drawing machines (metalworking), A-45.
Drawings & specifications, N-26.
Driers, dehydrators, and anhydrators, N-13, N-24, AF-6, D-7.
Driers, thermal, A-32, N-3, N-24, D-7.
Drilling machines, A-45, N-6, N-24, N-27a, AF-5, D-4.
Drill bits, counterbores and countersinks, N-24, AF-1, AF-5.
Drills, twist, A-45, AF-1.
Drives, ballistic, A-45.
Drones, N-12, AF-3b, AF-4.
Drugs, A-2, A-12, A-13, N-21, N-26, D-1.
Drums and cans (5 gallon, 55 gallon), AF-4, D-4.
Dry cleaning equipment, N-3, D-4.
Dry cleaning fluid, D-6.
Drydocks, floating, N-4.
Duck and webbing, D-1.
Duplicating services, N-14, N-26, AF-1.
Dyes, A-45, D-4.
Dynamite, A-45.

Earth moving and excavating equipment, D-7.
Ecclesiastical equipment & supplies, N-24, N-26, D-4.
Electric lighting fixtures (See Lighting fixtures).
Electric portable and handlighting equipment, AF-4, D-4.
Electric starters, A-11, A-31, A-32, N-9, N-11, N-26, D-4, D-7.
Electric vehicular lights and fixtures, A-31, A-32, D-4.
Electrical appliance & extension cords (See Extension cords).
Electrical contact brushes & electrodes, N-12, AF-3, D-4.
Electrical control equipment, AF-3, D-4.
Electrical hardware & supplies, A-2, A-4, A-11, A-31, A-32, A-45, N-6, N-11, N-12, N-19, N-21, N-24, N-26, N-27, N-27a, N-29, N-29b, AF-1, AF-3, AF-7, AF-14, AF-17, D-4, CG-2, CG-3, CG-4, CG-5, CG-6.
Electrical insulators & insulating materials, N-24, AF-3, D-4.
Electrical rectifying equipment, A-11, N-6, N-9, N-11, N-12, N-14, N-19, N-24, N-26, N-27, N-29, N-29b, AF-3, AF-1.
Electrical & electronic equipment components, A-11, N-9, N-11, N-12, N-14, N-24, N-26, N-27, N-27a, N-29a, N-29b, CG-2.
Electrodes, A-11, A-45, N-11, N-19, N-26, D-4.
Electrodes, lighting, AF-3.
Electrodes, welding, A-45, N-24, D-4.
Electron beam studies, advanced, AF-8.
Electron tubes, transistors & rectifying crystals, A-11, A-45, N-11, N-12, N-19, N-24, N-25, N-26, N-27, N-27a, AF-1b, AF-3, D-9, AF-17.
Electronic assemblies, A-11, N-10, N-26.
Electronic counter measures equipment, N-1, N-8, N-9, N-12, AF-1, AF-14, AF-17, N-19, N-27, N-29c, AF-5, AF-1, AF-12.
Electronic data processing, A-4, A-11, N-1, N-3, N-9, N-12, N-19, N-26, CG-1, AF-1, AF-17.
Electronic installation services, N-24.
Electronic items, components spare parts, systems, etc., A-2, A-11, A-44, A-45, A-61, N-3, N-5, N-6, N-8, N-9, N-11, N-12, N-14, N-19, N-24, N-26, N-27, N-27a, N-29a, N-29b, N-29c, N-30, AF-1b, AF-3, AF-7, AF-17, D-9, CG-1, CG-2.
Elevators and escalators, A-32, AF-5.
Elevators, passenger & freight, A-32, N-3, N-4.
End items for analysis & testing, miscellaneous, N-1.
Engine accessories, miscellaneous, A-2, A-31, A-32, N-9, D-7, N-11, N-14, N-24, N-26, AF-2, AF-4, AF-6, D-7, CG-6, D-5.
Engine air & oil filters, strainers & cleaners, aircraft, A-2, N-9, AF-2, AF-4, D-5.
Engine air & oil filters, strainers & cleaners, non-aircraft, AF-4, D-7, CG-6.
Engine components, A-2, A-32, N-9, N-11, N-12, N-14, N-24, N-25, D-7, AF-2, AF-4, CG-6.
Engine cooling system components, aircraft, AF-2, AF-4, D-5.
Engine cooling system components, non-aircraft, A-2, AF-4, D-7, CG-6.
Engine dynafocal suspension mounts, A-11, A-32, N-9, AF-4, CG-6.
Engine electrical system components, aircraft, A-32, N-9, N-14, AF-2, AF-4, AF-6, CG-1, CG-4, D-5.
Engine electrical system components, non-aircraft, A-31, AF-4, D-7.
Engine instruments, A-2, A-31, A-32, D-4, N-1, N-9, N-26, AF-2, AF-4, AF-6, CG-6.
Engine fuel system components, aircraft, A-32, N-9, AF-4, CG-4, D-5.

Engine fuel system components, non-aircraft, A-2, A-31, AF-4, D-7, CG-6.
Engine generators, A-31, A-32, N-9.
Engine valves, A-31, A-32, N-9, D-7, CG-3, CG-6.
Engineering services (electronic), A-11, A-61, N-1, N-3, N-4, N-8, N-12, N-24, N-26, N-27, CG-1.
Engineering services (marine), N-3, N-4, N-12, N-24, N-25, N-27, CG-1.
Engineering services (specialized) (ASW, AAW), N-12, N-14, N-26.
Engineering tests, N-1, N-4, N-12, CG-1.
Engines, aircraft, maintenance, overhaul, and repair of, A-32, N-1, N-26, AF-2, AF-4, CG-1, CG-4.
Engines, auto (gasoline), A-2, A-31, A-32.
Engines, auto (diesel), A-2, A-31, A-32, D-7.
Engines, diesel (locomotive), A-32, D-7.
Engines, diesel (marine use only), A-32, N-3, N-24, AF-4, D-7, CG-1.
Engines, gasoline reciprocating (aircraft), A-32, N-1, AF-4b.
Engines, gasoline reciprocating, (except aircraft), A-2, A-31, A-32, N-3, N-4, AF-4, D-7, CG-1.
Engines, gasoline reciprocating, (marine use only), A-32, N-24, N-13, D-7, CG-1.
Engines, gas turbine & jet, aircraft & components, A-32, N-9, AF-1d, AF-2c, AF-4, AF-6, CG-1, CG-4.
Engines, gas turbine & jet, non-aircraft & components, N-3, CG-1.
Engines, jet, N-1, AF-1d, AF-2c, AF-4b, CG-1, CG-4.
Engines, multi fueled, A-31.
Engines, steam (locomotive) A-32.
Engines, steam (marine use only), A-32, N-3.
Environmental control equipment, AF-5.
Environmental test equipment, N-6, N-14, N-19, N-24, N-27, N-27a, N-29a, AF-4.
Epoxy Tank coating, N-14, N-24.
Erosion machines, electrical & ultrasonic, N-6, AF-5.
Excavating machinery, N-5, D-7.
Excavating machinery, miscellaneous repair parts & attachments, N-31, D-7.
Exhaust systems (aircraft), AF-3, AF-5.
Exhibits/Display, A-4.
Expansion joints, N-14.
Explosive charges, high, nuclear ordnance, AF-1, AF-4, AF-16.
Explosive ordnance disposal tools, N-2, AF-1a.
Explosives & bulk propellants, A-45, N-11, AF-1a, AF-16.
Extension & appliance cords, A-2, N-6, N-21, N-21a, N-25, D-4.
Eye glasses, prescription, N-14, AF-7, D-1.

Fabric, plastic nylon reinforced, N-25.
Fabricated materials, glass (See Glass fabricated materials).
Fabricated materials, nonmetallic, miscellaneous (See Nonmetallic materials, miscellaneous, fabricated).
Fabricated metal products, general, A-45, N-6, N-9, N-11, N-14, N-19, N-24, N-26, N-27, N-27a, N-29a, CG-1, CG-2, CG-3, CG-4, CG-5, CG-6, AF-1, AF-2, AF-7, D-4.
Facial tissues, A-2, N-21, N-21a, D-4, CG-3, CG-4, CG-5, CG-6.
Facsimile equipment (non-airborne), AF-3.
Face shields, clear plastic, N-31, D-4.
Fairinas, plastic periscope, N-14, N-25.
Fair leads, aluminum or magnesium, D-5, D-7.
Fan & blower equipment, thermal, A-32, N-3, N-11, N-12, N-24, AF-4, D-4.
Fans, A-2, A-32, N-3, N-14, N-24, N-26, AF-4, D-4.
Fastening devices, A-2, A-31, A-32, A-45, N-6, N-26, N-27, AF-1, AF-3, AF-4, AF-17, D-5.
Fences, A-77, N-4, N-5, N-31, D-7.
Fencing, A-77, N-4, N-24, N-31, AF-17, D-7.
Fertilizers, A-2, A-32, N-26, N-28, AF-7, AF-13, AF-17.
Fibers, raw wool & cotton, D-1.
Fiber, vegetable, (see vegetable fibers).
Film, A-2, A-4, A-21, N-19, AF-1, AF-7, AF-17, CG-1, CG-5, CG-6.
Film, Medical, X-ray, D-1.
Film strips, CG-1, CG-5, CG-6.
Filters, air, aircraft, (see Air filters).
Filters, air, automotive, (see Air filters).
Filters, air & nitrogen service, A-45, N-3, N-11, N-24.
Filters, gasoline & oil, A-2, A-31, A-32, N-3, N-9, N-24, D-7.
Filters & networks, N-11, N-19, N-27, AF-1b, AF-6, D-9.
Filters, pressure, D-7.
Filters, radio interference, N-11, N-27, D-9.
Filters, (resistors, capacitors, or coil), AF-3.
Finders, range, A-45.
Findings, apparel and notions, A-2, D-1.
Fire control equipment, aviation, ordnance, A-45, N-1, N-9, N-12, N-29c, AF-5, AF-6, D-7.
Fire control equipment, Army armament, A-45, AF-5, D-7.
Fire control equipment, shipboard, N-2, N-12, N-14, N-27, N-27a.
Fire control equipment, synchros and synchro systems & servometers, (See synchros and synchro systems).
Fire control maintenance and repair equipment, A-45, N-12, AF-1, AF-5.
Fire extinguishers, A-2, A-31, A-32, N-5, N-24, AF-4, AF-7, D-7.
Firefighting equipment, mobile, A-32, N-29a, AF-5, D-7.
Firefighting equipment, other, A-32, N-4, N-5, N-9, N-24, AF-5, D-7.
Fireman's protective clothing, A-32, N-24, D-1.
Fireworks (see Pyrotechnics).
Firing and fuzing devices, nuclear ordnance, AF-4, AF-16.
Fishing equipment, A-2, A-32.
Fittings, ferrous and nonferrous, N-24, N-25, N-27, N-28, D-7, AF-17.
Fittings, marine special, N-24, N-29b.
Fittings for rope, cable & chain, A-32, N-9, N-11, N-24, N-29b, D-5, AF-17, CG-1, CG-2, CG-3.
Flags & Pennants, A-2, N-26, D-1, CG-2.
Flame cutting equipment, A-45, N-3, N-5, N-6, N-24, N-25, N-30, AF-5, D-4.
Flamethrowers, A-45.
Flares, (See Pyrotechnics).
Flashers, A-3.
Flashlights, A-2, N-21a, AF-4, D-4, CG-2.
Flight indicators, (See Indicators, flight).
Floats, (lifesaving equipment), A-32, N-11, D-7.
Floodlights, N-4, N-5, N-14, N-24, N-26, N-27, AF-4, CG-1, D-4.
Floor coverings, A-2, A-4, N-6, N-21, N-24, N-28, D-4.
Floor polishers, N-6, N-21, N-24, N-26, D-4.
Floor sanders, N-6, D-4.
Fluids, hydraulic, D-6, AF-1.
Foil, nonferrous base, A-31, A-32, A-45, AF-5.
Food, A-2, A-62, N-21, N-21a, N-26, N-28, D-1, CG-3, CG-4, CG-5, CG-6.
Food catering service, N-14.
Food products machinery & equipment, N-21, N-24, N-26, CG-5.
Food, cooking, baking & warming equipment, aircraft (See Aircraft).
Food, cooking & warming equipment, A-2, A-32, N-21, N-21a, N-24, N-26, N-28, D-4, CG-5.
Food preparation & serving equipment, A-2, N-14, N-21, N-21a, N-24, N-26, N-28, N-29, D-4, AF-5, AF-7, CG-5.
Footwear, men's, A-2, N-21, N-21a, D-1, CG-2.
Footwear, women's, A-2, N-21, D-1.
Forging machinery & hammers (metalworking), A-45, N-6, AF-5, D-4.
Forgings (machined), A-32, A-45, N-24, N-25, N-27, N-27a, N-29a, AF-1, AF-2, D-5.
Forming & bending machines (metalworking), A-45, N-6, N-24, AF-5, AF-7, D-4, CG-3, CG-4.
Forms, intermediate & nonferrous base metal refinery, AF-5.
Foundry equipment & supplies, A-32, A-45, N-24, N-25.
Fuel burning equipment units, A-32, D-7.
Fuel cells (aircraft), AF-1, AF-3.
Fuel dispensing equipment, A-31, A-32, A-45, N-3, N-5, N-9, N-21, N-21a, N-24, N-31, D-7, CG-1, CG-3, CG-4, CG-5, CG-6, AF-1.
Fuel oils, (See Oils, fuel).
Fuel system components, aircraft, A-32, AF-1, AF-2, AF-3, N-9, AF-4, CG-4.
Fuel system components, automotive, A-2, A-31, N-31, D-8.
Fuel system components, locomotive, A-32, N-13.
Fuel system components, marine, A-32, N-11, N-24, CG-1, CG-3, CG-6.
Fuel tanks, aircraft auxiliary, (See Aircraft).
Fuel tanks, engine, (except aircraft), A-2, A-31, D-7.
Fuels, gases, (See Gases, fuel).
Fuels, high energy, AF-4, AF-16.
Fuels, jet, D-6, AF-1.
Fuels, solid, D-6.
Fuels, turbine, D-6.
Fur material, D-1.
Furnaces, industrial, A-32, N-3, N-5, N-6, N-12, N-14, N-19, N-24, D-7, N-26, N-27, N-27a, AF-5.
Furniture, hospital, N-24, N-26, AF-7, D-1.
* Furniture, household & office, A-2, A-4, N-6, N-21, N-24, N-28, N-31, AF-7, AF-17, D-4.
Furniture, metal, A-2, N-6, N-21, N-28, AF-7, AF-17, D-4.
Furniture repair, A-4.
Furniture, shipboard, N-11, N-12, N-14, N-24, N-25, AF-17.
Furs, (for specialized AF requirements), D-1.
Fuze components, A-45, N-12, N-24, N-27, N-27a, AF-1.
Fuzes, A-2, A-11, A-32, A-45, N-11, N-12, N-13, N-27, N-27a, AF-1, AF-16.
Fuzes, missile ordnance, N-2, AF-16.

Gages, inspection, A-11, A-45, N-12, N-24, AF-4, AF-1, AF-5.
Gages, oil pressures, N-9, AF-1c.
Gages, plug ring and thread, N-25.
Gages, pressure, (See Pressure gages).

*Mainly procured for Department of Defense by General Services Administration. See Code 440 in listing of Federal Civilian Purchasing Offices, Page 81.

Galvanizing service, N-14, N-24, N-25.
Galvanometers, A-11, A-45, N-11, N-24, AF-4.
Games, toys & wheeled goods, A-2, D-4, CG-3, CG-4, CG-5, CG-6.
Garbage grinders, shipboard, N-3, N-24, N-25, CG-1.
Gardening implements and tools, A-2.
Gas cylinders, compressed gases, A-45, N-3, N-11, AF-1, AF-2, AF-4, AF-7, D-4.
Gas detecting devices, A-44, A-45, N-3, AF-4.
Gas flow measuring instruments, A-32, A-45, AF-4, AF-17.
Gas generating equipment, A-11, A-32, N-3, AF-4, D-4.
Gas masks & accessories, A-43.
Gases, compressed & liquefied, N-19, N-24, N-25, N-27, N-28, N-29, N-29c, AF-4, D-4.
Gases, fuel, AF-4, D-6.
Gaskets, A-2, A-31, A-32, N-11, N-25, N-29a, AF-1, AF-4, D-5.
Gasoline & components, A-2, N-21, N-21a, D-6.
Gasoline Reciprocating Engines, except aircraft; and components, D-7.
Gasoline Reciprocating Engines, aircraft; and components, D-5.
Gas turbines & jet engines, aircraft & components, A-32, AF-2, AF-4, AF-6, D-5.
Gas turbines and jet engines except aircraft and components, D-5.
Gates (for fences), A-77.
Gauges & meters, A-2, A-11, A-32, A-45, N-3, N-9, N-11, N-12, N-24, N-25, N-26, AF-4, AF-5, D-4.
Gear cutting & finishing machines, A-45, N-6, N-24, AF-5.
Gears, pulleys, sprockets, & transmission chain, A-31, N-29a, AF-4, D-7.
Gears, shipboard type, N-11, N-24, CG-1.
Gears, unassembled, A-32, N-6, N-9, N-11, N-24, N-27.
Generators, A-4, A-31, A-32, A-45, N-3, N-4, N-6, N-9, N-11, N-24, N-25, N-26, N-27a, AF-1, AF-7, AF-14, AF-17, D-4, D-7, CG-1, CG-2.
Generator sets, gasoline diesel, steam engine and steam turbine, A-32, N-3, N-4, N-5, N-9, N-12, N-14, N-24, N-28, N-29c, AF-3, D-4, CG-1, CG-2, AF-17.
Generators and generator sets, electrical, A-11, A-32, A-45, N-3, N-4, N-6, N-9, N-11, N-12, N-19, N-24, N-26, N-27, N-27a, N-29a, AF-1, AF-3, AF-6, AF-17, D-4, CG-1, CG-2.
Generators, signal, A-11, N-5, N-8, N-11, N-12, N-14, N-19, N-24, N-27, AF-4, AF-7, AF-13, AF-17, CG-1.
Geophysical instruments, A-11, N-29b, AF-4, D-4, AF-17.
Glass, building, (See Building glass).
Glass, fabricated materials, A-45, D-4, AF-5.
Glass, industries machinery, A-32, D-4, N-19.
Glass, plate, N-24, D-7.
Goggles and sun glasses, A-2, D-1, D-4, AF-6.
Graphics, artwork, displays, exhibits and advertising, and publicity, publications, A-2, A-4, N-2, N-3, N-5, N-6, N-14, N-19, N-19a, N-24, N-27, N-81, AF-7, CG-1.
Graphnels, A-32, N-24, CG-2.
Gravel, (See Construftion materials).
Greases, lubricating, D-6.
Grenade launchers, A-32.
Grenades, A-45, AF-1a.
Grinding machines, A-32, A-45, N-6, N-14, N-24, N-26, AF-5, D-4.
Grit, mineral, N-14.
Ground handling equipment, missiles, A-32, N-3, N-9, N-12, N-29a, AF-1b, AF-16, AF-5b.
Guard services, A-4.
Gums, crude, D-6.
Guided missile handling and servicing equipment, D-7.
Gun mounts, A-31, N-27, N-27a.
Guns & howitzers, towed field, anti-aircraft & anti-tank, A-32.
Guns, 30mm. & under, including mechanisms, mounts, attachments, accessories, & components, A-32, AF-1, AF-5, D-7.
Guns, Naval Ordnance type (including mounts & components), N-27.
Guns, over 30mm. through 300mm. caliber, A-32, D-7.
Gutters, D-7.
Gyrocompasses, N-3, CG-1.
Gyro-components, airborne, N-1, N-9, N-12, AF-2, AF-6, AF-13, D-4.
Gyroscopic systems, N-1, N-3, N-12, AF-13.

Haberdashery items, A-2, N-21, N-21a, D-1, CG-3, CG-4, CG-5, CG-6.
Hammers & forging machinery (metalworking), A-45, A-84, N-6, D-4, CG-3, CG-4.
Handcarts, N-6, D-4.
Handling devices, warehead (guided missiles & rockets), A-45, N-27, AF-1b, AF-5a, AF-16.
Handwear items, A-2, D-1, CG-3, CG-4, CG-5, CG-6.
Harbor defense equipment, N-3.
Hardware, aircraft, A-32, N-9, AF-1c, D-5, CG-4.
Hardware, commercial, A-2, A-32, A-45, N-9, N-12, N-21, N-24, N-26, N-27, N-27a, AF-1, D-5, CG-2, CG-3, CG-4, CG-5, CG-6.
Hardware, electrical, A-2, N-9, AF-7, AF-3, D-4, AF-1, AF-17.
Hardware, marine, A-32, N-11, N-12, N-24, N-25, N-29b, CG-2, CG-3.
Hardware, miscellaneous, A-2, N-24, N-26, N-27a, AF-4, AF-7, AF-14, D-4.
Hardware, railway, A-32, D-7.
Harness & wire assemblies, A-31, A-32, A-45, N-9, N-24, N-27, N-27a, AF-1, AF-16.
Harvesting equipment, A-32, D-7.
Hatches, A-32, N-11, N-14, N-25.
Hawse pipes, A-32.
Hazard detecting instruments, miscellaneous, A-32, A-45, D-4, N-3, AF-4, AF-16.
Head-sets (including components & accessories), A-11, A-45, N-9, D-9, CG-1, CG-4, AF-17.
Headwear items, A-2, D-1, CG-3, CG-4, CG-5, CG-6.
Heat exchangers, A-32, N-3, N-14, N-19, N-24, N-25, AF-5, CG-3, CG-4, AF-2, AF-17.
Heat treating equipment, metal, A-45, N-24, AF-1, AF-5, D-4, CG-4.
Heaters, aircraft, cabin & cockpits, (See Aircraft).
Heaters, marine, (See Marine heaters).
Heaters, vehicular, A-31, D-7.
Heaters, water, domestic, (See Water heaters, domestic).
Heating equipment, space, A-32, N-11, N-24, AF-5, AF-7, AF-14, D-7.
Heating equipment, miscellaneous, A-31, N-3, N-5, N-11, N-12, AF-1, N-24, N-26, N-29, N-31, D-7.
Heatsink, electronic, AF-1, AF-3.
Helicopter parts & components, A-32, N-9, CG-1, CG-4, AF-5.
Helicopter rotor blades, drive mechanisms and components, D-7.
Helicopters, A-45, N-1, CG-1, AF-6.
Helmet, various, D-1.
Hoists, (marine use), N-3, N-4, N-11, N-14, N-23, N-24, N-25, N-26, N-27, D-7, CG-3.
Hose, air, N-9, D-7.
Hose, assemblies, N-9, D-7, AF-17.
Hose, fittings & specialties, A-31, A-32, A-45, N-11, N-19, N-26, N-27a, N-31, D-7, CG-3, AF-1, AF-15, AF-17.
Hose, flexible, A-31, A-32, A-45, N-5, N-9, N-11, N-24, N-25, N-27, N-31, AF-1, AF-4, AF-17, D-7.
Hose, flexible, metallic and nonmetallic, N-2, N-9, D-7, AF-17.
Hose, hydraulic, A-32, N-9, D-7, AF-15, AF-17.
Hosiery, men's & women's, A-2, N-21, D-1, CG-3, CG-4, CG-5, CG-6.
Hospital equipment, A-12, A-13, N-14, N-26, AF-7, AF-14, D-1.
Household equipment, A-2, N-21, N-21a, AF-15.
Household furnishings (textiles), A-2, N-21, N-24, N-21a, D-1, AF-15.
Housekeeping items & services, N-21, N-24, N-29, D-4.
Housewares & accessories, A-2, N-21, N-21a, D-4.
Howitzers, A-45, A-84.
Hull items, A-32, N-3, N-11, N-12, CG-3.
Humidity measuring & controlling instruments, A-11, A-32, A-45, N-1, N-3, N-19, N-24, N-27a, N-29b, AF-4, AF-6, D-4.
Hydraulic equipment, A-45, N-12, N-19, N-26, AF-2, AF-17.
Hydrophones, N-3, N-11, N-19, N-27, N-27a, N-29b.

Ice cream machines, N-14, N-21, N-24.
Ignitors, A-45, N-12, N-27, N-27a, AF-4.
Ignition coils, A-2, A-11, A-31, A-32, D-7, D-9.
Ignition harness assemblies, A-11, A-31, A-32, A-45, N-9, N-24, N-31, D-7, AF-4.
Impregnating equipment, A-45, N-6.
Indexing, A-4, N-6.
Indicator assembly, fire control, A-45.
Indicator panel, N-27.
Indicators, air speed, N-9, AF-6.
Indicators, altimeter setting, N-9, AF-6.
Indicators, flight, A-32, N-1, N-9, N-26, N-29b, AF-2, AF-6, D-4.
Indicators, flight, gyro horizon, navigational, N-9, AF-6.
Indicators, ship's use, N-3.
Inflatable shelters, AF-7.
Infrared equipment, A-11, A-45, N-1, N-8, N-12, N-19, AF-6.
Ingots, copper & nickel, N-14, N-24, N-25.
Ingots, nickel, aluminum, bronze, N-14.
Initiators, pad, A-45.
Insignia, decorative & identification items, D-1, CG-2, CG-3, CG-4, CG-5, CG-6.
Instrument lights, A-31, A-32, A-45, AF-1.
Instruments, chemical analyses, A-45, N-24, AF-4, D-2.
Instruments, chemical composition determining, (See Chemical composition determining instruments).
Instruments, combination & miscellaneous, AF-1, AF-4, D-4.
Instruments, electrical & electronic properties measuring & testing A-11, A-32, A-45,

A-61, N-6, N-11, N-12, N-19, N-24, N-25, N-27, N-27a, N-28, N-29b, AF-4, AF-5, CG-1, AF-1, AF-14, AF-16, AF-17.
Instruments, engine, pressure measuring, N-9, AF-6.
Instruments, equipment and supplies, D-1.
Instruments, flight, A-32, N-1, N-9, N-29c, AF-1, AF-2, AF-6, CG-4.
Instruments, gas flow measuring, (See Gas flow measuring instruments).
Instruments, hazard detecting, miscellaneous, (See Hazard detecting instruments).
Instruments, humidity measuring & controlling, (See Humidity measuring & controlling instruments).
Instruments, liquid flow measuring, (See Liquid flow measuring instruments).
Instruments, liquid level measuring, (See Liqid level measuring instruments).
Instruments, mechanical motion measuring, (See Mechanical motion instruments).
Instruments, medical & dental, N-24, N-29, D-1, AF-14.
Instruments, miscellaneous nautical, (includes navigational instruments), N-1, N-3, N-9, N-11, N-24, N-27, N-29b, N-29c.
Instruments, Navigation, AF-1, AF-2, AF-6, D-4.
Instruments, pressure measuring & controlling, A-45, N-1, N-3, N-9, N-12, N-14, N-29b, AF-4, AF-6, AF-17, D-4.
Instruments, temperature measuring & controlling, (See Temperature measuring & controlling instruments).
Instruments, time measuring, (See Time measuring instruments).
Insulating materials, electrical, A-11, N-11, N-24, D-4.
Insulating materials, electronic, AF-3.
Insulation materials, (construction), A-77, N-14, N-24, N-77, D-7.
Insulators, electrical, A-11, A-45, N-10, N-24, D-4, CG-1.
Insulators, electronic, AF-3.
Intercommunication equipment, A-2, A-4, A-11, N-1, N-3, N-9, N-11, N-24, N-26, AF-2, AF-5, AF-6, CG-1.
Intercommunication systems, aircraft type, N-9, D-9, AF-6.
Intercommunication systems, (non-airborne), AF-3.
Interior decorating, shipboard, N-14.
Interpreter, translation services, A-4.
Iron & steel primary & semifinished products, A-31, A-45, A-82, A-84, N-6, N-12, N-24, N-27a, D-5.

Jamming systems, A-11, A-44, N-1, N-3, N-8, N-19, AF-6.
Janitorial cleaning supplies & equipment, A-2, A-4, AF-1, N-21, D-4.
Janitorial services, A-4.
Jars, N-8, D-4.
Jewelry, A-2, N-21, N-21a, D-4, CG-3, CG-4, CG-5, CG-6.
Jigs & fixtures, A-45, N-25, N-27.

Keys, A-2, A-4, A-31, A-45, D-5.
Kilns, industrial, N-3, AF-5, D-7.
Kitchen equipment & appliances, miscellaneous, A-2, A-4, N-6, N-14, N-21, N-24, N-26, D-4, CG-3, CG-4, CG-5, CG-6.
Kits, demolition, A-45.
Kits, kitchen, hand tools & equipment, D-4.
Kits, survivors', N-9, AF-4.
Knobs & pointers, N-9, N-10, AF-1, AF-4, D-5.

Laboratories, chemical, assembled outfits, A-45.
Laboratory equipment & supplies, miscellaneous, A-45, N-6, N-14, N-19, N-24, N-26, N-27, N-27a, N-28, N-29b, D-1, AF-4, AF-7, AF-12, AF-17.
Ladders, A-2, A-33, N-14, N-24, D-7.
Ladders, rope, N-11.
Lamps & lamp assemblies, A-2, N-6, N-9, N-21, N-21a, N-24, AF-4, D-4.
Lamp holders, starters & ballasts, N-13, N-24, AF-4.
Landing mats & accessories, N-5, D-7.
Landscaping services, A-4.
Language instruction, including tapes & records, A-4.
Lanterns, electric, N-31, AF-4, D-4.
Laser devices, AF-1, AF-3, AF-16.
Lathes, A-45, N-6, N-14, N-27, N-29, N-31, AF-5, D-4.
Laundry equipment, A-32, N-12, N-14, N-21, N-31, N-36, N-36, N-30, D-4.
Laundry equipment, commercial, (bath & fumigation), A-32, N-5, N-6, N-21, N-24, N-31, D-4.
Laundry equipment, commercial (impregnation sets & impregnation machines for fixed and mobile impregnating plants only), A-45, N-14, N-21, N-24, N-26, D-4.
Laundry service, N-6, N-12, N-14, N-24, N-25, N-26, N-27a, N-29.
Laundry supplies, N-21, N-21a, N-28, D-4.
Leather, D-1.
Leather, tanning & working industries machinery, A-32.
Lehrs, industrial, AF-5, D-7.
Life boats, rubber, inflatable, N-9.
Life preservers, A-2, A-32, N-9, D-7.
Life rafts, N-9.
Life saving equipment, marine, A-32, N-9, D-7, AF-5.
Lifting plugs, A-45.
Lighting fixtures, aircraft, A-31, N-9, D-4, CG-4.
Lighting fixtures, automotive, (parts, attachments & accessories), A-2, A-31, N-31, D-4.
Lighting fixtures, automotive type, A-31, D-4.
Lighting fixtures, aviation, sealane & carrier deck, N-9, N-11, N-14, N-29a.
Lighting fixtures, electric, aviation ground type, N-14, N-24, N-26, N-29a.
Lighting fixtures, electric, commercial, A-2, N-14, N-24, N-27, N-27a, N-31, D-4.
Lighting fixtures, electric, marine types, A-32, N-14, N-24, N-25, D-4.
Lighting fixtures, non-electric, AF-4.
Lighting fixtures, railroad & rapid-transit type, A-32, D-4.
Lightning arrestors, A-32, N-10, N-24, AF-3, D-9.
Lights, instrument, A-31, A-32, A-45, AF-1.
Limbers for guns & howitzers, A-45.
Lime, chlorinated, A-45.
Linen supply service, A-4, N-26, AF-7.
Line-throwing devices & accessories, A-32, N-24.
Links, cartridge, A-45, N-11.
Link trainers, A-32, AF-1, AF-6.
Liquid flow measuring instruments, A-32, A-45, N-1, N-3, N-12, N-14, N-29b, AF-4, AF-6, D-4, AF-17.
Liquid level measuring instruments, A-32, A-45, N-1, N-3, N-12, N-14, N-25, N-29b, AF-4, AF-6, D-4, AF-17.
Liquid propellant fuels & oxidizers, chemical base, AF-4, AF-16.
Lithographic equipment & supplies, N-81, D-4.

Lithographing, N-81.
Live animals, not raised for food, A-43, AF-4.
Loaders for guns (towed) anti-aircraft, A-45.
*Lockers, wall, metal, N-5, N-6, N-24, D-4.
Locomotive cranes & parts, A-32.
Locomotive fuel system components (See Fuel system components).
Locomotive and Rail car accessories and Components D-7.
Locomotives, A-32.
Lubricants, cutting, N-29c, D-6.
Lubricating oils (See Oils, lubricating).
Lubrication & fuel dispensing equipment, A-31, A-32, N-3, N-5, AF-4, D-7.
Luggage & leather goods, A-2, N-21, N-21a, D-1, CG-3, CG-4, CG-5, CG-6.
Lugs, terminals & terminal strips, N-9, N-11, N-19, N-27, AF-1b, AF-3, D-4.
**Lumber, N-14, N-24, N-25, N-26, N-27, N-27a, N-28, N-29, D-7.
Machines, arc welding, N-24, N-25, N-27a, D-4.
Machine guns, A-45, N-27.
Machine shop items, A-45, N-24, N-25, N-27, N-27a, N-28, N-29a, D-4, AF-1.
Machine tool accessories, A-45, N-6, N-24, N-27, N-27a, AF-5, D-4, CG-3, AF-1.
Machine tools, A-2, A-31, A-32, A-45, N-6, N-19, N-24, N-27, AF-1, AF-5, D-4, CG-3.
Machine work, N-19, N-24, N-25, N-27, N-27a, AF-1.
Magazines (See Periodicals).
Magnetic tape, N-6, N-24, N-27, N-29b, AF-1, AF-7, AF-13, AF-17.
Magnetic tape equipment, A-4, N-1, N-3, N-6, N-11, N-12, N-19, N-24, N-27, N-29b, AF-1, AF-13.
Magnetos, A-11, A-31, A-32, N-9, D-7.
Magnetostriction elements, AF-3.
Magnets, permanent, AF-3.
Maintenance and repair shop specialized equipment, miscellaneous, A-32, A-45, N-6, N-9, N-11, N-24, AF-4, D-7.
Maintenance, overhaul & repair of aircraft engines, A-32, N-1, N-9, N-12, N-26, AF-2, AF-4.
Maintenance, overhaul & repair of communications & radar equipment, A-4, A-11, N-12, N-14, N-19, N-24, AF-13, AF-16.
Maintenance, overhaul & repair of photographic equipment, A-4, N-12, AF-1.
Management engineering services, A-4, N-1, N-3, N-4, N-6, N-24, N-29a, CG-1, AF-6.
Manholes, A-32.
Manifolds, A-11, A-31, A-32, N-11, N-24, CG-6.
Manometers, N-26.
Mapping instruments, AF-4.
Maps.
Marine fule system components (See Fuel system components).
Marine Hardware and hull items, D-5.
Marine heaters, A-32, N-3, N-8, N-11, N-12, N-25.
Marine life saving & diving equipment, N-6, N-12, D-7.
Marine types lighting fixtures (See Lighting fixtures).

***Mainly procured for Department of Defense by General Services Administration. See Code 440 in listing of Federal Civilian Agency Purchasing Offices.**
****See also *Sales of Federal Timber*, Part VII of Directory.**

Marking devices (Stamp pads; stamps, rubber; stamps, metal including marking dies, seal presses; steel letters, figures & numerals; branding irons; & stencils), A-2, A-61, N-27, N-29b, D-4, AF-1, AF-7.
Maser devices, AF-3.
Mast & boom fittings, A-32, N-24, CG-3.
Masts, A-32, N-11, CG-3.
Material handling equipment, A-2, A-4, A-45, N-3, N-4, N-6, N-9, N-21, N-24, N-27a, D-4, D-7, CG-1, CG-2, CG-3, CG-4, CG-6, AF-1, AF-6, AF-17.
Material identification, stock numbering and inventory processing services, N-6.
Matting, rubber, condutive, N-27a.
Mattresses, N-24, D-1.
Mechanical motion measuring instruments, A-45, N-2, N-6, N-12, AF-4, AF-17.
Mechanical assemblies, small precision & parts, A-45, N-11, N-29a, AF-1, AF-4.
Medical books (See Books, Medical).
Medical equipment & supplies, A-12, A-13, N-6, D-1, AF-14.
Medical sets, kits & outfits, A-12, D-1.
Medicine, A-12, A-13, D-1.
Memorials; Cemeterial & Mortuary equipment & supplies, D-4.
Mess attendant services, N-6, N-12, N-14, N-24, N-25, N-26.
Metal castings, A-42, A-45, N-6, N-9, N-24, N-25, N-26, N-27, N-27a, N-29a, D-5, AF-1.
Metal findings, D-5.
Metal finishing equipment, A-45, N-6, N-24, AF-5.
Metal, additive & master alloys, AF-5, D-5.
Metal products, architectural & related (See Architectural & related metal products).
Metal ware (See Silverware, plated ware & similar metal ware).
Metal working machinery, A-45, N-6, N-24, N-27, AF-5, AF-7, D-4.
Metalizing equipment, A-45, N-26, AF-5, D-4.
Metallurgical testing equipment, A-45, N-6, N-19, D-4.
Metals, steel, copper, brass, bronze, lead, aluminum & magnesium alloys, (purchased in rods, bars, shapes, sheets, plates, discs, ingots, castings & forgings), A-43, A-45, N-6, N-12, N-14, N-19, N-24, N-25, N-26, N-27, N-27a, N-28, AF-1, AF-5, AF-7, AF-17, D-5, CG-3, CG-4.
Metals, precious, A-45, D-1, D-5, AF-1.
Meteorological instruments & apparatus, A-11, A-45, N-1, N-9, N-29b, AF-3, AF-17, D-4.
Meters, miscellaneous, aircraft, A-32, N-1, N-9, CG-1, AF-1, AF-4.
Meters, other, A-11, A-45, N-3, N-5, N-6, N-11, N-14, N-24, N-27, N-31, D-4, CG-1, AF-1, AF-4.
Microelectric circuit devices, D-9, AF-1, AF-3.
Microfilming, A-2, A-4, A-11, A-32, N-6, N-14, CG-1.
Micrographics, A-4.
Micrometers, N-6, N-25.
Micro-nodules, A-11.
Microphones & speakers (including components & accessories), A-2, A-11, N-3, N-9, N-11, AF-3, D-9.
Microscopes, A-45, N-6, N-19, AF-4.
Mill, pulverizing type, electric motor drive, N-6.
Milling machines, A-45, N-6, N-19, N-27, N-29, AF-5, D-4.
Millwork, N-14, D-7.
Mine, anti-personnel, anti-tanks, metal parts, A-45.
Mine, anti-personnel, anti-tank, plastic, A-45.
Mine detecting sets, N-3.
Mine laying equipment, N-29c.
Mine, practice, metal, A-45, A-63.
Mine, practice, plastic, A-45, A-63.
Minerals, natural & synthetic, A-32, D-5, D-6.
Mineral construction material bulk, D-7.
Mines, amphibious, A-45.
Mines, land, A-45, A-63, AF-1a.
Mines, underwater, & components, N-2, N-27, AF-1a.
Minesweeping equipment, N-3, N-11, N-27, N-29c.
Mining machinery, D-7, AF-16.
Mining machinery, miscellaneous repair parts & attachments, D-7.
Mining, rock drilling, earth boring and related equipment, D-7.
Mirrors, A-2, N-19, D-4, D-7.
Miscellaneous Aircraft Accessories and Components, D-5.
Miscellaneous special industry machinery, A-45, N-24, N-27a, D-7.
Miscellaneus power transmission equipment, N-24, D-7.
Missile components, A-21, N-3, N-12, N-27, AF-1b, AF-2a, AF-3a, AF-5a, AF-16.
Missile guidance equipment, A-21, N-3, N-12, N-29c, AF-1b, AF-16, AF-17.
Missile, guided, A-21, N-1, N-3, AF-1b, AF-2a, AF-5a, AF-6, AF-16.
Missile handling equipment, A-32, N-3, N-9, N-12, N-27, AF-1b, AF-3a, AF-5a, AF-16.
Missile items, A-21, A-45, N-1, N-3, N-23, N-27, AF-1b, AF-16.
Missile launchers, A-21, A-45, D-4, N-1, N-3, N-11, N-12, N-27, AF-1b, AF-3, AF-5a, AF-16.
Missile maintenance, repair & check out specialized equipment, A-21, N-12, AF-1b, AF-26, AF-3, AF-5b, AF-16.
Missile propulsion units, A-21, AF-1a, AF-16.
Missile remote control systems, A-45, AF-1b, AF-3a, AF-5a, AF-6, AF-16.
Missile spare parts replenishment, A-21, N-11, N-12, AF-1b, AF-2a, AF-5, AF-16.
Missile support equipment, A-45, N-1, N-3, N-9, N-11, N-12, AF-1, AF-2a, AF-16.
Missile systems, ballistic, A-21, N-1, N-3, AF-1, AF-2a, AF-16.
Missile system, ballistic missile defense, A-21, AF-16.
Missile systems, guided, A-21, N-1, N-3, AF-2a, AF-1, AF-5, AF-16.
Missile test equipment, A-21, A-32, A-45, N-3, N-12, AF-1, AF-2a, AF-16.
Missile tracking devices, N-1, N-3, N-12, N-19, AF-2a, AF-16.
Missile trailers, A-31, N-27, N-29a, AF-1, AF-5, AF-16.
Missile warheads & explosive units, A-45, N-3, N-27a, AF-1a, AF-2, AF-16.
Missiles, guided, A-21, N-1, N-3, AF-1b, AF-2a, AF-5a.
Mixing machines, D-4, D-7.
Mops, A-2, N-21, N-21a, D-4.
Mortuary services, N-12, N-14, N-24, N-26, AF-7.
Motion picture production, A-21, N-6, N-12, N-27, AF-9.
Motion, mechanical, measuring instruments, N-12, AF-4, D-4.
Motor generators, A-45, N-3, N-4, N-6, N-12, N-14, N-24, N-29a, N-30, N-31, AF-4, D-4, CG-1, CG-2, AF-1.
Motor vehicle components & parts, A-2, A-31, N-28, D-7, AF-1.
Motor vehicles maintenance & repair shop equipment, A-31, AF-4, D-7.
Motor vehicles (specialized purpose only), A-31, AF-1.
Motor vehicles, amphibious, military (landing vehicles, tracked), A-31, N-3.
Motor vehicles, amphibious, military (excludes landing vehicles, tracked), A-31.
Motors, electrical, A-2, A-11, A-32, N-3, N-5, N-6, N-9, N-11, N-14, N-24, N-25, N-27, N-27a, N-28, N-29a, AF-1, AF-3, D-4.
Mounts, fire control, A-5, N-12.
Moving & storage services, A-98, N-12, N-14, N-24, N-25, N-27a, N-28, AF-7, AF-14, AF-17.
Music, sheet & book, A-32, N-24, D-4.
Musical instruments, A-2, A-32, N-6, N-21, N-24, N-28, D-4.
Musical instrument repair services, N-6, N-28.

Nails, A-2, A-31, A-45, D-5.
Nameplates, charts, dials & scales, A-2, A-4, A-11, A-45.
Navigation equipment, N-8, N-9, N-11, AF-2, AF-6.
Navigation systems, aircraft and missiles, N-1, N-3, N-19, AF-2, AF-5, AF-6, AF-16.
Navigation systems, shipboard, N-3, N-19, N-29c.
Nets, N-9.
Nets & booms, harbor defense only, N-27.
Networks, N-11, AF-1b, AF-3, D-9.
Newspapers, A-2, A-4, N-24, AF-7.
Nonelectrical lighting fixtures, AF-4, D-4.
Nonferrous base metal refining & intermediate forms, A-31, A-45, N-11, N-24, AF-5, D-5.
Nonmetallic materials, miscellaneous, fabricated, N-5, N-9, N-24, N-27a, N-31, AF-5, AF-7, D-4.
Notions, A-2, N-21, N-21a, D-1, CG-3, CG-4, CG-5, CG-6.
Nuclear components, AF-1b, AF-3a, AF-5a.
Nuclear demolition charges, AF-1a.
Nuclear reactors, A-32, N-3.
Nuclear warheads & sections, AF-1a, AF-16.
Nuts, A-2, A-31, A-32, N-9, N-24, N-25, N-27, N-27a, N-29a, AF-1, AF-4, D-5.

Oarlocks, N-9, N-11.
Oars, A-33, N-11.
Ocean transportation, N-79.
Oceanographic devices, N-1, N-3, N-12, N-19, N-24, N-29b, CG-1.
*Office devices, and accessories, A-2, A-4, D-4.
*Office machines, except automatic data processing equipment, A-2, A-4, AF-15, D-4.
Office supplies, A-2, A-4, N-21, N-24, N-20, N-29b, D-4, AF-1, AF-15.
Oil field producing equipment, D-7.
Oil filters, aircraft, A-32, N-9, AF-2, AF-4.
Oil filters, automotive, A-2, A-31, A-32, D-7.
Oil, road, (See construction materials).
Oil, shale, crude, (See Shale oil, crude).
Oils, cutting, A-45, D-4, D-6.
Oils, electrical insulating, D-6.
Oils, fuel, D-6.
Oils, hydraulic, A-45, D-4, D-6.
Oils, industrial, A-45, D-6.

*Mainly procured for Department of Defense by General Services Administration. See Code 440 in listing of Federal Civilian Purchasing Offices, Page 81.

Oils, lubricating, A-2, A-45, D-4, N-14, N-21, N-21a, D-6, AF-1.
Optical accessories & components, A-45, N-11, N-12, N-19, N-24, N-27a, AF-1.
Optical instruments, miscellaneous, A-45, D-4, N-3, N-6, N-11, N-12, N-19, N-24, N-27, N-27a, AF-1, AF-4, AF-12.
Optical items, spheres, flats, prisms, reticles, etc., A-45, N-10, N-12, N-25, AF-1.
Oscillators, N-6, N-9, N-11, N-12, N-14, N-24, N-27, N-27a, AF-4, AF-6, AF-14, AF-17.
Oscillographs, A-11, A-45, N-1, N-11, N-19, N-24, AF-13, N-27a, AF-4, CG-1.
Oscilloscopes, A-11, A-45, A-61, N-1, N-5, N-6, N-11, N-14, N-19, N-24, N-26, N-27, N-27a, N-29, AF-4, AF-6, AF-7, AF-13, AF-17, CG-1.
Ovens, industrial, A-45, N-3, N-6, N-12, N-14, N-19, N-24, D-7, N-26, N-27a, AF-5, AF-13.
Overhaul & rehabilitation of aircraft components, A-32, N-9, AF-1, AF-2.

Packaging, A-2, A-11, A-45, N-2, N-24, D-4, AF-1.
Packaging & wrapping machinery, N-6, D-4, AF-1.
Packing & gasket material, A-31, A-32, A-45, N-9, N-11, N-25, N-27, N-29a, AF-4, D-5, AF-1.
Packing & packaging bulk materials, A-45, N-27, N-31, D-4, AF-1, AF-5.
Packing, crating, storage, household goods, A-61, A-98, N-12, N-14, N-24, N-25, N-26, N-28, AF-1, AF-7, AF-17.
Padding, D-1.
Paints, A-2, AF-17, CG-2.
Pallet adaptors, N-11.
Pallet racks (steel & wood), A-2, A-4, N-24, D-4, AF-1.
Pallets, steel & wood, A-2, A-32, N-11, N-24, N-27a, D-4, AF-1, AF-6, CG-2, CG-4, CG-6.
Pallets, wire, N-11, AF-1.
Pamphlets, AF-7.
Paper, A-2, A-45, N-24, N-31, D-4, AF-1, AF-5.
Paper, blueprint, N-14.
Paperboard, N-31, D-4, AF-5.
Paper building (See Building paper).
Parachute canopies, A-32, N-9, AF-4.
Parachutes & aerial pickup, delivery and cargo tie downs, A-32, AF-4, AF-5, D-5.
Parachutes, cargo, personnel, & parts, A-32, N-5, N-9, N-12, N-24, AF-4, AF-5, AF-7, AF-13, CG-4.
Parrafin, chlorinated, A-45.
Passenger, ocean transport, N-79.
Perfumes, A-2, N-21, N-21a, CG-3, CG-4, CG-5, CG-6.
Periodicals, A-2, A-4, A-43, A-45, N-5, N-14, N-19, N-24, N-26, N-27, N-28, N-29, AF-1, AF-7, D-4, CG-1, CG-2, CG-3, CG-4, CG-5, CG-6.
Periscopes, A-45, N-3.
Pest control agents, A-2, A-45, D-4, AF-17.
Pest, disease and frost control equipment, D-7.
Petroleum, crude, D-6.
Petroleum production & distribution equipment, A-32, D-7.
Petroleum products, miscellaneous, A-2, D-6, AF-1.
Phonographs, radios, and television sets, household type, A-2, N-21, D-4, CG-3, CG-4, CG-5, CG-6.
Phonograph records, A-2, D-4, AF-7, CG-3, CG-4, CG-5, CG-6.
Phosphoric acid, A-45.
Photographic equipment, A-2, A-4, D-4, N-1, N-6, N-12, N-14, N-19, N-21, N-21a, N-24, N-26, N-27, N-29b, AF-1, AF-7, AF-14, AF-17, D-7, CG-1, CG-4, CG-5, CG-6.
Photographic services, A-4, A-21, A-45, A-61, N-1, N-6, N-12, N-14, N-27, AF-1, AF-7.
Photographic supplies, A-2, A-4, A-21, A-45, A-61, N-6, N-9, N-14, N-21, N-21a, N-24, N-27, N-31, AF-1, AF-7, D-4, CG-1, CG-4, CG-5, CG-6, AF-17.
Photogaphic work, CG-1.
Photostat machines & equipment, D-4.
Pictorial services, motion picture, A-21.
Pilotage services, N-26.
Pilot mechanism, automatic, N-1, N-9, AF-2, AF-6.
Pins, A-2, A-31, A-32, A-45, D-5
Pins, retainers (See Retainer, pins).
Pins, wrist, (See Wrist pins).
Pipe, fittings & specialties, N-9, N-11, N-12, N-14, N-24, N-25, N-27, N-29a, N-31, AF-3, D-7.
Pipe, metal, A-32, A-45, N-6, N-11, N-14, N-24, N-25, N-27, D-7.
Pipe, nonmetallic, A-45, N-11, N-23, N-25, N-29, D-7.
Pipes & tubes, A-45, N-6, N-14, N-24, N-25, D-7.
Piston rings, A-31, A-32, N-9, N-11, D-7, CG-6.
Pistons, A-31, A-32, N-9, N-11, D-7, CG-6.
Planers & shapers, A-45, N-6, N-24, N-27, AF-5, D-4.
Plastic fabricated materials, A-45, N-3, N-9, N-11, N-14, N-24, N-27, N-27a, N-31, AF-1, AF-5, D-4.
Plastics, A-11, A-45, N-24, N-27a, N-29c, D-4, AF-1.
Plate, iron & steel, A-31, A-45, N-6, N-12, N-24, N-25, N-27, AF-1, AF-5, D-5.
Plate, metal, nonferrous base, A-31, A-32, A-45, N-19, N-24, N-25, N-27, N-31, AF-1, AF-5, D-5.
Plates & emblems, auto distinguishing, D-1.
Plugs, base, N-27a.
Platform, maintenance and test, N-9.
Plumbing equipment, miscellaneous, N-12, N-24, N-28, AF-7, AF-14, D-7.
Plumbing fixtures & accessories, N-14, N-24, N-26, N-28, AF-5, AF-7, D-7.
Plywood, N-25, N-26, D-7.
Pointers & knobs, AF-4, D-5, AF-1.
Polishers, floor (See Floor polishers).
Polishes, A-2, D-4.
Polishing compounds & preparations, N-26, D-4.
Pontoons, floating docks & components, A-32, N-12.
Posters, N-14, D-4, CG-1.
Power equipment, electrical, miscellaneous, N-3, N-24, N-27, AF-1, AF-3, AF-4.
Power supplies, electrical & electronic, A-11, A-45, N-3, N-6, N-11, N-12, N-14, N-19, N-24, N-27, N-27a, N-29b, AF-2, AF-4, D-4.
Power tools, A-2, A-4, A-45, N-25, AF-1, AF-5, AF-6, AF-7, AF-17.
Power transmission equipment, miscellaneous, A-32, AF-4, D-7.
Precision layout tools, AF-5.
Prefabricated building panels (See Building panels prefabricated).
Prefabricated buildings, N-14, N-19, N-24, D-7, AF-5.
Prefabricated & portable buildings, N-14, N-24, N-27a, D-7, AF-5.
Pre-heaters, welding, N-24, N-25.
Preservatives, D-6.
Presses, manual, D-4.
Presses, power driven (metalworking), A-45, N-6, AF-5, D-4.
Pressure gages, A-11, A-45, N-3, N-9, N-11, N-14, N-24, N-25, N-27, N-29a, AF-1, AF-2, AF-4, AF-6, D-4.
Pressurizing equipment, aircraft, AF-2, AF-6.
Primers, A-45, N-24, AF-1a.
Printing & duplication & bookbinding equipment, A-1, A-2, A-4, D-4.
*Printing & related products, A-1, N-24, N-81.
*Printing matter, miscellaneous, A-1, D-4.
*Printing services, A-1, A-2, A-21, N-6, N-14, N-24, N-25, N-81.
Production & design studies, N-1, N-3, N-12, N-24, N-27
Propellant actuated devices and component parts, A-45, AF-1a, AF-6, AF-16.
Propellant fuels & oxidizers, liquid, chemical base, AF-4, AF-16.
Propellants, A-45, N-2, AF-1a, AF-5, AF-16, D-6.
Propellers, ship, N-3, N-6, N-11, N-24, AF-5, CG-1, CG-3.
Propulsion shafting, A-32, N-3, N-11, N-24, CG-1, CG-3.
Protective equipment, chemical-biological-radiological, A-45, N-24, N-29c, D-1, AF-6.
Public address systems, A-2, A-4, A-11, A-45, N-3, N-6, N-10, N-24, AF-3, AF-5, CG-1.
Publications, miscellaneous, A-1, A-2, A-4, A-21, N-3, N-6, N-14, N-24, N-26, N-D-4, CG-1.
Pulleys (Hardware), N-9, D-4, CG-3.
Pulp & paper industries machinery, A-62.
Pump bucket, lubricating, N-31.
Pump, service station, N-21.
Pumps and compressors (for industrial and shipboard use), N-12, N-14, N-24, N-25, D-7.
Pumps, hand, AF-3, AF-17, AF-5, D-7.
Pumps, power-driven, A-32, N-3, N-6, N-11, N-12, N-14, N-24, N-25, N-26, N-29a, AF-1, AF-5, D-7, CG-1, CG-3, D-7.
Pumps, rotary, power-driven, A-32, D-7.
Pumps, vacuum, A-32, N-3, N-6, N-9, N-11, N-12, N-19, N-24, N-26, N-27, N-27a, AF-1, AF-5, AF-12, D-7.
Pumps, water, all types, A-32, N-3, N-6, N-11, N-12, N-24, N-27, N-27a, N-31, D-7, CG-6.
Punch card service, (sorting, listing & collating), A-4, N-3, N-6, N-24, N-25, N-27.
Punched card systems machines, A-4, N-6.
Punching & shearing machines (metalworking), A-45, N-6, N-14, N-27, AF-5, D-4.
Purifiers, oil, centrifugal, N-3.
Pushcarts, N-21, N-24, D-4.
Pylons (Aircraft), AF-1, AF-3, AF-6.
Pyrotechnic launchers, AF-1, AF-5, AF-6.
Pyrotechnics (flares, signals, fireworks), A-45, D-4, N-11, N-24, N-27a, AF-1a, AF-6, CG-1.

Quadrants, A-45.

*Printing and binding services are not purchased by the Government procurement offices except on waiver issued by the Government Printing Office.

Radar equipment, A-11, N-3, N-6, N-8, N-9, N-11, N-12, N-14, N-19, N-24, N-29c, AF-1, AF-3, AF-12, AF-13, AF-14, AF-17, CG-1.
Radar equipment, airborne, N-1, N-12, N-19, N-24, N-29c, AF-5, AF-6, CG-1, AF-1, AF-12, AF-13, AF-17.
Radar equipment, missile & weapon control, N-3, N-12, N-27, AF-1, AF-16, AF-17.
Radarsonde sets, AF-3.
Radar test sets, N-9, N-12, AF-1, AF-12, AF-13.
Radiac equipment, A-11, A-45, N-1, N-8, N-10, N-12, N-19.
Radio communication equipment, A-11, N-1, N-5, N-8, N-9, N-11, N-12, N-14, N-19, N-24, N-26, N-27, N-27a, N-29c, N-31, AF-2, AF-3, AF-7, D-9, CG-1, AF-1, AF-5, AF-6, AF-12, AF-13, AF-16, AF-17.
Radio interference filters, A-11, N-11, N-24.
Radio navigation equipment, A-11, N-8, N-11, N-19, N-24, N-29b, N-29c, AF-2, AF-1, AF-3, AF-6, D-9, CG-1.
Radio navigation equipment, airborne, N-1, N-19, AF-1, AF-5, AF-6, AF-1b, CG-1.
Radio test sets, N-9.
Radiological instruments, A-11, A-45, N-1, N-9, N-13, N-24, CG-1.
Radiological protective equipment, (See Protective equipment).
Radiosondes, N-9, AF-3.
Radiosondes, recorder, N-9.
Radomes, A-21, N-3, N-9, N-11, N-29c, D-9, AF-1, AF-17.
Rafts, A-32, D-7, CG-2, AF-6.
Rail cars, including self-propelled cars, A-32, D-7.
Rail transportation maintenance & repair-shop equipment, A-32.
Railroad and rapid-transit-type lighting fixtures (See Lighting Fixtures).
Railroad right of way construction & maintenance equipment, D-7.
Railroad signal & warning devices (See Signal & warning devices, railroad).
Railroad transportation equipment parts, including non-machine castings, A-32.
Rails & tracks accessories, A-32, N-27a.
Railway hardware (See Hardware).
Receivers (radios) aircraft, N-9, AF-6, AF-17.
Recorder, humidity, temperature and electrical resistance, N-27, N-29b.
Recording & reproducing equipment (See Sound recording & reproducing equipment).
Recordings, motion picture sound, A-21.
Recreational equipment, A-2, N-5, N-21, N-21a, N-30, N-31, AF-1, AF-7, D-4, CG-3, CG-4, CG-5, CG-6.
Rectifying equipment, electrical (See Electrical rectifying equipment).
Reels (wire), D-9, AF-5, D-4.
Refractories & fire surfacing materials, D-4, AF-5.
Refrigeration equipment, A-2, A-32, A-77, N-3, N-5, N-6, N-9, N-11, N-12, N-19, N-24, N-26, N-27a, N-28, N-31, AF-1, AF-4, AF-15, D-4.
Relays, contractors & solenoids, A-11, A-45, N-11, N-12, N-24, N-27, N-27c, AF-1b, AF-3, D-4, D-9.
Repair & maintenance of aircraft engines, A-32, N-1, N-26, AF-2, AF-4.
Repair & maintenance of rail cars, A-32.
Repair, overhaul & inspection of aircraft, A-32, N-1, N-12, N-14, N-26, AF-1, AF-2, AF-3, AF-4, AF-5.
Research & development, See Part V.
Resale merchandise, A-1, N-21, N-21a, CG-2, CG-3, CG-4, CG-5, CG-6.
Resistors, A-11, A-32, A-45, N-9, N-11, N-24, N-27, N-27a, N-29b, AF-1, AF-3, D-9, CG-2.
Resolvers, electronic, AF-1, AF-3.
Respirators, A-32, A-45, D-4.
Retainer pins, A-11, A-31, A-32, AF-3, AF-4.
Reticles, A-45, N-11.
Rifles, recoilless, A-45.
Rigging, A-32, N-6, N-24, N-25, D-5.
Rigging & rigging gear, A-32, N-11, N-24, N-25, D-5.
Right of way construction & maintenance equipment, railroad, D-7.
Rings (for optical components), A-45.
Rings, connecting and retaining, D-5.
Riveting machines, N-6, N-26, AF-5, D-4.
Rivets, A-32, D-5.
Road cleaning & clearing equipment & parts, A-32, D-7.
Rocket items, A-45, N-1, N-3, N-11, N-12, AF-1, AF-16.
Rocket launchers, A-21, A-45, N-1, N-3, N-11, N-27, AF-1, AF-5, AF-16.
Rocket engines & components, N-12, AF-1, AF-3, AF-16, D-5.
Rockets, A-21, A-45, AF-1, AF-16.
Rods, cleaning, A-45.
Rods, iron & steel, A-45, N-24, N-25, N-26, D-5, CG-3.
Rods, nonferrous base, A-31, A-32, A-42, A-45, A-82, A-84, N-24, N-25, D-5, CG-5.
Roofing materials, N-26.
Rope, cable, chain and fittings, N-24, AF-17.
Rope, fiber, A-32, N-14, N-24, D-5, CG-2.
Rubber fabricated materials, A-32, A-45, N-5, N-9, N-11, N-19, N-27, N-27a, N-31, D-1, D-4.

Saddlery, harness whips, & related animal furnishings, A-32, D-7.
Safety awards, N-6.
Safety glasses, N-14, N-19, N-24, N-27, N-29a, AF-1, D-1, CG-3, CG-4.
Safety & rescue equipment, A-45, N-24, AF-5, D-4.
Sail booms, CG-5.
Sails, CG-5.
Salvage apparatus, N-3, N-9.
Sand (See Construction materials, minerals).
Sanitation equipment, miscellaneous, D-7.
Saw blades, concrete, N-6.
Saw blades, masonry, N-6.
Saw blades, metalworking, A-32, A-45, N-6, N-25, N-27.
Saw blades, plastic, A-32, N-6.
Saw blades, wood, A-32, A-45, N-6.
Saws, hand, various types, A-2, N-6, AF-5.
Saws, masonry, A-32, N-6.
Saws, power, A-2, N-14, D-4.
Sawmill machinery, A-32, D-4.
Scabbards, A-45.
Scaffolding equipment, N-12, N-24, N-25, N-26, AF-5, D-7, CG-4, CG-6.
Scaler, Needle, N-14.
Scales, A-2, A-32, A-45, N-6, N-14, N-26, AF-4, D-4.
Scrap, Iron and Steel, non-ferrous, D-5.
Screen, projection, photo, A-2, A-4, A-21, AF-1.
Screening, metal, D-5.
Screw machine products, A-45, N-27, N-27a, N-29a, D-5.
Screw machines, A-45, N-6.
Screws, A-2, A-31, A-33, A-45, N-9, N-24, N-25, N-27, N-27a, D-5, AF-1.
Scuppers, N-25.
Scuttles, N-11, N-14, N-25.
Sea chests, N-25, CG-3.
Sea cocks, N-25, CG-3.
Sealane lighting fixtures (See Lighting fixtures).
Seals, oils & grease, A-31, A-32, A-45, N-9, N-11, N-27, AF-1.
Searchlights, A-45, N-11, D-4, CG-1, CG-3.
Security guard services, A-2, N-6, N-12, N-14, N-24.
Seeds & nursery stock, A-32, N-28.
Semiconductors, A-11, N-9, N-11, N-19, N-27, N-27a, N-29b, D-9, AF-1.
Service & trade equipment, miscellaneous, N-24, D-4.
Services, data processing & card punching, N-3, N-6, N-9, N-14, N-19, N-24, N-25, N-27, N-29b, N-29c, AF-1.
Services, galvanizing, N-14, N-24, N-25.
Services, janitorial, A-2, A-61, N-24, N-25, AF-1, AF-14, AF-17.
Services, mess attendant, N-6, N-12, N-14, N-24, N-25, AF-17.
Services of consultants, management, technical engineering, etc., A-4, A-17, A-21, A-31, A-32, A-100, N-1, N-3, N-4, N-6, N-8, N-12, N-14, N-24, N-29a, AF-1, AF-6, AF-7, AF-16, CG-1.
Services, radioactive waste disposal, N-24, N-25, N-29.
Sets, kits & outfits, food preparation & serving, D-4.
Sets, kits & outfits of measuring tools, D-4.
Sewage treatment equipment, N-3, N-6, D-7, CG-1.
Sewing machines, industrial, N-6, D-4.
Sextants, N-9, N-11, AF-1.
Shafting, flexible & parts, N-11.
Shale, oil, crude, D-6.
Shapers & planers, (See Planers and shapers).
Shearing machines & punches (metalworking), A-45, N-6, N-14, N-27, D-4, AF-7.
Sheet metal, nonferrous base, A-31, A-45, N-6, N-24, N-27, AF-1, AF-5, D-5, CG-4.
Sheet metal products, A-45, N-14, N-24, N-27, N-27a, D-4, AF-1, AF-2, AF-4.
Sheet & strip, iron & steel, A-32, A-45, N-6, N-24, N-25, N-26, N-27, D-5, AF-1.
Shell components, A-45.
Sheets, plastic copper clad and plain, N-27.
Shelters, electric, equipment (light weight), A-11, A-45, N-19, N-24, N-29a, AF-1, AF-2.
*Shelving, metal, A-2, N-6, N-14, N-24, N-26, AF-1, D-4.
Ship & marine equipment, miscellaneous, A-32, D-4, D-7, N-3, N-11, N-12, N-24, N-25, N-27, N-29b, D-7, CG-1, CG-3.
Ship propellers, A-32, N-3, N-11, N-24, CG-1, CG-3.
Ship propulsion components, A-32, N-3, N-11, N-12, N-24, N-25, CG-1, CG-3, D-7.
Ship repair, A-32, N-3, N-12, N-13, N-24, N-29a, CG-5, CG-6.
Ship ventilators, A-32, N-3, N-11, N-12, N-24, CG-3.
Ships, N-3, CG-1.
Shoe-repairing equipment, N-21, D-4, CG-5.
Shoe findings & soling materials, D-1, CG-5.
Shoes, men's & women's A-2, N-21, N-21a, D-1, CG-3, CG-4, CG-5, CG-6.
Shot preening, equipment, N-26.
Siding materials, N-29a.
Signal & warning devices, railroad, A-32, D-4.

Mainly procured for Department of Defense by General Services Administration. See Code 440 in listing of Federal Civilian Purchasing Offices, Page 81.

Signals, (See Pyrotechnics).
Signs, advertising, displays & identification plates, D-4, AF-5, CG-1.
Silver recovery from used film, N-14, N-24, AF-1.
Silverware, plated ware & similar metal ware, A-2, D-4.
Simulated radiation devices AF-3.
Slings, A-32, N-14, N-24, N-26, N-27, D-5.
Slings, aerial delivery, A-32, N-5, N-9, AF-4.
Slings, steel, A-31, A-32, N-11, N-24, D-5.
Small arms, rifle, carbines, pistols, revolvers, submachine guns, shot guns, pyrotechnic projectors, A-2, A-45, CG-1.
Small craft, A-32, N-3, CG-1, CG-6.
Smoke generators, A-45.
Smoker's articles, A-2, N-21, N-21a, D-4, CG-3, CG-4, CG-5, CG-6.
Snaps, steel wire, D-5.
Soap, laundry, A-2, D-4.
Soap, powder, A-2, D-4.
Soap, scouring, A-2, D-4.
Soap, toilet, A-2, N-21, N-21a, D-4.
Sodium hexametaphosphate, A-45, N-14, D-4.
Sodium orthosilicate, A-45, D-4.
Sodium phosphate, A-45, N-14, D-4.
Soil preparation equipment, A-32, D-7.
Solders, solid, N-11, D-4.
Solenoids, A-11, A-45, N-5, N-9, N-11, N-27, N-27a, AF-1b, AF-3, D-4, D-9.
Solvents, N-27, D-6.
Solvents and degreasers, N-26, N-27.
Sonobuoys, N-1, N-19, N-27, N-29b, N-29c.
Sound equipment, underwater (SONAR), N-1, N-3, N-8, N-9, N-11, N-12, N-14, N-19, N-24, N-27, N-29b, AF-3, CG-1.
Sound recording & reproducing equipment, A-2, A-4, A-11, A-45, N-3, N-6, N-8, N-9, N-10, N-12, N-14, N-19, N-24, N-27, AF-1, AF-2, AF-3, D-9, AF-17, CG-1.
Space systems & components, N-19, AF-3, AF-8, AF-16.
Space survival equipment, A-32.
Spacers, sleeve, D-5.
Spare parts, aeronautical & missile, A-21, N-9, AF-1, AF-2, AF-4, AF-16, AF-17, CG-4.
Spare parts, electronic equipment, A-2, A-11, N-9, N-11, N-24, N-29b, N-31, D-9, CG-2, AF-1, AF-2, AF-14.
Spare parts, ordnance equipment, A-45, AF-1, CG-2.
Spare parts, ships' propulsion & hull equipment, A-32, N-6, N-11, N-12, N-24, CG-3, CG-5, CG-6.
Spark plugs, A-2, A-31, A-32, N-9, N-21, AF-4.
Special service vessels & repair parts, A-32, N-27.
Speed changes, N-5, N-6, N-9.
Sponges, A-2, N-29, D-4.
Spools (wire), A-11, D-4.
Springs, A-31, A-32, A-45, N-9, N-11, N-27, N-27a, N-29a, D-5.
Sprockets, AF-4, D-7.
Stackers, industrial, materials, handling, N-6.
Stampings (large & small) A-45, N-27a, D-5, AF-4.
Stationery & Supplies, A-2, N-21, N-21a, D-4, CG-3, CG-4, CG-5, CG-6.
Steam condensers, A-32.
Steam turbines and components D-7.
Steel plates, sheets, strips, various, A-31, A-32, A-45, N-6, N-24, N-25, N-26, N-27, AF-5, D-5, CG-3, AF-15.
Steel stripping & hardware, D-5, CG-3.
Steering gears & controls, A-32, N-3, D-7, CG-1, CG-3.
Stenographic reporting, A-4.
Stern tubes, CG-3.
Stevedoring & related services & supplies, A-98, N-24.
Strainers, oil and water, N-14.
Strips, metal, nonferrous base, A-31, A-32, A-45, N-14, N-24, D-5, CG-3, AF-1.
Structural shapes, iron & steel, A-31, A-32, A-45, N-6, N-24, AF-1, AF-5, D-5, CG-3.
Structural shapes, nonferrous base, A-31, A-45, N-24, N-25, D-5.
Studies, A-4, N-4, N-6, N-12, CG-1, AF-1.
Also see Part V, since studies are often performed in conjunction with Research and Development.
Studs, A-11, A-31, A-32, A-41, N-25, N-29a, AF-4, D-5.
Studs, welding, N-14.
Stuffing materials, D-1.
Submarine & reactor parts, N-3, N-11, N-24.
Subsistence, A-2, N-21, N-21a, N-24, N-26, D-1.
Surgical equipment & supplies, N-24, D-1.
Surveying instruments, N-5, N-29b, AF-4.
Survival equipment, aircraft, N-9, N-29c, AF-4, AF-6, CG-1.
Survival equipment shipboard, N-9, N-11, D-7, CG-1, CG-3.
Switchboards, A-11, N-2, N-11, N-14, N-19, N-24, N-26.
Switches, A-11, A-32, A-45, N-9, N-11, N-14, N-24, N-27, N-29a, AF-1b, AF-3, AF-4, AF-6, AF-17, D-4, D-7, D-9, CG-1, CG-4.
Switches, pressure, N-27, N-27a, AF-1, AF-4.
Synchros & resolvers, A-45, N-11, N-27, AF-1, D-9.
Synchros & synchro systems & servometers, fire control, A-11, A-45, A-14, A-40, N-9, N-11, N-24, N-27a, N-29c, AF-1, AF-3.

Tableware, A-2, N-21, N-28, D-4, CG-2, CG-3, CG-4, CG-5, CG-6.
Tacan equipment and systems, N-9.
Tanks, A-45, N-14, AF-1.
Tanks, fuel (aircraft) AF-1, AF-3, AF-5, AF-6.
Tanks, liquid fuel, collapsible, N-5, D-4.
Tanks, storage, A-32, A-45, N-4, N-5, N-11, N-14, N-24, N-25, N-26, N-77, D-7, AF-1.
Tape, magnetic, A-2, N-13, N-14, N-19, N-27, N-29b, AF-1, AF-5, AF-13, AF-17.
Tape, pressure sensitive, A-2, N-25, N-29b, AF-1.
Taps, dies & collets, A-45, N-24, N-25, AF-5.
Target carriers, steel, N-5.
Target drones, aircraft (See Aircraft).
Targets, bull's eye, silhouette, etc., A-45.
Tarpaulins, A-32, N-24, D-1, D-4.
Technical data manuals & handbooks, A-2, A-4, A-11, A-21, A-31, A-32, A-45, A-100, N-3, N-6, N-9, N-14, N-19a, N-24, N-25, N-27, N-80, AF-1, AF-2, AF-4, CG-1.
Technical services, N-12, N-14, N-19, N-24, AF-1, AF-6, CG-1.
Technical writing, A-4, A-11, A-21, A-31, A-32, A-45, N-3, N-6, N-14, N-19a, N-24, N-27, AF-1, AF-4, AF-5, AF-6, AF-16.
Telegraph equipment, military, A-11, N-10, AF-2, AF-3, CG-1.
Telemetering equipment (nonairborne), AF-3, AF-13, AF-14, AF-17.
Telephone equipment, AF-3.
Telescope, A-45, AF-4, D-9.
Teletype and facsimile equipment, A-2, A-4, A-11, N-6, N-10, N-27, AF-1, AF-3, CG-1, D-9.
Television communication equipment, A-2, A-4, A-11, N-1, N-3, N-5, N-6, N-9, N-10, N-12, N-19, N-24, AF-1, AF-3, D-9, AF-14, CG-1.
Television production, video tape & film, A-21.
Temperature measuring & controlling instruments, A-45, N-1, N-3, N-6, N-9, N-11, N-24, N-27a, N-29b, AF-1, AF-4, AF-6, D-4, CG-1.
Templates, A-45, D-4, N-29.
Tents, D-1.
Terminal operation, petroleum products, D-6.
Terminals & terminal strips (See Lugs, terminals & terminal boards).
Test equipment, electronic, A-4, A-11, A-45, N-3, N-6, N-8, N-11, N-14, N-19, N-21, N-24, N-27, N-27a, N-29b, AF-1, AF-4, AF-6, AF-16, AF-17.
Test equipment, specialized, N-6, N-27a, D-4, AF-1, AF-6, AF-17.
Tester, internal combustion engine, N-30, AF-4.
Testing equipment, physical properties, A-11, A-32, A-45, N-5, N-6, N-9, N-14, N-19, N-24, N-25, N-27, N-27a, N-29b, N-31, AF-1, AF-4, D-4.
Testing instruments, electrical & electronic properties, A-11, A-32, A-45, N-6, N-12, N-19, N-24, N-27, N-27a, N-29b, AF-1, AF-4, AF-6, D-9, CG-1, CG-2, CG-3, CG-4, CG-5.
Test sets, communications, radar, radio, N-9, N-12, N-27a, AF-1, AF-17.
Test stands, A-32, A-45, N-6, N-14, N-24, N-26, N-27a, N-29a, AF-1, AF-4, AF-6, AF-13.
Textile fabrics, D-1.
Textile household furnishings, A-2, N-21, N-21a, N-24, D-1.
Textiles (For specialized aviation requirements), N-9, N-29c, D-1.
Textiles, industries machinery, A-32.
Thermal insulation materials, N-24, N-25, AF-1.
Thermistors, AF-3.
Thermometers, chemical/clinical, N-14, D-1.
Thermonuclear systems, N-1, N-3.
Thermocouples, A-45, N-11, N-14, AF-1, AF-4.
Thinners, dope, paint, enamel & lacquer, N-25, CG-2.
Thread, A-2, N-21, N-21a, D-1.
Tile, N-23, N-28, N-29, D-4.
Tile, plastic vibration damping, N-25.
Tile, quarry, N-14, N-26.
Tile, rubber air lead, N-25.
Time measuring instruments, A-45, N-9, N-11, AF-4, D-4.
Tires & tubes (except aircraft), A-2, A-31, A-32, N-21.
Tires & tubes, aircraft, A-32, AF-1, N-9.
Tires, recapping and repairing, A-31, N-9, AF-1.
Tire rebuilding materials, A-2, A-31.
Tire retreading materials, A-31.
Tobacco & accessories, A-2, N-21, N-21a, D-1, CG-3, CG-4, CG-5, CG-6.
Toilet paper, A-2, N-21, N-21a, D-4.
Toiletries, A-2, N-21, N-21a, D-4, CG-3, CG-4, CG-5, CG-6.
Toiletry paper products, A-2, N-21, N-21a, D-4.
Tools, cutting (machine tools), A-2, A-45, N-6, N-24, N-27, N-27a, D-4, AF-1.
Tools, explosive ordnance disposal (See explosive ordnance disposal tools).

LOCAL PURCHASES BY MILITARY INSTALLATIONS

LOCAL PURCHASES BY MILITARY INSTALLATIONS

Military installations are authorized to make local purchases and to contract for various services. Local purchases usually can be made under the following conditions: (1) the purchase is small (usually $25,000 or less); (2) the items to be purchased are perishable; (3) the items are required for maintenance and repair of buildings of the installation; (4) the items are required for the maintenance, rehabilitation and/or repair of military equipment stocked, issued and stored at the installation (depot); or (5) the items are not available through Government supply channels and are needed in carrying out the installation's mission or, in the case of a supply distribution depot, are needed by installations which rely upon the depot to supply them such items.

Examples of items purchased locally are automotive spare parts and supplies, tools and equipment, and office supplies; perishable food items for troop meals; items sold in ships' stores; those sold in commissaries (perishable and nonperishable food items); and furniture, equipment and supplies for officers' and noncommissioned officers' clubs. Services contracted for include laundry, dry cleaning, custodial service, refuse collection, mess attendant services; tailoring, shoe, watch and automotive repairs; construction, repair and maintenance jobs; training aids, job lot printing, packaging, packing and marking; and van and rail shipments.

The military installations listed below are in addition to those listed in the section, "Major Military Purchasing Offices." A firm desiring to supply purchases made by these installations, or by the major installations previously listed, should contact those in the area it can serve, specify the items or services it wishes to sell, and ask to be considered when future purchases are made.

ALABAMA

Anniston

U.S. Army School Training Center (A), Ft. McClellan, 36201, Mr. George Hudson, AC 205/238-3622

Anniston Army Depot (A), ATTN: SDSAN-SB, 36201, Mrs. Kathryn Cagle, AC 205/238-7346

Montgomery

Base Contracts Office (AF), Maxwell AFB, 36112, Ms. Mary W. Whittle, AC 205/293-6113

National Guard (A) (AF), c/o USPFO, Alabama, P.O. Box 3715, 36193, Col. Max S. Bowdoin, AC 205/272-6450

Ozark

U.S. Army Aviation Center (A), Fort Rucker, 36362, Mrs. Betty Stinson, AC 205/255-3404

ALASKA

Anchorage

U.S. Army Engineer District (A), P. O. Box 7002, 99501, Mr. Thomas L. Carter, AC 907/552-3518

Contracting Office (A), Ft. Richardson, 99505, Mr. Hazen Kramer, AC 907/863-4101

National Guard (A) (AF), c/o USPFO Alaska, Camp Denali Pouch B, Ft. Richardson, 99505, Col. Edward M. Johnson, AC 907/428-6100

ARIZONA

National Guard (A) (AF), c/o USPFO, Arizona, 5636 E. McDowell Road, 85008, Col. Simon C. Krevitsky, AC 602/273-9812 or 9814

Marine Corps Air Station, Yuma
Naval Air Facility, Phoenix
United States Property and Fiscal Office, State of Arizona, 747 West Van Buren Street, Phoenix
Williams Air Force Base, Chandler
Yuma Proving Ground, Yuma

ARKANSAS

National Guard (A) (AF), c/o USPFO, Arkansas, P.O. Box 677, 72115, Col. Wallace B. Shaw, AC 501/758-4053, Ext. 232

Little Rock Air Force Base, Little Rock
Pine Bluff Arsenal, Pine Bluff
United States Property and Fiscal Office, State of Arkansas, Camp Joseph T. Robinson, Little Rock

CALIFORNIA

Alameda Administration Center, 2155 Webster Avenue, Alameda
Beale Air Force Base, Marysville
Castle Air Force Base, Merced
Edwards Air Force Base, Edwards
Fort Irwin, Barstow
Fort MacArthur, San Pedro
Fort Ord, Monterey

CALIFORNIA—Continued

George Air Force Base, Victorville
Letterman General Hospital, Presidio of San Francisco

Lathrop

Sharp Army Depot (A), ATTN: SDSSH-C-SH, 95331, Ms. Essie Ford, AC 209/982-2115

Directorate of Industrial Operations, Contracting Division (A), Building 650, Presidio of San Francisco, 94129, Mr. Michael Adelman, AC 415/561-4716

Sacramento Army Depot (A), ATTN: SDSSA-PS-9, 95813, Mr. Clarence Roberts*, AC 916/388-2510

March Air Force Base, Riverside
Marine Corps Air Station, El Toro
Marine Corps Base, Camp Pendleton
Marine Corps Base, Twenty-nine Palms
Marine Corps Recruit Depot, San Diego
Mather Air Force Base, Sacramento
McClellan Air Force Base, Sacramento
Naval Air Facility, El Centro
Naval Air Station, Alameda
Naval Air Station, Imperial Beach
Naval Air Station, Lemoore
Naval Air Station, Miramar
Naval Air Station, Moffett Field
Naval Air Station, North Island, San Diego
Naval Ammunition and Net Depot, Seal Beach
Naval Ammunition Depot, Concord
Naval Ammunition Depot, Fallbrook

CALIFORNIA—Continued

Naval Amphibious Base, Coronado
Naval Construction Battalion Center, Port Hueneme
Naval Hospital, Camp Pendleton
Naval Hospital, Long Beach
Naval Hospital, Oakland
Naval Hospital, San Diego
Naval Missile Facility, Point Arguello

San Luis Obispo
National Guard (A) (AF), P.O. Box G, Camp San Luis Obispo, 93406, Col. Theodore M. Robin, AC 805/544-4900

Naval Ordnance Laboratory, Corona
Naval Post Graduate School, Monterey
Naval Repair Facility, San Diego
Naval Station, Treasure Island, San Francisco
Naval Supply Center, Oakland
Naval Training Center, San Diego
Naval Weapons Center, China Lake
Naval Weapons Station, Seal Beach
Norton Air Force Base, San Bernardino
Pacific Missile Range, Point Mugu
Presidio of San Francisco, San Francisco
Sacramento Army Depot, Sacramento
Sharpe Army Depot, Lathrop
Travis Air Force Base, Fairfield
United States Property and Fiscal Office, State of California, P.O. Box 1139, Sacramento
Vandenberg Air Force Base, Lompoc
Western Area, Military Traffic Management Command, Oakland Army Base, Oakland 94626

COLORADO

Air Force Academy, Colorado Springs
Fitzsimmons General Hospital, Denver

Fort Carson
Contracting Office (A), Ft. Carson, 80913, Mr. Jack Smart, AC 303/579-5040

Golden
National Guard (A) (AF), Camp George West, 80401, Col. Donald S. Hightower, AC 303/279-2511, Ext. 204

Lowry Air Force Base, Denver
Peterson Air Force Base, Colorado Springs
Procurement Division, Rocky Mountain Arsenal, Denver
United States Property and Fiscal Office, State of Colorado, Camp George West, Golden

CONNECTICUT

Naval Underwater Systems Center, New London Laboratory, Fort Trumbull, New London
United States Property and Fiscal Office, State of Connecticut, State Armory, 360 Broad Street, Hartford

DELAWARE

Dover Air Force Base, Dover
New Castle County Airport, Wilmington
United States Property and Fiscal Office, State of Delaware, P.O. Box 607, Wilmington

DISTRICT OF COLUMBIA

Naval Air Facility, Washington, D.C.

DISTRICT OF COLUMBIA—Continued

Naval Communications Station, Washington, D.C.
Naval Dispensary, Washington, D.C.
Naval Research Laboratory, 4555 Overlook Avenue, S.W., Washington, D.C. 20390
Naval Security Station, Washington, D.C.
Naval Station, Washington, D.C.
National Guard Bureau, Room 3D165, Pentagon, Washington, D.C.
National War College, Ft. Lesley J. McNair, Washington, D.C. 20315
Office of the Surgeon General, Department of the Army, Washington, D.C. 20315
Office of the Chief of Naval Operations, Navy Department, Procurement Branch, Room 3D 757, Pentagon Bldg., Washington, D.C. 20350
United States Property and Fiscal Office, District of Columbia, 2001 East Capitol Street, Washington, D.C.
Walter Reed Army Medical Center, Washington, D.C.
Washington National Airport, Washington, D.C. (Gravelly Point, Va.)

FLORIDA

Eglin Air Force Base, Valparaiso
Eglin Air Force Base Auxilliary, Hurlburt Field #9, Valparaiso
Florida Group, Atlantic Reserve Fleet, Green Cove Springs
Homestead Air Force Base, Homestead
MacDill Air Force Base, Tampa
Miami International Airport, Miami
Naval Air Station, Cecil Field
Naval Air Station, Key West
Naval Aviation Medical Center, Pensacola
Naval Hospital, Key West
Naval Station, Mayport
Naval Research Laboratory, Underwater Sound Reference Division, Orlando
Naval Training Equipment Center, Orlando

St. Augustine
National Guard (A) (AF), State Arsenal, 32084, Col. George H. Mosley, AC 904/824-8461, Ext. 501

Patrick Air Force Base, Cocoa Beach
Tyndall Air Force Base, Panama City
United States Property and Fiscal Office, State of Florida, State Arsenal, St. Augustine

GEORGIA

Dobbins Air Force Base, Marietta
Fort Benning, Columbus
Fort Gordon, Augusta

Atlanta
U.S. Army Forces Command (A), Ft. McPherson, 30330, Mr. Jerry L. Blaydes*, AC 404/752-4153

Moody Air Force Base, Valdosta

Contracting Officer (A), Ft. McPherson, 30330, Mr. Tom Corley, AC 404/752-3316

Augusta
U.S. Army signal Center (A), Ft. Gordon, 30905, Mr. John R. Drummond, AC 404/791-3320

Columbus
HQ U.S. Army Infantry Center (A), Fort Benning, 31905, Ms. Judith Davidson, AC 404/545-5171

GUAM

National Guard (A) (AF), Dept. of Military Affairs, P.O. Box GG, Agana, 96910, LTC John R. D'Araujo, AC 671/477-9941

HAWAII

Procurement Division, DIO USASUPCOM, Honolulu, 96810
District Army Engineer, Honolulu
Hickam Air Force Base, Hickham AFB
Marine Corps Air Station, Kaneohe, Oahu
Naval Supply Center, Pearl Harbor
Naval Air Station, Barbers Point, Oahu
Pearl Harbor Naval Shipyard, Pearl Harbor

U.S. Army Support Command (A), 96858, Mr. Salvatore T. Tobacco, AC 808/438-9205

National Guard (A) (AF), 3949 Diamond Head Road, 96816, Col. Thomas S. Ito, AC 808/737-8073

Fort Shafter
Assistant Chief of Staff for Acquisition Management (A), U.S. Army Western Command, 96858, Mr. Richard D. Young, AC 808/438-2233

IDAHO

Mountain Home Air Force Base, Mountain Home
United States Property and Fiscal Office, State of Idaho, Box 1098, Boise

ILLINOIS

Chanute Air Force Base, Rantoul

Fort Sheridan
Contracting Office (A), Fort Sheridan, 60037, Mr. Dan Babarik, AC 618/452-4356

Mid-Western Regional Office, U.S. Army Signal Supply Agency, 400 South Jefferson Street, Chicago
Naval Air Station, Glenview
Naval Hospital, Great Lakes
O'Hare International Airport, Chicago
Rock Island Arsenal, Rock Island
Scott Air Force Base, Belleville
U.S. Army Headquarters and distribution Support Activity, Granite City
United States Property and Fiscal Office, State of Illinois, Illinois
National Guard General Depot, Box 459, Springfield

Springfield
National Guard (A) (AF), 1301 N. MacArthur Blvd., 62702, Col. Gene W. Blade, AC 217/785-3544

Indianapolis
DCASMA, Indianapolis (DLA), Bldg. 1, Fort Benjamin Harrison (A) 46249, Mr. Charles Loch*, AC 317/542-2015

INDIANA

Fort Benjamin Harrison (A) 46216, Ms. Norma J. Gill, AC 317/542-2783 or 2784

Grissom Air Force Base, Peru
Fort Benjamin Harrison, Indianapolis
Jefferson Proving Ground, Madison
Indiana Army Ammunition Plant, Charlestown

National Guard (A) (AF), P.O. Box 41346, 46241, Col. Byron L. Dukes, AC 317/247-3304

INDIANA—Continued

United States Property and Fiscal Office, State of Indiana, Stout Field, W-I Station, Indianapolis
Wabash River Army Ammunition Plant, Newport

Grimes
National Guard (A) (AF), Camp Dodge, RR#1, 50111, Col. Franklin D. Peterson, AC 515/278-9247

IOWA

Sioux City Municipal Airport, Sioux City
United States Property and Fiscal Office, State of Iowa, Camp Dodge, Grimes

KANSAS

Fort Leavenworth
Combined Arms Center (A), Fort Leavenworth, 66027, Mr. Donald C. Jewell, AC 913/684-2572

Fort Riley
Contracting Office (A), 66442, Ms. Edna Van Lieu, AC 913/239-3238

McConnell Air Force Base, Wichita
United States Property and Fiscal Office, State of Kansas, 27th and Kansas Avenue, Topeka

Topeka
National Guard (A) (AF), P.O. Box 2099, 66601, Col. Clayton H. Bowman, AC 913/233-7416

KENTUCKY

Fort Knox
U.S. Army Armor Center (A), 40121, Mr. William Mahanna, AC 502/624-7152 or 5454

Frankfort
National Guard (A) (AF), Boone National Guard Center, 40601, Col. Edward H. Milburn, AC 502/564-8466

Fort Campbell
Contracting Office (A), 42223, Ms. Jane Evans, AC 502/798-7126

United States Property and Fiscal Office, State of Kentucky, Box AA, Cherokee Station, Louisville

LOUISIANA

Barksdale Air Force Base, Shreveport
England Air Force Base, Alexandria
Fort Polk, Leesville
Louisiana Army Ammunition Plant, Shreveport
Headquarters, Naval Support Activity, New Orleans
Naval Air Station, New Orleans
Naval Auxiliary Air Station, New Iberia
United States Property and Fiscal Office, State of Louisiana, Jackson Barracks, New Orleans

National Guard (A) (AF), Jackson Barracks, 70146, Col. Edwin P. Roux, AC 504/271-6262, Ext. 421

MAINE

Loring Air Force Base, Limestone
Naval Air Station, Brunswick
United States Property and Fiscal Office, State of Maine, Camp Keyes, Augusta

MAINE—Continued

Augusta
National Guard (A) (AF), Camp Keyes, 04333, Col. Richard D. Sylvain, AC 207/622-9331, Ext. 51

MARIANAS ISLANDS

U.S. Naval Supply Depot, Guam

MARYLAND

Fort George G. Meade
U.S. Army Troop Support Agency (A), Northeast Commissary Region, ATTN: DALO-TAN-C, 20755, Mr. Hugh Roper, AC 301/677-4411

Maryland Procurement Office (A), Code L413, 9800 Savage Road, 20755, Ms. Ruth P. Craig*, AC 301/688-6974

Contracting Office (A), 20755, Mr. Val Rogolino, AC 301/677-4570

Havre DeGrace
National Guard (A) (AF), Station Military Reservation, 21078, Col. James M. McFall, AC 301/939-3366 or 3367

U.S. Army Harry Diamond Laboratories, 2800 Powder Mill Road, Adelphi
U.S. Army Intelligence Center and Fort Helabird, Dundalk
U.S. Army Medical Material Agency, Fort Detrick
U.S. Army STRATCOM-CONUS, Fort Ritchie, Maryland 21719
United States Property and Fiscal Office, State of Maryland, State Military Reservation, Havre de Grace

MASSACHUSETTS

Fort Devens
Contracting Office (A), Fort Devens, 01433, Ms. Frances Rafferty, AC 617/796-2430

Naval Air Station, S. Weymouth
Naval Ammunition Depot, Hingham
Naval Hospital, Chelsea
Naval Station, Boston
United States Property and Fiscal Office, State of Massachusetts, 905 Commonwealth Avenue, Boston
Westover Air Force Base, Chicopee Falls

MICHIGAN

K. I. Sawyer Air Force Base, Gwinn
Naval Air Station, Grosse Ile
United States Property and Fiscal Office, State of Michigan, P.O. Box 958, Lansing
Wurtsmith Air Force Base, Oscoda

MINNESOTA

Duluth International Airport, Duluth
Minneapolis-St. Paul International Airport, Minneapolis
Naval Air Station, Minneapolis
Twin Cities Army Ammunition Plant, Minneapolis
United States Property and Fiscal Office, State of Minnesota, Camp Ripley Military Reservation, Little Falls

Little Falls
National Guard (A) (AF), P.O. Box 288, Camp Ripley, 56345, Col. William S. Mahling, AC 612/632-6631, Ext. 331

MISSISSIPPI

Jackson
National Guard (A) (AF), P.O. Box 4447, Fondren Station, 39216, Col. Robert M. Dent, Jr., AC 601/939-8661

Columbus Air Force Base, Columbus
Naval Construction Battalion Center, Gulfport
Keesler Air Force Base, Biloxi
Naval Auxiliary Air Station, Meridan
United States Property and Fiscal Office, State of Mississippi, P.O. Box 1220, Jackson

MISSOURI

Aeronautical Chart and Information Center
Fort Leonard Wood
Fort Leonard Wood (A), 65473, Mr. Daniel Jakovich, Jr., AC 314/368-3914

Department of Defense Military Personnel Records Center, 9700 Page Boulevard, St. Louis 32
Kansas City Records Center, Kansas City
Lake City Army Ammunition Plant, Independence
Richards-Gebaur Air Force Base, Grandview
United States Property and Fiscal Office, State of Missouri, 1701 Industrial Avenue, Jefferson City
Whiteman Air Force Base, Knobnoster

MONTANA

Glasgow Air Force Base, Glasgow
Malmstrom Air Force Base, Great Falls
United States Property and Fiscal Office, State of Montana, 1100 North Main Street, Helena

Helena
National Guard (A) (AF), P.O. Box 1157, 59601, Col. Peter Tyanich, AC 406/449-2672

NEBRASKA

Naval Ammunition Depot, Hastings
Offutt Air Force Base, Omaha
United States Property and Fiscal Office, State of Nebraska, Building 1154, Huskerville, Lincoln

NEVADA

Camp Desert Rock, Las Vegas

Carson City
National Guard (A) (AF), 2601 S. Carson Street, 89701, Col. Willis Garretson, AC 702/883-7111

Nellis Air Force Base, Las Vegas
United States Property and Fiscal Office, State of Nevada, 406 East 2nd Street, Carson City

NEW HAMPSHIRE

Concord
National Guard (A) (AF), P.O. Box 2003, 03301, Col. Russell J. Grady, AC 603/228-1135

Pease Air Force Base, Portsmouth
United States Property and Fiscal Office, State of New Hampshire, State Military Reservation, Concord

New Jersey

Eastern Area Military Traffic Management Command, Bayonne

Fort Dix
Fort Dix (A), 08640, Mrs. Dolores E. Hargrove, AC 609/562-6657 or 3456

McGuire Air Force Base, Wrightstown
Naval Air Station, Lakehurst
Naval Air Turbine Test Station, Trenton

Trenton
National Guard (A) (AF), P.O. Box 2000, 08607, Col. Edward F. Barth, AC 609/883-6700

Naval Ammunition Depot, Earle
Naval Supply Center, Bayonne
United States Property and Fiscal Office, State of New Jersey, The Armory, Armory Drive, Trenton

New Mexico

Field Command, Defense Atomic Support Agency, P.O. Box 5100, Albuquerque
Cannon Air Force Base, Clovis
Holloman Air Force Base, Alamogordo
Kirtland Air Force Base, Albuquerque
Naval Ordnance Missile Test Facility, Proving Ground, Las Cruces
United States Property and Fiscal Office, State of New Mexico, Kirtland Air Force Base, Box 495, Albuquerque
White Sands Missile Range, White Sands

Santa Fe
National Guard (A) (AF), P.O. Box 4277, 87501, Col. Antonio Martinez, AC 505/471-7838, Ext. 278

New York

Camp Drum, Watertown
Eastern Area, Military Traffic Management and Terminal Service, First Avenue & 58th Street, Brooklyn 11250
First United States Army Medical Laboratory, New York
Fort Hamilton, Brooklyn
Griffiss Air Force Base, Rome
Naval Correspondence Center, Scotia

Albany
National Guard (A) (AF), State Campus, Building No. 4, 12226, Col. Lloyd E. Haas, AC 518/457-1109

Watertown
Contracting Office (A), Fort Drum, 13602, Mr. Bruce Ferguson, AC 315/782-2396

Niagara Falls Municipal Airport, Niagara Falls
Niagara Falls Army Chemical Plant, Niagara Falls
Plattsburgh Air Force Base, Plattsburgh
Staten Island Terminal, Staten Island
United States Military Academy, West Point
United States Naval Hospital, St. Albans, Long Island
United States Property and Fiscal Office, State of New York, 201—64th Street, Brooklyn
Watervliet Arsenal, Watervliet

North Carolina

Camp Mackall, Hoffman

Fayetteville
Contracting Office (A), Fort Bragg, 28306, Mr. Larry Travis, AC 919/396-9133

North Carolina—Continued

Marine Corps Air Facility, New River
Marine Corps Air Station, Cherry Point
Marine Corps Base, Camp Lejeune
Naval Hospital, Camp Lejeune
Naval Medical Field Research Laboratory, Camp Lejeune
Pope Air Force Base, Fort Bragg
Seymour Johnson Air Force Base, Goldsboro
United States Property and Fiscal Office, State of North Carolina, P.O. Box 791, Raleigh

Raleigh
National Guard (A) (AF), P.O. Box 26328, 27611, Col. Earl B. Huie, AC 919/733-3770, Ext. 200

North Dakota

Grand Forks Air Force Base, Grand Forks
Minot Air Force Base, Minot
United States Property and Fiscal Office, State of North Dakota, Fraine Barracks, Bismarck

Bismark
National Guard (A) (AF), P.O. Box 1817, 58505, Col. Earl D. Holly, AC 701/224-5230

Ohio

Engineer Maintenance Center, Corps of Engineers, United States Army, P.O. Box 119, 52 Starling Street, Columbus
Rickenbacker Air Force Base, Columbus
Marion Engineer Depot, Corps of Engineers, United States Army, Marion
Navy Finance Center, Cleveland
Newark Air Force Station, Newark
United States Property and Fiscal Office, State of Ohio, Building 101, Fort Hayes, Columbus
Wright-Patterson Air Force Base, Dayton
Youngstown Municipal Airport, Youngstown

Worthington
National Guard (A) (AF), 2811 West Granville Road, 43085, Col. Thomas S. Farrell, AC 614/889-7200

Oklahoma

Altus Air Force Base, Altus

Fort Sill
U.S. Army Artillery Center (A), Fort Sill, 73503, Mr. Eugene Darnell, AC 405/351-1264 or 1267

National Guard (A) (AF), 3501 Military Circle, N.E., 73111, Col. James M. Bullock, Jr., AC 405/427-8371

United States Property & Fiscal Office, State of Oklahoma, 2205 N. Central, Oklahoma City
Vance Air Force Base, Enid

Oregon

Kingsley Field, Klamath Falls

Salem
National Guard (A) (AF), 2150 Fairgrounds Road, N.E., 97303, Col. Hugh B. Nelson, AC 503/378-3943

United States Property and Fiscal Office, State of Oregon, Room 504, State Office Building, Salem

Pennsylvania

Greater Pittsburgh Airport, Pittsburgh
Naval Air Station, Willow Grove
Naval Hospital, Philadelphia

New Cumberland
New Cumberland Army Depot (A), ATTN: SDSNC-SP, 17070, Ms. Patricia Ebersole, AC 717/782-6109

Annville
Contracting Office (A), Fort Indiantown Gap, 17003, Mr. James Cowhey, AC 717/273-2146

National Guard (A) (AF), Dept. of Military Affairs, 17003, Col. Richard H. Houser, AC 717/787-7243 or 7254

Carlisle
Carlisle Barracks (A), 17013, Chief, Contracting Division, AC 717/245-4816

Chambersburg
Letterkenny Army Depot (A), ATTN: SDSLE-S, 17201, Ms. Jane Fryberger*, AC 717/263-6386

United States Property and Fiscal Office, State of Pennsylvania
U.S. Army War College and Carlisle Barracks, Carlisle Barracks
Valley Forge General Hospital, Phoenixville
Willow Grove Air Reserve Facility, Willow Grove

Tobyhanna
Tobyhanna Army Depot (A), ATTN: SDSTO-CB, 18466, Mr. John Liberty*, AC 717/894-8301, Ext. 9234

Rhode Island

Providence
National Guard (A) (AF), 51 Stenton Avenue, 02906, Col. John B. Altieri, AC 401/861-7460

United States Naval Construction Battalion Center, Davisville
United States Property and Fiscal Office, State of Rhode Island, 51 Stenton Avenue, Providence
Naval Underwater Systems Center, Newport
Naval Underwater Systems Center, Newport Laboratory, Newport

South Carolina

Charleston Air Force Base, Charleston

National Guard (A) (AF), P.O. Box 1090, 29202, Col. Catha L. Ridgeway, Jr., AC 803/748-4299

Fort Jackson, Columbia
Marine Corps Air Station, Beaufort
Marine Corps Recruit Depot, Parris Island
Myrtle Beach Air Force Base, Myrtle Beach
Naval Hospital, Beaufort
Naval Hospital, Charleston
Naval Weapons Annex, Charleston
Shaw Air Force Base, Sumter
United States Property and Fiscal Office, State of South Carolina, Room 107, Wade Hampton Street Office Building, Columbia

Columbia
U.S. Army Training Center (A), Fort Jackson, 29207, Mr. Thomas J. Cooper, AC 803/751-5231

SOUTH DAKOTA

Rapid City

Base Contracting Division (AF), Ellsworth AFB, 57706, Mr. Richard D. Rasmussen, AC 605/399-2464

National Guard (A) (AF), Camp Rapid, 57701, Col. Lowell M. Davis, AC 605/394-6740

United States Property and Fiscal Office, State of South Dakota, Camp Rapid, Rapid City

TENNESSEE

Arnold Air Force Station, 37389
Holston Army Ammunition Plant, Kingsport
McGhee-Tyson Municipal Airport, Knoxville
Memphis Defense Depot, (DSA), Memphis
Memphis Municipal Airport, Memphis
Milan Army Ammunition Plant, Milan
Naval Hospital, Memphis
National Guard (A) (AF), Powell Avenue, P.O. Box 40748, 37204, Col. Billy F. Alderson, AC 615/244-5812
United States Property and Fiscal Office, State of Tennessee, Vultee Boulevard, Nashville

TEXAS

National Guard (A) (AF), P.O. Box 5218, 78763, Col. Vernon M. Scofield, AC 512/465-5186

Bergstrom Air Force Base, Austin
Brooke Army Medical Center, Fort Sam Houston
Brooks Air Force Base, San Antonio
Carswell Air Force Base, Fort Worth
Dyess Air Force Base, Abilene

Corpus Christi Army Depot (A), ATTN: SDSCC-EP, 78419, Mr. William Majewski, AC 512/939-3913

Red River Army Depot (A), ATTN: SDSRR-AB, 75501, Mr. Howard Knight, AC 214/838-2656

Fort Bliss, El Paso
Fort Hood, Killeen

Contracting Office (A), Fort Sam Houston, 78234, Mr. Don Furru, AC 512/221-2930

Fort Walters, Mineral Wells
Goodfellow Air Force Base, San Angelo
Headquarters, VII Corps, 708 Colorado Street, Austin
Kelly Air Force Base, San Antonio
Lackland Air Force Base, San Antonio
Laughlin Air Force Base, Del Rio
Lone Star Army Ammunition Plant, Texarkana
Longhorn Army Ammunition Plant, Marshall
Naval Auxiliary Air Station, Chase Field, Beeville
Naval Auxiliary Air Station, Kingsville
Naval Hospital, Corpus Christi
Pantex Ordnance Plant, Amarillo
Randolph Air Force Base, San Antonio
Red River Army Depot, Texarkana
Reese Air Force Base, Lubbock
San Jacinto Ammonia Works, San Jacinto Ordnance Depot
Sheppard Air Force Base, Wichita Falls
Texas Group, Atlantic Reserve Fleet, Orange
United States Naval Hospital, Corpus Christi

TEXAS—Continued

United States Property and Fiscal Office, State of Texas, P.O. Box 5218, West Austin Station, Austin
Webb Air Force Base, Big Spring
William Beaumont General Hospital, El Paso

UTAH

Dugway Procurement Division, U.S. Army Support Detachment, Dugway
Hill Air Force Base, Ogden
Naval Oceanographic Distribution Office, Clearfield, Ogden

Tooele

Tooele Army Depot (A), ATTN: SDSTE-SEP, 84074, Mr. Milton H. Sevy, AC 801/833-2606

United States Property and Fiscal Office, State of Utah, Building 104, Fort Douglas
Ogden Defense Depot, (DSA), Ogden

National Guard (A) (AF), P.O. Box 8000, 84108, Col. Wayne H. Holt, AC 801/524-4047

VERMONT

United States Property and Fiscal Office, State of Vermont, Building #1, Camp Johnson, Winooski

Winooski

National Guard (A) (AF), Building 1, Camp Johnson, 05404, Col. William C. Wilson, AC 802/655-0270

VIRGINIA

Arlington Hall Station, Arlington
Armed Forces Staff College, Norfolk

Office, Chief, National Guard Bureau (A), Room 2E379, The Pentagon, Washington, D.C. 20310, Mr. Jack Hauslein, AC 202/695-1002

Cameron Station, 5010 Duke Street, Alexandria 22314
Fort Belvoir, 22060
Fort Lee, Petersburg 23801

Fort Monroe

Hq. U.S. Army Training & Doctrine Command (A), ATTN: SADBU, DCS PAL, 23651, Mr. Ed Manning*, AC 804/727-3291

Fort Monroe, (A), 23651, Mr. Heschel A. Shelby, AC 804/727-2630

Langley Air Force Base, Hampton
Marine Corps Air Station, Quantico
Marine Corps Schools, Quantico
Naval Air Station, Norfolk
Naval Air Station, Oceana, Virginia Beach
Naval Ammunition Depot, St. Juliens Creek, Portsmouth
Naval Amphibious Base, Little Creek, Norfolk
Naval Hospital, Portsmouth
Naval Hospital, Quantico
Naval Weapons Station, Yorktown
Radford Army Ammunition Plant, Radford

National Guard (A) (AF), 401 East Main Street, 23219, Col. Horace Mann, III, AC 804/786-2266

U.S. Army Aviation Materiel Laboratories, Ft. Eustis, Va. 23604

VIRGINIA—Continued

The Judge Advocate School, Charlottesville
United States Fleet Anti-Air Warfare Training Center, Damneck, Virginia Beach
United States Property and Fiscal Office, State of Virginia, Room 107, State Office Building, Richmond
Vint Hill Farms Station, Warrenton
Washington Procurement Office, 5001 Eisenhower Avenue, Alexandria

Fort Eustis

U.S. Army Air Mobility Research and Technology Laboratories (A), 23604, Mr. Gene McGraw, AC 804/878-4828

U.S. Army Training Support Center (A), 23604, Mr. Richard Potter*, AC 804/878-5943

WASHINGTON

Fairchild Air Force Base, Spokane

Tacoma

Contracting Office (A), Fort Lewis, 98433, Mrs. Laura Rahn, AC 206/967-2151

National Guard (A) (AF), Camp Murray, 98430, Col. Gerald A. Dines, AC 206/964-6291

Madigan General Hospital, Tacoma
McChord Air Force Base, Tacoma
Naval Air Station, Whidbey Island, Oak Harbor
Paine Field, Everett
Seattle Army Terminal, 1519 South Alaskan Way, Seattle
Tulalip Back-Up Storage Area, Marysville
United States Property and Fiscal Office, State of Washington, Camp Murray, Fort Lewis, Tacoma

WEST VIRGINIA

United States Property and Fiscal Office, State of West Virginia, Point Pleasant

Buckhannon

National Guard (A) (AF), 26201, Col. Zane H. Summers, AC 304/472-2670 or 2671

WISCONSIN

Camp Douglas

National Guard (A) (AF), 54618, Col. John M. Spaulding, AC 608/427-3321

Fort McCoy

Contracting Office (A), 54656, Mrs. Gary Freidl, AC 608/388-3818

General Billy Mitchell Field, Milwaukee
United States Property and Fiscal Office, State of Wisconsin, Camp Douglas

WYOMING

Francis E. Warren Air Force Base, Cheyenne
United States Property and Fiscal Office, State of Wyoming, 604 East 25th Street, Cheyenne

National Guard (A) (AF), P.O. Box 1709, 5500 Bishop Boulevard, 82001, Col. Robert E. Latta, AC 307/772-6271/6272

PRODUCTS AND SERVICES BOUGHT BY THE MAJOR FEDERAL CIVILIAN PURCHASING OFFICES

MAJOR FEDERAL CIVILIAN PURCHASING OFFICE LOCATOR

Agency	Purchasing Office	Number Code
Action	Contracts and Grants Management Division	635
	Regional Offices	635a
Agriculture, Department of	Office of Operations	101
	Regional Foresters	102
	Director of Administrative Services	102a
	Soil Conservations Service	103
	State and Other Administrative Purchasing Offices Using Dept. of Agriculture Funds.	104
	Agriculture Research Service Field Offices	106
	Forest and Ranger Experiment Stations	107
	Agriculture Marketing Service	108
	Agriculture Stabilization and Conservation Service	109
	Agriculture Research Services	110 through 110.8
	Rural Electrification Administration	110.9
	National Agricultural Library	110.10
	Economic Management Support Center	110.11
Commerce, Department of	Office of Procurement Operations	145
	Property and Supply Branch, Bureau of the Census	150
	National Oceanic and Atmospheric Adm. (NOAA) Headquarters	165
	NOAA—National Weather Service Regional Procurement Offices	166
	NOAA—Regional Procurement Office—Seattle, Washington	167
	NOAA—National Marine Fisheries Service	168
	NOAA—National Regional Procurement Office	169
	NOAA—Environmental Research Laboratories Regional Procurement Offices.	170
	NOAA—Environmental Data Services Regional Procurement Offices	171
	NOAA—Office of Ocean Engineering	172
	National Bureau of Standards	520
Community Services Administration	Procurement Division	625
D.C. Government	Bureau of Material Management	200
Education, Department of		412
Energy, Department of		380
Environmental Protection Agency		530
Federal Communication Commission	Procurement Division	485
Federal Energy Administration		626
General Services Administration		440
Government Printing Office, US	Materials Management Service	450
	Printing Procurement Division	451
Health and Human Services, Department of.	Division of Contract and Grant Operations Office of Management Services.	410
	Division of Contracting and Procurement, Social Security Administration	413
	Contract Branch, Division of General Services, Social and Rehabilitation Service.	414
	Administrative Services Center, Public Health Service	418
	Food and Drug Adm. Public Health Service	418a
	National Institutes of Health, Division of Administrative Services, Material Management, Procurement Branch.	418b
	Federal Health Programs Service (USPHS Hospitals)	418c
	Regional Offices, Dept. of Health and Human Services	419
Housing and Urban Development, Department of.	Assistant Secretary for Housing Management	455
	Contracts and Agreements Division, Office of General Services	457
	Reconditioning and Contracting Division, Office of Property Disposition	458
Information Agency, US		305
Interior, Department of	Bureau of Reclamation	511
	Bureau of Indian Affairs	512
	Bureau of Land Management	513
	National Park Service Offices	514

Agency	Purchasing Office	Number Code
	Bureau of Mines	515
	U.S. Fish and Wildlife Service	516
	Geological Survey	517
	Office of Surface Mining Reclamation and Enforcement	518
	Minerals Management Service	519
	Office of Administrative Services	519a
	Office of Aircraft Services	519b
Justice, Department of	Procurement and Contracts Staff	251
	Bureau of Prisons	252
	Bureau of Prisons (Field)	253
	Federal Prison Industries (Field)	254
	Office of Justice Assistance, Research and Statistics	255
	Drug Enforcement Administration	256
	U.S. Marshals Service	257
	Federal Bureau of Investigation	279
	Immigration and Naturalization Service	280
Labor, Department of	Office of Administrative Services	600
	Regional Administrators for ETA	627
	Division of Procurement ETA	628
	Mine Safety & Health Administration	628(a)
National Aeronautics and Space Adm.		285
Nuclear Regulatory Commission, U.S.		634
Panama Canal Co.		475
Postal Service, U.S.		490
Small Business Administration		633
Smithsonian Institution		210
State, Department of	Office of Supply and Transportation	300
	Director for Foreign Buildings	303
Tennesee Valley Authority	Division of Purchasing	480
Transportation, Department of	Contracts Division, Logistics Service, Federal Aviation Adm. (FAA)	160
	Contracts Division (FAA)	161
	Procurement Division, Aeronautical Center (FAA)	162
	Contracts Service Branch FAA Technical Center (FAA)	164
	Office of Contracts and Procurement, Federal Highway Administration	175
	Federal Railroad Adm.	629
	Office of Management Services and Procurement—Maritime Adm.	190
	Maritime Administration Field Offices	191
	U.S. Merchant Marine Academy	192
	National Highway Traffic Safety Adm., Office of Contracts and Procurement.	630
	Procurement Operations Division	631
	Research and Special Programs Administration	632
Treasury, Department of	Manager, Printing Procurement Publications Branch, Internal Revenue Service.	349
	Procurement Officer, Bureau of Engraving and Printing	350
	Bureau of the Mint Purchasing Offices	351
	Contracting Officer Bureau of Governmental Financial Operations	352
	Logistics Management Division, U.S. Customs	353
	Contracts and Procurement Branch, Internal Revenue Service	354
	Procurement Branch, Bureau of the Public Debt	355
Veterans Administration	Office of Procurement & Supply	500
	Veterans Administration Medical Centers	501
	Marketing Center	502
	Supply Depot	503
	Veterans Canteen Service Department of Medicine and Surgery	504
	Department of Veterans Benefits	505
	Department of Memorial Affairs	506
	Office of Construction	507
	Veterans Administration Field Stations	508

MAJOR FEDERAL CIVILIAN PURCHASING OFFICES

101. Office of Operations, Procurement Division, U.S. Department of Agriculture, Room 1567, South Building, Washington, D.C. 20250.

102. Contact one or more of the Forest Service Regional Offices listed below. Address as: Regional Forester, Forest Service, U.S. Department of Agriculture—

517 Gold Avenue SW Albuquerque, New Mexico 87102	310 West Wisconsin Avenue Milwaukee, Wisconsin 53203
1720 PeachTree Rd., NW Atlanta, Georgia, 30367	324 25th Street Ogden, Utah 84401
11177 West 8th Avenue Lakewood, Colorado 80225	319 S.W. Pine Street Portland, Oregon 97208
P.O. Box 1628 Juneau, Alaska 99802	630 Sansome Street San Francisco, California 94111
P.O. Box 7669 Missoula, Montana 59807	

102a. Director of Administrative Services, Forest Service, U.S. Department of Agriculture, 1621 North Kent Street, Arlington, Virginia 22209.

103. Soil Conservation Service, Administrative Services Division, Procurement Management Branch, P.O. Box 2890, U.S. Department of Agriculture, Washington, D.C. 20013.

104. Write to Administrative Services Division, Soil Conservation Service, U.S. Department of Agriculture, Washington, D.C. 20013, for a list of the State and other administrative offices which do purchasing.

106. Contact one or more of the Agriculture Research Service field offices listed below. Address as Agriculture Research Service, U.S. Department of Agriculture Administrative Office.

Eastern Regional Research Center 600 East Mermaid Lane, Philadelphia, PA 19118	Northern Regional Research Center, 1815 N University, Peoria, IL 61605
Richard B. Russell Research Center P.O. Box 5677 College Station Rd., Athens, GA 30613	National Animal Disease Center, P.O. Box 70, Ames, IA 50010
P.O. Box EC, College Station, TX 77841	Western Regional Research Center, 800 Buchanan Street, Berkeley, CA 94710
Delta States Research Center, P.O. Box 225 Stoneville, MS 38776	301 South Howes, P.O. Box E, Ft. Collins, CO 80522

107. Contact one or more of the Forest and Range Experiment Stations listed below. Address as: Forest Service, U.S. Department of Agriculture—

Intermountain Experiment Station 507 25th Street Ogdon, UT 84401	Pacific Southwest Experiment Station 1960 Addison Street P.O. Box 245 Berkeley, CA 94701
North Central Experiment Station 1992 Folwell Avenue St. Paul, MN 55108	Rocky Mountain Experiment Station 240 West Prospect Avenue Fort Collins, CO 80526
Northeastern Experiment Station 370 Reed Road, Broomall, PA 19008	Southeastern Experiment Station 200 Weaver Boulevard Asheville, NC 28804
Pacific Northwest Experiment Station 809 N.W. 6th Avenue Portland, OR 97232	Southern Experiment Station Room T-10210 701 Loyola Avenue, New Orleans, LA 70113

Also contact:

Director, Forest Products Laboratory, U.S. Department of Agriculture, P.O. Box 5130, Madison, WI 53705.

Director, Institute of Tropical Forestry, U.S. Department of Agriculture, P.O. Box AQ, Rio Piedras, Puerto Rico 00928.

108. Agricultural Marketing Service, Administrative Services Division, Property and Procurement Branch, U.S. Department of Agriculture, Washington, D.C. 20250.

109. Agriculture Stabilization and Conservation Service, Management Services Division, Procurement and Contracting Branch, U.S. Department of Agriculture, Washington, D.C. 20250.

Agricultural Stabilization and Conservation Service, Management Field Office, P.O. Box 205, Kansas City, Missouri 64141.

110. U.S. Department of Agriculture, Agricultural Research Service Administrative Office, 4th Floor NAL Building, Beltsville, MD 20705.

110.1. USDA Animal and Plant Health Inspection Service, Procurement and Engineering Branch, Federal Building, 6505 Belcrest Road, Hyattsville, MD 20782.

USDA Animal and Plant Health Inspection Service, Field Servicing Office, Butler Square West, 5th Floor, 100 North 6th Street, Minneapolis, MN 55403.

110.2. USDA Estension Service, Management Services Branch, Room 019 West Auditors Building, Washington, D.C. 20250.

110.3. USDA Farmers Home Administration, Directives and Services Division, Property and Procurement Management Branch, Washington, D.C. 20250.

USDA Farmers Home Administration, Business Services Branch, 1520 Market Street, St. Louis, MO 63103.

110.4. USDA Federal Crop Insurance Corporation, Administrative Management Division, Administrative Services Branch, Washington, D.C. 20250.

110.5.

110.6. USDA Food and Nutrition Service, Administrative Services Division, Procurement and Property Branch, 3101 Park Center Drive, Room 903, Alexandria, VA 22302.

Contact one or more of the Food and Nutrition Service Regional Offices listed below. Address as: Office Services, Food and Nutrition Service, Department of Agriculture—

Mid-Atlantic Region 1 Vahlsing Center Robbinsville, NJ 08691	Western Region 550 Kearny Street San Francisco, CA 94108
Southeast Region 1100 Spring Street, N.W. Atlanta, GA 30309	New England Region 33 North Avenue Burlington, MA 01803
Mid-West Region 536 South Clark Street Chicago, IL 60605	Mountain Plains Region 2420 W. 26th Avenue, Suite 415-D Denver, CO 80211
Southwest Region 1100 Commerce Street Dallas, TX 75242	

110.7. USDA, Food Safety and Inspection Service, Administrative Services. Division, Program Services Branch, Butler Square West, 100 North 6th St., Minneapolis, MN 55403.

USDA, Food Safety and Inspection Service, Administrative Services Division, Procurement and Property Branch, 14th and Independence Avenue, S.W., Washington, DC 20250.

110.8. Foreign Agricultural Service Management Services Division,

U.S. Department of Agriculture, Washington, D.C. 20250.

110.9. Rural Electrification Administration, Management Services Division, Management Analysis and Services Branch, Supply and Space Management Section, U.S. Department of Agriculture, Washington, D.C. 20250.

110.10. National Agricultural Library, Acquisition Division, U.S. Department of Agriculture, Beltsville, Maryland 20705.

110.11. Economics Management Staff, Administrative Service Division, Procurement and Property Management Branch, Room 1364-South Building, Washington, DC 20250.

145. Office of Procurement and Federal Assistance, U.S. Department of Commerce, Room 6855 HCHB, Washington, DC 20230.

150. Property and Supply Branch, Bureau of the Census, Federal Office Building No. 4, Room 1021, Suitland, Maryland (Mail Address: Washington, D.C. 20230).

160. Contracts Division, Logistics Service, Federal Aviation, Administration, Washington, D.C. 20590.

161, 162, 164. National Headquarters (Purchases on a National Basis): Federal Aviation Administration, Contracts Division, ALG-380, 800 Independence Avenue, S.W., Washington, D.C. 20591, Telephone: (202) 426-8230.

Metropolitan Washington Airports: Federal Aviation Administration, Metropolitan Washington Airports, Contracts Branch, AMA-54, West Bldg., Washington, D.C. 20001, Telephone: (703) 557-1394.

New England Region (Maine, Vermont, New Hampshire, Massachusetts, Connecticut, and Rhode Island): Federal Aviation Administration Procurement Branch, ANE-55, 12 New England Executive Park, Burlington, Massachusetts 01803, Telephone: (617) 273-7362.

Great Lakes Region (Minnesota, Wisconsin, Michigan, Illinois, Indiana, Ohio, North Dakota, and South Dakota): Federal Aviation Administration, Procurement Branch, ACL-57, O'Hare Lake Office Center, 2300 East Devon Avenue, Des Plaines, Illinois 60018, Telephone: (312) 694-7232.

Central Region (Nebraska, Iowa, Kansas, and Missouri): Federal Aviation Administration, Procurement Branch, ACE-55, 601 East 12th Street, Federal Building, Kansas City, Missouri 64106, Telephone: (816) 374-3401.

Eastern Region (New York, New Jersey, Pennsylvania, Delaware, Maryland, Virginia, and West Virginia): Federal Aviation Administration, Procurement Branch, AEA-55, Federal Building, JFK International Airport, Jamaica, New York 11430, Telephone: (212) 917-1086.

Southern Region (Kentucky, Tennessee, North Carolina, South Carolina, Mississippi, Alabama, Georgia, Florida, Puerto Rico, Canal Zone, and Virgin Islands): Federal Aviation, Administration, Procurement Branch, ASO-55, Post Office Box 20636, Atlanta, Georgia 30320, Telephone: (404) 763-7321.

Southwest Region (Arkansas, Louisiana, Oklahoma, Texas, and New Mexico): Federal Aviation Administration, Procurement Branch, ASW-55, Post Office Box 1689, Fort Worth, Texas 76101, Telephone: (817) 877-2000.

Western-Pacific Region (Nevada, Arizona, California, Hawaii, Samoa, and Guam): Federal Aviation Administration, AWP-55, Post Office Box 92007, World Way Postal Center, Los Angeles, California 90009, Telephone: (213) 536-6170.

Northwest-Mountain Region (Idaho, Oregon, Washington, Montana, Wyoming, Colorado, and Utah): Federal Aviation Administration, Procurement Branch, ANW-55, 17900 Pacific Hwy. So., P.O. C 68968, Seattle, WA 98168, (206) 431-2055.

Alaska Region: Federal Aviation Administration, Procurement Branch, AAL-55, 701 C Street, Box 14, Anchorage, Alaska 99513, Telephone: (907) 271-5866.

Aeronautical Center (Purchases on a National Basis): Federal Aviation Administration, Mike Monroney Aeronautical Center, AAC-70, Procurement Division, P.O. Box 20582, Oklahoma City, Oklahoma 73125, Telephone: (405) 686-4774.

FAA Technical Center (Purchases on a National Basis): Federal Aviation Administration, FAA Technical Center, Contracts Services Branch, ACT-51, Atlantic City Airport, New Jersey 08405, Telephone: (609) 484-4000, Ext. 3335.

165. National Oceanic and Atmospheric Administration (NOAA), Chief, Acquisition and Grants Management Branch, AT/GGMI, 6010 Executive Boulevard, Rockville, Maryland 20852.

The principal operating elements of NOAA are as follows:

The National Weather Service (NWS)
The National Ocean Service (NOS)
The National Marine Fisheries Service (NMFS)
The National Environmental Satellite, Data and Information Service (NESDIS)
The Office of Oceanic and Atmospheric Research (OAR)

166. NOAA—National Weather Service Regional Procurement Offices: Contact the Chief, Procurement and Supply Branch at the following addresses:

National Weather Service, Alsaka Region, 632 6th Avenue, Anchorage, Alaska 99501.

National Weather Service, Pacific Region, 1149 Bethel Street—Bethel-Pauahi Building, Honolulu, Hawaii, 96813.

National Weather Service, Western Region, Box 11188, Federal Building, 125 South State Street, Salt Lake City, Utah 84111.

National Weather Service, Central Region, 601 East 12th Street, Kansas City, Missouri 64106.

National Weather Service, Southern Region, 819 Taylor Street, Fort Worth, Texas 76102.

National Weather Service, Eastern Region, 585 Stewart Avenue, Garden City, New York 11530.

167. NOAA—Regional Procurement Office, Northwest, Administrative Office, (NASO), Lake Union Building, 1700 Westlake Avenue, Seattle, Washington 98109; Attn: Chief, Administrative Operations Division.

168. NOAA—National Marine Fisheries Service Regional Procurement Offices: Contact the Chief, Procurement and General Services at the following addresses:

National Marine Fisheries Service, Northeast Region, 14 Elm Street—Federal Building, Gloucester, Massachusetts 01930.

National Marine Fisheries Service, Southeast Region, Federal Office Building, 6th Floor, 114 First Avenue, South, St. Petersburg, Florida 33701.

169. NOAA—National Ocean Service Procurement Office: Atlantic Marine Center, NOS, Chief, Procurement & Supply Division, 439 West York Street, Norfolk, Virginia 23510.

170. NOAA—Environmental Research Laboratories Regional Procurement Offices: Contact the following: Environmental Research Laboratories, Headquarters—Research Building 3, East University Campus, Boulder, Colorado 80302, Attention: Director, Office of Research Support Services.

The procurement mission for the Environmental Research Laboratories is performed on-site by the Procurement Division, National Bureau of Standards, 325 South Broadway, Boulder, Colorado 80202.

Marine Minerals Technology Center, 3150 Paradise Drive, Tiburon, California 94920.

171. NOAA—Environmental Data Service Regional Field Procurement, Offices: Contact the following: National Climatic Center, Federal Building, Room 301-D, Asheville, North Carolina 28801.

172. NOAA—Office of Ocean Engineering, Regional Procurement Office: NOAA Data Buoy Office, OE, National Space Technology Laboratories, Bay St. Louis, Mississippi 39520.

Note: Major contracting support is provided by: National Aeronautics and Space Administration (NASA), NSTL, Bay St. Louis, Mississippi.

175. Office of Contracts and Procurement, Federal Highway Administration, Department of Transportation, 400 7th Street, S.W., Washington, D.C. 20590.

190. Office of Management Services and Procurement, Maritime Administration, U.S. Department of Transportation, Washington, D.C., 20590.

191. Contact one or more of the Maritime Administration field offices listed below: Address as: Maritime Administration, U.S. Department of Transportation.

ITM Building, 2 Canal Street, New Orleans, Louisiana 70130.
26 Federal Plaza, New York, N.Y. 10007.
450 Golden Gate Avenue, San Francisco, California 94102.

192. U.S. Merchant Marine Academy, Department of Administrative Services and Procurement, Kings Point, N.Y. 11024.

200. D.C. Government, Bureau of Materiel Management, Department of General Services, 613 G Street, N.W., Washington, D.C. 20001.
210. Office of Supply Services, Smithsonian Institution, 955 L'Enfant Plaza, S.W., Suite 3120, Washington, D.C. 20024.
251. Department of Justice, Procurement and Contracts Staff, 10th & Constitution Avenue, N.W., Washington, D.C. 20530.
252. Bureau of Prisons, U.S. Department of Justice, 320 First Street, N.W., Washington, D.C. 20534.
253. Bureau of Prisons (Field), Contact one or more of the Federal Penal and Correctional Institutions listed below:
Metropolitan Correctional Centers
Chicago, Illinois 60605: 71 W. Van Buren Street.
New York, N.Y. 10007: 150 Park Row.
San Diego, California 92101: 808 Union Street.
United States Penitentiaries
Altanta, Georgia 30315.
Leavenworth, Kansas 66048.
Lewisburg, Pennsylvania 17837.
Miami, Florida 33177: 15801 S.W., 137th Avenue.
Terre Haute, Indiana 47808.
Federal Correctional Institutions
Alderson, West Virginia 24910.
Ashland, Kentucky 41101.
Bestnop, Texas 78602.
Butner, North Carolina 27509: Old North Carolina Highway 75.
Danbury, Connecticut 06801.
El Reno, Oklahoma 73036.
Englewood, Colorado 80110.
Fort Worth, Texas 76119.
La Tura (Anthony, N.M.), Texas 88021.
Lexington, Kentucky 40507.
Lompoc, California 93436.
Memphis, Tennessee 38134: 1101 John Denies Road
Milan, Michigan 48160.
Morgantown, West Virginia 26505.
Oxford, Wisconsin 53952.
Petersburg, Virginia 23803.
Phoenix, Arizona 85029.
Pleasanton, California 94566.
Ray Brook, New York 12977.
Sandstone, Minnesota 55072.
Seagoville, Texas 75159.
Talladega, Alabama 35160.
Tallahassee, Florida 32031.
Terminal Island, California 90731.
Texarkana, Texas 75501.
Federal Prison Camps
Allenwood—Montgomery, Pennsylvania 17752.
Big Spring, Texas 79720.
Boron, California 93516.
Duluth, Minnesota 55814.
Eglin Air Force Base, Florida 32542.
Maxwell Air Force Base, Montgomery, Alabama 36112.
Safford, Arizona 85546.
U.S. Medical Center for Federal Prisoners
Springfield, Missouri 65802.
Federal Detention Centers
El Paso, Texas 79925.
254. Federal Prison Industries (Field), contact one or more of the field offices located in the Federal Penal and Correctional Institutions listed under 253. Address is UNICOR Federal Prison Industries, Inc., c/o the particular institution.
255. Office of Justice Assistance, Research and Statistics, U.S. Department of Justice, Office of the Comptroller, Contracts Branch, 633 Indiana Avenue, NW, Washington, D.C. 20531.
The Office of Justice Assistance, Research and Statistics assists State and local governments in strengthening and improving law enforcement and criminal justice at every level by Federal assistance. Assistance may be given by grant, contract, or cooperative agreement. Functional areas include courts, police, corrections and juvenile justice. In addition, techncial assistance is available covering a multitude of skilled areas and professions, surveys, studies, ADP and telecommunications, evaluations, research and development, training, etc.
256. Drug Enforcement Administration, U.S. Department of Justice, 1405 I Street, N.W., Washington, D.C. 20537.
257. U.S. Marshals Service, U.S. Department of Justice, 1 Tysons Corner Center, Attn: Procurement and Property Management Division, McLean, Virginia 22102.
279. Federal Bureau of Investigation, U.S. Department of Justice, Property Procurement and Management Section, Procurement and Management Section Room 6823, 9th and Pennsylvania Avenue, NW, Washington, D.C. 20535.
280. Contact one or more of the Immigration and Naturalization Service offices listed below. Address as:
Immigration and Naturalization Service—
Immigration and Naturalization Service, U.S. Department of Justice, Contracting and Procurement Branch, 425 I Street, NW, Room 2102, Washington, D.C. 20536.
Immigration and Naturalization Service, U.S. Department of Justice, Eastern Regional Office, ATTN: ARC/PMP, Federal Building, Burlington, Vermont 05402.
Immigration and Naturalization Service, U.S. Department of Justice, Northern Regional Office, ATTN: ARC/PMP, Federal Building, Fort Snelling, Twin Cities, Mn. 55111.
Immigration and Naturalization Service, U.S. Department of Justice, Southern Regional Office, ATTN: ARC/PMP, Skyline Center, Building C, 311 North Stemmons Freeway, Dallas, Tx. 75207.
Immigration and Naturalization Service, U.S. Department of Justice, Western Regional Office, ATTN: ARC/PMP, Terminal Island, San Pedro, Ca. 90731.
285. Contact one or more of the offices listed below. Address as:
Headquarters, National Aeronautics and Space Administration, Washington, DC 20546.
Ames Research Center, NASA, Moffett Field, CA 94035.
Goddard Space Flight Center, NASA, Greenbelt, MD 20771.
Jet Propulsion Laboratory*, 4800 Oak Drive, Pasadena, CA 91109.
Lyndon B. Johnson Space Center, NASA, Houston, TX 77058.
John F. Kennedy Space Center, NASA, Kennedy Space Center, FL 32899.
Langley Research Center, NASA, Hampton, VA 23665.
Lewis Research Center, NASA, 21000 Brookpark Rd., Cleveland, OH 44135.
George C. Marshall Space Flight Center, NASA, Marshall Space Flight Center, AL 35812.
National Space Technology Laboratories, NASA, NSTL, MS 39529.
300. Procurement Branch, Office Supply Transportation Division and Procurement, Department of State, Washington, D.C. 20520.
303. Director For Foreign Buildings, Department of State, Washington, D.C. 20520.
305. United States Information Agency, Office of Contracts, Washington, D.C. 20547.
349. Manager, Printing Procurement, Publications Branch, Internal Revenue Service, The Department of the Treasury, Washington, D.C. 20224.
350. Procurement Officer, Bureau of Engraving and Printing, The Department of the Treasury, Washington, D.C. 20228.
351. Contact one or more of the Bureau of the Mint Purchasing Offices listed below. Address as: Purchasing Office, Bureau of the Mint, The Department of the Treasury—
Denver, Colorado 80201.
Philadelphia, Pennsylvania 19105.
San Francisco, California 94102.
Washington, D.C. 20220.
352. Contracting Officer, Bureau of Government Financial Operations, The Department of the Treasury, Madison Place and Pennsylvania Avenue, N.W. Room 139, Washington, D.C. 20226.
353. *Washington Office:* Office of Logistics Management, U.S. Customs Service, The Department of the Treasury, 1301 Constitution Avenue, N.W., Washington, D.C. 20229.
Regional Offices: Address as: Deputy Assistant Regional Commissioner Logistics Management, U.S. Customs Service,

* The Jet Propulsion Laboratory (JPL) of the California Institute of Technology is operated under contract to NASA.

The Department of the Treasury,
100 Summer Street, Suite 1819, Boston, MA 02110.
U.S. Customhouse, Room 715, 6 World Trade Center, New York, New York 10048.
7370 N.W. 36th Street, Suite 300, Miami, Florida 33166.
Canal-LaSalle Bldg., Suite 2400, 1400 Canal Street, New Orleans, LA 70112.
5850 San Felipe, Houston, Texas 77057.
300 No. Los Angeles Street, P.O. Box 2071, Los Angeles, California 90053.
211 Main Street, Suite 1000, San Francisco, California 94105.
55 E. Monroe Street, Suite 1501, Chicago, Illinois 60603.

354. Contract and Procurement Branch, Internal Revenue Service, The Department of the Treasury, 1111 Constitution Avenue, N.W., Room 1320, Washington, D.C. 20224.

355. Procurement Branch, Bureau of the Public Debt, The Department of the Treasury, Washington, D.C. 20226.

380. Department of Energy (DOE) procurement activities cover a wide variety of services and supplies. These fall into the following general categories:

(a) Material, Equipment and Supplies:
These include all industrial classifications and constitute the great majority of the purchases made by contractors operating DOE-owned plants and laboratories. Except for a limited number of orders to meet initial equipment requirements for new DOE-owned facilities, large production run orders are not characteristic of DOE procurement. DOE procurement is made up of many small orders for standard, semi-standard, and off-the-shelf items, as well as specialized, unique equipments and components for use in its research and development activities.

(b) Construction and Architect-Engineering Services:
All types of construction and design, ranging from administrative and auxiliary support buildings to complex industrial facilities, are required by DOE.

(c) Management and Operating Contractor Services:
These services are required for the management, operation, and maintenance of a Government-owned or controlled research, development, special production or testing establishment. In addition, DOE and its management and operating contractors have requirements for the services of support contractors to assist in accomplishing their primary mission functions.

(d) Fuel Processing, Fabrication, and Recovery Services:
DOE requires services for the processing of uranium, thorium, or plutonium compounds and alloys, fabrication of fuel elements, and the recovery of special nulcear material from scrap.

The items listed may or may not be purchased on a repetitive basis. For further information regarding selling to DOE and its contractors, contact the Purchasing Office of the nearest DOE office listed below:

Manager, Albuquerque Operations Office, U.S. Department of Energy, P.O. Box 5400, Albuquerque, NM 87115.
Manager, Chicago Operations Office, U.S. Department of Energy, 9800 South Cass Avenue, Argonne, IL 60439.
Manager, Idaho Operations Office, U.S. Department of Energy, 550 Second Street, Idaho Falls, ID 83401.
Manager, Oak Ridge Operations Office, U.S. Department of Energy, P.O. Box E, Oak Ridge, TN 37830.
Manager, Nevada Operations Office, U.S. Department of Energy, P.O. Box 14100, Las Vegas, NV 89114.
Manager, Pittsburgh Naval Reactors Office, U.S. Department of Energy, P.O. Box 109, West Mifflin, PA 15122.
Manager, Richland Operations Office, U.S. Department of Energy, P.O. Box 550, Richland, WA 99352.
Manager, San Francisco Operations Office, U.S. Department of Energy, 1333 Broadway, Oakland, CA 94612.
Manager, Savannah River Operations Office, U.S. Department of Energy, P.O. Box A, Aiken, SC 29801.
Manager, Schenectady Naval Reactors Office, U.S. Department of Energy, P.O. Box 1069, Schenectady, NY 12301.
Director, Morgantown Energy Technology Center, U.S. Department of Energy, P.O. Box 880, Morgantown, WV 26505.
Director, Pittsburgh Energy Technology Center, U.S. Department of Energy, P.O. Box 10940, Pittsburgh, PA 15236.
Project Manager, Strategic Petroleum Reserve Project Management Office, 900 Commerce Road East, New Orleans, LA 70123.
Director, Naval Petroleum Reserves, U.S. Department of Energy, P.O. Box 11, Tupman, CA 93276.
Director, Naval Petroleum and Oil Shale Reserves, U.S. Department of Energy, 800 Werner Court, Suite 342, Casper, WY 82601.
Administrator, Alaska Power Administration, U.S. Department of Energy, P.O. Box 50, Juneau, AK 99802.
Administrator, Bonneville Power Administration, U.S. Department of Energy, P.O. Box 3621, Portland, OR 97208.
Administrator, Southeastern Power Administration, U.S. Department of Energy, Samuel Elbert Building, Elberton, CA 30635.
Administrator, Southwestern Power Administration, U.S. Department of Energy, P.O. Box 1619, Tulsa, OK 74104.
Administrator, Western Area Power Administration, U.S. Department of Energy, P.O. Box 3402, Golden, CO 80401.
Director, Office of Procurement Operations, U.S. Department of Energy, 1000 Independence Avenue, S.W., Washington, D.C. 20585.

410. Division of Contract and Grant Operations, Office of Management Services, Office of the Secretary, Department of Health and Human Services, Room 443-H SP, 200 Independence Avenue, S.W., Washington, D.C. 20201.

412. Assistance Management and Procurement Service, U.S. Department of Education, 400 Maryland Avenue, S.W., Washington, D.C. 20202.

413. Division of Contracting and Procurement, Social Security Administration, P.O. Box 7696, Baltimore, Maryland 21207.

414. Contract Branch, Division of General Services, Social and Rehabilitation Service, 330 Independence Avenue, S.W., Washington, D.C. 20201.

418. Administrative Services Center, Public Health Service, 5600 Fishers Lane, Room 3B-26, Rockville, Maryland 20857.

418a. Food and Drug Administration, Public Health Service, Negotiated Contracts Branch, 5600 Fishers Lane, HFA-510, Rockville, Maryland 20857.

418b. National Institutes of Health, Division of Administrative Services, Material Management, Procurement Branch, Building 13, Room 2W34, 9000 Rockville Pike, Bethesda, Maryland 20014.

418c. Federal Health Programs Service (USPHS Hospitals)
General Supply Officer, USPHS Hospital, 3100 Wyman Park Drive, Baltimore, Maryland 21211.
General Services Officer, USPHS Hospital, 15th Avenue and Lake Street, San Francisco, California 94118.
Office Service Manager, USPHS Hospital, 210 State Street, New Orleans, Louisiana 70118.
General Supply Officer, USPHS Hospital, Carville, Louisiana 70721.
Supply Management Officer, USPHS Hospital, Bay and Vanderbilt Street, Stapleton, Staten Island, New York 10304.
General Supply Officer, USPHS Hospital, 4400 Avenue M, Galveston, Texas 77550.
General Supply Officer, USPHS Hospital, 77 Warren Street, Boston, Massachusetts 02135.
General Supply Officer, USPHS Hospital, 6500 Hampton Blvd., Norfolk, Virginia.
General Supply Officer, USPHS Hospital, 1131-14th Avenue, South, Seattle, Washington 98114.

419. Regional Offices, Department of Health and Human Services:
Region I
Department of Health and Human Services, Office Services Manager, John F. Kennedy Federal Building, Government Center, Boston, Massachusetts 02203.
Region II
Department of Health and Human Services, Office Services Manager, Federal Building, 26 Federal Plaza, New York, New York 10007.
Region III
Department of Health and Human Services, Office Serv-

ices Manager, P.O. Box 12900, Philadelphia, Pennsylvania 19108.

Region IV

Department of Health and Human Services, Financial Management Officer, Room 404, 50 Seventh Street, N.E., Atlanta, Georgia 30323.

Region V

Department of Health and Human Services, Office Services Manager, Room 712, New Post Office Building, 433 West Van Buren Street, Chicago, Illinois 60607.

Region VI

Department of Health and Human Services, Office Services Manager, 114 Commerce Street, Dallas, Texas 75202.

Region VII

Department of Health and Human Services, Office Services Manager, 601 East 12th Street, Kansas City, Missouri 64106.

Region VIII

Department of Health and Human Services, Office Services Manager, 9017 Federal Office Building, 19th and Stout Streets, Denver, Colorado 80202.

Region IX

Department of Health and Human Services, Office Services Manager, Federal Office Building, 50 Fulton Street, San Francisco, California 94102.

Region X

Department of Health and Human Services, Office Services Manager, Arcade Building, 1320 Second Avenue, Seattle, Washington 98101.

440. General Services Administration. The basic procurement programs of GSA are as follows:

1. Federal Supply Service of GSA purchases thousands of common-use supply, equipment, and service items for which the various Federal agencies have recurring needs; These purchases are made under regional and national contracts, in accordance with the best interests of the Government, and include:
   a. Stock replenishment and new items for the Retail Supply System;
   b. Federal Supply Schedule contracts;
   c. Consolidated purchases of selected items which are not feasible for inclusion under programs "a" and "b" above; and
   d. Purchases of a wide variety of products and services on request of Federal agencies, as needed, including many items required in connection with civil defense, disaster relief, foreign aid, etc.
   e. Procurement of transportation of freight and passengers by contract, Government bill of lading, Government transportation request, and other means.
2. Federal Property Resource Service purchases of strategic and critical raw and industrial materials; rotation of stocks of crude rubber, fibers, vegetable and other oils; upgrading of stockpile materials; and related services for all of the above. Procurement of strategic and critical materials for the National Stockpile is performed solely by the Federal Property Resource Service from its headquarters location in Washington, D.C.
3. Public Buildings Service of GSA leases real property; and purchases commodities and services for management, design, construction, remodeling, repair, maintenance and protection of Government buildings, and public utilities.
3. The Office of Information Resource Management of GSA contracts for ADP equipment and services and communications services.

It should be noted that GSA's purchases under 1.b. includes a majority of the items in the Part IV of the Directory and that under 1.d. additional items not available under the other three programs may be purchased.

For assistance regarding the various GSA procurement programs and to have a firm's name added to a specific bidders list, requests should be directed to the Regional Service Center at the offices listed below:

REGION 1

Business Service Center, General Services Administration, John W. McCormick Post Office and Courthouse, Boston, MA 02109: Connecticut, Maine, Vermont, New Hampshire, Massachusetts, and Rhode Island

REGION 2

Business Service Center, General Services Administration, 26 Federal Plaza, New York, N.Y. 10007: New Jersey, New York, Puerto Rico, and Virgin Islands

National Capitol Region

Regional Director of Business Affairs, Business Service Center, General Services Administration, 7th & D Streets, S.W., Room 1050, Washington, D.C. 20407: District of Columbia and nearby Maryland and Virginia

REGION 3

Business Service Center, General Services Administration, Ninth and Market Sts., Philadelphia, PA 19107: Pennsylvania, Delaware, Virginia, Maryland and West Virginia

REGION 4

Business Service Center, General Services Administration, 1776 Peachtree Street, N.W., Atlanta, Georgia 30309: Alabama, Florida, Georgia, Kentucky, Mississippi, North Carolina, South Carolina, and Tennessee

REGION 5

Business Service Center, General Services Administration, 230 South Dearborn Street, Chicago, IL 60604: Illinois, Indiana, Ohio, Michigan, Minnesota, and Wisconsin

REGION 6

Business Service Center, General Services Administration, 1500 East Bannister Road, Kansas City, MO 64131: Iowa, Kansas, Missouri, and Nebraska

REGION 7

Business Service Center, General Services Administration, 819 Taylor Street, Fort Worth, TX 76102: Arkansas, Louisiana, Texas, New Mexico, and Oklahoma

Gulf Coast Business Service Center, General Services Administration, FOB Courthouse, 515 Rusk Street, Houston, TX 77002: Gulf Coast from Brownsville, Texas, to New Orleans, Louisiana

REGION 8

Business Service Center, General Services Administration, Building 41, Denver Federal Center, Denver, CO 80225: Colorado, North Dakota, Utah, South Dakota, Montana, and Wyoming

REGION 9

Business Service Center, General Services Administration, 525 Market Street, San Francisco, CA 94105: Northern California, Hawaii, and all of Nevada except Clark County

Business Service Center, General Services Administration, 300 North Los Angeles Street, Los Angeles, CA 90012: Los Angeles, Southern, California, Clark County, Nevada, and Arizona

REGION 10

Business Service Center, General Services Administration, 440 Federal Building, 915 Second Avenue, Seattle, WA 98174: Alaska, Idaho, Oregon, and Washington

450. U.S. Government Printing Office, Materials Management Service, North Capitol and H Streets, N.W., Washington, D.C. 20401

Central Office

451. U.S. Government Printing Office, Printing Procurement Department, North Capitol and H Streets, N.W., Washington, D.C. 20401

REGION 1

U.S. Government Printing Office, Regional Printing Procurement Office, John W. McCormack Post Office and Court House Post Office Square, Room 1400, Boston, Massachusetts 02109: Connecticut, Massachusetts, Maine, New Hampshire, Rhode Island, and Vermont

REGION 2

U.S. Government Printing Office, Regional Printing Procurement Office, 8001 Roosevelt Blvd., Room 306,

Philadelphia, Pa. 19152: Delaware, New Jersey, Pennsylvania

REGION 2(II)
U.S. Government Printing and Procurement Office, 201 Varick Street, 7th Floor, New York, New York 10014: New York, New Jersey, (Commercial zone of New York City)

REGION 3
U.S. Government Printing Office, Regional Printing Procurement Office, Building 720B, Langley AFB VA, 23665: Southern Virginia, North Carolina

REGION 4
U.S. Government Printing Office, Regional Printing Procurement Office, R.B. Russell Federal Office Building, Room 788, 75 Spring St., Atlanta, GA 30303: Alabama, Florida, Georgia, Mississippi, North Carolina, South Carolina, Tennessee

REGION 5(I)
U.S. Government Printing and Procurement Office, 610 South Canal Street, Room 1051, Chicago, Illinois 60607: Illinois, Indiana, Michigan, Wisconsin

REGION 5(II)
U.S. Government Printing Office, Regional Printing Procurement Office, 200 North High Street, Federal Bldg., Room 34, Columbus, Ohio 43215: Ohio, Kentucky, West Virginia

REGION 6
U.S. Government Printing Office, Regional Printing Procurement Office, 210 North Tucker Blvd., Room 1466, St Louis, Missouri 63101: Iowa, Kansas, Minnesota, Missouri, Nebraska, North Dakota, South Dakota

REGION 7
U.S. Government Printing Office, 1100 Commerce Street, Room 3B7, Dallas, Texas 75242: Arkansas, Louisana, Oklahoma, Texas

REGION 8
U.S. Government Printing and Procurement Office, Denver Federal Center, Building 53, Room H-1004, Denver, Colorado 80225: Colorado, New Mexico, Utah, Wyoming

REGION 9(I)
U.S. Government Printing and Regional Printing Procurement Office, 15000 Aviation Blvd., Room 2E26, Federal Office Building, Lawndale, California 90261: California (southern), Nevada (southern), Arizona

REGION 9(II)
U.S. Government Printing and Procurement Office, 620 Folsom Street, San Francisco, California 94107: California (northern), Nevada (northern)

REGION 10
U.S. Government Printing and Procurement Office, 4735 East Marginal Way South, Seattle, Washington 98134: Idaho, Montana, Oregon, Washington

455 Assistant Secretary for Public and Indian Housing. The Consolidated Supply Program (CSP) is a HUD sponsored program in which HUD identifies and prequalifies potential vendors interested in selling their products to local Public Housing Authorities (PHAs). The main idea of the CSP is to have consolidated bidding on a national basis for items commonly used by PHAs. HUD advertises the bids, negotiates prices, and lists the qualified firms on the CSP listing. This gives the PHAs the ability to choose the product which best serves their needs.

Interested contractors should contact local PHAs or HUD headquarters or local offices. HUD headquarters inquiries should be directed to the Department of Housing and Urban Development, Consolidated Supply Program, 451 7th Street, S.W., Room 6240, Washington, D.C. 20410.

457 Office of Procurement and Contracts, Department of Housing and Urban Development, 451 7th Street, S.W., Room 5260, Washington, D.C. 20410.

458 Reconditioning and Contracting Division, Office of Housing Management, Assistant Secretary for Housing, Department of Housing and Urban Development, Room 6182, 451 7th Street, S.W., Washington, D.C. 20410. Purchases for the repair and rehabilitation of acquired properties; real estate management and maintenance.

475 Chief, Procurement Division, Panana Canal Company, 4400 Dauphine Street, New Orleans, Louisiana 70140.

480 Division of Purchasing, Tennessee Valley Authority, Chattanooga, Tennessee 37401.

485 Procurement Branch Federal Communications Commission, Room 326, Brown Building, 1200 19th Street N.W., Washington, D.C. 20554.

490 The Office of Contracts at USPS Headquarters in Washington, DC, handles centralized procurements (national contracts), as well as the buying for headquarters offices.

Office of Contracts, Procurement and Supply Department, United States Postal Service, 475 L'Enfant Plaza, SW, Washington, DC 20260-6230.

The Postal Service is divided into 5 regions. A Procurement Division, located at each regional headquarters, buys supplies, services, and equipment for that region.

Contract and Supply Management Branch Procurement Division, U.S. Postal Service, 1633 Broadway, New York, NY 10098-0531

Contract and Supply Mangement Branch Procurement Division, U.S. Postal Service, 1845 Walnut Street, P. O. Box 8601, Philadelphia, PA 19197-0531

Contract and Supply Management Branch, Procurement Division, U.S. Postal Service, 1407 Union Avenue, Memphis, TN 38166-0531

Contract and Supply Management Branch, Procurement Division, U.S. Postal Service, 433 West Van Buren Street, Chicago, IL 60699-5301

Contract and Supply Management Branch, Procurement Division, U.S. Postal Service, 850 Cherry Avenue, San Bruno, CA 94099-0531

Each region is made up of districts. Supplies, services, and equipment that are not bought under national or regional contracts are bought at the district level by Procurement Services Offices (PSO's). A PSO may combine several purchases for different offices under one contract.

For the address or phone number of the PSO serving a particular area, contact the regional office (listed above) closest to that area.

Real Estate and Buildings

The Postal Service has an ongoing building program administered by the Real Estate and Buildings Department. Architect-engineer firms interested in working on Postal Service construction projects should submit a Standard Form 254 to the office with jurisdiction over the project (explained below).

Construction projects costing over $5 million are handled by Postal Service Headquarters. You can get specific information by writing to the General Manager, Facilities Procurement Division, Real Estate and Buildings Department, 475 L'Enfant Plaza, SW, Washington, DC 20260-6411. Projects costing less than $5 million are handled by the regions. Contact the Director, Real Estate and Buildings Department, at the nearest regional address (listed above, under Supplies and Services—but use "0200" as the last 4 digits of the ZIP + 4).

Mail Transportation

The Postal Service relies on numerous contractors to move mail over the highways. This is a specialized service with its own regulations and procedures, differing markedly from those of the Federal agencies. Contracts usually run for 4 years (and may run to 6 in special cases). They may also be renewed. All types and sizes of vehicles are used.

The Postal Service also contracts to transport mail by air. If scheduled airline service is inadequate, the Postal Service may contract with air-taxi operators holding valid FAA Air Taxi Operator's Certificates (and whose aircraft are included within the limitations in CAB Economic Regulation 298). These contracts do not exceed 4 years.

The Postal Service also uses contractors to carry mail by boat, ship, rail, and certified air carrier.

For further information, contact the General Manager, Logistics Division, at any of the regional offices listed above (under Supplies and Services—but use "0410" as the last 4 digits of the ZIP + 4) or the Director, Transportation and International Services, Mail Processing Department, U.S. Postal Service, Washington, DC 20260-7130.

500 Veterans Administration, Office of Procurement & Supply (90), 810 Vermont Avenue, N.W., Washington, D.C. 20420.

501 Veterans Administration Medical Centers. Each of our 172 medical centers purchases a considerable amount of its requirements locally. These items, generally speaking, are maintenance supplies; perishable foodstuffs; off-the-shelf items of drugs, medical supplies, etc.; maintenance and repairs to building and equipment; and books. Contact the Chief, Supply Service, at the locations shown in list of Veterans Administration Medical Centers.

502 Veterans Administration, Marketing Center, P.O. Box 76, Hines, Illinois 60141

The Marketing Center, P.O. Box 76, Hines, Illinois 60141, located on the Hines Veterans Administration Reservation in building Number 50, is the national purchasing arm of VA. The center consists of six marketing divisions, each handling a major commodity essential to the overall VA Medical Program as follows: (i) M-1, Subsistence; (ii) M-2 Medical Supplies; (iii) M-3, Federal Supply Schedules; (iv) M-4, Requirements and Inventory Management; (v) M-5, Pharmaceutical Products; and (vi) M-6, Medical Equipment.

Each division determines acquisition source and method of distribution, procures depot stock plus special items of equipment and supplies when requested, assists customer installations by providing product and commodity information and renders procurement assistance to other Government agencies on an individual basis.

The marketing divisions use both competitive sealed bids and negotiation in their procurement actions. Depending upon the commodity, most of the contracts are definite quantity, fixed price with definite delivery dates, or call type contracts with delivery orders placed as the need arises. Much of the purchasing performed results in large quantity deliveries to our Supply Depots located in New Jersey, Illinois, and California.

The center maintans an active bidder's list and commodity index file indicating the various items offered by prospective bidders in each marketing division. Should you desire to have your firm placed on such a list, the center, at your request, will be pleased to furnish Standard Form 129, which should be completed in detail and signed by an officer of the company authorized to execute contracts.

503 Veterans Administration Supply Depot, Somerville, New Jersey 08876

504 Veterans Canteen Service, Department of Medicine and Surgery, Veterans Administration, Washington, D.C. 20420.

Price agreements with manufacturers are negotiated by the Procurement Section located in the Office of the Director of Veterans Canteen Service, Washington, D.C. 20420.

Firms which want to be listed with the Veterans Canteen Service should contact the Chief, Procurement, and should furnish all the necessary information with reference to cost, terms, shipping, weight, samples, etc.

Canteens are permitted to purchase (a) only from authorized sources, and (b) only those items which are listed.

Vendors or their representatives are discouraged from calling on the individual canteens.

505 Veterans Administration, Department of Veterans Benefits, Washington, D.C. 20420.

VA regional offices and centers having loan guaranty divisions make purchases for the repair and maintenance of acquired single family residential properties.

506 Veterans Administration, Department of Memorial Affairs, is the national purchasing arm of the Veterans Administration for headstones and grave markers (upright and flat marble, flat granite and flat bronze). Department of Memorial Affairs receives and processes the application for a headstone or marker, and places the order with the applicable VA contractor to manufacture and ship the monument. All contracts are requirements type, with indefinite quantities, firm fixed price (with the exception of bronze, which has an economic price adjustment clause based upon the price of Bronze ingot 245 as published in the American Metal Market Newspaper), with definite delivery dates, and with delivery orders placed as the need arises.

Department of Memorial Affairs maintains an active bidder's list indicating the various types (marble, granite and/or bronze) of monuments offered by prospective bidders. Should you desire to have your firm placed on such a list, write to the Chief Memorial Affairs Director (40), Veterans Administration, 810 Vermont Avenue, N.W., Washington, D.C. 20420, and he will furnish Standard Form 129, which should be completed in detail and signed by an officer of the company authorized to execute contracts.

507. Office of Construction, Veterans Administration, Washington, D.C. 20420.

The Office of Construction is responsible for the planning and development of criteria; design and construction of new buildings additions and alterations; major repairs of existing buildings and structures at nearly 280 medical centers, domiciliaries, nursing homes; and master planning and development of 107 cemeteries located throughout the United States. It is also responsible for management of all real property including acquisition, disposal and space management for the agency.

508. Contact one or more of the Veterans Administration field stations listed below. Address as: Director, Veterans Administration Medical Center; Director, Veterans Administration Regional Office, Director, Veterans Administration Medical Centers, Supply Service, which services the Veterans Administration Cemeteries in its area; and so forth, as appropriate:

VA Regional Offices

Director, VA Regional Office, Arnor Building, 474 South Court Street, Montgomery, Alabama 36104.

Director, VA Regional Office, 235 East 8th Avenue, Anchorage, Alaska 99501.

Director, VA Regional Office, 3225 North Central Avenue, Phoenix, Arizona 85012.

Director, VA Regional Office, 1200 West 3rd Street, Little Rock, Arkansas 72201.

Director, VA Regional Office, 655 First Avenue North, Fargo, North Dakota 58102.

Director, VA Regional Office, Federal Building & U.S. Courthouse, 550 West Fort Street, Box 044, Boise, Idaho.

Director, VA Regional Office, 536 South Clark Street, Chicago, Illinois 6068C.

Director, VA Regional Office, 575 North Pennsylvania Street, Indianapolis, Indiana 46204.

Director, VA Regional Office, 210 Walnut Street, Des Moines, Iowa 50309.

Director, VA Regional Office, 321 South Main Street, Providence, Rhode Island 02903.

Director, VA Regional & Medical Center, Southport Office Building, 100 West Capitol Street, Jackson, Mississippi 39269.

Director, VA Regional Office, Federal Building, 1520 Market Street, St. Louis, Missouri 63103.

Director, VA Regional & Medical Center, Fort Harrison, Montana 59236.

Director, VA Regional Office, 100 Centennial Mall North, Lincoln, Nebraska 68508.

Director, VA Regional Office, Federal Building, 275 Chestnut Street, Manchester, New Hampshire 03104.

Director, VA Regional Office, 20 Washington Place, Newark, New Jersey 07102.

Director, VA Regional Office, 500 Gold Avenue, S.W., Albuquerque, New Mexico 87101.

Director, VA Regional Office, Federal Building, 111 West Huron Street, Buffalo, New York 14202.

Director, VA Regional Office, 252 Seventh Avenue @ 24th Street, New York, New York 10010.
Director, VA Regional Office, Federal Building, 1220 S.W. 3rd Avenue, Portland, Oregon 97204.
Director, VA Regional & Medical Center, P.O. Box 8079, Philadelphia, Pennsylvania 19101.
Director, VA Regional Office, 1000 Liberty Avenue, Pittsburgh, Pennsylvania 15222.
Director, VA Regional Office, 1131 Roxas Boulevard, Manila, Phillippines.
Director, VA Regional & Medical Center, GPO Box 4867, San Juan, Puerto Rico 00936.
Director, VA Regional Office, 1801 Assembly Street, Columbia, South Carolina 29201.
Director, VA Regional Office, 110 Ninth Avenue South, Nashville, Tennessee 37203.
Director, VA Regional Office, 2515 Murworth Drive, Houston, Texas 77054.
Director, VA Regional Office, 1400 North Valley Mills Drive, Waco, Texas 76710.
Director, VA Regional Office, Federal Office Building, West Los Angeles, 11000 Wilshire Boulevard, Los Angeles, California 90024.
Director, VA Regional Office, 211 Main Street, San Francisco, California 94105.
Director, VA Regional Office, Denver Federal Center, Denver, Colorado 80225.
Director, VA Regional Office, 450 Main Street, Hartford, Connecticut 06103.
Director, VA Regional Office, 941 North Capitol Street, Washington, D.C. 20421.
Director, VA Regional Office, P.O. Box 1437, St. Petersburg, Florida 33731.
Director, VA Regional Office, 730 Peachtree Street N.E., Atlanta, Georgia 30308.
Director, VA Regional Office, P.O. Box 50188, 96850, Honolulu, Hawaii 96813.
Director, VA Regional & Medical Center, 5500 East Kellog, Wichita, Kansas 67218.
Director, VA Regional Office, 600 Federal Place, Louisville, Kentucky 40202.
Director, VA Regional Office, 701 Loyala Avenue, New Orleans, Louisiana 70113.
Director, VA Regional & Medical Center, Togus, Maine 04330.
Director, VA Regional Office, Federal Building, 31 Hopkins Plaza, Baltimore, Maryland 21202.
Director, VA Regional Office, J.F.K. Building, Government Center, Boston, Massachusetts 02203.
Director, VA Regional Office, Federal Building, 477 Michigan Avenue, Detroit, Michigan 48226.
Director, VA Regional & Medical Center, Federal Building—Fort Snelling, St. Paul, Minnesota 55111.
Director, VA Regional Office, Federal Building, 251 North Maine Street, Winston-Salem, North Carolina 27102.
Director, VA Regional Office, Federal Building, 1240 East 9th Street, Cleveland, Ohio 44199.
Director, VA Regional Office, Federal Building, 125 South Main Street, Muskogee, Oklahoma 74401.
Director, VA Regional Office, 640 4th Avenue, Huntington, West Virginia 25701.
Director, VA Regional Office, Federal Building, 125 South State Street, Salt Lake City, Utah 84138.
Director, VA Regional & Medical Center, White River Junction, Vermont 05001.
Director, VA Regional Office, 210 Franklin Road, S.W., Roanoke, Virginia 24011.
Director, VA Regional Office, Federal Building, 915 Second Avenue, Seattle, Washington 98174.
Director, VA Regional Office, 342 North Water Street, Milwaukee, Wisconsin 53202.

VA Medical Centers Location

ALABAMA
Birmingham 35233 (700 South 19th Street).
Montgomery 36109 (215 Perry Hill Road).
Tuscaloosa 35401.
Tuskegee 36083.
ARIZONA
Phoenix 85012 (Seventh St. & Indian School Rd.).
Prescott 86301.
Tucson 85723.
ARKANSAS
Fayetteville 72701.
Little Rock 72206 (300 East Roosevelt Rd.).
North Little Rock.
CALIFORNIA
Fresno 93703 (2615 Clinton Ave.).
Livermore 94550.
Loma Linda 92354.
Long Beach 90801 (5901 East Seventh Street).
Los Angeles 90073 (Brentwood).
Los Angeles 90073 (Wadsworth).
Martinez 94553 (150 Muir Road).
Palo Alto 94304 (3801 Miranda Ave.).
Menlo Park Division.
Palo Alto Division.
San Diego 92161 (3350 La Jolla Village Drive).
San Francisco 94121 (4150 Clement Street).
epulveda 91343.
COLORADO
Denver 80220 (1055 Clermont Street).
Fort Lyon 81038.
Grand Junction 81501.
CONNECTICUT
Newington 06111 (555 Willard Avenue).
West Haven 06516 (West Spring Street).
DELAWARE
Wilmington 19085 (1601 Kirkwood Highway).
DISTRICT OF COLUMBIA
Washington 20422 (50 Irving Street, N.W.).
FLORIDA
Bay Pines 33504.
Gainesville 32602 (Archer Road).
Lake City 32055.
Miami 33125 (1201 Northwest 16th Street).
Tampa 33612 (13000 North 30th St.).
GEORGIA
Augusta 30904.
Downtown Division.
Lenwood Division.
Decatur 30033 (1670 Clairmont Road) (VAH, Atlanta).
Dublin 31021.
IDAHO
Boise 83702 (Fifth and Fort Sts.).
ILLINOIS
Chicago 60611 (333 East Huron St.) (Research).
Chicago (South Side).
Chicago 60680 (820 South Damen Ave.) (West Side) PO Box 8195.
Danville 61832.
Downey 60064.
Hines 60141.
Marion 62959.
INDIANA
Fort Wayne 46805 (1600 Randalia Dr.).
Indianapolis 46202 (1481 West 10th St.).
Cold Spring Road Division.
Tenth Street Division.
Marion 46952.
IOWA
Des Moines 50310 (30th & Euclid Avenue).
Iowa City 52240.
Knoxville 50138.
KANSAS
Leavenworth 66048.
Topeka 66622 (2200 Gage Blvd.).
Wichita 67218 (5500 East Kellogg).
KENTUCKY
Lexington 40507.
Cooper Drive Division.
Leestown Division.
Louisville 40202 (800 Zorn Avenue).
LOUISIANA
Alexandria 71301.
New Orleans 70146 (1601 Peridido St.).
Shreveport 71130 (510 East Stoner Avenue).
MAINE
Togus 04330.
MARYLAND
Baltimore 21218 (3900 Lock Raven Blvd.).
Fort Howard 21052.
Perry Point 21902.
MASSACHUSETTS
Bedford 01730 (200 Springs Road).
Boston 02130 (150 South Huntington Avenue).
Brockton 02401.
Northampton 01060.
West Roxbury 02132 (1400 Veterans of Foreign Wars Parkway).
MICHIGAN
Allen Park 48101.
Ann Arbor 48105 (2215 Fuller Road).
Battle Creek 49016.
Iron Mountain 49801.
Saginaw 48602 (1500 Weiss St.).
MINNESOTA
Minneapolis 55417 (54th St. & 48th Ave., South).
St. Cloud 56301.
MISSISSIPPI
Biloxi 39531.
Biloxi Division.
Gulfport Division.
Jackson 39216 (1500 East Woodrow Wilson Avenue).
MISSOURI
Columbia 65201 (800 Stadium Road).
Kansas City 64128 (4801 Linwood Blvd.).
Poplar Bluff 63901.
St. Louis 63125.
John Cockran Division.
Jefferson Barracks Division.
MONTANA
Fort Harrison 59636.
Miles City 59301.
NEBRASKA
Grand Island 68801.
Lincoln 68510 (600 South 70th

Street).
Omaha 68105 (4101 Woolworth Avenue).

NEVADA

Reno 89502 (1000 Locust St.).

NEW HAMPSHIRE

Manchester 03104 (718 Smyth Rd.).

NEW JERSEY

East Orange 07019.
Lyons 07939.

NEW MEXICO

Albuquerque 87108 (2100 Ridgecrest Dr., S.E.).

NEW YORK

Albany 12208.
Batavia 14020.
Bath 14810.
Bronx 10468 (130 West Kingsbridge Road).
Brooklyn 11209 (800 Poly Place).
Buffalo 14215 (3495 Bailey Avenue).
Canandaigua 14424.
Castle Point 12511.
Montrose 10548.
New York 10010 (First Avenue at East 24th Street).
Northport 11768.
St. Albans 11425 (Linden Blvd. & 179 Street).
Syracuse 13210 (Irving Avenue & University Place).

NORTH CAROLINA

Durham 27705 (508 Fulton Street).
Fayetteville 28301 (2300 Ramsey St.).
Asheville 28805.
Salisbury 28144.

NORTH DAKOTA

Fargo 58102.

OHIO

Chillicothe 45601.
Cincinnati 45220 (3200 Vine St.).
Cleveland 44106 (10701 East Blvd.).
Wade Park Division.
Brecksville Division.
Dayton 45428.

OKLAHOMA

Muskogee 74401 (Memorial Station. Honor Heights Dr.).
Oklahoma City 73104 (921 Northeast 13th Street).

OREGON

Portland 97207 (Sam Jackson Park).
Roseburg 97470.
White City 97501.

PENNSYLVANIA

Altoona 16603.
Butler 16001.
Coatesville 19320.
Erie 16501 (135 East 38th St. Blvd.).
Lebanon 17042.
Philadelphia 19104 (University & Woodland Aves.).
Pittsburgh 15206 (Leech Farm Rd.).
Pittsburgh 15240 (University Drive C).
Aspinwall Division.
Pittsburgh Division.
Wilkes-Barre 18711 (1111 East End Blvd.).

PUERTO RICO, COMMONWEALTH OF

(Including the Virgin Islands).
Rio Piedras 00921 (Barrio Monacillos).

RHODE ISLAND

Providence 02908 (Davis Park).

SOUTH CAROLINA

Charleston 29403 (109 Bee St.).
Columbia 29201.

SOUTH DAKOTA

Fort Meade 57741.
Hot Springs 57747.
Sioux Falls 57101.

TENNESSEE

Memphis 38104 (1030 Jefferson Avenue).
Mountain Home 37684. (MAIL: VAMC, Johnson City).
Murfreesboro 37130.
Nashville 37203 (1310 24th Avenue, South).

TEXAS

Amarillo 79106 (6010 Amarillo Blvd. W.).
Big Spring 79720.
Bonham 75418.
Dallas 75216 (4500 South Lancaster Road).
Houston 77031 (2002 Holcombe Blvd.).
Kerrville 78028.
Marlin 76661.
San Antonio 78284 (7400 Merton Minter Blvd.).
Temple 76501.
Waco 76703 (Memorial Drive).

UTAH

Salt Lake City 84113.

VERMONT

White River Junction 05001.

VIRGINIA

Hampton 23667.
Richmond 23249 (1201 Broad Rock Rd.).
Salem 24153.

WASHINGTON

American Lake, Tacoma 98493.
Seattle 98108 (4435 Beacon Avenue., So.).
Spokane 99208 (North 4815 Assembly Street).
Vancouver 98661.
Walla Walla 99362 (77 Wainwright Dr.).

WEST VIRGINIA

Beckley 25801 (200 Veterans Ave.).
Clarksburg 26301.
Huntington 25701 (1540 Spring Valley Drive).
Martinsburg 25401.

WISCONSIN

Madison 53705 (2500 Overlook Terrace).
Tomah 54660.
Wood 53193 (5000 West National Avenue).

WYOMING

Cheyenne 82001 (2360 East Pershing Blvd.).
Sheridan 82801.

VA Cemeteries

Servicing Station	*Cemetery/Location*
VAMC Albuquerque	Fort Bayard, Fort Bayard, N. Mex. 88036.
	Fort Bliss, Fort Bliss, Tex. 79906.
	Santa Fe, Santa Fe, N. Mex. 87501.
VAMC Alexandria	Alexandria, Pineville, La. 71360.
VAMC Atlanta (Decatur)	Marietta, Marietta, Ga. 30060.
	National Cemetery Supervising Office, Atlanta, Ga. 30308.
VAMC Baltimore	Annapolis, Annapolis, Md. 21401.
	Baltimore, Baltimore, Md. 21228.
	Loudon Park, Baltimore, Md. 21229.
VAC Bath	Bath, Bath, N.Y. 14810.
	Woodlawn, Elmira, N.Y. 14901.
VAC Bay Pines	Bay Pines, Bay Pines, Fla. 33504.
VAC Biloxi	Barrancas, Pensacola, Fla. 32508.
	Biloxi, Biloxi, Miss. 39531.
	Mobile, Mobile, Ala. 36604.
VAMC Brockton	National Cemetery of Massachusetts, Bourne, Mass.
VAMC Brooklyn	Cypress Hills, Brooklyn, N.Y. 11208.
VAMC Charleston	Beaufort, Beaufort S.C. 29902.
VAMC Clarksburg	Grafton, Grafton, W. Va. 26354.
VAMC Columbia, Mo.	Jefferson City, Jeffson City, Mo. 65101.
VAMC Columbia, S.C.	Florence, Florence, S.C. 29501.
VAMC Danville	Camp Butler, Springfield, Ill. 62707.
	Danville, Danville, Ill.
VAC Dayton	Dayton, Dayton, Ohio 45428.
VAMC Denver	Fort Logan, Denver, Colo. 80235.
VAMC Durham	Raleigh, Raleigh, N.C. 27610.
VAMC Fayetteville, Ark.	Fayetteville, Fayetteville, Ark. 72701.
VAMC Fayetteville, N.C.	New Bern, New Bern, N.C. 28560.
	Wilmington, Wilmington, N.C. 28401.
VAMC Fort Lyon	Fort Lyon, Fort Lyon, Colo. 81038.
VAMC Fort Meade	Black Hills, Sturgis, S.C. 57785.
	Fort Meade, Fort Meade, S.C. 57741.
VAMC Gainesville	St. Augustine, St. Augustine, Fla. 32084.
VAMC Grand Island	Fort McPherson, Maxwell, Nebr. 69151.
VAC Hampton	Hampton, Hampton, Va. 23669.
	Hampton (VAC), Hampton, Va. 23667.
VARO Honolulu	National Memorial Cemetery of the Pacific.
	Honolulu, Hawaii 96813.
VAC Hot Springs	Hot Springs, Hot Springs, S. Dak. 57747.
VAMC Houston	Houston, Houston, Tex. 77088.
VAMC Indianapolis	Crown Hill, Indianapolis, Ind. 46208.
VAMC Iowa City	Keokuk, Keokuk, Iowa 52632.
	Quincy, Quincy, Ill. 62301.
	Rock Island, Rock Island, Ill. 61201.
VAC Jackson	Natchez, Natchez, Miss. 39120.
VAMC Kerrville	Kerrville, Kerrville, Tex. 78028.
VAC Leavenworth	Forth Leavenworth, Fort Leavenworth, Kans. 66027.
	Fort Scott, Fort Scott, Kans. 66701.
	Leavenworth, Leavenworth, Kans. 66084.
*VAMC Lebanon	Indiantown Gap, Indiantown Gap, Pa.
VAMC Lexington	Camp Nelson, Nicholasville, Ky. 40508.
	Danville, Danville, Ky. 40442.
	Lebanon, Lebanon, Ky. 40033.
	Lexington, Lexington, Ky. 40508.
	Mills Springs, Nancy, Ky. 42544.
	Perryville, Perryville, Ky. 40468.
VAMC Livermore	National Cemetery Supervising Office.
VAMC Little Rock	Fort Smith, Fort Smith, Ark. 72901.
	Little Rock, Little Rock, Ark. 72206.

*New cemeteries under construction.

Servicing Station	*Cemetery/Location*
VAMC Louisville	Cave Hill, Louisville, Ky. 40204.
	New Albany, New Albany, Ind. 47150.
	Zachary Taylor, Louisville, Ky. 40207.
VAMC Marion, Ill.	Mound City, Mound City, Ill. 62963.
VAMC Marion, Ind.	Marion, Marion, Ind. 46952.
VAC Martinsburg	Culpeper, Culpeper, Va. 22701.
	Winchester, Winchester, Va. 22601.
VAMC Memphis	Corinth, Corinth, Miss. 38834.
	Memphis, Memphis, Tenn. 38122.
VAMC Minneapolis	Fort Snelling, St. Paul, Minn. 55111.
VAC Mountain Home	Mountain Home, Mountain Home, Tenn. 37684.
VAMC Muskogee	Fort Gibson, Fort Gibson, Okla. 74434.
VAMC Nashville	Chattanooga, Chattanooga, Tenn. 37404.
	Knoxville, Knoxville, Tenn. 37917.
	Nashville, Madison, Tenn. 37115.
VAMC New Orleans	Baton Rouge, Baton Rouge, La. 70806.
	Port Hudson, Zachary, La. 70791.
*VAMC Northport	Long Island, Farmingdale, N.Y. 11735.
	*Calverton, Calverton, Long Island, N.Y.
VAMC Philadelphia	Beverly, Beverly, N.J. 08010.
	Philadelphia, Philadelphia, Pa. 19138.
	National Cemetery Supervising Office 19106.
VAMC Poplar Bluff	Springfield, Springfield, Mo. 65804.
VAMC Portland	Willamette, Portland, Oreg. 97266.
VAC Prescott	Prescott, Prescott, Ariz. 86313.
VAMC Richmond	City Point, Hopewell, Va. 23860.
	Cold Harbor, Mechanicsville, Va. 23111.
	Fort Harrison, Richmond, Va. 23231.
	Glendale, Richmond, Va. 23231.
	Richmond, Richmond Va. 23231.
	Seven Pines, Sandston, Va. 23150.
VAMC Roseburg	Roseburg, Roseburg, Oreg. 97470.
VAMC Salem	Danville, Danville, Va. 24541.
	Staunton, Staunton, Va. 24401.
VAMC Salisbury	Salisbury, Salisbury, N.C. 28144.
VAMC San Antonio	Fort Sam Houston, San Antonio, Tex. 78209.
	San Antonio, San Antonio, Tex. 78202.
VAMC San Diego	Fort Rosecrans, San Diego, Calif. 92106.
VAMC San Francisco	Golden Gate, San Bruno, Calif. 94066.
	San Francisco, San Francisco, Calif. 94129.
VAC San Juan	Puerto Rico, Bayamon, Puerto Rico 00619.
VAMC St. Louis	Alton, Alton, Ill. 62003.
	Jefferson Barracks, St. Louis, Mo. 63125.
VAMC Seattle	Sitka, Sitka, AK 99835.
VAC Togus	Togus, Togus, Maine 04330.
*VAMC Wadsworth	Los Angeles, Los Angeles, Calif. 90049
	*Riverside, Riverside, Calif.
*VAMC Washington	Alexandria, Alexandria, Va. 22314.
	Balls Bluff, Leesburg, Va. 22075.
	*Quantico, Quantico, Va.
VAD White City	White City, White City, Oreg. 97501.
VAC Wilmington	Finn's Point, Salem, N.J. 08079.
VAC Wood	Wood, Wis. 53193.

511. Contact one or more of the Bureau of Reclamation offices listed below. Address as: Bureau of Reclamation, U.S. Department of the Interior—

*New cemeteries under construction.

Washington Contracting Office, 18th & C Streets, N.W., Washington, D.C. 20240.
Denver Federal Center, Building 67, P.O. Box 25007, Denver, CO 80225.
Federal Building, P.O. Box 043, 550 W. Fort, Boise, ID 83724.
Federal Building, 2800 Cottage Way, Sacramento, CA 95825.
Federal Building, 125 South State Street, P.O. Box 11568, Salt Lake City, UT 84111.
Herring Plaza, Box H-4377, Amarillo, TX 79101.
Federal Building, P.O. Box 2553, Billings, MT 59103.
Denver Federal Center, Building 20, Denver, CO 80225.
P.O. Box 427, Boulder City, NV 89005.

512. Contact one or more of the Bureau of Indian Affairs area offices listed below. Address as: Director of Area Office, Bureau of Indian Affairs, U.S. Department of the Interior—
Contracting and Grants Administration Staff, Branch of General Service, 1951 Constitution Avenue, N.W., Washington, D.C. 20240.
Field Administration Office, P.O. Box 2088, 500 Gold Avenue, Albuquerque, NM 87103.
Eastern Area Office, 1000 N. Glebe Road, Arlington, VA 22201.
Aberdeen Area Office, 115 4th Avenue, S.E., Aberdeen, SD 57401.
Albuquerque Area Office, 5301 Central Avenue, N.E., Albuquerque, NM 87103.
Anadarko Area Office, P.O. Box 368, Anadarko, OK 73005.
Minneapolis Area Office, 15 S. Fifth Street, Minneapolis, MN 55402.
Federal Building, Muskogee Building, Muskogee, OK 74401.
Navajo Area Office, P.O. Box 1060, Gallup, NM 87301.
Billings Area Office, 316 North 26th Street, Billings, MT 59101.
Juneau Area Office, Box 3-8000, Juneau, AK 99801.
Phoenix Area Office, 3030 N. Central Building, P.O. Box 7007, Phoenix, AZ 85011.
Portland Area Office, 1425 Irving Street, N.E., P.O. Box 3785, Portland, OR 97208.
Division of Facilities Engineering, P.O. Box 1248, Albuquerque, NM 87103.

513. Contact one or more of the Bureau of Land Management Offices listed below. Address as: Bureau of Land Management, U.S. Department of the Interior—
Administrative Services, Washington Office, 18th & C Street, N.W., Washington, D.C. 20240.
Denver Federal Center, Building 41, Denver, CO 80225.
Division of Contracting, 2400 Valley Bank Center, Phoenix, AZ 85073.
Federal Building, Room 398, 550 West Fort Street, Box 042, Boise, ID 83724.
701 C Street, Box 13, Anchorage, AK 99513.
Granite Tower, 222 N. 32nd Street, P.O. Box 30157, Billings, MT 30157.
Federal Building, Room 3008, 300 Booth Street, Reno, NV 89509.
Federal Office Building, Room E-2841, 2800 Cottage Way, Sacramento, CA 95825.
Colorado State Bank Building, 1600 Broadway, Room 700, Denver, CO 80202.
U.S. Post Office and Federal Building, South Federal Place, P.O. Box 1449, Sante Fe, NM 87501.
729 N.E. Oregon Street, P.O. Box 2965, Portland, OR 97208.
University Club Building, 135 East South Temple, Salt Lake City, UT 84111.
2515 Warren Avenue, P.O. Box 1828, Cheyenne, WY 82001.
Eastern States Office, 350 S. Pickett Street, Alexandria, VA 22304.
Boise Interagency Fire Center, 3905 Vista Avenue, Boise, ID 83705.
800 A Street, P.O. Box 1159, Anchorage, AK 99510.

514. Contact one or more of the National Park Service Offices listed below. Address as:

Concessions Management Division, 1100 L Street, Room 3317, Washington, D.C. 20240.
General Services and Contracting Division, 18th and C Streets, N.W., Washington, D.C. 20240.
Contract Administration Division, Denver Service Center, P.O. Box 25287, 755 Parfet Street, Denver, CO 80225.
Contracting and Property Management Division, Midwest Region, 1709 Jackson Street, Omaha, NE 68102.
Contracting and Property Management Division, Western Region, 450 Golden Gate Avenue, P.O. Box 36063, San Francisco, CA 94102.
Contracting and Property Management Division, Southwest Region, P.O. Box 728, Santa Fe, NM 87501.
Contracting and Property Management Division, Pacific Northwest Region, 601 Fourth and Pike Building, Seattle, WA 98101.
Contracting and Property Management Division, Rocky Mountain Region, P.O. Box 25287, 655 Parfet Street, Denver, CO 80225.
Contracting and Property Management Division, 75 Spring Street, S.W., Atlanta, GA 30303.
Harpers Ferry Service Center, Harpers Ferry, West Virginia 25425.

515. Contact one or more of the Bureau of Mines Procurement Offices listed below:
Section of Procurement—Denver, Denver Federal Center, Building 20, Denver, CO 80225.
Branch of Procurement, 2401 E Street, N.W., Washington, D.C. 20241.
Section of Procurement and Property Management, 4800 Forbes Avenue, Pittsburgh, Pa. 15213.
Helium Operations, Box H, 4372 Herring Plaza, Amarillo, TX 79101.
Wilkes-Barre Office, Room 3323 Peen Place, 20 North Pennsylvania, Wilkes-Barre, Pa. 18701.
Twins Cities Research Center, P.O. Box 1660, Twins Cities, MN 55111.
Tuscaloosa Research Center, P.O. Box L, University of Alabama, Tuscaloosa, AL 35486.
Alaska Field Operations Center, P.O. Box 550, Juneau, AK 99402.
Avondale Research Center, Avondale, MD 20470.
Rolla Research Center, P.O. Box 280, Rolla, MO 65401.
Reno Research Center, 1605 Evans Avenue, Reno, NV 89520.
Albany Research Center, P.O. Box 70, Albany, OR 97321.
Boulder City Engineering Laboratory, 500 Date Street, Boulder City, NV 89005.
Salt Lake City Research Center, 1600 East 1st South, Salt Lake City, UT 84112.
Spokane Research Center, 315 E. Montgomery Avenue, Spokane, WA 99207.

516. Contact one or more of the following offices of the U.S. Fish and Wildlife Service, U.S. Department of the Interior—
Division of Contracting and General Services, Branch of Contracts, 18th and C Streets, N.W., Washington, D.C. 20240.
Lloyd 500 Building, Suite 1692, 500 N.E. Multnomah Street, Portland, OR 97232.
P.O. Box 1306, Albuquerque, NM 87103.
Federal Building, Fort Snelling, Twin Cities, MN 55111.
Richard B. Russell Federal Building, 75 Spring Street, S.W., Atlanta, GA 30303.
One Gateway Center, Suite 700, Newton Corner, MA 02158.
Denver Federal Center, P.O. Box 25486, Denver, CO 80225.
1011 East Tudor Road, Anchorage, AK 99503.

517. Contact one or more of the following offices of the Geological Survey, U.S. Department of the Interior:
Branch of Procurement and Contracts, 12201 Sunrise Valley Drive, Mail Stop 205, Reston, VA 22090.
Eastern Region Procurement Section, 12201 Sunrise Valley Drive, Mail Stop 291, Reston, VA 22090.
Central Region Procurement Section, Box 25046, Mail Stop 204, Denver, CO 80225.
Western Region Procurement Section, 345 Middlefield Road, Mail Stop 85, Menlo Park, CA 94025.

518. Contact the following Procurement Office of the Office of Surface Mining listed below:
Division of Administrative Services, 1951 Constitution Avenue, N.W., Washington, D.C. 20240.

519. Contact one or more of the Minerals Management Service Procurement Offices listed below:
Procurement and General Services Division, 12203 Sunrise Valley Drive, Mail Stop 635, Reston, VA 22091.
Central Administrative Service Center, Procurement Operations Branch, P.O. Box 25165, Lakewood, CO 80225.
Southern Administrative Service Center, Procurement and General Services Branch, P.O. Box 7944, Metairie, LA 70010.
Western Administrative Service Center, Procurement and General Service Branch, P.O. Box 1159, Anchorage, AK 99510.

519a. Contact the following Procurement Office of the Office of Administrative Services listed below:
18th and C Streets, N.W., Washington, D.C. 20240.
Office of Aircraft Services

519b. Contact one or more of the following Procurement Offices of the Office of Aircraft Services listed below:
Division of Contracting, 3905 Vista Avenue, Boise, ID 83705.
4343 Aircraft Drive, Anchorage, AK 99503.
Denver Region, Lake Plaza North, 134 Union Boulevard, Suite 520, Lakewood, CO 80228.
Atlanta Region—South, 75 Spring Street, S.W., Atlanta, GA 30303.

520. National Bureau of Standards (NBS) Headquarters, Office Management Division, Room B128, Building 301, Washington, D.C. 20234.
National Bureau of Standards, Boulder Laboratory, Procurement Section, Boulder, Colo. 80302.

530. U.S. Environmental Protection Agency. Contact one or more following offices:
Headquarters Contract Operations, U.S. Environmental Protection Agency, Washington, D.C. 20460.
Contracts Management Division, U.S. Environmental Protection Agency, 26 West St. Clair Street, Cincinnati, Ohio 45268.
Contracts Management Division, U.S. Environmental Protection Agency, Research Triangle Park, NC 27711.

600. U.S. Department of Labor, Office of Administrative Services, Division of Procurement, 200 Constitution Avenue, N.W., Washington, D.C. 20210.

625. Community Services Administration, Procurement Division, 1200 19th Street, N.W., Washington, D.C. 20506.

626. Federal Energy Administration, Washington, D.C. 20461, Headquarters.
Region I—Analex Building—Room 700, 150 Causeway Street, Boston, MA 02114.
Region II—26 Federal Plaza, Room 3206, New York, NY 10007.
Region III—1421 Cherry Street—Room 1001, Philadelphia, PA 19102.
Region IV—1655 Peachtree Street, N.E., 8th Floor, Atlanta, Georgia 30309.
Region V—175 West Jackson Boulevard, Room A-333, Chicago, IL 60604.
Region VI—P.O. Box 35228, 2626 West Mockingbird Lane, Dallas, TX 75235.
Region VII—1150 Grande Avenue, Kansas City, MO 64106.
Region VIII—P.O. Box 26247, Belmar Branch, 1075 South Yukon Street, Lakewood, CO 80226.
Region IX—111 Pine Street, Third Floor, San Francisco, CA 94111.
Region X—1992 Federal Building, 915 Second Avenue, Seattle, WA 98174.

627. Address as follows: Regional Administrator for ETA, U.S. Department of Labor—
Room 1703, John F. Kennedy Building, Boston, MA 02203.
Room 3713, 1515 Broadway, New York, NY 10036.
P.O. Box 8796, Philadelphia, PA 19101.
Room 405, 1371 Peachtree Street, N.E., Atlanta, GA 30309.

6th Floor, 230 South Dearborn, Chicago, IL 60604.
Room 316, 555 Griffin Square Bldg., Dallas, TX 75202.
Federal Building, Room 1000, 911 Walnut Street, Kansas City, MO 64106.
16122 Federal Office Bldg., 1961 Stout Street, Denver, CO 80202.
Box 36084, San Francisco, CA 94102.
Rom 1145, Federal Office Bldg., 909 First Avenue, Seattle, WA 98174.

628. Division of Procurement, U.S. Department of Labor, 7122 Patrick Henry Drive, Washington, D.C. 20213.

628a. Contracts and Grants Branch, Mine Safety and Health Administration, U.S. Department of Labor, 4015 Wilson Blvd., Arlington, VA 22203.

629. Federal Railroad Administration, Office of Procurement, Room 8226, Nasif Building, 400 7th Street, S.W., Washington, D.C. 20590.

630. National Highway Traffic Safety Administration, Office of Contracts and Procurement (NAD-30), 400 7th Street, S.W., Washington, D.C. 20590.

631. Procurement Operations Division, M-43, Office of the Secretary of Transportation, Washington, D.C. 20590.

632. Research and Special Programs Administration, Procurement Division, DMA-14, 400 7th Street, S.W., Washington, DC, 20590, Telephone: (202) 426-2620.
Transportation Systems Center, Acquisition Division, DTS-85, Kendall Square, Cambridge, MA, 02142, Telephone: (617) 494-2144.
Transportation Safety Institute, 6500 South MacArthur Blvd., Attn: DMA-61, Oklahoma City, OK, 73125, Telephone: (405) 686-2159.

633. Small Business Administration, Office of External Awards, 1441 L Street, N.W., Washington, D.C. 20416.

634. U.S. Nuclear Regulatory Commission, Division of Contracts, Washington, D.C. 20555.
U.S. Nuclear Regulatory Commission, Region I, 631 Park Avenue, King of Prussia, Pennsylvania 19406.
U.S. Nuclear Regulatory Commission, Region II, 230 Peachtree Street, N.W., Suite 818, Atlanta, Georgia 30303.
U.S. Nuclear Regulatory Commission, Region III, 799 Roosevelt Road, Glen Ellyn, Illinois 60137.
U.S. Nuclear Regulatory Commission, Region IV, 611 Ryan Plaza Drive, Suite 1000, Arlington, Texas 76012.
U.S. Nuclear Regulatory Commission, Region V, 1900 North California Blvd., Suite 202, Walnut Creek, California 94596.

635. Director, Contracts and Grants Management Division, ACTION, Washington, D.C. 20525.

635a. Contracts and Grants Officer, ACTION Regional Office:
441 Stewart Street, 9th Floor, Boston, MA 02116.
26 Federal Plaza, 16th Floor, Suite 1611, New York, New York 10007.
2nd & Chestnut Streets, Room 108, Philadelphia, Pennsylvania 19106.
101 Marietta Street, N.W., Room 1003, Atlanta, Georgia 30303.
10 W Jackson Boulevard, 3rd Floor, Chicago, Illinois 60604.
1100 Commerce Street, Room 6-B-11, Dallas, TX 75242.
II Gateway Center, Suite 330, 4th and State, Kansas City, Kansas 66101.
1845 Sherman Street, Room 201, Denver, Colorado 80203.
211 Main Street, 5th Floor, San Francisco, California 94105.
1111 3rd Ave., Room 330, Seattle, Washington 98101.

PRODUCTS AND SERVICES BOUGHT BY THE MAJOR FEDERAL CIVILIAN PURCHASING OFFICES

Ablative heat shields, 285.
Abrasive belts, 253, 254, 285, 380, 440, 475, 480, 515.
Abrasive cloth, 253, 254, 285, 380, 440, 480.
Abrasive cutting machines, 200, 285, 380, 450.
Abrasive disks, except dental, 253, 254, 285, 380, 414, 440, 450, 520.
Abrasive materials, except dental, 150, 200, 253, 254, 285, 380, 440, 450, 475, 480, 508.
Abrasive papers, except dental, 252, 253, 254, 285, 380, 440, 475, 480, 520.
Abrasive polishing compounds, except dental, 253, 285, 380, 440, 480.
Abrasive powders, except dental, 200, 285, 380, 440, 480.
Abrasive rouge, except dental, 285, 380, 440.
Abrasive stones, except dental, 253, 285, 380, 440, 450, 480.
Abrasive wheels, except dental, 253, 254, 285, 380, 440, 450, 475, 480, 490, 515.
Abrasives, dental, 200, 418c, 440, 502, 508.
Abrasives, metal finishing, 200, 253, 285, 380, 440, 475, 480.
Absorbant for oil, 520.
Accelerometers, 145, 160, 285.
Accounting machines, 145, 200, 280, 285, 352, 380, 410, 418, 440, 475, 512, 515
Accumulators, aircraft, 285.
Acetate, plastic, 104, 110.1, 110.3, 150, 200, 285, 380, 440, 450, 475, 502, 516, 517.
Acetone, 150, 285, 380, 440, 450, 475, 480, 502, 520.
Acids, inorganic, 200, 285, 380, 440, 450, 480.
Acrylite, 380, 502.
Actinic (ultraviolet) commercial processing units, 380.
Activated Carbon, 475, 516.
Actuators, hydraulic, aircraft, 285.
Actuators, electric motor, pneumatic, rotary, solenoid, thermal, 285, 440, 475.
Adapters, electrical, 150, 160, 162, 165, 166, 200, 285, 380, 440, 475, 480, 512, 520.
Adding machine repair, 150, 512, 516.
Additive metallic materials, 380, 440.
Address plate frames, mounting, 355, 380, 440.
Addressing machine plate embossing service, 109, 380, 440, 475.
Addressing machines, 150, 200, 253, 254, 380, 418, 440, 508, 515.
Adhesive cements, 150, 200, 253, 254, 285, 380, 440, 480, 504, 520
Adhesives, 102, 110.1, 150, 200, 253, 254, 285, 350, 380, 440, 450, 475, 480, 490, 502, 515, 520.
Advertising displays, 150, 380, 413, 440, 480, 516.
Aerial cameras, motion picture, 285, 410, 418, 440.
Aerial cameras, still picture, 170, 285, 380, 440, 517.
Aerial fertilization, 513.
Aerial photography, 102, 102a, 103, 107, 109, 150, 285, 380, 480, 511, 513, 514, 516, 517, 518.
Aerial Spraying, 102, 106, 380, 480, 512, 513, 514, 518.
Aggregate (sand, cement, gravel), 440, 480, 513, 516.
Agriculture implements, supplies and equipment, 102, 103, 104, 106, 107, 110.1, 110.5, 200, 253, 285, 380, 440, 480, 512, 513, 516.
Agricultural products, crude, 200, 380, 440, 512.
Agricultural supplies, 440.
Air circulators, nonindustrial, 102, 107, 285, 350, 380, 440, 480, 508, 515.
Air cleaners, engine, 102, 200, 280, 380, 440, 475.
Air-conditioning integral self-contained units, 102, 106, 107, 110.1, 160, 162, 165, 166, 200, 252, 253, 285, 380, 413, 440, 475, 480, 485, 515, 516, 517.
Air-conditioning room-type units, 104, 106, 107, 108, 110, 160, 162, 165, 166, 167, 168, 200, 280, 285, 351, 380, 413, 418, 440, 475, 430, 485, 490, 512, 515, 516.
Air-conditioning store-type units, 380, 440, 480.
Air-conditioning system components, 106, 107, 200, 210, 251, 285, 300, 351, 380, 440, 475, 480, 508, 512.
Air-conditioning units, 106, 107, 160, 161, 162, 164, 165, 166, 167, 168, 200, 280, 285, 350, 380, 413, 440, 475, 480, 490, 512, 515, 516.
Air-conditioning units, aircraft, 280, 285.
Air-conditioning units, vehicular, 380, 440, 475.
Air-conditioning window-type units, 102, 106, 107, 108, 167, 168, 200, 280, 285, 300, 380, 413, 418, 440, 480, 490, 514, 516.
Air filters, aircraft, 160, 161, 162, 285, 475.
Air filters, engine, 160, 161, 162, 200, 280, 380, 440, 475, 480.
Air ground operating console, 160, 162.
Air hose, 175, 190, 191, 200, 254, 280, 380, 440, 475, 480.
Air purification equipment, 145, 285, 380, 440, 450, 480.
Air quality analyses, 513.
Air taxi service, 634, 519b.
Air brushes artists', 380, 440, 480, 508.
Aircraft, 165, 170, 256, 280, 353, 516, 519b.
Aircraft accessories and components, miscellaneous, 160, 161, 162, 170, 280, 285, 380, 440, 516, 519b.
Aircraft accumulators, 285.
Aircraft actuators, hydraulic, 285.
Aircraft arresting and barrier equipment, 160, 161, 162, 519b.
Aircraft electrical system components, 160, 162, 285, 353.
Aircraft, fixed wing, 102a, 110, 280, 285, 353, 480, 513, 516, 518, 519b.
Aircraft floats, 102, 513, 516, 519b.
Aircraft gyroscopes, 160, 162, 515.
Aircraft hardware, 170, 280, 285, 380, 519b.
Aircraft hydraulic actuators, 285.
Aircraft instruments, 106, 160, 162, 170, 280, 285, 353, 380, 519b.
Aircraft landing systems, 160, 161, 162, 380.
Aircraft, lighter-than-air.
Aircraft maintenance, engine checks and repairs, 102, 107, 160, 162, 165, 169, 170, 256, 280, 285, 353, 380, 480, 516, 517, 518, 519b.
Aircraft maintenance specialized tools, 160, 161, 162, 170, 285, 519b.
Aircraft receivers, (radio) 110, 160, 162, 280, 285, 353, 380, 516, 519b.
Aircraft rental and storage, 102, 160, 162, 165, 170, 285, 353, 380, 480, 514, 519b.
Aircraft, rotary wing, 280, 480, 519b.
Aircraft skills, 516, 519b.
Aircraft-type intercommunication systems, 170, 280, 285.
Airframe structural components, 102, 107, 285.
Alarm and signal sounding devices, 200, 251, 256, 280, 285, 380, 440, 450, 475, 480, 508, 520.
Alarm and signal systems, aircraft, 160, 162, 285, 300, 480.
Alarm systems, burglar, 200, 280, 285, 380, 440, 475, 490.
Alarm systems, police, 200, 251, 285, 380, 440, 475, 480.
Alarms, fire, 200, 285, 380, 440, 450, 475, 480, 508.
Alarms, gas, 380, 440.
Albumen, egg, 450.
Alcohol, 106, 145, 150, 165, 166, 200, 285, 380, 440, 450, 475, 480, 520, 530.
Alcohol denatured, 150, 165, 166, 350, 440, 450.
Alcohol, anti-freeze, 165, 166, 200, 280, 285, 380, 440, 480.
Alcoholic beverages, 502, 508.
Alidades, 380, 440, 517.
Aligners, wheel, motor vehicle, 160, 175, 200, 280, 380, 440, 475, 490, 508.
Alloys, master, 515.
Altar cloths, 440, 508.
Altars, 440, 508.
Alternators, motors, 160, 162, 200, 280, 285, 380, 440, 475, 480, 516.
Altimeter setting indicators, 106, 145, 160, 162, 165, 166, 167, 169, 285, 475.
Altimeters (flight instrument), 160, 162, 285, 353, 480.
Altimeters, surveying, 145, 200, 380, 440, 475, 517, 518.
Altitude gyro indicators, 160, 162, 285.
Aluminum and aluminum alloys, 145, 150, 165, 166, 167, 169, 200, 285, 380, 418, 440, 450, 475, 480, 517, 520.

Aluminum litho plates, 440, 450, 517.
Aluminum, strip, 150, 200, 380, 440, 480, 490.
Aluminum sulphate, 475, 520.
Ambulances, 200, 380, 440, 475.
Ammeters, 160, 162, 165, 200, 285, 380, 440, 475, 480, 485, 508, 517, 518.
Ammonium hydroxide, 380, 440, 502.
Ammunition, components, through 15.2 mm. (cal. .60), 285, 349, 512.
Ammunition, miscellaneous, 200, 251, 256, 279, 280, 285, 353, 380, 450, 475, 480, 490.
Ammunition, through 15.2 mm. (cal. .60), 200, 251, 280, 285, 353, 380, 512.
Amplifiers, audio, 145, 160, 162, 165, 166, 200, 251, 285, 380, 413, 440, 475, 480, 520.
Amplifiers, direct current, 160, 162, 165, 166, 200, 285, 440, 485.
Amplifiers, radio, 145, 165, 166, 251, 279, 280, 285, 380, 440, 480, 485.
Amplifiers, radio frequency, 160, 162, 165, 166, 200, 251, 280, 285, 440, 485, 520.
Amplifiers, synchro, gyrocompass, 280, 285.
Amplitude and phase control equipment, 160, 162, 285, 480, 485.
Analog data acquisition systems, 145, 165, 166, 167, 168, 169, 170, 171, 172, 285, 440.
Analog data analysis systems, 145, 285, 440.
Analog data conversion systems, 145, 285, 440.
Analog data reduction systems, 145, 285, 440.
Analyzers, gas, 145, 285, 380, 440, 475, 480, 515, 517, 520, 530.
Analyzers, sound, 145, 160, 161, 162, 164, 285, 520.
Anchors, marine, 252, 440, 475.
Anchors, piping, 380, 440, 480.
Anemometers, 440, 515, 520.
Anesthesia apparatus, 200, 253, 380, 440, 475, 480, 502.
Angledozers, 102, 102a, 104, 175, 200, 380, 440, 480, 508, 516.
Angles, nonferrous base metal, 200, 475, 480, 520.
Anhydrators, 380, 480.
Animal Feed, 418b.
Animal furnishings, 380, 418, 418a, 440, 475, 508.
Animal Housing and Maintenance 418b.
Animals, live not raised for food, 380, 411a, 418, 418b, 440, 508.
Annunciators, 285, 480.
Anodes, graphite, 190, 191, 440, 475.
Anodes, nickel and copper, 350, 440, 450, 475.
Anodizing equipment, 285, 380, 440.
Antenna and related equipment, 145, 160, 161, 162, 164, 165, 200, 251, 253, 256, 279, 280, 285, 300, 305, 380, 440, 475, 480, 485, 508, 516, 520.
Antifreeze compounds, 200, 380, 440, 520.
Anti-instrusion alarm systems, 251, 280, 380, 440, 475, 480.
Anti-seizing compounds, 380, 440, 480, 520.
Apparel, children's and infant's, 200, 440.
Apparel, safety, personal, 102, 150, 200, 280, 285, 350, 380, 440, 475, 480, 508, 515.
Appliance cords, 380, 440, 475, 480, 508.
Appraisal Services, 102, 145, 160, 166, 175, 251, 252, 440, 458, 490, 500, 511, 512, 513, 514, 516.
Aprons, leather, 440.
Aprons, oilskin, 440.
Aprons, rubber, 440.
Arch supports, 440, 506.
Architectural and engineering services, 102, 104, 110, 110.1, 110.9, 145, 160, 161, 162, 164, 165, 167, 168, 175, 192, 200, 280, 285, 303, 305, 380, 410, 418, 440, 450, 480, 485, 507, 508, 511, 512, 514, 516, 518, 519, 626, 627.
Architectural and related metal products, 200, 285, 380, 440, 480, 508, 512, 518.
Argon, missile checkout, 440.
Arresters, lighting, 160, 161, 162, 164, 166, 200, 380, 440, 475, 480, 508, 511, 518, 519.
Art goods, stamped, for embroidery and art needlework, 414, 440, 508.
Art supplies, 150, 200, 256, 280, 285, 305, 380, 418, 440, 450, 480, 508, 512, 520, 530, 600, 627.
Artificial eyes, 200, 508.
Artificial limbs, 200, 418c, 502.
Artists: accessories, 150, 200, 285, 380, 418, 440, 450, 480, 502, 508.
Artist's airbrushes, 285, 380, 440, 480, 508.
Asbestos, 200, 285, 380, 440, 518, 520.
Asbestos fabricated materials, 200, 285, 380, 418, 440, 475, 480, 508.
Ash trays, 150, 380, 418, 440, 502, 504, 508, 516, 520.
Asphalt, 175, 200, 280, 440, 475, 480, 508, 514, 516.
Asphalt distributors, 102a, 175, 380, 440, 475.
Asphalt elevators, 440, 475.
Asphalt heaters, 175, 380, 440, 475, 480.
Asphalt kettles, 175, 380, 440, 475, 480.
Asphalt transfers, 380, 475.
Assay laboratory equipment and supplies, 380, 440.
Athletic clothing, 192, 200, 253, 256, 440, 475, 502, 508, 512, 516.
Athletic footwear, 192, 200, 256, 418, 440, 475, 502, 508, 512.
Athletic and sporting goods, 192, 200, 253, 440, 475, 508, 512, 516.
Atlases, 150, 192, 200, 252, 380, 410, 418, 440, 475, 485, 512.
Atomic energy ammunition, 380.
Attenuators, resistive, 160, 161, 162, 164, 285, 380, 440, 485.
Audio oscillators, 160, 161, 162, 164, 285, 440, 485, 517.
Audio visual show & components, 600, 627.
Audit services, 600.
Autoclaves, 285, 530.
Automotives, sedan, 380, 440, 516.
Automotive electric lighting fixtures, 200, 285, 380, 440, 475, 480, 490, 518.
Automotive lifts, 200, 285, 380, 440, 475, 480.
Automotive maintenance specialized tools, 175, 200, 280, 285, 380, 440, 475, 480, 490, 516, 518.
Automotive parts, 418.
Awnings, 166, 200, 285, 380, 418, 440, 508.
Axes, except fire, 102, 200, 380, 440, 480.
Axes, fire, 102, 200, 380, 440, 475, 480, 506, 512.
Axle components, vehicular, 200, 380, 440, 475, 480.
Azimuths, 285, 485.

Bacteriological culture media, 106, 200, 285, 380, 440, 480, 530.
Badges, 200, 251, 256, 279, 280, 285, 353, 354, 380, 418, 440, 450, 480, 490, 502, 508, 512, 520.
Bags, burlap, cotton, jute, paper, 108, 150, 200, 380, 440, 480, 512.
Bags, duffel, 380.
Bags (garment, laundry, club, furlough), 440, 504, 512.
Bags, glassine, 108, 280, 380, 440, 475.
Bags, mail carriers, 440.
Bags (packaging material), 145, 280, 380, 440, 450, 475, 480, 490.
Bags, paper, 150, 200, 285, 300, 380, 418, 440, 475, 504, 520.
Bags, plastic (packaging), 145, 355, 440.
Bags, sand, 200, 380, 440.
Bags, sleeping, 380, 440.
Bakers, field (ovens), 102.
Bakers, mobile (ovens), 102.
Balances, 103, 104, 106, 107, 108, 285, 380, 440, 475, 502, 515, 530.
Balances, household, 440, 502.
Balances, industrial, 285, 330, 440, 475, 502.
Balances, laboratory, 103, 104, 106, 107, 108, 110, 145, 150, 167, 168, 200, 252, 285, 380, 418c, 440, 450, 480, 502, 515, 516, 517, 520, 530.
Balances, postal, 102, 103, 104, 150, 380, 440, 450, 475, 480, 490.
Baling bands, 161, 162, 253, 254, 380, 440, 450.
Bailing ties, 380, 440, 450, 490.
Bailing wire, 161, 350, 380, 440, 450, 490.
Bail cocks, 380, 440.
Ball point pens, 380, 440, 450, 475, 480, 504, 512, 516.
Ballast, 102, 253, 440, 450, 480, 520.
Ballast tubes, resistive, 440, 480.
Balloons, meteorological, 145, 165, 166, 285, 380.
Balls, for use in ball bearings, 150, 253, 254, 285, 380, 440.
Barber chairs, 200, 380, 440, 502, 508.
Barber-shop equipment, 200, 253, 380, 440, 502, 504.
Barges, piledriver, 285, 480.
Barographs, 440.
Barrels, 167, 168, 380, 440.
Barrier paper, moisture-vaporproof, 200, 380, 440, 480.
Bars, glass, 380, 440.
Bars, iron, 175, 200, 285, 350, 380, 440, 475, 480, 518, 520.
Bars, nonferrous base metal, 200, 285, 380, 440, 450, 475, 480, 515, 516, 517, 518.
Bars, pinch and crow, 380, 440.
Bars, precious metals, 285, 380, 440.
Bars, steel, 175, 200, 253, 254, 285, 380, 440, 450, 475, 480, 518.
Bars, wrecking, 380, 440, 480, 520.
Baseball equipment, 200, 440, 475, 502.
Basketballs, 192, 200, 440, 475, 502.
Baskets, household, 200, 440.
Batching plants, 175, 380, 475, 514.
Batteries, dry, 145, 150, 165, 166, 200, 279, 280, 285, 300, 353, 380, 418, 440, 475, 480, 502, 504, 516, 520.
Batteries for hearing devices, 440, 475, 502.
Batteries, wet, 145, 280, 285, 353, 380, 418, 440, 450, 475, 480, 508, 520.
Battery charging equipment, nonrotating, 200, 280, 285, 353, 380, 413, 418, 440, 450, 475, 480, 490, 506, 511, 518.
Batting, cotton, 200, 440, 475, 502, 506.
Batts, glass wool, 102, 380, 440, 480, 508.
Beacons, 36" rotating, 160, 162.
Bead insulating materials, 380, 440, 475.
Bearing Hanger units, 380.
Beakers, 520.
Bearing piles, 480.
Bearing pillow blocks, 450, 480.
Bearing step box units, 380.
Bearings, antifriction, mounted, 253, 254, 285, 380, 440, 480.
Bearings, antifriction, unmounted, 150, 285, 380, 440, 450, 480.
Bearings, ball, unmounted, 150, 253, 254, 285, 380, 440, 450, 520.
Bearings, demountable, 440, 475.

Bearings, plain, unmounted and mounted units, 150, 285, 380, 440, 480.
Bearings, roller, unmounted, 254, 285, 380, 440, 450, 480.
Bearings, sleeve, mounted and unmounted, 150, 285, 440, 450, 480.
Bearings, split, 285, 380, 440, 475.
Bearings, washer-type, 150, 285, 380, 440.
Beaters, fire, 192, 380, 440, 480.
Beauty-shop equipment, 502.
Bedpans, 200, 253, 418c, 440, 502.
Bed pillows, 200, 303, 418c, 440, 475, 502, 512.
Bedding, 200, 303, 380, 418c, 440, 502, 508, 512, 516.
*Beds, 200, 280, 418, 440, 475, 512, 516.
*Beds, fracture, hospital, 200, 254, 418c, 440, 502, 508.
Bedsprings, 200, 380, 440, 502, 512.
Beeswax, technical, 440, 450.
Bell jars, 520.
Bellows, stainless steel, 285, 520.
Belts, accessories, power transmission, 200, 280, 285, 380, 440, 490.
Belt dressings, 200, 285, 380, 440, 480, 502, 520.
Belts, drive, 150, 200, 254, 280, 285, 380, 440, 480, 508, 520.
Belts, fan, internal combustion engine, 150, 161, 162, 200, 280, 285, 380, 440, 480.
Belts, flagstaff, 440.
Belts, men's, 200, 253, 380, 440, 502, 504.
Belts, women's, 200, 380, 440.
Benches, work, 145, 150, 165, 200, 285, 380, 440, 450, 475, 480, 490, 520.
Bending machines, 254, 285, 350, 380, 440, 475, 480.
Bentonite clay (for waterproofing ponds or fire retardant), 380, 513.
Beverage, nonalcoholic, 200, 380, 418, 440, 475, 504, 508.
Bicycles, except children's, 285, 380, 440.
Billets, steel, 285, 380, 440, 475.
Billfolds, 440, 504.
Billing machines, 150, 380, 440.
Binding machines, plastic element, 150, 380, 418, 440.
Binding posts, 150, 380, 440, 485, 520.
Binding services, library, 145, 150, 165, 200, 210, 380, 410, 418, 440.
Binoculars, 102, 200, 256, 279, 280, 285, 353, 380, 440, 480, 502, 516.
Binoculars, prismatic, 102, 106, 285, 440.
Bins, 150, 285, 380, 418, 440, 475, 480.
Biological indicators, 285, 380, 440.
Biological products, 285, 380, 418c, 440, 502, 530.
Biological stains, 380, 440, 480, 502.
Biomedical instruments, 285, 440.
Birds not raised for food, 418.
Birds, game, 475.
Black plate, 380, 480.
Blackboards, 150, 161, 162, 200, 380, 413, 418, 440, 480, 512, 516.
Blades, cutting, 150, 254, 285, 380, 418, 440, 480, 520.
Blades, hacksaw, 150, 253, 254, 285, 380, 418, 440, 475, 480, 520.
*Blankets, 200, 280, 350, 380, 440, 502, 512, 516.
Blankets, lithographic, 109, 145, 165, 169, 350, 418, 440, 450, 480.
Blanks, glass, optical, 285, 440, 520.

*Mandatory for purchase by United States agencies from Federal Prison Industries or Blind Made Products. When not available from these, purchase is made on the open market.

Blasting materials, 161, 162, 175, 285, 380, 440, 475, 480, 515.
Bleachers, prefabricated, 200, 380, 440, 475, 502.
Bleaching compounds, 200, 380, 440.
Blinds, venetian, 200, 285, 303, 380, 440, 450, 480, 490, 516.
Block, building, 102, 253, 380, 418, 440, 480, 508.
Block, building, glass, 102, 252, 253, 380, 440, 480, 508.
Block, cinder, 102, 200, 253, 380, 440, 480, 508.
Block, concrete, building, 102, 200, 252, 253, 380, 440, 480, 508, 515, 516, 518.
Block, slag, 102, 200, 253, 380.
Blocks, fuse, 161, 162, 164, 380, 440, 475, 480.
Blocks, gage, 380, 508.
Blocks, pillow, bearing, 480.
Blocks, tackle, 380, 440, 480.
Blocks, wood (currency packing), 350.
Blood-plasma cabinets, 200, 380, 440, 508.
Blood transfusion apparatus, 200, 253, 380, 418c, 440, 475, 480, 502.
Blooms, steel, 380, 475.
Blower equipment, industrial, 200, 285, 350, 380, 440, 475, 480, 506, 515.
Bluing, household, 380, 440, 475.
Board, ceiling, 102, 200, 253, 380, 440, 480, 508.
Board, gypsum, 102, 161, 162, 200, 253, 380, 440, 480, 508.
Board illustrating, 150, 380, 418, 440, 516.
Board, insulating, 102, 161, 200, 253, 380, 440, 475, 480, 508.
Board, soundproofing, 102, 253, 380, 440, 475, 480, 508.
Boards, bulletin, 150, 200, 251, 253, 256, 285, 380, 413, 418, 440, 450, 480, 490, 516.
Boards, flight progress, 160, 162.
Boat hooks and poles, 191, 192, 200, 380, 440, 514, 516, 530.
Boat manufacturing equipment, 191, 192, 200.
Boat propulsion components, 145, 190, 191, 192, 200, 252, 253, 353, 380, 440, 475, 530.
Boats, 191, 192, 200, 280, 353, 380, 418a, 440, 475, 480, 513, 514, 516, 530.
Boats, lifesaving, 190, 191, 192, 200, 440, 480.
Boilers, stationary (over 15 pounds WSP), 200, 440, 480, 508.
Boilers, steam (over 15 pounds WSP), 200, 252, 380, 440, 480, 508.
Bolometers, 285.
Bolts (hardware), 150, 200, 253, 254, 380, 440, 450, 475, 480, 490.
Bolts, railroad, 380, 440, 475, 480.
Book music, 192, 200, 380, 440, 508.
Book paper stock, 280, 285, 305, 380, 418, 440, 450, 475, 480, 490.
Bookbinding equipment, 440.
Bookbinder's leather, 200, 285, 380, 450.
Bookbinding machinery, 200, 254, 285, 350, 380, 410, 440, 450, 480.
Bookbinding services, 418, 512.
Books and pamphlets, nontechnical (excludes book music), 103, 106, 145, 150, 165, 167, 168, 169, 170, 171, 175, 200, 210, 251, 252, 253, 254, 256, 280, 285, 300, 351, 354, 380, 410, 418, 440, 475, 480, 485, 511, 512, 515, 516, 518, 530.
Books and pamphlets, technical (excludes book music), 145, 150, 165, 166, 167, 168, 169, 170, 171, 175, 200, 210, 251, 253, 254, 216, 280, 285, 300, 305, 354, 380, 410, 418, 440, 475, 480, 511, 512, 515, 516, 518, 520, 530.
Books, rare, 380, 418, 503, 527.
Books, record, 150, 280, 380, 440, 475, 480, 508.

Boom fittings, ship, 254, 380.
Booms, crane and shovel, 175, 380, 440, 475, 480.
Borate, 440.
Boring equipment, earth, 103, 104, 175, 200, 254, 285, 380, 440, 475, 480, 512, 515, 518, 519.
Boring machines, 175, 200, 254, 285, 380, 440, 450, 475.
Boron, Nitride, 285, 440.
Bottle washers, 200, 380, 440, 502, 520.
Bottled gas service, 285, 380, 440, 450, 455.
Bottles, vacuum, 285, 380, 418c, 440, 475, 480, 502.
Bottles, glass, water cooler, 440.
Bouillons, 380, 502.
Box Blanks (paperboard), 172, 350.
Box liners, 102, 108, 109, 172, 380, 440.
Box shook, 172, 200, 254, 380.
Boxes, 108, 109, 150, 165, 166, 172, 200, 210, 253, 254, 255, 280, 285, 300, 380, 418, 440, 450, 490, 508.
Boxes, burial, 172, 440, 475.
Boxes, cash and stamp, 172, 380, 440, 490.
Boxes, corrugated (paperboard), 150, 172, 280, 350, 351, 352, 355, 380, 413, 418, 440, 450, 475, 490, 251, 512.
Boxes, tool, 150, 172, 380, 440, 475.
Boxes, wooden packing, 172, 305, 351, 440.
Braces, medical, 172, 200, 252, 253, 440, 475, 508.
Braces, orthopedic, 172, 200, 253, 440, 475, 508.
Braces, surgical, 172, 200, 253, 440, 475, 508.
Brackets, vehicular, 172, 440, 475.
Brads (hardware), 150, 166, 172, 200, 253, 254, 255, 380, 440, 520.
Brake components, vehicular, 172, 280, 285, 440, 450, 475, 480.
Brake service equipment, automotive, 172, 175, 200, 280, 285, 380, 440, 480, 490, 516.
Brass, rod and rolled, 172, 200, 285, 351, 380, 440, 450, 480, 490, 520.
Breathing apparatus, rescue, 172, 200, 252, 253, 380, 440, 475, 480, 515, 516.
Brick building, 102, 172, 253, 380, 440, 450, 480, 508.
Brick, fire, clay, 172, 440, 475.
Brief cases, 150, 172, 380, 440, 480, 516, 520.
Briquettes, 172, 200.
Bristles, 172, 200, 254, 440.
Broaches, metalworking, 380, 440, 475, 502.
Broaching machines, 285, 380, 440, 475.
Brokerage Services, Real Estate and Property Maintenance, 458.
Broom manufacturing equipment, 200, 254.
Broom manufacturing material, 200, 254.
*Brooms, cleaning, 161, 200, 380, 440, 516, 520.
*Brooms, whisk, 200, 380, 440, 475, 480.
Brush fibers, vegetable, 254, 285.
Brush manufacturing equipment, 254, 285.
Brushes, artists', 150, 200, 285, 380, 418, 440, 450, 480, 502, 508, 520.
*Brushes, cleaning, 150, 200, 285, 380, 440, 475, 480, 508, 520.
Brushes, hair, 380, 440, 504.
Brushes, nail, 440, 502, 504.
*Brushes, paint, 161, 162, 200, 285, 380, 440, 450, 480, 520.
Brushes, wire, 200, 285, 380, 440, 450, 475, 480, 508, 520.
Buckets, 200, 380, 440, 475, 480, 520.

*Mandatory for purchase by United States agencies from Federal Prison Industries or Blind Made Products. When not available from these, purchase is made on the open market.

Buckets, crane and shovel, 175, 200, 380, 440, 475, 480, 516.
Buckles, ratchet, 350.
Buffing wheels, 253, 254, 285, 380, 440, 450, 475, 480, 508.
Building block, 102, 253, 380, 440, 480, 508.
Building construction contracts, 102, 145, 160, 161, 162, 164, 175, 191, 192, 280, 285, 303, 350, 353, 380, 410, 440, 475, 485, 507, 512, 513, 514, 516, 518, 519.
Building glass, 102, 200, 252, 253, 380, 440, 475, 480, 508.
Building paper, 102, 200, 253, 380, 440, 475, 480, 508.
Building tile, 102, 200, 253, 285, 380, 440, 450, 480, 508.
Building, prefabricated, 102, 145, 160, 161, 162, 164, 165, 166, 167, 168, 175, 280, 285, 380, 440, 475, 480, 511, 513, 514.
Bulbs, photoflash, 109, 280, 285, 353, 380, 418, 440, 475, 502, 504, 508, 520.
Bulbs, resistance, 285, 380, 440, 480, 508.
Bulldozers, 102, 104, 107, 100, 175, 200, 205, 380, 440, 480, 508, 511, 512, 513, 514, 516, 518.
Bulletin boards, 150, 251, 253, 285, 380, 413, 418, 440, 450, 480, 490, 512, 520.
Bunker "C" commercial grade fuels, 380, 475, 480, 508, 516.
Bunting, 254, 440, 480.
Buoy and lighthouse electric timers and flashers, 172, 475.
Buoys, 145, 172, 200, 475, 480, 514, 530.
Burial boxes, 440, 475.
Burlap, 440.
Burners, fuel oil, 200, 380, 440, 455, 480, 508.
Bus, Shuttle Service, 516, 634.
Buses (motor), 200, 280, 285, 380, 440, 475, 515.
Bushings Sealing, 160, 162, 440, 520.
Business forms, 150, 220, 251, 280, 285, 300, 349, 380, 413, 418, 440, 450, 475, 480, 515.
Button blanks, 440.
Buttons, 253, 380, 418, 440, 520.
Buzzers 520.

Cabinet hardware, 102, 200, 253, 254, 380, 418, 440, 480, 502, 508, 515.
*Cabinets, 150, 160, 161, 162, 163, 164, 165, 166, 200, 250, 251, 280, 380, 413, 418, 440, 450, 475, 480, 490, 502, 508, 520.
Cabinets, blood-plasma, 440, 506.
Cabinets, enclosed check, 20-drawer, 4" x 8" ID drawers, 352, 440.
*Cabinets, filing, 150, 200, 279, 280, 380, 418, 440, 450, 475, 516, 520.
Cabinets, ice cream, 253, 380, 440, 508.
Cabinets, instrument, 145, 165, 166, 200, 252, 253, 280, 285, 380, 418, 440, 480, 502, 508, 519, 520.
Cabinets, kitchen, 161, 200, 380, 418, 440, 502, 508.
Cable, accessories, 145, 160, 161, 162, 164, 165, 166, 169, 200, 251, 285, 300, 380, 440, 480, 518.
Cable, coaxial, 160, 161, 162, 164, 165, 166, 169, 251, 280, 285, 300, 305, 380, 440, 475, 480, 485, 508, 518.
Cable, electrical, insulated, 145, 150, 160, 161, 162, 164, 165, 166, 190, 191, 200, 251, 285, 305, 350, 380, 440, 450, 475, 480, 485, 490, 511, 518, 519, 520.

*Mandatory for purchase by United States agencies from Federal Prison Industries or Blind Made Products. When not available from these, purchase is made on the open market.

Cable, electrical, non-insulated, 145, 160, 161, 162, 164, 165, 166, 169, 200, 251, 285, 380, 440, 475, 480, 485, 511, 518, 519.
Cable, fabricated, power, with attachments, 145, 160, 161, 162, 164, 165, 166, 169, 200, 285, 380, 440, 475, 480, 485, 511, 518, 519.
Cable fittings, 150, 160, 161, 162, 164, 190, 200, 253, 285, 380, 440, 475, 480, 485, 518, 520.
Cable terminating (potheads), 110, 160, 161, 162, 164, 285, 440, 480, 485, 511, 518.
Cable, twinax, 165, 166, 169, 440.
Cadastrial surveys, 513.
Cafeteria equipment and supplies, 192, 200, 380, 418, 440, 450, 475, 502, 504, 512.
Cages, small animal, 285, 418, 440.
Calcium chloride, 200, 285, 380, 440, 475.
Calculating Machine Repair, 251, 512, 516.
Calendar pads, 150, 251, 285, 380, 418, 440, 475, 512, 520.
Calipers, 285, 380, 440, 450, 480, 520
Calorimeters, 285, 440, 520.
Cambric, varnished, insulating, 000, 475, 400.
Camelback, 175, 440, 475.
Camera accessories, motion picture, 102, 103, 109, 279, 285, 380, 418, 440, 475, 480, 508, 516, 520.
Camera accessories, still picture, 102, 103, 104, 106, 109, 251, 256, 279, 280, 285, 350, 380, 418, 440, 475, 480, 504, 508, 515, 516, 520.
Cameras, copy, lithographic, 440.
Cameras, motion picture, 102, 103, 109, 145, 279, 285, 353, 380, 418, 440, 475, 480, 504, 508, 515, 516, 520.
Cameras, still picture, 102, 103, 104, 109, 256, 279, 280, 285, 350, 353, 380, 418, 440, 450, 475, 480, 504, 515, 516, 517, 520.
Camaflage and deception equipment, 380.
Camp equipment, 102, 440.
Can openers, 252, 253, 380, 418, 440, 504.
Cancelers, 380, 440, 490.
Canceling machines, 380, 440, 490.
Candelabra, ecclesiastical, 440, 500.
Candy, 200, 253, 380, 440, 503a, 508.
Canning equipment, 253, 254.
Canning material, 253, 254.
Cans, garbage and trash, 150, 285, 380, 416, 440, 455, 475, 508, 520.
Cans, film, 150, 285, 305, 418, 440.
Cans, milk, 440.
Cans, oil, 440, 520.
Cans, gasoline, 440, 475, 520.
Canteens, 440.
*Canvas materials, 200, 285, 380, 440, 450, 475, 480, 490, 502, 508.
Canvas specialty manufacturing equipment, 254, 440.
Cap screws, 200, 380, 440, 480, 506, 520.
Capacitors, 145, 150, 160, 161, 162, 164, 165, 166, 279, 285, 300, 305, 380, 475, 480, 485, 518, 519, 520.
Caps, detonating, 175, 380, 440, 480.
Carbon, activated, 475.
Carbon brush stock, 380, 450, 475, 480.
Carbon dioxide, 285, 380, 440.
Carbon electrodes, 285, 380, 475, 480, 508.
Carbons, 380, 450, 475, 520, 580.
Carbons, photo, 109, 450, 517.
Carboys, 285, 380.
Carburetors, 200, 285, 380, 440, 475.
Cards, guide, 150, 418, 440, 520.
Cards, playing, 440, 502, 504.
Cargo trailers, 102, 102a, 166, 380, 440, 475, 480, 490, 516.
Cargo vessels, 190, 516.
Carpet sweepers, 200, 380, 440, 475.

Carpets, 145, 150, 200, 256, 280, 285, 380, 410, 418, 440, 475, 480, 508, 512.
Cars, railroad, 440, 475.
Cartographic services, 513.
Carts, food, 200, 252, 380, 418, 440, 475, 502, 504.
Cases (card, photo, pass, eyeglass) 440, 504, 520.
Cases, exhibition, 210, 380, 440, 475.
Cases, index card, transfer, 150, 380, 418, 440, 475.
Cases, museum, 210, 514.
Cases, musical instrument, 200, 440, 475, 502.
Cases, specimen, 210, 440, 514.
Caskets, 200, 300, 440, 475.
Casters, 150, 285, 440, 450, 475, 480, 490, 502, 508, 520.
Castings and forgings, iron and steel, 145, 165, 166, 169, 200, 285, 351, 380, 440, 450, 475, 480.
Castings, ferrous and nonferrous metal, 145, 165, 166, 169, 200, 285, 351, 380, 440, 475, 480.
Cataloging, 160, 161, 162, 285, 380.
Catches, 520.
Catgut, 380, 418c, 440.
Cattle guards, 440, 512, 513.
Caulking compounds, 380, 440, 480, 502, 508, 520.
Caustic soda, 145, 380, 440, 475.
Ceiling board, 102, 200, 253, 380, 418, 440, 450, 480, 508.
Cellophane, 350, 380, 440.
Cells, fuel, 285.
Cells, photoconductive, 520.
Cellulose acetate, 150, 285, 380, 440, 450, 485, 502.
Cement, 102, 106, 161, 175, 200, 253, 285, 380, 440, 475, 480, 508, 511, 513, 520.
Cements, adhesive, 150, 200, 253, 254, 285, 380, 418, 440, 450, 480, 508, 520.
Cemeterial equipment, 440, 506.
Cemeterial supplies, 440, 506.
Çentrifugals, 106, 200, 285, 380, 418, 440, 520.
Ceramic tile, 102, 200, 253, 285, 380, 418, 440, 450, 475, 480, 508.
Chain, 200, 285, 380, 440, 450, 475, 480, 490, 520.
Chain fittings, 254, 380, 440, 475, 480.
Chain ladder, 200, 380.
Chain, load, 380, 475, 480.
Chain pipes, ship, 254.
Chain, power transmission, 480.
Chain, wire, 380, 475, 480.
Chaining, 513.
Chains, surveyors', 161, 380, 440, 475, 480.
Chairs, folding, 200, 280, 285, 380, 418, 440, 475, 480, 508.
Chairs, operating, dental, 200, 252, 418, 440, 502.
Chairs, wheel, 200, 253, 380, 418, 440, 475, 502.
Chalices, 440, 502.
Chalk, 150, 380, 440, 520.
Chambers, environmental, 145, 165, 166, 285, 440.
Chamois, 380, 440, 520.
Change purses, 504.
Channels, nonferrous base metal, 285, 480, 520.
Charcoal, 200, 380, 440, 480, 508.

*Mandatory for purchase by United States agencies from Federal Prison Industries or Blind Made Products. When not available from these, purchase is made on the open market.

Construction materials, mineral, bulk, 102, 106, 107, 110, 200, 252, 253, 285, 380, 440, 480, 508, 511, 518.
Construction materials, miscellaneous, 102, 167, 168, 197, 200, 252, 253, 285, 303, 380, 418, 440, 450, 475, 480, 508, 511, 512, 513, 515, 516, 518.
Construction of irrigation canals, 380, 440, 511.
Construction of radio transmitters and relay stations, 145, 160, 161, 162, 164, 165, 166, 280, 305, 380, 518, 519.
Construction of roads, 102, 175, 200, 380, 511, 512, 513, 516.
Construction of transmission lines, 305, 380, 511, 518, 519.
Construction of transmission lines (including towers and equipment substations, etc.), 165, 166, 305, 380, 511, 518, 519.
Consultant services, 109, 110.1, 110.2, 110.4, 110.6, 145, 150, 160, 161, 162, 164, 165, 166, 167, 168, 169, 170, 171, 172, 210, 251, 280, 285, 352, 380, 410, 413, 418, 440, 450, 480, 485, 511, 512, 513, 516, 518, 519, 530, 600, 628, 633.
Containers, 102, 150, 251, 253, 254, 285, 380, 418, 440, 450, 502, 508.
Contractors' jacks, 200, 380, 440, 475, 480.
Control equipment, amplitude and phase, 160, 161, 162, 164, 285, 480, 485.
Control units, landline remote, 160, 161.
Controllers, motor, electrical, 150, 200, 285, 380, 440, 450, 475, 480, 508.
Converters, electrical, 150, 160, 161, 162, 164, 165, 285, 350, 380, 440, 450, 480, 485, 508, 518, 520
Converters, phase, 285, 380, 440, 450, 480, 485, 518.
Converters, synchronous, 285, 380, 440, 450, 480, 485, 518.
Conveyors, 175, 200, 285, 351, 380, 440, 450, 475, 480, 490, 502, 515.
Cooking equipment, food, 162, 200, 252, 253, 380, 418, 440, 502, 504.
Coolers, liquid, 200, 252, 253, 254, 285, 380, 440, 475, 480, 508.
Coolers, air evaporator type, 440.
Copper, 520.
Copyholders, 150, 280, 380, 413, 440, 480, 508, 520.
Cordage, 440.
Cord, lacing, 440, 480, 490.
Cord, venetian blind and window shade, 200, 380, 440, 480, 520.
Cords, extension, 200, 380, 440, 475, 480, 508, 520.
Core drilling, 103, 380, 440, 475, 517.
Core paste, 200, 254, 380, 440.
Correct time service, 440.
Cosmetics, 200, 504.
Cotton batting, 200, 440, 502, 508.
Cotton fibers, 254, 440.
Cotton ginning machinery, 106, 440.
Cotton twine, 200, 380, 440, 450, 475, 490, 508.
Cotton batting, 254, 440, 502, 508.
Cotton waste, 440, 475.
Counterpoise and framing, 160, 162.
Counter, pulse video, 160, 162, 164, 485.
Counters, electronic, 145, 160, 161, 162, 164, 165, 285, 380, 418a, 440, 450, 485, 517, 520.
Counters, revolution, 165, 440, 475, 480, 485.
Counters (shoe findings), 253, 254, 380, 414.
Counting machines, coin, 351, 380, 440, 490.
Counting machines, paper, 350, 440, 450.
Couplings, fluid, 285, 380, 480, 520.
Couplings, nonvehicular, 380, 480, 520.
Covers, seat, automobile, 200, 380, 440, 480, 508.
Covers and steps manhole, 440.
Craftsman's levels, 380, 440, 480, 502, 508.
Crane and shovel attachments, 102, 104, 175, 200, 380, 440, 475, 480, 508, 516, 518.
Cranes, convertible, tracklaying and wheeled, construction-type, 175, 380, 440, 480, 516, 518.
Cranes, fixed, 351, 380, 440, 480.
Cranes, materials handling, mobile, 175, 200, 285, 380, 440, 450, 475, 480, 502, 508, 511, 518.
Cranes, rail, 285, 351, 380, 440, 475.
Cranes, traveling, 200, 285, 380, 475, 480, 511.
Cranes, warehouse, 200, 285, 380, 440, 450, 480, 502.
Cranes, wrecking, mounted, 200, 440.
Crane-shovel, basic and complete units, 102, 104, 175, 200, 380, 440, 475, 480, 516.
Crash trucks, 160, 161, 162, 164, 285, 380, 440.
Crate shook, 353, 380.
Crates, 253, 254, 285, 380, 440, 475.
Crayons, 200, 380, 440, 490, 504, 508, 520.
Crop thinners, 440, 480.
Crushing equipment, stone, 102, 102a, 104, 175, 200, 380, 440, 475, 516.
Crucibles, 520.
Crutches, 145, 200, 440, 502.
Cryogenic equipment, 285, 485.
Cryptographic equipment, 256, 300, 380.
Crystals, 160, 161, 162, 164, 166, 280, 285, 380, 440, 475, 485.
Culture media, bacteriological, 110, 200, 380, 418c, 480, 501.
Culture resource studies, 513.
Cups, paper, 200, 285, 380, 418, 440, 475, 480, 502, 504, 508.
Cups, tableware, 200, 252, 253, 254, 380, 440, 502, 504.
Currency machines, 352, 480.
Current limiters, 380, 475, 480.
Curtain hardware, 303, 380.
Curtains, 380, 440, 508.
Cushioning material, 380, 418, 440.
Cushions, chair, 380, 418, 440, 508, 520.
Cuspidors, 440.
Cutouts, electrical, 160, 161, 162, 164, 380, 480.
Cutouts, 380, 475.
Cutters, glass, 380, 440, 520.
Cutters, paper, manual, 150, 280, 380, 440, 450, 475, 480, 508, 520.
Cutters, pipe, 200, 285, 380, 440, 450, 475, 490, 508, 518, 520.
Cutting and forming tools for metalworking machinery, 150, 165, 166, 169, 200, 254, 380, 440, 450, 475, 480, 490, 517.
Cutting oils, 200, 254, 285, 380, 450, 475, 480, 508.
Cylinder covers, duplicating machines, 165, 166, 410.
Cylinders, gas (empty), 285, 380, 418, 440, 475, 480, 515.
Cylinders, sound recording, 380, 440.

Dairy equipment, 110, 200, 252, 253, 254, 380, 440.
Data processing machines, electronic, 109, 110.3, 110.5, 110.7, 145, 160, 165, 170, 171, 210, 251, 256, 280, 285, 300, 305, 353, 354, 380, 410, 413, 418, 440, 450, 475, 485, 500, 511, 512, 520, 600, 626, 627, 628, 633.
Data Processing Services, 251, 256, 418, 512, 519, 600, 626, 627, 628, 628b, 633.
Davits, boat, 254, 300, 305.
Decalcomanias, 160, 200, 252, 280, 285, 349, 380, 418, 440, 450, 480.
Decking Steel, 160, 162.
Deck machinery, ship, 145, 166, 167, 168, 169, 190.
Decontaminating equipment, 285, 380.
Decorative ware, 502.
Dehumidifiers, 440, 450, 475.
Dehydrators, air-conditioning, 285, 380, 440, 450, 480, 508.
Dehydrators, furnace, 380, 440.
Dehydrators, refrigeration, 285, 380, 440, 508.
Dehydrators, steam plant, 285, 380, 440.
De-icer boots, 160, 161, 162, 164.
Delivery Services, 145, 305.
Demographic Geographic Survey, 626.
Demodulator-modulators (radio), 160, 161, 162, 164, 285.
Dental abrasives, 265, 418c, 440, 475, 502, 506.
Dental engines, 418c, 502.
Dental equipment, 200, 252, 253, 418c, 440, 502.
Dental floss, 418c, 440, 502, 504, 520.
Dental instruments, 200, 252, 253, 418c, 440, 502.
Dental laboratory equipment, 200, 252, 418c, 440, 475, 502, 517.
Dental operating chairs, 200, 252, 418c, 475, 502.
Dental precious metals, 440, 502.
Dental supplies, 200, 418c, 440, 502.
Dental X-ray equipment, 200, 252, 418c, 440, 502.
Dental X-ray supplies, 200, 252, 253, 418c, 440, 502.
Dentrifrices, 440, 475, 508.
Deodorants, 440, 475, 503a, 504, 508.
Derricks, 380, 440, 480.
Desk sets, 145, 150, 380, 440, 515.
Desicators, chemistry glass, 520.
Detecting equipment, gas, 285, 380, 513, 515.
Detectors, probe (UHF)—(VHF), 160, 161, 285, 485.
Detectors, pulse power—frequency measuring unit, 160, 161, 480, 485.
Detectors, radio (field and course), 160, 161, 162, 164, 485.
Detergents, 440, 475, 520.
Detonating caps, 285, 380, 440, 480.
Detonators, 285, 380, 440, 475, 480.
Developing and printing, photographic, 256, 280, 285, 380, 410, 440, 485.
Deways, storage, 285.
Dextrine, foundry, 380, 440.
Dextrines, 350, 440, 450, 502.
Diagnostic compounds, mixtures and reagents, 200, 253, 380, 440, 480, 502.
Dials, 145, 165, 166, 380, 520.
Diamond dust, 380.
Diamonds, industrial, 380, 440, 475, 480.
Dictating machines, 200, 251, 256, 280, 285, 349, 380, 410, 418, 440, 485, 508, 515.
Die cast products, 160, 285, 380, 440.
Die casting machines, 254, 440.
Die-impressed stencil, 380, 440.
Dies, metalworking, 200, 254, 380, 440, 450, 475.
Diesel engines (all types), 160, 161, 162, 164, 165, 166, 167, 168, 169, 175, 200, 254, 285, 305, 380, 440, 475, 480, 512, 513, 515, 516.
Digital data acquisition systems, 145, 150, [illegible], 285, 440.
Digital data analysis systems, 145, 251, 285, 440.
Digital data conversion systems, 145, 251, 285, 440.

Digital data reduction systems, 145, 251, 285, 440.
Digging, exploratory, 380, 517.
Dinnerware, glass and plastic, 200, 380, 440, 502, 504.
Diodes, 285, 520.
Diplex teletype receiving keyers, 160, 162, 485.
Direction finders, automatic VHF, 160, 162, 165, 166, 485.
Discriminators, 285.
Disease control equipment, 440, 480.
Dishes, soap, 380, 440.
Dishwashing machines, 200, 252, 418, 440, 502, 504, 508.
Disinfectants, 200, 252, 253, 254, 380, 418, 440, 450, 475, 480, 508.
Dispensers, drinking water, 440.
Dispensers, liquid, 200, 380, 440, 475, 480, 502, 504.
Dispensers, soap, 200, 380, 418, 440, 475, 502, 520.
Dispensers, tape, 200, 380, 440, 450, 475, 520.
Dispensers, towel, 200, 380, 440, 450, 520.
Display cases, refrigerated, 380, 475, 504.
Display forms, 440, 504.
Displays, advertising, 413, 418, 440, 480.
Distributors, ignition, 280, 380, 440, 475, 480.
Ditchers, 102, 104, 175, 380, 440, 475, 480.
Divers suits, 353, 380, 440.
Diving apparatus, 145, 353, 380, 440, 475.
Document distribution service, 634.
Dollies, nonpowered, 280, 285, 352, 380, 440, 480, 508.
Dollies, semitrailer, 285, 380, 440, 475, 513, 516.
Door closers, 102, 200, 380, 440, 480, 508.
Door frames, metal, 102, 200, 252, 380, 440, 480, 506.
Door frames, wood, 102, 200, 252, 380, 440, 480, 508.
Doors, watertight, ship, 254.
Doors, wooden, 102, 200, 380, 440, 508.
Dowel pins, 254, 380, 440, 480, 508, 520.
Down spouts, metal, 102, 200, 252, 380, 440, 480, 508.
Downs and feathers, processed, 418.
Drafting instruments, 103, 104, 145, 150, 160, 161, 162, 164, 175, 200, 252, 280, 285, 380, 418, 440, 475, 480, 485, 508, 515.
Drafting service (mechanical, topographical, etc.), 200, 280, 285, 380, 512.
Drafting tables, 145, 150, 200, 251, 256, 280, 285, 380, 418, 440, 518.
Drafting tools, 150, 160, 161, 162, 164, 200, 280, 285, 380, 418, 440, 450, 475, 480, 507, 508, 515.
Drain tile, 102, 253, 380, 480, 508.
Draperies, 145, 150, 200, 251, 256, 280, 303, 380, 410, 418, 440, 508, 516, 520, 600, 627.
Drapery hardware, 150, 200, 256, 280, 300, 380, 410, 418, 440, 508.
Drawing instruments, 103, 104, 145, 160, 161, 162, 200, 280, 285, 380, 418, 440, 475, 480, 508, 515, 520.
Drawing machines, 285, 380, 440, 475, 480, 518.
Drawings (technical), 285, 380, 440, 512.
Dredges, 475.
Dressing material surgical, 200, 253, 380, 440, 475, 480, 502.
Dressings, belt, 200, 380, 440, 450, 480, 520.
Dressings, surgical, 200, 253, 380, 440, 475, 480, 502.
Driers, (paint) 102, 160, 161, 162, 164, 285, 380, 440, 480, 502.
Driers, thermal, 380, 480, 502.
Driftmeters, 380.
Drilling core, 103, 380, 440, 517.
Drilling equipment, rock, 175, 200, 380, 440, 475, 480, 514.
Drilling Machines (machine tools), 145, 165, 166, 175, 200, 254, 285, 380, 440, 450, 475, 480, 502, 508.
Drilling machines, portable, 175, 200, 254, 285, 351, 380, 440, 450, 475, 480, 502, 508, 517.
Drilling, well, 380, 511, 512, 513, 517.
Drills, core, power-driven, 103, 480.
Drills, metalworking, 150, 161, 162, 164, 175, 200, 254, 285, 380, 440, 475, 480, 490, 502, 508.
Drills, power-driven, 145, 165, 166, 175, 200, 254, 285, 380, 440, 450, 475, 480, 490, 508, 520.
Droppers, medicine, 520.
*Drugs, 200, 251, 256, 380, 418c, 440, 475, 480, 490, 502.
Drums, boiler, 200, 480, 508.
Drums, steel, 285, 380, 440, 475.
Dry-cleaning equipment, commercial, 200, 254, 380, 440, 508.
Dry-cleaning solvent, 200, 380, 440, 475.
Dryers, home laundry, 440.
Dryers, photographic, 109, 165, 166, 200, 280, 285, 380, 410, 440, 450, 480, 502.
Ducts, Air ventilating units, 160, 162.
Duplicating equipment, office type, 145, 150, 175, 200, 280, 285, 380, 410, 418, 440, 485, 508, 512, 515, 520, 600, 628b.
Duplicating Services, 166, 634.
Dust-collection equipment, 285, 350, 380, 480, 506.
Dyes, 200, 350, 380, 440, 450, 508.
Dynamite, 440, 475.
Dynamometers, 145, 285, 380, 475, 480.
Dynamotors, 165, 166, 167, 168, 169, 380, 480.

Earth boring equipment, 103, 175, 200, 254, 285, 380, 440, 480, 512, 515, 518, 519.
Earth moving equipment, 102, 104, 175, 200, 380, 440, 475, 480, 508, 511, 512, 513, 516, 518.
Earth moving, specialized attachments for mounting or attachment on trucks or tractors, 102, 104, 175, 200, 380, 440, 480, 508, 513, 516, 518.
Earthenware, 252, 502.
Earths, artificially activated, 380, 480.
Easels, artists, 200, 380, 475, 502, 508.
Ecclesiastical equipment, 440, 502.
Ecclesiastical supplies, 440, 502.
Economic development studies, 145, 410, 440.
Economic Impact Studies, 519, 626.
Educational Equipment and Supplies, 354, 512.
Elastic hosiery, 200, 440, 508.
Electric motor-operated valves, powered, 285, 380, 475, 480.
Electric motors, 150, 160, 161, 162, 164, 175, 200, 253, 254, 280, 285, 300, 350, 380, 440, 450, 475, 480, 490, 508, 511, 512, 515, 518, 520.
Electric power and distribution equipment, miscellaneous, 145, 160, 161, 162, 164, 165, 166, 200, 254, 285, 305, 350, 351, 380, 450, 475, 480, 508, 511, 515, 518, 519, 520.
Electric shavers and accessories, 504.
Electric signs, 200, 380.
Electric adapters, 160, 162, 200, 285, 380, 440, 480, 508, 520.
Electrical control equipment, miscellaneous, 106, 110, 145, 165, 166, 200, 285, 305, 350, 380, 440, 450, 475, 480, 485, 508, 511, 515, 518, 519, 520.
Electrical cooking ranges, 200, 380, 418, 440, 475, 504.
Electrical cutout, 160, 161, 162, 164, 380, 440, 480.
Electrical equipment components, miscellaneous, 145, 150, 160, 161, 162, 164, 165, 166, 167, 168, 169, 170, 171, 200, 285, 350, 380, 418, 440, 450, 475, 480, 508, 515, 518, 519, 520, 530.
Electrical hardware, 145, 150, 160, 161, 162, 164, 166, 167, 168, 169, 170, 171, 200, 285, 380, 418, 440, 450, 475, 480, 485, 490, 508, 511, 518, 519, 520.
Electrical installation contracts, 145, 160, 161, 162, 164, 166, 167, 168, 169, 170, 200, 285, 350, 380, 418, 440, 511, 512, 514, 518, 519.
Electrical insulating materials, 160, 161, 162, 164, 200, 285, 380, 440, 450, 475, 480, 485, 508, 518.
Electrical insulators, 160, 161, 162, 164, 200, 285, 380, 440, 450, 475, 480, 485, 508, 511, 518, 519, 530.
Electrical properties measuring instruments, 145, 160, 161, 162, 164, 165, 166, 167, 168, 169, 170, 200, 285, 380, 475, 480, 485, 508, 511, 517, 518, 519, 520, 530.
Electrical properties testing instruments, 145, 160, 161, 162, 164, 165, 166, 167, 168, 169, 170, 200, 285, 380, 475, 480, 485, 511, 517, 518, 519, 520.
Electrical supplies, 106, 145, 150, 160, 161, 162, 164, 166, 167, 168, 169, 170, 200, 253, 256, 280, 285, 305, 350, 380, 418, 440, 450, 475, 480, 485, 508, 511, 515, 516, 518, 519, 520.
Electrodes, welding, 175, 200, 253, 254, 285, 380, 440, 450, 475, 480, 502, 508.
Electromagnets, lifting, for cranes and shovels, 380, 440, 475, 480.
Electro-magnetic systems, 285.
Electron tubes, 145, 160, 162, 165, 166, 167, 168, 169, 170, 200, 280, 285, 305, 380, 440, 450, 475, 480, 485, 508, 518, 520.
Electronic accounting machines, rental, 352, 410, 440.
Electronic counters, 145, 150, 160, 161, 162, 164, 165, 166, 167, 168, 169, 170, 285, 350, 352, 380, 440, 450, 485, 517.
Electronic computer services, 102, 109, 145, 150, 160, 166, 167, 168, 169, 170, 200, 280, 285, 305, 352, 353, 380, 410, 440, 457, 480, 511, 513, 530.
Electronic data processing, 104, 109, 145, 150, 160, 166, 167, 168, 169, 170, 200, 251, 256, 280, 285, 305, 352, 353, 354, 380, 410, 413, 440, 457, 511, 513, 514, 600, 627, 628, 628a.
Electronic equipment components, miscellaneous, 109, 145; 150, 160, 161, 162, 164, 165, 166, 167, 168, 169, 170, 200, 256, 279, 280, 285, 305, 352, 380, 418, 440, 480, 485, 517, 520.
Electronic filters, 160, 380, 480, 485.
Electronic items, components, spare parts, systems, etc., 145, 150, 160, 161, 162, 165, 166, 167, 168, 169, 170, 256, 285, 300, 305, 380, 475, 480, 485, 508, 517.
Electronic precipitrons, 380, 480.
Electronic properties measuring instruments, 145, 160, 161, 162, 164, 165, 166, 167, 168, 169, 170, 200, 285, 305, 380, 440, 475, 480, 485, 508, 511, 517, 518, 520, 530.
Electronic properties testing instruments, 145, 160, 161, 162, 164, 165, 166, 167, 168, 169, 170, 200, 285, 305, 380, 475, 480, 485, 508, 511, 517, 518, 520, 530.

*Drugs, 503—The Veterans Administration has the purchase assignment to contract for the drug requirements of civilian agencies.

Electronic quantity measuring instruments, 145, 160, 161, 162, 164, 165, 166, 167, 168, 169, 170, 200, 285, 300, 380, 475, 480, 485, 502, 508, 511, 520, 530.
Electroplating equipment, 285, 380, 440, 450, 475.
Element, Heating, 520.
Elevator inspection service, 106, 200, 380, 440, 480, 514.
Elevators, 110, 200, 285, 380, 440, 450, 475, 480, 508, 511.
Elevators, aggregate, 102, 175, 380, 440, 475, 480, 508.
Elevators, asphalt, 380, 440, 475.
Enamelware, 200, 380, 475.
Enamel, wire, 160, 161.
Encoders, 288.
Energy absorption devices, 285.
Energy conservation 626.
Engine acessories, miscellaneous (nonaircraft), 280, 440.
Engine components, 175, 280, 300, 380, 440, 176, 100, 500.
Energy raw material sources, 626.
Engine electrical system components, 285, 380, 440, 475, 508.
Engine fuel system components, 380, 440, 475.
Engine generators, 160, 161, 162, 164, 305, 380, 440, 518.
Engine instruments, 380, 440, 475, 480, 508.
Engine instruments, marine, 254.
Engine instruments, vehicular-type, 280, 380, 440, 508.
Engine thermometers, 200, 380, 440, 475, 508.
Engineering and architectural services, 145, 280, 285, 300, 303, 380, 440, 450, 511, 512, 628.
Engineering scales, 160, 161, 162, 164, 175, 285, 380, 475, 480, 508, 517.
Engines, aircraft, internal combustion, 160, 162, 280, 285, 353, 480.
Engines, compressed air, 200, 380, 508, 513.
Engines, dental, 440, 502.
Engines, diesel (all types), 160, 161, 162, 164, 165, 166, 167, 168, 169, 170, 171, 175, 254, 285, 380, 440, 475, 480, 512, 513, 515, 516.
Engines, gas reciprocating, 160, 161, 285, 380, 440, 475, 480, 512, 513, 515.
Engines, internal combustion, except aircraft, 380, 440, 480.
Engines, miscellaneous, 175, 305, 380, 440, 475, 480.
Engines, semidiesel (all types), 175, 380.
Engines, steam, 380, 440.
Envelopes, 150, 200, 256, 280, 380, 413, 418, 440, 450, 475, 485, 490, 504, 508, 520.
Environmental Impact Studies, Environmental Studies, 513, 519, 626.
Erasers, 200, 380, 440, 475, 480, 508, 520.
Epoxey's, 285, 440, 475, 520.
Erasers, blackboard, 200, 380, 440, 475, 520.
Essential oils, 380, 475, 508.
Evaluations, educational program, 410, 412.
Evaporators, 285, 380, 480, 508.
Excavating equipment, 102, 104, 175, 200, 285, 380, 440, 475, 480, 508, 516.
Excavating, specialized attachments for mounting or attachment on trucks, or tractors, 102, 104, 175, 200, 285, 380, 440, 480, 508, 516, 518.
Excelsior, 380, 440.
Exhaust heads, 380.
Exhaust systems, vehicular, 380, 440.
Exhibits, design and construction, 145, 150, 165, 166, 170, 210, 285, 305, 353, 354, 380, 410, 413, 440, 511, 514.
Expansion joints, piping, 285, 380, 440, 480, 508.
Exploratory digging, 380, 517.
Explosives, 200, 380, 440, 475, 480, 508, 515.
Extension cords, 200, 380, 440, 475, 480, 508, 520.
Extermination service, 191, 200, 285, 380, 440, 480, 508.
Extinguishers, fire, 160, 161, 162, 164, 200, 285, 380, 418, 440, 450, 475, 480, 508, 511, 513.
Extractors, commercial laundry, 200, 252, 254, 380, 418, 508.
Extractors, glass, 520.
Extrusion, metal, 160, 285, 380, 480.
Eyelet (hardware), 102, 253, 254, 285, 380, 440, 450, 508, 520.
Eyelets, (shoe findings), 253, 254, 450.

Fabricated metal products, general, 145, 150, 165, 166, 167, 168, 200, 256, 285, 380, 413, 440, 480.
Fabrics, plastic, 145, 165, 166, 167, 168, 169, 170, 171, 200, 285, 380, 440, 450, 475.
Fabrics, textile (excludes carpeting), 200, 254, 285, 351, 380, 440, 450, 502, 508.
Fabrics, textile (rubber-coated), 350, 380, 440.
Fabrics, upholstery, 254, 303, 380, 440, 508.
Face plates, electrical, 285, 380, 440, 475, 508, 520.
Facial tissues, 200, 253, 380, 440, 502, 504, 520.
Facsimile equipment, 145, 165, 166, 167, 168, 169, 170, 256, 280, 352, 353, 418, 440, 512.
Fairleads, crane and shovel, 175, 380, 480.
Fan equipment, industrial, 200, 252, 285, 351, 380, 440, 475, 480, 508.
Fans, attic-type exhaust, 200, 380, 440, 450, 475.
Fans, cooling, internal combustion engine, 160, 161, 162, 164, 285, 380, 440, 475.
Fans, floor, 160, 161, 162, 200, 280, 285, 380, 440, 475, 480, 508.
Fans, household type, 160, 161, 162, 164, 200, 280, 380, 440, 475, 480, 508.
Fans, nonindustrial, 160, 161, 162, 164, 380, 440, 475, 480.
Fans, pedestal-type, 160, 161, 162, 164, 200, 280, 380, 440, 450, 475, 480, 508.
Farm tractors, 103, 104, 200, 253, 380, 440, 480, 516.
Fasteners, paper, 280, 285, 380, 440, 450, 475, 508, 520.
Fasteners, slide (hardware), 102, 253, 254, 285, 380, 440, 475, 480, 508.
Fasteners, slide (notions), 253, 254, 380, 475, 508.
Fasteners, snap, 254, 380, 440, 480.
Fats, food, 102, 253, 380, 475, 502.
Faucets, 253, 380, 440, 475, 508, 520.
Feed, manufactured, 106, 200, 253, 380, 418a, 440, 475.
Feed, unprocessed, 253, 380, 440, 480.
Felt, (textile), 285, 380, 440, 475, 480, 502, 520.
Felt, roofing, 102, 200, 253, 380, 440, 450, 475, 508.
Fences, metal, 102, 175, 200, 252, 285, 380, 440, 475, 480, 508, 516, 519.
Fences, wood, 102, 285, 380, 508, 514.
Fencing masks, 380, 440.
Fencing metal, 102, 160, 161, 162, 164, 200, 252, 253, 280, 285, 350, 380, 440, 475, 480, 508, 513, 516, 518.
Fencing, wood, 102, 380, 440, 506, 513.
Fenders, ship, 254, 475.
Fenders, rubber, dock, 475.
Ferrous metals, all kinds, 160, 200, 285, 380, 450, 480, 508, 518.
Fertilizer spreaders, 200, 254, 380, 508.
Fertilizers, natural, 102, 106, 200, 252, 253, 380, 440, 508, 516.
Fertilizers, synthetic, 102, 106, 200, 252, 253, 380, 440, 480, 508.
Fiber, rope, 254, 285, 380, 440, 475, 480, 508.
Fiberboard, hardboard, 160, 380, 440.
Fiberglass products, 145, 160, 165, 166, 285, 380, 440, 480, 508, 520.
Fibers, animal, 200, 254, 440.
Fibers, synthetic, 200, 254, 380, 440, 502, 508.
Fibers, vegetable, 254, 440.
File folders, 145, 150, 160, 161, 162, 164, 200, 280, 380, 440, 450, 485, 508, 520.
Files, 102, 161, 162, 200, 280, 380, 440, 450, 480, 485, 508, 520.
Files, metalworking, 161, 162, 200, 285, 380, 440, 520.
Files, nail, 440, 502, 504.
Files, suspended folder type, 150, 280, 380, 418, 440, 520.
*Filing cabinets, 145, 150, 175, 200, 279, 280, 380, 418, 440, 450, 508, 512, 520.
Filing systems, 145, 280, 285, 353, 380, 418, 440.
Fillers, wall, 380, 440.
Fillers, wood, 102, 106, 254, 380, 440, 480, 508.
Filling machines, 380, 480.
Film and graphic arts, 626.
Film, processed, except training and educational, 145, 185, 280, 353, 354, 380, 413, 418, 440, 508, 517.
Film, training, 150, 279, 280, 353, 354, 380, 410, 418, 440, 480, 490, 508, 520, 600.
Film, unprocessed, photographic, 104, 109, 145, 150, 160, 161, 162, 165, 166, 200, 256, 280, 285, 380, 418, 440, 450, 475, 480, 485, 504, 508, 516, 520.
Film X-ray, medical, 200, 380, 418, 440, 475, 480, 502.
Films, information, 410, 440, 520, 600.
Filters, air, aircraft, 160, 161, 162, 164, 170, 285, 380.
Filters, air, engine, 160, 161, 162, 380, 440, 475, 480.
Filters, air, furnace, 380, 440, 455, 520.
Filters, electronic, 160, 161, 162, 164, 285, 380, 480, 485.
Filters, interference, 285, 380, 508.
Filters, oil, engine, 160, 161, 162, 164, 285, 380, 440, 480, 508.
Filters, photographic, 109, 280, 285, 380, 418, 440, 480, 508.
Filters, pressure, 285, 380, 480.
Filters, RF (Radio frequency), 485.
Filters, vacuum, 285, 380, 480.
Filtration equipment, 285, 380, 440, 475, 480, 508, 519.
Findings, apparel, 253, 254.
Findings, jewelers', 508.
Findings, shoe, 253, 254, 418, 475, 508.
Fingerprinting equipment 253, 279, 280, 380, 440, 475, 480, 490, 508, 520.
Firearms, maintainance and repair, 200, 251.
Fire beaters, 102, 380, 440, 480.
Fire boats, 200.
Fire control computing sights and devices, 285, 380, 440.
Fire control designating and indicating equipment, 380, 440.
Fire control directors, 380, 440.
Fire control equipment, miscellaneous, 285, 380, 440, 475, 508.
Fire control radar equipment, 380.

*Mandatory for purchase by United States agencies from Federal Prison Industries or Blind Made Products. When not available from these, purchase is made on the open market.

Fire control systems, complete, 285, 380, 508.
Fire escapes, metal, 102, 380, 418, 480, 507, 508.
Fire extinguishing fluorcarbons, 440.
Fire extinguishers, 161, 162, 164, 200, 285, 380, 418a, 440, 450, 475, 480, 508, 511.
Fire fighting equipment, 102, 160, 161, 162, 164, 200, 285, 380, 440, 475, 480, 512, 513, 514, 518.
Fire hose (bulk), 102, 200, 380, 440, 450, 475, 480, 508, 512.
Fire hose fittings, 102, 200, 380, 440, 475, 480, 508, 512.
Fire hose reels, 102, 380, 440, 450, 480, 508, 512.
Fire hose (with fittings), 102, 200, 380, 440, 450, 475, 480, 508, 512, 516.
Fire hydrants, 102, 200, 380, 440, 480, 508.
Fire rakes, 102, 380, 440, 508.
Fire-resistant compounds, 380, 440, 475, 480, 508.
Fire surfacing materials, 380, 480.
Fire trucks, 102, 160, 161, 162, 164, 200, 380, 440, 475, 480, 513.
Firemen's protective clothing, 102, 200, 285, 380, 440, 475, 480, 508.
Fireplace sets, 303, 440.
First Aid kits, 280, 380, 440, 508.
Fish, 102, 200, 253, 380, 418, 475, 502.
Fishing tackle, except commercial, 440.
Fittings, cable, 160, 161, 162, 164, 253, 254, 285, 380, 475, 480, 508, 518.
Fittings, chain, 254, 385, 380, 440, 450, 475, 480, 508.
Fittings, fuel line, 160, 161, 162, 380.
Fittings, hose, 285, 380, 440, 480, 508.
Fittings, mast and boom, 380.
Fittings, obstruction light, 160, 161, 162, 440.
Fittings, pipe, 102, 106, 200, 253, 285, 380, 418, 440, 450, 475, 480, 508, 520.
Fittings, plumbing, 106, 200, 285, 380, 418, 440, 450, 475, 480, 508, 520.
Fittings, rope, 285, 380, 475, 480, 508.
Fittings, tube, 285, 380, 418, 440, 480, 508, 520.
Flag poles, 200, 380, 418, 480, 508, 514.
Flags and pennants, 160, 165, 166, 167, 168, 169, 170, 200, 251, 280, 300, 352, 380, 410, 418, 440, 475, 490, 502, 508.
Flags, signaling, 440.
Flagstaffs, 200, 380, 418, 440, 480, 508.
Flanges, vacuum and high pressure, 520.
Flare guns, 380.
Flares, 285, 380, 440.
Flash ranging sets, 380.
Flashlights, 285, 300, 440, 504, 520.
Flasks, chemistry, 520.
Flavoring materials, 380, 440, 502.
Flight displays, 285.
Flight progress boards, 160, 162.
Floodlight fixtures, photo, 109, 145, 165, 166, 167, 168, 380, 410, 440, 480, 508.
Floodlight, electric, except photo, 285, 380, 440, 475, 480, 508.
Floor coverings, 200, 253, 380, 418, 440, 450, 480, 508.
Floor oils, 380, 440.
Floor plate, steel, 285, 380, 450, 475, 480.
Floor polishers, 200, 380, 418, 440, 450, 475, 480, 490, 508.
Floor sanders, 200, 285, 380, 440, 450, 475, 480, 502, 508.
Flooring wood, 102, 200, 253, 254, 380, 440, 450, 475, 480, 508.
Flour, 102, 200, 253, 380, 440, 502, 520.
Flow nozzles, 145, 165, 166, 167, 168, 169, 380, 440, 480.
Flowmeter, 520.
Flow-pressure instruments, 200, 285, 380, 480, 520.
Fluid couplings, 285, 380, 480.
Fluid jets, 480.
Fluid motors, 285, 380.
Fluorescent lamps, 160, 161, 162, 164, 200, 285, 303, 380, 440, 475, 502, 508, 515, 520.
Flux, 520.
Flywheels, 380.
Foil, nonferrous base metal, 380, 450, 480.
Foil, precious metals, 380, 450, 480.
Folders, file, 280, 380, 418, 440, 506.
Food, 102, 169, 170, 200, 252, 253, 380, 418, 440, 475, 500, 502, 503, 504, 508, 512, 513, 520.
Food carts, 200, 252, 380, 418, 440, 475, 502, 504.
Food, dietary, 440.
Food, dog, 440.
Food industry ovens, 200, 252, 253, 380, 440, 502, 504, 508.
Food paring machines, 200, 253, 380, 440, 502, 508.
Food peeling machines, 200, 253, 254, 380, 418, 440, 475, 502, 508.
Food products machinery and equipment, 200, 380, 440, 475.
Food slicing machines, 200, 252, 253, 254, 418, 440, 475, 502, 504, 508.
Food specialty preparations, 102, 253.
Food storage, utensils, 380, 440, 508.
Food warming equiment, 200, 252, 253, 380, 418, 440, 502, 504.
Foot lockers 200, 380, 440, 504.
Footwear, athletic, 200, 256, 440, 508.
Footwear, childrens', 200, 440, 475.
Footwear, infants', 200, 440.
Footwear, men's (excluding athletic footwear and safety footwear), 200, 380, 440, 504.
Footwear, rubber, men's, 200, 380, 440, 480, 504, 508.
Footwear, rubber, women's, 200, 380, 440, 475, 508.
Footwear, women's (excludes athletic foot-wear and safety footwear), 200, 380, 440, 508.
Forage, 102, 200, 253, 440, 475.
Forceps, 520.
Foreign Language Translations, 418.
Forges, metal working 440.
Forgings and castings, iron and steel, 165, 200, 285, 351, 380, 440, 475, 480.
Forging machinery, 285, 380, 440, 475, 508.
Forklifts, 145, 150, 165, 166, 167, 168, 200, 210, 254, 285, 300, 350, 351, 380, 410, 413, 418, 440, 450, 475, 480, 490, 502, 508, 512, 513, 516, 517, 518.
Forks (handtools), 380, 440, 475, 508.
Forks, cooks', 252, 253, 380, 440, 502, 504, 508.
Forks, table, 161, 200, 252, 253, 380, 440, 475, 502, 504, 508.
Forks, tuning, 440, 508.
Forks, wooden, 252, 440, 480.
Forming machines, wire, 285, 380.
Forms, business, 200, 251, 280, 300, 349, 380, 410, 413, 418, 440, 475, 480, 485, 515.
Forms, intermediate, base metal, nonferrous, 380.
Forms, record, 200, 285, 380, 440, 450, 480, 508, 515.
Foundry dextrine, 200, 380.
Foundry equipment, 200, 254, 285, 380, 475.
Foundry handtools, specialized, 254, 380, 440, 475.
Foundry supplies, 200, 254, 285, 380, 475.
Fountain pens, 160, 161, 162, 200, 380, 440, 504, 508.
Fracture beds, hospital, 200, 254, 380, 418c, 440, 502, 508.
Frames, airfilter, sheetmetal, 160, 161, 162.
Frames, spectacle, 253, 380, 440.
Frames, window, wood, 102, 380, 508.
Framing, floor steel, 160, 162.
Freezers, home, 200, 380, 440, 502, 508.
Freezing machines, ice cream, 200, 253, 440, 508.
Frequency, counters, 485.
Frequency meters, 145, 160, 161, 162, 164, 165, 166, 167, 168, 169, 170, 200, 279, 285, 353, 380, 475, 480, 485, 513, 518, 519, 520.
Frequency shift exciter, 160, 162, 485.
Frequency standard, 485.
Friction tape, 161, 162, 163, 190, 191, 380, 440, 475, 502, 508.
Frost control equipment, 102, 480, 508.
Frozen food equipment, 380, 508.
Fruits, 102, 200, 253, 254, 380, 440, 502, 508.
Fuel burning equipment units, 165, 166, 167, 168, 169, 170, 380, 508.
Fuel cells, 285.
Fuel dispensing equipment, 380, 440, 475, 480, 508.
Fuel gases, 285, 380, 440, 480, 508, 520.
Fuel hose, 102, 200, 285, 380, 440, 475, 480, 508.
Fuel, JP-1 jet and kerosene, 160, 162, 380, 480.
Fuel, JP-4 jet and kerosene, 170, 285.
Fuel, JP-5 jet and kerosene, 170, 380.
Fuel line fittings, 160, 161, 162, 164, 285, 380.
Fuel lines, fabricated engine, 285, 380.
Fuel nuclear, 480.
Fuel oils, 161, 162, 200, 380, 440, 450, 480, 508, 513, 520.
Fuel pressure gauges, 285, 380, 440, 450, 475, 480.
Fuel pumps, engine, 102, 200, 380, 440, 475, 480.
Fuel system components, engine, 380, 440, 475.
Fuel tanks (steel), 110, 160, 161, 162, 200, 513, 518.
Fuel tanks, vehicular, 380, 440.
Fuels, black (boiler type), 380, 440, 508.
Fuels, bunker "C" commercial grade, 380, 475, 480, 508, 516.
Fuels, diesel, 161, 162, 164, 175, 200, 380, 480, 485, 520.
Fuels, heavy burner, 285, 380.
Fuels, light burner, 380, 480, 485.
Fuels, solid, 253, 285, 380, 440, 480, 490.
Fungicides, 106, 380, 440, 475, 480, 508.
Funnels, 440, 520.
Furnaces, heat treating, 285, 351, 380, 440, 508, 515.
Furnaces, industrial, 200, 285, 350, 380, 440, 480.
Furnaces, metal melting, 254, 285, 351, 380, 440, 515.
Furnaces, metallurgical, 285, 351, 380, 515, 520.
Furnaces, pipe, warm air, 380, 508.
Furnaces, pipeless, warm air, 380, 508.
Furnaces, warm air, 380, 508.
Furniture and fixtures, miscellaneous, 145, 160, 161, 162, 165, 166, 167, 168, 169, 170, 171, 200, 251, 256, 280, 285, 303, 380, 418, 440, 450, 457, 485, 490, 508, 600, 627.
Furniture, auditorium, 200, 285, 380, 413, 418, 440, 502, 508, 514.
Furniture, church, 200, 380, 440, 502.
*Furniture, household, 145, 161, 200, 256,

*Mandatory for purchase by United States agencies from Federal Prison Industries or Blind Made Products. When not available from these, purchase is made on the open market.

280, 300, 303, 380, 418, 440, 502, 508.
Furniture, industrial, 200, 285, 380, 440.
Furniture, laboratory, 106, 110, 145, 165, 170, 200, 210, 285, 380, 413, 418, 418c, 440, 480, 502, 515, 516, 517.
Furniture, library, 145, 165, 166, 170, 200, 380, 440, 457, 475, 508.
Furniture manufacturing equipment, fiber, metal, and wood, 254.
Furniture, meteorological, specialized, 145, 165, 166, 167, 169.
Furniture, office, 145, 150, 160, 161, 162, 200, 256, 280, 285, 300, 353, 354, 380, 410, 413, 418, 418a, 440, 450, 475, 480, 485, 508, 512.
Furniture, park, 440.
Furniture, porch, 300, 303, 380, 440.
Furniture, print shop, 200, 254, 380, 440, 450.
Furniture, professional, 200, 380, 440, 502, 506.
Furniture, public building, 200, 380, 418, 440, 457, 475, 490, 508, 515.
Furniture, restaurant, 200, 253, 380, 440, 475, 502, 504a.
Furniture, school, 200, 253, 380, 440, 475, 508, 512.
Furniture, specialized, hospital, 200, 252, 253, 380, 418, 440, 475, 502.
Furniture, theater, 200, 380, 418, 440, 502, 507, 508.
Fuse blocks, 161, 162, 285, 380, 440, 475, 480, 506, 508.
Fuse boxes, 161, 162, 200, 285, 380, 440, 475, 480, 508.
Fuse holders, 160, 161, 162, 200, 285, 380, 440, 475, 480, 508.
Fuse limiter links, 285, 380, 440, 475, 480, 508, 511, 518.
Fuse posts, 380, 440, 475, 480, 508.
Fuse wire, 380, 440, 475, 480, 508.
Fuses, 160, 161, 162, 164, 200, 285, 380, 440, 475, 480, 508, 520.
Fuses, detonating, 380, 440, 475, 480.
Fuses, electric, 160, 161, 162, 164, 285, 380, 440, 520.
Fuses, holders, power, 160, 162, 200, 380, 440, 480, 508, 511, 518.
Fuses, power, 200, 380, 440, 480, 508, 511, 518.
Fuses, safety, 161, 162, 200, 380, 440, 508.
Fuses, warning, highway flare, 440.

Gage blocks, 285, 380, 440, 520.
Gage kits, 285, 380.
Gage, outfits, 285, 380.
Gage, water stage, 517.
Gage sets, 145, 165, 166, 167, 168, 169, 170, 171, 380, 440.
Gages, fabrication, 285, 380.
Gages, fuel pressure, 285, 380, 440, 450, 480, 508.
Gages, length, go and not-go, 380.
Gages, line printing, 254, 280, 380, 450.
Gages, manifold pressure, 285, 380, 440, 480.
Gages, oil pressure, 285, 380, 440, 450, 480, 508.
Gages, plug, go and not-go, 285, 380.
Gages pressure, 145, 165, 166, 167, 168, 169, 170, 171, 285, 380, 440, 450, 480, 508, 520.
Gages, rain and snow, 380, 440.
Gages, ring, go and not-go, 380.
Gages, snap, go and not-go, 380.
Gages, special, 145, 165, 166, 167, 168, 169, 350, 380.
Gages, thread, go and not-go, 285, 380.
Galley equipment, 440.
Galley kits, 102, 200, 440.
Galley outfits, 200, 440.
Galley sets, 200.
Games, 200, 380, 440, 502, 504, 508.
Gantries, 285.
Garage service for Government-owned cars, 279, 280, 380, 418a, 440, 508.
Garbage disposal machines, household, 440.
Garbage and trash cans, 200, 380, 440, 455, 475, 504, 508, 520.
Garden tractors, 106, 200, 380, 440, 475.
Garden tractors, walking type, 200, 253, 475, 490, 508.
Gardening implements, 200, 253, 380, 440, 480, 508.
Garter's men's, 504.
Gas burners, 200, 380, 440, 508.
Gas cylinders (empty), 285, 380, 418, 440, 480, 515.
Gas detecting equipment, 200, 285, 380, 440.
Gas engines, reciprocating, 160, 161, 162, 164, 279, 380, 440, 475, 480, 512, 515.
Gas generating equipment, 200, 285, 440.
Gas service, bottled, 285, 380, 440, 455.
Gases, compressed, 106, 145, 165, 166, 200, 285, 380, 418, 440, 475, 480, 508, 515, 520.
Gases, fuel, 285, 380, 440, 480, 508, 512, 520.
Gases, industrial, 285, 380, 440.
Gases, liquefied, 145, 200, 285, 380, 440, 475, 480, 508, 520.
Gases, medicinal, 200, 380, 417, 440, 480, 508.
Gases, refrigerant, 200, 285, 380, 440, 475.
Gaskets, cylinder head, 161, 162, 254, 380, 440, 480, 508.
Gaskets, fabricated, 285, 380, 440, 475, 480, 508.
Gasoline, 161, 162, 200, 285, 380, 440, 475, 480, 485, 508, 513, 516.
Gasoline, automotive, 175, 200, 280, 285, 380, 440, 475, 480, 485, 508.
Gasoline, aviation, 170, 280, 285, 480.
Gates, metal, 192, 380, 475, 480, 511.
Gates, railroad, 380, 475.
Gates, wood, 102, 380.
Gauze, 520.
Gear cutting and finishing machines, 351, 380, 475.
Gears (power transmission), 380, 440, 450, 480.
Gears, reduction, 285, 440, 450, 475, 480.
Geiger counters, 200, 380, 440, 515.
Gelatin, inedible, 475.
Generator sets, electrical, 145, 160, 161, 162, 165, 166, 167, 168, 169, 170, 171, 200, 279, 285, 305, 350, 351, 380, 440, 475, 480, 508, 515, 518, 519, 520.
Generator sets, engine-driven, 145, 160, 161, 162, 165, 166, 167, 168, 169, 170, 175, 190, 191, 200, 285, 300, 305, 353, 380, 440, 475, 480, 485, 508, 513, 515, 518.
Generator sets, motor, 160, 161, 162, 165, 166, 167, 168, 169, 170, 200, 279, 285, 300, 305, 351, 380, 440, 475, 480, 485, 508, 517, 518, 519.
Generator sets, turbine-driven, 285, 380, 440, 475, 480, 511.
Generator sets, wind-driven, 145, 165, 166, 167, 168, 169, 170, 171, 440, 511.
Generators, automotive-type, 200, 380, 440, 475.
Generators, electrical, 145, 160, 161, 162, 165, 166, 167, 168, 169, 170, 200, 285, 305, 350, 351, 353, 380, 440, 450, 475, 480, 508, 511, 517.
Generators, signal RF, 440, 485.
Generators, steam, 440.
Geodetic instruments, 145, 165, 166, 169, 380, 440, 480, 517.
Geology and energy mineral analyses and studies, 513.
Geophysical instruments, 145, 165, 166, 169, 285, 440, 515, 517.
Girdles, women's, 200, 440, 504.
Glass bars, 380, 440, 508.
Glass, building, 102, 252, 253, 380, 440, 475, 480, 508.
Glass, building block, 102, 252, 253, 380, 440, 480, 508.
Glass cutters, 380, 440.
Glass-fabricated materials, 285, 380, 440.
Glass, rods, 380, 440, 508.
Glass, structural, 102, 252, 253, 380, 440, 480, 508.
Glass tubes, 285, 380, 440, 450, 502, 508.
Glass tubing, 285, 380, 440, 450, 480, 502, 508.
Glass, window 380, 440, 450, 475, 480, 508, 520.
Glass wool batts, 102, 380, 440, 480, 508.
Glassware, 200, 252, 253, 303, 380, 440, 502, 504.
Glassware, laboratory, 102, 103, 104, 106, 107, 108, 200, 285, 351, 380, 418c, 440, 450, 475, 480, 502, 515, 520.
Glazing compounds, 102, 252, 253, 254, 380, 440, 480.
Glide slope projector, 160.
Globes, 200, 380, 440.
Globes, prismatic (market lamps), 160, 162, 440.
Glove, leather, 254, 380, 440, 504.
Glove manufacturing equipment, 253.
*Gloves, leather, 200, 380, 440, 520.
Gloves, rubber, surgical, 200, 285, 380, 418c, 440, 475.
Gloves, welders', 200, 285, 380, 440, 450, 475, 480.
*Gloves, work, 285, 380, 440, 504, 520.
Glue, 254, 285, 380, 440, 450, 475, 480, 504, 520.
Glue, ground gelatin, 350, 355, 380, 440.
Goggles, safety, 200, 254, 285, 380, 440, 475, 480, 508, 520.
Goggles, welders, 200, 252, 254, 285, 380, 440, 475, 480, 502, 508, 520.
Goniometers, 160, 162, 517.
Graders, (earth-moving), 102a, 104, 175, 200, 380, 440, 480, 511, 512, 513.
Grandstands, prefabricated, 200, 380, 440, 508.
Graphics, art work, displays, exhibits, and advertising and publicity publications, 102, 145, 165, 166, 210, 256, 280, 285, 353, 380, 410, 413, 418B, 440, 480, 508, 513, 514, 520, 600, 627.
Graphite, 200, 285, 380, 440, 450, 480, 508, 520.
Graters, food, 200, 252, 254, 380, 440, 502.
Gratings, metal, 102, 160, 161, 162, 200, 285, 380, 440, 475, 480.
Grave markers, 440, 504.
Gravel, 102, 110, 200, 253, 285, 380, 440, 475, 480, 508, 513, 518.
Grease, 200, 285, 380, 440, 508, 520.
Grease dispensers, 200, 285, 380, 440, 480, 508.
Grease guns, hand, 285, 380, 440, 450, 475, 480, 508, 520.
Greeting and local view cards, 504.
Grenades, 440.
Grilles, concrete, 102, 380, 440.
Grilles, metal, 102, 253, 380, 450, 480, 508, 514.
Grills, sandwich 200, 380, 440, 504.
Grinders, portable, 175, 200, 254, 285, 380, 440, 450, 475, 480, 490, 502.

*Mandatory for purchase by United States agencies from Federal Prison Industries or Blind Made Products. When not available from these, purchase is made on the open market.

Grinding machines, 175, 200, 254, 285, 351, 380, 440, 450, 475, 480, 490, 502, 520.
Grinding wheels, 520.
Grips, 520.
Grommets, 254, 285, 380, 440, 475, 490, 520.
Grounds Maintenance, 418, 511.
Guide dogs, 440, 500, 508.
Guiding systems, 285.
Gum, chewing, 475, 504.
Gummed-paper tape, 280, 285, 380, 440, 450, 475, 490.
Guns, flare, 200, 250, 380, 440.
Guns, machine, 200, 279, 280.
Guns, signal, 160, 161, 162, 200, 380.
Guns, through 15.2 mm (cal. 60), 200, 251, 252, 256, 279, 280, 285, 300, 380, 480, 490, 512.
Guns, tear gas, 251, 280, 440.
Gutters, metal, 102, 254, 380, 480.
Gymnastic equipment, 410, 440.
Gypsum board, 102, 161, 162, 200, 253, 285, 380, 440, 475, 480, 508.
Gyro components, airborne, 160, 285.
Gyroscopes (aircraft), 160, 161, 162, 164, 285.

Hair dryers, 440.
Hair nets, 504.
Halyards, 440, 475.
Hammers, 380, 440, 475, 480, 520.
Hampers, clothes, 200, 380, 440, 508.
Handcarts, 200, 285, 380, 418, 440, 450, 502, 508.
Handcrafts, 280, 353.
Handcuffs, 256, 353, 440.
Handkerchiefs, mens', 200, 253, 414, 440, 502, 504.
Handkerchiefs, womens', 200, 440, 504.
Handles, 200, 380, 440, 490, 520.
Hand oilers, 285, 380, 440, 480.
Hand tool kits, 102, 150, 160, 161, 162, 175, 200, 253, 254, 285, 380, 440, 480, 508.
Hand tool outfits, 161, 162, 175, 200, 380, 440, 480, 502, 508.
Hand tool sets, 161, 162, 173, 175, 200, 285, 380, 440, 480, 508.
Hand tools, edged, nonpowered, 161, 162, 175, 200, 253, 254, 285, 380, 418, 440, 450, 475, 480, 508.
Handtools, kitchen, 102, 161, 200, 252, 253, 285, 380, 440, 504, 508.
Handtools, non-edged, non-powered, 161, 175, 200, 253, 254, 285, 380, 418, 440, 475, 480, 508.
Handtools, power driven, 102, 161, 175, 200, 253, 254, 285, 351, 380, 418, 440, 450, 475, 480, 508, 513, 520.
Handtools, specialized, 161, 175, 200, 253, 254, 285, 380, 418, 440, 475, 480, 508, 513.
Hand trucks, 150, 200, 253, 254, 280, 285, 350, 380, 418, 440, 450, 475, 480, 490, 502, 504, 508, 520.
Handwear, men's, 380, 440, 480, 502, 508.
Hanger units, bearing, 380, 508.
Hangers, garment, 440, 520.
Hangers, piping, 380, 440, 475, 480, 508, 520.
Hardness testers, 106, 285, 351, 380, 480, 515, 520.
Hardware, aircraft, 280, 285, 380.
Hardware, cabinet, 102, 200, 253, 254, 285, 380, 413, 440, 480, 502, 508, 515.
Hardware, capacitor mounting, 285, 380, 480, 508.
Hardware, curtain, 202, 380.
Hardware, drapery, 200, 280, 380, 508.
Hardware electrical, 150, 160, 161, 162, 200, 285, 300, 351, 380, 425, 440, 450, 475, 480, 490, 508, 511, 512, 518, 519, 520.
Hardware, finishing, 440, 475.
Hardware, marine, 166, 167, 168, 169, 285, 475.
Hardware, miscellaneous, 102, 160, 161, 162, 163, 165, 166, 167, 168, 169, 170, 171, 200, 253, 254, 280, 285, 351, 380, 418, 440, 450, 475, 480, 502, 508, 518, 530.
Hardware, pole line, 160, 161, 162, 380, 440, 480, 508, 511, 518, 519.
Hardware, railroad, 475.
Hardware, window shade, 200, 440, 508.
Harness, 102, 285, 440.
Harness, assemblies, ignition, 285, 380, 440.
Harvesting equipment, 102, 200, 254, 440, 516.
Hasps, 520.
Hatchets, 102, 380, 440, 480, 508, 520.
Hauling services (drayage), Local, 280, 285, 440, 450.
Hay, 106, 110, 200, 440, 475, 513.
Hazard-detecting equipment, 285, 380, 440, 485, 508.
Headphones, 160, 162, 440, 502, 508.
Headsets, 160, 162, 251, 252, 253, 280, 440, 475, 502.
Headwear, civilian, men's, 418, 440, 502.
Headwear, nonmilitary uniform men's, 200, 380, 440, 450, 502.
Headwear, special purpose, 200, 251, 380, 440, 475, 480, 508.
Healthcare delivery services, 418e, 600, 628b.
Hearing devices, 200, 418c, 440, 502.
Hearses, 440, 475.
Heat exchanger equipment, air conditioning, 106, 107, 110, 200, 285, 380, 440, 480, 508, 520.
Heat exchanger equipment, refrigeration, 200, 285, 380, 440, 508.
Heat exchangers, except air conditioning and refrigeration, 200, 285, 350, 380, 440, 480, 515.
Heat sink, 520.
Heat treating equipment, metal, 285, 351, 380, 480, 515.
Heat treating furnaces, 285, 351, 380, 508, 515.
Heaters, asphalt, 175, 200, 380, 475, 480, 508.
Heaters, domestic, water, 200, 380, 440, 455, 475, 480, 508.
Heaters, space electric, 161, 162, 200, 380, 440, 455, 475, 480, 508.
Heaters, space, nonelectric, 161, 162, 380, 440, 455, 480.
Heaters, vehicular, 380, 440, 508.
Heating and air conditioning equipment, ventilating, 102, 110, 160, 161, 162, 200, 210, 285, 350, 351, 380, 440, 450, 480, 508, 516, 519.
Heating equipment, hot water, 200, 380, 418, 440, 455, 475, 480, 508.
Heating equipment, steam, 200, 380, 418, 440, 480, 508.
Hedge trimmers, 200, 440, 475, 508.
Helicopter parts and components, 280, 285, 440, 480.
Helicopter service, 102, 160, 162, 353, 380, 440, 480, 513, 517, 518, 519.
Helicopters, 280, 285, 353, 480, 518.
Helium, 165, 440, 520.
Helmets, welders, 200, 254, 285, 380, 440, 480, 508.
Hides, 508.
Highway contract transportation, 440, 490.
Highway maintenance equipment, 175, 440, 475.
High speed tractors, 380, 440.
Hinges, 102, 253, 254, 285, 380, 440, 450, 480, 508, 520.
Hobby craft items, 504.
Hoists, 102, 175, 200, 285, 351, 380, 440, 450, 475, 480, 490, 508, 511.
Holders, copy, 280, 380, 413, 418, 440, 480, 508, 520.
Holders, fuse, 160, 162, 285, 380, 440, 475, 480, 508, 520.
Holders, fuses, power, 160, 162, 285, 440, 480, 508, 511, 518.
Holders, toilet paper, 200, 380, 440.
Holsters, revolver, 200, 251, 253, 279, 280, 350, 490.
Home appliances, miscellaneous, 162, 200, 300, 440, 475.
Home freezers, 200, 440, 502, 508.
Honey, 102, 253, 440, 502.
Hood, weather, metal, 160, 162.
Hood, weather, plastic, 160, 162.
Hooks, plate, printing equipment, 254, 280, 380, 508.
Horizon seekers, 285.
Horsehair, 200, 254, 418, 440.
Horsemeat, 440.
Hose, air, 200, 254, 280, 285, 380, 440, 475, 480, 502, 508.
Hose assemblies, 102, 200, 285, 380, 440, 480.
Hose, chemical, 102, 200, 380, 440, 475, 480, 520.
Hose, fire (bulk), 102, 200, 380, 440, 475, 480, 512, 518.
Hose, fire (with fittings), 102, 191, 200, 285, 380, 440, 450, 475, 480, 506, 512, 514, 516.
Hose fittings, plumbing, 380, 440, 480, 508.
Hose fittings, fire, 102, 200, 380, 440, 475, 480, 508, 512, 513.
Hose, flexible, metallic, 102, 285, 380, 440, 450, 475, 480, 508.
Hose, fuel, 102, 200, 285, 380, 440, 450, 475, 480, 508.
Hose, hydraulic, 102, 150, 285, 380, 440, 480.
Hose, nonmetallic, flexible, 102, 285, 380, 440, 450, 475, 480, 508, 513.
Hose, oil, 102, 380, 440, 475, 480.
Hose, water, 102, 200, 380, 440, 450, 475, 480, 508.
Hose, water assemblies, fabricated, internal combustion engine, 380, 440, 475.
Hosiery, elastic, 440, 508.
Hosiery, men's, 200, 440, 502, 504.
Hosiery, women's, 200, 440, 504.
Hospital equipment, 200, 252, 253, 380, 418, 440, 450, 475, 480, 502, 508.
Hospital furniture, specialized, 200, 252, 253, 380, 418c, 440, 475, 502, 508.
Hospital operating lamps, 200, 380, 418c, 440, 475, 502.
Hospital & sanatorium care, 200, 502.
Hot water heating equipment, 200, 380, 418, 440, 455, 475, 480, 508.
Hotel equipment and supplies, 380, 418, 475.
Household equipment, miscellaneous, 162, 200, 380, 418, 440, 475, 502, 508.
Household furnishings, 163, 200, 280, 303, 380, 418, 440, 475, 502, 508.
*Household furniture, 161, 200, 256, 280, 303, 380, 418, 440, 475, 502, 508.
Housing construction, college, 456.
Humidity controlling instruments, 145, 165, 166, 167, 168, 169, 170, 171, 285, 380, 440, 450, 475, 508, 520.
Humidity measuring instruments, 165, 285, 380, 440, 450, 475, 480, 508, 520.
Hydrants, fire, 102, 200, 380, 475, 480, 508.
Hydraulic presses, 200, 254, 285, 350, 351, 380, 440, 475, 480.

*Mandatory for purchase by United States agencies from Federal Prison Industries or Blind Made Products. When not available from these, purchase is made on the open market.

Hydraulic pumps, aircraft, 285.
Hydraulic rams, 102, 106, 285, 380.
Hydraulic tubing, 285, 380, 480.
Hydrometers, 380, 440, 480, 520.
Hydrostatic lubrications, 380.

Ice cream, 102, 200, 418, 440, 508.
Ice cream cabinets, 200, 253, 440, 508.
Ice cream freezing machines, 200, 253, 380, 440.
Ice cream mixes, 200, 253, 418, 440, 508.
Ice making machines, 440.
Ices, 200, 440, 508.
Ignition coils, 200, 280, 380, 440.
Ignition distributors, 200, 280, 285, 380, 440.
Ignition harness, assemblies, 285, 380, 440.
Implements, agricultural, supplies & equipment, 102, 103, 104, 106, 160, 200, 253, 380, 440, 480, 508, 512.
Incinerators, 200, 380, 440, 508.
Indicators, air position, 285, 380.
Indicators, air speed, 440.
Indicators, altimeter setting, 110, 145, 160, 102, 105, 100, 107, 100, 205.
Indicators, altitude gyro, 285.
Indicators, biological, 380, 502.
Indicators, flight, 160, 162.
Indicators, fuel mixture, 285, 380, 480.
Indicators, gyro horizon, 280, 285.
Indicators, navigational, 285.
Indicators, power level, 160, 162, 285.
Indicators, volume, 160, 162, 285.
Indicators, wind direction, 145, 160, 162, 166, 440.
Industrial diamonds, 380, 440, 480.
Inertial guidance systems, 285.
Inductors, Radio Frequency, 520.
Industrial Hygien Implementation, 628.
Infants accessories, 200, 440.
Information systems, 410, 412, 418.
Ingots, iron, 200, 475.
Ingots, nonferrous base metal, 145, 200, 380.
Ingots, precious metal, 145, 380.
Ink, cancelling, 440, 490.
Ink, printing, 145, 200, 253, 254, 256, 280, 285, 305, 350, 380, 440, 450, 480, 485, 508, 517, 520.
Ink, writing, 200, 280, 285, 380, 440, 475, 480, 508, 520.
Inking pads, duplicating, 280, 440.
Insects, 418b.
Insect repellants, 102, 106, 285, 440, 480, 508.
Insect screening metal, 440, 475, 508.
Insecticides, 102, 106, 107, 200, 253, 254, 285, 380, 418, 440, 450, 475, 480, 508, 520.
Insignia, 145, 200, 251, 252, 280, 285, 440, 480, 502.
Instrument cabinets, 145, 165, 166, 167, 168, 169, 170, 171, 200, 252, 253, 280, 285, 380, 418, 480, 502, 508, 519.
Instrument shelter support, 145, 165.
Instruments, alkalinity measuring, 380, 440, 480, 502, 508, 517.
Instruments, chemical composition determining, 102, 103, 104, 106, 107, 108, 145, 252, 285, 380, 440, 475, 480.
Instruments, combination temperature pressure, 145, 165, 285, 380, 440, 480, 508.
Instruments, dental, 200, 252, 253, 418, 440, 502.
Instruments, drafting, 103, 104, 145, 150, 160, 161, 162, 200, 252, 280, 285, 380, 418, 440, 480, 508, 515.
Instruments, drawing, 103, 104, 160, 161, 162, 200, 280, 285, 380, 418, 440, 480, 508, 515, 520.
Instruments, electrical properties measuring, 145, 160, 161, 162, 165, 166, 169, 170, 285, 380, 475, 480, 485, 508, 511, 517, 518, 519, 520.
Instruments, electrical properties testing, 145, 160, 161, 162, 164, 165, 166, 169, 170, 200, 285, 380, 475, 480, 485, 511, 518, 519, 520.
Instruments, electronic properties measuring, 145, 160, 161, 162, 164, 165, 166, 169, 170, 285, 380, 440, 475, 480, 485, 508, 511, 517, 518, 520.
Instruments, electronic properties testing, 145, 160, 161, 162, 164, 165, 166, 169, 170, 200, 285, 380, 475, 480, 485, 506, 511, 517, 518, 520.
Instruments, electronic quantity measuring, 145, 160, 161, 162, 164, 165, 166, 169, 170, 200, 285, 380, 440, 475, 480, 485, 502, 503, 508, 511, 530.
Instruments, engine, 280, 380, 440, 475, 480, 508.
Instruments, flight, 280, 440.
Instruments, flow-pressure, 145, 285, 380, 480, 511.
Instruments, fluid flow measuring, 145, 285, 380, 475, 480, 511, 517.
Instruments, geodetic, 145, 285, 440, 480, 517.
Instruments, geophysical, 145, 285, 440, 515, 517.
Instruments, humidity controlling, 285, 380, 440, 520.
Instruments, humidity measuring, 145, 165, 166, 167, 285, 380, 440, 475, 480, 508, 520.
Instruments, liquid level float, 102, 285, 380, 440, 475, 480, 508.
Instruments, liquid level measuring, 145, 285, 380, 440, 475, 480, 508, 520.
Instruments, mapping, 145, 169, 380, 440, 480, 511, 513, 517.
Instruments, mechanical motion measuring, 145, 285, 380, 440, 475, 480, 508.
Instruments, medical, 200, 252, 253, 413, 418c, 440, 450, 475, 480, 508, 520, 530.
Instruments, meteorological, 145, 165, 166, 285, 440, 511.
Instruments, miscellaneous, 145, 165, 166, 167, 168, 169, 170, 171, 200, 285, 380, 440, 450, 508, 530.
Instruments, musical (excludes phonographs, radios, television sets), 200, 440, 475, 502.
Instruments, navigational, 145, 160, 162, 169, 190, 191, 285, 440, 475, 516.
Instruments, oceanographic, 145, 167, 169, 170, 172, 475, 516, 517.
Instruments, optical, 145, 200, 285, 380, 440, 480, 502, 517.
Instruments, opticians', 200, 440, 475, 502, 508.
Instruments, optometrists', 440, 502, 508.
Instruments, photogrammetric, 145, 480, 511, 513, 517.
Instruments, pressure controlling, 145, 165, 166, 285, 380, 440, 480, 508, 520.
Instruments, pressure measuring, 145, 165, 166, 285, 380, 440, 480, 508, 520.
Instruments, radiation detection, 110, 145, 285, 380, 440, 480, 485, 600.
Instruments, rotation measuring, 145, 380, 475, 480, 508.
Instruments, seismographic, 103, 145, 166, 169, 170, 285, 380, 517.
Instruments, surgical, 200, 253, 380, 418c, 440, 475, 480, 502.
Instruments, surveying, 103, 104, 145, 161, 166, 175, 200, 440, 480, 511, 513, 517, 518.
Instruments, temperature controlling, 145, 160, 162, 165, 166, 167, 168, 169, 170, 200, 285, 351, 380, 440, 450, 475, 480, 508, 515, 520.
Instruments, temperature measuring, 145, 161, 162, 165, 200, 285, 351, 380, 440, 475, 480, 508, 515, 520.
Instruments, time measuring, 145, 160, 162, 165, 166, 170, 200, 285, 380, 440, 480, 508.
Instruments, vehicular-type engine, 280, 380, 440.
Instruments, veterinary, 200, 440.
Insulating board, 102, 161, 162, 200, 253, 380, 440, 475, 480, 508.
Insulating materials, electrical, 160, 161, 162, 200, 285, 380, 440, 475, 480, 508, 518.
Insulation materials, 102, 145, 165, 166, 167, 168, 169, 170, 171, 200, 253, 254, 285, 380, 440, 450, 475, 480, 508, 520.
Insulators, electrical, 160, 161, 162, 200, 305, 380, 440, 475, 480, 508, 511, 518, 519, 520.
Insulators, strain, 160, 518.
Insulators, transmission line, 160, 161, 162, 164, 480, 511, 518, 519.
Integrators, 285, 450.
Intercommunication equipment, 145, 150, 160, 161, 162, 165, 166, 167, 168, 169, 170, 200, 279, 280, 285, 305, 380, 413, 418, 440, 475, 100, 100, 500.
Intercommunication systems, aircraft type, 170, 280.
Intercommunication systems, office-type, 145, 279, 285, 413, 418, 440, 480, 485, 490, 508, 517.
Intercommunication systems, wired, audio, 145, 165, 166, 167, 168, 169, 170, 279, 285, 305, 380, 440, 480, 502, 508.
Interference filters, 285, 380, 508.
Inverters, 285.
Ionization chambers, 285, 380.
Iron bars, 175, 200, 285, 351, 380, 440, 475, 480, 518.
Iron ingots, 200, 440.
Iron lungs, 440, 502.
Iron pigs, 200, 254, 475.
Iron pipe (rigid only), 102, 161, 162, 200, 253, 380, 440, 450, 475, 480, 508, 518.
Iron plate, 200, 285, 380, 450, 475, 480, 508, 518.
Iron primary and semifinished products, 351, 380, 440, 475, 508.
Iron rods for wire, 285, 380, 440, 475.
Iron scrap, 200, 254, 440.
Iron strip, 285, 380, 440, 475, 480.
Iron structural shapes (3 inches and over), 285, 350, 380, 440, 475, 480, 508, 518.
Iron tube (rigid only), 380, 418, 440, 475, 480, 508, 518.
Iron wire, nonelectrical, 380, 440, 450, 475, 480, 508.
Ironers, commercial laundry, 253, 254, 414, 502, 508.
Irons, waffle, 440, 502.
Irrigation canal construction, 440, 511.
Irrigation gates, 440.

Jacks, including contractors', 200, 285, 380, 440, 450, 475, 480, 508, 518, 520.
Janitorial equipment and supplies, 200, 285, 380, 418, 440, 450, 480, 520.
Janitorial services, 166, 167, 168, 169, 170, 285, 305, 330, 353, 354, 411, 418b, 440, 511, 512, 513, 530.
Jars, glass, canning, 440.
Jewelers' findings, 285, 508.
Jewelers' specialized handtools, 285, 440, 502, 508.
Jewelry, 502.
Jewelry emblematic, length-of-service buttons and pins, 440, 450.
Job recording devices, 480, 502.
Joint bars, railroad, 480.
Joints, piping, 380, 440, 480, 508.

Livestock equipment, 102, 440.
Load banks, resistor type, 160, 162.
Load chain, 380, 475, 480.
Loaders (construction equipment), 102a, 175, 200, 285, 380, 440, 475, 480, 508, 514.
Local hauling (drayage) services, 280, 305, 440.
Lock boxes with wood nestings, 490.
Lock boxes with steel nestings, 490.
*Lockers, except foot, 191, 200, 285, 380, 440, 480, 490.
Lockers, foot, 200, 380, 440, 504.
Locknuts, 285, 440, 480.
Locks, hardware, 101, 102, 165, 166, 253, 254, 285, 380, 440, 450, 475, 480, 490, 502, 508, 520.
Lockwashers, 254, 285, 380, 440, 475, 480, 520.
Locomotive components, 200, 380, 440, 475.
Locomotives, 200, 380, 440, 475, 480.
Logging equipment, 440.
Logistics & warehousing services, 285.
Loofa sponges, 502.
Loom, insulating, 440, 475.
Looms, textile, 254, 440, 502.
Loud speakers, 160, 285, 440.
Louvers, sheet metal, 160, 162.
Lubricants, 200, 285, 351, 380, 440, 475, 480.
Lubricating oils, 104, 161, 162, 200, 253, 254, 280, 285, 380, 440, 450, 480, 508, 520.
Lubrication dispensing equipment, 175, 200, 285, 380, 440, 480, 490, 508.
Lubrication systems, centralized, 285, 380, 440, 475, 480.
Lubrications, hydrostatic, 285, 380, 440.
Lubricators, sight feed, 508.
Luggage, 440.
Lugs, 380, 440, 475, 520.
**Lumber, dimensional, 102, 106, 161, 167, 168, 200, 210, 252, 253, 254, 285, 380, 418, 440, 450, 475, 480, 508, 516, 518, 520.
*Lumber, rough, 102, 106, 161, 167, 168, 200, 252, 253, 254, 380, 440, 450, 475, 480, 508, 516.
Lunar equipment systems, 285.

Machetes, 102, 440, 475, 480.
Machine guns, 200, 279, 280.
Machine repair services, 200, 280, 418, 475, 504, 520.
Machine screws, 200, 253, 254, 285, 380, 440, 480, 490, 502, 508.
Machine shop items, 106, 150, 160, 162, 200, 253, 285, 380, 440, 480.
Machine shop kits, 200, 285, 380, 440, 502, 508.
Machine shop outfits, 200, 254, 380, 440, 475, 502, 508.
Machine shop sets, 200, 285, 380, 440, 475, 502, 508.
Machine shop trucks, 351, 380, 440.
Machine shop work, 285, 380, 440.
Machine tools, miscellaneous, 145, 150, 161, 162, 175, 200, 210, 254, 280, 285, 380, 418, 440, 450, 475, 480, 490, 502, 508, 515, 517.
Machine tools, portable, 161, 162, 175, 200, 253, 254, 285, 380, 418, 440, 450, 475, 480, 502, 508, 515.
Machinery, construction, 440, 475.
Machinery maintenance, specialized tools, 106, 175, 200, 285, 351, 380, 440, 475, 502, 508.

*Mandatory for purchase by United States agencies from Federal Prison Industries or Blind Made Products. When not available from these, purchase is made on the open market.

** See also Sales of Federal Timber, Part IV of this directory.

Machinery, industrial, 440.
Machinery, planting, seeding, fertilizing, 200, 380, 440, 480.
Magnet wire, 200, 285, 380, 450, 475, 480.
Magnetometers, 285, 517.
Magnetos, engine, 160, 161, 162, 380, 440, 475.
Magnetrons, 285.
Magnets, 440, 520.
Magnifiers, 150, 285, 380, 440, 475, 480, 490, 520.
Mailing machines, 150, 200, 354, 380, 418, 440, 450, 480, 502.
Maintenance and repair-shop specialized equipment, 160, 161, 162, 164, 175, 200, 253, 254, 285, 380, 418, 440, 475, 480, 508, 518.
Maintenance contracts, office machines, 145, 200, 280, 285, 300, 380, 410, 440, 480, 508, 633.
Maintenance, engine checks, repairs, aircraft, 160, 165, 166, 167, 280, 285, 353, 480, 517, 519b.
Maintenance equipment, specialized, motor vehicle, 161, 162, 175, 200, 251, 253, 280, 285, 380, 440, 475, 480, 490, 508, 513, 518.
Management consulting, 145, 160, 162, 165, 166, 167, 168, 169, 170, 200, 251, 280, 285, 353, 380, 410, 417, 440, 511, 512, 514, 519, 626.
Management engineering services, 160, 161, 162, 164, 165, 166, 167, 168, 169, 170, 200, 285, 380, 410, 440, 511, 512, 519.
Manicure implements, 504.
Mannequins, 210, 285.
Manometers, 285, 517.
Map files, 145, 280, 285, 440, 480.
Mapping cameras, motion-picture, 145, 285, 380, 440, 480.
Mapping instruments, 145, 285, 380, 440, 480, 513, 517.
Mapping, topographic, 285, 380, 440, 511, 517.
Maps, except training-aid maps, 145, 252, 253, 256, 280, 285, 380, 440, 480.
Maps, training-aid, 252, 253, 254, 280, 285, 440.
Marine electric lighting fixtures, 254, 380, 475.
Marine equipment, miscellaneous, 145, 285, 353, 440, 475.
Marine hardware, 167, 169, 200, 353, 440, 475.
Marine organisms, 418.
Marine rigging and rigging gear, 253.
Markets, grave, 440, 502.
Markers, survey, 160, 161, 165, 166, 167, 169, 380, 480, 517.
Market and trade studies, 145, 165, 168.
Markets, traffic, 440.
Marking devices (stamp pads, stamps, rubber, stamps, metal, including marking dies; seal presses; steel letters, figures and numerals; branding irons; and stencils), 280, 285, 300, 380, 410, 440, 450, 480, 485, 490, 520.
Marking machines, commercial laundry, 200, 253, 254, 418, 440, 502.
Masers, 285.
Mashers, food, 252, 253, 440, 502.
Masks, fencing, 380, 440, 475.
Mast fittings, 380.
Matches, 440, 504, 520.
Materials handling cranes, mobile, 175, 200, 285, 380, 440, 475, 480, 508, 511, 518.
Materials handling equipment, nonpowered, 145, 165, 166, 280, 285, 350, 380, 410, 413, 418, 440, 450, 475, 480, 502, 508, 518.
Materials handling rigging, 285, 380, 440, 518.
Mats, cocoa and rubber, 380, 440, 450, 520.

Mattress covers, 200, 380, 440, 475, 512.
*Mattresses, 162, 200, 303, 380, 440, 475, 502, 512.
Mattress manufacturing equipment, 254.
Meals and Lodging, 285, 380, 440, 508.
Measuring apparatus, rotation, 475.
Measuring equipment, distance (electronic), 145, 160, 285, 485, 511, 513, 517.
Measuring instruments, acidity (ph), 380, 440, 480, 502, 515.
Measuring instruments, alkalinity, 380, 440, 475, 480, 502, 508, 517.
Measuring instruments, fluid flow, 145, 285, 380, 440, 475, 480, 517.
Measuring instruments, liquid level, 145, 285, 380, 440, 475, 480, 508.
Measuring instruments, mechanical motion, 145, 380, 440, 475, 480, 508.
Measuring instruments, rotation, 145, 285, 380, 440, 475, 480, 508.
Measuring tools, craftsman's, 285, 380, 440, 480, 508, 520.
Medical braces, 200, 252, 253, 418c, 440, 508.
Medical consultants, 418c.
Medical equipment, 200, 252, 253, 285, 380, 415, 418c, 440, 450, 475, 480, 503, 530.
Medical instruments, 200, 252, 253, 380, 411a, 418c, 440, 450, 480.
Medical kits, 252, 253, 280, 440, 450, 502, 503.
Medical outfits, 252, 253, 440.
Medical research, 285, 380, 440, 500.
Medical sets, 252, 253, 440.
Medical supplies, 200, 252, 253, 285, 380, 411a, 418c, 440, 450, 475, 480, 502, 520.
Medical X-ray equipment, 200, 252, 253, 285, 380, 418c, 440, 450, 475, 480, 502.
Medical X-ray supplies, 200, 252, 253, 285, 380, 418c, 440, 450, 475, 480, 502.
Medical X-ray tubes, 200, 252, 253, 285, 380, 411a, 418c, 440, 450, 480, 502, 504.
Medicinal chemicals, 200, 252, 253, 280, 380, 418c, 440, 450, 480, 502.
Magameters, 380, 475, 480.
Memory cells, 285.
Mercury, 285, 380, 480.
Mercury lamps, 161, 165, 166, 200, 285, 380, 440, 475, 502.
Mesh, metal, industrial, 102, 253, 380, 475, 480.
Mess tables, 380, 440.
Metal castings, 145, 165, 166, 169, 200, 285, 351, 380, 440, 475, 480.
Metal cloth, industrial, 254, 380, 440, 475, 480, 502, 508.
Metal, electrotype backing, 450.
Metal extrusions, 160, 380, 480.
Metal, ferrous, all kinds, 102, 106, 110, 285, 380, 440, 450, 480, 518.
Metal finishing equipment, 254, 285, 351, 380, 440, 475.
Metal forming and cutting machines, 145, 165, 166, 169, 200, 254, 285, 350, 351, 380, 440, 450, 475, 480, 490.
Metal forming machines, primary, 200, 254, 351, 380, 440, 475, 490.
Metal lath, 200, 440, 475, 480.
Metal melting furnaces, 254, 351, 380, 515.
Metal, non-ferrous, all kinds, 102, 106, 285, 351, 380, 440, 480, 518, 520.
Metal products, fabricated, general, 145, 165, 166, 285, 380, 413, 440, 480.
Metal scrap, 254, 440.

*Mandatory for purchase by United States agencies from Federal Prison Industries or Blind Made Products. When not available from these, purchase is made on the open market.

Office machines (other than typewriters), rental, repair, maintenance, and reconditioning, 145, 165, 166, 190, 191, 192, 200, 256, 280, 285, 380, 410, 413, 418, 440, 475, 480, 485, 508, 512, 520.
Office machines, miscellaneous, 145, 150, 165, 166, 200, 251, 253, 254, 256, 280, 285, 300, 380, 410, 413, 418, 440, 450, 480, 490, 504, 508, 512, 515, 520.
Office moving services, 145, 150, 165, 256, 280, 410, 440, 512.
Office supplies, 145, 150, 165, 190, 191, 192, 200, 253, 254, 256, 280, 285, 380, 418, 440, 450, 475, 480, 490, 508, 512, 520.
Office trailers, 104, 165, 166, 285, 380, 440, 480, 513, 518.
Offset blankets, 145, 165, 169, 170, 418, 440.
Offset duplicating plates, regraining, 145, 165, 169, 170, 280, 418, 440, 450, 508.
Offset presses (10- x 15- inch printing area or less), 145, 165, 170, 254, 285, 380, 440, 450, 480, 485, 502, 508, 515.
Offset presses (over 10- x 15- inch printing area), 145, 165, 166, 169, 251, 254, 285, 350, 380, 440, 450, 508, 515.
Ohmeters, 160, 161, 162, 285, 380, 440, 475, 480, 485, 508.
Oil burners, 200, 380, 480, 508.
Oil filters, engine, 161, 280, 380, 440, 450, 480, 508.
Oil measures, 380, 440, 480, 508.
Oil retainers, 380, 475, 480, 508.
Oil strainers, engine, 285, 380, 508.
Oil tubing, 285, 380, 480, 508.
Oilcloth, 285, 440.
Oilers, hand, 285, 380, 440, 480, 508.
Oils, cutting, 200, 254, 380, 440, 450, 480, 508.
Oils, food, 102, 253, 380, 440, 475, 502, 504.
Oils, illuminating, 380.
Oils, lubricating, 104, 161, 200, 253, 254, 285, 380, 440, 450, 475, 480, 508, 520.
Oils, nonfood, 475.
Omnirange equipment, 160, 162.
Ophthalmological equipment, 200, 418c, 440.
Optical glass blanks, 285, 440.
Optical instruments, 145, 200, 285, 380, 418c, 440, 475, 480, 502, 517, 520.
Optical lenses, 285, 440, 517, 520.
Optical mirrors, 285, 440, 502.
Opticians' equipment, 200, 285, 440, 475, 508.
Opticians' instruments, 285, 440, 502, 508.
Opticians' supplies, 285, 440, 508.
Optometrists' equipment, 440, 475.
Optometrists' instruments, 440, 502, 508.
Orthopedic braces, 200, 253, 440, 475, 500, 508.
Orthopedic equipment, 200, 440, 500.
Orthopedic and prosthetic appliances, and their repair, 200, 418c, 440, 475, 500, 508.
Orthopedic shoes, 200, 440, 502, 508.
Orthopedic supplies, 200, 440, 475, 500, 508.
Oscillators, audio, 160, 162, 165, 166, 285, 440, 485, 517.
Oscillographs, 285, 440, 518.
Oscilloscopes, 145, 150, 160, 161, 162, 165, 166, 200, 285, 380, 418C, 440, 475, 480, 485, 513, 517, 518, 520.
Outboard engines, 440, 475, 480, 514, 516.
Outerwear, civilian, men's, 200, 380, 440, 480, 504.
Outerwear, civilian, women's, 200, 380, 440.
Outlet boxes, electrical, 160, 161, 162, 253, 254, 285, 380, 440, 475, 480, 508, 520.
Ovens, food industry, 200, 252, 253, 380, 440, 502, 504, 508.
Ovens, industrial, 200, 285, 380, 440.
Ovens, laboratory (soils), 103, 285, 380, 440.
Oxygen apparatus, 200, 252, 253, 285, 380, 440, 475, 480, 502, 508, 515.
Oxygen warning devices, aircraft, 285.

Package sealing machines, 256, 440, 450.
Packaging machinery, 350, 353, 354, 440, 475.
Packaging materials, 150, 253, 254, 280, 285, 350, 351, 380, 418, 440, 450, 520.
Packing, fabricated, 285, 418, 440, 475, 480.
Packing materials, bulk, specialized, 253, 254, 285, 351, 440, 475.
Padding materials, except feathers, and downs, unprocessed, 254, 285, 440, 508.
Padding stock (tire repair), 254.
Padlocks, 440, 503a, 517, 520.
Pads, composition, 285, 440, 490, 520.
Pads, rubber, 160, 162, 285, 380, 418c, 440, 490, 508, 520.
Pads, rug, 280, 285, 380, 418, 440, 480, 502, 508, 515.
Pads, shoulder, 253, 254, 440.
Pads, stamp, 280, 380, 440, 480, 490, 520.
Pads, typewriter, 200, 253, 380, 440, 508.
Pails, 200, 380, 440, 480.
Paint sealers, 102, 106, 200, 252, 253, 254, 285, 380, 440, 450, 480, 502, 508.
Paintspraying equipment, 190, 191, 200, 252, 254, 285, 380, 440, 450, 475, 480, 490, 502, 508.
Paints, 102, 106, 161, 175, 190, 200, 253, 254, 285, 380, 418, 440, 450, 455, 475, 480, 490, 502, 508, 518, 520.
Paints, oil, 102, 106, 145, 161, 190, 200, 252, 253, 254, 285, 380, 440, 450, 455, 475, 480, 502, 508, 516, 518.
Paints, water, 102, 106, 161, 200, 285, 440, 455, 480, 502, 508.
*Pallets, 200, 285, 380, 440, 450, 475, 480, 490, 502.
Pamphlets and books, nontechnical (excludes book music), 103, 145, 165, 167, 168, 169, 170, 171, 200, 251, 252, 253, 280, 285, 300, 305, 351, 380, 410, 418, 440, 480, 485, 503, 512, 515, 516, 518.
Pamphlets and books, technical (excludes book music), 145, 165, 166, 167, 168, 169, 170, 171, 200, 251, 253, 254, 280, 285, 380, 410, 415, 418, 440, 480, 503, 512, 515, 516, 518, 520.
Panelboards and wiring devices, 200, 285, 349, 350, 380, 440, 450, 475, 480, 511, 518, 519, 520.
Paneling, wood, 352.
Panels, electric distribution, 160, 162, 200, 285, 350, 380, 480, 511, 518, 520.
Panels, patch, 160, 162.
Panels, plywood, 102, 200, 253, 254, 285, 380, 440, 475, 508, 518.
Panels, prefabricated, 160, 162, 380, 418, 440, 480.
Panels, resectoring, 160, 162.
Panels, veneered, 102, 253, 254, 380, 440, 506.
Pans, cooking, 252, 253, 380, 440, 502, 504, 520.
Paper, 160, 161, 162, 254, 280, 285, 300, 305, 350, 380, 418, 440, 450, 475, 480, 490, 508, 520.
Paper, building, 102, 253, 380, 418, 440, 475, 480, 508.
Paper, chart recording, 145, 165, 166, 169, 285, 380, 418, 440, 520.
Paper, corrugated, 102, 200, 253, 254, 280, 285, 440, 475, 490, 502, 508.
Paper, counting machines, 110, 350, 380, 450.

*Mandatory for purchase by United States agencies from Federal Prison Industries or Blind Made Products. When not available from these, purchase is made on the open market.

Paper cups, 200, 380, 418, 440, 475, 480, 502, 504, 508.
Paper cutters, manual, 280, 285, 380, 440, 450, 475, 480, 508, 520.
Paper cutting machines, 145, 285, 350, 440, 450.
Paper facsimiles, 145, 165, 166, 256, 285, 440.
Paper fasteners, 280, 380, 440, 508, 520.
Paper materials, bulk, 145, 165, 166, 167, 168, 169, 170, 254, 285, 380, 508.
Paper, moisture vapor barrier, 285, 380, 440, 480, 508.
Paper plates, 380, 440, 475, 504.
Paper, printing, white copy, dry electrostatic process, 145, 165, 166, 169, 251, 285, 440.
Paper products, toiletry, 200, 285, 380, 440, 475.
Paper pulping machines, 440.
Paper pulverizing machines, 440.
Paper shredding machines, 256, 280, 440, 520.
Paper stock, book, 145, 165, 166, 169, 170, 280, 305, 418, 440, 450, 480, 490.
Paper, tar, 253, 380, 440, 475, 508.
Paper, toilet, 161, 163, 200, 285, 380, 440, 450, 475, 508.
Paper towels, 200, 285, 380, 418, 440, 450, 475, 508.
Paper tubing, 285, 380, 440.
Paper wrapping, 280, 350, 380, 440, 475, 480, 504, 508.
Paperboard, 350, 380, 440, 490.
Paperboard box blanks, 350, 440.
Paperboard corrugated boxes, 145, 150, 280, 285, 350, 418, 440, 475, 502.
Parachutes, 145, 165, 166, 285, 440.
Paraffin 520.
Paramedical Services, 418c.
Parcel Delivery 418.
Paring machines, food, 200, 253, 440, 508.
Parking meters, 200.
Passenger trailers, 380, 440, 517.
Passenger transport vessels, 190, 440.
Paste, core, 200, 254, 380, 440.
Patches, vulcanizing, 253, 254, 380, 440, 508.
Paulins, 165, 285, 380, 440, 480, 508.
Pavers, bituminous, 175, 200, 380, 440, 475.
Pavers, concrete, 175, 440, 475.
Peat, 440.
Pedicure implements, 508.
Peeling machines, food, 200, 253, 254, 380, 418, 440, 475, 508.
Pencils, 200, 380, 440, 475, 480, 504, 516, 520.
Pencil sharpeners, 285, 352, 380, 418, 440, 475, 516, 520.
Pennants and flags, 145, 165, 166, 167, 168, 169, 200, 280, 300, 380, 410, 418, 440, 475, 490, 502, 508.
Pen points, 200, 380, 440, 450, 475, 520.
Pens, ball point, 200, 285, 380, 440, 450, 475, 490, 504, 520.
Pens, fountain, 200, 285, 380, 440, 475, 504.
Penholders, 285, 380, 440.
Percale, 440.
Perfumes, 440.
Periodicals, 145, 160, 161, 162, 164, 165, 166, 167, 168, 169, 170, 171, 200, 210, 252, 253, 280, 285, 300, 305, 352, 380, 410, 418, 440, 475, 480, 503, 512, 513.
Periscopes, 285, 380, 440.
Personal safety equipment, 102, 165, 200, 254, 280, 285, 380, 418, 440, 450, 475, 480, 508.
Pest control agents, 200, 285, 380, 414, 440, 480, 508.
Pest control equipment, 200, 285, 414, 440, 480, 508.
Petrolatum, 440, 502.
Petroleum waxes, 380, 440, 480.
Paramaceuticals, 418.

Phonograph records, 200, 440, 475, 508.
Phonographs, home type, 440.
Photo carbons, 109, 285, 517.
Photo floodlight fixtures, 109, 145, 165, 166, 380, 440, 480, 508.
Photo-interpretation kits, 109, 253, 280.
Photocopy cameras, 109, 145, 150, 165, 166, 167, 168, 169, 170, 200, 280, 380, 410, 480, 508, 511, 515.
Photocopy machines, 256, 440, 485, 512.
Photoelectric cells, 285, 380, 475.
Photoengraving machinery, 350, 475.
Photoengraving & process cameras, 109, 145, 165, 166, 251, 440.
Photoflash bulbs, 109, 280, 285, 380, 418, 440, 475, 504, 508, 520.
Photogrammetric instruments, 145, 440, 480, 513, 517.
Photographic accessories, 104, 109, 145, 160, 161, 162, 166, 169, 200, 251, 256, 279, 280, 285, 350, 353, 380, 418, 440, 450, 475, 480, 508, 515, 520.
Photographic chemicals, specially packaged, 104, 109, 145, 150, 200, 253, 256, 280, 285, 379, 380, 418, 440, 475, 502, 508.
Photographic developing equipment, 104, 109, 145, 150, 200, 251, 253, 279, 280, 285, 380, 410, 413, 418, 440, 475, 480, 502.
Photographic dryers, 109, 145, 165, 166, 167, 168, 169, 170, 280, 285, 349, 380, 418, 440, 480, 502, 508.
Photographic editing equipment, 109, 145, 166, 167, 168, 169, 170, 251, 280, 285, 380, 418, 440, 480, 508.
Photographic enlarging equipment, 109, 145, 166, 167, 168, 169, 170, 251, 280, 285, 380, 418, 440, 480, 508, 515.
Photographic equipment, 145, 150, 166, 169, 256, 280, 418b, 450, 305, 516.
Photographic filters, 109, 280, 285, 380, 418, 440, 480, 508.
Photographic film processing, 411, 513.
Photographic finishing equipment, 109, 145, 165, 166, 167, 168, 169, 170, 251, 280, 285, 380, 418, 440, 475, 480, 508.
Photographic kits, 109, 285, 380, 418, 440, 508.
Photographic light meters, 103, 104, 109, 285, 380, 418, 440, 480, 508.
Photographic presses, 109, 440.
Photographic printers, 104, 109, 251, 253, 280, 285, 440, 508.
Photographic projection equipment, 103, 104, 109, 145, 160, 162, 165, 166, 169, 200, 251, 256, 280, 285, 380, 418, 440, 475, 480, 502, 508.
Photographic range finders, 103, 104, 109, 251, 280, 380, 413, 440.
Photographic refrigerators, 145, 285, 440.
Photographic screens, 104, 109, 200, 285, 380, 418, 440, 450, 475, 480, 508.
Photographic sensitized paper, 104, 109, 145, 150, 160, 162, 200, 280, 285, 380, 418, 440, 450, 475, 480, 502.
Photographic sets, 109, 285, 380, 410, 440.
Photographic supplies, 109, 145, 150, 160, 161, 162, 165, 166, 169, 200, 256, 280, 285, 380, 418, 440, 450, 475, 480, 502, 508, 515, 520.
Photographic tripods, 103, 104, 109, 285, 380, 418, 440, 506.
Photographic viewers, 109, 285, 380, 475, 508, 520.
Photographic washers, 102, 109, 165, 166, 169, 285, 380, 440, 502.
Photographic work, 280, 380, 410, 506.
Photomap projectors, 109, 145.
Photostat machines, 279, 280, 349, 380, 410, 418, 440, 450, 502, 508, 515.
Photostat service, 279, 410, 418, 440.
Physical properties inspecting equipment, 145, 380, 480.
Physical properties testing equipment, 145, 175, 200, 380, 440, 480.
Physical therapy equipment, 200, 251, 502.
Pick-up and delivery services, 256, 280, 300, 305.
Picks, 102, 253, 380, 440, 475, 480.
Pig iron, 200, 254, 440, 475.
Pigments, dry, 350, 440, 450.
Pigments, flushed, 350.
Pigments for coloring, 102, 106, 200, 440, 480, 508.
Pigs, steel, 200.
Piledriver barges, 475, 480.
Piledriving attachments, 175, 380, 475, 480, 511.
Piles, sheet metal, 285, 380, 480.
Piling, creosote, 475.
Piling, sheet, 175, 475, 480.
Piling, wood, 380, 440, 480.
Pilot, automatic, electric, for aircraft, 160, 162.
Pilot devices, electrical, 475, 480.
Pilot plant construction, for research in mineral and fuel fields, 380.
Pilot mechanism, automatic, 160, 285.
Pins, (hardware), 380, 440, 475, 480, 520.
Pins, (notions), 253, 254, 440, 504, 520.
Pins, leader, 475.
Pins, shafting, 254, 380, 475, 480.
Pins, tent, 440, 480.
Pins, wrist, engine, 380, 440, 513.
Pipe, cement, 520.
Pipe, clay, 102, 200, 253, 380, 440, 480, 508.
Pipe, concrete, 102, 175, 200, 285, 380, 440, 480, 508, 513, 518.
Pipe covering, 102, 200, 253, 380, 440, 480, 508, 520.
Pipe cutters, 200, 285, 380, 413, 440, 480, 508, 518.
Pipe fittings, 102, 106, 200, 253, 285, 380, 418, 440, 475, 480, 508, 513, 520.
Pipe furnaces, warm air, 380, 455, 508.
Pipe, iron (rigid), 102, 106, 161, 162, 200, 253, 380, 418, 440, 475, 480, 508, 513.
Pipe, nonferrous base metal (rigid), 102, 106, 161, 200, 254, 380, 475, 508, 513, 520.
Pipe, nonmetallic, 102, 106, 200, 380, 440, 480, 508, 513, 520.
Pipe, reamers, 380, 440, 475, 480, 508.
Pipe, steel (rigid only), 106, 161, 162, 175, 200, 285, 380, 440, 450, 475, 480, 508, 513, 515, 518.
Pipe, transite, cement, asbestos, 513.
Pipeless furnaces, warm air, 380, 506.
Pipeline assemblies, 440.
Pipes, clay, 440, 475, 508.
Piping anchors, 200, 440, 480, 508.
Piping expansion joints, 285, 380, 480, 508, 520.
Piping hangers, 380, 440, 480, 508, 520.
Piping joints, 380, 418, 440, 480, 508, 520.
Piping specialties, 380, 480, 508.
Piping supports, 380, 418, 440, 480, 508.
Piping traps, except plumbing, 380, 480.
Pistols, very, 200, 380.
Piston rings, 253, 440, 508.
Pistons, engine, 253, 380, 440.
Pitot tubes, 380.
Planners, 145, 175, 254, 285, 350, 351, 440, 475, 480, 508.
Plane tables, 480.
Planing mill machinery 440, 475.
Plant materials, crude grades, 380.
Plasterboard, 102, 253, 380, 440, 475, 480.
Plaster, gypsum, magnesia, 440.
Plastic, acetate, 104, 285, 380, 440, 450, 502, 517, 520.
Plastic fabricated materials, 145, 165, 166, 167, 169, 285, 380, 440, 480, 502, 508.
Plastic fabrics, 145, 165, 166, 167, 169, 200, 285, 380, 440, 450, 475.
Plastic, mylar, 280, 285, 300, 350, 440, 450, 502, 513, 517.
Plastic netting, 285, 440, 475.
Plastic pails, 350, 440.
Plastic products (molded), 160, 162, 285, 350, 380, 418, 440, 502.
Plastic sheeting, 104, 285, 380, 418, 440.
Plastic, surgical tape, 520.
Plastic tubs, 350, 440.
Plastic, vinyl, 104, 380, 418, 440, 450, 502, 517.
Plasticizer (Dioctyl Phthalate), 350.
Plasticizers (Polyvinyl Chloride Resin), 350.
Plastics, 160, 162, 285, 380, 440, 450.
Plastics, pipe and fittings, 285, 440, 475, 518.
Plate, black, 380, 440, 480, 518.
Plate, floor, steel, 285, 380, 475, 480, 518.
Plate, hooks, printing equipment, 254, 380, 440.
Plate, iron, 200, 285, 380, 440, 450, 475, 480, 518.
Plate, nonferrous base metal, 285, 350, 380, 440, 475, 480, 518.
Plate, pedestal mounting and ribframe assembly, 160, 162.
Plate, precious metals, 285, 380.
Plate, steel, 165, 166, 200, 254, 285, 350, 380, 440, 450, 475, 480, 518.
Plates, aluminum, litho, 380, 440, 450, 517.
Plates, lithographic, paper and metal, 150, 285, 380, 440, 450.
Plates, paper, 380, 440, 475, 504.
Plates, screw, 380, 440, 475.
Plates, tableware, 252, 380, 440, 502, 504.
Platform, maintenance and text, 160, 162.
Platform trucks, 145, 165, 166, 200, 350, 351, 380, 418, 440, 450, 475, 480, 490.
Platinum ware, 380, 517.
Playground equipment, 200, 440, 455, 475, 502, 508.
Playing cards, 200, 440, 502, 504.
Plexiglass, 285, 380, 418, 440, 450, 475, 480, 502, 520.
Pliers, 285, 380, 440, 475, 480, 490, 502, 508, 520.
Plotting boards, 145, 165, 166, 167, 169, 285, 380.
Plowing, 513.
Plugs, electrical, 161, 166, 285, 380, 440, 475, 508, 520.
Plumb bobs, 380, 440, 480, 508.
Plumbing accessories, 106, 192, 200, 285, 351, 380, 418, 440, 455, 475, 480, 508, 520.
Plumbing fittings, 106, 192, 200, 285, 351, 380, 418, 440, 450, 475, 480, 508, 520.
Plumbing fixtures, 106, 161, 192, 200, 285, 351, 380, 418, 440, 450, 455, 475, 480, 508.
Plumbing fixtures, trim, 192, 200, 285, 351, 380, 418, 440, 475, 480, 508.
Plumbing and heating equipment, miscellaneous, 106, 161, 162, 191, 192, 200, 285, 350, 351, 380, 418, 440, 450, 455, 480, 508.
Plywood, 102, 106, 200, 210, 253, 254, 285, 352, 418, 440, 450, 475, 480, 508, 518.
Plywood, panels, 102, 110, 200, 253, 254, 285, 380, 440, 475, 508, 518.
Pneumatic tub systems, 285, 380.
Pointers (electrical and electronic equipment), 380.
Pole line hardware, 160, 161, 380, 440, 480, 511, 518, 519.
Poles, wood, 200, 380, 440, 475, 480, 485, 511, 513, 518, 519.

Police equipment, 200, 251, 256, 280, 380, 440, 512.
Polishers, floor, 200, 380, 418, 440, 450, 475, 480, 490, 508.
Polishing compounds and preparations, 200, 253, 254, 285, 380, 440, 480, 502, 508, 520.
Polishing wheels, except dental, 285, 380, 440, 502, 605.
Pool equipment (tables), 165, 166, 440, 508.
Post, fence, steel, 165, 166, 285, 380, 440, 480, 513, 516.
Postage meters, 165, 166, 200, 380, 440, 480, 490.
Postal balances, 102, 103, 104, 440, 480, 490.
Postal scales, 280, 440, 480, 490, 508.
Posters, printed, 252, 253, 380, 440.
Posts, fuse, 165, 166, 285, 380, 475, 480, 508.
Potato chips, 200, 253, 440, 503a, 508.
Potheads, cable terminating, 110, 160, 162, 480, 511, 518.
Pots, cooking, 162, 200, 252, 253, 380, 418, 440, 502, 504.
Potters' supplies, 502.
Pountry equipment, 110.
Powders, scouring, 200, 252, 253, 254, 380, 440, 475, 480, 490, 508.
Powders, toilet, 380, 440.
Power fuses, 285, 440, 480, 511, 518.
Power and distribution equipment, electric, miscellaneous, 145, 160, 161, 162, 165, 166, 167, 169, 191, 192, 200, 254, 285, 305, 350, 351, 380, 440, 450, 455, 475, 480, 508, 511, 515, 518, 519, 520.
Power and distribution switchgear, 160, 162, 165, 166, 200, 254, 285, 305, 350, 380, 440, 475, 480, 508, 511, 518, 519.
Power level indicators products (molder) plastic, 160, 162, 440.
Power pumps, centrifugal, 175, 200, 285, 350, 380, 440, 450, 475, 480, 508, 511.
Power transmission equipment, miscellaneous, 165, 166, 285, 380, 440, 450, 480, 508, 518, 519.
Powerstats, 145, 165, 166, 167, 169, 440, 480, 508.
Precious metals, 145, 285, 380, 440, 450, 502.
Precious metals, primary forms, except dental, 380, 440.
Precipitrons, electronic, 380, 480.
Precision tapes, 285, 380, 440, 450.
Prefabricated buildings, 102, 160, 161, 162, 164, 165, 166, 175, 285, 380, 440, 475, 480, 485, 513.
Prefabricated structures, 145, 165, 166, 175, 280, 285, 380, 440, 480, 485, 513.
Preservative compounds, 190, 285, 380, 440, 480, 508.
Preservatives, wood, 440, 475, 480, 508.
Press clipping services, 150, 256, 285, 380, 410, 440, 634.
Pressers, photograhpic, 440.
Presses, coin (metal forming and cutting machines), 351, 440.
Presses, commercial dry cleaning, 200, 253, 254, 380, 418, 440, 502, 508.
Presses, hydraulic, 200, 254, 285, 350, 351, 380, 440, 450, 475, 480.
Presses, offset (10- x 15- inch printing area or less), 145, 165, 169, 254, 285, 349, 380, 440, 450, 480, 485, 502, 506, 515, 517.
Presses, offset (over 10- x 15-inch printing area), 165, 169, 251, 254, 285, 350, 380, 440, 450, 485, 508, 515, 517.
Presses, printing, all other, 165, 169, 440, 450, 475.
Pressure controlling instruments, 145, 165, 166, 167, 169, 170, 285, 380, 440, 475, 480, 508.
Pressure filters, 285, 380, 440, 480.
Pressure gages, 145, 165, 166, 167, 169, 170, 285, 380, 440, 450, 475, 480, 508, 520.
Pressure gun fittings, 285, 440, 480.
Pressure measuring instruments, 145, 165, 166, 167, 169, 170, 200, 285, 380, 440, 475, 480, 508, 520.
Pressure suits, 285.
Pressure tank enclosures, 285, 380.
Pressure transducers, 285.
Preventive compound, corrosion, 440, 475.
Primary and semifinished products, iron, 165, 166, 167, 169, 351, 380, 475.
Print shop furniture, 254, 380, 440, 450.
Printed circuits, 520.
Printed matter, miscellaneous, 145, 165, 169, 280, 285, 349, 380, 418, 440, 450, 503.
Printed posters, 252, 285, 380, 418, 440, 450, 451, 508.
Printed signs, 165, 166, 285, 380, 418, 440, 450, 451, 508.
Printers, photographic, 104, 109, 251, 253, 280, 285, 440.
*Printing and binding services (typesetting, printing, photoengraving, platemaking & bookbinding), 145, 200, 280, 349, 380, 410, 418, 440, 451, 508, 512.
Printing industries machinery and equipment, 169, 200, 254, 300, 350, 380, 413, 440, 450, 475, 502, 508, 515.
Printing leads, 254, 280, 380, 450, 502, 508.
Printing plate hooks, 254, 280, 380, 508.
Printing quoins, 254, 380, 450, 502.
Printing rules, 254, 380, 440, 450.
Printing slugs, 254, 380, 450, 502, 508.
Printing type, 254, 450, 502, 508, 515.
Probe (UHF)--(VHF) detectors, 160, 162, 165, 166.
Programming services, special, 145, 160, 165, 285, 410, 440, 450.
Projector, glide slope, 160, 440.
Projectors, photomap, 109, 440.
Propellants, bulk, 285, 380.
Propeller, aircraft, 516.
Propellers, ship, 475.
Property leasing, 165, 166, 280, 285, 440.
Prosthetic and orthopedic appliances and their repair, 440, 508.
Public address systems, 285, 380, 440, 480, 508.
Pulleys, 285, 380, 440, 450, 480, 508.
Pulse power frequency measuring unit detectors, 160, 162, 480, 485.
Pulse video counter, 160, 485.
Pulverizing equipment, minerals, 480.
Pumps, centrifugal, mixed-flow, 200, 285, 380, 440, 508, 511, 530.
Pumps, centrifugal, power, 175, 200, 285, 350, 351, 380, 440, 450, 475, 480, 508, 511, 530.
Pumps, centrifugal, propeller-type, 106, 175, 200, 380, 440, 475, 508, 511.
Pumps, fuel oil dispensing, 102, 106, 380, 440, 480, 508.
Pumps, fuel engine, 102, 200, 380, 440, 450, 475, 480, 508.
Pumps, gasoline dispensing, 102, 106, 285, 380, 440, 450, 475, 480, 490, 508, 516.
Pumps, gear, 285, 380, 480, 508, 511.
Pumps, hand, 102, 380, 440, 450, 475, 480, 508.
Pumps, miscellaneous, 102, 106, 190, 200, 285, 351, 380, 440, 450, 475, 480, 508, 530.
Pumps, oil dispensing, 102, 106, 380, 450, 490, 508.
Pumps, peripheral, 380, 440.

***Printing and binding services are not purchased by Government procurement offices except on waiver issued by the Government Printing Office.**

Pumps, reciprocating, piston-type, 102, 106, 200, 285, 380, 440, 475, 508.
Pumps, reciprocating, plunger-type, 102, 106, 200, 380, 440, 480, 508.
Pumps, reciprocating, power, 102, 106, 200, 285, 380, 440, 450, 475, 508.
Pumps, rotary, power, 102, 106, 285, 380, 440, 450, 475, 480, 508, 530.
Pumps, screw, 102, 106, 285, 380, 508.
Pumps, turbine, closed, 102, 106, 380, 440, 480, 508, 511.
Pumps, vacuum, except aircraft, 102, 106, 145, 165, 166, 167, 169, 200, 285, 380, 440, 450, 480, 508, 520.
Pumps, vane, 102, 106, 380, 440.
Pumps, water, internal combustion engine, 102, 106, 161, 285, 380, 440, 475, 480, 502, 508, 516.
Punch card service, 160, 200, 280, 285, 380, 410, 418, 440, 512.
Punch-card system machines, 145, 200, 280, 285, 380, 418, 440, 450, 480, 508.
Punches, office-type, 280, 285, 380, 440, 480, 508.
Punching machines (metalworking), 175, 254, 285, 351, 380, 440, 450, 475.
Punching machines, plastic element, 418, 440.
Purses, change, 504.
Pushcarts, 285, 418, 440, 480.
Putties, 440, 480, 508, 520.
Pyrotechnic signals, 200, 516.

Quarrying equipment, stone, 102, 104, 175.
Quartz, crystals, 440.
Quions (printing equipment), 254, 380, 450.

Races, bearing, 480.
Raceways, electrical, 380, 440, 475, 480, 508.
Racks (relay), 160, 162, 480, 518, 520.
Racks, film storage, steel, 285, 418, 440, 503.
Racks, (tier), carton storage, 352.
Racks, towel, 380, 440, 475, 480, 508.
Radar detecting trainers, 516.
Radar equipment, 145, 160, 161, 162, 165, 166, 167, 169, 170, 280, 285, 353, 475.
Radar test sets, 145, 160, 161, 162, 165, 166, 167, 169, 170, 280, 285, 380.
Radiation detection instruments, 110, 145, 285, 380, 440, 480, 485, 600.
Radiation protective clothing, 285, 380, 440.
Radiation shielding, 145, 285, 440, 520.
Radiators, 253, 440, 508.
Radiators, cooling system, internal combustion engine, 161, 253, 380, 440, 475, 480.
Radio communication equipment, 102, 102a, 145, 160, 161, 162, 164, 165, 166, 167, 168, 169, 200, 251, 252, 256, 279, 280, 285, 300, 305, 353, 354, 380, 440, 475, 480, 485, 508, 511, 512, 513, 516, 518, 519, 520.
Radio (field and course) dectors, 160, 162, 353, 380, 485.
Radio frequency amplifiers, 160, 162, 285, 300, 380, 485, 520.
Radio meters, 285, 485.
Radio test sets, 160, 161, 162, 164, 165, 166, 167, 168, 169, 170, 200, 279, 280, 285, 475, 480, 485, 502, 508, 513, 520.
Radio transmitters and relay stations, construction, 280, 300, 305, 380, 513, 518, 519.
Radio tubes, 102, 160, 162, 200, 285, 305, 380, 440, 475, 480, 508, 518, 520.
Radiological instruments, 285, 380, 440.
Radios, home-type, 165, 166, 200, 440, 502.
Radiosondes, 145, 165, 166.
Radiosondes, recorder, 145, 165, 166.
Radome, antenna shelter, plastic or fiber glass, 145, 160, 162, 165, 166, 353.
Railing, plastic, 160, 162.

Railroad cars, 440, 475.
Railroad gates, 475.
Railroad hardware, 200, 380, 475.
Railroad joint bars, 440, 480.
Railroad rails, 380, 475, 480.
Railroad signal and warning devices, 475.
Railroad spikes, 380, 440, 475, 480.
Railroad tie plates, 380, 440, 475, 480.
Railroad ties, wood, 200, 380, 440, 475, 480.
Rails, railroad, 380, 440, 475, 480.
Railway equipment, 440, 475.
Rainwear, plastic, 504.
Rakes, except fire and garden, 380, 440, 508.
Rakes, fire, 102, 380, 440, 514.
Rakes, garden, 200, 253, 380, 440.
Rams, hydraulic, 102, 106, 380.
Range finders, fire control, 514.
Range finders, photographic, 103, 104, 109, 251, 280, 285, 380, 410, 440.
Ranges, cooking, electrical, 200, 380, 440, 455, 475, 503a, 514.
Ranges, cooking, gas, 380, 440, 455.
Rasps, 380, 440, 475, 480, 502, 520.
Rayon fibers, 254.
Razor blades, 440, 475, 504.
Razors (all kinds), 440, 475, 502, 504, 508.
Reactors, nuclear, 480.
Real property, 440.
Reamers, metal working, 175, 200, 254, 380, 440, 475, 480, 502, 508.
Reamers, pipe, 380, 440, 450, 508, 580.
Recapping and repairing of tires, 200, 280, 380, 440, 475.
Receivers (radios) aircraft, 110, 160, 162, 285, 513, 516.
Receivers (radio) LF/MF, VHF, UHF, 102, 110, 145, 160, 162, 200, 251, 285, 300, 305, 485, 511, 513, 516, 517, 518, 519.
Receptacles, electrical, 150, 165, 166, 285, 380, 440, 475, 480, 508, 520.
Receptacles, wastepaper, 280, 380, 418, 440, 504, 508, 520.
Record equipment, visible, 150, 280, 285, 380, 418, 440, 480, 508, 515.
Record forms, 150, 200, 380, 440, 480, 508, 515.
Recorders, digital, 145, 285, 517, 520.
Recorders, film, 440.
Recorders, radiosonde, 145, 165, 166.
Recorders, liquid level, 440, 475.
Recorders, tape, 280, 353, 440, 503a, 512, 520.
Recording equipment, sound, 150, 160, 161, 162, 164, 253, 256, 279, 280, 285, 353, 380, 413, 440, 450, 502, 508, 512.
Recording, paper, chart, 145, 165, 166, 285, 380, 418, 440, 520.
Recording and transcription service, 145, 251, 280, 285, 410, 418, 440, 508.
Records, phonograph, 200, 440, 475, 502.
Recreational equipment, 253, 380, 440, 455, 475, 502, 508.
Rectifying equipment, electrical, 145, 160, 161, 165, 166, 167, 169, 170, 190, 285, 350, 380, 475, 480, 490, 508.
Rectifying equipment, rotating, electrical, 285, 380, 475.
Rectifying tubes, 160, 161, 162, 200, 285, 380, 475, 480, 508.
Reducers, line voltage, 145, 165, 166, 169, 285, 380, 450, 475, 480, 508.
Reels, fire hose, 102, 380, 440, 480, 508, 512.
Reels, film, 285, 305, 418, 440.
Reels, recording tape, magnetic oxide coated, 150, 285, 305, 418, 440.
Refinery machines, 351, 440.
Reflector, microwave, 160, 162, 285, 485.
Refractories, 380, 440, 475, 480, 508.
Refrigerant strainers, 380, 508.
Refrigerated display cases, 440, 475, 504.
Refrigeration equipment, commercial, 106, 110, 253, 380, 440, 508.
Refrigeration equipment, industrial, 200, 285, 380, 440, 450, 475, 508.
Refrigeration system components, 106, 110, 285, 475.
Refrigerators, household, 161, 200, 380, 418, 440, 455.
Refrigerators, mortuary, 440, 508.
Refrigerators, photographic, 280, 285, 440.
Refrigerators, professional, 106, 285, 440, 475.
Refrigerators, scientific, 106, 165, 166, 167, 169, 170, 192, 200, 285, 380, 418a, 440, 475, 508, 530.
Registers, cash, 440, 475.
Registers, wind velocity, 440.
Regraining of offset duplicating plates, 165, 169, 280, 440, 450.
Regulators, substation assembly, 160, 162.
Regulators, turbosupercharger, 380.
Regulators, voltage, engine, 160, 161, 162, 165, 166, 380, 440, 475, 485, 508, 520.
Rehabilitative services, 415.
Relays, 150, 160, 161, 162, 165, 166, 167, 168, 169, 170, 171, 285, 380, 440, 475, 480, 485, 508, 518, 520.
Remote sensing, 513.
Removers, wax, paint, varnish, 285, 440.
Rental, storage (aircraft), 102, 160, 161, 162, 165, 167, 480, 513, 518.
Rental of microphotographic equipment, 145, 150, 440, 508.
Rental of tabulating equipment, 145, 160, 161, 162, 164, 165, 166, 167, 168, 169, 170, 171, 172, 280, 285, 440, 450, 480, 500.
Repair-shop equipment, specialized (and Maintenance), 161, 162, 165, 166, 175, 200, 253, 254, 280, 380, 440, 475, 490, 508, 516, 518.
Repairs, building, 165, 166, 167, 168, 191, 192, 200, 210, 285, 300, 303, 440, 458, 512, 514.
Repair, maintenance and rehabilitation of public buildings, 440, 458, 512.
Repairs, motor vehicle body and fender, glass, and painting, 280, 380, 440, 514.
Reproducing equipment, sound, 160, 161, 162, 285, 300, 305, 380, 418, 440, 502, 503, 508.
Research and development; See part V.
Rescue equipment, 102, 303, 380, 440, 475, 480, 515.
Resin, polyvinyl chloride, 285, 350, 440.
Resistance bulbs, 380, 440, 480, 508.
Resistance wire, 285, 380, 440, 475, 480, 508.
Resistive attenuators, 285, 380, 485.
Resistive ballast tubes, 440, 480, 508.
Resistors, 150, 160, 161, 162, 285, 380, 440, 475, 480, 506, 520.
Respirators, 200, 285, 380, 440, 480, 520.
Restaurant equipment, 380, 475, 502, 504.
Retainers, oil, 285, 380, 475, 480, 508.
Revolution counters, 145, 165, 166, 380, 440, 475, 480.
Revolver holsters, 200, 251, 253, 256, 279, 280, 350, 380, 490, 512.
Rheostats, 440.
Ribbons, office machine, 150, 280, 285, 352, 380, 413, 418, 440, 450, 475, 480, 490, 508, 512, 520.
Ribbons, printer, 145, 150, 280, 300, 410, 440.
Ribbons, teletypewriter, 145, 150, 165, 166, 167, 168, 169, 170, 171, 256, 285, 300, 380, 418, 440, 475.
Rigging, materials, handling, 285, 380, 518.
Rings, cast iron, 520.
Rings, cork, 520.
Rings, piston, 253, 380, 440, 508.
Rippers, road, 102a, 175, 516.
Riveters, power-driven, 200, 285, 440, 475.
Rivets, 150, 200, 285, 380, 440, 480, 490, 520.
Road Construction, 102, 175, 191, 192, 200, 380, 455, 511, 512, 513, 514, 516, 518.
Road construction and repair equipment, 102, 104, 175, 200, 380, 440, 475, 480, 512, 514, 516.
Road Scrapers, 102, 104, 175, 200, 380, 440, 475, 480, 512, 516.
Rodenticides, 102, 200, 253, 285, 440, 480, 508.
Rods, glass, 285, 380, 440, 520.
Rods, ground, 160, 161, 162, 285, 440, 518.
Rods, hanger, 520.
Rods, level, 103, 104, 160, 161, 162, 380, 440, 475, 480, 517.
Rods, nonferrous base metal, 285, 380, 440, 450, 475, 480, 517.
Rods, plastic, 418.
Rods, precious metals, 380, 440, 502.
Rods, welding, 175, 200, 253, 254, 285, 380, 418, 440, 450, 475, 480, 502, 508.
Rods, for wire, iron, 380, 440, 475.
Rods for wire, steel, 380, 440, 475, 480.
Rollers, printing, rubber (recovering of), 350, 440.
Rollers, sheepsfoot, 175, 380, 440.
Rollers, tread, rubber, 175, 440, 450.
Rolling mills, 351, 380.
Roofing (all materials), 102, 161, 162, 200, 253, 285, 303, 380, 440, 450, 455, 475, 480, 520.
Roofing, felt, 102, 191, 192, 200, 253, 285, 380, 440, 450, 475, 508.
Roofing, sheet metal, 102, 161, 162, 200, 253, 254, 285, 380, 440, 475, 480, 508.
Roofing tile, 102, 180, 200, 253, 440, 508.
Rooters, 175, 380.
Rope, fiber, 254, 380, 440, 475, 480, 508, 520.
Rope fittings, 380, 440, 480, 508.
Rope, manila, 285, 380, 440, 475, 480.
Rope, nylon, 285, 475, 520.
Rope, textile, 254, 285, 380, 440, 480, 502.
Rope, wire, 175, 200, 285, 380, 440, 475, 480, 508, 514, 516, 518.
Rotating rectifying equipment, electrical, 285, 380, 475.
Rotation measuring apparatus, 475.
Rotation measuring instruments, 145, 285, 380, 475, 480, 508.
Rubber footwear, men's, 380, 440, 480, 503a, 508.
Rubber footwear, women's, 380, 440, 504.
Rubber mats, 285, 380, 418, 440, 480, 508.
Rubber, natural fabricated materials, 285, 380, 440, 480, 508.
Rubber, (recovering of printing rollers), 285, 350.
Rubber regroovers, 285, 440, 508.
Rubber sheeting, 200, 253, 285, 380, 440, 475, 480, 508.
Rubber synthetic, fabricated materials, 145, 285, 380, 440, 502.
Rubber tile, 102, 253, 285, 440, 475, 508.
Rubber vulcanizing machinery, 175, 508.
Rug pads, 280, 285, 418, 440, 480, 502, 508, 515.
Rugs, 150, 200, 280, 285, 300, 303, 380, 418, 440, 502, 508, 515.
Rulers, hardware, 520.
Rulers, office-type, 150, 200, 280, 285, 380, 440, 520.
Rules, printing, 150, 254, 285, 380, 440, 450, 502.
Rules, slide, 150, 285, 380, 440.
Rust-preventive compounds, 190, 285, 380, 440, 475, 480, 508.

Sacks, Jiffey bags, 520.
Safes, 280, 285, 380, 440, 475, 480, 490.
Safety apparel, personal, 102, 190, 191, 192, 200, 280, 285, 380, 418, 440, 450, 475, 480, 508.
Safety equipment, 102, 165, 191, 192, 200, 254, 285, 300, 303, 380, 418, 440, 450, 475, 480, 508, 515, 600.
Safety equipment, personal, 102, 165, 191, 192, 200, 254, 280, 380, 418, 440, 450, 475, 480, 508.
Safety fuses, 161, 285, 380, 440, 508.
Safety hats, 285, 418, 475.
Safety shoes, 200, 285, 380, 418, 440, 475, 480, 508.
Salvage apparatus, 475.
Sampling services, 410, 440.
Sand, 102, 106, 200, 285, 380, 440, 475, 480, 513.
Salt-water evaporator and distiller, 190.
Sanders, floor, 200, 380, 440, 450, 475, 480, 502, 508.
Sandwich grille, 200, 440, 475, 504.
Sanitation equipment, 440, 475.
Sash, window, metal, 102, 253, 380, 440, 475, 480, 508.
Sash, window, wood, 102, 253, 380, 440, 508.
Satchels, letter carriers, 440, 490.
Saw blades, concrete, 285, 440.
Saw blades, masonry, 285, 440.
Saw blades, plastic, 285, 440.
Saw blades, metalworking, 150, 285, 380, 440, 480, 520.
Saw blades, wood, 150, 285, 380, 440, 520.
Sawmill machinery, 440, 475.
Saws, hand, 102, 200, 285, 380, 440, 475, 508, 520.
Saws, masonry, 440.
Saws, metalworking machine, 145, 150, 175, 200, 254, 285, 351, 380, 440, 475, 480, 502, 508, 520.
Saws, portable, electric, 150, 166, 175, 200, 254, 285, 351, 380, 418, 440, 450, 475, 480, 502, 508, 514, 520.
Scaffolding equipment, 200, 285, 380, 418, 440, 475, 480, 508.
Scale models (training aids), 285, 380, 440.
Scales, architectural, 280, 440, 480, 508.
Scales, engineering, 160, 161, 162, 175, 280, 285, 380, 440, 480, 508, 517.
Scales, household, 200, 440, 502.
Scales, industrial, 200, 253, 285, 380, 440, 475, 480.
Scales, laboratory, 102, 103, 104, 106, 107, 108, 145, 165, 166, 167, 169, 170, 171, 175, 200, 252, 256, 285, 351, 380, 418, 440, 450, 475, 480, 502, 515, 516, 520.
Scales, postal, 280, 440, 450, 480, 490, 508.
School equipment and supplies, 200, 253, 440, 475, 508.
School furniture, 200, 253, 380, 440, 475, 508.
Scientific and Technical Studies, 145, 165, 166, 167, 168, 169, 170, 519.
Scooters, motorized, 440, 475, 480, 513.
Scouring powders, 200, 252, 253, 254, 285, 380, 440, 475, 480, 490, 508, 520.
Scows, 475.
Scrap, iron, 200, 254, 440.
Scrapers, road, 102, 104, 175, 440, 475, 480, 512, 516.
Screen cloth, 200, 285, 380, 440, 455, 475, 480.
Screening equipment, 102, 104, 200, 380, 440, 480.
Screening, metal, 102, 160, 161, 162, 200, 253, 285, 380, 418, 440, 475, 508.
Screening, plastic, 160, 162.
Screens, photographic, 104, 109, 200, 380, 418, 440, 450, 475, 480.
Screw drivers, 150, 253, 254, 285, 380, 440, 475, 480, 502, 508, 520.
Screw machine products, 160, 162, 285, 380, 440, 480.
Screw plates, 380, 440, 475.
Screws, 102, 150, 200, 253, 285, 380, 440, 450, 475, 480, 502, 508, 520.
Screws, machine, 200, 253, 254, 285, 380, 440, 475, 480, 490.
Scriptwriting service, 354, 380, 410, 513.
Sealers, paint, 102, 106, 200, 252, 253, 254, 285, 380, 440, 480, 502, 508.
Sealing compound, 102, 106, 253, 285, 380, 440, 450, 475, 480, 502, 508, 520.
Seals, fabricated, 285, 440, 475, 520.
Seals, lead, 101, 285, 355, 440, 450, 475, 490.
Seals, metal-band, 285, 440, 450, 475, 490.
Seals, shipping, 101, 109, 285, 380, 440, 480.
Searchlights, electric, 380, 440, 475, 480.
Seasonings, 102, 253, 440, 502.
Seat belts, 440, 475.
Seat covers, automobile, 200, 380, 440, 480, 508.
Seats, water closet, 380, 440, 455.
Secondary metal-forming and cutting machines, 380, 480, 502, 508.
Sectional shelving, 166, 200, 280, 285, 380, 418, 440, 480, 490, 508, 515, 517.
Security equipment and supplies, 110, 160, 192, 280, 285, 300, 354, 380, 418, 440, 508.
Security guard services, 280, 285, 512.
Seed drilling, 513.
Seed stock, 102, 192, 200, 253, 285, 440, 475, 480, 508, 513.
Seeders, lawn, 192, 200, 380, 440, 508.
Seedlings, tree, 440, 513.
Seismographic instruments, 145, 285, 380, 517.
Self-propelled cars, rail, 440, 475.
Semidiesel engines (all types), 175, 190, 380, 440.
Semitrailers, 175, 380, 440, 475, 513, 516.
Sensitized paper, photographic, 104, 109, 150, 160, 200, 280, 285, 380, 418, 440, 450, 475, 480, 502, 508.
Sensors, altitude, 285.
Separating equipment, 102, 380.
Separators, 252, 253, 285, 380, 450, 508.
Separators (packing materials), 102.
Septic tanks, 480, 506.
Services, Accounting and Auditing, 512, 626.
Services, building maintenance and operation, 280, 285, 305, 380, 440, 512.
Services, editorial, 410, 412, 440.
Services of consultants, management, technical engineering, etc., 103, 145, 160, 161, 162, 164, 200, 251, 285, 380, 410, 412, 413, 418, 440, 480, 485, 512, 514, 519, 600.
Services, pickup and delivery, 305.
Servomechanisms, 145, 285, 380.
Sewage treatment equipment, 165, 167, 168, 169, 200, 380, 440, 450, 514, 530.
Sewing machines, household, 200, 418, 440, 502.
Sewing machines, industrial, 200, 254, 351, 380, 418, 440, 450, 475, 490, 502.
Sewing machines, shoe, 200, 502.
Sextants, 475.
Shackles, 475, 480.
Shades, window, 200, 418, 440, 455, 508.
Shafting keys, 380, 475, 480, 508.
Shafting pins, 380, 475, 480.
Shafting propulsion, ship, 475.
Shafts, power transmission, 380.
Shapes, precious metals, 380.
Sharpeners, pencil, 150, 380, 440, 475, 520.
Shaving preparations, 440, 503, 504.
Shaving soap, 440, 475.
Shearing machines (metalworking), 145, 254, 285, 351, 380, 440, 475.
Shears and scissors, hand, 150, 169, 440, 520.
Sheepsfoot rollers, 166, 167, 175, 380, 440.
Sheet bar, steel, 150, 200, 254, 285, 380, 440, 450, 480, 508, 518.
Sheet, iron, 150, 200, 254, 380, 440, 475, 480, 508, 518.
Sheet metal, 150, 200, 254, 285, 350, 380, 418, 440, 450, 475, 480, 518.
Sheet metal piles, 380, 440, 475, 480.
Sheet metal products, 150, 354, 440.
Sheet metal roofing, 102, 161, 200, 253, 254, 380, 440, 475, 480, 508.
Sheet music, 200, 502, 508.
Sheet, nonferrous base metal, 200, 285, 380, 440, 450, 475, 480.
Sheet piling, 175, 380, 440, 475, 480.
Sheet, precious metals, 285, 380, 440, 502.
Sheet steel, 150, 200, 253, 254, 285, 380, 418, 440, 450, 475, 480, 502, 508, 518.
Sheeting, plastic, 104, 150, 285, 440.
Sheeting, rubber, 200, 253, 285, 380, 440, 475, 480, 508.
Shelter supports, instruments, 145, 166, 167.
Shelter, instrument, 167, 168, 169, 285, 440.
Shelter mounting, steel fixture, 160, 162.
Shellfish, 102, 200, 253, 475, 508.
Shelving, 165, 200, 210, 280, 285, 380, 418, 440, 450, 475, 480, 490, 508, 520.
Shin guards, hockey, 200, 440, 475.
Shingles, 102, 200, 253, 380, 440, 508.
Ship equipment, miscellaneous, 145, 191, 192.
Ship models, all kinds, 145, 190, 210.
Ship propellers, 475.
Ship stores, 475.
Shipping seals, 101, 380, 440, 480.
Shipping tags, 280, 285, 380, 440, 450, 475, 480, 490, 508.
Shirts, nonuniform, men's, 200, 253, 440, 502, 504.
Shirts, nonuniform, women's, 200, 440.
Shock absorbers, vehicular, 280, 380, 475, 508.
Shoe care items, 440, 504.
Shoe findings, 253, 254, 418, 440, 508.
Shoelaces, 253, 254, 440, 450, 503a, 508.
Shoe leather, 200, 253, 254, 418, 440, 502.
Shoemaking machinery, 200, 254, 440.
Shoe-manufacturing equipment, 254.
Shoe-repairing equipment, 200, 440.
Shoe-sewing machines, 200, 502.
Shoe-soling materials, 253, 254, 414.
Shoes, orthopedic, 200, 440, 508.
Shoes, safety, 175, 200, 285, 380, 418, 440, 450, 475, 480, 508, 520.
Shook, box, 200, 254, 380.
Shook, crate, 380.
Shop desks, 440.
Shoulder pads, 200, 253, 254, 440.
Shovel, convertible tracklaying and wheeled construction type, 175, 380, 440, 516.
Shovels, 102, 192, 200, 285, 380, 440, 475, 480, 508.
Shovels, for attachment on excavators, 102, 104, 175, 200, 380, 440, 516.
Shovels, power, 102, 175, 200, 285, 380, 440, 480, 514, 516.
Shower heads, 380, 440, 450, 508.
Siding materials, 120, 253, 440, 475, 480.
Sign boards, 150, 440.
Signal guns, 160, 162, 200.
Signal systems, traffic and transit, except railroad, 200, 380, 475.

Signals, pryotechnic, 516.
*Signs, 109, 165, 166, 280, 285, 380, 418, 440, 480, 516.
*Signs, metal, 102, 109, 160, 161, 162, 165, 166, 285, 380, 418, 440, 480, 508, 511, 518.
Silicofloride, 475.
Simulators, 285.
Siphons, iron, 520.
Skids, 145, 166, 167, 169, 285, 440, 450, 490.
Skis, 440.
Skis, aircraft, 516.
Skull crackers, crane and shovel, 102, 104, 175.
Slabs, nonferrous base metal, 380.
Slag block, 102, 200, 253, 380.
Sleeves, desiccator, 520.
Sleds, 440.
Sleeping pads, insulated, 508.
Slicing machines, food, 200, 252, 253, 254, 380, 418, 440, 475, 502, 504, 508.
Slide fasteners (hardware), 102, 253, 254, 285, 380, 440, 450, 475, 480, 508.
Slide fasteners (notions), 253, 254, 380, 475, 508.
Slide rules, 285, 380, 440.
Slides, recreational equipment, 440, 508.
Slings, 285, 440, 475.
Slotters and shapers, portable, 254, 475.
Slugs, printing equipment, 254, 380, 508.
Small arms, 280, 300, 353, 354, 440.
Small craft, 165, 166, 170, 190, 191, 192, 475, 480, 514.
Smokers' articles, 440, 504, 508.
Snake bite kits, 440.
Snap fasteners, 254, 285, 380, 440, 480.
Snaps (notions), 254, 440.
Snowplows, 175, 380, 440, 490.
Snuff, 440, 504.
Soap dispensers, 200, 285, 380, 440, 475, 502.
Soap, laundry, 200, 254, 380, 440.
Soap, paste, 418, 440.
Soap, powder, 200, 254, 380, 418, 440, 475, 504.
Soap, shaving, 440, 502, 504.
Soap stock, 380, 440, 480.
Soap, toilet, 200, 380, 440, 450, 503a, 508.
Sockets, tube, electrical, 285, 380, 440, 475, 480, 508, 520.
Socks, windcone, 160, 161, 162, 285.
Sod for landscaping, 200, 380, 440, 514.
Soda fountain equipment, 440, 475, 508.
Sodium hydroxide, 165, 440.
Sodium lamps, 380, 440.
Soft drinks, 200, 440, 475.
Soil preparation equipment, 106, 107, 253, 440, 480, 513.
Soil Surveys, 513.
Solar Energy Conversion Equipment, 285.
Solder, 380, 440, 520.
Sole pattern lasts (shoe findings), 253, 254, 418.
Solenoids, 285, 300, 380, 475.
Solid fuels, 253, 285, 380, 440, 480, 490, 508.
Soling materials, shoe, 253, 254, 418.
Solvent (trichloroethylene) 285, 350, 380, 440, 450.
Solvents, naptha, 254, 285, 440, 450, 480, 508.
Sorters (office machines), 150, 200, 380, 418, 440, 508, 515.
Sound equipment, underwater, 165, 167, 169, 170, 172, 285.
Sound recording equipment, except motion-pictures, 145, 150, 160, 161, 162, 164, 253, 279, 280, 285, 305, 418, 440, 508.

*Mandatory for purchase by United States agencies from Federal Prison Industries or Blind Made Products. When not available from these, purchase is made on the open market.

Sound reproducing equipment, 145, 160, 161, 162, 164, 285, 300, 305, 418, 440, 502, 503, 506.
Sounding devices, alarm and signal, 200, 251, 280, 285, 350, 380, 418, 440, 475, 480.
Soundproofing board, 102, 253, 380, 440, 450, 470, 475, 480, 508.
Spacecraft concepts, 285.
Space heating equipment, 160, 161, 162, 380, 440, 455, 508.
Spark plugs, suppressors, 380, 440, 475, 508.
Spark plugs, 161, 162, 200, 280, 380, 440, 475, 508.
Spatulas, 520.
Speakers, 160, 161, 162, 253, 280, 285, 380, 418, 440, 475, 502, 508, 520.
Special industry machinery, miscellaneous, 145, 253, 254, 285, 350, 380, 440.
Specialized attachments for earth moving and excavating trucks, 102, 104, 165, 175, 200, 380, 440, 480, 508, 516, 518.
Specifications, 285, 380, 480, 502, 503, 508.
Spectacle frames, 253, 440, 502.
Spectrophotometers, 145, 285, 440, 502, 517, 520, 530.
Spectrometers, 145, 285, 440, 502, 515, 520, 530.
Spectrum analyzers, 440, 485.
Splints, 380, 440, 480, 508.
Sponges, 380, 440, 450, 490.
Sporting and athletic goods, 200, 253, 440, 475, 508.
Spraying equipment, metal, 200, 254, 285, 380, 440, 480, 502.
Spraying equipment, paint, 166, 200, 252, 254, 285, 380, 440, 450, 475, 480, 490, 502, 508.
Spreaders, fertilizer, 200, 254, 440, 508, 513.
Spring and mattresses, 200, 303, 380, 440, 475.
Springs, valve, engine, 380, 440.
Springs, vehicular, 380, 440.
Springs, wire, 254, 285, 380, 440, 450, 480, 518.
Sprinkler heads, 192, 380, 440, 450, 480.
Sprinklers, lawn, 192, 440, 508.
Sprockets, 285, 440, 475, 480, 508.
Squares, 285, 380, 440, 480, 502.
Squilgees, 380, 440, 475, 508.
Stabilizing equipment, earth, 102, 104, 175.
Stains, (paint), 102, 106, 150, 200, 285, 380, 440, 475, 480, 502, 508.
Staircases, metal, 285, 440.
Stamp pads, 150, 280, 285, 352, 380, 440, 480, 490, 520.
Stamps, rubber, 150, 280, 285, 352, 380, 410, 418, 440, 450, 480, 485, 490, 508, 520.
Stands, calendar, 150, 285, 440.
Stands, music, 440, 475, 502.
Staplers, office-type, 150, 256, 280, 285, 380, 440, 508, 515, 520.
Staples, non-office-type, 102, 253, 254, 280, 285, 380, 418, 440, 475, 502, 520.
Staples, packaging, 150, 280, 285, 380, 418, 440.
Stapling machines, except office-type, 280, 285, 380, 418, 440, 450, 508, 517, 520.
Starches, 102, 200, 253, 254, 350, 440, 475, 502.
Starching machines, commercial laundry, 253, 254, 380, 508.
Starters, engine, electrical, 380, 440, 450, 508.
Starters, fire, 440.
Starters, fluorescent lamp, 440, 475.
Starting motors, engine, 160, 161, 162, 380, 440.
Station wagons, 440.
Stationery, 285, 352, 380, 440, 480, 490, 504, 515.

Steam cleaners, 175, 200, 285, 440, 475, 480.
Steam heating equipment, 200, 380, 418, 440, 455, 480, 508.
Steam tables, 200, 252, 253, 380, 418, 440, 503a, 508.
Steam turbines, 380, 440, 480, 508.
Steel bars, 200, 253, 254, 285, 350, 380, 440, 450, 475, 480, 518.
Steel billets, 285, 440, 475.
Steel blooms, 475.
Steel drums, 285, 380, 440.
Steel pigs, 200, 440.
Steel pipe (rigid), 106, 150, 161, 162, 175, 200, 285, 380, 418, 440, 450, 475, 480, 508, 515, 518.
Steel plate, 106, 150, 200, 254, 285, 350, 380, 418, 440, 450, 475, 480, 508, 518, 520.
Steel primary and semifinished products, 200, 285, 351, 380, 440, 508.
Steel rods for wire, 285, 380, 440, 475, 480.
Steel sheet, 106, 150, 200, 253, 254, 285, 380, 440, 450, 475, 480, 502, 508, 518.
Steel sheet bar, 106, 200, 254, 285, 380, 440, 450, 480, 508, 518, 520.
Steel strapping, 150, 253, 254, 285, 350, 380, 440, 450, 475, 480, 490, 508.
Steel strip, 106, 254, 285, 380, 440, 450, 475, 480, 490, 508, 518.
Steel tube (rigid), 106, 150, 254, 285, 380, 418, 440, 450, 475, 480, 508, 518.
Steel wire, nonelectrical, 150, 200, 254, 285, 380, 440, 475, 480, 490, 508, 519.
Steel wool, 285, 380, 440, 475, 490, 520.
Steering components, vehicular, 380, 440.
Stencil machines, office-type, 280, 285, 380, 418, 440, 508.
Stencils, die-impressed, 380, 440.
Stencils, duplicating machine, 285, 300, 305, 380, 418, 440, 485.
Stenographic reporting service, 101, 150, 160, 165, 190, 200, 251, 256, 280, 285, 300, 380, 410, 413, 418, 440, 485, 490, 513.
Sterilizers, 200, 380, 418, 440, 475, 480, 502, 508.
Stevedoring services (unloading, handling & storage), 440.
Stirrers, 520.
Stitching machines, 440, 450.
Stokers, 165, 167, 168, 169.
Stone, cut, 102, 200, 440.
Stone, cut, polished, 102, 440.
Stone, rough dimension, 102, 200, 440.
Stone-quarrying equipment, 102, 104, 175, 440, 475.
Storage tanks assembled, except water, 106, 160, 161, 162, 285, 380, 440, 480, 508, 518.
Storage tanks, oil, 380, 440.
Storage tanks, unassembled, except water, 106, 380, 440.
Storage tanks, water, 106, 167, 169, 200, 253, 380, 440, 480, 508, 513.
Stoves and ranges, domestic (except electric), 200, 300, 440.
Strain and standoff insulators, 160, 161, 162, 475, 480, 508.
Strainers, oil, engine, 380, 440, 475, 508.
Stainers, refrigerant, 380, 440, 508.
Strapping machines, 285, 380, 418, 440, 450, 490.
Strapping steel, 253, 254, 285, 380, 418, 440, 450, 480, 490.
Straw, 150, 200, 440, 480.
Straws, drinking, 440.
Strip, iron, 106, 380, 440, 475, 480.
Strip, nonferrous base metal, 106, 200, 380, 440, 475, 480, 490, 508.
Strip, precious metal, 285, 380, 440.
Strips, rubber, 285, 440.

Strips, terminal, 160, 161, 162, 285, 380, 475.
Structural glass, 102, 252, 253, 285, 380, 480, 508.
Structural shapes, nonferrous base metal, 106, 285, 380, 480, 518, 519.
Structural shapes (3 inches and over), steel, 175, 200, 254, 285, 380, 475, 480, 511, 518, 519.
Structural steel, fabricated, 106, 165, 166, 167, 168, 169, 285, 380, 480, 518, 519.
Structures, prefabricated, 165, 166, 167, 168, 175, 285, 380, 440, 480, 513.
Studies, See Part V, since studies are often performed in conjunction with Research and Development.
Studies, economic development, 145, 175, 300, 410, 440, 512, 633.
Studies, scientific and technical, 145, 175, 230, 285, 440, 511, 530, 633
Studies, trade and market, 145, 300, 440, 633.
Studies, Transportation, 160, 175, 629, 630, 631, 632.
Studio cameras, still-picture, 253, 285, 418, 440.
Studio equipment, radio and television, 285, 305, 418, 440.
Studs, (hardware), 285, 380, 440, 475, 480.
Studs, terminal (electrical), 160, 161, 162, 380, 475, 480.
Submersible vehicles, 145.
Substation assemblies, 160, 162.
Suitcases, 440, 475.
Summary boards and racks, 440.
Sunglasses, 440, 503a.
Supports for antenna and randome, 145, 160, 161, 162, 163.
Support, instrument shelter, 145, 165, 166, 167, 285.
Support, wind equipment, 145, 165, 166, 167, 285.
Supports, piping, 285, 380, 418, 480, 508.
Suppressors, spark plug, 380, 440, 475, 508.
Surgical braces, 200, 253, 440, 475, 506.
Surgical dressing material, 200, 253, 380, 440, 475, 480, 502.
Surgical dressings, 200, 253, 380, 418, 475, 480, 502.
Surgical equipment, 200, 253, 380, 418, 440, 450, 475, 480, 502.
Surgical instruments, 200, 253, 380, 418, 440, 450, 475, 480, 502.
Surgical supplies, 200, 253, 380, 418, 440, 450, 475, 480, 502.
Survey markers, 160, 162, 165, 166, 167, 169, 200, 380, 440, 475, 480, 513, 517, 518.
Surveying altimeters, 380, 440, 517, 518.
Surveying instruments, 103, 104, 145, 161, 162, 165, 166, 167, 169, 175, 200, 380, 440, 475, 480, 508, 511, 513, 517, 518.
Surveyors' chains, 161, 162, 200, 380, 440, 475, 480.
Surveyors' levels, 103, 104, 161, 162, 175, 200, 380, 440, 475, 480, 508, 517.
Surveyors' tapes, 161, 162, 200, 380, 440, 475, 480, 508.
Surveys, statistical 165, 175, 410, 412.
Survival equipment, 285, 475.
Suspenders, 418, 440, 504.
Swabs, deck, 440.
Sweepers, carpet, 200, 440, 475.
Swings (recreational equipment), 200, 440, 475.
Switches, electrical, 150, 160, 161, 162, 165, 166, 200, 285, 380, 440, 450, 475, 480, 485, 490, 508, 511, 518, 519, 520.
Switches, knife, 160, 161, 162, 285, 380, 440, 475, 480, 508, 520.
Switches, mercury, 285, 380, 440, 475, 480, 502, 508.
Switches, oil, 160, 161, 162, 285, 440, 480, 511, 518.
Switches, pushbutton, 440, 475, 480, 508.
Switches, rotary, electrical, 160, 161, 162, 165, 166, 285, 380, 440, 450, 475, 480.
Switches, safety, 160, 161, 162, 285, 440, 480.
Switches, toggle, 161, 285, 440, 475, 480, 490, 508, 520.
Switches, tumbler, 160, 161, 162, 285, 440.
Switchgear, power and distribution, 145, 160, 161, 254, 285, 305, 350, 380, 440, 475, 480, 508, 511, 518, 519.
Synthetic fibers, 200, 254, 440.
Systems equipment, Tacan, 160, 162.

Tablecloths, 200, 440, 500.
Tables, billiard, 440, 508.
Tables, mess, 200, 380, 440.
Tables, pool, 440, 508.
Tables, rate of return, 285.
Tables, steam, 200, 252, 253, 380, 440, 503a, 508.
Tables, work, kitchen, 161, 200, 252, 253, 380, 440, 475, 502, 504, 508.
Tableware, 200, 252, 253, 303, 380, 440, 475, 502, 504.
Tabulating cards, 145, 150, 256, 280, 410, 440, 520.
Tabulating equipment, rental, 160, 161, 162, 164, 280, 285, 410, 418, 440, 450, 485, 508.
Tabulators (office machines), 200, 280, 285, 380, 410, 418, 440, 485, 508.
Tacan equipment and systems, 160, 162.
Tachometers, 145, 165, 166, 167, 169, 170, 285, 380, 440, 475, 480, 508.
Tackle (materials handling), 380, 440.
Tackle blocks, 380, 440, 475, 480, 508.
Tacks, 253, 254, 380, 440, 475, 480, 502, 508, 520.
Tags, shipping, 150, 280, 285, 380, 440, 450, 480, 490, 508.
Tank, pressure, enclosures, 285, 380, 508.
Tank, stock watering, 513.
Tank, vacuum, enclosures, 285, 380, 508.
Tanks, fuel (steel), 160, 161, 162, 380, 440, 518.
Tanks, fuel, vehicular, 380, 440.
Tanks, oil storage, 380.
Tanks, septic, 167, 169, 480, 508.
Tanks storage, assembled, 160, 161, 162, 285, 380, 480, 508, 518.
Tanks, storage, unassembled, 380, 508.
Tanks, water storage, 167, 169, 200, 253, 380, 440, 480, 508, 513.
Tape dispensers, 150, 200, 285, 380, 440, 450, 505, 508, 516, 520.
Tape, friction, 153, 161, 162, 285, 380, 440, 475, 502, 508, 520.
Tape, gummed-paper, 150, 280, 285, 350, 380, 440, 450, 490, 508.
Tape, masking, 150, 285, 380, 440, 520.
Tape, plastic, insulation, 285, 440, 520.
Tape, pressure sensitive (all types), 145, 150, 165, 166, 256, 280, 285, 350, 418, 440, 450, 520.
Tape recorders 150, 256, 280, 353, 504, 512, 516, 520.
Tape recording, instrumentation, magnetic, oxide, coated, 145, 150, 280, 285, 418, 440.
Tape, sound recording magnetic oxide coated, 150, 285, 300, 418, 440.
Tape teletypewriter, 150, 256, 285, 418, 440, 475.
Tape measuring, all types, 150, 285, 380, 440, 490, 520.
Tapes, precision, 285, 380, 440, 450, 475.
Tapes, surveyors', 161, 162, 165, 166, 200, 440, 475, 480.
Tapes, metalworking, 254, 285, 380, 440, 475.
Tape, (shoe findings), 253, 254.
Tar, 440.
Tar paper, 253, 380, 440, 475, 508.
*Tarpaulins, 200, 285, 380, 440.
Taximeters, 380.
Technical and scientific studies, 145, 165, 166, 167, 168, 170, 172, 192, 411, 440.
Technical books and pamphlets, 145, 150, 165, 166, 167, 168, 169, 170, 171, 192, 200, 251, 253, 254, 280, 285, 300, 305, 380, 410, 418, 440, 475, 480, 485, 503, 512, 515, 516, 518, 520, 530.
Technical editing, 103, 192, 410, 411.
Technical writing, 210, 285, 380, 410, 418, 440, 626.
Tees, nonferrous base metal, 285, 380, 440, 480, 508.
Teeth, 200, 253, 440, 508.
Teflon, 520.
Telegraph equipment, 300, 380, 440.
Telemetering equipment, 145, 165, 166, 285, 380, 480, 511, 518, 519, 520.
Telephone equipment, 145, 165, 166, 200, 285, 380, 418, 440, 475, 480, 511, 512.
Telephone test sets, 380, 475, 480.
Teletype equipment, 145, 150, 160, 162, 165, 166, 252, 256, 280, 285, 300, 305, 380, 418, 440, 475, 480, 485.
Teletype news ticker service, 285, 305, 418, 440.
Teletype receiving keyers, diplex, 160, 162.
Teletypewriter ribbons, 145, 150, 165, 166, 285, 380, 418, 440, 475, 485.
Television, closed circuit, 256, 280, 285, 440, 450, 490.
Television, video tape, 256, 440, 490
Television communication equipment, 160, 164, 165, 166, 200, 252, 256, 285, 305, 380, 418, 440, 485.
Television productions, video tape and film, 145, 353, 354, 440.
Television sets, home-type 200, 418, 440.
Television test equipment, 440, 485.
Temperature controlling instruments, 145, 160, 161, 162, 165, 166, 169, 285, 380, 440, 450, 475, 480, 508, 515, 520.
Temperature measuring instruments, 145, 161, 162, 165, 166, 169, 200, 285, 380, 440, 475, 480, 508, 515, 520, 530.
Templates, 150, 280, 285, 380, 440.
Tenoners, 254, 475.
Tent materials, 380, 480, 513.
Tent pins, 440, 480.
*Tents, 380, 440.
Terminal strips (electrical), 161, 162, 285, 380, 475, 480.
Terminal studs (electrical), 161, 162, 285, 380, 475, 480.
Terminals (electrical), 145, 161, 285, 380, 475, 480, 520
Terra cotta, architectural, 102, 200, 253, 475.
Test clips, 285, 380, 475, 480.
Test sets, cable, 380, 418, 475, 480.
Test sets, communications, 160, 161, 162, 164, 279, 285, 380, 475, 480, 508.
Test sets, radar, 145, 160, 161, 162, 164, 165, 166, 167, 169, 285, 380.
Test sets, radio, 160, 161, 162, 164, 165, 166, 167, 168, 169, 200, 279, 280, 285, 353, 380, 475, 480, 502, 508, 513.
Test sets, telephone, 380, 475, 480.

*Mandatory for purchase by United States agencies from Federal Prison Industries or Blind Made Products. When not available from these, purchase is made on the open market.

Transmission assemblies, vehicular, 380, 440.
Transmission line construction, 380, 455, 511, 518, 519.
Transmission line construction (including towers and equipment, substations, etc.), 380, 511, 518, 519.
Transmitters, communication, 165, 166, 305, 485.
Transmitters, navigational instrument, 145, 160, 162.
Transponders, 145, 285.
Transportation of motion picture films, 145, 165.
Transportation, air, bus, ocean, rail, and truck, 145, 150, 280, 285, 380, 440, 450, 632.
Transportation, energy interface, 626.
Transportation, highway, contract, 440, 490.
Transportation of motion picture films, 508.
Transportation of passengers and baggage, 165, 200, 285, 418, 440.
Traps, game, rodent, 440.
Traps, piping, except plumbing, 380, 480, 520.
Trays, food and serving, 200, 380, 440, 504.
Tread rollers, rubber, 175, 450.
Treads, tracklaying rubber, 508.
Tree planting, 513.
Tree thinning, 513.
Tripods, used in chemistry, 520.
Tripods, photographic, 104, 109, 166, 285, 380, 410, 418, 440, 508.
Trophies, 440.
Truck attachments for earth moving and excavating, 102, 103, 104, 165, 175, 200, 440, 480, 508, 516, 518.
Truck, chasis only, 200.
Truck, Compactor, Refuse, 200.
Trucks, crash, 160, 161, 162, 164, 440.
Trucks, fire, 102, 200, 285, 380, 440, 475, 480, 513, 514.
Trucks, fuel servicing, 380, 440, 475.
Trucks, garbage, 200, 380, 440, 475, 508.
Trucks, hand, 200, 253, 254, 285, 350, 351, 380, 418, 440, 450, 475, 480, 490, 502, 504, 508, 520.
Trucks, industrial, 200, 285, 350, 380, 413, 440, 450, 480.
Trucks, special construction (earth and rock hauling), 102, 104, 175, 200, 350, 440, 475.
Trucks, specialized (X-ray laboratory, medical laboratory, machine shop, dormitory), 175, 417, 440, 450.
Trucks, tank, 145, 175, 380, 440, 475, 480.
Trucks, warehouse, 165, 200, 254, 285, 380, 410, 413, 418, 440, 450, 475, 480, 490.
Trucks, wrecker, 200, 380, 440.
Truck-tractor and trailer combinations, 102a, 175, 200, 380, 440, 490, 514, 516.
Truck-tractors, 175, 200, 380, 440, 475, 480, 514, 516.
Tube fittings, 285, 380, 418, 440, 480.
Tube, iron, (rigid), 285, 350, 380, 418, 480.
Tube repair kits, 380, 440, 508.
Tube repair materials, 380, 508.
Tube rounds, 285, 380.
Tube sockets, electrical, 285, 380, 440, 475, 480, 508.
Tube, steel (rigid), 150, 165, 254, 285, 380, 418, 450, 475, 480, 508, 518.
Tube, systems, pneumatic, 380, 450, 508.
Tubes, ballast, resistive, 440, 480, 508.
Tubes, electron, except medical, 145, 160, 162, 165, 200, 279, 280, 285, 305, 380, 418, 440, 450, 475, 480, 508, 518, 520.
Tubes, glass, 285, 380, 418, 440, 450, 502, 508, 520.
Tubes, inner, aircraft, 440.
Tubes, inner, except aircraft, 380, 440.
Tubes, insulating, 380, 440, 475, 508, 520.
Tubes, pilot, 380, 440.
Tubes, radio, 102, 160, 161, 165, 166, 200, 285, 305, 380, 440, 475, 480, 508, 518.
Tubes, rectifying, 160, 161, 162, 165, 166, 200, 285, 380, 418, 475, 480, 508.
Tubes, relief, aircraft, 285.
Tubes, tire, 440.
Tubes, venturi, 285, 380, 480.
Tubes, X-ray, medical, 200, 252, 253, 285, 380, 418, 440, 450, 480, 502, 508.
Tubing, air, flexible, nonmetallic, 102, 253, 254, 380, 440, 480, 508.
Tubing, chemical, flexible, nonmetallic, 102, 285, 380, 440, 480, 502, 508.
Tubing, flexible, metallic, 102, 200, 285, 380, 440, 450, 480, 508, 518.
Tubing, fuel, flexible, nonmetallic, 102, 285, 475, 508.
Tubing, glass, 285, 380, 440, 450, 480, 502, 508, 520.
Tubing, hydraulic, flexible, nonmetallic, 285, 380, 440, 502.
Tubing, nonmetallic, flexible, 165, 200, 285, 380, 440, 480, 508.
Tubing, oil, flexible, nonmetallic, 285, 380, 440, 508.
Tubing, paper, 380, 440, 520.
Tubing, precious metals, 380.
Tubing, water, flexible, nonmetallic, 102, 285, 480, 508.
Tugs, 475.
Tumblers, drying (commercial laundry), 254, 418, 440, 502, 508.
Tumbling mills, 254, 351.
Tung oil, 440.
Tuning forks, 440, 508.
Turbine components, 285, 413, 480.
Turbines, gas, except aircraft, 380, 440, 480.
Turbines, steam, 285, 380, 440, 480, 508.
Turbines, water, 285, 440, 480, 511.
Turnbuckles, 380, 440, 475, 480, 508, 520.
Turpentine, 380, 440, 475, 502, 508, 520.
Twinax cable, 165.
Twine & cordage, 200, 280, 380, 410, 440, 450, 508.
Twine, cotton & jute, 200, 440, 450, 475, 490, 508, 520.
Type, printing, 254, 440, 450, 515.
Typesetting machinery, 200, 254, 450, 475.
Typewriters, 145, 150, 190, 191, 192, 200, 256, 280, 285, 300, 352, 353, 380, 410, 418, 440, 475, 508, 512, 515, 520.
Typewriters, electric: Maintenance and reconditioning, 145, 150, 190, 191, 192, 251, 256, 260, 285, 353, 380, 418, 440, 475, 485, 508, 512, 515, 520.
Typewriters, manual: Repair, maintenance & reconditioning, 145, 280, 300, 352, 418, 440, 485, 508, 515, 520.

Ultraviolet (actinic) commercial processing units, 380.
Underwater log equipment, 475.
Underwater sound equipment, 285.
Underwear, men's 200, 440, 502.
Underwear, women's, 200, 440.
Uniform shirts, nonmilitary, men's, 200, 210, 353, 380, 440, 480, 516.
Uniforms, nonmilitary, men's, 200, 210, 353, 380, 418, 440, 475, 480, 516.
Uniforms, nonmilitary, women's, 200, 210, 351, 353, 418, 440, 480.
Universal joints, vehicular, 380, 508.
Upholstery fabrics, 254, 303, 418, 440, 508.
Upholstery leather, 254, 418, 440, 502, 508.
Urns, burial, 440, 475, 508.
Utensils, kitchen, 102, 161, 200, 252, 253, 303, 380, 418, 440, 475, 502, 504, 508.
Utility kits, 440, 504.

Vacuum bottles, 285, 380, 418, 440, 480, 502.
Vacuum cleaners, domestic, 200, 440, 450, 475, 520.
Vacuum cleaners, industrial, 192, 200, 380, 418, 440, 480, 490.
Vacuum filters, 285, 380, 480, 520.
Vacuum jugs, 285, 502.
Vacuum pumps, except aircraft, 102, 106, 145, 150, 165, 200, 285, 380, 440, 480, 508, 520.
Vacuum tank enclosures, 285, 380, 508.
Vacuum tube test sets, 160, 162, 165, 285, 380, 440, 475, 480.
Valve cocks, 285, 380, 440, 475, 480.
Valve cores, inner tube, 380, 440, 508.
Valve springs, engine, 380, 440.
Valves, air radiator, 440.
Valves, angle, 285, 380, 440, 450, 475, 480, 508, 520.
Valves, automatic, non-powered, 285, 380, 418, 440, 450, 480, 508.
Valves, check, 200, 285, 380, 440, 450, 475, 480, 508, 511.
Valves, engine, 380, 440, 450, 508.
Valves, external pilot-operated, 285, 380, 440, 475, 480, 508.
Valves, flush, plumbing, 285, 380, 440, 450, 475, 480, 508, 520.
Valves, gate, 200, 285, 380, 440, 450, 475, 480, 508, 511.
Valves, globe, 200, 285, 380, 440, 450, 475, 480, 508, 511.
Valves, hydraulic-operated, 285, 380, 440, 475, 480.
Valves, inner tube, 380, 440, 475, 508.
Valves, instrument-operated, 285, 380, 418, 440, 480, 508.
Valves, mechanically operated, 285, 380, 440, 475, 480, 508.
Valves, non-powered, 285, 380, 413, 440, 480, 508.
Valves, powered, 285, 380, 440, 475, 480, 508, 511.
Valves, relief, 106, 110, 285, 380, 440, 450, 475, 480, 508.
Valves, solenoid-operated, 285, 380, 450, 475, 480, 508, 511.
Valves, stop, plumbing, 380, 440, 475.
Varitype machines, 280, 380, 418, 440, 450.
Varnished cambric, insulating, 380, 475, 480.
Varnishes, 102, 106, 161, 162, 200, 253, 254, 285, 380, 440, 450, 475, 480, 520.
Varnishes, lithographic, 350, 440, 450.
Vegetable fibers, except brush fibers, 254, 440.
Vehicles, over-snow traveling, 103, 104, 280, 440, 514.
Vehicle maintenance, 513.
Vehicles, special purpose, 145, 280, 285, 440.
Vehicular accessories, 175, 200, 285, 380, 440, 450, 475, 480.
Vending machines, 200, 475, 490, 504.
Veneer, 102, 200, 253, 254, 440.
Veneer lathes, 254.
Veneered panels, 102, 253, 254, 285, 440, 508.
Venetian blind hardware, 200, 440, 475, 508.
Venetian blinds, 200, 285, 380, 418, 440, 450, 475, 480, 490.
Ventilating, heating, and air conditioning equipment, 102, 110, 160, 161, 162, 192, 285, 350, 351, 380, 440, 475, 480, 508.
Ventilators, ship, 274.
Venturi tubes, 285, 380, 480.
Very pistols, 200, 380.
Vessel, charter, trawler w/fishing equipment, 166.

Veterinary equipment, 106, 110, 440, 475.
Veterinary instruments, 106, 110, 440, 475.
Veterinary services, 200, 440.
Veterinary supplies, 106, 110, 440, 475.
Veterinary X-ray equipment, 440.
Vibrators, concrete, 102, 104, 175, 285, 380, 475, 480.
Vibrators, electrical, 285.
Video tape transfer, 305.
Viewers, photographic, 109, 150, 285, 380, 418, 475, 485, 508.
Vinyl, plastic, 104, 285, 450, 502, 517, 520.
Vises and clamps, 285, 440, 450, 475, 520.
Visible light communication equipment, 160, 160a, 285, 380.
Visible record equipment, 150, 256, 280, 285, 380, 418, 440, 480, 508, 515.
Voltmeters, 150, 160, 161, 162, 165, 166, 167, 169, 285, 380, 440, 475, 480, 518, 520.
Vulcanizing machinery, rubber, 440, 508.
Vulcanizing patches, 253, 254, 380, 440, 508.

Wadding, cotton, 200, 254, 285, 440, 502, 508.
Wagons, 102, 285.
Wagons, farm, 440.
Wall fillers, 380, 440.
Wallboard, 102, 161, 162, 200, 253, 285, 380, 440, 475, 480, 508.
Warehouse cranes, 285, 380, 440, 480.
Warehouse tractors, 200, 285, 380, 440, 475, 480, 490.
Warehouse trailers, 285, 380, 440, 475, 490.
Warehouse trucks, 145, 165, 166, 200, 254, 285, 380, 410, 418, 440, 450, 475, 480, 490.
Warehousing service, 280, 285, 353, 440.
Warm air furnaces, 380, 440, 508.
Warming equipment, food, 200, 252, 253, 380, 418, 440, 502, 504.
Washers (hardware), 200, 253, 254, 285, 380, 440, 480, 508, 520.
Washers, bottle, 106, 200, 285, 380, 440, 502.
Washers, commercial laundry, 200, 253, 254, 418, 440, 502, 508.
Washers, home laundry, 200, 440, 475.
Washers, photographic, 102, 109, 145, 165, 166, 169, 285, 380, 410, 440, 508.
Washing compounds, 200, 252, 253, 254, 285, 380, 440, 480, 508.
Waste, cotton, 285, 440, 475.
*Wastepaper receptacles, 280, 285, 380, 418, 440, 504, 508, 520.
Watch bands, 440, 504.
Watch glass, 520.
Watch movements, 165, 166, 167, 169, 170, 480.
Watches, 165, 166, 167, 169, 170, 285, 380, 440, 480, 504, 517, 520.
Water columns, 380.
Water coolers, 200, 285, 380, 440, 450, 475.
Water distillation equipment, 106, 145, 285, 380, 418a, 480, 530.
Water gates, 513.
Water guzzlers, 513.
Water heaters, domestic, 200, 380, 440, 455, 475, 480, 508.
Water-purification equipment, 285, 380, 440, 450, 475, 480, 508, 530.
Water-purifying compounds, 285, 380, 440, 475, 480, 508, 530.
Water-resistant compounds, 285, 380, 440, 480, 503, 508.
Water-softening compounds, 380, 418, 440, 480, 503, 508.
Water supply systems, automatic, 440.

*Mandatory for purchase by United States agencies from Federal Prison Industries or Blind Made Products. When not available from these, purchase is made on the open market.

Water turbines, 440, 480, 511.
Wattmeters, 165, 166, 285, 380, 475, 480, 485, 508, 518, 520.
Waveguides & related equipment, 160, 165, 285, 380.
Waxes, non-petroleum, 200, 285, 380, 440, 520.
Waxes, petroleum, 285, 380, 440, 480, 520.
Weatherstripping, 380, 440, 475.
Weather-resistant compounds, 285, 380, 440, 480, 508, 513.
Weather stations, 513.
Webbing, 350, 440.
Weed killers, 102, 106, 253, 380, 440, 475, 480, 508, 513, 516, 518.
Wedges, steel, 520.
Weeders, 440, 480.
Weighing services, 440.
Welders, engine-driven, 102a, 285, 380, 475.
*Welders' gloves, 200, 285, 380, 440, 450, 475, 480, 508, 516.
Welders' helmets, 200, 254, 285, 380, 440, 450, 475, 480, 508, 516.
Welding electrodes, 175, 253, 254, 285, 380, 440, 450, 475, 480, 502, 508.
Welding equipoment, 106, 150, 175, 200, 253, 254, 285, 380, 418, 440, 450, 475, 480, 490, 502, 508, 516, 520.
Welding rods, 175, 200, 253, 254, 285, 380, 418, 440, 450, 475, 480, 502, 508, 516.
Welding supplies, 106, 150, 175, 200, 253, 254, 285, 380, 440, 450, 475, 480.
Well drilling, 380, 512, 513, 514, 517.
Well drilling equipment, 440.
Wheel aligners, motor vehicle, 175, 200, 280, 380, 440, 475, 490, 508.
Wheel chairs, 200, 253, 418, 440, 475, 502, 508.
Wheelbarrows, 380, 440, 475, 508, 516.
*Whiskbrooms, 200, 380, 440, 480.
Whistles, air and steam, 380.
Wicks, cotton, 520.
Winches, 175, 380, 440, 475, 480.
Wind engines, 513.
Wind equipment support, 145, 165, 166, 285.
Windcone socks, 160, 161, 162, 285.
Windlasses, 440, 475, 480.
Windmill, complete, 440, 513.
Window frames, wood, 102, 380, 440, 508.
Window glass, 150, 200, 285, 380, 440, 450, 475, 480, 508.
Window sash, metal, 102, 107, 253, 380, 440, 475, 480, 508.
Window sash, wood, 102, 107, 253, 285, 380, 440, 508.
Window shade hardware, 200, 285, 380, 440, 508.
Windshield wipers, vehicular, 200, 380, 440, 475, 515.
Wine, 502.
Wiping cloths, 285, 351, 380, 418, 440, 450, 475, 480, 490.
Wiping cloths service, 150, 200, 254, 285, 410, 440, 450, 480, 485, 508, 514, 515.
Wire, antenna, 145, 160, 161, 162, 165, 166, 253, 280, 285, 380, 440, 475, 480, 508.
Wire, barbed, 380, 440, 475.
Wire, bare copper, 160, 161, 162, 285, 380, 440, 480, 518.
Wire, bookbinders', 350, 440, 450.
Wire brush wheels, 285, 380, 440, 475, 480.
Wire chain, 380, 440, 475, 480.
Wire cloth, 160, 161, 162, 285, 380, 440, 450, 475, 480.

*Mandatory for purchase by United States agencies from Federal Prison Industries or Blind Made Products. When not available from these, purchase is made on the open market.

Wire, electrical, insulated, 150, 160, 161, 162, 165, 166, 167, 168, 169, 170, 171, 200, 285, 305, 380, 440, 450, 475, 480, 490, 508, 511, 515, 516, 518, 519, 520.
Wire, electrical, non-insulated, 145, 150, 160, 161, 162, 166, 167, 168, 169, 170, 200, 285, 305, 380, 440, 475, 480, 508, 511, 518, 519, 520.
Wire, electronic, 145, 150, 165, 166, 167, 168, 169, 170, 285, 380, 440, 475, 480, 508, 514, 516, 518, 520.
Wire, enamel, 160, 161, 162.
Wire forming machines, 380.
Wire, fuse, 285, 380, 440, 475, 480, 508.
Wire, iron, nonelectrical, 285, 380, 440, 475, 480, 508.
Wire, magnet, 200, 285, 380, 450, 475, 480, 520.
Wire, nonferrous base metal, nonelectrical, 200, 285, 350, 380, 440, 475, 480, 490.
Wire, resistance, 285, 380, 475, 480, 508.
Wire rope, 175, 200, 285, 380, 440, 475, 480, 508, 514, 516, 518.
Wire springs, 254, 285, 380, 450, 475, 480, 508, 520.
Wire steel, 160, 161, 162, 285, 380.
Wire steel, nonelectrical, 200, 254, 285, 380, 440, 475, 480, 490, 508, 519.
Wire, thermocouple, 285.
Wiring devices and panelboards, 160, 162, 200, 285, 304, 349, 350, 380, 440, 450, 475, 480, 511, 518, 519, 520.
Wood blocks (currency packing), 350.
Wood fillers, 102, 106, 254, 380, 440, 480, 508, 520.
Wood materials, basic, 102, 253, 254, 285, 380, 450, 480.
Wood piling, 380, 480.
Wood preservatives, 285, 380, 440, 475, 480, 508.
Wood products, 200, 285, 380, 440.
Woodworking machines, 165, 166, 169, 200, 253, 254, 285, 350, 380, 440, 450, 475, 490, 502, 508, 514, 520.
Wool fibers, 254, 440.
Wool suiting, 440.
Word processing, 600, 627, 628, 628(a).
Work benches, 165, 166, 169, 256, 285, 380, 440, 475, 480, 490.
Work clothing, 200, 285, 380, 440, 480, 502, 504, 516.
Work tables, kitchen, 161, 200, 252, 253, 418, 440, 502, 504, 508, 516.
Wrapping machinery, 350, 353, 354, 440, 450.
Wrapping materials, 285, 350, 351, 410, 440, 450, 490, 508.
Wrecking bars, 285, 380, 440, 480, 508.
Wringers, commercial laundry, 200, 253, 380, 440, 508.
Wristpins, engine, 380, 440.
Writing, script, 285.

X-ray equipment, 353, 440.
X-ray equipment, dental, 200, 252, 380, 418, 440, 502.
X-ray equipment, medical, 106, 200, 252, 253, 285, 380, 413, 418c, 440, 450, 480, 502.
X-ray equipment, veterinary, 106, 440.
X-ray film, medical, 200, 285, 380, 417, 440, 480, 502.
X-ray machines, industrial, 200, 285, 380, 440, 480, 517.
X-ray supplies, dental, 200, 252, 253, 418, 440, 502.
X-ray supplies, medical, 200, 252, 253, 285, 380, 413, 418, 440, 475, 480, 502.
X-ray tubes, medical, 200, 252, 253, 380, 418, 440, 480, 502, 508.